ABSTRACTS OF PERRY COUNTY DEEDS

BOOKS 1-4, 1821-1844

Abstracted by Bill Eddleman

To Hope and Chris, for their patience with my genealogical Pursuits

Southern Historical Press, Inc.
Greenville, South Carolina

Copyright © 2004 by:

Southern Historical Press, Inc.

All rights reserved. No part of this publication may be reproduced, stored in a retrieval system or transmitted in any form or by any means without the prior written permission of the author.

Please direct All correspondence and Orders to:

Southern Historical Press, Inc.
PO Box 1267
Greenville, SC   29602

ISBN #0-89308-800-5

Printed in the United States of America

Abstracts of Perry County Deeds, Books 1-4, 1821-1844

This book contains abstracts of deeds from Deed Books 1-4 of Perry County, Missouri. The deed abstracts were prepared from microfilm of the original books contained in the Perry County Recorder's Office, filmed by the Church of Jesus Christ of Latter Day Saints, and available from the LDS Family History Library in Salt Lake City, its local branches, and the Missouri State Archives, film numbers C5114 (Book 1), C5115 (Book 2), C5116 (Book 3), and C5117 (Book 4). The plats included were copied from the microfilm.

All names mentioned in the deeds are included, except for the clerk's name listed as recording the deed. Land title transfers constitute the bulk of the abstracts, but land patents, mortgages, powers of attorney, wills, personal property transfers, agreements to pay debts, posting of bonds, depositions, and estate partitions are among the types of transactions included. Spellings are as they appear in the deed, so check for alternate spellings. Question marks (?) are used to indicate when the abstractor was unsure of some of the information. Some additional information from other sources is used where it helps to clarify land descriptions, and is included in [ ]. One should always examine the microfilm or original deed books to insure accuracy and to see complete land descriptions, especially where metes and bounds descriptions are used to delineate property.

The abstracts include the following information:

1. A number assigned by the abstractor for indexing purposes only
2. Beginning page in the original deed book
3. Date the deed was executed
4. Grantor(s), including county of residence (Perry County or not given if not indicated). The word "same" is used if the grantor is repeated from the previous deed.
5. Grantee(s), including county of residence (Perry County or not given if not indicated). The word "same" is used if the grantor is repeated from the previous deed.
6. Consideration paid and the amount if given
7. Type of deed, if given (most are warranty deeds)
8. Number of acres of land, with __ indicating the information is not given in the deed
9. Location of land, water course, lot number, survey number, description of property, or neighbors if given
10. Explanation for mortgages or deeds executed at court order
11. Signature of grantor(s). An "x" is inserted between the given name and surname if the grantor signed with a mark. Also indicated is whether the wife of the grantor relinquished her right of dower (amount to 1/3 of the property).
12. Witnesses or those who attested to the deed, including official witness(es)
13. Recording date
14. Satisfaction information for mortgages

The index uses the deed numbers assigned by the abstractor, not page numbers. Indices include an every name index, a slave index, and a location index. Slaves are indexed under "negro" in the every name index, and under the grantor's and grantee's names in the slave index.

Abbreviations used in the abstracts:

Admr - administrator
Atty - attorney
JCC - justice of County Court
Co. - county
Directions - abbreviated using 1 or 2 capital letters (e. g. N for north, NE for northeast)
Execr - executor
JP - justice of the peace
RD - relinquished dower rights

Rng - Range
Sd - said
Sec - section
St - street
Twp - township

Getting Land in Perry County

Perry County lies on the eastern boundary of Missouri, on the Mississippi River (Fig. 1). It is bounded on the east by the Mississippi River, north by Ste. Genevieve County, west by St. Francis and Madison counties, and south by Bollinger and Cape Girardeau counties.

Missouri is mostly a public land state, with first title being purchased by individuals from the U. S. Government. However, original titles to land in the county were also obtained by a number of methods outside the public land offices. Researchers thus need to be aware of the varied locations that must be sought to provide original title information on their ancestors.

Perry County is among a number of eastern Missouri counties that was settled prior to the Louisiana purchase. These settlers often obtained Spanish and French land grants, and such grants were a major inducement to settlement during the late 1700s and early 1800s. The location and brief histories of the Spanish land grants of Perry County has been summarized (Perry Co. Historical Society 1984). Many are also referred to in the abstracts in this book.

The policy of the U. S. government after the Louisiana Purchase in 1803 was to transfer land to individuals. However, claims by those who had received Spanish land grants had to be settled before the land could be sold. The land also had to be surveyed in order to provide orderly transfer of title. Some land claims were settled by the First Board of Land Commissioners, which issued its final report in However, a large number of claims were not settled by this Commissioner, necessitating a Second Board of Commissioners, which did not finalize its work until 1836.

Missouri lands were then surveyed by government surveyors, using the rectangular or U. S. Public Land Office system. Briefly, this involved surveying 36 square mile divisions, 6 miles on a side and called Townships, from a primary meridian (the 5th Principal Meridian), running north-south through the center of Missouri, and an east-west baseline in Arkansas. The north-south component is also called the Township, and the east-west component is the Range. Township 35 N is thus 35 Townships north of the baseline, and Range 11 East is 11 townships east of the 5th Principal Meridian. Each 36-square-mile township is further subdivided into 36, 1-square-mile units termed Sections. For a complete description of the U. S. Public Land Office system, see Greenwood (1990) or Luebking (1997).

Surveyed lands were sold through local land offices. The first of these was opened at St. Louis, but most land sales from Perry Co. were handled through the U. S. Land Office at Jackson, Missouri (in Cape Girardeau Co.), which opened on December 31, 1826 (Ozarks Genealogical Society 1985). Land sales for Perry Co. have been summarized (Eddleman 2000). In addition, a summary of U. S. Land office sales can be found online at the U. S. Bureau of Land Management's land sales website: http://www.glorecords.blm.gov

A few Perry County residents obtained land by cashing in warrants given to veterans as payment for military service. These records are sometimes referred to in deeds, but a full accounting would require that a researcher obtain the bounty land file of the veteran who obtained the warrant. Warrants could be sold, and frequently the individual who cashed in the warrant was not the veteran.

Before public lands were offered for sale, Section 16 (and sometimes parts of other section) of each township was transferred to local school districts for the benefit of the schools. Local school boards sold these lands, with interest from the proceeds being used to fund schools. These records may be found in county courthouses, and are also located in the Missouri State Archives (Kliethermes 1987).

Lands that were considered swamp or overflow lands (wetlands) were often considered worthless for sale through the land offices. These lands were of such low value that the U. S. Government finally transferred title to the states in 1850 (Hibbard 1939). Sale of these parcels was done through a land office at Benton, Missouri at that time. Later, the state of Missouri transferred title to unsold swamp and overflow lands to the counties, and sale of the land continued through offices of the county. These records should be in the Perry County Courthouse in Perryville.

A Brief History of Perry County

The first settlers in what is now Perry County were a few Frenchman from the Ste. Genevieve area, none of whom were permanent settlers. The earliest settlements in the area were in Bois Brule Bottom and The Barrens area near Perryville, in about 1800 (Goodspeed 1888). Those who settled in Bois Brule were from Pennsylvania, and included Michael Burns and his sons Barnabas, William, and James, and his sons-in-law, Thomas Allen, Thomas Cochran, John and Joel Kinnison, William Flynn, Alexander Patterson, Archibald Camster, and Alexander McConoche. The first settlers in The Barrens came from southwestern Kentucky, and were nearly all Catholics (Goodspeed 1888). These included the Tucker family (Joseph and his nine sons), the Moores, the Laytons, and the Hagans. Since these families and other early settlers arrived prior to the Louisiana Purchase, they received Spanish land grants (Perry Co. Historical Society 1984). Many settlers who arrived in the county in the 1820s through 1840s were second, third, and fourth generation English, German, and Scotch-Irish immigrants from western North Carolina. The southeastern part of Perry County was settled largely by German immigrants, the Saxon Lutherans, in the early 1840s.

At the time of settlement by American emigrants, Perry County was part of the Ste. Genevieve District. This area was later organized as Ste. Genevieve County, and Perry County was organized from Ste. Genevieve County on May 21, 1821 (Goodspeed 1888). The county was initially divided into three townships: Brazeau, between Apple Creek and Cinque Hommes Creek; Bois Brule, the northeastern part of the county; and Cinque Hommes, including the remainder. The deeds abstracted in this book include some deeds transacted when the area was part of Ste. Genevieve County, and recorded after 1821, and all deeds transacted and recorded after 1821. Those researching this area prior to 1820 should also consult land and other records of Ste. Genevieve County

Eddleman, Bill. 2000. Original land patentees of Perry County, Missouri. Perry County Historical Society, Perryville, Mo.
Goodspeed Publishing Company. 1888. History of Southeast Missouri. The Goodspeed Publishing Co., Chicago, Ill. [Reprinted 1990 by Southern Historical Press, Inc., Greenville, S. Car.].
Greenwood, Val D. The researcher's guide to American genealogy. 2nd edition. Genealogical Publishing Co., Baltimore, Md.
Hibbard, Benjamin Horace. 1939. A history of public land policies. Peter Smith, New York, N. Y.
Kliethermes, Sharon A. 1987. Missouri school land sales. Dogwood Publications, Loose Creek, Mo.
Luebking, Sandra H. 1997. Research in land and tax records. Pages 241-288 in Loretto D. Szucs, editor. The source--a guidebook of American genealogy. Ancestry, Inc., Salt Lake City, Utah.
Ozarks Genealogical Society. 1985. Index of purchasers, United States Land Sales in Missouri, 1818-1827. Volume 1. Springfield, Mo.
Perry County Historical Society. 1984. The Spanish land grants of our own Perry County, Missouri. Perry Co. Historical Society, Perryville, Mo.

Index to Map of Perry County in 1821-1844

A
Altenburg, J6
Apple Creek, E6, F6-7, G6-7, H7, I7, J7, K7

B
Barren Settlement, F4
Belgique, G2
Biehle, F6
Birmingham, K7
Blue Spring Branch, E2-3, F2-3
Bois Brule Bottom, F1-2, G1-3, H2-3, I3-4
Bois Brule Creek, E2, F2, G2-3, H3
Bollinger County B7, C7, D7, E7, F7
Brazeau, I5
Brazeau Creek, I6, J5-6, K5-6
Brewer, E3

C
Cape Girardeau County F7, G7, H7, I7, J7, K7
Cedar Fork, C4, D3-4
Christenson Branch, F3, G3
Cinque Hommes Creek, F4-5, G3-4, H3-4, I4
Claryville, F1
Clines Branch, I5, J4
Crosstown, H4

D
Dry Fork, D4, G4-5, H4-5

E
Falls Branch, E2, F2
Farrar, H5
Friedenburg, G5
Frohna, I6

G
Giboney, D3
Goose Creek, D3-4

H
Highland, E6
Highland Creek, F5
Huber Branch, F3, G3
Hunt Branch, E4-5

I
Indian Creek, H5-6, I6-7

J
Jackson County, Illinois I3-4, J3-4, K3-7, L3-7
Jordan Branch, C5

L
Lithium, F2
Longtown, G5

M
Madison County A6-A7
McBride, F2

McClanahans Creek, G3
Menfro, H3
Millheim, F6
Mississippi River, F1, G1-2, H2-3, I3-4, J4-5, K5-7

N
Nations Creek, C5-6
Neece Branch, C6
North Fork Apple Creek, E6, F6

O
Omete Creek, H4-5, I4
Owl Creek, J5, K5

P
Parker Lake, C5
Patton Creek, J6, K6
Perryville, F4-5
Point Rest, H3

R
Randolph County, Illinois G1, H1-2, I1-2, J1-2, K1-2, L1-2

S
Ste. Genevieve County A1-A5, B1-B5, C1-C4, D1-D2
St. Laurant Creek, E2
St. Marys, E2
Saline Creek, C3, D1-3
Saline Junction, F3
Schawanee Springs Branch, F5
Sereno, F3
Seventy-Six, J4
Silver Lake, J4
South Fork Apple Creek, E6-7, F6-7
South Fork Saline Creek, B5, C5, D3, D5, E3-5
Streile Branch, F3, G3

T
Tyler Branch, E5, F5

U
Union County, Illinois K7, L7
Uniontown, H6

W
Whitewater River, B5-6, C6-7
Wittenberg, K6

Y
Yount, C6

Figure Captions

Figure 1. Perry County, Missouri, showing major streams and settlements.

Figure 2. Survey number 956, granted to Simon Duval under Joseph Tucker senior, and conveyed to George W. Hudson on 27 December 1831 (Book 3, Page 6).

Figure 3. Plat of the partition of 7056 arpents in Perry and Ste. Genevieve Counties granted to Francois Valle senior (Book 3, Page 85).

Figure 4. Plat of the partition of John Manning's survey No. 2173, part of which was sold by Robert S. Manning to Johann Gorge Gube on June 11, 1839 (Book 3, Page 107).

Figure 5. Division of a tract confirmed to James Thompson, the lower part of which was conveyed from John Logan to William Cox on March 12, 1839 (Book 3, Pages 301-302, No. 947).

Figure 6. Part of the land conveyed by Henry McAtee and Maria, his wife, to James McCauley on April 18, 1840 (Book 3, Page 303, No. 948).

Figure 7. Plat of the partition of Survey No. 447, granted to James Newsom, and partitioned by Commissioners on April 18, 1840 (Book 3, Page 385, No. 1018).

Figure 8. Plat of the Partition of Claim No. 2137, granted to James Moore, and partitioned by Commissioners on October 14, 1841 (Book 4, Page 74, No. 1251).

Figure 9. Plat of the division of land owned by A. H. Puckett and George Camster, about January 24, 1836 (Book 4, Page 146, No. 1315).

Figure 10. Plat of 5 acres conveyed by Daniel O'Meara to Ann Hagan on August 3, 1837 (Book 4, Page 192, No. 1354).

Figure 11. Plat of the partition of land of William Flynn by Commissioners on February 5, 1842 (Book 4, Pages 279-281, No. 1418).

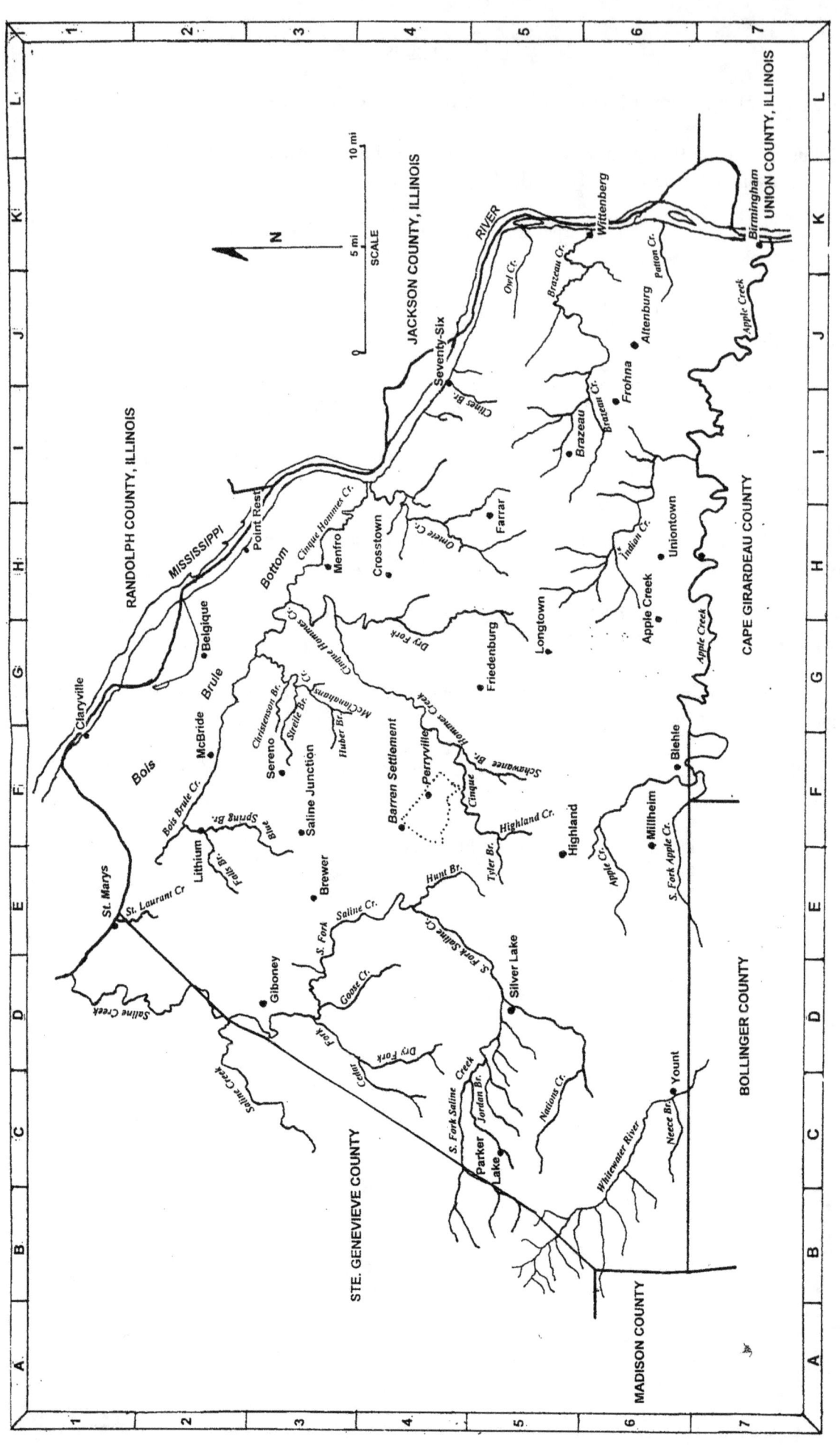

3:6
Figure 2

County who is personally known to me to be the persons
to the foregoing instrument of writing as subscribing w
Mariann Duvall whoes name is subscribed to the sa
as grantor, is one of the real persons who executed the s
Mariann Duvall subscribed, sealed and delivered th
and acknowledged the same to be her act and deed fo
therein mentioned and that the said Tresia Layton
subscribed said deed as witness in the presence and as
Taken and certified and subscribed and sworn to t
aforesaid. Teresia Layton before James Rice Just

T 35 N. R. 10 E.

Sec 30   N 43 E. 80.00 Survey N° 956 Simon Duval under Joseph Tucker Sen. 640 acres   S 47 E. 80.00   Sec 29

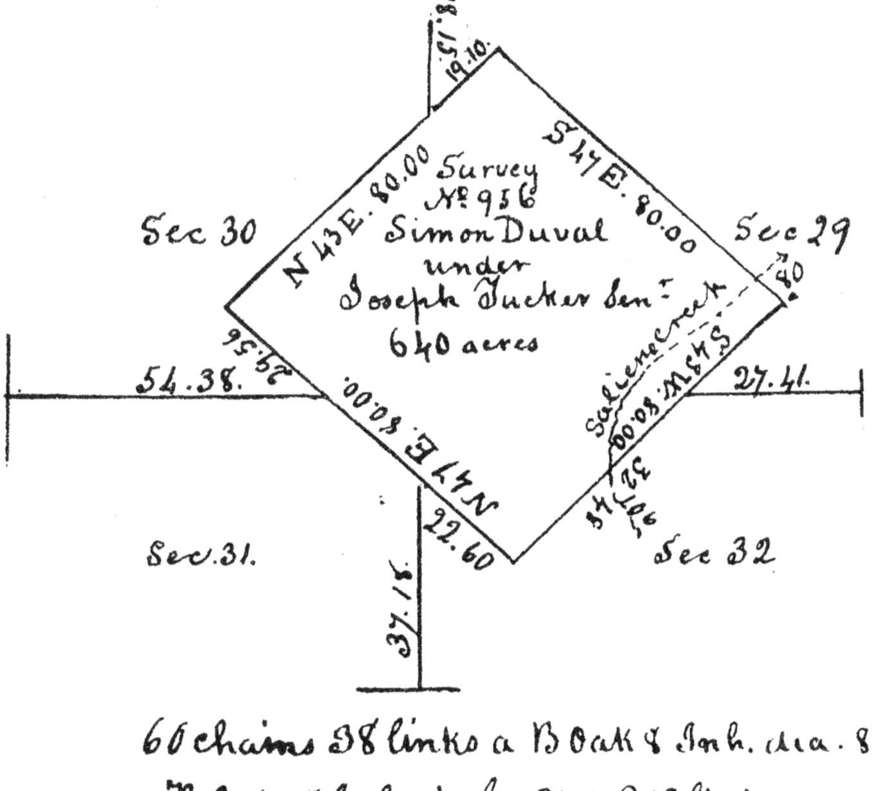

Sec 31   54.38   27.41   Sec 32

Survey N°
Surveyed for Simon
light of Joseph Tu
752 32/100 arpents Be
a B Oak 10 Inh. dia
Oak 10 Inh. dia.
10 46 chains 00 li
Creeke 106 links u
00 links set post cor
Walnut 14 Inh. di
B. Oak 6 Inh. dia
47 W. 20 chains 8.

60 chains 38 links a B Oak 8 Inh. dia. 80 chains 00 links set po
a B. Oak 8 Inh dia br. S 79 E 18 links and a B Oak 10 Inh. dia. br. N
E 36 chains 00 links, a B. Oak 12 Inh dia 62 chains 14 links a
00 links set a post corner of survey from which a W oak 10 Inh.
a W oak 20 Inh. dia. brs. N 47 E 40 lks Thence S 47 E 28 chains 40
chains 10 link a W oak 12 Inh dia 74 chains 50 links Saline cre
80 chains 00 links Intersected the post at the beginning. Surveye

3:85 40, E 200 chs 50 lks to corner of _____
figure N 70 cha. to creek thence with the Creek meandering up the creek, till
3 it intersects the Northern boundary of Lot No 4. thence S. 47° 20, E 135. chs
to the eastern corner of No 5 Thence S 42° 40 W. 95 chains Thence S 47.
60 chains to beginning.

Plat of Survey Referred to and Made Part of this deed of Partition

N. 47°. 20. E 245.00

No 2	Emilie Wilkinson No 1
Robert J. Brown	847 100/100 Acres
397 100/100 acres	190.50

54.44

No 3
Francois Valle
655 74/100
acres

No 6
2444. Acres & 45/100 of an acre

Robert J. Brown

49.50   135.50

104.41   80.59

No 4   No 5
            965 60/100 acres
991 22/100 acres
Joseph Pratte   Joseph Pratte

104.41   80.95 hill   60.00

S. 47°. 20. E 245.00

State of Missouri County of Perry. Set. Be it Remembered
Term of the County Court begun and held at Perryville in sa.
County and State aforesaid on the 6th day of May in the year of
1839. before the Justices thereof in Open Court, personally app-
-d. Brown and Catharine Brown his wife, Francois Valle, Sr.
and Marie Pratte his wife, and Emilie Wilkinson, Who ar-
-ally known to the court to be the persons whose names are su-
the foregoing Instrument of Writing as having executed the sa-

B:107 Figure 4

wife who hereby relinquishes her right of Dower in the said lands & premises have hereunto set our hands and seals this Eleventh day of June in the Year of Our Lord One thousand eight hundred and thirty nine. Robert S. Manning (seal) Anna x her Manning (seal) Signed sealed & delivered in presence of Fred'k C. Hase.

Plat of John Mannings Survey No. 2173 in Township No. 34 North of Base Line Range No. 13 & 14 East of the 5th P.M. as subdivided

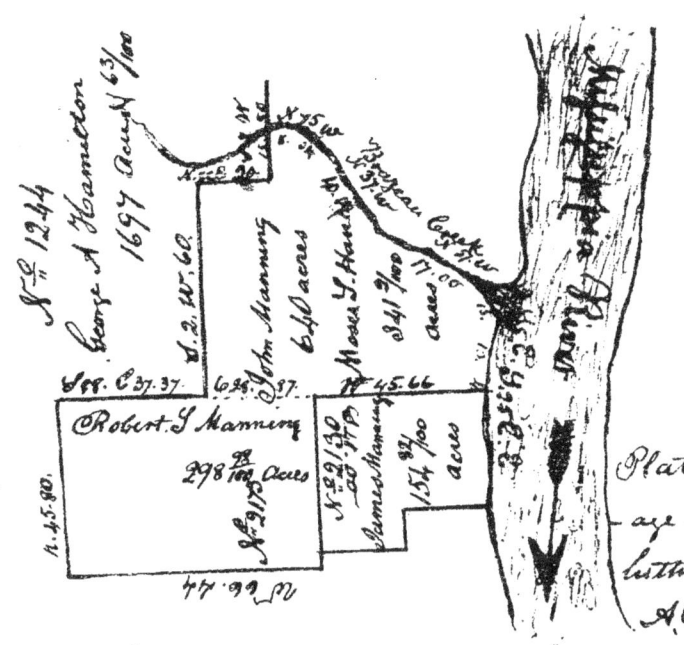

Plat and Surveyed by H.C. Bi—
age Agent for the Evangelical
Lutheran Congregation at Bar
A.D. 1839 in May June 10 A.D.

State of Missouri County of Perry ss: Be it Remembered that on Eleventh day of June in the the Year of Our Lord eighteen hundred thirty nine, Before Me Frederick C. Hase clerk of the circuit Court within and for the County aforesaid Personally Appeared Robert Manning and Anna Manning his wife who are both personally known to Me to be the persons whose Names are subscribed to the foregoing Instrument of writing as having executed the same and severally acknowledged the same to be their act and deed for the purposes therein Mentioned. She the said Anna Manning Wife of the said Robert S. Manning being by Me first Made acquainted with the contents

3:302 Figure 5

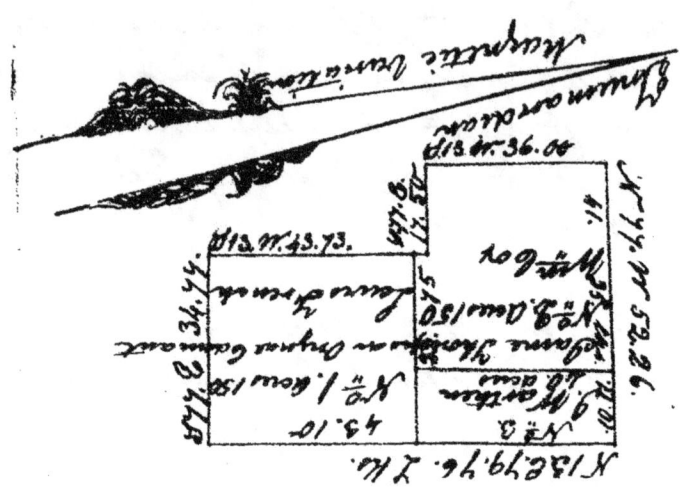

State of Missouri Cou-
bred that on this day
of our Lord eighte
Me Frederick C Hase
Within and for the
Wm Coy and Lewis
known to me to be the
cribe on the foregoin
been Executed by their order and Mutual Consent,
line between them as their act and deed as set [of]
Testimony Whereof I Frederick C Hase clerk as
My hand and Affixe the Seal of said Court,
May A.D. 1840. Fred'k C Hase clk. Recor

Frd'k C Hase clk
By His Sepu

Henry McAtee
to
James McCauley

N° 948 J.

This Indenture M[ade]
one thousand Eight hundred and forty, by
and Martha his Wife of the County of Trny
first part and James McCauley of the [second]
Witnesseth that the said Henry McAtee and
the sum of three hundred

3:30½
Figure 6

of And Examined Seperate and apart,
she executed the said deed And Relinqu
tenements therein Mentioned voluntar
ion or undue influence of her said hus
that she executed said deed And Relin
and tenements therein Mentioned Volun
pulsion or undue influence of her sa
the day and year before Written by Re
court of Perry County M. O.   The foll
and by the forgoing deed layed down
inch.   I do hereby certify to have s 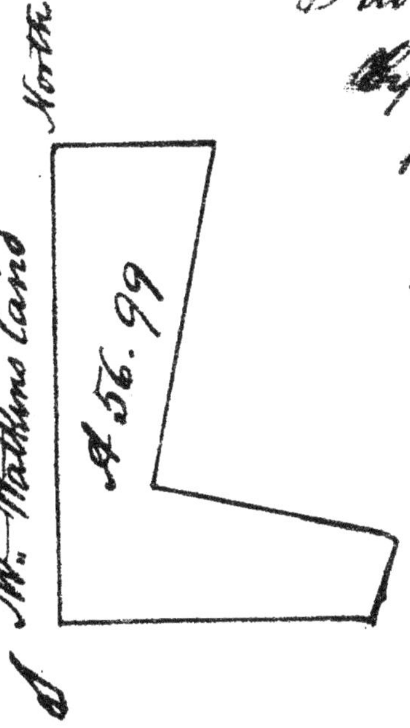
           by the Anexed plat, S
           11. to east South East fr
           for James McCaule
           on the township li
           second corner N.
           to W. Ook 24 inc
           Horey 14 inche
           the third co
           from Which

North
Mrs Mathins land
A 56.99

links S 89. W. And to W. Oak 24 inches di
the fourth corner Adjoining J. Presto
to the corner of the intersection of A
post from which to B. Oak 36. inc
Oak 30. inches 82 chs. S 21 W. Thence D.
Township line; At Which there is a
ameter 11 chs davis to B. oak 24 inches diameter
S 73. E. Thence to the place

without compulsion ...
nowledged And declared that She Executed the Sa
quished her dower to the lands And tenements
Voluntarily freely And Without Compulsion Or
her Said Husband. Taken And certified the day
Robert Trotter J. P. Recorded August 18th

3:385
Figure 7.

Fred.k C. Hase Clk & Ex Of
By his Deputy

Commissioners Report No. 1118

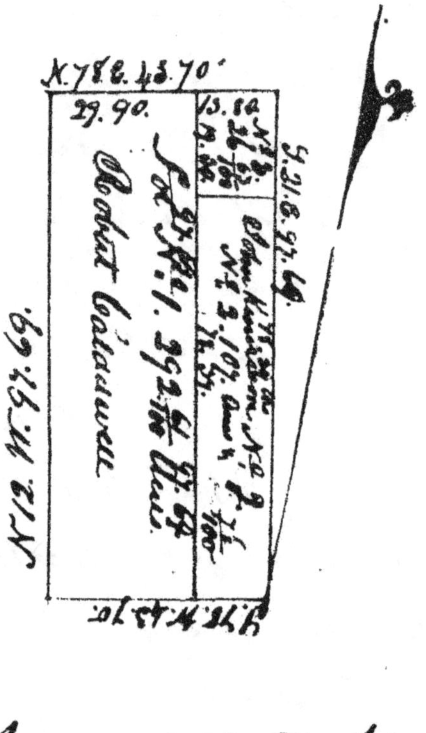

State of Missouri County of
Order of the Circuit Court
the Case of Robert Caldwell
And Sina his Wife And the
B. Newsom deceased the Una
have this day Surveyed the
of land it being the tract Na
the Said tract Was Granted to
containing 502 Arpens Equal to
Survey 447 & Situated in bois brule Bottom on both
creek, And We have Made Partition of

...which is respectfully submitted. As witness our hands this 14th day of October 1841. John [Sim?] [Seal] Peter H. Pratt [Seal] [...] Clark [Seal] — Exhibit A. Part of the Commissioners Report is in the words and figures "to wit." Plat of A Claim No 215, in Town No 35 N. Range 11 East of 5th P.M. containing 640 acres. Originally to James Moore. Subdivision of the land.

4.74 Figure 8

[Plat diagram showing Lots No. 1 through 7 with acreages:
Lot No. 1 — 89.12 A
Lot No. 2 — 100 Acres
Lot No. 3 — 86.25 A
Lot No. 4 — 88.64 A
Lot No. 5 — 50.00 A
Lot No. 6 — 60.12 A
Lot No. 7 — 164.37 A]

It is hereby certified that the above [plat] of Subdivisions as ordered by the [...] pointed by the Circuit Court [Sury] September A.D. 1841. Jeffrey [Dover]

Plat is a correct and [...] commissioners for this [...] ville Perry County State [...] Surveyor by Henry C. B[...]

State of Missouri County of Perry [SS] Be it Remembered that At a Term of the Circuit

Daniel O'meara
To } N° 1354 Certified plate
Ann Hagan } of 5 acres sold by said O'meara to said Ann Hagan

Projected by a scale
of 20 perches to
One Inch

```
         E. 1000 links 40 perches
    ┌─────────────────────────┐
    │                         │
  N.500 links 20 perches      │
 W  │         5 acres         │ E
    │                         │
    └─────────────────────────┘
              S
```

I do hereby Certify the above to be a platt of 5 acres of land situated in the south west Corner of the lot of 40 acres which belongs to Daniel O'meara being the the South west quarter of South east quarter of Section N° 27 Township 35 North Range 10 east which lot of five acres he ceded to Ann Hagan and is bounded on the South by Ann Hagan's Own land On the west by the Publick, and On the North & east by Daniel O'meara's land

Jeffrey Power Perry County 3rd of August 1837
Recorded April 30th 1842
John W Noell Clerk and
Ex officio Recorder. P.C.M.

Vincent Hagan
To } N° 1355 Deed }
James Dunn   This Indenture made and entered
into this thirtieth day of April A.D. 1842 between Vincent Hagan of the county of Perry and State of Missouri of the One part and James Dunn of the County and State aforesaid Of the Other part Witnesseth, that the said Vincent Hagan for and in consideration of the Sum of Twenty five dollars to him in hand paid by the said James Dunn, the receipt whereof is hereby acknowledged, he hath given, Granted, bargained and sold, and by these presents doth, give, Grant bargain, Sell, alien, Convey and Confirm, unto the said James Dunn the following described tract

PERRY COUNTY DEED BOOK 1

1. Page 1. 5 Jan 1821. Alexander **McNair**, Governor of Mo., to Cornelius M. **Slattery**, Esq. Appointment as Clerk of Perry Co. Circuit Court. Signed A. **McNair** by Joshua **Barton**, Sec. of State. Cornelius M. **Slattery** takes the oath of office. Signed Corns. M. **Slattery**. Wit Thos. **McGuire** (JP). Rec 26 Mar 1821.

2. Page 1. 12 Dec 1820. Cornelius M. **Slattery**, Jeremiah **Conner**, and Thomas **McGuire**, all of St. Louis, Mo., to Alexander **McNair**, Governor of Mo. For the sum of $3000, bond to guarantee that sd **Slattery** will perform the duties of Circuit Court Clerk of Perry Co. Signed Corns. M. **Slattery**, Jerh. **Conner**, Thomas **McGuire**. Wit Isidore **Moore**, R. S. **Thomas**, Judge of 4th Judicial Circuit. Rec 26 Mar 1821.

3. Page 1. 6 Mar 1821. Alexander **McNair**, Governor of Mo., to Cornelius M. **Slattery**. Appointment as Clerk of Perry Co. Court. Signed A. **McNair** by Joshua **Barton**, Sec. of State. Cornelius M. **Slattery** takes the oath of office. Signed Corns. M. **Slattery**. Wit Thos. **McGuire** (JP). Rec 26 Mar 1821.

4. Page 2. 5 Feb 1821. Cornelius M. **Slattery** and Jeremiah **Conner**, both of St. Louis, Mo., to Alexander **McNair**, Governor of Mo. For the sum of $1000, bond to guarantee that sd **Slattery** will perform the duties of Perry Co. Court Clerk. Signed Corns. M. **Slattery**, Jerh. **Conner**. Wit I. **Moore**, Aquila **Hagan**, Joshua **Barton**, R. T. **Brown**. Approved by Lewis **Cissell**, D. L. **Caldwell**, Samuel **Anders**, Justices of Perry Co. Court. Rec 26 Mar 1821.

5. Page 2. 1 Jan 1821. Alexander **McNair**, Governor of Mo., to Robert T. **Brown**. Appointment as Sheriff of Perry Co. until the next general election. Signed A. **McNair** by Joshua **Barton**, Sec. of State. Certified by Barnabas **Burns** (JP). Rec 26 Mar 1821.

6. Page 3. 29 Jan 1821. Robert T. **Brown**, Walter **Wilkinson**, and Charles C. **Valle** to Alexander **McNair**, Governor of Mo. For the sum of $8000, bond to guarantee that sd **Brown** shall perform the duties of the office of Sheriff of Perry Co. Signed R. T. **Brown**, W. **Wilkinson**, Cns. C. **Valle**. Wit Favis **Valle**, R. S. **Thomas**, Judge of 4th Judicial Circuit. Rec 26 Mar 1821.

7. Page 3. 8 Dec 1820. Alexander **McNair**, Governor of Mo., to Lewis **Cissell**, Esq. Appointment as Justice of Perry Co. Court for four years. Signed A. **McNair** by Joshua **Barton**, Sec. of State. Lewis **Cissell** takes the oath of office. Signed Lewis **Cissell**. Wit John **Layton** (JP). Rec 26 Mar 1821.

8. Page 3. 8 Dec 1820. Same to Samuel **Anderson**, Esq. Appointment as Justice of Perry Co. Court for four years. Signed A. **McNair** by Joshua **Barton**, Sec. of State. Samuel **Anderson** takes the oath of office. Signed Saml. **Anderson**. Wit John **Layton** (JP). Rec 26 Mar 1821.

9. Page 4. 8 Dec 1820. Same to David L. **Caldwell**, Esq. Appointment as Justice of Perry Co. Court for four years. Signed A. **McNair** by Joshua **Barton**, Sec. of State. David S. **Caldwell** takes the oath of office. Signed D. L. **Caldwell**. Wit John **Layton** (JP). Rec 26 Mar 1821.

10. Page 4. 21 Nov 1820. Same to Benjamin **Davis**. Appointment as JP for Cinque Hommes Twp for four years. Signed A. **McNair** by Joshua **Barton**, Sec. of State. Benjamin **Davis** takes the oath of office. Signed Benjamin **Davis**. Wit Barnabas **Burns** (JP). Rec 26 Mar 1821.

11. Page 5. 21 Nov 1820. Same to James J. **Fenwick**. Appointment as JP for Cinque Hommes Twp for four years. Signed A. **McNair** by Joshua **Barton**, Sec. of State. James J. **Fenwick** takes the oath of office. Signed James J. **Fenwick**. Wit John **Layton** (JP). Rec 26 Mar 1821.

12. Page 5. 2 Dec 1820. Peter **Tucker** and Christeney, his wife, Thomas **Tucker** and Susanah, his wife, Nicholas **Tucker** and Mary, his wife, James **Tucker** and Treacy, his wife, William **Tucker** and Sary, his wife, John **Tucker** and Eleanor, his wife, and Francis **Tucker** and Sary, his wife; all legal representatives of Joseph **Tucker** Sr., decd, and all of Ste. Genevieve Co.; to Joseph **Tucker**. For the sum of $600, 95 arpens, more or less, on the Mississippi River above the mouth of Obrasaw, granted to Thomas **Tucker** and sold by him to Joseph **Tucker** Sr., decd. Signed Peter **Tucker**, Christeney **Tucker**, Thomas **Tucker** and Susanah (x) **Tucker**, Nicholas **Tucker**, Mary (x) **Tucker**, James **Tucker**, Tresey (x) **Tucker**,, William **Tucker**, Sary (x) **Tucker**, John **Tucker**, Eleanor (x) **Tucker**, Francis **Tucker**, Sary (x) **Tucker**. Wit Daniel **Killian**, Thomas **Layton**, D. L. **Caldwell**, JP in Ste. Genevieve Co. Rec 9 Apr 1821.

13. Page 6. 3 Aug 1819. William **Harrison**, William **Hinkson** and Jane, his wife, Andrew **Miller** and Cathrine, his wife, Julius **Harrison**, Mary **Harrison**, and Aris **Harrison**, all of Washington Co., Mo., children and legal heirs of Benjamin **Harrison**, decd, late of Ste. Genevieve Co. to William **Burns**. For the sum of $150, their right to __ acres on the bank of the Mississippi River, on which Benjamin **Harrison** settled before Feb 1813. Sd heirs have right of preference in purchasing the land from the U. S., and transfer that right to sd **Burns**. Signed W. **Harrison**, W. **Hinkson**, A. **Miller**, Mary **Harrison**, Ginney **Harrison**, Cathrine **Miller**, Julius **Harrison**. Wit John C. **Brickey**, Dep Clerk of Washington Co., Mo., Jms. **Andrews**, JP in Washington Co., Mo., John **Jones**, Clerk of Washington Co., Mo. [Cathrine **Miller** is too sick to attend at the clerk's office.] Rec 12 Apr 1821.

14. Page 8. 3 Aug 1819. William **Harrison** for Aris **Harrison** to same. For $__, the right to the land in the preceding deed (1:6) when sd Aris reaches his majority. Signed W. **Harrison**. Wit Jno. Rice **Jones**, B. **Anthony**. Rec 12 Apr 1821.

15. Page 8. 10 Jun 1820. Heirs of John **Layton**, decd, to Peter **Tucker**, Simon **Duvall**, and Joseph **Cissell**, arbitrators for the division of land of sd decd. For the sum of $300, bond to abide by the decision of sd arbitrators in the division of 470 acres belonging to sd John **Layton**, part of 640 acres granted to sd decd less 200 arpens (about 170 acres) that was previously sold. Signed Zachariah **Layton**, Clement **Cissell**, Joseph **Manning**, Wilfred **Layton**, John **Layton**, Walter **Layton**, Bernard **Layton**, William **McLain**, Michael **Hagan**. Wit Corns. M. **Slattery**, Clerk. Rec 14 Apr 1821.

16. Page 9. 26 Jan 1816. Thomas **Fenwick** to Clare **Hamilton**, both of Ste. Genevieve Co., Mo. For the sum of $1500, two tracts and several negroes; 500 arpens on the Mississippi River about four miles above the Grand Tower, bounded on the N by Joseph

Fenwick and S by Mark **Manning**; 500 arpens on Brazoe Creek, including George A. **Hamilton**'s improvement; a negro woman named **Lett** about 30 years old, and her children **Grandison**, **Henry**, etc.; and a negro boy named **Ned** about 18 years old. The property is to be divided upon the death of sd Clare among her surviving children: Josiah **Hamilton**, Austin F. **Hamilton**, Matilda **Hamilton**, Wile **Hamilton**, Leo **Hamilton**, Walter **Hamilton**, and George **Hamilton**. Signed Thos. **Fenwick**. Wit James J. **Fenwick**, E. **Fenwick**, Benjamin **Davis** (JP). Rec 5 May 1821.

17. Page 10. 23 Feb 1821. William **Tucker** to Michael **Warren**, both of Barren Settlement, Perry Co. For the sum of $2, preemption right to fractional 1/4 Sec 26, Rng 10, Twp 36, Sec 26; that he purchased from William **Dunn**. Signed William **Tucker**, Michael **Warren**. Wit Benjamin **Roberts**, John **Layton** (JP). Rec 14 May 1821.

18. Page 10. 26 Feb 1821. Andrew **Dunks** Sr. of St. Landry Parish, La. to Henry **Clark** of Ste. Genevieve Co., Mo. For the sum of $400, 640 acres in Bois Brule Bottom; adjoining land conveyed by sd **Dunks** to sd **Clark**, Solomon **Morgan**, and Mark **Brooks**; and confirmed to John **Dunks**, decd, to whom Andrew **Dunks** is sole heir. Signed Andrew (x) **Dunks**, Henry **Clark**. Wit James **Ray**, David **Bell**, Geo. **King**, Parish Judge. Rec 15 May 1821.

19. Page 11. 26 Feb 1821. Same to same. For the sum of $400, 640 acres in Bois Brule Bottom, adjoined on one side by Solomon **Morgan**, and the other side by Mark **Brooks**; confirmed to the seller by the Board of Commissioners. Signed Andrew (x) **Dunks**, Henry **Clark**. Wit James **Ray**, David **Bell**, Geo. **King**, Parish Judge. Rec 15 May 1821.

20. Page 11. 2 Dec 1820. Francis **Tucker** and Sarah, his wife, to Equilla **Hagin**, all of Ste. Genevieve Co., Mo. For the sum of $5, their interest in __ acres on the Mississippi River just above the mouth of Obraso, belonging to the heirs of Joseph **Tucker** Sr., decd. Signed Francis **Tucker**, Sarah (x) **Tucker**. Test Peter **Tucker**, D. L. **Caldwell** (JP). Rec 17 May 1821.

21. Page 12. 28 Apr 1821. Benjamin **Hagan** to Barnard **Layton**. For the sum of $75 he owes sd **Layton**, mortgage on a bay mare, one feather bead, two cous, one calf, two three-year-old stears, and two heipher yearlings. Signed Benjamin **Hagan**. Wit John **Layton** (JP). Rec 19 May 1821.

22. Page 12. 9 Mar 1821. William **Morris** to Joseph R. **Bland**. For the sum of $200, 20 acres in Bois Brule Bottom, being the lower part of 100 acres that is the upper part of 640 acres granted to Archibald **Morgan**; beginning on the Mississippi River; sold by sd **Morgan** to Jackson **Taylor** on 29 Aug 1818, by sd **Taylor** to Charles **Ellis** and by sd **Ellis** to William **Morris** on 12 Oct 1818. Signed William (U) **Morris**. Wit William **Leatherberry**, W. **Searcy**, Barnabas **Burns** (JP). Rec 11 Jun 1821.

23. Page 13. 4 Jun 1821. William **Berry** of Cinque Hommes Twp to Little Berry **Lewis**. For the sum of $100, 18 hogs, one black horse, a sorrel mare, one mottled faced cow & calf, Buoyshear plow, five geese, one rifle gun, one feather bed and furniture, two straw beds, and all his household furniture. Sd **Berry** has placed sd **Lewis** in possession of same before John **Morris** on about 4 Jun 1821. Signed William **Berry**. Wit John **Morris**, Ansel (x) **Ferrel**, C. M. **Slattery**, Clerk. Rec 20 Jun 1821.

24. Page 13. 23 Oct 1811. George and Rebecca **Miller**, both of the Ste. Genevieve Dist, to Thomas **Donohue**. For the sum of $200, their interest in a tract of James **Newsom**, decd, where they now reside, adjoining **Lewis**(?) **Coty** & **Bovus** land. The further bind themselves for $400 to make a deed to sd **Donohue** when sd tract is divided. Signed George (x) **Miller**, Rebeckah (x) **Miller**. Wit Henry **Dickinson**, Mark **Brooks** (as to sd **Dickinson**), D. L. **Caldwell**, JCC. Rec 23 Jun 1821.

25. Page 14. 6 Jun 1821. Alexander **McNair**, Governor of Mo., to John F. **Henry**. Appointment as JP of Bois Brulet for four years. Signed A. **McNair** by Joshua **Barton**, Sec. of State. John F. **Henry** takes the oath of office before Barnabas **Burns** (JP). Rec 12 Jul 1821.

26. Page 14. 4 Aug 1821. William **Dunn** and Elizabeth, his wife, to Clement **Knott**. For the sum of $276, 597 1/2 acres, more or less, on the S fork of McClenahans Creek, granted to them by the U. S. A. in consequence of their inhabiting and cultivating the same before 20 Dec 1803; and adjoining the estate of James **Samuels**. Signed William **Dunn**, Elizabeth (x) **Dunn**. Test John **Layton** (JP), Corns. M. **Slattery**. Rec 6 Aug 1821.

27. Page 15. 31 Jul 1821. Ignatius **Layton** and Elizabeth, his wife, and Nicholas **Miles** and Elizabeth, his wife, to Nicholas **Moore**. For the sum of $49, 39.22 acres on the S fork of Saline Creek in the N corner of a tract they purchased from Michael **Tucker**, including the place where sd **Moore** now lives; beginning at a sycamore sapling marked NM. Signed Ignatius **Layton**, Elizabeth (x) **Layton**, Nicholas **Miles**, Elizabeth **Miles**. Wit Isidore **Moore**, John **Layton** (JP). Rec 6 Aug 1821.

28. Page 16. 8 Aug 1821. Walter **Wilkinson** to Robert T. **Brown**. For securing his wife's personal property and for the sum of $1, deed of trust on personal property, by an agreement made 10 Nov 1813 between sd **Wilkinson** and Emilie **Valle** in contemplation of their marriage. Before the marriage was solemnized, it was agreed that personal property, to wit, negroes descended to her from her father Francis **Valle**, decd, (in as much as sd **Wilkinson** was not seized of an estate sufficient to equal her fortune) should be conveyed by sd Walter to be at her own disposal, to wit, one negro man named **Pierre**, one negroe man named **Voluntine**, one negro boy named **Charles**, one negro woman named **Grace** and her two children named **Mary** and **Pierre**, on negro woman named **Aura** and her two children named **Catharine** and **Louise**, and one negro girl named **Therese**. Also one negro man named **Phrisby** alias **Frisby**; 30 cattle including 15 milk cows and calves; 100 hed of hogs of different sizes; 23 sheep; one yoke of oxen and cart; 7 horses; one waggon and geer; 4 horses; one Dearborn carriage and harness; 3 beds, bedsteads, and furniture; one settee and 14 chairs (windsor); one secretary (desk); one side board; all the household & kitchen furniture; three ploughs and all other utensils for plantation work; two cherry dining tables; two breakfast tables; one beureau; and one cloths press. Sd **Brown** is to hold the property in trust for sd Emilie. Signed Walter **Wilkinson**. Wit Tho. **Oliver**, JP in Ste. Genevieve Co., Mo., Barnabas **Burns** (JP). Rec 13 Aug 1821.

29. Page 17. 23 Jul 1821. Robert **Caldwell** and George **Camster** to Walter **Wilkinson**. For the sum of $300, 640 acres on the Mississippi River in Bois Brule Bottom, confirmed to Joseph **Allan** by the U. S. A., and purchased by sd **Caldwell** and sd

Camster from Reubin **Sutton**, Rachel **Sutton**, and Rachel **Allan**. Signed Robt. **Caldwell**, George **Camster**. Wit D. L. **Caldwell**, JCC, R. T. **Brown**. Rec 25 Aug 1821.

30. Page 18. 6 May 1821. Thomas **Fenwick**, Ezekiel **Fenwick**, Martin **Fenwick**, Clare **Hamilton**, James J. **Fenwick**, and Leo **Fenwick**; all heirs of Walter **Fenwick**, late of Ste. Genevieve, Mo.; to George **Fleming** of Cape Girardeau Co., Mo. For the sum of $250, 640 acres on the W bank of the Mississippi River just below the Grand Tower, granted to James **Huchins** and confirmed to Walter **Fenwick**. Signed Thos. **Fenwick**, E. **Fenwick**, Clear **Hamilton**, James J. **Fenwick**, Leo **Fenwick** by his atty Jas. J. **Fenwick**. Wit Matthew **Duncan**, Josiah F. **Hamilton**, Saml. **Anderson**, JCC. Rec 28 Aug 1821.

31. Page 18. 5 Sep 1821. Cornelius **Rhodes** to John **Layton**, both of Cinque Hommes Twp. For the sum of $150, mortgage on one negro woman named **Reachel**. Sd **Rhodes** owes the debt to sd **Layton** by 5 Sep next without interest. Signed Cornelius **Rhodes**. Wit Cons. M. **Slattery**, Clerk, William **Tucker**. Rec 17 Sep 1821.

32. Page 19. 3 Aug 1818. Guy **Gaylord** of Bois Brule Bottom in Ste. Genevieve Co. to Hezekiah **Johnson**, late of Pittsburgh, Pa. For the sum of $837.80, mortgage on about 116 acres in sd bottom on the lower end of Horse Island, part of 360 arpens supposed to have been confirmed to William **Flynn**, decd, under James **Dutton**, then possessed by Thomas **Ramsey**, and which sd **Gaylord** purchased from Charles **Ellis**, and which sd **Ellis** purchased from William **Flynn**, son of William **Flynn**, decd. Thomas **Maddin** now owns 200 acres of the original grant, where the town of Maddinsboro was advertised to be laid out. Sd **Gaylord** owes a note to sd **Johnson**, payable on demand. Signed Guy **Gaylord**. Wit Rufus **Easton**, T. **Quarles**, A. **Gamble**, Clerk of St. Louis Co. Circuit Court. Rec 20 Sep 1821.

33. Page 20. 23 Jan 1811. Jean Baptiste Ste Geme **Beauvais**. Division of property amongst his children; sd property being community property of him and his wife Therese **Lasondrais**, decd, who died 30 April 1807. All children are to receive equal shares to be determined in the fairest and most equitable way possible by his family: Raphael **Beauvais**; Vital Ste Gemes **Beauvais**; Berthelemy Ste Gemes **Beauvais**; Joseph **Beauvais**; Jean Baptiste Ste Gemes **Beauvais**; Auguste Ste Gemes **Beauvais**; Marie Louise **Beauvais**; Louis **Bolduc**; Pascal **Delehemendy**, on behalf of Marie Therese Ste Geme **Beauvais**; Bazile **Meplais** on behalf of Julie Ste Gemes **Beauvais**;and Eleonore Ste Geme **Beauvais**, aged 17 years, one month, 13 days, all heirs of the deceased Therese **Lasoudrais**, their mother. The inventory and valuation is to be made by Mr. Vital **Beauvais**, their uncle, and Pierre **Menard** and Jean Bapte **Valle**, their honest friends. After the sd inventory and division of property is made, neither the aforesaid heirs nor their children can make any appeal in any court about the inheritance. Signed J. S. G. **Beauvais**, Barthelemy **Ste Gemes**, Ste Gemes **Beauvais**, Mr. Louis **Bolduc**, P. **Delehemendy**, Bazile **Mesplais**, Raphael **Beauvais**, Mr. **Ste Gemmes**, Jph. **Beauvais**, Augus **Ste Gemes**. Wit Vitale **Beauvais**, Pr. **Menard**, J. Bte. **Valle**, A. **Langlois**. 29 Jan 1811. The two hundred and sixth item is entered on the Inventory Book as follows to wit: concession of 25 arpens by 40 deep, making a total of 1000 arpens located at Bois Brule, which belonged to the property with Vital **Beauvais** of the said concession, the division having been made with 100 arpens left as the property of Jean Bapte. Ste Gemme **Beauvais** and Therese **Lasaudrais**, decd. Signed J. S. G. **Beauvais**, Raphael **Beauvais**, Mr. **Ste Gemmes**, Berthelemy **Ste Gemes**, Jph. Beauvais **Ste Gemes**, Louis **Bolduc**, P. **Delehemeny**, Bazile Mesplais **Ste Gemme**, August **Ste Gemes**. Wit Vitale **Beauvais**, J. Bte. **Valle**, Pierre **Menard**, A. **Langlois**, Tho. **Oliver**, Clerk of Ste. Genevieve Co., Mo. Court. Rec 1 Oct 1821.

34. Page 21. 8 Aug 1821. George **Preston**, James **Preston**, and Ann **Preston** to Joseph Zachariah **Wimsatt**. For the sum of $350, 280 acres; bounded on the E by Bede **Moore**, S by John **Duvall**, W by Elisha **Belsha**, and N by Clement **Knott** and the U. S. A.. Signed James (x) **Preston**, George **Preston**, Ann (x) **Preston**. Wit Corns. M. **Slattery**, Clerk, Barnabas **Burns**. Rec 1 Oct 1821.

35. Page 22. 2 Dec 1820. James **Tucker** and Treasy, his wife, to Nicholas **Tucker**. For the sum of $40, 50 arpens adjoining sd Nicholas **Tucker**'s claim on the S line of Joseph **Tucker** Sr.'s survey. Signed James **Tucker**, Tareasea **Tucker**. Test Joseph **Tucker**, D. L. **Caldwell** (JP). Rec 2 Oct 1821.

36. Page 22. 28 Jul 1821. John **Logan** to Martin **Rodney** of Cape Girardeau Co., Mo. For the sum of $300, a mulatto woman named **July**, about 22 years old, and her three children, **Austin** about 8 years old, **Jack** about 6 years old, and **Betsey** about 2 years old. Signed John **Logan**. Test Thos. S. **Rodney**, Isaac **Devore**, John **Akin**, JP in Byrd Twp, Cape Girardeau Co., Mo. Rec 8 Oct 1821.

37. Page 23. 6 Aug 1821. Alexander **Chesley** to Alfred **Bird**. For the sum of $1 and securing five notes, mortgage on __ acres that sd **Chesley** bought from sd **Bird** on this day. Sd **Bird** holds five promissory notes for $200 each from sd **Chesley**, totaling $1000, and due in one, two, three, four, and five years. Signed A. C. **Chesley**. Wit John F. **Henry** (JP). Rec 22 Oct 1821. [Marginal note: Alfred **Bird** transfers the notes to Louisa Jane **Oklap**, daughter of John **Oklap**, on 14 Sep 1819. Signed A. **Bird**. Wit Thos. **Oliver**. Full satisfaction received on 9 Dec 1822. Signed John **Oklap** for Louisa Jane **Oklap** by James **Clark**, atty in fact.]

38. Page 23. 15 Nov 1821. Luke Edward **Lawless** to Thomas **Hanly**, both of St. Louis. For the sum of $__, 640 acres, more or less, on the waters of Brazeau Creek in St. Genevieve Co.; sold to Reuben **Smith** by Henry **Dodge**, Sheriff of sd county, at the suit of John **Smith** against Robert **Henthston**, and sold to sd **Lawless** by Reuben **Smith** on 14 Dec 1819. Signed L. E. **Lawless**. Wit Jerh. **Connor**, Archibald **Gamble**, Clerk of St. Louis Co. Court. Rec 21 Nov 1821.

39. Page 24. 6 Aug 1821. Alfred **Bird** to Alexander **Chesley**. For the sum of $1200, 100 acres, part of a tract devised to sd **Bird** by the will of Amos **Bird** on 19 Feb 1821; beginning on the point on the river at the line between Joseph **Dennichea** Sr. and Alfred **Bird**. Signed A. **Bird**. Wit John F. **Henry** (JP). Rec 5 Nov 1821.

40. Page 24. 8 Sep 1821. Susan **Hayden** of Washington Co., Ky. to Guy **Elder**. Power of atty to sue for, recover, and receive property from the estate of her decd father Clement **Hayden**, late of Perry Co. Signed Susanna **Hayden**. Wit Jesse **Abell**, James H. **Tucker**, both JP in Washington Co., Ky., Thomas **Cull**, Presiding JP for Washington Co., Ky. Rec 26 Nov 1821.

41. Page 25. 8 Sep 1821. Cecelia **Miles** of Washington Co., Ky. to same. Power of atty to sue for, recover, and receive property from the estate of her decd father Joseph **Miles**, late of Perry Co.

Signed Ceclia **Miles**. Wit Jesse **Abell**, James H. **Tucker**, both JP in Washington Co., Ky., Thomas **Cull**, Presiding JP for Washington Co., Ky. Rec 26 Nov 1821.

42. Page 26. 22 Oct 1821. Thomas **Allen** to Aequila **Hagan**. For the sum of $100, 200 acres near the head waters of McClenehans Creek, beginning at the SW corner of sd **Allen**'s survey. Signed Thomas **Allen**. Test John **Layton** (JP), James C. **Moore**. Rec 26 Nov 1821.

43. Page 26. 6 Oct 1821. Joseph **Bland** to William **Morris**. For the sum of $200, 20 acres in Bois Brule Bottom; the lower part of 100 acres of the upper part of 640 acres originally granted to Archibald **Morgan**, and on the Mississippi River; sold by sd **Morgan** to Jackson **Taylor** on 29 Aug 1818, and by sd **Taylor** to Charles **Ellis**, and by sd **Ellis** to William **Morris** on 12 Oct 1818, and by sd **Morris** to sd **Bland** on 9 Mar 1821. Signed Joseph R. **Bland**. Test D. L. **Caldwell**, JCC, Mark **Brooks**. Rec 10 Dec 1821.

44. Page 27. 24 Oct 1821. Alexander **McNair**, Governor of Mo., to Cornelius M. **Slattery**. Appointment as JP for Cinque Hommes Twp. Signed A. **McNair** by Wm. G **Pettus**, Sec. of State. Cornelius M. **Slattery** takes the oath of office. Signed Corns. M. **Slattery**. Wit Thos. **McGuire** (JP). Rec 26 Oct 1821.

45. Page 27. 3 Apr 1821. Francis **Bartheaum** to John **Logan**. For the sum of $800, all his title, claim, and interest to the estate of his father Francis **Bartheamne**, decd. Signed Frances ( ) **Barthume**. Wit Wm. **Lively**, Benjamin **Davis** (JP). Rec 10 Dec 1821.

46. Page 28. 20 Dec 1821. Martin **Rodney** to John **Logan**. For the sum of $300 repaid to sd **Rodney**, a negro woman named **Julia** and her children named **Austin**, **Jack**, and **Betsy**. Sd negroes were security for the debt. Signed Martin **Rodney**. Wit John Rice **Jones**, Justice of Mo. Supreme Court. Rec 9 Jan 1822.

47. Page 28. 17 Nov 1821. Thomas **Donohue** and Polly, his wife, to John **Duvall**. For the sum of $200, 34 acres, more or less, on the Mississippi River; part of a tract belonging to the estate of Joseph **Donohue**, decd, and that Thomas **Donohue** purchased from Perry **Evans**. Signed Thos. **Donnohue**, Polly (x) **Donnohue**. Test Thomas **Wright**, D. L. **Caldwell**, JCC. Rec 22 Jan 1822.

48. Page 28. 22 Jan 1822. James **Tucker** and Treacey, his wife, to Thomas **Cody**. For the sum of $__, 71 1/9 acres; bounded on the W by Aequila **Hagan**, S by Joseph **Tucker** Sr., and E by James **Moore** Sr. Sd Treacey is heir and legal representative of Joseph **Hagan**, decd. Signed James **Tucker**, Treacey (x) **Tucker**. Wit Corns. M. **Slattery** (JP), James **Rice**. Rec 8 Feb 1822.

49. Page 30. 13 Dec 1821. Thomas **Hanly** to the State of Mo. For the sum of $1000, mortgage on 640 acres on Brazoe Creek, Brazoe Settlement, which he bought from L. E. **Lawless**; assessed to him at $2180. Sd mortgage is due on 1 Sep 1822. Signed Th. **Hanly**. Wit R. **Paul**, Cornelius **Slattery**, Clerk. Rec 4 Mar 1822.

50. Page 30. 8 Mar 1822. Locious **Reed**, Benjamin **Reed**, and Matilda **Reed** to James J. **Fenwick**. For the sum of $145, their undivided interest in 100 acres, more or less, on the Mississippi River at the mouth of Brazoe, which they hold as heirs of their father William **Reed**; granted and confirmed to William **Reed**.

Signed Aloysius **Reed**, Benjamin **Reed**, Matilda **Reed**. Wit John **Layton** (JP), Benjamin (x) **Hagan**. Rec 11 Mar 1822.

51. Page 31. 24 Oct 1821. Thomas **Allen** to John W. **Stewart**. For the sum of $120, 120 acres on the waters of McClannahan's Creek, being the SE corner of his survey of 640 acres. Signed Thomas **Allen**. Wit M. **Amoureux**, John F. **Henry** (JP). Rec 18 Mar 1822.

52. Page 31. 2 Mar 1822. John W. **Stewart** and Lidia, his wife, to Ansel **Ferrel**. For the sum of $120, 120 acres as described in the preceding deed (1:31); joining 200 acres sold to Aequila **Hagan** by sd **Allen**. Signed John W. **Stewart**, Lidia **Stewart**. Wit Barnabas **Burns** (JP), Michael **Burns**. Rec 18 Mar 1822.

53. Page 32. 6 Oct 1821. Benajah **Morgan** and Elizabeth, his wife, to Joseph R. **Bland**. For the sum of $400, __ acres in Bois Brule Bottom, which they claim as heirs of John **Morgan**, decd; being their part of 640 acres granted to John **Morgan** as his settlement right. Signed Benajah **Morgan**, Elizabeth (x) **Morgan**. Test William **Boyd**, D. L. **Caldwell**, JCC. Rec 18 Mar 1822.

54. Page 32. 14 May 1821. John **Logan** by Sheriff Robert T. **Brown** to Robert **Caldwell**, agent for Joab **Waters** Sr. For the sum of $50, 150 arpens within 1/2 mile of the Mississippi River near the mouth of Apple Creek; bounded on the lower side by Benjamin **Davis** and on the upper side by Lewis **Alfemous**. Sold on 5 Jun 1821 on an execution issued 29 Mar 1821 by Ste. Genevieve Co. Circuit Court in a suit for Alexander **McConahue** and against sd **Logan** impleaded with Ezekiel **Abel** for $104 debt and $22.30 damages. Signed Robert T. **Brown**, Sheriff. Wit Corns. M. **Slattery**, Clerk. Rec 19 Mar 1822.

55. Page 34. 27 Mar 1822. Henry B. **Newsom** to the State of Mo. For the sum of $750, mortgage on 506 arpents in Boyee Rule Bottom where he now resides; bounded on the N by William **Shannon**, W by Logan **Caldwell**, and E by Roland **Meredith**. The debt is due with 6% interest per annum from 27 Mar 1823. Signed H. B. **Newsom**. Wit Wm. **McGuire**, Corns. M. **Slattery**, Clerk. Rec 29 Mar 1822.

56. Page 34. 8 Apr 1822. Aquila **Hagan** and Mary, his wife, to Rebeckah and James **Moore**. For love and good will they bear toward their daughter and her husband, 50 acres, part of 640 acres where they now live; beginning at a stone at the N corner of the survey. Signed Aquila **Hagan**, Mary (x) **Hagan**. Wit Corns. M. **Slattery** (JP), Elizabeth (x) **Hagan**. Rec 8 Apr 1822.

57. Page 35. 10 Apr 1822. George **Cockram** and Mariah, his wife, to Samuel **Mansico**. For the sum of $550, 100 arpens, more or less, being the undivided 1/6 share of land in Bois Brule Bottom on the Mississippi River; sd tract was devised by Absolum **Kennison**, decd, to his son John **Kinnison**, and deeded to sd **Cockram** by John **Kinnison** on 23 May 1818 (Book O, folio 50-51). Signed George **Cochran**, Mariah (x) **Cochran**. Wit Barnabas **Burns** (JP), John (x) Grant **Gittar**. Rec 17 Apr 1822.

58. Page 36. 10 May 1822. Thomas **Donnohue** to David L. **Caldwell** and Roland **Boid**. For serving as security for $200 sd **Donnohue** borrowed at the Loan Office, 68 acres, more or less, in Bois Brulle Bottom on the Mississippi River, confirmed to his father Joseph **Donohue**, now belonging to his heirs and being where he resided at his death. The deed to be void if Thomas

Donnohue repays the Loan Office. Signed Thos. **Donnohue**. Wit Benedict **Riley**, Corns. M. **Slattery** (JP). Rec 13 May 1822.

59. Page 36. 1 Mar 1822. Walter **Wilkinson** to Robert T. **Brown**. For the sum of $2000, 640 acres in Bobruly Bottom, sold by Joseph **Allair** to Ezekiel **Abel**, and purchased by sd **Wilkinson** from Samuel **Campbell**, atty in fact for sd **Abel** [record in Ste. Genevieve Co.]. Signed Walter **Wilkinson**. Wit Corns. M. **Slattery** (JP), Ryder(?) A. **Ball**. Rec 14 May 1822.

60. Page 37. 11 May 1822. Thomas **Tucker** to Joseph **Manning**. For the sum of $150, quit claim to 640 acres on Brazeau Creek, except 95 acres. Signed Thomas (x) **Tucker**. Wit W. **Wilkinson**, Corns. M. **Slattery**, Clerk. Rec 14 May 1822.

61. Page 38. 8 May 1821. Bernard **Layton** and Mary, his wife, of Cinque Hommes Twp, to Robert T. **Brown**, Joseph **Tucker** Sr., and Thomas **Riney**, Commissioners of the Courthouse and Goal. For one of the lots to be laid off on the land described (not to cover the spring nor to front on the public square) or cash for the same, 51 acres in a square beginning at a point one pole N and two poles E of a spring called the Pond Spring. Signed Bernard **Layton**, Mary (x) **Layton**; John **Layton**, Simon **Duvall**, Benjamin **Davis**, Commissioners appointed by the General Assembly to find a seat of justice for Perry Co. Wit Corns. M. **Slattery**, Clerk. Rec 14 May 1822.

62. Page 39. 28 Mar 1822. James **Reed** and Lucy, his wife, to James **Brewer**. For the sum of $20, their interest to a floating claim, of which William M. **Reed** could not obtain more than 108 acres by reason of other surveys and the Mississippi River surrounding him on every side. Signed James **Reed**, Lucy (x) **Reed**. Test John **Layton** (JP), John P. **Tucker**. Rec 27 May 1822.

63. Page 40. 1 Jun 1822. Joseph **Manning** and Mary, his wife, to John **Moranville**, all of Cinque Hommes Twp. In exchange for land purchased by sd **Manning** and sd **Moranville** of Thomas **Tucker** on 11 May 1822 (1:37) in the name of sd **Manning**, 272 1/2 acres, more or less, bounded on the E by sd **Manning**, S by William **DeBurgh**, W by Joseph **James**, and N by public land; including sd **Moranville**'s improvements. The exchange is to be void if either tract is taken away or they are evicted. Signed Joseph **Manning**, Mary (x) **Manning**, John B. **Moranville**. Wit Corns. M. **Slattery** (JP), Mark **Manning**. Rec __ Jun 1822.

64. Page 41. 21 May 1822. Thomas **Hanly** and Mary, his wife, to Arthur **Magenis** [McGinnis]. For the sum of $200, 640 acres, more or less, on Brazoe Creek that was originally confirmed to Robert **Hinckston** as his settlement right; sold under an execution against sd **Hinckston** at the suit of John **Smith** by the Sheriff of Ste. Genevieve Co. to Ruben **Smith**, and assigned to sd **Hanly**. The tract is subject to a mortgage of $1000 with interest to the State of Mo., and another not to exceed $250 to John **Scott**. Signed Th. **Hanly**, Mary **Hanly**. Wit Arthur **Magenis**, Patrick **Shearman**, Jno. Rice **Jones**, Mo. Supreme Court Justice. Rec __ Jun 1822.

65. Page 42. 6 Jun 1822. Levy **Hagan** and Mary Ann, his wife, Benjamin **Reed** and Matilda, his wife, Vincent **Greeny** and Mary, his wife, and Elosius **Reed** to Ignatius **Layton** and John **Layton**. For the sum of $160, 432 acres and 68 poles, part of the land confirmed to William M. **Reed**, decd. The grantors are heirs of sd decd. Signed Levi (x) **Hagan**, Mary Ann (x) **Hagan**, Benjamin **Reed**, Matelda (x) **Reed**, Vincent (x) **Greeny**, Mary (x) **Greeny**, Aloysius **Reed**. Wit Corns. M. **Slattery** (JP), Lewis **Moore**. [No recording date]

66. Page 42. 30 July 1822. Thomas **Donohue** to Henry **Dodge** of Ste. Genevieve Co. For securing a debt for $103 to the Branch Bank of Missouri, mortgage on the undivided moiety of __ acres on the bank of the Mississippi in Bois Brulla Bottom, where Joseph **Donohue** resided at the time of his death, and which stands mortgaged to David L. **Caldwell** and Rowland **Boyd** as security for payment of $200; also all the hogs sd **Donohue** has under his mark. Signed Thos. **Donnohue**. Wit D. L. **Caldwell**, Corns. M. **Slattery** (JP). Rec 13 Jul 1822.

67. Page 43. 15 Jul 1822. Richard S. **Thomas** of Cape Girardeau Co. to William **McCasland** and Andrew M. **McCasland**. For the sum of $400, 200 acres in the Bois Brulle Bottom, part of 640 acres confirmed to William **Hickman**; beginning at the SE corner of a tract confirmed to sd **Hickman**, also the corner of Joseph **Allair**; and also bounded by Alexander **Mordock**. Signed Richard S. **Thomas**. Wit Timothy **Davis**, Corns. M. **Slattery** (JP). Rec 15 Jul 1822.

68. Page 44. 6 Dec 1820. Gustavus A. **Bird** of Ste. Genevieve, Mo. to William P. **McArthur**, John M. **McArthur**, Lewis L. **McArthur**, and Theodosia M. **McArthur**, minor children of John and Mary Ann **McArthur**. To confirm an earlier transaction, one undivided half of 450 arpens in Bois Brulle Bottom on the waters of Cape Cinq Hommes Creek, which was confirmed to Mary **Lockard**, and conveyed by her and James **Lockard** to David **Holly** and James **McLane**, and 1/2 of same conveyed to sd **Bird** by sd **Holly**. Sd **Bird** had previously conveyed the land to William **Linn** for $800, and sd **Linn** requires sd **Bird** to convey the tract to the parties of the second part. Signed G. A. **Bird**. Wit Thomas **Gholson**, Richard S. **Thomas**, Judge of 4th Judicial Circuit. Rec 2 Sep 1822.

69. Page 45. 27 Dec 1821. John F. **Henry** to Lewis F. **Linn** of Ste. Genevieve, Mo. For the sum of $2000, bond to make a deed to 300 arpens in Bois Brulle Bottom by 27 Dec 1826, being the upper half of a confirmed Spanish grant made to Alexander **McConnoahue**, and conveyed by sd **McConnohue** to __ **Robinson**, and by sd **Robinson** to John A. **Saunders**. Sd **Linn** is to take possession by 1 Mar next, and he binds himself to pay sd **Henry** $2000 within 10 years, with 6% interest, and agrees to set out an apple orchard of selected fruit, containing 400 trees set 40 feet apart, within two years. Sd tract to be sold at public sale if sd **Linn** does not pay the debt, and any excess from the sale is to go to sd **Linn**. Signed John F. **Henry**, Lewis F. **Linn**. Wit Beverley **Allen**, Henry **Millard**, Tho. **Oliver** (JP). Rec 3 Sep 1822.

70. Page 46. 13 Feb 1820. Will of Joseph **Moore** Sr. To his daughter Elizabeth for her natural life: 100 acres in the NW corner of his survey, surveyed as near as possible to the line between him and Mr. **Tucker**; after her natural life to descend to his daughter Barbara, provided she comes within seven years, and whom he appoints as guardian to his daughter Elizabeth, and to her eldest son if she does not come. To his daughter Elizabeth: the bed and furniture where he now lies, also choice of two cows, a mare, two ewes and lambs, all his pot metal, pewter, wheels, and cards; all to descend to son James and daughter Ann at her death. To his granddaughter Matilda: his loom and tackling. To his granddaughter Maria: his other bed and furniture. To his eight grandchildren Matilda, Maria, Thomas, Sabina, James, Ann, William, and Ignatius [children of his son James]: the remainder of his land. All other personal property to be sold to pay debts and educate the boys, except a certain shotgun to his grandson Thomas and books of devotion. Isidore **Moore** is appointed executor. Signed James **Moore** Sr. Wit Richard F. **Spalding**, Cornelius **Rhodes**, John (x) **May**. 8 Jul 1822. Codicil. To his granddaughter Matilda: 50 acres of the tract where he now lives, surveyed in a square from the corner next to Henry **Miles**; in lieu of her 1/8 portion. She and her husband shall not have the power to dispose of the land, but it shall descend to her children. Also, if his daughter Barbara or her eldest son shall not come to enjoy the part of the land intended for them, then it shall be equally distributed among the children of his son James after the death of his daughter Elizabeth. Signed James (x) **Moore**. Wit Joseph **Tucker**, Nicholas **Tucker**, Isidore **Moore**, Corns. M. **Slattery**, Clerk. 1 Aug 1822. Codicil. If his daughter Barbara does not come to reside on the land intended for her or her oldest son, then they shall not dispose of it, but remain for the benefit of the other heirs. John [covered] is appointed guardian of his daughter Elizabeth, is empowered to sell perishable property for her support, and provide her with sufficient pork, bacon, or hogs to support her for one year after the death of sd **Moore**, with any excess to go to his grandchildren. Should his granddaughter Matilda die without issue, then the 50 acres shall return to her brothers and sisters or their representatives. Signed James (x) **Moore**. Wit John **O'Conner**, John **May**, Isidore **Moore**, Corns. M. **Slattery**, Clerk. Rec 5 Sep 1822.

71. Page 48. 10 Oct 1822. Ezekiel B. **Herrick** to Gustavus A. **Bird**, both of Ste. Genevieve Co. For the sum of $480, mortgage on 300 acres, more or less, at the mouth of St. Laurent, devised to him by his uncle Amos **Bird**, decd; also negroes acquired by the same will: **Mylat**(?), **Oretia** and her children. A debt of $196 is due with interest in one year; sd **Bird** is security for a note by sd **Herrick** and sd **Bird** to Stephen [covered] for about $102, and a note is due to the State of Mo. Loan Office for $192. Signed E. B. **Herrick**. Test J. T. **Sprigg**, Corns. M. **Slattery** (JP). Rec 14 Oct 1822. [Marginal note: Full satisfaction received on 25 Mar 1825. Signed G. A. **Bird**.]

72. Page 49. 1 Oct 1822. John **Logan** to Henry **Seybert**. For the sum of $3000, 1/2 of 640 acres on Apple Creek, confirmed to Frances **Barthieme**; beginning at a post on the N bank of Apple Creek; including 1/2 of the mill on sd parcel, and the dwelling houses and 30 acres attached thereto, to include the cleared land E of the houses. Signed John **Logan**, Marier **Logan**. Wit Philip **Davis**, Benjamin **Davis** (JP). Rec 30 Oct 1822.

73. Page 50. 7 Oct 1822. James **Henderson** to Francis **Kenner** and William **Hondcock**. For the sum of $640, __ acres on the Cedar Fork of Saline, lying above Roland **Boid**'s survey; originally settled by Henry **Tucker**, and sold by sd **Tucker** to James **Henderson**. Signed James (x) **Henderson**. Wit Roland **Boid**, Phlip **Painter**, Corns. M. **Slattery** (JP). Rec 19 Nov 1822.

74. Page 51. 19 Nov 1822. Luke Edward **Lawless** by Sheriff Robert T. **Brown** to Aristides **Auduze**. For the sum of $305.86 1/2, 640 acres on the waters of Brazeau Creek, originally confirmed to Robert **Hinkston**. Sold on 19 Nov 1822 on decree of Circuit Court issued Jul 1822 in favor of John **Scott** and against sd **Lawless**. Signed R. T. **Brown**, Sheriff. Wit Corns. M. **Slattery**, Clerk. Rec 19 Nov 1822.

75. Page 51. 24 Jul 1822. Thomas **Riney** and Sarah, his wife, to Bernard **Brown**. For the sum of $340, 240 acres in Cinque Hommes Twp, on which sd **Brown** resides; beginning at a stone on the line of a survey confirmed to John **Grenewalt**; also bounded by sd **Riney**. Signed Thomas **Riney**, Sary (x) **Riney**. Wit Corns. M. **Slattery** (JP). Rec 25 Nov 1822.

76. Page 52. 25 Nov 1822. Bernard **Brown** to Thomas **Riney**. Release for a bond to convey 100 acres posted by sd **Riney** on 3 Dec 1807, and recorded in Ste. Genevieve Co. Deed Book A:207 (see 1:51). Signed Bernard (x) **Brown**. Wit Corns. M. **Slattery** (JP). Rec 25 Nov 1822.

77. Page 52. 18 Jan 1816. Charles **Ellis** and Sarah, his wife, to John **Burget**, all of Ste. Genevieve Co. For the sum of $250, __ acres in Bois Brulle Bottom known as the Pr_aria tract; adjoining Mark **Brooks** and by the _igg Pond; heretofore leased to Joseph **Donohue** Esq., decd, to Samuel **McCall**, and by sd **McCall** to John **Williams**, blacksmith; and being claimed by sd **Ellis** and Sarah **Ellis** as heirs by will of John **Newsom** Sr., decd. Signed Charles **Ellis**, Salley **Ellis**. Wit A. **Bird**, Daniel T. **Counsil**, Corns. M. **Slattery** (JP). Rec 30 Nov 1822.

78. Page 53. 9 Dec 1822. Alexander C. **Chesley** to Louisa Jane **Oklap** by her father John **Oklap**, of Ste. Genevieve Co. For the sum of $1000, 100 acres in Bois Brulle Bottom; that sd **Chesley** purchased from Alfred **Bird** on about 6 Aug 1821. Signed A. C. **Chesley**. Wit Corns. M. **Slattery** (JP). Rec 9 Dec 1822.

79. Page 54. 8 Dec 1822. John **Oklap**, father and guardian of Louisa Jane **Chesley**, to James **Clark**, both of Ste. Genevieve Co. Power of attorney to discharge a mortgage for $1000 paid by Alexander C. **Chesley**. The mortgage, dated 6 Aug 1821, was originally in favor of Alfred **Bird**, and was transferred to sd Louisa Jane (1:23). Signed John **Oklap**. Wit Thomas **Oliver**, Notary Public. Rec 9 Dec 1822.

80. Page 54. 10 Jun 1822. William **Russell** of St. Louis Co. and Henry **Elliott** of Ste. Genevieve Co. Deed of partition for 640 acres in Bois Brulle Bottom confirmed to John **Smith** Sr. Sd **Elliot** receives 315 acres, beginning at the N corner on the Mississippi River; and sd **Russell** receives 325 acres. Signed Wm. **Russell**, Henry **Elliott**. Wit Joshua **Barton**, R. **Easton**, N. B. **Tucker**, Judge of 3rd Judicial Circuit. Rec 24 Dec 1822.

81. Page 55. 7 Dec 1822. John **Logan** to Henry **Seibert**. For the sum of $2500, 640 acres, less 100 acres deeded to John **Logan** Sr., being 1/2 of a tract on Apple Creek confirmed to Francis **Barthume**; beginning at a stake on the N bank of Apple Creek. Signed John **Logan**, Marier **Logan** (RD). Wit Isaac **Cadwallader**, Benjamin **Davis** (JP). Rec 4 Jan 1823.

82. Page 56. 21 Oct 1822. Henry **Seibert** [and Katharine, his wife] to Isaac **Cadwallader**. For the sum of $2300, mortgage on 1/2 of 640 acres as described in 1:49. The debt is due in five payments: $700 due by 1 Apr 1823, $400 due by 1 Oct 1824, $400 due by 1 Oct 1825, $400 due by 1 Oct 1826, and $400 due by 1 Oct 1827. Otherwise, the tract to be sold by sd **Cadwallader** at public sale. Signed Henry **Seibert**, Katharine (x) **Seibert**. Wit Benjamin **Davis** (JP), Philip **Davis**. Rec 4 Jan 1823.

83. Page 58. 15 Apr 1822. John **Logan** Jr. [and Maria, his wife] to John **Logan** Sr. For the sum of $200, 100 acres on the waters of Apple Creek, part of a tract confirmed to Francis **Barchume**, and adjoining the SE line of sd survey, beginning at the NE corner of the survey. Signed John **Logan**. Wit Benjamin **Davis** (JP). Rec 24 Jan 1823.

84. Page 59. 22 Feb 1823. Henry J. **Rhodes** and Mitilda, his wife, to James B. **May**. For the sum of $85, 80 acres in the survey of James **Moore** Jr., decd, the father of sd Matilda; adjoined on the E by land confirmed to Bede **Moore**, and W by the confirmation of James **More**, son of Nicholas **More**. Signed Henry J. (x) **Rhodes**, Matilda (x) **Rhodes**. Wit Corns. M. **Slattery** (JP). Rec 22 Feb 1823.

85. Page 60. 5 Nov 1812. Isaac **Kester** to Francis **Kenner** of the Ste. Genevieve Dist. For the sum of $__, 640 acres on the N branch of the S fork of Saline Creek, that was first settled by Henry **Tucker**, and sold by him to James **Henderson**, by sd **Henderson** to Archibald **Huddleston**, and by sd **Huddleston** to sd **Kester**; 250 arpens was confirmed to sd **Kester** by the U. S. Commissioners. Sd **Kester** binds himself for $1000 to keep the deed good and safe. Signed Isaac **Kester**. Wit Joseph **Tucker**, William (x) **Cozens**, Tho. **Oliver**, Recorder (Ste. Genevieve Co. Book B, folio 298-299). Title is assigned to William **Hancock** and Britten **West** for value received on 19 Aug 1819. Signed Francis **Kenner**. Test Alexr. **Richard**, Tho. **Oliver**, Clerk. Britten **West** is released from the debt for the sum of $1 paid by Francis **Kenner**, and reconveys his claim to sd **Kenner**. Signed Britten **West**. Wit Thos **Oliver** (JP). Rec 24 Feb 1823.

86. Page 61. 11 Dec 1822. William **Searsy** and Rosanna Wallace **Searcy**, his wife, to William **Shannon** of Ste. Genevieve Co. For the sum of $1500, two tracts; the undivided 1/2 of 800 arpens fronting on the Mississippi in Bois Brulle Bottom; the settlement right of John **Smith** Sr., which he conveyed to William **Russell** (Ste. Genevieve Co. Book B:365); and which sd **Russell** conveyed to sd **Smith** (C:85), and which sd **Smith** conveyed to sd **Searcy** on 9 Nov 1818 (C:126); adjoined by land that Robert **Smith** conveyed to Henry **Elliott** and that is the original claim of Isaac **Devee**; and 1/2 of 640 acres in Brooks Prairie in Bois Brulle Bottom, being the share of sd **Searcy** in land that he and sd **Shannon** hold jointly, purchased from Thomas **Donohue** (C:164), who purchased from Roland **Meredith** in his lifetime (B:308), and being the original claim of sd **Meredith**. Signed W. **Searcy**, Rosannah W. **Searcy**. Wit Tho. **Oliver**, Clerk of Ste. Genevieve Co., H. B. **Newsom**. Corns. M. **Slattery**, Clerk. Rec 25 Feb 1823.

87. Page 62. 19 Feb 1823. John **Donohue** of Ste. Genevieve Co. to George F. **Strother** of St. Louis. For the sum of $479, mortgage on 640 acres on Cape Cinque Hommes Creek, confirmed to Benjamin **Cox** as his settlement right. Sd **Strother** has been appointed the attorney of the U. S. to collect a debt owed by the Bank of Missouri, to which sd **Donohue** has become indebted, the debt due with interest in one year. Signed John **Donohue**. Wit Tho. **Oliver**, JP in Ste. Genevieve Co., Timothy **Davis**. Rec 18 Mar 1823.

88. Page 63. 22 Mar 1823. Henry **Clark** to John **Logan** Jr. For the sum of $62.50, 50 acres in Bois Brulle Twp, part of land confirmed to sd **Clark**; bounded on the N by Francis **Clark**'s heirs, E by land confirmed to John **Graham**, S by a line yet to be run, and W by the original line of the survey. Signed Henry **Clark**. Wit H_____ **Caldwell**, D. L. **Caldwell**, JCC. Rec 1 Apr 1823.

89. Page 64. 14 Sep 1820. Will of Alexander **Patterson** [Sr.]. To his wife Rebecca: his home plantation for her life, with sufficient firewood and timber to keep the same in repair, also his cattle, horses, hogs, farming utensils and household furniture, and stock of sheep. To his eldest son William: 100 acres adjoining his plantation below on the Mississippi River, whereon he has cleared a two-acre field according to a survey made by Henry **Clark** which is either lost, mislaid, or destroyed. To his eldest daughter Mary **Guitar**, 100 acres below him on the Mississippi River according to the running of Henry **Clark**, adjoining Isaac **Meredith** on the lower side. To his second daughter Sarah **Kennedy**, 100 acres adjoining the land given to his son William on the lower side and between that land and the land given to Mary **Guitar**, and where she and her husband now live, but she nor her husband can never dispose of the same, and it should descend to her children at her death. To his second son Alexander, 100 acres on the back part of his land, adjoining sd **Meredith**, being 1/2 of 200 acres run by sd **Clark**. To his youngest son John, 100 acres of his home plantation after the death of his wife Rebecca. His sons William and John are to dispose of the 40 acres of his house plantation not heretofore bequeathed, and the remaining 100 acres of his land to be equally divided among his children if he does not sell it during his lifetime. His son William **Patterson** to be executor. Signed Alexander (x) **Patterson**. Wit Joab **Waters** senr., Joab **Waters** Jr., Daniel **Meredith**. 12 Mar 1823. Codicil. To his second son Alexander: 200 acres assessed by Henry **Clark** at the back of sd **Patterson**'s survey. Signed Alexander (x) **Patterson**. Test Joab **Waters** senr. Joab **Waters** Junr., Mos. A. **Massey**, Corns. M. **Slattery**, Clerk. Rec 8 Apr 1823.

90. Page 65. 24 Jun 1820. Archibald **Morgan** to Mark **Brooks**, both of Ste. Genevieve Co. For the sum of $2000, bond to make a deed on 200 acres in Bois Brulle Bottoms, part of a tract confirmed to John **Morgan**, decd; bounded on the S by Benajah **Morgan** and David **Morgan**, E & W by vacant land, and N by the heirs of John **Morgan**, decd. The tract has been sold for $1200, $900 paid by Oct next, and $300 by Oct 1821; the deed to be made upon full payment. Signed A. **Morgan**. Wit A. **Bird**, D. L. **Caldwell**, JP in Ste. Genevieve Co., John (x) **Morgan**, R. T. **Brown**. Rec 12 May 1823.

91. Page 66. 4 Apr 1823. William **Girty** and Charity, his wife, of Scott Co., Mo. to George **Camster**. For the sum of $840, 420 arpents; bounded on the N by the Mississippi River, E by Neal **Hornback**, and W by Alexander **McConnohue**; confirmed to William **FitzGibbons**. Signed William (x) **Girty**, Charrity (x) **Girty**. Wit H. **Clark** (JP), J. P. **Graham**. Rec 12 May 1823.

92. Page 66. 7 Dec 1822. Henry **Seibert** [and Kathran, his wife] to John **Logan**. For the sum of $2500, mortgage on 1/2 of 640 acres on Apple Creek confirmed to Francis **Barthume**, less 100 acres sold to John **Logan** senior; beginning at a corner post on the N bank of Apple Creek. The debt to be paid as $500 due 7 Dec next, $500 in good merchantable whiskey at the market price due 7 Dec 1824, $500 in whiskey due 7 Dec 1825, $500 in whiskey due 7 Dec 1826, and $500 in whiskey due 7 Dec 1827. Signed Henry **Seibert** [in German]. Wit Benjamin **Davis** (JP). Rec 23 May 1823. [Marginal note: Full satisfaction received by John **Logan** on 4 Dec 1851, and recorded in Book 8:13.]

93. Page 68. 13 May 1823. Robert T. **Brown**, Joseph **Tucker**, and Thomas **Riney**, Commissioners of Perryville, to David **Bollinger**. For the sum of $15.50, Lot No. 56 in Perryville. Signed R. T. **Brown**, Thomas **Riney**, Joseph **Tucker** senr., Commissioners. Wit Corns. M. **Slattery** (JP). Rec 23 May 1823.

94. Page 68. 24 May 1823. Same to Aequila **Hagan**. For the sum of $41, Lot No. 63 in Perryville. Signed R. T. **Brown**, Joseph **Tucker** senr., Thomas **Riney**, Commissioners. Wit Corns. M. **Slattery** (JP). Rec 24 May 1823.

95. Page 69. 24 May 1823. Same to Isidore **Moore**. For the sum of $79, Lot Nos. 9 & 33 in Perryville. Signed R. T. **Brown**, Joseph **Tucker** senr., Thomas **Riney**, Commissioners. Wit Corns. M. **Slattery** (JP). Rec 24 May 1823.

96. Page 70. 24 May 1823. Same to James C. **Moore**. For the sum of $21, Lot Nos. 12 & 27 in Perryville. Signed R. T. **Brown**, Joseph **Tucker** senr., Thomas **Riney**, Commissioners. Wit Corns. M. **Slattery** (JP). Rec 24 May 1823.

97. Page 70. 24 May 1823. Same to Joseph Z. **Wimsatt**. For the sum of $30.25, Lot No. 43 in Perryville. Signed R. T. **Brown**, Joseph **Tucker** senr., Thomas **Riney**, Commissioners. Wit Corns. M. **Slattery** (JP). Rec 24 May 1823.

98. Page 71. 24 May 1823. Same to William **McLane** and Wilfred **Layton**. For the sum of $32.25, Lot No. 42 in Perryville. Signed R. T. **Brown**, Joseph **Tucker** senr., Thomas **Riney**, Commissioners. Wit Corns. M. **Slattery** (JP). Rec 24 May 1823.

99. Page 72. 24 May 1823. Same to John **May**. For the sum of $12.25, Lot No. 11 in Perryville. Signed R. T. **Brown**, Joseph **Tucker** senr., Thomas **Riney**, Commissioners. Wit Corns. M. **Slattery** (JP). Rec 24 May 1823.

100. Page 72. 24 May 1823. Same to Robert **Abernathy**. For the sum of $27.25, Lot No. 49 in Perryville. Signed R. T. **Brown**, Joseph **Tucker** senr., Thomas **Riney**, Commissioners. Wit Corns. M. **Slattery** (JP). Rec 24 May 1823.

101. Page 73. 24 May 1823. Same to James F. **Abernathy** and George **Rutledge**. For the sum of $61.12 1/2, Lot Nos. 61 & 62 in Perryville. Signed R. T. **Brown**, Joseph **Tucker** senr., Thomas **Riney**, Commissioners. Wit Corns. M. **Slattery** (JP). Rec 24 May 1823.

102. Page 73. 24 May 1823. Same to Joseph **Snearbush**. For the sum of $13.25, Lot Nos. 13 & 15 in Perryville. Signed R. T. **Brown**, Joseph **Tucker** senr., Thomas **Riney**, Commissioners. Wit Corns. M. **Slattery** (JP). Rec 24 May 1823.

103. Page 74. 24 May 1823. Same to Rezin L. **Bishop**. For the sum of $19, Lot No. 10 in Perryville. Signed R. T. **Brown**, Joseph **Tucker** senr., Thomas **Riney**, Commissioners. Wit Corns. M. **Slattery** (JP). Rec 24 May 1823.

104. Page 75. 9 Jun 1823. Same to Barnabas **Burns**. For the sum of $71, Lot Nos. 34 & 58 in Perryville. Signed R. T. **Brown**, Joseph **Tucker** senr., Thomas **Riney**, Commissioners. Wit Corns. M. **Slattery** (JP). Rec 24 May 1823.

105. Page 75. 11 Aug 1823. John **Morgan** and Martha, his wife, to the heirs of Archibald **Morgan**, all of Bois Brulle Twp. For the sum of $524.75, 160 acres in Bois Brulle Twp, part of a tract confirmed to sd **Morgan**; bounded on the E by land confirmed to Andrew **Dunks**, S by land confirmed to the heirs of John **Morgan**, and W by Congress land. Signed John (x) **Morgan**, Martha (x) **Morgan**. Test D. L. **Caldwell**, Corns. M. **Slattery** (JP). Rec 11 Aug 1823.

106. Page 76. 28 Aug 1823. Frederick C. **Hase** to Joseph **Rosati**. In consideration of the conditions below and the sum of $1, 640 acres in Cinque Hommes Twp which sd **Hase** now occupies, and through which the road from Ste. Genevieve to Jackson runs; as confirmed to William **Middleton**. Sold to sd **Hase** for $500 on 3 Jul 1821, as sd **Rosati** is empowered to sell the land by a deed of trust dated 8 Mar 1820, and recorded in Ste. Genevieve Co., Book C:300-301. Signed Fredk. C. **Hase**. Wit Corns M. **Slattery** (JP). Rec 28 Aug 1823.

107. Page 77. 28 Aug 1823. Joseph **Rosati** to Frederick C. **Hase**. For the sum of $500, the land described in the preceding deed (1:76). Signed Joseph **Rosati**. Wit Corns. M. **Slattery** (JP). Rec 28 Aug 1823.

108. Page 78. 6 Sep 1823. Commissioners of Perryville to George **Hoar**. For the sum of $34.75, Lot Nos. 3, 25, & 26 in Perryville. Signed R. T. **Brown**, Thomas **Riney**, Joseph **Tucker**, Commissioners. Wit Corns. M. **Slattery** (JP). Rec 6 Sep 1823.

109. Page 78. 23 Jan 1812. James **Heydon** and Mary, his wife, to George **Fenwick**, all of the Ste. Genevieve Dist. For the sum of $111, all the land allowed them from the estate of sd **Heydon**'s father. Signed James **Hayden**, Mary (x) **Hayden**. Test Zachariah **Layton**, William **Tucker**, Corns. M. **Slattery** (JP). Rec 13 Sep 1823.

110. Page 79. 4 Oct 1823. Wilfred **Layton** and Susanna, his wife, to John Baptist **Layton**. For the sum of $37.75, 400 arpens on the S fork of Saline Creek, including part of the branch that descends from Nicholas **Tucker**'s spring; purchased from Maj. John **Hawkins** and Rebeckah, his wife on 15 Oct 1808 by Joseph **Layton**, decd, from Washington Co., Ky., of whom the contracting parties are two of the heirs. Signed Wilfred **Layton**, Susanna (x) **Layton**. Wit Alby **McLain**, Corns. M. **Slattery** (JP). Rec 4 Oct 1823.

111. Page 80. 25 Jul 1823. Cecili **Miles** to Henry **Miles**. For the sum of $26.25, 21 1/9 acres, being an undivided part of 640 acres granted to Joseph **Miles**, and the same tract where sd Henry now lives. Signed Ceilia **Miles**. Wit John **Layton** (JP). Rec 15 Oct 1823.

112. Page 80. 4 Apr 1823. William **Girty** and Charrity, his wife, of Scott Co., Mo. to George **Camster**. For the sum of $840, 420 arpens, French measure, confirmed to William **FitzGibbons**; bounded on the N by the Mississippi River, E by land confirmed to Noel **Hornbeck**, and W by Alexander **McConnohue**. Signed William (x) **Girty**, Charrity **Girty**. Wit H. **Clark** (JP), J. P. **Graham**, Corns. M. **Slattery** (JP). Rec 23 Oct 1823.

113. Page 81. 8 Sep 1823. Thomas **Dodge** to Lewis Paul **Dezier** of Madison Co., Mo. For the sum of $120, mortgage on one bay mare, three cows, and three yearlings. The debt is due by 25 Dec

1823 in a note of even date. Signed Thos. **Dodge**. Wit W. **Wilkinson**, JCC. Rec 26 Oct 1823.

114. Page 82. 12 Nov 1823. Thomas **Allen** to Aequila **Hagan**. For the sum of $155, 320 acres in Cinque Hommes Twp; being 1/2 of a tract confirmed to sd **Allen**, with the line to run through the center of the survey; bounded on the N, W & S by public land, and E by Ansel **Ferrell** and land purchased by sd **Hagan** of sd **Allen** on 22 Oct 1821 (1:26). Signed Thomas **Allen**. Wit James C. **Moore**, Corns. M. **Slattery** (JP). Rec 12 Nov 1823.

115. Page 83. 17 Nov 1823. John F. **Henry**, now of Christian Co., Ky., and Lewis F. **Linn** of Ste. Genevieve Co. Articles of agreement between the two parties dated 27 Dec 1821 (1:45) are null and void. Signed John F. **Henry**, Lewis F. **Linn**. Wit Tho. **Oliver**, JP in Ste. Genevieve Co. Rec 21 Nov 1823.

116. Page 83. 19 Jun 1823. Matthew **Duncan** by Ste. Genevieve Co. Sheriff Francis **Valle** to Lewis F. **Linn** and John **Oklap**. For the sum of $9.50, 350 arpens on the N side of Saline Creek, part of 500 acres originally claimed by James **Maxwell**. Sold on the first Monday of Nov 1821 to pay $6 of delinquent taxes assessed by former Ste. Genevieve Co. Sheriff Henry **Dodge**. Signed Frois **Valli**, Sheriff. Wit Tho. **Oliver**, Circuit Court Clerk, Ste. Genevieve Co. Rec 21 Aug 1823.

117. Page 84. [marked through] Henry **Seibert** to Gustavus A. **Bird** and John **Logan** of Apple Creek. For the sum of $2500, quit claim to a tract they hold as tenants in common [end of entry; see next deed].

118. Page 85. 7 Dec 1822. John **Logan** to Henry **Seibert**. For the sum of $2500, 1/2 of 640 acres on Apple Creek, confirmed to Francis **Barthume**, less 100 acres sold to John **Logan**, senor; beginning at a stake on the N bank of Apple Creek. Signed John **Logan**, Marier **Logan**. Wit Isaac **Cadwallader**, Benjamin **Davis** (JP). __ Nov 1823. Henry **Seibert** to Gustavus A. **Bird** and John **Logan**. For the sum of $2500, quit claim to the tract described above, conveyed to sd **Seibert** by sd **Logan** and wife. His wife RD. Signed Henry **Seibert**. Wit T. **Davis**, E. **Walsh**, Corns. M. **Slattery** (JP). Rec 21 Nov 1823.

119. Page 86. 19 Sep 1823. William **Polk** of Cape Girardeau Co. to [his son] John **Polk**. For the sum of $50. 100 acres, more or less, on Whitewater, part of a 640 acre survey; beginning on William **Polk**'s corner near the stone chimney. Signed William **Polk**. Wit Daniel **Killian**, William **Polk** Junr, Corns. M. **Slattery** (JP). Rec 29 Nov 1823.

120. Page 87. 1 Dec 1823. John **Logan** of Apple Creek to Gustavus A. **Bird**, atty at law. For the sum of $1050, 1/4 part of 540 acres in Perry & Cape Girardeau counties, part of a tract of 640 acres confirmed to Francis **Bartheaum**, decd, of which 100 acres was sold to John **Logan** Sr., and on which there are a saw mill and small grist mill; the interest conveyed to John **Logan** [Jr.] by Henry **Seibert**. Signed John **Logan**, James **Russell**. Wit Richard S. **Thomas**, Judge of 4th Judicial Circuit. Rec 3 Dec 1823.

121. Page 88. 5 Dec 1823. Tunas **Quick** and Nancy, his wife, to Clement **Knott**. For the sum of $426, 213 acres and 25 perches in The Barrens, part of their Spanish settlement grant; beginning at the SW corner of the survey. Signed Tunis **Quick**, Nancy (x) **Quick**. Wit Isidore **Moore**, Corns. M. **Slattery** (JP). Rec 5 Dec 1823.

122. Page 89. 9 Dec 1823. Daniel **Donnohue** of Clarke Co., Ky. to Thomas **Wright**. For the sum of $102, 34 acres, more or less, bounded on the N by the Mississippi River at or near the head of Boisbrula Bottom; part of a grant to Joseph **Donnohue**, ancestor of sd Daniel, and being the part that descended to Daniel **Donnohue** as an heir of Joseph **Donnohue**, decd. Should the land be lost to a better claim, then the purchase price is to be refunded. Signed Daniel **Donnohue**. Test Robert D. **Hart**, Dep Clerk of Clarke Co., Ky., David B. **Young**. Rec 31 Dec 1823.

123. Page 89. 2 Feb 1824. Joseph Z. **Wimsatt** to James & Benedict **McCauley**, children and heirs of William **McCauley**. For natural love and affection and the sum of $1, two feather beds, four coverlets and the furniture to them belonging; one sete of cooper's tools; one anville No. 314 weight 98 pounds; one still containing about 90 gallons; 20 still tubs; five cows; three yearlings; three two year old steers next spring; one gray horse; three chopping axes; one pot; one oven; one stew kettle; one sett tea cups & saucers; one sett teaspoons; 1 dozen crocks; one sett pewter plates and two basons of pewter ware; one sett knives and forks; four hoes; three briddles & two saddles. Signed Joseph Z. **Wimsatt**. Wit James **Hayden**, Robert **Wimsatt**, R. T. **Brown**, Corns. M. **Slattery** (JP). Rec 2 Feb 1824.

124. Page 90. 16 Feb 1824. Bernard **Layton** and Mary, his wife, to Joseph **James** Junr. For the sum of $75, part of a lot in Perryville, beginning at a stake at the SE corner of Lot No. 3; bounded by George **Hore** and sd **Layton**. Signed Bernard **Layton**, Mary (x) **Layton**. Wit Corns. M. **Slattery** (JP). Rec 16 Feb 1824.

125. Page 91. 6 Feb 1824. Same and same to Joseph **Cissell**. For the sum of $175, 140 acres and 9 perches on the waters of Cinque Hommes Creek, part of a tract donated to the County for the seat of justice; beginning at a set stone on the SE line of the original survey, and bounded by William **McLane**. Signed Bernard **Layton**, Mary (x) **Layton**. Wit Joseph **James** Jur., Corns. M. **Slattery** (JP). Rec 26 Feb 1824.

126. Page 92. 28 Dec 1822. Francis **Valle** of Ste. Genevieve, Mo. to Charles C. **Valle**. For the sum of $2000, negro slaves; **Gabriel** age about 40, **Catharine** age about 29, **Adiel** age about 14, **Marceler** age about 10, **Paul** age about 4, and **Henry** age about 2. Signed Frois **Valle**. Wit Corns. M. **Slattery** (JP), R. T. **Brown**. Rec 27 Feb 1824.

127. Page 93. 27 Feb 1824. John **Harris** to Thomas **Wilson**. For the sum of $360, two negro boys named **Bob** and **Jim**. Signed John **Harris**. Test A. **Burns**, Corns. M. **Slattery** (JP). Rec 13 Mar 1824.

128. Page 93. 21 Feb 1824. Richard S. **Thomas** and Frances, his wife, to Claiborne S. **Thomas**, all of Cape Girardeau Co. For the sum of $880, 440 acres in Bois Brulle Bottom, part of a tract confirmed to William **Hickman**, and transferred by him to Robert **Reynolds**, and by sd **Reynolds** to Richard S. **Thomas**; the remainder of the tract was previously conveyed to William **McCasland** and ___ **McCasland**. Signed Richard S. **Thomas**, Frances **Thomas**. Wit Eliza Ann **Thomas**, David **Armour**, JP in Cape Girardeau Co. Rec 7 Apr 1824.

129. Page 94. 27 Feb 1824. Claiborne S. **Thomas** to John **Juden** Junior, both of Cape Girardeau Co. For the sum of $1320, 440 acres as described in the preceding deed (1:93). Signed Claiborne S. **Thomas**. Wit Peter R. **Garrett**, JP in Cape Girardeau Co. Rec 7 Apr 1824.

130. Page 95. 26 Apr 1824. Bernard **Layton** and Mary, his wife, of Cape Girardeau Co., to Benjamin **Wilson**. For 160 acres in Cape Girardeau Co., and the sum of $100, 266 acres in Cinque Hommes Twp, confirmed to sd **Layton** by the Commissioners; beginning at the NE corner of the original survey, and bounded by Ignatius **Layton**, John **Layton**, William **McLane**, ___ **Duvall**, Joseph **Cissell**, Joseph **James** Jr., George **Hoare**, and the town of Perryville. Signed Bernard **Layton**, Mary (x) **Layton**. Wit John **Layton** (JP), Ignatius **Layton**. Rec 1 May 1824.

131. Page 97. 1 Oct 1823. Thomas **Oliver** of Ste. Genevieve Co. to John **Huston**, late of Ky. and now of Ind. For the sum of $50, quit claim to the preemption right of Isaac **Beard** in Bois Brule Bottom opposite the head of Cape Cinque Hommes Island, that sd **Huston** and sd **Oliver** purchased from John **Stewart** on 16 Jun 1819; also to any other land he holds in common with sd **Huston** and that he purchased from sd **Stewart** and that he promised to procure from the heirs of David **Stuart**, decd, at the head of Cape Cinque Hommes Island. Signed Tho. **Oliver**. Wit Jos. D. **Grafton**, JCC in Ste. Genevieve Co. Rec 1 May 1824.

132. Page 97. 2 Sep 1823. Will of Rosannah **Caldwell**. All her stock and other property except the negroes and items disposed of in the will to be sold and the money divided as directed. To her daughter Margaret **Tuttle**: all her household furniture except one bed and furniture, which is to go to her son Robert. To her daughter Rosannah Wallace **Searcy**: one choice cow. To her daughter Margaret **Tuttle**, son Robert, and son James: $400 each to be paid in negroes at their valuation. To her son David L.: $800 to be paid in negros at their valuation. To her daughter Margaret **Tuttle** and son Robert: 1/6 part each of the balance of her negroes, money arising from sale of stock, and other property. To her daughter Polly Ann Elizabeth **Waters**: 1/6 part of same for her natural life, and to be divided equally among her children, except James L. **Waters**, at her death. To her son David L.: 1/3 part of same. To her son James C.: 1/6 part of same. Sons Robert and David L. are appointed executors. Signed Rosannah **Caldwell**. Wit William **Boyd**, Francis **Clark**, William **Flynn**, Corns. M. **Slattery**, Clerk. Rec 1 May 1824.

133. Page 98. 4 May 1824. Alfred **Bird** to Thomas **Oliver** for the use of John **Oklap** and James **Clark** of Ste. Genevieve Co. For securing a debt and the sum of $1, deed of trust on 157 acres, more on less, on the Mississippi River in Bois Brule Bottom; joined on the upper side (N) by land heretofore conveyed to Louisa Jane **Oklap**, daughter of sd **Oklap**, S by William **Morris**, and W by Lawrence **Clark** and others; also two negro girls, **Leah** above 10 years old, and **Lucretia** about 7 years old. Sd **Bird** is indebted to sd **Oklap** and sd **Clark** for $263 in two notes dated 4 May 1824, one for $100 due by 4 Oct next, the other for $163 due on the same date with 10% interest per annum. Sd notes are delivered to Thomas **Oliver** as trustee, who is to sell the property at public sale if the debt is not paid. Signed A. **Bird**. Wit Thomas **Oliver**, Clerk of Ste. Genevieve Co. Rec 5 May 1824.

134. Page 99. 1 Mar 1822. Medical Society of Lexington, University of Transylvania. This is to certify that Richard S. **Dorsey** was admitted a younger fellow (member) of the Medical Society of Lexington, and is recommended to every friend of Philosophy and Medicine. Signed H. **Miller**, President, H. Glen(?) **Doyle**, Secret. Rec 5 May 1824.

135. Page 100. 19 Aug 1823. Elisha **Bellsha** and Mary, his wife, to James **Phillips**. For the sum of $90, 50 acres, part of a tract sold by Johnathan **Preston** to Wm. **Hooks**, and sold by sd **Hooks** to sd **Bellsha**; beginning at the SW corner of a survey confirmed to sd **Preston**. Signed Elisha **Bellsha**, Poley (x) **Bellsha**. Wit John **Layton** (JP). Rec 1 Jun 1824.

136. Page 101. 23 Jun 1824. William **McGuire** to Claiborne S. **Thomas**, both of Cape Girardeau Co., Mo. For the sum of $500, bond to convey 134.15 acres, being 1/2 of 270. 30 acres in 6 tracts in Twp 36 N, Rng 12 E, purchased from the U. S. jointly with John **Juden** Jr.: NW fractional 1/4, Sec 16 (75 acres); SE fractional 1/4, Sec __ (22.74 acres); NE fractional 1/4, Sec 17 (48.59 acres); NW fractional 1/4, Sec 21 (31.57 acres); N fractional 1.2, Sec 22 (41.84 acres); and W fractional 1/2, Sec 26 (50.47 acres). Sold to sd **Thomas** at the rate of $2/acre, and to be conveyed when sd **McGuire** receives the patents for sd tracts. Signed Wm. **McGuire**. Wit Peter R. **Garrett**, JP in Cape Girardeau Co. Rec 25 Jun 1824.

137. Page 101. 31 May 1822. Samuel **Mansker** [and Nancy, his wife] of Randolph Co., Ill. to Presley **Kennison**. For the sum of $750, 100 acres, more or less, being an undivided 1/6 of 600 arpens in Bois Brulle Bottom on the Mississippi River; being formerly owned by Absolum **Kennison**, decd, and devised by him to his son John, sold by him to George **Cockrane** (Ste. Genevieve Co. Book C:50), and by sd **Cockran** and Mariah, his wife, to sd **Mansker** on 7 Apr 1822. Signed Samuel **Mansker**, Nancy **Mansker**. Wit George **Camster**, Elisha **Eggers**, Barnabas **Burns** (JP). Rec 10 Aug 1824.

138. Page 102. 16 Aug 1821. Abner **Kennison** and Louisa, his wife, of Cape Girardeau Co. to same. For the sum of $600, 150 arpens in Bois Brulle Bottom, 100 of which was willed to sd Abner by his father Absolom **Kennison**, and 50 of which was purchased from Joel **Kennison**. Signed Abner **Kennison**. Wit John F. **Henry** (JP). Rec 10 Aug 1824.

139. Page 103. 9 Aug 1824. Joseph **Manning** and Mary, his wife, to Rezin L. **Bishop**, all of Cinque Hommes Twp. For the sum of $190, 96 1/4 acres and 24 perches, part of a tract confirmed to John **Layton**, decd, father-in-law of sd **Manning** and father of Mary, his wife, agreeable to a survey made by Isidore **Moore**; beginning at a stake S of the quarter post; and bounded by Ignatius **Layton**. Signed Joseph **Manning**, Mary (x) **Manning**. Wit Corns. M. **Slattery**, Clerk, David L. **Caldwell**, Lewis **Cissell**, Walr. **Wilkinson**, Esq, JCC. Rec 10 Aug 1824.

140. Page 104. 20 Jul 1824. James **Fenwick** to Levi **Hagan**. For the sum of $197.29 1/2, mortgage on 500 arpens on the waters of Apple Creek, where Daniel **Cunningham** now resides; being James **Fenwick**'s part of 3000 arpens granted by the Spanish Government to his father Joseph **Fenwick**. The debt is the balance of a note for $300 dated 15 Jan 1818 and due in 18 months. Signed James J. **Fenwick**. Test Josiah F. **Hamilton**, John **Layton** (JP). Rec 19 Sep 1824.

141. Page 105. 8 Jul 1824. William **McLane** to Mark **Manning**. For the sum of $100, mortgage on 160 acres, more or less, , part of Bernard **Layton**'s old survey and where sd **McLane** now resides. The debt is due in a note of even date. Signed William (x) **McLane**. Test John **Layton**, Corns. M. **Slattery** (JP). Rec 23 Sep 1824. [Marginal note: CUT OFF OF FILM IN PART Signed Alexues **Manning**, Execr of Mark **Manning**, decd, _____ widow of Mark **Manning**, decd.]

142. Page 105. 16 Mar 1824. Henry **Clark** by Sheriff Robert T. **Brown** to Timothy **Davis**. For the sum of $72, two tracts in Bois Brulle Township; 640 acres, more or less, on the Mississippi River, said to have been confirmed to John **Dunks**; and 640 acres, more or less, said to have been confirmed to Andrew **Dunks**. Sold on 18 Nov 1823 on a writ of execution from Circuit Court dated 18 Oct 1823 in favor of John **Morgan** and against Francis **Clark** and Henry **Clark** for $114. Signed R. T. **Brown**, Sheriff. Wit Corns. M. **Slattery**, Clerk. Rec 21 Oct 1824.

143. Page 106. 15 Oct 1824. Timothy **Davis** and Nancy, his wife, to John **Scott** and Beverley **Allen**, all of Ste. Genevieve Co., Mo. For the sum of $90, the two tracts described in the preceding deed (1:105). Signed Timothy **Davis**, Nancy W. **Davis**, John **Scott**, Beverly **Allen**. Wit Tho. **Oliver**, Clerk of Ste. Genevieve Co. Court. Rec 21 Oct 1824.

144. Page 107. 9 Jun 1824. John **Duvall** and Penelope **Bird**. Marriage contract. Penelope **Bird** shall retain all power, right, and authority for her own separate use and benefit to her property and effects, and anything she may acquire or accrue because of sd property. Each shall be liable for their own separate debts and responsibilities, and no debt shall accrue to both of them except by signed document. Sd **Duvall** is also not liable for any accident, waste, destitution, or decay of her property. Should she survive him, she is entitled to a dower, or 1/3, of all of the property he acquires during her marriage, and should he survive her, she may disposed of the same by will. Signed John **Duvall**, Penelope (x) **Bird**. Wit R. T. **Brown**, T. **Wright**, Timothy **Davis**, Corns. M. **Slattery**, Clerk. Rec 21 Oct 1824.

145. Page 108. 13 Apr 1824. James C. **Caldwell** to Robert **Caldwell**, both of Catahoula Parish, La. Power of attorney to demand his share of the estate of and from the execrs of the last will and testament of Rosannah **Caldwell**, decd. Signed James C. **Caldwell**, G. W. **Matthews**, S. M. **Heakins**, Sam. **Lightner**, Parish Judge of Catahoula Parish, La. Rec 7 Dec 1824.

146. Page 109. 13 Nov 1824. John **Duvall** to Ann Arpy **Abernathy**, wife of Robert **Abernathy**. For love, affection, and good will to his daughter, equal 1/2 of 200 arpents, valued at $500, originally granted to sd **Duvall**; beginning at the SW corner of the survey. This land is to be deducted from her portion of the estate of sd **Duvall**. Signed John **Duvall**. Wit Rezin L. **Bishop**, John **Layton** (JP). Rec 7 Dec 1824.

147. Page 110. 13 Nov 1824. Same to his son Joseph **Duvall**. For love, affection, and good will, 200 arpents on the head of the McLenahan's Creek, the W branch of Cinque Hommes Creek; originally granted to William **Boyce** by concession, and adjoined on the W by sd John **Duvall**'s grant; valued at $500, and being an advancement on his portion of the estate of sd **Duvall**. Signed John **Duvall**. Wit John **Layton** (JP), Rezin L. **Bishop**. Rec 11 Dec 1824.

148. Page 110. 23 Jul 1824. John **Donohue** by Sheriff Robert T. **Brown** to Timothy **Davis**. For the sum of $61, 340 acres, more or less, on the waters of Cape Cinque Hommes Creek; part of a tract of 640 acres confirmed to Benjamin **Cox**. Sold on 16 Mar 1823 on a writ of execution issued by Ste. Genevieve Co. Circuit Court on 17 Nov 1823, in favor of Henry B. **Newsom**, and against sd **Donohue** for $126.54 1/2 damages for nonperformance of certain promises. Signed R. T. **Brown**, Sheriff. Wit Cornelius M. **Slattery**, Clerk. Rec 11 Dec 1824.

149. Page 112. 30 Dec 1824. Commissioners of Perryville to Thomas **Cody**. For the sum of $32.75, Lot Nos. 51, 50, & 94 in Perryville. Signed R. T. **Brown**, Thomas **Riney**, Joseph **Tucker** senr., Commissioners. Wit Edw. **Walsh**, Corns. M. **Slattery** (JP). Rec 30 Dec 1824.

150. Page 113. 2 Aug 1823. Commissioners of Perryville to Clement **Knott**. For the sum of $43, Lot No. 64 in Perryville. Signed R. T. **Brown**, Joseph **Tucker** senr., Thomas **Riney**, Commissioners. Wit Corns. M. **Slattery** (JP). Rec 30 Dec 1824.

151. Page 113. 30 Dec 1824. Commissioners of Perryville to Thomas **Riney**. For the sum of $21, Lot No. 68 in Perryville. Signed R. T. **Brown**, Joseph **Tucker** senr., Commissioners. Wit Edwd. **Walsh**, Corns. M. **Slattery** (JP). Rec 30 Dec 1824.

152. Page 114. 30 Dec 1824. Commissioners of Perryville to John **Layton**. For the sum of $69, Lot Nos. 46 & 59 in Perryville. Signed R. T. **Brown**, Thomas **Riney**, Joseph **Tucker** senr., Commissioners. Wit Corns. M. **Slattery** (JP). Rec 30 Dec 1824.

153. Page 114. 30 Dec 1824. Commissioners of Perryville to Joseph **James** Jr. For the sum of $15, Lot No. 24 in Perryville. Signed R. T. **Brown**, Thomas **Riney**, Joseph **Tucker** senr., Commissioners. Wit Corns. M. **Slattery** (JP). Rec 30 Dec 1824.

154. Page 115. 7 Jun 1824. Joseph **James** Jr. and Elizabeth, his wife, to Tunis **Quick**. For the sum of $25, Lot No. 24 in Perryville, purchased from the Commissioners on 11 May 1822 [but see previous deed, 1:114]. Signed Joseph **James** Jr., Elizabeth (x) **James**. Wit Corns. M. **Slattery** (JP). Rec 30 Dec 1824.

155. Page 116. 8 Nov 1824. Lewis **Thorp** [and Ann, his wife,] to Joseph Z. **Wimsatt**. For the sum of $123, 92 1/3 acres, bounded on the E by Bede **Moore**, S by John **Duvawl**, W by Elisha **Belsha**, and N by Clement **Knott** and the U. S. A. Signed Lewis **Thorp**, Ann (x) **Thorp**. Wit Corns. M. **Slattery**, Clerk. Rec 30 Dec 1824.

156. Page 117. 24 Jan 1825. John **May** to Richard S. **Dorsey**. For the sum of $12, Lot No. 11 in Perryville. Signed John **May**. Wit Corns. M. **Slattery** (JP). Rec 24 Jan 1825.

157. Page 117. 7 Jan 1825. George **Hore** to Robert T. **Brown**. For the sum of $110, two tracts; 2 acres in Cinque Hommes Twp which sd **Hore** purchased from Bernard **Layton** and Mary, his wife, including a tanyard, dwelling house, and improvements; and 19 acres, 2 roods, and 31 perches that he bought from Joseph **James** Jr., who bought it from sd **Layton** and wife on 16 Feb 1824 (1:90), adjoining Perryville and beginning at a stake at the SE corner of Lot No. 3 in Perryville, and agreeable to Isidore

Moore's survey. Signed George **Hore**. Wit Corns. M. **Slattery** (JP). Rec 27 Jan 1825.

158. Page 118. 18 Aug 1824. Zar **Sturdivant** and Rachel, his wife, to Allieus **Tucker**. For the sum of $$200, 100 acres on St. Laurent Creek, to be run off the SE end of the tract where they now live; purchased from Thomas **Donohue**. Signed Zar **Sturdevant**, Rachael (x) **Sturdevant**. Test A. **Bird**, D. L. **Caldwell**, JCC. Rec 16 Feb 1825.

159. Page 119. 30 Oct 1824. Joseph B. **Davis** [and Margaret H., his wife] to Benjamin **Davis**. For the sum of $170, 80 acres on the waters of Apple Creek, being Lot No. 2 E, Sec 2, Twp 33, Rng 13 E. Signed Joseph B. **Davis**, Margaret H. **Davis** (RD). Test James **Logan**, Thomas **Harris**, James J. **Fenwick** (JP). Rec 26 Feb 1825.

160. Page 120. 22 Mar 1825. Cornelius M. **Slattery**, Joab **Waters** senr., Robert T. **Brown**, and Frederick C. **Hase** to Frederick **Bates**, Governor of Mo. For the sum of $3000, bond to insure that sd **Slattery** shall perform the duties of Circuit Court Clerk of Perry Co. Signed Corns. M. **Slattery**, R. T. **Brown**, Joab **Waters**, Fredk. C. **Hase**. Wit John D. **Cook**, Judge of 4th Judicial Circuit. Rec 22 Mar 1825.

161. Page 120. 31 Mar 1825. James J. **Fenwick** and Ann, his wife, to Martin **LePare** of St. Louis Co., Mo. For the sum of $240, 500 arpens, more or less, on Indian Creek, being the share of sd James of the real estate of his father Joseph **Fenwick**; beginning 156 chains, 66 2/3 links from the lower SW corner of sd survey (see Ste. Genevieve Co. Book B:333). Signed James J. **Fenwick**, Ann **Fenwick**. Test Lewis **Moore**, Thomas **Tucker**, John **Layton** (JP). Rec 6 Apr 1825.

162. Page 121. 15 Apr 1825. Commissioners of Perryville to Ignatius **Layton**. For the sum of $65, Lot Nos. 8, 19, & 31 in Perryville. Signed Thomas **Riney**, Joseph **Tucker** senr., R. T. **Brown**, Commissioners. Wit Corns. M. **Slattery** (JP). Rec 15 Apr 1825.

163. Page 122. 16 Mar 1824. Thomas **Fenwick** by Sheriff Robert T. **Brown** to Robert S. **Manning**. For the sum of $140, 840 acres in Brazoe Twp on the waters of Apple Creek. Sold on 18 Nov 1823 on a writ of execution issued by Circuit Court in favor of sd **Manning** and against sd **Fenwick** and Ezekiel **Fenwick** for $158.87. Signed R. T. **Brown**, Sheriff. Wit Corns. M. **Slattery**, Clerk. Rec 15 Apr 1825.

164. Page 123. 19 Mar 1825. Timothy **Davis** and Nancy, his wife, to John **Duvall**. For the sum of $85, the balance of 640 acres on Cape Cinque Hommes Creek; confirmed as the settlement right of Benjamin **Cox**, Sr., and sold by him to John **Donohue**, and being the part that sd **Donohue** had not heretofore sold to sd **Duvall**. Signed Timothy **Davis**, Nancy **Davis** (RD). Wit John D. **Cook**, Judge of 4th Judicial Circuit. Rec 9 May 1825.

165. Page 123. 8 Jan 1825. Nicholas **Miles** and Elizabeth, his wife, and John **Moore** and Sarah, his wife, to Henry **Miles**. For the sum of $52.50, 42 2/9 acres in Cinque Hommes Twp, part of a section confirmed by the Commissioners to Joseph **Miles**, decd, in his lifetime; being 2/9 of 190 acres of sd section. Signed Nicholas **Miles**, Elizabeth (x) **Miles**, John **Moore**, Sarah (x) **Moore**. Wit Corns. M. **Slattery** (JP), Owen **Evans**. Joab **Waters** senr., Benjamin **Davis**, James **Mattingley**, Esqs., JCC, attest to Sarah **Moore**. Rec 9 May 1825.

166. Page 125. 26 Mar 1824. U. S. A. to Joseph **James**. Confirmation of his claim of 640 acres on Brazeau Creek; being Survey No. 2112; beginning at a post. Signed James **Monroe**, President. Wit Geo. **Graham**, Commissioner of the General Land Office. Rec 9 May 1825.

167. Page 125. 9 May 1825. Commissioners of Perryville to Benjamin **Davis**. For the sum of $23, Lot No. 6 in Perryville. Signed R. T. **Brown**, Thomas **Riney**, Joseph **Tucker** senr., Commissioners. Wit Corns. M. **Slattery** (JP). Rec 9 May 1825.

168. Page 126. 18 Jul 1825. Josiah F. **Hamilton**, for himself and his minor brothers and sisters, and Fenwick **Hamilton** to James **Evans**. For the sum of $1, bond to make a quit claim deed to 160 acres. Sd Evans was employed as attorney for the grantors in a suit in Circuit Court to obtain a decree for title to a tract granted to Charles **Duncaster**, of which the 160 acres is a part. Signed Josiah F. **Hamilton**, Fenwick **Hamilton**. Test Corns. M. **Slattery**, Clerk. Rec 20 Jul 1825.

169. Page 126. 26 Mar 1825. Henry **McAtee** and Ann, his wife, to Perry **Evans**. For the sum of $185, 150 acres, more or less, on Thompsons Fork of McClanahans Creek; the lower part of a survey established by Henry **Elliott**, U. S. Surveyor, and confirmed as the Spanish grant of James **Thompson**; running up the creek two hollows near Long's old improvement. Signed Henry (x) **McAtee**, Ann (x) **McAtee**. Test John **Layton** (JP), Lewis **Moore**. Rec 20 Jul 1825.

170. Page 127. 1 Aug 1825. William **Tucker** and Sarah, his wife, John **Hayden** and Elenor, his wife, Benedict **Hayden** and Mary, his wife, Benedict **Riley** and Ann, his wife, James **Hayden** and Mary, his wife, George **Fenwick** and Margaret, his wife, Susanna **Hayden**, Clement **Hayden**, and Sarah **Hayden**, all heirs of Clement **Hayden**, decd (Sarah **Hayden** being the widow), to Peter **Holzer**. In consideration of an agreement entered into by Clement **Hayden** and sd Holzer on 20 Mar 1811, 510.42 acres, so as to include a spring and branch some distance about the falls of the Big Rocks, being Survey No. 2062; purchased by sd **Hayden** of John **Grenewalt**, and confirmed to sd **Hayden**. beginning at a post. Signed William **Tucker**, Sarah **Tucker**, John **Hayden**, Elenor (x) **Hayden**, Benedict **Hayden**, Mary (x) **Hayden**, Benedict **Riley**, Ann (x) **Riley**, George **Fenwick**, Margaret (x) **Fenwick**, Sarah **Hayden**, Susanna **Hayden**, Clement **Hayden**, Mary **Harris** (late wife of Jas. **Hayden**, decd). Wit Corns. M. **Slattery** (JP), Thomas **Hayden**; Joab **Waters**, Benjamin **Davis**, James **Mattingley**, JCC. Rec 3 Aug 1825.

171. Page 128. 27 Jun 1825. Commissioners of Perryville to Henry **Tucker**. For the sum of $6.50, Lot No. 40 in Perryville. Signed R. T. **Brown**, Joseph **Tucker** senr., Commissioners. Wit Corns. M. **Slattery** (JP). Rec 3 Aug 1825.

172. Page 129. 27 Jun 1825. Commissioners of Perryville to James N. **Moore**. For the sum of $11, Lot No. 28 in Perryville. Signed R. T. **Brown**, Joseph **Tucker** senr., Commissioners. Wit Corns. M. **Slattery** (JP). Rec 3 Aug 1825.

173. Page 129. 10 Aug 1825. Stephen **Sanders** to Moses **Harris** in trust for Emilie **Dickerson**. In contemplation of the marriage of sd **Sanders** and sd **Dickerson**, agreement that she shall have sole control over __ acres in Bois Brulle Twp., confirmed to [COVERED] **Clark**, on which stands a tanyard, and which sd **Sanders** bought from John **Logan** on 15 Jan 1825. Signed Stn. **Sanders**. Wit Corns. M. **Slattery**, John **Layton** (JP). Rec 10 Aug 1825

174. Page 130. 11 May 1825. U.S.A. to Clement **Hayden** under John **Greenwalt**. Confirmation of a claim of 510.42 acres; beginning at a post; being Survey No. 2062 held under Certificate No. 750. Signed J. Q. **Adams**, President. Wit Geo. **Graham**, Commissioner of the General Land Office. Rec 10 Aug 1825.

175. Page 131. 6 Apr 1825. Walter **Layton** and Mary Elenor, his wife, William **McLane** and Lucey, his wife and late Lucey **Layton**, and John **Layton**, atty for Mary **Layton**, to Joseph **Hines**. For the sum of $113.25, 113 1/4 acres, more or less, on Saline Creek, allotted to the grantors as heirs of Joseph **Layton**, decd; beginning at a post oak, and bounded in part by Joseph **Tucker**'s spring branch and Saline Creek. Signed John **Layton**, atty for Mary **Layton**, William (x) **McLane**, Walter **Layton**, Mary Elenor (x) **Layton**, Alley (x) **McLane**. Wit Corns. M. **Slattery** (JP); Joab **Waters**, Benjamin **Davis**, James **Mattingley**, JCC. Rec 10 Aug 1825.

176. Page 132. 22 Jun 1825. Thomas and James **Underwood** to John **Hahn**, all of Cape Girardeau Co., Mo. For the sum of $66.66 2/3, __ acres, being 2/3 of the W 1/2, SW 1/4, Sec 36, Twp 35 N, Rng 9 E. Signed Thos. **Underwood**, James **Underwood**. Wit John L. **Conrad**, Jemerson(?) **Underwood**, John D. **Cook**, Judge of 4th Judicial Circuit. Rec 12 Sep 1825.

177. Page 133. 13 Nov 1825. Commissioners of Perryville to Robert T. **Brown**. For the sum of $67.25, Lot Nos. 65 & 47 in Perryville. Signed Thomas **Riney**, Joseph **Tucker** senr., Commissioners. Wit Corns. M. **Slattery**, Clerk. Rec 30 Nov 1825.

178. Page 134. 30 Nov 1825. Commissioners of Perryville to Bernard **Brown**. For the sum of $116.50, Lot Nos. 5, 6, 35, & 22 in Perryville. Signed R. T. **Brown**, Thomas **Riney**, Joseph **Tucker** senr., Commissioners. Wit Corns. M. **Slattery** (JP). Rec 30 Nov 1825.

179. Page 134. 1 Sep 1825. Commissioners of Perryville to Thomas **Riney** and Zachariah **Layton**. For the sum of $206.25, Lot Nos. 32, 66, 78, 77, 86, 26, 97, 96, & 14 in Perryville. Signed R. T. **Brown**, Joseph **Tucker** senr., Commissioners. Wit Corns. M. **Slattery** (JP). Rec 30 Nov 1825.

180. Page 135. 1 Dec 1825. Commissioners of Perryville to Joseph **Tucker** senr. For the sum of $104.62 1/2, Lot Nos. 30, 18, 36, & 37 in Perryville. Signed R. T. **Brown**, Thomas **Riney**, Joseph **Tucker** senr., Commissioners. Wit Corns. M. **Slattery** (JP). Rec 1 Dec 1825.

181. Page 136. 24 Oct 1825. Robert T. **Brown** to Joab **Waters** senior. For the sum of $900, 640 acres in Bois Brulle Bottom on the Mississippi River; adjoined on the S by Alexander **Patterson**, decd, and N by Absolum **Kennison**, decd; being known as the Allen Tract and deeded to sd **Brown** by Walter **Wilkinson**. Signed R. T. **Brown**. Wit D. L. **Caldwell** (JP), J. J. **Wilkenson**. Rec 12 Dec 1825.

182. Page 137. 14 Sep 1825. William **Tucker** and Sarah, his wife, to James **Manning**. For the sum of $79.37 1/2, 63 1/2 acres, the SE end of a tract confirmed to Clement **Hayden** under John **Greenwalt**; beginning at a post between two w. oaks; and bounded in part by Susanah **Hayden** and sd **Tucker**. Signed William **Tucker**, Sarah (x) **Tucker**. Test John **Layton** (JP), Zachariah **Layton**. Rec 13 Dec 1825.

183. Page 137. 22 Oct 1825. Susannah **Hayden** to same. For the sum of $110, 127 acres, her undivided share of land as legal heir of Clement **Hayden**, decd; beginning at a white oak; and adjoined on the S by sd **Manning** and Benedict **Hayden**, W by Bernard **Brown**, N by Peter **Holzer** senr, and E by public land. Signed Susanna **Hayden**. Wit John **Layton** (JP), John **Tucker**. Rec 13 Dec 1825.

184. Page 138. 28 Nov 1825. John **Cox** and Andrew **Cox** Junior, heirs of Andrew **Cox** senr, decd, to Nancy **Burge**. For the sum of $96, 400 arpens near the mouth of St. Louret, on or near the boundary between Perry and Ste. Genevieve Cos.; bounded by the deduction of a concession made to Andrew **Cox** senr on 20 Jan 1798, W by **Pernshe**'s(?) survey, and E by River St. Louret. It is understood that this deed does not include 48 acres, which is another heir's part. Signed John **Cox**, Andrew **Cox**. Test John **Layton** (JP). Rec 26 Dec 1825.

185. Page 139. 23 Aug 1825. James **Caldwell** and Mecka, his wife, and James W. **Smith** and Lucinda, his wife, all of St. Francois Co., Mo. to Elias **Barber**. For the sum of $800, 640 acres on the S fork of Abrasos or Obrazo Creek, five or six miles from the Mississippi; confirmed to Charles **Duncaster** as his head right, and conveyed by him to William **Hinkston**, and by sd **Hinkston** to Jacob **Pettett** as atty in fact, and by sd **Pettett** to sd **Caldwell** and sd **Smith**, as recorded in Ste. Genevieve Co. Signed James **Caldwell**, Mecke **Caldwell**, James W. **Smith**., Lucinda C. **Smith**. Wit Jno. D. **Peers**, Circuit Court Clerk of St. Francois Co., Mo. Rec 26 Dec 1825.

186. Page 140. 4 Jan 1826. Raphel **Tucker**, one of the heirs of Joseph **Tucker** senr, decd, of Washington Co., Ky. to John **Tucker**. For the sum of $30, 95 arpens, more or less, on the Mississippi above the mouth of Obrasaw; granted to Thomas **Tucker**, and sold to Joseph **Tucker** senr, decd; beginning and running with the survey line of Thomas **Tucker**. Signed Ralphael **Tucker**. Wit Joseph **Tucker** senr., Joab **Waters** (JP). Rec 4 Jan 1826.

187. Page 140. 4 Jan 1826. Same to Joseph **Tucker** senr. For the sum of $25, part of 150 arpens on the road from Ste. Genevieve to Cape Girardeau, granted to Joseph **Tucker** senr, decd, and as much as was bequeathed to Raphel **Tucker**, without touching or interfering with parcels left by sd decd to Nicholas **Tucker** and James **Tucker**, and agreeable to the last will and testament of Joseph **Tucker** senr, decd, and a deed of gift from sd decd to Nicholas **Tucker**; bounded on the W by Aquila **Hagan**, N by Joseph **Hagan**, decd, and E by James **Moore** ser. Signed Ralphael **Tucker**. Wit John **Tucker**, Joab **Waters** (JP). Rec 4 Jan 1826.

188. Page 141. 18 Nov 1825. Josiah F. **Hamelton** of Brazoe Twp to Wm. P. **Lacey** of Cape Girardeau Co., Mo. For the sum of $65, 65 acres, more or less, on the Mississippi River in Brazoe Twp, being Lot No. 7 in the plat of the commissioners to divide land between the heirs of George A. **Hamelton**, decd. Signed Josiah L.

Hamelton. Wit James **Davis**, Henry **Jones**, John D. **Cook**, Judge of 4th Judicial Circuit. Rec 28 Feb 1826.

189. Page 142. 28 Feb 1826. William P. **Lacey** and Emely M., his wife, of Cape Girardeau Co., Mo. to Harrison **Young**. For the sum of $195, 65 acres and 88 poles or perches as described in the preceding deed and laid out in Record Book A, folio 99-101 of the 4th Judicial Circuit. Signed Wm. P. **Lacey**, Emily M. **Lacey**. Wit Benjamin **Wilson**, Corns. M. **Slattery**, Clerk. Rec 28 Feb 1826.

190. Page 143. 6 Jan 1826. John **Moore** and Sarah, his wife, to Nicholas **Tucker**. For the sum of $300, 200 1/2 acres and 20 perches in the Barren Settlement, the SE corner of a survey granted to Josephius **Tucker**; beginning at a stone corner of the original survey on a line of James **Moore** son of Nicholas. Signed John **More**, Sary (x) **Moore** (RD). Test John **Layton** (JP), Henry **Miles**. Rec 28 Feb 1826.

191. Page 144. 28 Feb 1826. Joseph **Tucker** senr and Eleanor, his wife, to Peter T. **Tucker**, all of Cinque Hommes Twp. For the sum of $25 and the tender love they have for their son, 188 acres, more or less, on the waters of Saline Creek, beginning at a rock marked with letters P. T. Signed Joseph **Tucker** senr, Eleanor **Tucker** (RD). Wit John **Layton** (JP). Rec 27 Mar 1826.

192. Page 145. 15 Feb 1825. Richard S. **Dorsey** and Louvecy, his wife, to Stephen **Dalson**. For the sum of $100, Lot Nos. 10, 11, 13, & 15 in Perryville. Signed R. S. **Dorsey**, Louvecy **Dorsey**. Test John **Logan** (JP). Rec 12 May 1826.

193. Page 145. 18 Aug 1825. Gustavus A. **Bird** and Hannah L., his wife, to John **Logan** of Ill. For the sum of $1000, 1/4 of 540 acres confirmed to Francis **Bartheaume**, which sd **Logan** conveyed to sd **Bird** on 1 Sep 1823. Signed G. A. **Bird**, Hannah L. **Bird**. Wit Gor. **Maize**, J. J. **DLashmutt**, John D. **Cook**, Judge of 4th Judicial Circuit. Rec 3 Jun 1826.

194. Page 146. 27 Apr 1826. Nicholas **Tucker** and Mary, his wife, to Francis **Miles**. For the sum of $21, 21 1/9 acres in Cinque Hommes Twp; being 1/9 of 190 acres, and part of a section of land confirmed to Joseph **Miles**, decd, in his lifetime by the Commissioners. Signed Nicholas **Tucker**, Mary Ann (x) **Tucker**. Wit Corns. M. **Slattery**, Clerk. Rec 5 Jun 1826.

195. Page 147. 14 Feb 1826. Aristideze **Anduze**, Rector, of St. James Parish, La. to Edmond **Saulnier** of St. Louis, Mo. Power of attorney to sell 640 arpens on Brazeau Creek. Signed A. **Anduze**. Wit Christover **de Armas**, Notary Public in New Orleans, New Orleans Parish, La., Jn. Bp. **Lameth**, L. H. **Ferand**, Henry **Johnson**, Governor of La. Rec 15 Jun 1926.

196. Page 148. 27 May 1826. Edmond **Saulnier**, atty in fact for Aristides **Anduze**, rector, of St. James Parish La., to Thomas **Biddle** and Thomas H. **Benton** in trust for Virginia **Lawless**, wife of Luke Edward **Lawless** of St. Louis, Mo. For the sum of $200, undivided moiety of 640 arpens on Brazeau Creek; confirmed to Robert **Hinckston**, and conveyed by the Sheriff of Ste. Genevieve Co. to Reuben **Smith** on 16 Aug 1815 (Book B:433). Signed Edm. **Saulnier**. Wit M. Philip **Ledue**, Probate Judge in St. Louis Co., Mo. Rec 15 Jun 1826.

197. Page 149. 26 Dec 1825. Roland **Boyd** and Julian, his wife, to Joseph **Shoults** of Cape Girardeau Co., Mo. For the sum of $500, 400 acres, more or less, joined on the S by Lunsford **Ellis**, and N by Guy **Elder**; being where sd **Boyd** now lives. Sd **Boyd** and sd **Shoults** shall have joint and equal interest in any lead or mineral discovered on sd tract. Signed Roland (x) **Boyd**, Juliet **Boyd** (RD). Wit Timothy **Davis**., W. **Wilkinson** (JP). Rec 17 Jun 1826.

198. Page 150. 8 Nov 1825. Clement **Cissell** and Ann, his wife, to John Baptist **Layton**. For the sum of $50, their right to 400 arpens on the S fork of Saline Creek, which they hold as heirs to sd tract; purchased from Major John **Hawkins** and Rebeckah, his wife, on 15 Oct 1808 by Joseph **Layton**, decd, who was then an inhabitant of Washington Co., Ky., and to whom the grantors are heirs. Signed Clement **Cissell**, Ann **Cissell**. Wit William **McLane**, Ignatius **Layton**, Corns. M. **Slattery**, Clerk. Rec 18 Jul 1826.

199. Page 151. 2 May 1826. Rezin L. **Bishop** and Rebecca, his wife, to James and Benedict **McCauley**. For the sum of $80, 40 acres, part of a tract conveyed by Joseph **Manning** and Mary, his wife, to sd **Bishop**; beginning at a stake on the NW corner of sd tract, and bounded in part by a line run by Isidore **Moore** for making partition among the heirs of John **Layton**, decd, the original claimant. Signed Rezin L. **Bishop**, Rebecca **Bishop** (RD). Wit John **Layton** (JP). Rec 17 Aug 1826.

200. Page 152. 11 Aug 1826. John **Gutau** and Mary, his wife, to John **Burns**, all of Bois Brulle Twp. For the sum of $157, 100 acres in Bois Brulle Bottom on the Mississippi River, willed by Alexander **Patterson** senr., decd, to his daughter Mary **Guitau**; being the lower part of a survey confirmed to sd **Patterson**, bounded on the SE by Isaac **Meredith** and NW by Sarah **Kennedy**, daughter of sd **Patterson**. Signed John **Guitau**, Mary (x) **Guitau** (RD). Wit Joab **Waters**, Corns. M. **Slattery**, Clerk. Rec 14 Aug 1826.

201. Page 153. 16 Nov 1826. Joseph **Pratte** of Ste. Genevieve Co., Mo. to Walter **Wilkinson**. Loan of a negro man **Jim Evon**(?), one boy **Charles**, one girl **Maria**, and one girl **Lucy**. Signed Jos. **Pratte**. Wit Thomas **Hayden**, Corns. M. **Slattery**, Clerk. Rec 16 Nov 1826.

202. Page 153. 4 Nov 1826. Robert T. **Brown** to same. Loan of the following negro slaves: one man **Nace**(?), one man **Ben Dainold**, one boy **George**, one boy **Sam**, one woman **Minty**, one woman **Sarah**, and one girl **Nelly**. Signed Robt. T. **Brown**. Wit Thomas **Hayden**, Corns. M. **Slattery**, Clerk. Rec 16 Nov 1826.

203. Page 154. 4 Nov 1826. Charles C. **Valle** to same. Loan of negro slaves: one man **Nace** and one boy **Dick**. Signed Charles C. **Valle**. Wit Thomas **Hayden**, Corns. M. **Slattery**, Clerk. Rec 16 Nov 1826.

204. Page 154. 9 Jun 1826. Isaac **Cadwaller** of Jefferson Co., Mo. to Benjamin **Davis**. For diverse good causes and considerations, power of attorney to receive money and perform all kinds of business. Signed Isaac **Cadwallader**. Wit Saml. W. **Lewis**, JP in Jefferson Co., Mo., Henry **Seibert**. Rec 1 Nov 1826.

205. Page 155. 9 Sep 1826. Ansel **Ferrel** and Esther, his wife, to George **Preston**. For the sum of $200, 120 acres on the waters of McChlanehan's Creek; part of a tract confirmed to Thomas **Allen**, and in the SE corner of sd tract; adjoining 200 acres sold by sd **Allen** to Aquila **Hagan**. Signed Ansel (x) **Ferrel**, Esther (x) **Ferrel** (RD). Wit John **Layton** (JP). Rec 2 Nov 1826.

206. Page 156. 15 May 1826. Ulila **Hamilton** of Fleuresante, St. Louis Co., Mo. to Fenwick **Hamilton**, her brother. Power of attorney to sell her interest in 1000 acres, bounded on the N by land formerly owned by Thomas **Fenwick**, S by widow **Manning**, W by land formerly owned by **Hinkston**, and E by the Mississippi River. Signed Regis Eulalie **Hamilton**. Wit Leo F. **Hamilton**, Odaria **Berthold**, religeont of the sacred heart, Hugh **Neil**, JP in St. Louis Co., Mo. Rec 6 Nov 1826.

207. Page 157. 6 Nov 1826. Same by her atty in fact Fenwick **Hamilton** to Harrison **Young**. For the sum of $132, 44 acres and 65 poles, fronting on the Mississippi River, her share of 1000 acres as described in Circuit Court Book A:100; bounded on the E by Fenwick **Hamilton** and S by Matilda **Hamilton**. Signed Fenwick J. **Hamilton**. Wit Corns. M. **Slattery**, Clerk, D. L. **Caldwell**. Rec 6 Nov 1826.

208. Page 158. 20 Nov 1826. Rezin L. **Bishop** and Rebecca, his wife, to David **Evans** of Cape Girardeau Co., Mo. For the sum of $50, undivided 1/3 part of 103 acres in Madison Co., Ky. on the waters of Silver Creek, the plantation where William **Morehead** died, and which was devised to his son John after the death of his mother, and after the death of sd John to Rebecca, then Rebecca **Howell**, to Polly **Collier** (and said?) **Evans**; as described in a deed from Caleb **Williams** to William **Morehead**. Signed Rezin L. **Bishop**, Rebecca (x) **Bishop** (RD). Wit Joab **Waters**, John **Layton**, Corns. M. **Slattery**, Clerk. Rec 24 Nov 1826.

209. Page 159. 21 Mar 1826. Fenwick J. **Hamilton** to Harrison **Young**. For the sum of $132, 44 acres on the Mississippi River near the mouth of Obrzoe Creek and above land granted to Mark **Manning**, being Lot No. 2 as divided by the Commissioners to partition land among the heirs of George A. **Hamilton**, decd. Signed Fenwick J. **Hamilton**. Wit Isidore **Moore**, J. **Abernathy** (JP). Rec 6 Nov 1826.

210. Page 159. 21 Mar 1826. Isidore **Moore** to same. Quit claim to 44 acres, being Lot No. 2 purchased at sheriff's sale of the property of Fenwick J. **Hamilton**. Signed Isidore **Moore**. Wit J. **Abernathy** (JP). Rec 6 Nov 1826.

211. Page 160. 20 Apr 1824. Rev. Louis William **Dubourg** of New Orleans, La. to Rev. Joseph **Rosati**. Power of attorney to manage his affairs and concerns in Mo., to administer property, sell property, and settle accounts. Signed L. Wm. (x) **DuBourg**. Wit Greenbury Ridgely **Stringer**, Notary Public, John **Stringer**, John **Petukin**(?), Thomas Bollinger **Robertson**, Gov. of La., Archibald **Gamble**, Recorder of St. Louis Co., Mo. Rec 13 Dec 1826.

212. Page 161. 20 Dec 1826. Bishop Lewis William **DuBourg** by Joseph **Rosati**, atty in fact, to Rev. Francis Xavier **Dahmen** of Ste. Genevieve, Mo., [Rev.] John **Odin**, and [Rev.] Joseph **Paquin**. For the sum of $1, 38 3/4 acres and 39 perches on the S fork of Saline Creek, part of a tract originally granted to Michael **Tucker**; beginning at a small sugar tree, hickory, and ironwood standing in a branch. Signed Lewis William **DuBourg** by Joseph **Rosati**, atty in fact. Wit Martin **Blanka**, John **Bosoni**, John **Layton** (JP). Rec 13 Dec 1826.

213. Page 162. 12 Dec 1826. Same by same to same, same, and same. For the sum of $1, 640 acres upon which the seminary is built, which was conveyed to sd **DuBourg** by Ignatius **Layton** and Elisabeth, his wife; joining Joseph **Manning** and John **Layton**. Signed Lewis William **DuBourg** by Joseph **Rosati**, atty in fact. Wit Martin **Blanka**, John **Bosoni**, John **Layton** (JP). Rec 13 Dec 1826.

214. Page 163. 12 Dec 1826. Same by same to same, same, and same. For the sum of $1, __ acres on the waters of Apple Creek; being all the right of the late Clair **Hamilton**'s 1/6 part of 3000 arpents, which she claimed as heir of her deceased father Joseph **Fenwick**, and which she sold to sd **DuBourg** on 9 Aug 1819. Signed Lewis William **DuBourg** by Joseph **Rosati**, atty in fact. Wit Martin **Blanka**, John **Bosoni**, John **Layton** (JP). Rec 13 Dec 1826.

215. Page 164. 12 Dec 1826. Ignatius **Layton** and Elizabeth, his wife, to Bishop Lewis William **DuBourg**. For the sum of $900, 640 acres or 752.32 arpens according to Survey No. 845 made 23 Mar 1818 by Henry **Elliot**, Dep Surveyor and recorded in St. Louis in Book E:12; which is patented in Certificate No. 1049 dated 22 Sep 1826; beginning at a corner of Joseph **Manning**'s survey. Signed Ignatius **Layton**, Elizabeth (x) **Layton** (RD). Test Lewis **Tucker**, Frances **Jourdain**, John **Layton** (JP). Rec 13 Dec 1826.

216. Page 166. 5 Oct 1826. Stephen **Dolson** and Elizebeth, his wife, of Cinque Hommes Twp to Rezin L. **Bishop**. For the sum of $125, Lot Nos. 10, 11, 13, & 15 in Perryville. Signed Stephen **Dolson**, Elizabeth **Dolson** (RD). Wit John **Layton** (RD), Wm. **Lacey**. Rec 26 Feb 1827.

217. Page 167. 6 Mar 1827. Ignatius **Layton** and Elizabeth, his wife, to Richd. S. **Dorsey**. For the sum of $100, 20 acres, beginning at a stake, **McGinises** second corner in the old line of John **Layton**, decd. Signed Ignatius **Layton**, Elizabeth (x) **Layton** (RD). Wit John **Layton** (JP). Rec 6 Mar 1827.

218. Page 168. 19 Mar 1827. Cornelius M. **Slattery** and Lucretia, his wife, to Charles C. **Valie**. For the sum of $81, 640 acres on the waters of Brazoe Creek, a tract purchased at sheriff's sale as the property of Walter **Wilkinson** and Emilie, his wife. Signed Cornelius M. **Slattery**, Lucretia **Slattery** (RD). Wit James **Nagle**, Walter **Wilkinson** (JP). Rec 19 Mar 1827.

219. Page 168. 14 Nov 1826. Commissioners of Perryville to George **Hoar**. For the sum of $54.25, Lot Nos. 71, 53, 72, & 84 in Perryville. Signed R. T. **Brown**, Thomas **Riney**, Joseph **Tucker** senr., Commissioners. Wit John **Layton** (JP). Rec 21 Mar 1827.

220. Page 169. 16 Apr 1827. Aquila **Hagan** and Mary, his wife, to their daughter Ann **Brewer** and her husband John. For love and good will, 50 acres and 30 perches, part of the tract whereon they now live; beginning at a stone set on a line of the original survey at James **Moore**'s W corner. Signed Aquila **Hagan**, Mary (x) **Hagan** (RD). Test F. J. **Hamilton**, John **Layton** (JP). Rec 27 Sep 1827.

221. Page 170. 31 Mar 1827. Rezin L. **Bishop** and Rebecca, his wife, of Cinque Hommes Twp to Joseph **Shoults**. For the sum of $125, Lot Nos. 10, 11, & 13 in Perryville. Signed R. L. **Bishop**, Rebecca (x) **Bishop** (RD). Wit John **Layton** (JP), James B. **May**. Rec 27 Sep 1827.

222. Page 171. 26 Feb 1827. Treasury Department, Auditor's Office, Missouri, City of Jefferson. Delinquent tax list, to be paid by 7 May 1827, or to be sold for the tax and penalties at 5% per month from Dec 1826.

To Whom Assessed	Original Claimant	Where situated	No. of acres
Bird, Alfred	---	Mississippi	225
Dodge, Henry, for estate of	James **Samuels**	Cinq hommes	640
Flemming, George	James **Hutchings**	Mississippi	640
Horrel, Benj. & John	Joseph **Fenwick**	Apple Creek	425
Lane & **Relfe**	Sol. **Morgan**	Mississippi	100
Madden, Thomas	**Flynn, Kelly**, & others	Mississippi	1683
Rhodes, Jedthson	James **Moore** senr.	Saline	50

Signed E. **Barcroft**, Auditor, N. **Simonds**, Treasurer. Rec 27 Sep 1827.

223. Page 171. 12 Mar 1827. Lunsford **Ellis** and Keziah, his wife, to Clement **Cissell** and Bernard **Cissell**. For the sum of $250, 200 acres, more or less, on a branch of the S fork of Saline Creek; the upper part of a tract of 640 acres on which sd **Boyd**(?) now lives; beginning at a white oak six inches in diameter. Signed Lunsford (x) **Ellis**, Keziah **Ellis** (RD). Wit Lewis **Cissell**, Lewis **Duvall**, John **Layton** (JP). Rec 27 Sep 1827.

224. Page 172. 18 Jun 1827. Robert **Manning** and Nancy, his wife, James **Mattingly** and Nancy, his wife, William **Mattingly** and Elizabeth, his wife, Lewis **French** and Polly, his wife, and Anastasia **Manning**, widow of John **Manning** senr., decd, (sd Robert **Manning**, Nancy **Mattingly**, Elizabeth **Mattingly**, and Polly **French** being heirs of John **Manning** junr., decd) to Moses **Harris**. For the sum of $200, their undivided shares of 340.02 acres [on Brazoe Creek and the Mississippi River]; beginning at the upper corner of James **Manning**'s survey to his NW corner; part of a tract of 640 acres confirmed to John **Manning** on 30 Mar 1826, recorded in General Land Office Book 5:228-230, plat dated 30 Nov 1826; and bequeathed to his sons John and Robert in his will dated 27 Dec 1813 (Ste. Genevieve Co. Will Book). Signed Robert S. **Manning**, Nancy **Manning** (RD), James **Mattingly**, William **Mattingly**, Lewis (x) **French**, Anastasia (x) **Manning**, Nancy (x) **Mattingly**, Elizabeth (x) **Mattingly**, Polly (x) **French**. Wit John **Layton** (JP), John F. **Hase**, Clerk pro tem. Rec 27 Sep 1827.

225. Page 174. 3 Oct 1827. Henry B. **Newsom** by Robert T. **Brown**, former Collector of Perry Co., to Joab **Waters** senr. For the sum of $7.62 1/2 and 10% per annum thereon in back taxes, 426 acres in Bois Brulle Twp. Sold on 28 Mar 1824 at the house of Bede **Moore** in Cinque Hommes Twp, to pay taxes that were due in 1823. Signed R. T. **Brown**, late Collector. Wit W. **Wilkinson** (JP). Rec 26 Nov 1827.

226. Page 175. 9 Oct 1827. Heirs of Edward **Hempstead**, decd. Deed of partition for property in Mo. made on order of Lincoln Co., Mo. Circuit Court in Chancery, issued 1 Oct 1823 in case of Thomas **Hempstead**, William **Hempstead**, Edward L. **Hempstead**, Albert G. **Hempstead**, Mary Lisa **Beebe**, Sarah **Beebe**, and Joseph **Hempstead** against Charles S. **Hempstead**; Thomas, Stephen, & Samuel **Hempstead**, infant children of Joseph **Hempstead**; Joseph, Mary, Clarissa, & Cornelia, infant children of Stephen **Hempstead**; Edward H. & Mary H. **Beebe**, infant children of Sally **Beebe**; and Charles Edward H. **Pratiot**, infant children of Susan **Pratiot**; all the infants by their guardian Charles S. **Hempstead**. In 1817, Edward **Hempstead**, brother of Thomas, William, Mary, Sarah, and Joseph and uncle of Edward L. and Albert, died seized of all the land described. In his will, after providing for his wife and several legacies, he left the residue in eight shares to his brother William, sister Mary Lisa should she be a widow at the time of his death (she was), brother Charles, the children of Joseph **Hempstead** (Edward L. and Albert, now adults, John & Christopher, infants and since decd without issue, and Thomas, Stephen, & Samuel, still infants), children of brother Stephen **Hempstead** (Joseph, Mary, Clarissa, & Cornelia, all infants), children of Sally **Beebe** (Edward H. & Mary H., infants and now living, and Charles & William, then infants and since decd without issue), and children of his sister Susan **Pratiot** (Charles and Edward H., infants). All live in Mo. except Thomas, Stephen, and Samuel, sons of Joseph **Hempstead**, who reside in Conn. Thomas and Charles have assigned their parts in trust to Robert **Wash** and Spencer **Pettis**, Esqs., to secure a debt due to the Bank of Mo., and the parts of Edward L. and Albert G. **Hempstead** have been sold and assigned to sd William **Hempstead**. Clarissa, widow of sd Edward **Hempstead**, died in 1825, and her interest ceased, being only a life estate. All allocations are to be held as joint tenants and not tenants in common. To Mary Lisa: 160 arpens, more or less, about four and a half miles N of St. Louis, the S part of a grant confirmed to Antoine **Morin**, decd; part of one lot in St. Louis on Church or Second Main St and bounded on the S by Myette St and W by Second St and a lot late of R. H. **Price**, E by John **Smith**, Grocer, formerly **Keesackers**, and N by Lot No. 2, being Lot No. 3 of sd lot; and 120 arpens, more or less, about four miles W from St. Louis, confirmed to Edward **Hempstead** under Susannah **Dubrenil**. To Joseph **Hempstead** and Stephen, Thomas, and Samuel, infant children of sd Joseph: 200 1/2 acres in St. Louis Co., on the Mississippi River about 13 miles from St. Louis, the upper or N moiety of 401 acres confirmed to John **Graham**; and 600 arpens in Lincoln Co., part of a concession of 800 arpens granted to Joseph **Bessonnette**, bounded by the grants of Paul **Prims** and Charles **Bissonnette**. To Charles and Edward H. **Pratiot**, infant children of Susan **Pratiot**: 100 arpens, more or less, at Beaver Ponds about six miles NW of St. Louis, originally granted to Joseph **Hortis** Jr. and sold to Edward **Hempstead** as Joseph **Lacroix**'s land; 80 arpens about five miles SW of St. Louis at Barriere des Noyers, originally granted to one "**Savarre**"; 40 arpens adjoining the last described tract, originally granted to one "**Dodier**"; 60 arpens in Barriere des Noyers originally granted to Alexis **Lalande**; part of a lot in St. Louis bounded on the W by Second Main or Church St, which separates the same from the lot of a free negress, N by Elen St, S by Lot No. 2, being Lot No. 1 and originally acquired by Edward **Hempstead** of the execr of Josoph **Robidoux**; 160 arpens on the Mississippi in St. Charles Co., originally granted to Joseph **Beauchemin**; 800 arpens near Bay de Roy in Lincoln Co., originally granted to Joseph **Brazeau**; and 800 arpens in Lincoln Co. on Bobs Creek, originally granted to James W. **Cochran**. To Sarah **Beebe**, surviving parent of Charles and William **Beebe**, to hold for her lifetime, and to Edward H. and Mary H. **Beebe**, infants (also to receive sd Sarah's half at her decease): 60 arpens in Grand Prairie three miles W of St. Louis, originally granted to **Morin**; 200 1/2 acres in St. Louis Co., being the lower, S moiety of 401 acres granted to John **Graham**; a lot in St. Louis, bounded on the W by Church St, N by Lot No. 1 allotted to S. **Pratiot**'s children, and S by Lot No. 3 allotted to sd Mary Lisa; and 40 arpens in common fields of St. Charles, originally granted to **Robidoux**. To Joseph, Mary, Clarissa, and Cornelia, infant children of Stephen **Hempstead**, Jr.: 1066 arpens about three miles from St. Charles, granted to Jaqque D. **Egler** and confirmed to Edward **Hempstead**; and two lots in the lower end of St. Charles, one originally granted to J. B. **Lesage**, the other to James **Croper** and confirmed to Edward **Hempstead**. To William **Hempstead** 800 arpens in Lincoln Co., originally granted to Pierre **Poims**; 800 arpens adjoining the first tract, originally granted to Charles **Bissonnette**, and 1600 arpens, more or less, in Pike Co., originally granted and confirmed to Joseph **Marie**, and sold by him to Edward **Hempstead**. To Robert **Wash** and Spencer **Pettis**, assignee of Charles S. **Hempstead**: 85 arpens, more or less, in St. Louis Co., originally granted to one **L'Esperance** and confirmed to Thomas Roy **Musick**(?); 288 arpens, more or less, in St. Charles Co., granted and confirmed to John **Cook**; 40 arpens, more or less, in the common fields of St. Charles, originally granted to Gregoire **Tiercorot** and confirmed to Edward **Hempstead**; 40 arpens, more or less, in the common fields of St. Charles, originally granted to Joseph **Girade** and confirmed to Edward **Hempstead**; 130 arpens, more or less, in St. Charles Co., being 1/2 of 260 arpens granted and confirmed to Francis **Dequette**; 2166 2/3 arpens, more or less, on Ramsey's Creek in Pike Co., part of 3000 arpens originally granted to Francis **Lesieur** and confirmed to Francis **Bonthelier**; 107 1/2 arpens in Pike Co., an undivided part of 430 arpens on Calumet originally granted and confirmed to Francis **Duquette**; 184.71 acres, more or less, in Perry Co., originally granted to Alexander **Murdock**; Lot Nos. 54, 68, & 104 in Potosi; 30 arpens, more or less, near St. Genevieve purchased from John **McArthur**; 320 acres, more or less, in Jefferson Co., originally granted to Joseph **Robidoux** and sold as the property of one **Lurial** to Edward **Hempstead**. To Robert **Wash** and Spencer **Pettis**, assignees of Thomas **Hempstead**: 80 arpens in common fields of St. Charles, originally granted to one "Barada" and confirmed to Edward **Hempstead**; 80 arpens adjoining the first tract, part of 240 arpens originally granted and confirmed to Francis **Duquette**; 60 arpens in common fields of St. Charles, originally granted to one "Bochamp"; 100 arpens in St. Charles Co., part of 400 arpens originally granted to Christian **Denny**; 800 arpens in Lincoln Co., originally granted to Paul **Primo**; 2000 arpens in Lincoln Co., being 1/2 of a grant of 4000 arpens originally granted to Andre **L'Andreville** and confirmed, with boundaries made in a partition between the devisees of Edward **Hempstead** and Alexander **Stuart** in Lincoln Co. Circuit Court. Signed Francis **Parker**, Lincoln Co., Mo. Circuit Court Clerk. Rec 18 Jan 1828.

227. Page 181. 10 Sep 1823. George **Camster** and Martha, his wife, to John **Patterson**, all of Bois Bruly Twp. For the sum of $185, 53 1/4 arpens in Bois Bruly Twp; bounded on the N by sd **Camster**, E by ___ **Thomas**, S by Katharine **Belsha**, and W by Joel **Kennison**. Signed George **Camster**. Martha **Camster**. Wit William **Boyd**, Henry **Camster**, Henry **Clark** (JP). Rec 28 Feb 1828.

228. Page 182. 8 Apr 1824. Thomas **Riney** and William **Mattingly**. Agreement for sd **Riney** to convey 640 acres on the S fork of Saline Creek about a mile and a half above Peter **Tucker**'s mill to sd **Mattingly**, provided sd **Mattingly** pays 2600 gallons of good proof whisky, delivered in good tite barrels, paid in six installments--434 gallons each in Jun of 1825, 1826, 1827, 1828, 1829, and 1830. Should sd **Mattingly** fail in any payment, he is to pay sd **Riney** 50 gallons of whisky for damages and interest. Sd **Riney** gives possession of the lower bottom field now, and the remainder on 1 Nov next. Signed Thomas **Riney**, William **Mattingly**. Test John B. **Cissell**, Martin J. (x) **Moore**, Frederick G. **Hase**, Clerk. Rec 20 Mar 1828.

229. Page 183. 22 Apr 1828. John **Shoultz** and Elizabeth, his wife, to John Anson **McLane** of Cape Girardeau Co., Mo. For the sum of $1000, undivided 1/2 of 103.48 acres, being Lot No. 7, NE 1/4, Sec 4, Twp 33, Rng 12 E; as patented on 6 Nov 1823; including 1/2 of the saw and grist mills. Signed John **Shultz**, Elizabeth (x) **Shultz**. Test Isidore **Moore**, William **Whitledge**, Henry **Shaner**, Benjamin **Davis** (JP). Rec 5 Jun 1828.

230. Page 184. 15 May 1828. James C. **Moore** and Rebecca, his wife, to William **Keyte**. For the sum of $7.50, Lot No. 27 in Perryville.; purchased by sd **Moore** of the Commissioners on 24 May 1823 (1:70). Signed James C. **Moore**, Rebecca **Moore** (RD). Wit John **Layton** (JP). Rec 12 Jun 1828.

231. Page 185. 8 Mar 1828. Treasury Department, Auditor's Office, Missouri, City of Jefferson. Delinquent tax list, to be paid by 2 Jun 1828, or to be sold for the tax and penalties at 5% per month from 1 Dec 1827.

To Whom Assessed	Original Claimant	Where situated	No. of acres	Total amt.
Camster, George	Archd. **Camster**	Miss.	480	2.71
Fowler, Thomas	Jno. **Townsend**	Brazoe	520	3.54
Fenwick, Martin	Jas. **Fenwick**	Apple Creek	425	3.01
Gill, James	Jas. **Manning**	Miss.	150	1.35
Hempstead, Charles S.		Miss.	375	2.67
Same for heirs of E. **Hempstead**		Miss.	148	1.72
James, Joseph	Jos. **James**	Brazoe	640	4.43
Lare & Relf	Saml. **Morgan**	Miss.	100	.99
Lawless, Virginia	Robt. **Kingston**	Brazoe	544	3.67
Prem, John		Apple Creek	80	.87
Russell, William	C. **Barnhart**	St. Law	640	2.71
Same	John **Smith**	Miss.	320	2.32
Same	Levi **Wiggins**	Miss.	640	3.49

Shaner, Jacob, for heirs   Benj. Harrison   Brazoe   640   3.61

Signed E. **Barcroft**, Auditor, N. **Simonds**, Treasurer. Rec 9 Jul 1828.

232. Page 186. 14 Jul 1828. Robert **Abernathy** and Ann Arpy, his wife, to William **Keyte**. For the sum of $35, Lot No. 49 in Perryville; sold to sd **Abernathy** for the Commissioners on 24 May 1823 (1:72). Signed Robert **Abernathy**, Ann Arpy **Abernathy** (RD). Wit James **Capper**, John **Burns**, Jonas **Abernathy** (JP). Rec 15 Jul 1828.

233. Page 187. 15 Jul 1825. U. S. A. to Frederick **Hase**. Patent for 159.90 acres, in Certificate No. 543; being SE fractional 1/4, Sec 18, Twp 35, Rng 11 E. Signed J. Q. **Adams**, President. Wit Geo. **Graham**, Commissioner of the General Land Office. Rec Vol. 1, page 583. Rec 19 Aug 1828.

234. Page 187. 30 Nov 1825. Commissioners of Perryville to Cornelius M. **Slattery**. For the sum of $30.07 1/2, Lot Nos. 29 & 52 in Perryville. Signed Joseph **Tucker** senr., R. T. **Brown**, Thomas **Riney**, Commissioners. Wit Thomas **Hayden**, John **Layton** (JP). Rec 19 Aug 1828.

235. Page 188. 22 Nov 1825. William C. **Carr**, adminr of Henry **Elliott**, decd, to same. For the sum of $7.75, 300 acres, more or less, fronting on the Mississippi River; joined on the S by Hezekiah P. **Harris**, and N by lands once claimed by Christian **Fenter**, and sold by him to Robert **Smith**, and which was also owned and transferred by John **Smith** senr. to Robert **Smith**. Sold on the third Monday of July 1825 on order of Circuit Court issued March Term 1825, to pay debts and demands due by sd estate. Signed Will. C. **Carr**, adminr of H. **Elliott**. Wit Jos. D. **Grafton**, Clerk of Ste. Genevieve Co. Circuit Court. Rec 19 Aug 1828.

236. Page 189. 30 Nov 1825. Commissioners of Perryville to James **Winfield**. For the sum of $22, Lot No. 17 in Perryville. Signed R. T. **Brown**, Thomas **Riney**, Joseph **Tucker** senr., Commissioners. Wit Corns. M. **Slattery** (JP). Rec 25 Aug 1828.

237. Page 190. 9 Aug 1828. James **Winfield** to George **Killian**. For the sum of $22, Lot No. 17 in Perryville. Wit James **Winfield**. Test John **Layton** (JP). Rec 25 Aug 1828.

238. Page 191. 28 Feb 1827. Ignatius **Layton** and Elizabeth, his wife, to same. For the sum of $75, 12 1/2 acres; beginning on the E side of Salin Creek at the Bishop's Corner on a black oak; bounded in part by Nicholas **Moor**. Signed Ignatius **Layton**, Elizabeth (x) **Layton** (RD). Test John **Layton** (JP). Rec 25 Aug 1828.

239. Page 192. 15 May 1828. James C. **Moore** and Rebecca, his wife, to Joseph **Shoults**. For the sum of $7.50, Lot No. 12 in Perryville; sold by the Commissioners to sd **Moore** on 24 May 1823 (1:70). Signed James C. **Moore**, Rebecca **Moore** (RD). Test John **Layton** (JP). Rec 4 Sep 1828.

240. Page 192. 11 Feb 1828. William **Shannon** to John **Townsend**. For the sum of $2000, mortgage on six tracts; 640 acres confirmed to Theophilus **Hickman** and patented to sd **Shannon** on 9 Dec 1822, called the Round Pond Tract; 1/2 of a tract on the Mississippi confirmed to John **Smith** senr. and William **Russell**, purchased from sd **Smith** by William **Searcy**, and conveyed by sd **Searcy** and wife to sd **Shannon** on 11 Dec 1822; a claim deeded to sd **Shannon** on 22 Nov 1825 by William C. **Carr**, adminr of Henry **Elliott**, decd; two fractional parts of Sec 28, Twp 37 N, Rng 11 E patented to sd **Shannon** and Isaac **Flinn** on 31 May 1824, of which sd **Shannon**'s part is 137.16 acres, and of which he purchased the presentation right from George **Camster**; and 1/2 of 300 arpens confirmed to Mark **Brooks**, conveyed by sd **Brooks** to Thomas **Oliver** and William **Searcy**, and conveyed by them to sd **Shannon** and Josephy **Bozy** on 21 Feb 1820 (Ste. Genevieve Co. record). Signed Wm. **Shannon**. Wit Andrew H. **Tucker**, Jacob J. **Everts**, W. **Wilkinson**, JCC. Rec 5 Sep 1828. [Marginal note: For deed of release of this mortgage, see 2:79.]

241. Page 193. 24 Mar 1828. Gustavus A. **Bird** by Sheriff David L. **Caldwell** to Henry **Seibert**. For the sum of $10.50, 270 acres on Apple Creek, originally claimed by Francois **Barchume**, part of a tract where Maj. Henry **Seibert** now lives. Sold on 26 Nov 1827 on an execution from Circuit Court issued in 15 Oct 1827 in favor of Egbart B. **Garfield** and against sd **Bird**, for $451 damages and $1.55 costs. Signed David L. **Caldwell**. Wit Frederick C. **Hase**, Clerk. Rec 25 Oct 1828.

242. Page 195. 27 Nov 1827. Thomas **Donohue** by same to Roland **Boyd**. For the sum of $20, 68 acres, more or less, in Bois Brule Twp on the bank of the Mississippi about one mile from the head of the bottom; part of a tract where Joseph **Donohue** lived at the time of his death. Sold on 1 Nov 1828 on an execution from Ste. Genevieve Circuit Court issued 16 Oct 1826 in favor of the State of Mo. and against sd **Donohue**, David L. **Caldwell**, and sd **Boid** for $235.66 damages. Signed David L. **Caldwell**. Wit Frederick C. **Hase**, Clerk. Rec 25 Oct 1828.

243. Page 196. 29 Nov 1828. Nicholas **Miles** and Elizabeth, his wife, to Francis **Miles**. For the sum of $62 1/2, 50 acres in Cinq Hommes Twp, part of the land confirmed to Joseph **Miles**, decd, by the Commissioners; adjoining where Francis **Miles** now lives. Signed Nicholas **Miles**, Elizabeth (x) **Miles** (RD). Wit John **Layton** (JP). Rec 26 Dec 1828.

244. Page 198. 18 Dec 1828. Elias **Barcroft**, Auditor of Public Accounts for Mo., to Jedthson **Rhodes**. For the sum of $1.62 1/2 in taxes for 1826, taxes for 1827, and $.38 taxes for 1828, paid on this day, redemption of 50 acres on Saline Creek sold for back taxes; originally claimed by James **Moore** senr. The same had been sold to Thomas **Hayden** on 7 May 1827 for back taxes. Signed E. **Barcroft**, Auditor. Rec 1 Jan 1829.

245. Page 198. 21 Oct 1823. Henry J. **Rhodes** and Matilda, his wife, to Thomas **Harte**. For the sum of $38, lease on 50 acres in the Barren Settlement, part of the survey of James **Moore** Senr., decd. Sd lease to run for the lifetime of sd Matilda, or until her youngest child reaches age 21. Signed Henry J. (x) **Rhodes**, Matilda (x) **Rhodes**. Test John **Layton** (JP), James C. **Moore**. Title is assigned to Thomas **Hayden** on 26 Nov 1829 for the sum of $75. Signed Thomas **Harte**. Wit John **Layton** (JP). Rec 19 Jan 1829.

246. Page 200. 6 Aug 1828. Commissioners of Perryville to Richard S. **Dorsey**. For the sum of $ 13.75, Lot No. 69 in

Perryville. Signed R. T. **Brown**, Thomas **Riney**, Joseph **Tucker** senr., Commissioners. Wit John **Layton** (JP). Rec 27 Jan 1829.

247. Page 200. 10 Jan 1829. Pius **Brewer** to Benjamin **Wilson**. For securing several debts, mortgage on two horses, nine cattle, six sheep, 18 hogs, all his farming utensils, all his beds and bedding, and all the household and kitchen furniture. Sd **Brewer** is indebted to sd **Wilson** in a note for $53.75 dated 15 Mar last and due on the first day instant; and $80 due to sd **Wilson** on 4 Mar next, $80 due on 4 Mar 1830, and $80 due on 4 Mar 1831. Sd property is to be sold at public sale if the debts are not paid. Signed Pius **Brewer**, Ben. **Wilson**. Wit Frederick C. **Hase**, John **Layton** (JP). Rec 27 Jan 1829.

248. Page 201. 30 Mar 1826. John **Patterson** and Nancy, his wife, to Hilliard **Fowler**, all of Bois Brule Twp. For the sum of $150, 53 1/4 arpens in Bois Brule Twp; bounded on the N by George **Camster**, E by Judge **Thomas**, S by Katharine **Belsha**, and W by Joel **Kinneson**. Signed John **Patterson**, Nancy **Patterson** (RD). Test Elisha **Eggers**, H. P. **Harris** (JP). Rec 16 Feb 1829.

249. Page 202. 12 Dec 1828. Hilliard **Fowler** and Naomy, his wife, to Lewis **Greeny**, all of Bois Brule Twp. For the sum of $150, 53 1/4 arpens as described in the preceding deed (1:201). Signed Hilliard **Fowler**, Naomy **Fowler** (RD). Test Joab **Waters** (JP), Joab **Waters** Junr. Rec 16 Feb 1829.

250. Page 203. 26 Jan 1829. Richard S. **Dorsey** to David **Burns**. For the sum of $__, one grey horse named Tom, one sorrel mare named Jenney, two cows and one calf, four red shoats, one black sow, all his household and kitchen furniture, and all debts and credits owed him for medicine and services rendered. Signed Richd. S. **Dorsey**. Test W. **Dorsey**, James **Burns**, Lidia **Burns**, Daniel **Bankson**, Frederick C. **Hase**, Clerk. Rec 2 Mar 1829.

251. Page 203. 3 Apr 1827. Joab **Waters** to Simon **Duvall**. For the sum of $400, one negro boy named **Price**, aged 15. Signed Joab **Waters**. Wit Frederick C. **Hase**, Clerk. Rec 4 Mar 1829.

252. Page 204. 18 Dec 1828. Elias **Barcroft**, Auditor of Public Accounts for Mo., to James **Gill**. For the sum of $1.69 in taxes for 1827, redemption of 151 acres on the Mississippi River, originally claimed by Jas. **Moore**. Signed E. **Barcroft**, Auditor. Rec 1 Jan 1829.

253. Page 204. 24 Mar 1829. James **Manning** and Elizabeth, his wife, formerly of Ste. Genevieve Co. and now of Perry Co. (as per title bond dated 24 Aug 1816), to George Washington **Gill** and Napoleon **Gill** of Ill. In consideration of a title bond to James **Gill** and the sum of $1, 150 acres, supposed to be 250 arpens, granted to him by the Commissioners, opposite Devil's Oven in Cinque Hommes Twp. An endorsement on sd bond states that the survey only had 150 acres, but James **Gill** signed that he was satisfied with the amount, on 6 Mar 1823. Signed James (x) **Manning**, Elizabeth (x) **Manning** (RD). Wit W. **Wilkinson** (JP). Rec 24 Mar 1829.

254. Page 205. 24 Mar 1829. Josiah F. **Hamilton** by Sheriff David L. **Caldwell** to Harrison **Young**. For the sum of $144, 65 acres and 88 perches in Brazo Bottom, being Lot No. 7 allotted to sd **Hamilton** by the Commissioners appointed to partition land of George A. **Hamilton**, decd. Sold on 24 Mar 1829 on an execution from Circuit Court issued 13 Jan 1829 in favor of the State of Mo. and against Fenwick **Hamilton**, Josiah F. **Hamilton**, and James J. **Fenwick** for $214.48 damages and costs. Signed D. L. **Caldwell**, Sheriff. Wit Frederick C. **Hase**, Clerk. Rec 24 Mar 1829.

255. Page 206. 19 Dec 1828. Catharine **McConnohue** of Vicksburg, Miss., widow of Alexander **McConohue**, decd, to John H. **Saunders** of Ken. Relinquishment of dower rights to 1/2 of 640 arpents in Bois Brule Bottom; the upper 1/2 of a concession by the Spanish Government to Alexander **McConohue**; which was sold by sd **McConohue** in his lifetime to George **Robinson**, and by sd **Robinson** to sd **Saunders** on 13 Apr 1819. Signed Chatharina (x) **McConohue**. Wit Lewis **McKlemarry**, JP in Warren Co., Miss., B. **Menn**, Clerk. Rec 22 Apr 1829.

256. Page 207. 30 Jul 1828. Richard S. **Dorsey** and Louvesy, his wife, to David **Burns**. For the sum of $300, bond to make deeds to any real estate that is part of their right in the estate of James **Burns**, decd. Signed R. S. **Dorsey**, Louisey **Dorsey**. Test John W. **Stewart**, John **Burns**, John **Layton** (JP). Rec 25 Apr 1829.

257. Page 208. 29 Apr 1829. Edward **McGennis** to Francis **Schools**. For the sum of $100, mortgage on one dun mare, two bridles, two saddles, two beds and bedings, two cows and calfs, one chest, one plough and all the Geers, 20 hogs, one table, three chairs, one wash kettle, three cooking pots, one dozen of knife and forks, eight hides in tan at **Logan**'s yard in Perryville, all household and kitchen furniture of all sorts and description, and 300 weight of bacon. The debt with interest is due by 28 Apr next. Signed Edward **McGennis**. Wit Frederick C. **Hase** (JP). Rec 29 Apr 1829.

258. Page 209. 27 Mar 1827. James **Rice** and Sabina, his wife and granddaughter of James **Moore** Senr, decd, to Thomas **Hayden**. For the sum of $55, their undivided share of a tract devised by sd **Moore** by his last will and testament to his grandchildren. Signed James **Rice**, Sabina (x) **Rice** (RD). Wit Benedict **Riley**, James B. **May**, Frederick C. **Hase**, Clerk. Rec 29 Apr 1829.

259. Page 210. 30 Apr 1829. W. **Searcy** to David L. **Caldwell**. For the sum of $100, two horses, eight cattle, one yoke of oxen, some hogs, a bed, and a horse named Turky; being all the property left in the last will and testament of Margaret **Tuttle** to Rosanna W. **Searcy**, and conveyed with sd Rosanna's consent. Signed W. **Searcy**. Wit W. **Wilkinson** (JP). Rec 4 May 1829.

260. Page 210. 9 Apr 1829. Commissioners of Perryville to George **Killian**. For the sum of $30, Lot No. 21 in Perryville. Signed R. T. **Brown**, Thomas **Riney**, Joseph **Tucker** senr., Commissioners. Wit W. **Wilkinson** (JP). Rec 5 May 1829.

261. Page 211. 11 Mar 1829. Hilliard **Fowler** and Naomah, his wife, of Bois Brule Twp, to Rueben **Tendall** of Randolph Co., Ill. Relinquishment of dower rights on 1/3 of 85 acres in Bois Brule Bottom where Francis **Seissall** died; adjoined on the N by Joseph **Bland**, and being where sd **Fowler** and wife now live. Sd Naomah, late Naomah **Seissall**, was entitled to a dower in sd land belonging to her late husband Francis **Seissall**. Signed Hilliard **Fowler**, Naomah (x) **Fowler** (RD). Wit Joab **Waters**, JCC, Polly Ann **Waters**. Rec 8 Jun 1829.

262. Page 212. 8 May 1829. Henry **Dodge** for the estate of James **Samuels** by Elias **Barcroft**, Auditor of Public Accounts for Mo., to James **Farquhar** and George E. **Jackson**. For the sum of $6, 640 acres on the waters of Cinque Hommes. Sold to pay back taxes and penalties for 1826. Signed E. **Barcroft**, Auditor. Wit Frederick C. **Hase**, Clerk. Rec 15 Jun 1829.

263. Page 213. 15 Apr 1828. William **McGuire** and Susan, his wife, and Claiborne S. **Thomas**, all of Cape Girardeau Co., Mo., to Lewis **Thorp**. For the sum of $39.46 1/4, 31.57 acres, being the NW fractional 1/4, Sec 21, Twp 36 N, Rng 12 E. Signed Wm. **McGuire**, Susan **McGuire** (RD), C. S. **Thomas**. Wit Peter R. **Garrett**, JP in Cape Girardeau Co., Mo. Rec 27 Jun 1829.

264. Page 214. 28 Jul 1829. James B. **May** by Sheriff David L. **Caldwell** to James **Rice**. For the sum of $20, 80 acres, an undivided part of 640 acres in Cinque Hommes Twp in The Barrens about one mile and a half E of Perryville; confirmed to James **Moore** Junr. Sold on 28 Jul 1829 on an execution issued 9 May 1829 by Circuit Court in favor of William M. **Newberry** and against sd **May** and George **Fenwick** for $90 damages and $14.51 1/4 costs and charges. Signed D. L. **Caldwell**, Sheriff. Wit Frederick C. **Hase**, Clerk. Rec 29 Jul 1829.

265. Page 215. 1 Aug 1829. Sally **Seargent** of Randolph Co., Ill. to David **Flynn**. For the sum of $ 125, 50 acres in Bois Brule Bottom, where sd **Seargent** resided, and which she bought from Archibald **Morgan** (Ste. Genevieve Co. records). Signed Sally (x) **Seargent**. Wit Joab **Waters** (JP), Isaac **Flynn**. Rec 3 Aug 1829.

266. Page 216. 27 Apr 1829. Ignatius **Layton** and Elizabeth, his wife, to John M. **Odin**. For the sum of $100, 50 acres on the waters of Cinque Hommes Creek, part of a tract divided among the heirs of John **Layton** senr, decd; beginning at the most E corner of the original survey, and bounded in part by Rezin L. **Bishop** and the heirs of Joseph **Layton**, decd. Signed Ignatius **Layton**, Elizabeth (x) **Layton** (RD). Wit John **Layton** (JP). Rec 15 Aug 1829.

267. Page 217. 10 Aug 1803. Sarah Ann **Abernathy** of Lincoln Co., N. Car. to her son-in-law John **Farrar**. For diverse good causes and considerations, one negro slave named **Milly** and her increase, after the decease of sd **Abernathy**; then to sd **Farrar** and his children by Elizabeth, the late daughter of sd **Abernathy**. Signed Sarah Ann (x) **Abernathy**. Wit R. J. **Miller**, jurat, Aaron **Abernathy**. Proved in open court at Oct 1804 sessions, Lincoln Co., N. Car., by sd **Miller**. Rec 7 Sep 1829.

268. Page 217. 27 Apr 1829. Delinquent tax list for 1828 taxes. The tax, plus 15% interest per annum, is due by 1 Aug 1829, or the property is to be sold.

To Whom Assessed or patentee	Original claimant	No. of acres & hundredths taxed	Part of sections or No. of survey	Twp	Rng	Amt. taxes etc. due	Years taxes
Able, Ezekiel	John **Townsend**	136.28	81	36	10	0.74	1828
Boggy & **Shannon**	John **O'Connor**	255.21	2063	36 & 37	11	2.03	do
Crips, David	David **Crips**	286.00	2186	36	10 & 11	1.88	do
Fenwick, Joseph	Joseph **Fenwick**	451.10	1243	33 & 34	12 & 13	3.25	do
Hinch, Saml. Senr.	Saml. **Hinch** senr	213.00	864	34	13	1.78	do
Hawkins, John	Alexr. **Murdock**	191.40	2109	36	11	1.65	do
Hamilton, Geo. A.	Geo. A. **Hamilton**	216.00	1244	34	13 & 14	1.89	do
Lockhart, Widow	Widow **Lockhart**	382.81	1884	36	11 & 12	1.43	do
McClanahan, Jms. legal reps.	Jms. **McClanahan**	170.14	661	36	11	1.02	do
Rolf, James H.	Solomon **Morgan**	100.00	2170	37	10 & 11	1.03	do
Smith, Henry C.	Henry C. **Smith**	170.14	2099	35 & 36	12	1.43	do

Signed E. **Barcroft**, Auditor of Public Accts. Wit Frederick C. **Hase**, Clerk. Rec 14 Sep 1829.

269. Page 218. 3 Nov 1828. Ignatius **Layton** and Elizabeth, his wife and daughter of Joseph **Miles**, decd, to John **Tucker**. For the sum of $89, their interest in an undivided part of 71 1/9 acres on Saline Creek; confirmed to sd **Miles**. Signed Ignatius **Layton**, Elizabeth (x) **Layton**. Wit Frederick C. **Hase**, Clerk pro tem. Rec 14 Sep 1829.

270. Page 219. 9 Apr 1825. Israel **Maddin** and Louisana, his wife, to Joseph **Bland**. For the sum of $100, 25 acres in Bois Brule Bottom, part of a settlement right granted to Solomon **Morgan** by the U. S. A., and sold by sd **Morgan** to James **McLease**, decd, and sold by his administrators to satisfy a judgment obtained against him by Amos **Bird** at Sheriff's sale to Gustavus A. **Bird**, and by him to sd **Maddin** to satisfy a judgment against the executors of Amos **Bird**; beginning where the SE line of James **McLean**'s concession would intersect Francis **Cissell**'s line. Signed Israel **Maddin**, Louisiana **Maddin**. Test D. L. **Caldwell** (JP). Rec 23 Sep 1829.

271. Page 220. 16 Oct 1828. Richard S. **Dorsey** and Louvesy, his wife, to Perry **Evans**. For the sum of $140, quit claim to 20 acres, more or less, beginning at a stake at **McGennis**'s second corner on the old line of John **Layton**, decd. Signed R. S. **Dorsey**, Louvesy **Dorsey** (RD). Wit John **Layton** (JP). Rec 6 Oct 1829.

272. Page 221. 1 Oct 1829. David L. **Caldwell** to William **Powell**. For the sum of $800, 196 2/3 acres, more or less, in Boise Brule Bottom, where sd **Caldwell** now lives; beginning near the bank of Newsom's Lake on the N side of Bois Brule Creek on an elm, hackberry, and hickory; bounded in part by land of **Newsom**, now owned by **Waters**. Signed David L. **Caldwell**. Wit Joab **Waters** (JP). Rec 2 Nov 1829.

273. Page 222. 1 Oct 1829. William **Powell** to David L. **Caldwell**. For the sum of $650, mortgage on 196 2/3 acres, more or less, in Bois Brule Bottom as described in the preceding deed (1:221), to secure the purchase of sd tract. The debt is due as $200 by 1 Oct

1830, $200 by 1 Oct 1831, and $250 by 1 Oct 1832. Signed Wm. **Powell**. Wit Joab **Waters** (JP), Frederick **Hase**. Rec 2 Nov 1829.

274. Page 223. 12 Sep 1828. James B. **May** and Maria, his wife, of Cinque Hommes Twp, to James **Rice** of Brazoe Twp. For the sum of $50, 80 acres, more or less, in Cinque Hommes Twp, confirmed to James **Moore** junior, decd; being the undivided share of Matilda, his daughter, and transferred by her and her husband, Henry J. **Rhodes**, to sd **May**. Signed James B. **May**, Maria (x) **May**. Wit John **Layton** (JP). Rec 16 Nov 1829.

275. Page 224. 28 Oct 1829. Samuel C. **McDaniel** to Frederick C. **Hase**. For the sum of $35, mortgage on one yoke of oxen, named Roben and Rock, and one other yoke; together with the yokes, rings, and steeples thereunto belonging. Sd **McDaniel** owes a note of equal date to sd **Hase**, due in six months; otherwise the property is to be sold at public sale. Signed Samuel C. **McDaniel**, Frederick C. **Hase**. Wit John **Layton** (JP). Rec 28 Oct 1829.

276. Page 225. 1 Nov 1829. Joseph **Brown** to same. To secure rent on a farm owned by sd **Hase** and rented by sd **Brown**, mortgage on three horses, seven cattle, 400 bushels of corn, 25 hogs, one yoke of oxen, one light waggon or Tearburn(?), all his farming utensils, all beds and beddings, and all the household and kitchen furniture. The property to be sold at public sale if the rent is not paid. Signed Joseph (x) **Brown**, Frederick C. **Hase**. Wit John **Logan**, JCC. Rec 21 Nov 1829.

277. Page 226. 20 Jul 1829. St. Gemme **Beauvis** of Ste. Genevieve Co., Mo. to David L. **Caldwell**, who claims under the heirs of Vital **Beauvis**, decd. For the sum of $5, quit claim to his right to 500 arpens, more or less, in Bois Brule Bottom; being the N half of 1000 arpens claimed by St. Gemme **Beauvis** and Vital **Beauvis** by virtue of a concession and settlement made under the Spanish Government, and confirmed to St. Gemme **Beauvis** by the U. S. A.; bounded on the N by sd **Caldwell**, originally John **Graham**, E by land originally owned by Jones **Newsom** Junr, W by land originally claimed by James **Davis**, now by the heirs of Henry **Dickason**, and S by the remainder of the tract; being the portion originally occupied by Vital **Beauvis** in his lifetime, then Joseph **Bogy**, and now occupied by William **Searcy**. Signed S. G. **Beauvis**. Wit Jos. D. **Grafton**, Clerk of Ste. Genevieve Co. Court. Rec 24 Nov 1829.

278. Page 227. 11 Jun 1829. Joseph **Bogy** and Mary, his wife, of Ste. Genevieve Co., Mo. to same. For the sum of $650, 500 arpens in Bois Brule Bottom, being Survey No. 442 and the N half of a tract of 1000 arpens as described in the preceding deed (1:226); which claim was relinquished by St. Gemme **Beauvis** to Vital **Beauvis** on 23 Jan 1811. One-third is conveyed in right of Mary, one of the daughters and heirs of Vital **Beauvis**, 1/3 was purchased from Nicholas **Jarrott** and Julie, his wife, sd Julie being another heir of sd Vital. Sd tract was divided by consent between St. Gemme and Vital **Beauvis**, and not running the lines. Signed Joseph **Bogy**, Maria **Bogy**. Wit John **Scott**, Jos. D. **Grafton**, Clerk of Ste. Genevieve Co., Mo. Rec 24 Nov 1829.

279. Page 228. 11 Jun 1829. David L. **Caldwell** to Joseph **Bogy** of Ste. Genevieve Co., Mo. For the sum of $550, mortgage on 500 arpens as described in the preceding two deeds (1:226, 1:227). The debt is due in two payments: $275 by 1 Oct 1830 and $275 by 1 Oct 1831. Signed D. L. **Caldwell**. Wit John **Scott**, W. **Wilkinson** (JP). Rec 24 Nov 1829.

280. Page 230. 24 Nov 1829. Commissioners of Perryville to Phineas **Block**. For the sum of $ 41.50, Lot No. 57 in Perryville. Signed R. T. **Brown**, Joseph **Tucker** senr., Thomas **Riney**, Commissioners. Wit W. **Wilkinson** (JP). Rec 24 Nov 1829.

281. Page 231. 9 Apr 1829. John **Morgan** and Patsy, his wife, of Washington Co., Ill. to Robert T. **Brown**. For the sum of $600, 480 acres, more or less, in Bois Brule Bottom; beginning on the bank of the Mississippi River at the corner of Thomas **Donohue**'s survey. Signed John (x) **Morgan**, Patsey (x) **Morgan** (RD). Wit Joab **Waters** (JP). Rec 16 Dec 1829.

282. Page 232. 28 Nov 1829. Robert T. **Brown** and Catherine, his wife, to Joseph **Paquin**. For the sum of $300, quit claim to their interest in an undivided half of 480 acres in Bois Brule Bottom, part of a tract purchased from John **Morgan**; beginning on the bank of the Mississippi River at the corner of Thomas **Donohue**'s survey. Signed R. T. **Brown**, Catharine **Brown** (RD). Wit Walter **Wilkinson** (JP). Rec 16 Dec 1829.

283. Page 233. 8 Apr 1824. Thomas **Riney** and William **Mattingly**. Agreement concerning land conveyance. Sd **Riney** has sold 640 acres on the S fork of Saline Creek about one and a half miles above Tuckers Mill to sd **Mattingly**. The purchase price to be paid as 2600 gallons of good proof whisky, delivered in good tight barrels in six installments of 434 gallons each: in Jun 1825, Jun 1826, Jun 1827, Jun 1828, Jun 1829, Jun 1830. Sd **Mattingly** is to pay an additional 434 gallons if he is late in any payment. Signed Thomas **Riney**, William **Mattingly**. Test John B. **Cissell**, Martin J. (x) **Moore**. Sd **Riney** has satisfied sd **Mattingley** for 640 acres as described in the deed, title is assigned to sd **Riney** on 9 Nov 1829. Signed William **Mattingly**. Wit James **Evans**, Frederick C. **Hase** (JP). Rec 16 Dec 1829.

284. Page 234. 5 Sep 1829. Treasury Department, Auditor's Office, Missouri, City of Jefferson. Delinquent tax list, to be paid by 14 Nov 1829, or to be sold for the tax and penalties at 5% per month from Dec 1828. Assessed to John **Layton** senr, 74 acres, Survey No. 844, in Twp 35 N, Rng 10 & 11 E, for $0.92. Signed E. **Barcroft**, Auditor of Public Accounts. Wit Frederick C. **Hase**, Clerk. Rec 30 Dec 1829.

285. Page 235. 7 May 1827. Alfred **Bird** by Elias **Barcroft**, Auditor of Public Accounts for Mo., to **Oakless & Clark**. For the sum of $3.54 in back taxes, 225 acres on the Mississippi River. Signed E. **Barcroft**, Auditor of Public Accounts. Wit Frederick C. **Hase**, Clerk. Rec 13 Jan 1830.

286. Page 236. 7 Nov 1829. Jonas **Winfield** and Elenor, his wife, to John **Moore**. For the sum of $45, 66 acres, being the N end, NE fractional 1/4, Sec 31, Twp 36 N, Rng 11 E; bounded on the S by Henry **McAttee** and E by Jonathan **Preston**. Signed Jonas **Winfield**, Eleonore **Winfield** (RD). Wit W. **Wilkinson** (JP). Rec 14 Jan 1830.

287. Page 237. 19 Oct 1827. Josiah F. **Hamilton** and Fanny, his wife, to Leo **Fenwick**. For the sum of $55, undivided 1/6 part of two tracts; 450 acres, part of 2000 arpens confirmed to George A. **Hamilton**, decd, and a part of the late widow Clare **Hamilton**'s dower land, wife of George A. **Hamilton**, bounded on the N by the tract where Joseph **Fenwick**, decd, last lived, W by poor barren, S & SW by 100 acres, more or less, owned by George A.

Hamilton and known as his hill land, and SE by 65 acres sold by Josiah F. **Hamilton** to one **Lacy**, now belonging to Harrison **Young**, and E by a line marking the W end of seven lots, six of 44 acres each, facing the Mississippi River three or four miles above the Grand Tower, and that once belonged to heirs of George A. **Hamilton**, decd, being Fenwick **Hamilton**, Matilda **Hamilton**, Ulila **Hamilton**, Leo F. **Hamilton**, Walter F. **Hamilton**, and George A. **Hamilton**, with the seventh lot being 76 acres, more or less, and is the other part of sd Clare **Hamilton**'s dower land and being the last residence of Clare **Sherry** and George A. **Hamilton**, her first husband; and 44 acres, more or less, which Josiah F. **Hamilton** holds as one of the heirs of his sister Matilda **Hamilton**, bounded on the N by the former lot of Ulila **Hamilton**, now Harrison **Young**, S by the lot formerly of Leo F. **Hamilton**, now John **Sherry**, and E by the Mississippi River. Signed Josiah F. **Hamilton**, Fanny (x) **Hamilton**. Wit Alexius **Manning**, Cornelius **Manning**, James **Mattingly** (JP). Rec 2 Feb 1830.

288. Page 238. 5 Dec 1827. Eulile **Hamilton** of St. Louis Co., Mo. by her atty Fenwick J. **Hamilton**, to same. For the sum of $55, her undivided 1/6 part of the two tracts described in the preceding deed (1:237); her portion of the first being Lot No. 3. Signed Fenwick J. **Hamilton**, agent for Eulile **Hamilton**. Test James J. **Fenwick**, Tho. **Fenwick**, James **Mattingly** (JP). Rec 2 Feb 1830.

289. Page 240. 5 Dec 1827. Fenwick J. **Hamilton** to same. For the sum of $55, his undivided 1/6 part of two tracts as described in 1:237; his portion of the first being Lot No. 2. Signed Fenwick J. **Hamilton**. Wit Thos. **Fenwick**, James J. **Fenwick**, James **Mattingly** (JP). Rec 2 Feb 1830.

290. Page 241. 9 Oct 1828. Leo F. **Hamilton** to same. For the sum of $55, his undivided right to two tracts as described in 1:237, the first between one and three miles above the mouth of Brazoe Creek, and the second being his share of Lot No. 4, allotted to his late sister Matilda. Signed Leo F. **Hamilton**. Wit Joseph **James**, Walter F. **Hamilton**, James J. **Fenwick** (JP). Rec 2 Feb 1830.

291. Page 242. 9 Oct 1828. Same to same. For the sum of $132, 44 acres and 65 poles, more or less, in the Mississippi River bottom between one and three miles above the mouth of Brazoe Creek; part of 2000 arpents that was confirmed to George A. **Hamilton**, his deceased father, and being Lot No. 5 which was drawn by the Commissioners appointed by Circuit Court to partition the real estate of George A. **Hamilton**; bounded on the E by the Mississippi River, S by Lot No. 6 for Walter F. **Hamilton**, W by 457 acres which was part of the dower land of the late Clare **Hamilton**, widow of George A. **Hamilton**, and N by Lot No. 4 for his deceased sister Matilda. Signed Leo F. **Hamilton**. Wit Joseph **James**, Walter F. **Hamilton**, James J. **Fenwick** (JP). Rec 2 Feb 1830.

292. Page 243. 4 Dec 1828. Fenwick J. **Hamilton** to same. For the sum of $33, all his share and Josiah F. **Hamilton**'s share of 457 acres set apart from the land of George A. **Hamilton**, decd, as the dower of his widow; being the NW corner of the original survey; bounded on the N by Joseph **Fenwick**, decd, W by public land, S by Lot Nos. 7 & 8, drawn for Josiah F. **Hamilton** and George A. **Hamilton**, and E by Lot Nos. 1-6 drawn for the heirs of George A. **Hamilton**, decd, and 76 acres, being the remainder of the widow's dower, and the land purchased by Fenwick J. **Hamilton** at Sheriff's sale on 26 Nov 1828. Signed Fenwick J. **Hamilton**. Test James J. **Fenwick** (JP). Rec 2 Feb 1830.

293. Page 244. 27 Jan 1830. Joseph **Shoults** and Elizabeth, his wife, to Isaac **Johnson**. For the sum of $400, 400 acres, more or less, on a branch of the S fork of Saline Creek; adjoined on the S by Bernard & Lewis **Cissell** and N by Rowland **Boyd**; where sd **Johnson** now resides. The lead and mineral rights are not transferred, and are reserved to sd **Boyd** and wife as per their deed to sd **Shoults** dated 6 Dec 1825; and sd **Shoults** reserves the right to cut timber NE of the top of the hill and NE of the house. Signed Joseph **Shoults**, Elizabeth (x) **Shoults** (RD). Wit Daniel **Killian**, Thos. **Allen**, Frederick C. **Hase** (JP). Rec 9 Feb 1830.

294. Page 246. 11 Feb 1830. John M. **Odin** to Valero **Fainia**. For the sum of $200, 50 acres in Cinq Hommes Twp, part of 640 acres confirmed to John **Layton** senr, decd, and divided among his heirs; conveyed by Ignatius **Layton** and Elizabeth, his wife, to sd **Odin** on 27 Apr 1829, and lately occupied by Edward **McGines**; beginning at the E corner of the original survey and bounded in part by Rezin **Bishop** and the heirs of Joseph **Layton**, decd. Signed J. M. **Odin**. Wit Alvan **Cook**, James **Hase**, Frederick C. **Hase** (JP). Rec 11 Feb 1830.

295. Page 247. 20 Feb 1830. Thomas **Riney** and Sarah, his wife, and Zachariah **Layton** and Mary, his wife, to George **Killian**. For the sum of $60, Lot No. 32 in Perryville, deeded to sd **Riney** and sd **Layton** by the Commissioners on 1 Sep 1825 (1:134). Signed Thomas **Riney**, Sarah (x) **Riney** (RD), Zachariah **Layton**, Mary (x) **Layton** (RD). Wit John **Layton** (JP). Rec 22 Feb 1830.

296. Page 248. 1 Sep 1829. Thomas **Cody** to William W. **Taylor**. For the sum of $20, Lot No. 51 in Perryville. Signed Thomas **Cody**. Wit James **Layton**. Test John **Layton** (JP). Rec 2 Mar 1830.

297. Page 248. 1 Nov 1828. James B. **May** and Maria, his wife, to James **Rice**. For the sum of $50, undivided part of 80 acres in the survey of James **Moore** Junr, decd, the father of sd Maria; adjoined on the E by land confirmed to Bede **Moore**, and W by land confirmed to James **Moore**, son of Nicholas **Moore**. Signed James B. **May**, Maria (x) **May**. Wit Henry **Miles**, Henry (x) **Miles**, [Jedson **Rhodes**], Frederick C. **Hase**, Clerk. Rec 15 Mar 1830.

298. Page 250. 17 Mar 1830. William **Hinkson** and Jane, his wife, to Jacob **Shaner**. For the sum of $320, the undivided moiety of 640 acres, more or less, on the waters of Brazeau, confirmed to Benjamin **Harrison** as Survey No. 2179; beginning at a post on the S boundary of Joseph **James**' survey. Signed Wm. **Hinkson**, Ginney **Hinkson** (RD). Wit Israel **McGready**, Clerk of Washington Co., Mo. Rec 19 Mar 1830.

299. Page 251. 14 Jun 1828. Commissioners of Perryville to Richd S. **Dorsey**. For the sum of $3.25, Lot No. 60 in Perryville. Signed R. T. **Brown**, Thomas **Riney**, Joseph **Tucker** senr., Commissioners. Wit W. **Wilkinson** (JP). Rec 1 Apr 1830.

300. Page 252. 7 Nov 1828. Richard S. **Dorsey** and Louvesy, his wife, to Bartholomew **Murphy**. For the sum of $7, Lot No. 60 in Perryville. Signed R. S. **Dorsey**, Louvecy **Dorsey** (RD). Wit John **Layton** (JP). Rec 1 Apr 1830.

301. Page 252. 1 Apr 1830. William A. **Keyte** to Elvis **Ragland**. For the sum of $5, lease on the NE corner of Lot No. 49, fronting on Main St, on which sd **Ragland** is building a blacksmith shop, for one year from 1 Dec last. Sd **Ragland** is not to transfer the lot during this time. Signed W. A. **Keyte**, Ann **Keyte** (RD). Wit James **Evans**, Frederick C. **Hase** (JP). Rec 1 Apr 1830.

302. Page 253. 22 Sep 1829. Isidore **Moore** and Leah, his wife, to Alfred H. **Puckett**. For a valuable consideration, Lot Nos. 9 & 33 in Perryville; Lot 9 having been obtained by deed on 24 May 1823. If any dispute should arise in the title in consequence of a patent not having been obtained by Bernard **Layton** when he conveyed land to the county, then there is to be no recourse against sd **Moore**, but against the county. Signed Isidore **Moore**, Leah (x) **Moore** (RD). Wit Austin **Moore**, Fredk. C. **Hase** (JP). Rec 9 Apr 1830.

303. Page 254. 23 Mar 1830. Commissioners of Perryville to Joseph **Manning** senr. For the sum of $ 67.12 1/2, Lot Nos. 4 & 48 in Perryville. Signed R. T. **Brown**, Thomas **Riney**, Joseph **Tucker** senr., Commissioners. Wit W. **Wilkinson** (JP). Rec 19 Apr 1830.

304. Page 255. 30 Mar 1830. Joseph **Manning** and Mary, his wife, to Joseph **Shoults**. For the sum of $111.50, Lot No. 48 in Perryville. Signed Joseph **Manning**, Mary (x) **Manning** (RD). Test John **Layton** (JP). Rec 19 Apr 1830.

305. Page 256. 18 Dec 1828. Elias **Barcroft**, Auditor of Public Accounts for Mo., to Joseph **James** by D. L. **Caldwell**. For the sum of $5.98 in back taxes and penalties for 1827, release of 640 acres on Brazeau, originally claimed by sd **James**. Signed E. **Barcroft**, Auditor of Public Accounts. Wit Frederick C. **Hase**, Clerk. Rec 27 Apr 1830.

306. Page 256. 23 Dec 1829. Rowland **Boyd** and Julie, his wife, to Joab **Waters**. For the sum of $1467, 640 acres on the Mississippi River near the lower end of Bois Brule Bottom, on what is called the cut off; part of the same confirmed to Charles **Ellis** senr by the U. S. A., and deeded by sd **Ellis** to Roling **Boyd** [Ste. Genevieve Co. records]; with the portion to be run off by Henry **Elliott**, and lies at the side of a concession granted to Joshua **Fisher**. Sd **Boyd** reserves 200 acres at the lower end of the original survey to himself, so as to take in more than half of the front of the cutoff. Signed Roland (x) **Boyd**, Julie (x) **Boyd** (RD). Wit W. **Wilkinson**, JCC. Rec 3 May 1830.

307. Page 258. 9 Jul 1830. Isidore **Moore** and Leah, his wife, to Levi **Block**, merchant. For the sum of $65, Lot No. 33 in Perryville, as deeded to him by the Commissioners on 24 May 1823. Signed Isidore **Moore**, Leah (x) **Moore** (RD). Wit Frederick C. **Hase** (JP). Rec 9 Jul 1830.

308. Page 259. 3 May 1830. Timothy **Davis**, adminr of Amos **Bird**, decd, to George **Petitt** of Ste. Genevieve Co., Mo. For the sum of $160, 640 acres of timbered land about one mile W of the residence of the decd at the time of his death; confirmed to Frederick **Woolford** and known as the Woolford Tract. Sold on the 4th Monday of Mar 1829 on order of Circuit Court issued Aug Term 1828 to sell sd land to pay debts of the estate. Signed Timothy **Davis**. Wit Frederick C. **Hase** (JP). Rec 9 Jul 1830.

309. Page 260. 6 Mar 1830. List of lands sold for taxes. Tax, penalties at the rate of 15% per annum, and 37 cents costs due by 17 May 1830, or the tracts are to be sold.

In whose name Assessed	Original Claimant or Patentee	Quantity	Parts of Sec. or Survey No.	Twp	Rng	Amt of of tax	No. of acres sold
Able, Ezekiel under	Jno. **Townsend**	340.28	81	36	10	$0.70	340.28
Fenwick, Joseph		5	part 1243	33 & 34	12 & 13	$0.40	5
Hagan, Joseph		204	852	35 & 36	10	$1.37	204
Hamilton, Geo. A.		620				$3.29	620
Hutchins, James		640	2175	34	14	$4.13	640
Hays, Jno. & Wm. **Garner**		80	W 1/2 SE, Sec 2	33	13	$0.94	80
Shannon & Boggy	Mark **Brooks**	255.21	2063	36 & 37	11	$1.57	255.21
"	under John **O'Connor**						
Tendo, Reuben		85				$0.74	85

Signed E. **Barcroft**, Auditor of Public Accounts. Wit Frederick C. **Hase**, Clerk. Rec 9 Jul 1830.

310. Page 260. 24 Jul 1830. James S. **Kelly** to John **Williams**. To secure a note of even date for $105 with interest, deed of trust on one bay mare, four cattle, 12 hogs, 10 sheep, and six spining wheels. The debt is due in 6 months, and the property is to be sold at public sale by sd **Williams** if the debt is not paid, with any surplus to go to sd **Kelly**. Signed James S. **Kelly**, John **Williams**. Wit Fredk. C. **Hase** (JP). Rec 24 Jul 1830.

311. Page 262. 7 Aug 1830. Robert **Wimsatt** and James **Wimsatt**, heirs of Joseph Z. **Wimsatt**, decd, and Mary **Wimsatt**, widow of sd decd, to Susan M. **Evans**. For the sum of $50, Lot No. 43 in Perryville; bounded on the N by St. Josephs St, and E, S, & W by lots; purchased by Joseph Z. **Wimsatt** of the Commissioners. Signed Robert **Wimsatt**, James **Wimsatt**, Mary (x) **Wimsatt**. Wit Frederick C. **Hase** (JP). Rec 7 Aug 1830.

312. Page 263. 16 Aug 1830. Henry **Welker** to David **Welker**. For the sum of $50, an improvement on Apple Creek where sd Henry now resides, one sorrel gelding four years old, two red cows, two white yearling heifers, one plough and geers. Signed Henry (x) **Welker**. Wit Pius **Brewer**, Alvan **Cook** (JP). Rec 16 Aug 1830.

313. Page 263. 1 Mar 1830. Barnabas **Burns** to Reddick **Eason**. For the sum of $100, Lot No. 58 in Perryville, purchased by sd **Burns** of the Commissioners on 9 Jun 1823 (1:75); being the SW corner lot of a flock fronting on the public square on Jackson St and St. Marys St. Signed Barnabas **Burns**. Test John **Layton** (JP), Isaac **Hill**. Rec 11 Oct 1830.

314. Page 264. 16 Sep 1830. John **Cox** to James **Roark**. For the sum of $50, on the waters of Bois Brule Creek; being an equal 1/3 part of 340 acres that came to sd **Cox** as an heir of Andrew **Cox**, decd; and being the settlement or head right of Elias **Cowen** and conveyed by him to Andrew **Cox**. Signed John **Cox**. Wit James **Evans**, Michael **Burns**, Fredk. C. **Hase** (JP). Rec 11 Oct 1830.

315. Page 265. 16 Mar 1830. William **Harrison** and Ann, his wife, Andrew **Miller** and Catharine, his wife, John **Swan** and Mary, his wife, Julias **Harrison**, and Aristides **Harrison**, all heirs of Benjamin **Harrison**, decd, to William **Hinkson**, all of Washington Co., Mo. For the sum of $320, undivided moiety of 640 acres on the waters of Brazeau, confirmed to Benjamin **Harrison** as Survey No. 2179; beginning at a post on the S boundary of Joseph **James**' survey. Signed Wm. **Harrison**, Ann (x) **Harrison** (RD), Andrew **Miller**, Catharine **Miller** (RD), John **Swan**, Mary **Swan** (RD), J. **Harrison**, Aristides **Harrison**. Wit Israel **McGready**, Clerk of Washington Co., Mo. Rec 14 Oct 1830.

316. Page 267. 16 Mar 1830. William **Harrison** and Ann, his wife, Andrew **Miller** and Catharine, his wife, William **Hinkson** and Jane, his wife, John **Swan** and Mary, his wife, Julias **Harrison**, and Aristides **Harrison**, all heirs of Benjamin **Harrison**, decd, all of Washington Co., Mo., to Jacob **Shaner**. For the sum of $640, undivided moiety of 640 acres described in the preceding deed (1:265). Signed Wm. **Harrison**, Ann (x) **Harrison** (RD), Andrew **Miller**, Catharine **Miller** (RD), William **Hinkson**, Ginne **Hinkson** (RD), John **Swan**, Mary **Swan** (RD), J. **Harrison**, Aristides **Harrison**. Wit Israel **McGready**, Clerk of Washington Co., Mo. Rec 14 Oct 1830.

317. Page 269. 19 Jul 1830. George **Camster** and Marthy, his wife, of Cape Girardeau Co., Mo. to George Washington **Sturdivant**. For the sum of $300, 200 acres, the lower part of 420 arpents confirmed to William **Fitz Gibbons**; bounded on the N by the Mississippi River, E by land confirmed to Neal **Hornback**, and W by Alexander **McConnohue**. Signed George **Camster**, Martha **Camster** (RD). Wit George **Henderson**, Justice of Cape Girardeau Co., Mo. Court. Rec 18 Oct 1830.

318. Page 269. 1 Sep 1830. Jonas **Winfield** and Elenor, his wife, to Lewis **French**. For the sum of $42.50, 6 3/4 acres on the N bank of Apple Creek, part of Sec 19, Rng 11, Twp 34; beginning at the dividing line between sd **Winfield** and sd **French** on the bank of the creek; agreeable to a bond dated 1 Jun 1829. Signed Jonas **Winfield**, Eleanor (x) **Winfield** (RD). Wit James **Evans**, Alvan **Cook** (JP), John **Layton** (JP). Rec 26 Oct 1830.

319. Page 271. 14 Jan 1830. Thomas **Cody** to Lot **Johnston**. For the sum of $100, 71 1/9 acres, more or less, part of a survey confirmed to Joseph **Hagan**, decd; including an improvement made by James **Tucker** senr. Signed Thomas **Cody**. Test John **Layton** (JP), James **Layton**. Rec 27 Oct 1830.

320. Page 271. 15 Jun 1830. James H. **Rolfe** and Mildred, his wife, to Thomas M. **Horine**, all of Washington Co., Mo. For the sum of $100, 100 acres in Bois Brule Bottom; taken off the upper end of a tract confirmed to James **McLane**, by a direct line from the Mississippi River drawn parallel to the lower boundary of the tract; and the same deeded by Thomas **Maddin**, adminr of the estate of sd **McLane** on 17 Feb 1821 to sd **Rolfe** and Harvey **Lane**, and by sd **Lane** for his interest to sd **Rolfe**. Signed James H. **Rolfe**, Mildred **Rolfe** (RD). Wit Amos J. **Bruce**, JCC in Washington Co., Mo., A. **Burt** Jr. Rec 1 Nov 1830.

321. Page 272. 17 Aug 1830. Elias **Barcroft**, Auditor of Public Accounts for Mo., to Hiram **Fowler**. For the sum of $14.98 in back taxes and penalties, release of 575 acres assessed in the name of sd **Fowler**, and situated at the Sweat House Spring, as described in the 1825 tax list. Signed E. **Barcroft**, Auditor of Public Accounts. Rec 2 Nov 1830.

322. Page 273. 27 Jul 1829. John **Polk** to William **Polk** Sr. For the sum of $60, 80 or 90 acres, more or less, on White Water, beginning on a stake near the stone chimney on Wm. **Polk**'s old corner. Signed John **Polk**. Test John W. **Miller**, JP in Madison Co., Mo., Henry **Powel**, Josias **Berryman**, JP in Madison Co. Rec 5 Nov 1830.

323. Page 274. 17 May 1830. Joseph **Hagan** by Elias **Barcroft**, Auditor of Public Accounts for Mo., to Michael **Hagan**. For the sum of $1.37 in back taxes and 5% interest per month from 1 Dec 1829, 204 acres, being Survey No. 852 in Twps 35 & 36, Rng 10. Sold to pay taxes for 1829, and which were not paid by 1 Dec 1829. Signed E. **Barcroft**, Auditor of Public Accounts. Wit Frederick C. **Hase**, Clerk. Rec 20 Nov 1830.

324. Page 275. 11 Apr 1829. James **Keyte** of St. Louis, Mo, and William A. **Keyte** of Perryville. Articles of agreement. W. A. is indebted to James for his stock of goods on hand in Perryville in his store, and conveys that stock to James, and all accounts, debts, and demands due to sd W. A. in sd store since 25 Dec last. Sd James appoints W. A. as his agent in sd store. W. A. shall convey to James two lots in Perryville, on one of which is the store and a dwelling now occupied by W. A., to secure the balance of accounts against sd W. A. W. A. covenants to discharge his duty as agent of sd James in the premises and account as stated, and to act in the interest of sd James and obey his instructions. This agreement is not to be considered a partnership. Signed William A. **Keyte**, James **Keyte**. Test J. R. **Browning**, J. C. **Garner**, JP in St. Louis Co., Mo. Rec 23 Nov 1830.

325. Page 276. 8 Jan 1829. Richard S. **Dorsey** and Louvecy, his wife, of Perryville to Robert T. **Brown**. For the sum of $200, 1/2 acre, more or less, being Lot No. 69 in Perryville. Signed R. S. **Dorsey**, Louvecy **Dorsey**. Wit Moses S. **Harris**, Thomas **Riney**, Jos. D. **Grafton**, W. **Wilkinson** (JP). Rec 15 Dec 1830.

326. Page 277. 14 Dec 1830. Roland **Boyd** and Juliet, his wife, to Isaac **Hill**. For the sum of $200, 155 acres, more or less, on the W side of Costerd Creek, a fork of Saline Creek; being where sd **Boyd** now resides. Signed Rowland (x) **Boyd**, Juliet **Boyd** (RD). Wit Frederk. C. **Hase** (JP), John **Modglin**, Joseph **Shoults**. Rec 18 Dec 1830.

327. Page 278. 8 Dec 1830. Robert T. **Brown** and Catharine, his wife, to Joseph **Paquin**. For the sum of $300, quit claim to the undivided half of 480 acres, more or less, purchased from John **Morgan**; beginning on the bank of the Mississippi River at the corner of Thomas **Donohue**'s survey. Signed R. T. **Brown**, Catharine **Brown** (RD). Wit W. **Wilkinson**, JCC. Rec 18 Dec 1830.

328. Page 279. 21 Dec 1830. Edward **McGinnes** and Margaret, his wife, to Alfred L. **Parker**. For the sum of $160, 80 acres, being the E 1/2, NE 1/4, Sec 28, Twp 34, Rng 12 E. Signed Edward (x) **McGinness**, Margaret **McGinness** (RD). Wit Elias **Barber** (JP). Rec 23 Dec 1830.

329. Page 280. 28 Aug 1829. John H. **Sanders** and Polly, his wife, of Henry Co., Ken. to Nathaniel P. **Robertson** of Nicholas Co., Ken. For the sum of $830, 300 arpents in Bois Brule Bottom; beginning at a stake on the lower corner on the Mississippi River; that Alexander **McConohue** sold to George **Robertson**, and that sd **Robertson** sold to sd **Sanders**; being the upper half of sd **McConohue**'s confirmation of 600 arpents. Sd **Sanders** only conveys such title as derived from George **Robertson**, and has no other than that derived from such title. Signed John H. **Sanders**, Polly C. **Sanders** (RD). Wit Danl. **Mayes**, Judge of Henry Co., Ken. Circuit, Edm. P. **Thomas**, Clerk of Henry Co., Ken. Rec 30 Dec 1830.

330. Page 281. 1 Jan 1831. Zachariah **Layton** and Mary, his wife, to Benedicta **Fenwick**, Superior of Bethlehem Convent in Perry Co. For the sum of $1, 4.57 acres, beginning where his W line cuts the N line of a 640-acre tract ceded to Bishop **DuBourg** by the congregation of this parish, at a stake which is at present in the field of Bethlehem Convent; also bounded by Joseph **Manning**. It is understood that there will be a lane between the convent lands and lands of sd **Layton**. Signed Zachariah **Layton**, Mary (x) **Layton** (RD). Test John **Timon**, SCM, John R. **Layton** (JP). Rec 25 Jan 1831.

331. Page 282. 30 Sep 1829. Edward **McGennis** and Margret, his wife, to Mathew **Dumphy**. For the sum of $8, Lot No. 44 in Perryville, sold by the Commissioners to sd **McGennis** on 4 Nov 1826. Signed Edward M. **McGinnes**, Marggret **McGinnes** (RD). Wit Fredk. C. **Hase**, Clerk. Rec 15 Mar 1831.

332. Page 283. 15 Mar 1831. Matthew **Dumphy** to Bartholomew **Murphy**. For the sum of $10, Lot No. 44 in Perryville as described in the preceding deed (1:283). Signed Matthew **Dumphy**. Wit Fredk. C. **Hase** (JP). Rec 15 Mar 1831.

333. Page 284. 29 Mar 1831. William A. **Keyte** and Ann, his wife, to James **Keyte** of Chariton Co., Mo. For the sum of $2000, two lots in Perryville; Lot No. 49, conveyed by Robert **Abernathy** to William **Keyte**, and where is erected a store and dwelling now occupied by sd **Keyte** as a tavern; and Lot No. 56 as sold by the Commissioners to sd **Keyte**, adjoining Lot No. 49, and on which is erected a house used for a stable. Signed W. A. **Keyte**, Ann **Keyte** (RD). Wit Greer W. **Davis**, Joab **Waters** (JP). Rec 29 Mar 1831.

334. Page 285. 5 Apr 1831. Bernard **Brown** and Ann, his wife, to Barnabas **Burns**. For the sum of $58.50, Lot No. 35 in Perryville, sold by the Commissioners to sd **Burns** on 30 Nov 1825. Signed Bernard (x) **Brown**, Ann (x) **Brown** (RD). Wit W. **Wilkinson**, JCC. Rec 13 Apr 1831.

335. Page 285. 9 Apr 1831. Same and same to Ambrose **Meagher**. For the sum of $20, Lot No. 6 in Perryville, sold to sd **Brown** on 20 Nov 1825. Signed Bernard (x) **Brown**, Ann (x) **Brown** (RD). Wit W. **Wilkinson**, JCC. Rec 13 Apr 1831.

336. Page 286. 13 Oct 1830. Lott **Johnson** and Matilda, his wife, to Michael **Hagan**. For the sum of $150, 71 1/9 acres, more or less, part of a survey confirmed to Joseph **Hagan**, decd, including an improvement made by James **Tucker** Senr. Signed Lott **Johnson**, Matilda (x) **Johnson** (RD). Wit John **Layton** (JP). Rec 19 Apr 1831.

337. Page 287. 29 Apr 1831. Edward **McGinnis** to William **Garner** of Cape Girardeau Co., Mo. For the sum of $150, mortgage on 80 acres, more or less, on Indian Creek, being the W 1/2, SE 1/4, Sec 26, Twp 34 N, Rng 12 E; conveyed to sd **McGinnis** by sd **Garner** on 4 Mar 1831. Sd **McGinnis** owes a note for $90 dated 15 Feb last, payable in 9 months, and also assigned a promissory note to sd **Garner** on Alfred L. **Parks** and Haly B. **Parks** for $60, dated 21 Dec 1830 and payable in 10 months. Signed Edward **McGinnis**. Wit Elias **Barber** (JP). Rec 2 May 1831.

338. Page 288. 13 Jun 1831. David L. **Caldwell**, Hezekiah P. **Harris**, Aquila **Hagan**, John **Layton**, and Jones **Abernathy**, Commissioners to partition the real estate of James **Burns**, decd, to Barnabas **Burns**. For the sum of $121.50, 255 acres, more or less, confirmed to James **Burns** as Survey No. 662. Sold on 4 May 1830 on order of Circuit Court continued from Mar Term 1829 to sell lands of sd decd. Signed D. L. **Caldwell**, H. P. **Harris**, Aquila **Hagan**. Wit Joab **Waters** (JP), Pious **Brewer**. Rec 13 Jun 1831.

339. Page 290. 9 Sep 1824. Joseph R. **Bland** and Sabrina, his wife, to William **Morris**. For the sum of $450, __ acres in Bois Brule Bottom, which sd **Bland** purchased from Benajah **Morgan** and Elizabeth, his wife, on 6 Oct 1821 (1:32). Signed Joseph R. **Bland**, Sabrina **Bland**. Wit D. L. **Caldwell**, JCC. Rec 13 Jun 1831.

340. Page 291. 7 Feb 1831. Joseph **Shoults** and Elizabeth, his wife, to Joseph J. **James**. For the sum of $200, Lot Nos. 11, 12, & 26 feet of Lot No. 10 (beginning at the SE corner) in Perryville. Signed Joseph **Shoults**, Elizabeth (x) **Shoults** (RD). Test James C. **Moore**, Aquila **Hagan**, John **Layton** (JP). Rec 25 Jun 1831.

341. Page 292. 31 May 1824. U. S. A. to Isaac **Flynn** and David **Flynn**. Patent for the 57.42 acres, the SW fractional 1/4, Sec 27, Twp 37 N, Rng 11 E. Signed James **Monroe**, President. Wit Geo. **Graham**, Commissioner of the General Land Office. Rec in Vol. 1, page 483. Rec 27 Jun 1831.

342. Page 292. 20 Jul 1831. George **Killian** and Matilda, his wife, to Hilarion **Manning**. For the sum of $26, Lot No. 17 in Perryville, conveyed by James **Winfield** to sd **Killian**, and on which is erected a dwelling house now occupied by Richard S. **Dorsey**. Signed George **Killian**, Matilda **Killian** (RD). Wit Fredk. C. **Hase** (JP). Rec 20 Jul 1831.

343. Page 293. 9 Mar 1831. List of lands sold for taxes. Tax, penalties at the rate of 15% per annum, and 37 cents costs due by 1 Jun 1831, or the tracts are to be sold.

In whose name Assessed	Original Claimant or Patentee	Quantity (acres/100ths)	Parts of Sec. or Survey No.	Twp	Rng	Amt of of tax	No. of acres sold
Henry, John F.	A. **McConohue**	300	147	37	11	$2.81	300

Logan, John senr	F. **Barcume**	100	1845	33 & 34	12	$0.86	100
Maddin, Thomas	Jas. **Dutton**	306.25	88	37	11	$3.44	306.25
Do	Jas. **Dodson**	232.81	440	37	11	$2.57	232.81
Do	A. **Morgan**	325	--			$2.33	325
Russell, William	Jno. **Smith**'s reps.	320	1886	36	11	$2.81	320
Shannon, William	T. **Hickman**	640	1867	36 & 37	11	$3.50	640
Do	Jno. **Smith**'s reps.	320	1886	36	11	$2.81	320

Signed E. **Barcroft**, Auditor of Public Accounts. Wit Frederick C. **Hase**, Clerk. Rec 20 Jul 1831.

344. Page 294. 20 Jun 1831. Absolum **Kennison** of Jackson Co., Ill. to Presly **Kennison**. For the sum of $100, an undivided 1/6 part of 640 acres or arpens in Bois Brule Bottom on the Mississippi River; being land confirmed to James **Murdock** and conveyed to Absolum **Kennison** senr from **Delassus**, and divided by the last will and testament of Absolum **Kennison** senr, decd, to sd Absolum **Kennison** Junr, his son. Signed Absalom **Kinnison**. Wit Joab **Waters** (JP), William P. **Kenaday**. Rec 20 Jul 1831.

345. Page 295. 26 Jul 1831. Henry B. **Newsom** by former Sheriff David L. **Caldwell** to Joab **Waters** senr. For the sum of $134, 506 arpens in Bois Brule Twp; bounded on the N by William **Shanon**, W by sd **Caldwell**, and E by Roland **Meredith**'s heirs; where sd **Waters** now resides. Sold on 28 Jul 1829 on an execution from Circuit Court issued 23 Mar 1829 against sd **Newsom** in foreclosure of mortgage of $750 with $381.53 interest, by the State of Mo. Signed D. L. **Caldwell**, Sheriff. Wit Frederick C. **Hase**, Clerk. Rec 26 Jul 1831.

346. Page 297. 3 Aug 1830. Timothy **Davis**, adminr de bonis non of Amos **Bird**, decd, to Joseph **Pratte** of Ste. Genevieve Co., Mo. For the sum of $2000, 600 acres, more or less, at the head of Bois Brule Bottom, including considerable improvements and a large and valuable orchard. Sold on the 4th Monday of Mar 1829 on decree of County Court to pay debts of the estate of sd **Bird**. Signed Timothy **Davis**. Wit Fredk. C. **Hase**, Clerk. Rec 2 Aug 1831.

347. Page 298. 3 Aug 1831. Barnabas **Burns**, adminr of John **Burns**, decd, to Isaac **Meredith**. For the sum of $215, 100 acres, more or less, on the bank of the Mississippi River in Bois Brule Bottom, part of a tract confirmed to Alexander **Patterson**. Sold on the 4th Monday of Jul 1831 on decree of County Court issued May Term 1831, to pay debts of the estate of sd **Burns**. Signed Barnabas **Burns**. Wit Dorsey F. **Dolan**, Frederick C. **Hase** (JP). Rec 6 Aug 1831.

348. Page 299. 23 Jun 1831. William **Reardon** to William **Rex**. For the sum of $150, all his interest in an undivided part of the tract whereon his mother, Lucretia **Reiorden**, now lives; confirmed to Amos **Roark**, and conveyed by him to Robert **Reardon**. Signed William (x) **Reiorden**. Wit Willis **Ellis**, Andrew H. **Tucker**, Fredk. C. **Hase** (JP). Rec 11 Aug 1831.

349. Page 300. 4 Nov 1826. Commissioners of Perryville to Edward **McGennis**. For the sum of $ 8, Lot No. 44 in Perryville. Signed R. T. **Brown**, Joseph **Tucker** senr., Thomas **Riney**, Commissioners. Test Fredk. C. **Hase** (JP). Rec 11 Aug 1831.

350. Page 301. 22 Aug 1831. Isaac **Hill** to Willis **Ellis**. For the sum of $125, 155 acres, more or less, on the W side of Custerds Creek, a fork of Saline Creek, being all the land owned by Roland **Boyd**, and conveyed by him and Juliett, his wife, to sd **Hill** on 14 Dec 1830 (1:278). Signed Isaac **Hill**. Wit Fredk. C. **Hase** (JP), Henry W. **Cooper**. Rec 22 Aug 1831.

351. Page 301. 18 Jan 1830. Last will and testament of Joab **Waters** senior, decd. To his daughter Anna **Burgee**: $1. To Henry G. **Waters**: $1. To Eleanor **Daviss**, late Eleanor **Burgee**: $1. To his daughter Jane **Phillips**: his house and lot in New Markett. To Miranda **Hyatt**: undivided moiety of a tract with William **Hobbs** of Samuel on Bennets Creek. To his sons Joab **Waters** Junr and John **Waters**, 2000 arpens, an undivided tract on Terre Blue with Joseph **Hertick**, purchased by him and sd **Hertick** of the representatives of John **Price**. To his beloved companion Polly Ann Elizabeth **Caldwell**, now called Polly Ann Elizabeth **Waters**: the farm where he now lives; 640 acres at the lower end of Bois Brule Bottom deeded to him by Robert T. **Brown**; 100 arpens bought from the Sheriff and sold by George **Camster** and **English**, adminrs of Abner **Kennison**, for payment of debts; 440 acres bought from Rowland **Boyd** on the cut off, confirmed to Charles **Ellis**; about 300 acres, being the concession of Joshua **Fisher**, deeded to him by **Vanburkelos** or **Boyd** or **Fisher**, which he does not recollect; all his negroes, stock, farming utensils, household and kitchen furniture, debts due him, and every other species of property. After her death, all the property is to descend to her children equally. Polly Ann Elizabeth **Waters** is appointed executrix. Postscript: His son Henry G. **Waters** of Frederick Co., Md. owes him about $3000 for sale of property in Md.; with the debt to be equally divided between sd Henry G., Anna **Burgee**, Joab **Waters** Junr, Ealenor **Gilbert** (late Ealenor **Burgee**), Jane **Phillips**, Miranda **Hyatt**, and John **Waters**; all sons and daughters of his first wife. Signed Joab **Waters**. Wit Jacob J. **Everts**, Rezin L. **Bishop**, John **Logan**, Frederick C. **Hase**, Clerk. Rec 14 Sep 1831.

352. Page 303. 9 Sep 1831. Solomon **Morgan** of Lafayette Parish, La. to William **Flynn**. For the sum of $60, __ acres in Bois Brule Bottom, confirmed to the heirs of John **Morgan** senr; bounded on the N by land confirmed to John **Morgan** Junr. and land confirmed to Archibald **Morgan**, E by Congress land and land confirmed to Andrew **Dunks**, and S & W by Congress land. Signed Solomon **Morgan**. Wit H. **Clark**, W. **Searcy** (JP). Rec 16 Sep 1831.

353. Page 304. 3 Nov 1831. James T. **Tucker** to Levi **Block**. For the sum of $57.68 1/4, deed of trust on one gray horse, one bay colt, two cows and calves, 18 hogs, two sheep, one whip saw, one cross cut saw, two feather beds, one bar shear plough, one chipping axe, 10 acres corn supposed to contain 300 bushels, 70 bushels of potatoes, six acres of cotton, and all farming utensils, household, and kitchen furniture. Sd **Tucker** owes a note of equal date to sd **Block**, with interest until paid, and due nine months after date; the property to be sold to pay the debt if it is not paid, with any surplus to go to sd **Tucker**. Signed James T. **Tucker**, Levi **Block**. Wit Fredk. C. **Hase** (JP). Rec 3 Nov 1831.

354. Page 305. 5 May 1828. William **Tucker** and Sarah, his wife, to James **Manning**. For the sum of $200, __ acres, beginning at a stone at the NE corner of a tract where sd **Tucker** now lives. Signed William **Tucker**, Sarah (x) **Tucker**. Wit Joseph **Cissell**, Simon **Duvall**. Rec 7 Nov 1831.

355. Page 306. 17 Nov 1831. Josephus **Tucker** and Ann, his wife, to Bernard **Brown**. Quit claim to 320 acres, more or less, being the upper or SE part of James **Thompson**'s survey, confirmed to sd **Tucker**. Signed Josephus (x) **Tucker**, Ann (x) **Tucker** (RD). Wit W. **Wilkinson**, John **Layton** (JP), James H. **Norfolk**, County Court Clerk. Rec 17 Nov 1831.

356. Page 306. 10 Nov 1831. Fredk. C. **Hase**, adminr of Cornl. M. **Slattery**, decd, to Luther **Taylor**. For the sum of $10.50, Lot No. 52 in Perryville, on Main St. Sold on the 1st Monday of Feb 1830 on order of County Court issued Nov term 1829 to pay debts due by sd estate. Signed Frederick C. **Hase**. Wit Isidore **Moore**, JCC. Rec 17 Nov 1831.

357. Page 308. 20 Sep 1830. Mary **Wimsatt** to Robert **Wimsatt**. For the sum of $100, bond to make a deed to her interest in 127 1/2 acres; adjoined on the E by Bede **Moore**'s land that he purchased from James **Berry**, W by Henry **McAtee** and Elisha **Belsha**, decd, N by Clement **Knott** and James J. **Moore**, and S by John **Duvall** and Joseph **Duvall**. Signed Mary (x) **Wimsatt**. Test Wm. **McCauley**, Fredk. C. **Hase** (JP). Rec 22 Nov 1831.

358. Page 308. 30 Sep 1825. Elisha **Belsha** and Mary, his wife, to Henry **McAtee** Junr. For the sum of $50, 28 acres in the Barren Settlement, part of a tract confirmed to Jonathan **Preston**; bounded on the N by James **Philips**, E by Clement **Knotts**, S by Joseph Z. **Wimsatt**, and W by Congress lands. Signed Elisha **Belsha**, Mary **Belsha** (RD). Test John **Layton** (JP), David **Long**. Rec 3 Dec 1831.

359. Page 309. 22 Oct 1825. Joseph Z. **Wimsatt** and Mary, his wife, to same. For the sum of $33, 22 acres, more or less, beginning at a stone set on the ground at two white oaks; bounded in part by Elisha **Belsha**. Signed Joseph Z. **Wimsatt**, Mary (x) **Wimsatt**. Test John **Layton** (JP), John **Tucker**. Rec 3 Dec 1831.

360. Page 310. 18 Oct 1830. Jonas **Winfield** and Elenor, his wife, to same. For the sum of $75, 30 acres, more or less, in the Barrens Settlement, part of the NE fractional 1/4, Sec 31, Twp 36 N, Rng 11 E on the S end of sd tract; beginning at the S corner of Jonathan **Preston**'s survey; bounded in part by John **Moore** and David **Watkins**. Signed Jonas **Winfield**, Elenor (x) **Winfield** (RD). Wit John **Layton** (JP). Rec 3 Dec 1831.

361. Page 311. 26 Aug 1831. Peter P. **Tucker** and Mary, his wife, to same. For the sum of $100, 65 acres, being the SE fractional 1/4, Sec 31, Twp 36 N, Rng 11 E. Signed Peter P. **Tucker**, Mary (x) **Tucker** (RD). Wit John **Layton** Senr (JP), James **Layton**. Rec 3 Dec 1831.

362. Page 312. 10 Apr 1830. Last will and testament of Barnabas **Burns**, decd. To his son Michael: 308 arpens whereon he now lives, and which he purchased from his brother William; and his negro boy **Stephen**. To his married daughter Nancy: $250. To his married daughter Margaret: a negro boy **Anderson**. To his son William: 400 arpens whereon he now lives and that he originally obtained from the Spanish Government; 100 arpens of the upper tract originally granted to Joseph **Boice**, to be laid off in a square adjoining the first tract; a negro man **Isaac** and negro boys **Martin** and **Lorenzo**; a house and lot in Perryville; his stock, farming utensils, household and kitchen furniture, distillery, etc. To his single daughter Mary: a negro woman **Sylvia** with her infant child **Elizabeth**, and her future increase; a side saddle, bed, and beding. To his grandson Barnabas, son of Michael: the remaining 500 arpens of the tract originally granted to sd **Boice**, a negro boy **Abraham**, and he enjoins his execr to give him a good English education in reading, writing, and the common rules of arithmetic. To his youngest daughters Margaret and Mary: his part of his father's estate, to be equally divided between them when a division of the estate is made. To his daughter Mary: a horse worth $65, a couple of good cows, and suitable cloathing and necessaries while she remains single. His son William is appointed execr. Signed Barnabas **Burns**. Test Isidore **Moore**, Leo **Moore**, Fredk. C. **Hase**, Clerk. Rec 8 Dec 1831.

363. Page 313. 4 May 1829. George **Fenwick** and Peggy, his wife, to Bernard **Smith**. For the sum of $200, 100 acres on the waters of the S fork of Saline Creek; beginning at Bernard **Brown**'s SW corner at a set stone. Signed George (x) **Fenwick**, Margret (x) **Fenwick**. Wit Frederick C. **Hase**, Clerk. Rec 16 Jan 1832.

364. Page 314. 22 Nov 1831. Bernard **Brown** and Ann, his wife, to Wilfred **Layton**. For the sum of $200, 320 acres, more or less, being the SE part of James **Thompson**'s survey, confirmed to Josephus **Tucker**. Signed Bernard (x) **Brown**, Ann (x) **Brown** (RD). Wit John **Layton** (JP). Rec 16 Jan 1832.

365. Page 315. 4 Mar 1831. William **Garner** of Cape Girardeau Co., Mo. to Edward **McGinnis**. For the sum of $150, 80 acres, more or less, on Indian Creek, being the W 1/2, SE 1/4, Sec 26, Twp 34 N, Rng 12 E; purchased by sd **Garner** of the U. S. A. Signed William **Garner**. Wit James C. **Steele**, John **Sheppard**, Elias **Barber** (JP). Rec 6 Feb 1832.

366. Page 316. 23 Jan 1832. Edward **McGinnis** and Margret, his wife, to George **Martin**. For the sum of $280, 80 acres as described in the preceding deed (1:315). Signed Edward **McGinnes**, Margret **McGinnis** (RD). Wit Elias **Barber** (JP). Rec 6 Feb 1832.

367. Page 317. 1 Apr 1831. Robt. T. **Brown** and Catiche, his wife, and Charles C. **Valle** and Melanie, his wife, to Charles **Gregoire** Junr. For the sum of $3000, the mills and seat on the S fork of Saline Creek, known as Brown & Valle's Mills, including enough land to erect any works for the security of the mills and abutments of the dam; the seat purchased by sd **Brown** and sd **Valle** of Robert **Riorden** and Lucretia, his wife, on 19 Aug 1820 (Ste. Genevieve Co. Book C:352). Signed R. T. **Brown**, Catharine **Brown** (RD), Chs. C. **Valle**, Milanie **Valle** (RD). Wit W. **Wilkinson** (JP). Rec 6 Feb 1832.

368. Page 318. 6 Feb 1832. Alfred H. **Puckett** and Emily, his wife, to Erastus **Davis** of Ste. Genevieve Co., Mo. For the sum of $500, mortgage on Lot No. 9 in Perryville, upon which a brick dwelling is built, where sd **Puckett** now resides and which is used as a saddler's shop. Sd **Puckett** owes a note of the same date, payable in one year with 10% interest per annum. Signed Alfred

H. **Puckett**, Emily B. **Puckett** (RD). Wit Alvan **Cook** (JP). Rec 7 Feb 1832. [Marginal note: Sd **Puckett** is to remain in possesson of the property until the condition of the bond is broken. Signed T. **Davis** for E. **Davis**.]

369. Page 319. 16 Feb 1832. John **Logan** senr of Jackson Co., Ill. to Benjamin **Davis**. For the sum of $150, 100 acres on the waters of Apple Creek, part of **Barthume**'s original survey; beginning at the NE corner of sd survey. Signed John (x) **Logan**. Wit Eliza **Davis**, Augustus **Davis**, Elias **Barber** (JP). Rec 18 Feb 1832.

370. Page 320. 10 Jun 1831. Lewis **Greene** and Winneyfred, his wife, to Joab W. **Burgee**, all of Bois Brule Twp. For the sum of $150, 53 1/4 arpens in Bois Brule Twp; bounded on the N by George **Camster**, E by land confirmed to **Hickman**, S by Katharine **Belsha**, and W by Joel **Kennison**. Signed Lewis (x) **Greene**, Winnefield (x) **Greene** (RD). Test Joab **Waters** (JP), Caleb (x) **Hatten**. Rec 6 Mar 1832.

371. Page 321. 4 Feb 1830. Obadiah **Scott** and Polly, his wife, of Ste. Genevieve Co., Mo. to Daniel **Cline**. For the sum of $300 paid to Robert **Cleveland**, 201 1/2 acres at the head of Obrazo Creek, part of a tract originally granted to Theophilus **Williams**; bounded on the E by land confirmed to C. S. **Hinch**, and also bounded in part by Charles **Scott**; and beginning on the E line of the original survey at a rock. Signed O. **Scott**, Polly **Scott** (RD). Wit W. **Wilkinson** (JP). Rec 6 Mar 1832.

372. Page 322. 7 Aug 1829. Last will and testament of Elisha **Belshey**. To his wife Polly: all the household furniture; her choice of two cows; six sheep; one horse colt two years old, being a pet colt; [the crop now growing and his hogs]; and the plantation where he now resides, for and during her life, provided she does not remarry or leave Mo. To his two nephews, Elisha, son of his brother James, decd, and Jerry, son of his brother Jeremiah: equal shares of the plantation where he now lives after the death of his wife Polly, or after her remarriage. To his three sisters, Ester, Jane, and Delilah: equal share of all the rest of his property. His trusty friend John **Duvall** is appointed execr. Signed Elisha **Belshey**. Wit Joab **Waters**, Thos. **Donnohue**, John **Logan**, Fredk. C. **Hase**, Clerk. Codicil, dated 17 Sep 1829. His wife Polly is also to have one bay horse, a plough & one set of geers, an ax with a swingle tree, and all the property that he gave her, except the plantation is to be her right and estate forever. His wife is also to give his three sisters $50 out of her share of the estate at her death. To his brother Jeremiah: his cart and apparatus. Signed Elisha **Bellsha**. Wit Joab **Waters**, Thos. **Donnohue**, Samuel C. **McDaniel**, Fredk. C. **Hase**, Clerk. Rec 21 Mar 1832.

373. Page 324. 16 Apr 1827. John **Tucker** and Eleanor, his wife, and Aquila **Hagan** and Mary, his wife, to William **Manning**. For the sum of $33, 95 arpens on the Mississippi above the mouth of Obrazeau; granted to Thomas **Tucker**, and sold by him to Joseph **Tucker** senr, decd; beginning and running with lines run when the land was surveyed to Thomas **Tucker**. John **Tucker** and sd **Hagan** have title to 2 1/2 shares out of 10 shares. Signed John **Tucker**, Eleonr (x) **Tucker**, Aquila **Hagan**, Mary **Hagan**. Test F. J. **Hamilton**, John **Layton** (JP), Frederick C. **Hase**, Clerk. Rec 26 Mar 1832.

374. Page 326. 15 Mar 1832. A. L. **Parks** to Joseph **Fulse** (Volz) senior. For the sum of $170, 80 acres, being the E 1/2, NE 1/4, Sec 28, Twp 34, Rng 12 E. Signed Alfred L. **Parks**. Wit James **Taylor**, Francis (x) **Snerbush**, Fredk. C. **Hase** (JP). Rec 26 Mar 1832.

375. Page 326. 23 Jan 1832. Bernard **Brown** and Ann, his wife, to Jacob **Conrad** and Joseph **Miller**. For the sum of $23, Lot No. 22 in Perryville. Signed Bernard (x) **Brown**, Ann (x) **Brown**. Wit Wilfred **Layton**, John **Layton** (JP). Rec 26 Mar 1832.

376. Page 327. 23 Jan 1832. Eve **Hahn** to Christian **Hahn**. For the sum of $150, 80 acres, being the W 1/2, NE 1/4, Sec 33, Twp 34 N, Rng 9; patented to Eve **Hahn** by the U. S. A. Signed Eve (x) **Hahn**. Test Joseph **Bess**, Joshua **Bess**, John **Layton** (JP). Rec 26 Mar 1832.

377. Page 328. 28 Mar 1832. James J. **Moore** to John **O'Conner**. For the sum of $40, his undivided share in his grandfather's survey in The Barrens, being Survey No. 2137 in Twp 35, Twp 10 E. Signed James J. **Moore**. Wit William **Burns**, James B. **May**, Fredk. C. **Hase** (JP). Rec 28 Mar 1832.

378. Page 329. 26 Mar 1832. James **Hutchins** and Barbary, his wife, to Robert T. **Brown**. For the sum of $100, 640 acres, more or less, opposite or near the Grand Tower on the Mississippi River; originally confirmed to sd **Hutchins** as Survey No. 2175 in Twp 34 N, Rng 14 E. Signed James (x) **Hutchings**, Barbara (x) **Hutchings** (RD). Wit Alvan **Cook** (JP). Rec 28 Mar 1832.

379. Page 330. 13 Feb 1832. Joseph **Tucker** ser and Eleanor, his wife, to Joseph **Tucker**. For the love and kindness they bear unto their child, __ acres, part of the tract where Joseph **Tucker** senr now lives; beginning at a white oak on Peter J. **Tucker**'s N line, marked with J. T.; also bounded by James **Moore** senr and Nicholas **Tucker**. Signed Joseph **Tucker** senr, Elenor **Tucker** (RD). Wit John **Layton** senr (JP). Rec 16 Apr 1832.

380. Page 331. 1 Nov 1831. Ignatius **Layton** and Elizabeth, his wife, to William H. **Keyte**. For the sum of $25, Lot No. 8 in Perryville. Signed Ignatius **Layton**, Elizabeth (x) **Layton** (RD). Wit John **Layton** (JP). Rec 25 Apr 1832.

381. Page 332. 9 May 1832. Rezin L. **Bishop** and Rebeckah, his wife, to Maurice **Bocktert**, all of Cinq Hommes Twp. For the sum of $150, 56 acres, one rood, and 24 square poles in Cinque Hommes Twp; part of a tract confirmed to John **Layton**, decd, the father-in-law of Joseph **Manning**, and father of Mary, his wife, who conveyed the same to sd **Bishop**, agreeable to a division made by Isidore **Moore**; bounded in part by the part of 40 acres sold to William **McCauley**. Signed Rezin L. **Bishop**, Rebecka (x) **Bishop** (RD). Wit John **Layton** senr (JP), James **Layton**. Rec 12 May 1832.

382. Page 333. 17 Feb 1832. Henry **Clark** to John **Scott** and Beverly **Allen**. Quit claim to two tracts in Bois Brule Bottom; 640 acres confirmed to John **Dunks**; and 640 acres confirmed to Andrew **Dunks**. Signed H. **Clark**. Wit Greer W. **Davis**, Hy. **Sanford**, Clerk of Cape Girardeau Co., Mo. Rec 18 Jun 1832.

383. Page 333. 11 Aug 1831. Samuel **Hinch** Sr. and John **Hawkins** by Elias **Barcroft**, Auditor of Public Accounts for Mo., to John **Logan**. For back taxes owed for 1828 and penalties, two tracts; 213 acres, being Survey No. 864 in Twp 34, Rng 13, assessed in the name of sd **Hinch**, the original claimant, for $1.78; and 191.40 acres assessed for $1.65 in the name of sd **Hawkins**

and originally claimed by Alexander **Murdock** as Survey No. 2109 in Twp 36, Rng 11. Sold on 1 Aug 1829. Signed Elias **Barcroft**, Auditor of Public Accounts. Wit Frederick C. **Hase**, Clerk. Rec 23 Jul 1832.

384. Page 335. 23 Jul 1832. John **Logan** to Milless R. **Anderson** and Pinkney K. **Anderson**. For the sum of $1, 106 1/2 acres, more or less, being 1/2 of 213 acres as described in the preceding deed (1:333). Signed John **Logan**. Wit Fredk. C. **Hase** (JP). Rec 23 Jul 1832.

385. Page 336. 24 Jul 1832. Fenwick **Hamilton** and Josiah F. **Hamilton** by Sheriff John **Logan** to Fenwick **Hamilton**. For the sum of $155, three tracts set aside by the Commissioners to partition lands of George A. **Hamilton**, decd; 457 acres, set aside as the widow's dower; 105 acres, Lot No. 9, assigned to Fenwick **Hamilton**; and 65 acres, Lot No. 2 assigned to Josiah F. **Hamilton**. Sold on 25 Nov 1828 by former Sheriff David L. **Caldwell** in his lifetime, on order of Circuit Court issued 4 Oct 1828 in favor of the State of Mo. and against Fenwick **Hamilton**, Josiah F. **Hamilton**, and James J. **Fenwick** for $214.48 damages and $12.40 costs. Signed John **Logan**, Sheriff. Wit Fredk. C. **Hase**, Clerk. Rec 24 Jul 1832.

386. Page 337. 24 Jul 1832. Fenwick J. **Hamilton**, for himself and as atty in fact for Eulile **Hamilton**, to Harrison **Young**. For the sum of $50, 3/6 part of 75.21 acres in the Mississippi Bottom, part of the undivided dower assigned to Clare **Hamilton**, decd, widow of George A. **Hamilton**, decd, including the mansion house and residence of sd decd; part of a larger tract of 2000 arpents confirmed to George A. **Hamilton**, decd; and being the parts of Josiah F., Fenwick J., and Eulilie **Hamilton**. Signed Fenwick J. **Hamilton**, Eulale **Hamilton** by Fenwick J. **Hamilton**, her atty in fact. Wit Fredk. C. **Hase** (JP). Rec 24 Jul 1832.

387. Page 338. 21 Jul 1832. Walter F. **Hamilton** to same. For the sum of $35, 44 acres and some poles in the Mississippi Bottom, being an undivided 1/6 part of Lot No. 4, drawn for his sister Matilda, decd, in the division of land formerly owned by his decd father George A. **Hamilton**; bounded on the E by the Mississippi River. Signed Walter F. **Hamilton**. Wit James **Evans**, Fredk. C. **Hase** (JP). Rec 24 Jul 1832.

388. Page 339. [no date given] Same to same. For the sum of $50, his right to about 76 acres that was allotted to his mother Clare **Sherry**, decd, as her dower of the land of his father George A. **Hamilton**, decd; except about 20 acres where James P. **Slaughter** now lives. Signed Walter F. **Hamilton**. Wit James **Evans**, Fredk. C. **Hase** (JP). Rec 24 Jul 1832.

389. Page 340. 24 Mar 1832. Peter J. **Tucker** and Mary, his wife, to John Baptist **Layton**. For the sum of $16, 8 acres, the W corner of a tract which formerly belonged to Joseph **Tucker** senr, decd; beginning at a white oak. Signed Peter J. **Tucker**, Mary (x) **Tucker** (RD). Wit John **Layton** senr (JP). Rec 24 Jul 1832.

390. Page 341. 15 Aug 1832. John **Kennison** and Sinah, his wife, to Thomas **Sanders**. For the sum of $200, 104 arpents, part of 640 arpents confirmed to Alexander **McConohoe**; beginning at a stake on the Mississippi River where it intersects the W boundary of 200 arpents where sd **Kinison** now lives; and including the place where sd **Sanders** now lives. Signed John **Kinnison**, Seniae **Kinnison**. Wit Frederick C. **Hase** (JP). Rec 1 Sep 1832.

391. Page 342. 29 Jul 1822. Joseph **Tucker** senr and Eleanor, his wife, to William **Manning** of Scott Co., Ken. For the sum of $262.50, seven and a half shares (of ten shares) of 95 arpents, more or less, on the Mississippi above the mouth of Obrasaw; granted to Thomas **Tucker**, and which Thomas **Tucker** sold to Joseph **Tucker** senr, decd; beginning and running with lines run when the land was surveyed for Thomas **Tucker**. Signed Joseph **Tucker** senr, Elenor (x) **Tucker**. Wit J. **Fenwick**, Cornelius M. **Slattery** (JP). Rec 13 Sep 1832.

392. Page 343. 30 Jul 1822. Mark **Manning** and Margaret, his wife, of Woodford Co., Ken. to same. For the sum of $600 in a note, 127 1/2 acres; bounded on the E by the Mississippi River, S by land confirmed to Thomas **Tucker**, N and W by land confirmed to George A. **Hamilton**. Signed Mark (x) **Manning**, Margret (x) **Manning**. Wit John **Layton** (JP). Rec 13 Sep 1832.

393. Page 344. 17 Oct 1832. Obadiah **Scott** and Polly, his wife, of Ste. Genevieve Co., Mo. to their son Charles **Scott** of Campbell Co., Ken. For the love and good will they bear toward their son, 203.55 acres on the head of Obrazo Creek, being originally granted to Theophilus **Williams**; bounded on the E by S. **Hinch** and S by Charles **Duncaster**; beginning at the SE corner of **Williams**' survey. Signed Obadiah **Scott**, Polly **Scott**. Wit Fredk. C. **Hase** (JP). Rec 17 Oct 1832.

394. Page 345. 9 May 1832. William **Rex** to Charles **Gregoire**. For the sum of $200, undivided 1/3 part of 550 acres on the S fork of Saline Creek known as the Grand Glaize Tract; joining lands of Frans. **Valle**, decd, and bounded on the S by Henry **Tucker**; transferred by Amos **Roark** to Robert **Riorden** (Ste. Genevieve Co. Book C:85). Signed William **Rex**. Wit W. **Searcy** (JP). Rec 5 Nov 1832.

395. Page 346. 10 Apr 1832. List of lands sold for taxes. Tax, penalties at the rate of 15% per annum, and 37 cents costs due by 15 Jun 1832, and the tracts were sold on 18 Jun 1832.

In whose name Assessed	Original Claimant or Patentee	Quantity (acres/100ths)	Parts of Sec. or Survey No.	Twp	Rng	Amt of of tax	No. of acres sold	To whom sold
Abel, Ezekiel	John **Townsend**	80		36	11	$1.00	80	State of Mo.
Girty, Wm. heirs	Noel **Hornback**	238.19	377	35 & 36	11	$2.23	238.19	Francis **Clark**
Hagan, Joseph	Joseph **Hagan**	83	852	35 & 36	10	$0.75	83	Michael **Hagan**
Maddin, Thomas	A. **Morgan**	325				$2.14	325	Francis **Clark**

Signed E. **Barcroft**, Auditor of Public Accounts. Wit Fredk C. **Hase**, Clerk. Rec 5 Nov 1832.

396. Page 346. 15 Apr 1831. Last will and testament of Zar **Sturdivant**. To his wife Rachel: 155 acres, the plantation on which he now resides, being deeded to him by Thomas **Donoho**, and all his personal property during her lifetime. The property is to be equally divided between his sons Zar and Homer **Sturdevant** after his wife's death, provided that they pay to his daughter Harriatt, after his decease, $120 in property at cash valuation, and that they pay his debts; should they fail to do so, then Harriatt is to have 1/3 part of the tract. To the heirs of his son Ira of Ohio: $5. To his son Washington G., $5. To his daughter Sabrina **Bland**: $5. To his son Homer: his rifle gun. To his wife Rachel: all his personal property during her lifetime; and after her death to his two sons Zar and Homer. Zar & Homer **Sturdivant** are named execrs. Signed Zar **Sturdivant**. Wit Walter **Wilkinson**, R. T. **Brown**, Fredk. C. **Hase**, Clerk. Rec 5 Nov 1832.

397. Page 348. 21 Nov 1832. Michael **Burns** and Rebbecca, his wife, to William **Burns**. For the sum of $400, 308 arpents, more or less, with both Bois Brule and McClanahan's Creeks running through it; adjoined on the W by the tract where the late Barnabas **Burns** resided, and S by a tract originally granted to John **McClanahan**; left to Michael **Burns** by the last will and testament of Barnabas **Burns**, decd (1:146). Signed Michael **Burns**, Rebecca (x) **Burns**. Wit Thomas **Long**, David **Burns**, JCC. Rec 22 Nov 1832.

398. Page 349. 27 Nov 1832. Robert S. **Manning** and Ann, his wife, to William **Manning**. For the sum of $500, 500 arpents on Indian Creek in Braseau Twp; being the W part of land assigned to Ezekiel and Thomas **Fenwick** out of 3000 arpents originally confirmed to Joseph **Fenwick**, and sold at Sheriff's sale on 16 Mar 1824; beginning on the W end of sd part. Signed Robert S. **Manning**, Ann **Manning**. Wit J. **Ranney**, R. S. **Dorsey** (JP). Rec 27 Nov 1832.

399. Page 350. 21 Nov 1832. Michael **Burns** and Rebecca, his wife, to William **Burns**. For the sum of $800, mortgage on 235 acres, more or less, an undivided share in Survey No. 662 in Bois Brule Bottom in Twp 36, Rng 11, purchased by Barnabas **Burns**, decd, from the commissioners to partition property of the heirs of John **Burns**, decd; undivided interest in Lot No. 35 in Perryville and a cotton gin; four horse creatures: one gray horse about 15 hands high and 7 or 8 years old, one mare about 15 hands high and about 15 years old, one bay horse two years old about 14 hands high, and one colt; 10 horned cattle; 50 hogs; and one wooden clock. The debt is due to William **Burns** when paid. Signed Michael **Burns**, Rebecca (x) **Burns** (RD). Wit Thomas **Long**, David **Burns**, JCC. Rec 14 Dec 1832.

400. Page 352. 17 Sep 1832. Henry **Welker** to George H. **Adinger**. For the sum of $53.12 1/2, mortgage on the SW 1/4, Sec 31, Twp 34 N, Rng 12 E. Sd **Welker** borrowed money from sd **Adinger** to enter the land at the land office, and the debt with 10% interest per annum is due in two years. Signed Henry (x) **Welker**. Wit Elias **Barber** (JP). Rec 27 Dec 1832.

401. Page 353. 11 Jan 1827. Last will and testament of Isaiah **Tucker**. To his wife Sarah: 1/3 of the balance of his estate after debts are paid. To the child with which sd Sarah is now pregnant, should it live: the remaining 2/3 of his estate. Should the child die before it reaches lawful age, the remaining 2/3 to be divided between his wife Sarah and her children by her first husband. His wife Sarah **Tucker** is appointed execx. Wit Joab **Waters** senr, William **Flynn**, Cornelius M. **Slattery**, Clerk of Probate Court, James H. **Norfolk**, Clerk. Rec 4 Jan 1833.

402. Page 354. 2 Jan 1833. Charles C. **Valle** and Melanie, his wife, of Ste. Genevieve Co., Mo. to Ezekiel **McNeely**. For the sum of $300, 640 acres on Brazoe Creek, as confirmed to William **Hinkson**. Signed Chls. C. **Valle**, Melanie **Valle** (RD). Wit Jos. D. **Grafton**, Clerk of Ste. Genevieve Co. Circuit Court. Rec 9 Jan 1833.

403. Page 355. 3 Jan 1832. Elizabeth **Riordan** to Charles **Gregoire** Jr. For the sum of $200, 550 arpens, more or less, on the S fork of Saline Creek; adjoining land of the heirs of Frs. **Valle**, decd, known as the Grand Glaise, deeded by Amos **Roark** to Robt. **Riardon** on 12 Aug 1818. Signed Elizabeth (x) **Reardin**. Wit Peter R. **Pratte**, William B. **Woodruff**, Frederick C. **Hase** (JP). Rec 18 Jan 1833.

404. Page 355. 7 Sep 1832. Jacob **Shaner** to John **Shaner**. For the sum of $240, 160 acres on Brazoe Creek in Rng 13 E, Twp 34 N, Sec 16; the NW 1/4 of 640 acres confirmed to Benjamin **Harrison**; joining the survey of Joseph **James**; with the creek being the line where sd 1/4 intersects it. Signed Jacob **Shaner**, Elizabeth **Shaner** (RD). Wit Henry **Seibert**, Elizabeth **Davis**, Benjamin **Davis** (JP). Rec 4 Feb 1833.

405. Page 357. 26 Mar 1833. Commissioners to partition land of William **Manning**, decd, to Robert **Manning**. For the sum of $800, 210 acres, more or less, in Brasoe Twp on the bank of the Mississippi River a short distance above the mouth of Brasoe Creek. Sold on the 1st Monday in Feb 1833 on order of Circuit Court on the petition of Elanor **Manning**, James C. **Manning**, George **Manning**, William **Manning**, John F. **Manning**, Robert **Manning**, Elisabeth **Quarles** (formerly **Manning**), Margaret M. **Caldwell** (formerly **Manning**), Julia **Kimmel** and Manning **Kimmel** (infant children of Caroline **Kimmel**, decd, formerly **Manning**) by their guardian Robert **Manning**; all heirs of William **Manning**, who died in 1823, leaving his widow Elanor and the other heirs. Signed John **Logan**, Moses **Farrar**, Mark **Manning**. Wit J. **Ranney**, Fredk. C. **Hase**, Clerk. Rec 26 Mar 1833.

406. Page 359. 26 Mar 1833. Robert S. **Manning** and Nancy, his wife, to Daniel **Cline**. For the sum of $500, 420 acres, being the E 1/2 of a tract purchased by sd **Manning** at Sheriff's sale, and the remainder of the tract which was not sold to William **Manning**, called the Poplar Flat. Signed Robert S. **Manning**, Ann (x) **Manning** (RD). Wit Greer W. **Davis**, A. H. **Puckett**, JCC. Rec 17 Apr 1833.

407. Page 360. 23 Apr 1833. Joseph **Layton** to Wilford **Layton**. For the sum of $108, two tracts; 40 acres, being the NW 1/4, SE 1/4, Sec 36, Twp 36 N, Rng 10 E; and 40 acres, being the NE 1/4, SW 1/4, Sec 36, Twp 36 N, Rng 10 E. Signed Joseph **Layton**. Wit Mats. **Barringer**, A. H. **Puckett**, JCC. Rec 23 Apr 1833.

408. Page 361. 17 Jun 1825. Benjamin S. **Mabry** and Delilah, his wife, of Wilson Co., Tenn. to Jane **Anderson**, Miley **Anderson**, Pinkney R. **Anderson**, Thomas **Anderson**, Arashee **Anderson**, Samuel A. Rickey **Anderson**, and Margaret **Anderson**, infant heirs of Samuel **Anderson**, decd. For the sum of $960, 320 acres on Obraso Creek in Brazo Twp, being 1/2 of 640 acres confirmed to Samuel **Hinch** senr as his settlement right. Signed Benjn. S. **Mabry**, Delilah (x) **Mabry** (RD). Wit John **Shaner**, Thomas (x)

Tucker, James Foster, JP in Wilson Co., Tenn., A. H. Puckett, JCC. Rec 23 Apr 1833.

409. Page 363. 15 Dec 1829. Lewis **Cissell** and Ann M., his wife, to Charles **Vessels**. For the sum of $300, two tracts; 150.27 acres, more or less, being the SE fractional 1/4, Sec 22, Twp 36 N, Rng 10 E; and 26 acres in Twp 36 N, Rng 10 E. Signed Lewis **Cissell**, Ann M. **Cissell** (RD). Test R. S. **Dorsey** (JP). Rec 23 Apr 1833.

410. Page 364. 25 Apr 1833. William **Evans** of Cape Girardeau Co., Mo. to Anna Clara **Welker**. For the sum of $120, 80 acres, being the N 1/2, NE 1/4, Sec 36, Twp 34 N, Rng 11 E. Signed William (x) **Evans**. Wit J. **Abernathy** (JP). Rec 27 Apr 1833.

411. Page 364. 25 Apr 1833. Anna Clara **Welker** to Isidore **Erstreicher**. For the sum of $170, 80 acres as described in the preceding deed (1:364). Signed Anne Clary (x) [**Welker**]. Wit J. **Abernathy** (JP). Rec 27 Apr 1833.

412. Page 365. 13 May 1833. Joseph J. **James** and Elizabeth, his wife, to John **Logan**. For the sum of $200, 19 acres, two roods, and 31 perches; beginning at a stake at the SE corner of Lot No. 3 in Perryville; bounded in part by George **Hore**'s lot (which he purchased from Bernard **Layton** and Mary, his wife), sd **Layton**'s original survey line, and the town line. Signed Joseph J. **James**, Elizabeth (x) **James** (RD). Wit R. S. **Dorsey** (JP). Rec 14 May 1833.

413. Page 366. 13 May 1833. Same and same to Warren **Clifton**. For the sum of $100, Lot Nos. 11, 12, and part of Lot No. 10 in Perryville; the SW part of Lot No. 10. Signed Joseph J. **James**, Elizabeth (x) **James** (RD). Test Richard S. **Dorsey** (JP). Rec 14 May 1833.

414. Page 367. 27 Dec 1831. Isaac **Hinkle** and Catherine, his wife, of Cape Girardeau Co., Mo. to Cullen **Penny**. For the sum of $352.50, 100.06 acres, being Lot No. 9, NW 1/4, Sec 6, Twp 33, Rng 12 E; that they purchased from the U. S. A. Signed Isaac (x) **Hinkle**, Catherine (x) **Hinkle** (RD). Received of Isaac **Hinkle**, $125.74, being in full for Lot No. 9, NW 1/4, Sec 6, Twp 33 N, Rng 12 E. Signed John **Hays**, Receiver. Wit Elias **Barber** (JP). Rec 1 Jun 1833.

415. Page 368. 18 Apr 1833. Francis **Shoults** to John A. **McLane**. For the sum of $250, relinquishment of dower rights in the estate of John **Shoults**, decd, including land on Apple Creek, and houses, mills, and other buildings on it; she being the widow of sd **Shoults**. Signed Francis (x) **Shoults**. Wit John **Whitledge**, William F. **Whitledge**, Elias **Barber** (JP). Rec 6 Jun 1833.

416. Page 369. 21 Dec 1832. Tunis **Quick** to John W. **Quick**. For the sum of $250, 200 acres, more or less, part of a claim of 640 acres confirmed to Tunis **Quick**; beginning at the most E corner. Signed Tunis **Quick**. Wit R. S. **Dorsey** (JP). Rec 5 Jul 1832.

417. Page 370. 17 May 1833. Joseph **Manning** to Juliana **Wathen**, Mother Superiour of Bethlehem Convent. For the sum of $130, 44.15 acres, beginning where the NE boundary of Joseph **Manning**'s land corners on Zachary **Layton**'s land, also bounded by the SW fractional 1/4, Sec 13, Twp 35, Rng 10 E, and the seminary land. Signed Joseph **Manning**. Wit John **Layton** (JP), John **Timon**. Rec 18 Jul 1833.

418. Page 371. 24 May 1833. Thomas **Maddin** of Washington Co., Mo. to Charles **Maddin** of Ste. Genevieve Co., Mo. For the sum of $10, 540 acres, more or less, in Bois Brule Bottom, being a tract he purchased from Archibald **Morgan**. Signed Thoms. **Maddin**. Test James **Maddin**, Malachi **Maddin**, A. H. **Puckett**, JCC. Rec 5 Aug 1833.

419. Page 372. 8 Aug 1833. Charles J. **Tucker** and Maria, his wife, Peter J. **Tucker** and Mary, his wife, and Joseph **Tucker** and Sarah Ann, his wife, to Edward **Walsh** of St. Louis Co., Mo., Valero **Frinia** of Perry Co., Guy T. **Elder** of Perry Co., and Apolnerius **Tucker** of St. Louis Co., Mo. For the sum of $195 paid to each of the men (total $585), their claim in the estate of Joseph **Tucker**, senior, decd; including 240 acres, more or less, in Survey No. 855 in Twp 35 N, Rng 10 E, confirmed to Joseph **Tucker** senior; and all horses, cattle, and other livestock, negroes, household and kitchen furniture, farming utensils, and the growing crop on the farm. Signed Charles J. **Tucker**, Maria (x) **Tucker** (RD), Peter J. **Tucker**, Mary (x) **Tucker** (RD), Joseph (x) **Tucker**, Sarah Ann (x) **Tucker** (RD). Wit James **Rice** (JP). Rec 8 Aug 1833.

420. Page 373. 18 Jan 1833. George **Killian** and Matilda, his wife, to Peter R. **Pratte**. For the sum of $400, two lots in Perryville; Lot No. 21, being sold to sd **Killian** by the Commissioners on 9 Apr 1829 (1:210); and Lot No. 32, sold to sd **Killian** by Thomas **Riney** and wife and Zachariah **Layton** and wife on 20 Feb 1830 (1:240); both bounded on the S by St. Mary's St, W by Main St, N by lots originally owned by Ignatius **Layton** and Bernard **Brown**, and E by Spring St. Signed George **Killian**, Matilda **Killian** (RD). Wit A. H. **Puckett**, JCC. Rec 19 Aug 1833.

421. Page 374. 26 Jul 1824. Gustavus A. **Bird** and Hannah L., his wife, of St. Louis, Mo. to Israel **Madden** for and on account of Charles & Philip **Madden** of Ste. Genevieve Co., Mo. For the sum of $550, 100 acres in Bois Brule Twp, purchased by sd **Bird** of the adminr of James **McLane**, decd; beginning at the line of a tract sold by sd adminr to Harvey **Lane** and James H. **Rolfe** near the NW corner of the tract; also bounded by a tract confirmed to Solomon **Morgan** on the Mississippi, and land conveyed by sd **McLane** to Francis **Cissel**, decd. Signed G. A. **Bird**, H. L. **Bird** (RD). Wit Archibald **Gamble**, Clerk of St. Louis Co. Rec 19 Aug 1833.

422. Page 376. 17 Oct 1832. Philip **Maddin**, Charles **Maddin**, and Malachi **Maddin** and Caroline, his wife, of St. Genevieve Co., Mo. to Thomas M. **Horine** of Washington Co., Mo. For the sum of $1933, three tracts in Bois Brule Bottom; 340.68 acres, confirmed to Thomas **Donohoe** by patent dated 12 May 1832, conveyed by him to Thomas **Maddin** senr on 20 Nov 1815, and willed by him to Philip and Charles **Maddin** on 9 Apr 1832; undivided part of 2/3 of 40 acres, part of a tract of 255.20 acres confirmed to James **McLane**, decd; 75 acres, part of 100 acres sold by Gustavus A. **Bird** to sd Philip & Charles on 31 Jul 1832, and part of 640 acres confirmed to James **McLane** under Solomon **Morgan**, to be taken off the upper end of the tract, the lower 25 acres having been sold by Israel **Madden** to Joseph **Bland**. Malachi **Maddin** and Caroline, his wife, for the sum of $215, convey to sd **Horine** the remaining undivided 1/3 of the 40 acres described above. Signed Philip **Maddin**, Charles **Maddin**, Malachi **Maddin**, Caroline **Maddin** (RD). Wit Maria **Field**, Henderson **Evans**, Emily **Black**, William **James**, JCC in Ste. Genevieve Co., Mo. Rec 19 Aug 1833.

423. Page 378. 23 Aug 1833. Aquila **Hagan** and Mary, his wife, to Daniel **Killian**. For the sum of $50, Lot No. 63 in Perryville, sold by the Commissioners to sd **Hagan** on 24 May 1823 (1:68); at the SW corner of the public square fronting on St. Joseph St and Jackson St. Signed Aquila **Hagan**, Mary (x) **Hagan** (RD). Wit John **Hagan**, John **Layton** (JP). Rec 24 Aug 1833.

424. Page 379. 29 Aug 1833. George Washington **Sturdivant** and Betsey, his wife, to Alfred Harrison **Puckett**. For the sum of $600, 200 acres in Bois Brule Bottom; the lower part of 420 arpens confirmed to William **Fitz Gibbons**, and the tract where sd **Sturdivant** now lives, and bought from George **Camster**; bounded on the N by the Mississippi River, and E by land confirmed to Alexander **McConahoe**; to include 1/2 of the front on the river. Signed George W. **Sturdivant**, Betsey **Sturdivant** (RD). Test Jacob J. **Everts** (JP). Rec 2 Sep 1833.

425. Page 380. 9 Sep 1833. William **McLane** and Ally Louisa, his wife, to Edward **McLane** and Walter **McLane** [brothers]. For the sum of $500, 160 acres, more or less, the SE corner of a tract confirmed to Barnard **Layton** as Survey No. 2129 in Twp 35 N, Rng 11 E; Lot Nos. 87, 88, 91, 92, & 93 in Perryville, being mainly on West St; six horse creatures: one brown bay horse about six years old, one sorrel mare four years old, one bay mare and sucking coalt, one horse colt bay colour, and one year old; one ox cart; 11 horned cattle; 13 sheep; 40 hogs; the growing crop on the above farm consisting of about 29 acres of corn and 50 bushels of wheat; and all our farming utensils, household, and kitchen furniture. Signed William (x) **McLane**, Alley L. **McLane** (RD). Wit James **Rice** (JP). Rec 12 Sep 1833.

426. Page 381. 12 Aug 1833. Samuel **Allen** [and Mahaly, his wife] to Moses **Farrar**. For the sum of $120, quit claim to his interest in two land receipts: No. 1495 dated 21 Mar 1833 for 138.22 acres, more or less, being the SE fractional 1/4, Sec 22, Twp 36 N, Rng 12 E; and No. 1477 dated 23 Mar 1833 for 5.22 acres, more or less, being fractional Sec 23, Twp 36 N, Rng 12 E. Signed Samuel (x) **Allen**, Mahaly (x) **Allen** (RD). Test A. H. **Puckett**, A. **Burns**, Joab W. **Burgee** (JP). Rec 20 Sep 1833.

427. Page 382. 23 Sep 1833. Alexander **Patterson** and Nancy, his wife, of St. Francies Co., Mo. to Thomas **Long** and Newton **Long**. For the sum of $150, 150 acres in Bois Brulla Bottom, being 1/2 of 300 acres left to sd **Patterson** by his father Alexander **Patterson**; confirmed to the elder Alexander **Patterson**; bounded on the NE by Daniel **Merideth**, so as to take 100 acres of the S corner of 640 acres of sd confirmation. Signed Alexander (x) **Patterson**, Nancy (x) **Patterson**. Test David **Pinkston**, Thomas **Hale**, JCC in St. Francois Co., Mo. Rec 26 Sep 1833.

428. Page 383. 20 Apr 1831. Joseph **Manning** and Mary, his wife, to John B. **Moranville**. For the sum of $281.25, 181 acres, more or less, part of a tract where sd **Manning** now lives, and which was granted to him as his settlement right, Survey No. 840; beginning at the NE corner of 85 acres sold to **James** and now owned by Joseph J. **James**. Signed Joseph **Manning**, Mary (x) **Manning** (RD). Wit John **Layton** (JP). Rec 28 Sep 1833.

429. Page 384. 30 Sep 1833. Benjamin S. **Mabry** and Delilah, his wife, of Wilson Co., Tenn. to William A. **Bull**. For the sum of $50, 80 acres in Brazoe Twp, part of 640 acres granted to Samuel **Hinch** senr, decd; bounded on the E by Joseph **James**, S by public land and **Smith** and **Caldwell**, W by land formerly owned by Theophilus **Williams**, and N by public land. Signed Benjamin S. **Mabry**, Delila (x) **Mabry** (RD). Test Wm. A. **Bull**, Elias **Barber** (JP). Rec 5 Oct 1833.

430. Page 385. 15 Oct 1831. Archabald **Mitchall** [and Eliza, his wife] to Thomas B. **Mitchel** and Matthew D. **Mitchel**. For the sum of $100, 80 acres on the waters of Brazoe Creek; being the E 1/2, NW 1/4, Sec 12, Twp 34 N, Rng 12 E, purchased by Archabald **Mitchel** from the U. S. A.; 30 acres on the N end of sd tract to Thomas B. **Mitchel** and the remaining 50 acres on the S end to be Matthew B. **Mitchel**'s. Signed Archabald **Michel**, Eliza **Mitchel** (RD). Wit Benjamin **Davis** (JP), Robert **Mitchel**. Rec 5 Oct 1833.

431. Page 386. 5 Oct 1833. Warren **Clifton** and Mary, his wife, to Matthias **Barringer**. For the sum of $200, Lot Nos. 11, 12, and the SW corner of Lot No. 10 in Perryville. Signed Warren **Clifton**, Mary (x) **Clifton** (RD). Wit Joab **Conen**(?), John **Layton** (JP). Rec 5 Oct 1833.

432. Page 387. 27 Mar 1833. Ann **Moore** to John **May**, son of James B. **May**. For the sum of $80, the undivided share of sd Ann to 80 acres, more or less, in Survey No. 2137 in Twp 35, Rng 10; a tract confirmed to James **Moore** Senior, decd. **Moore**. Signed Ann (x) **Moore**. Wit A. H. **Puckett**, JCC. Rec 7 Oct 1833.

433. Page 388. 23 Mar 1830. Commissioners of Perryville to David **Bolinger**. For the sum of $ 50.50, Lot No. 55 in Perryville. The original deed read Lot No. 56 by mistake, and Lot No. 56 was bid by Jos. A. **Moore**, who sold to D. L. **Caldwell**, who sold to William A. **Keyte**. This deed corrects the original deed. Signed R. T. **Brown**, Joseph **Tucker** senr., Thomas **Riney**, Commissioners. Wit W. **Wilkinson** (JP). Rec 12 Oct 1833.

434. Page 389. 10 Aug 1833. Joseph **Paquin** to John B. **Tornatori**. For the sum of $650, quit claim to 480 acres, more or less, being purchased from John **Morgan**; beginning on the banks of the Mississippi River at the corner of Thomas **Donahue**'s survey. Signed Joseph **Paquin**. Wit Joseph **Rolira**, John **Cotter**, John **Layton** (JP). Rec 18 Oct 1833.

435. Page 390. 10 Aug 1833. Jean Marie **Odin**, Joseph **Paquin**, and Xavier **Dahmen** to Jean Baptiste **Tornatore**. For the sum of $4000, 640 acres or 752.32 arpens, more or less, on which is the seminary of St. Mary's of the Barrens; another property known as the Bishop's Mill; and a tract on Braseau Creek; all tracts sold by Joseph **Rosati**, atty for the Right Reverend William **DuBourg**, to the grantors. Signed J. M. **Odin**, Joseph **Paquin**, Xavier **Dahmen**. Wit John **Layton** (JP). Rec 18 Oct 1833.

436. Page 391. 27 Apr 1833. Timothy **Davis** and Nancy, his wife, of Ste. Genevieve Co., Mo. to Thomas **Kennedy** of Campbell Co., Ken. For the sum of $400, 640 acres two miles SW of St. Maries Landing; beginning at a post; the SW corner of land formerly belonging to Thos. **Donohue** and C. **Barnhart**; and confirmed to Frederick **Woodford**. Signed Timothy **Davis**, Nancy **Davis**. Wit W. **Searcy** (JP). Rec 13 Nov 1833.

437. Page 392. 3 Aug 1833. Delinquent tax list. Tax, penalties at the rate of 15% per annum, and 37 cents costs due by 1 Jul 1833, or the tracts will be sold.

In whose name Assessed	Original Claimant or Patentee	Quantity (acres/100ths)	Parts of Sec. or Survey No.	Twp	Rng	To whom sold
Henry, John F.	Alexr. **McConehau**	300	147	37	11	Francis **Clark**
United States	Benjamin **Cox**	640	2146	36	10 & 11	Frederick C. **Hase**

Signed H. **Shurlds**, Auditor of Public Accounts for Missouri. Wit James A. C. **Hase**, Dep Clerk. Rec 18 Nov 1833.

438. Page 392. 21 Nov 1833. John **Layton** and Monica, his wife, to Francis **Schearer**. For the sum of $250, 50 acres, more or less, on the NE corner of 640 acres confirmed to sd **Layton**. Signed John **Layton**, Monaca **Layton** (RD). Wit R. S. **Dorsey** (JP). Rec 25 Nov 1833.

439. Page 393. __ May 1831. Commissioners to partition lands of James **Burns**, decd, to David **Burns**. For the sum of $375.25, 465 acres, being Survey No. 142 in Bois Brule Twp, confirmed to John R. **McLaughlin**; whereon James **Burns** lived at the time of his death. Sold on 4 May 1830 on order of Circuit Court issued Nov Term 1829 (continued from July Term 1828) on petition to partition real estate of sd heirs. Signed D. L. **Caldwell**, H. P. **Harris**, Aquila **Hagan**. Wit Joab **Waters** (JP), Pious **Brewer**. Rec 30 Nov 1833.

440. Page 396. 27 Mar 1830. Thomas **Riney** and Sarah, his wife, to Samuel **Shull**. For the sum of $40, Lot No. 68 in Perryville. Signed Thomas **Riney**, Sarah (x) **Riney** (RD). Test John **Layton** (JP), Benedict **Riley**. Rec 5 Dec 1833.

441. Page 397. 19 Nov 1833. Samuel **Shull** to Benjamin **Allbright**. For the sum of $250, Lot No. 68 in Perryville. Signed Samuel **Shull**. Wit James **Rice** (JP). Rec 5 Dec 1833.

442. Page 397. 16 Feb 1805. James **Thompson** to Jesse **Evans**, both of the Ste. Genevieve Dist. For the sum of $100, __ acres adjoining James **Burns**, thence to the road where it crosses to go to Mrs. Thomas **Allen**'s. Signed James **Thompson**. Wit James W. **Wright**, Beed **Moore**, J. **Donnehue**, JP in Ste. Genevieve Dist, Upper La. Rec 5 Dec 1833.

443. Page 398. 1 Jun 1831. U. S. A. to George **Welker**. Patent for 80 acres, being the W 1/2, NE 1/4, Sec 25, Twp 35 N, Rng 11 E. Signed Andrew **Jackson**, President. Wit Elijah **Haywood**, Commissioner of the General Land Office. Rec in Vol. 2, page 393. Rec 27 Dec 1833.

444. Page 399. 15 Jan 1833. George **Welker** to Paul **Hotop**, late of Germany. For the sum of $215, 80 acres as described in the preceding deed (1:398). Signed George (x) **Welker**. Wit Edward **Durning**, John **Hartle**, Joseph **Snobush**, Elias **Barber** (JP). Rec 27 Dec 1833.

445. Page 400. 29 Feb 1832. George **Killian** and Matilda, his wife, to Richard **Maddock** Senior. For the sum of $25, 12 1/2 acres, beginning on the E side of Saline Creek at a corner of Bishop **Dubourg**'s land at a black oak; also bounded by Nicholas **Moore**. Signed George **Killian**, Matilda **Killian**. Wit Fredk. C. **Hase**, Clerk. Rec 27 Dec 1833.

446. Page 401. 31 May 1824. U. S. A. to Thomas **Tucker**. Patent No. 9485 for 80 acres, being the W 1/2, NE 1/4, Sec 34, Twp 35 N, Rng 10 E. Signed James **Monroe**, President. Wit Geo. **Graham**, Commissioner of the General Land Office. Rec in Vol. 1, page 488. Rec 16 Jan 1834.

447. Page 401. 16 Jan 1834. Thomas **Tucker** and Susannah, his wife, to Levi **Hagan**. For the sum of $350, 80 acres as described in the preceding deed (1:401). Signed Thomas **Tucker**, Susannah **Tucker** (RD). Wit R. S. **Dorsey** (JP). Rec 16 Jan 1834.

448. Page 403. 18 Jan 1834. Charity **Gaty**, adminx of William **Gaty**, decd, to Timothy **Philips** of Washington Co., Mo. For the sum of $260, 420 arpens on the Mississippi River. Sold on 22 Mar 1830 on order of Scott Co., Mo. County Court issued 27 Oct 1829 to sell sd land. Signed Charity (x) **Gaty**, adminx of William **Gaty**, decd. George C. **Harbeson**, Clerk of Scott Co., Mo. Court. Rec 24 Jan 1834.

449. Page 404. 27 Jul 1833. William **Moore** to William **Manning**. For the sum of $70, 70 acres, more or less, in Survey No. 2137 in Twp 35, Rng 10; the undivided share of William **Moore** in part of the tract confirmed to James **Moore** Senior, decd. Signed William **Moore**. Wit James **Rice** (JP). Rec 29 Jan 1834.

450. Page 405. 1 Nov 1833. John **O'Conner** and Chatharine, his wife, to same. For the sum of $65, 70 acres, more or less, being their undivided share of land in Survey No. 2137, Twp 35, Rng 10 E; part of a tract originally belonging to James **Moore** Seigner, decd, and which fell to James J. **Moore**, son and heir of James **Moore** Senr, and was sold by him to sd **O'Conner**. Signed John **O'Conner**, Catharine **O'Connor** (RD). Wit John **Layton** Senr (JP), John **Layton** Jr. Rec 29 Jan 1834.

451. Page 405. 27 Apr 1833. George **Pettit** and Elizabeth, his wife, to Timothy **Davis** of Ste. Genevieve Co., Mo. For the sum of $200, 640 acres about two miles from the Mississippi, SW from St. Mary's Landing; confirmed to Frederick **Woolford**, and purchased by sd **Pettit** at a sale of lands of the estate of Amos **Bird**, decd. Signed George **Pettit**, E. **Pettit** (RD). Wit W. **Searcy** (JP). Rec 5 Feb 1834.

452. Page 406. 29 Mar 1834. Walter F. **Hamilton** to Robert **Manning**. For the sum of $50, __ acres, being the undivided 1/6 of 457 acres, in the NW corner of a tract originally granted to George A. **Hamilton**, and which was allotted to the widow of sd **Hamilton** as a portion of her dower commonly called the Hill Tract; and lying to the rear of Lot Nos. 1, 2, 3, 4, 5, 6, & 7. Signed Walter F. **Hamilton**. Wit R. S. **Dorsey** (JP). Rec 29 Mar 1834.

453. Page 407. 27 Mar 1834. Cullen **Penny** and Darcas, his wife, to Robert **Hinkle** of Cape Girardeau Co., Mo. For the sum of $300, 100.06 acres, being Lot No. 9, NW 1/4, Sec 6, Twp 33, Rng 12 E; purchased by sd **Penny** of Isaac **Hinkle** and Catharine, his wife. Signed Cullen **Penny**, Dorcas (x) **Penny** (RD). Wit Jonas **Abernathy** (JP). Rec 29 Mar 1834.

454. Page 408. 15 Mar 1834. Robert T. **Brown** and Catharine, his wife, to Ferdinand **Rozier** of Ste. Genevieve Co., Mo. For the sum of $350, Lot No. 69 in Perryville. Signed R. T. **Brown**, Catherin **Brown** (RD). Test R. S. **Dorsey** (JP). Rec 29 Mar 1834.

455. Page 409. 20 Mar 1830. Joseph **Duvall** and Evaline, his wife, to same, all of Ste. Genevieve Co., Mo. For the sum of $15, Lot No. 54 in Perryville. Signed Joseph **Duvall**, Evaline (x) **Duvall** (RD). Wit W. **Wilkinson** (JP). Rec 29 Mar 1834.

456. Page 410. 28 Mar 1834. Matthias **Barringer** to Warren **Clifton**. For the sum of $100, three lots in Perryville: Lot Nos. 11, 12, and the SW part of Lot No. 10. Signed Maths. **Barringer**. Test R. S. **Dorsey** (JP). Rec 29 Mar 1834.

457. Page 410. 21 Apr 1834. Charles **Maddin** of Ste. Genevieve Co., Mo. to Walter Bernard **Wilkinson** of St. Louis, Mo. For the sum of $400, 225 acres, more or less, in Bob Brule Bottom, the balance of 640 acres of a tract confirmed to Archibald **Morgan**; lying between James **Taylor** and St. Mary's Seminary; part of the land purchased from Thomas **Maddin** Senr. Signed Chs. **Maddin**. Wit W. **Searcy** (JP). Rec 3 May 1834.

458. Page 411. 27 Jan 1834. William **Boner** to William **McGuire**. For the sum of $229, mortgage on __ acres in Brazeau Twp where sd **Boner** and his family now live; the tanyard thereon; hides and unfinished leather in the vats and in and about the yard, house, and on sd land; bark and all the tools; and implements and means of sd trade on sd land. Sd **Boner** executed four writings obligatory to sd **McGuire**; one for $50 due in 12 months, one for $50 due in two years, one for $50 due in three years, and one for $79 due in four years. Signed Wm. **Boner**. Wit Johnson **Ranney**, Wm. C. **Ranney**, Dep Clerk of Cape Girardeau Co., Mo. Rec 28 May 1834.

459. Page 412. 26 Mar 1834. Henry **Seibert** to Isaac **Cadwallader** of Jefferson Co., Mo. For the sum of $400, deed of trust on 640 acres on the waters of Apple Creek; being Survey No. 1845 surveyed for Francis **Bearthune** in Twp 33 & 34 N, Rng 13 E; 100 acres is excepted and was sold to John **Logan** Senr. A debt of $400 with 10% interest is due in one year, or the land is to be sold at public sale. Signed Henry **Seibert**, Cathariner **Saibart** [in German] (RD). Wit Benjamin **Davis** (JP), Joseph **Morgan**, George **Seibert**. Rec 5 Jun 1834. [Marginal note: Satisfaction received of Henry **Seibert** on 10 Feb 1836. Signed Benjamin **Davis**, atty in fact for Isaac **Cadwallader**.]

460. Page 413. 4 Jun 1834. Bartholomew **Murphy** and Elleaner, his wife, to John **Logan**. For the sum of $120, mortgage on two lots in Perryville: Lot No. 44, conveyed to Edward **Maginnis** and wife, who conveyed it to Matthew **Dunphy**, who sold it to sd **Murphy**; and Lot No. 60, sold by the commissioners to Richard S. **Dorsey** and sold by him and wife to sd **Murphy**. The debt is due with interest until paid. Signed Bartholomew (x) **Murphy**, Elleanar (x) **Murphy** (RD). Wit James **Rice** (JP). Rec 7 Jun 1834.

461. Page 414. 21 Feb 1834. Timothy **Phelps** to James H. **Rolfe** and James C. **Johnson**, all of Washington Co., Mo. For the sum of $400, 238.19 acres, more or less, lately belonging to the heir of William **Girty** and originally claimed by Noel **Hornback**; being Survey No. 377. Signed Timothy **Phelps**, James H. **Rolfe**, J. C. **Johnson**. Wit Jno. S. **Bricky**, Isrial **McGready**, Clerk of Washington Co., Mo. Rec 1 Jul 1834.

462. Page 415. 15 Jul 1825. U. S. A. to Christopher **Hines**. Patent No. 602 for 65.45 acres, being fractional Sec 19, Twp 35 N, Rng 11 E. Signed John Quincy **Adams**, President. Wit Geo. **Graham**, Commissioner of the General Land Office. Rec in Vol. 2, page 25. Rec 7 Jul 1834.

463. Page 416. 11 Mar 1834. Christopher **Hines** and Treasa, his wife, to Augustin Zimmerman **Hase**. For the sum of $250, 65.45 acres as described in the preceding deed (1:415). Signed Christopher (x) **Hines**, Teresa (x) **Hines** (RD). Wit John **Layton** Siner (JP), Ignatius **Layton**. Rec 7 Jul 1834.

464. Page 417. 1 Jul 1830. Isidor **Moore** and Leah, his wife, to their son James **Moore**. For __, 255 acres, more or less, on Cinque Hommes Creek, being the NW 1/2 of 500.42 acres that they own by virtue of a patent from the U. S. A. dated 5 Nov 1821, and where they settled under the Spanish Government; beginning at the W corner of the original survey. Signed Isidore **Moore**, Leah (x) **Moore** (RD). Wit Samuel L. **Moore**, Leo **Moore**, Jas. **Rice** (JP). Rec 18 Jul 1834.

465. Page 418. 10 Mar 1834. Delinquent tax list for 1833. Tax, penalties at the rate of 15% per annum, and 37 cents costs due by 3 Jun 1834, or the tracts will be sold.

In whose name Assessed	Original Claimant or Patentee	Quantity (acres/100ths)	Parts of Sec. or Survey No.	Twp	Rng	To whom sold
Brown, Robert T.	Robert T. **Brown**		Lot No. 47 in Perryville			F. M. **Stevens**
Same Same	Same		Lot No. 65 in Perryville			State
James, Joseph	Jos. **James**		Lot No. 24 in Perryville			State
Lockhart, Widow	Widow **Lockhart**	382.81	1844	36	11	State
Layton, Bernard	Bernard **Layton**		Lot No. 75 in Perryville			State
Logan, James	James **Logan**		Lot No. 16 in Perryville			State
McLain, William	Wm. **McLain**		Lot No. 42 in Perryville			State
McCauley, William	Wm. **McCauley**		Lot No. 43 in Perryville			State
Schnarbush, Joseph	Jos. **Schnarbush**		Lot No. 13 in Perryville			State

Signed Henry **Shurlds**, Auditor of Public Accounts. Wit James A. C. **Hase**, Dep Clerk. Rec 18 Jul 1834.

466. Page 418. 29 May 1834. John **Brewer** and Ann, his wife, to James C. **Moore**. For 15.96 acres received in exchange, 15.96 acres, part of a 50 acre lot which Aquila **Hagan** and wife transferred to them in 1827; beginning on the N boundary of sd **Hagan**'s line at the intersection of a division line between sd **Brewer** and sd **Moore**. Signed John **Brewer**, Ann (x) **Brewer** (RD). Wit John **Layton** (JP), Henry **Dean**. Rec 22 Jul 1834.

467. Page 420. 31 Jul 1834. Leo **Fenwick** to Ralph **Guild**. For the sum of $300, mortgage on negros; a man **John** about 23 years old, a boy **Lloyd** about 15 years old, a woman **Peg** about 23 years old and her three children, a girl **Minty** about 18 years old, a girl **Dianah** about 16 years old, a girl **Bett** about 10 years old, and a girl **Polly** about 8 years old. Sd **Fenwick** is indebted to sd **Guild** for $200 and to sd **Guild** for the use of J & G. W. **Juden** for $100; the debts due by 1 Jan 1835. Signed Leo **Fenwick**. Test John **Scott**, James **Mattingly** (JP). Rec 31 Jul 1834. [Marginal note: Mortgage satisfied on 27 Nov 1838. Signed Ralph **Guild**.]

468. Page 421. 31 Jul 1834. John P. **Edinger** and Mary, his wife, of Cape Girardeau Co., to Jesse **Dickson**. For the sum of $256, three tracts; 40 acres, more or less, being Grant No. 1158 in Twp 35 N, Rng 13 E; and the undivided 1/4 of two other tracts as designated in a patent dated 31 May 1824 to the legal representatives of William **Burns**, decd, sd Mary being one of the heirs of sd decd: 98.39 acres on the Mississippi River, being the NE fractional 1/4, Sec 20, Twp 35 N, Rng 13 E; and 79.93 acres, being the E side of the NW fractional 1/4, Sec 20, Twp 35 N, Rng 13 E. Signed John P. **Edinger**, Mary (x) **Edinger**. Wit David **Burns**, Alexander **Baley**, Frederick C. **Hase**, Clerk. Rec 31 Jul 1834.

469. Page 422. 8 Jul 1834. Clement **Knott** and Elizabeth, his wife, to William **McCauley**. For the sum of $50, 67 1/2 acres and 16 perches on Cinque Hommes Creek; being all the lot where sd **McCauley** now resides, and that has a saw mill and grist mill that he erected in consequence of a contract entered into in Nov 1828; being the most E corner obtained by a settlement and cultivation prior to 20 Dec 1803. Signed Clement (x) **Knott**, Elizabeth (x) **Knott** (RD). Wit John **Layton** Senr (JP), Sarah (x) **Brown**. Rec 4 Aug 1834.

470. Page 424. 29 May 1834. James C. **Moore** and Rebeca, his wife, to John **Brewer**. In consideration of 15.96 acres received in exchange, 15 .96 acres, most of which is in the SE 1/4, NE 1/4, Sec 33, Twp 36 N, Rng 10 E; beginning on the boundary line of Aquilah **Hagan**. Signed James C. **Moore**, Rebecar **Moore** (RD). Wit John **Layton** (JP), Henry **Dean**. Rec 4 Aug 1834.

471. Page 425. 5 Aug 1834. Warren **Clifton** and Mary [his wife] to Charles **Stuart**. For the sum of $246, 3 lots in Perryville; being Lot Nos. 11, 12, and the SW part of Lot No. 10. Signed Warren **Clifton**, Mary **Clifton** (RD). Wit R. S. **Dorsey** (JP). Rec 5 Aug 1834.

472. Page 425. 23 Aug 1834. Simon **Duvall** and Mary [his wife] to William A. **Keyte**. For the sum of $25, Lot No. 7 in Perryville, fronting on Spring St and St. Marys St. Signed Simon **Duvall**, Mary **Duvall** (RD). Wit R. S. **Dorsey** (JP). Rec 23 Aug 1834.

473. Page 426. 29 Aug 1834. Richard **Harrison** to Kimmel & Taylor of Cape Girardeau Co., Mo. For the sum of $33.61, mortgage on a sorrel horse, a black & white heiffer, 2 sows and pigs, 2/3 of the crop of corn raised by sd **Harrison** on the plantation where he now lives and that belongs to John **Ross**. Sd **Harrison** owes the debt by 1 Nov next with 10% interest from date. Signed Richard **Harrison**. Wit William A. **Bull**, Elias **Barber** (JP). Rec 6 Sep 1834.

474. Page 427. 4 Feb 1833. Lewis **Grenier** and Winyfred, his wife, to Nathen **Pusey**. For the sum of $100, undivided moiety of 100 arpens in Bois Brule Bottom, sold by James **McLane**, decd, to Francis **Cissell**, decd; and part of a tract confirmed to Solomon **Morgan**, decd. Signed Lewis (x) **Greenier**, Winiffred (x) **Greeny**. Wit Fredk. C. **Hase**, Clerk. Rec 6 Sep 1834.

475. Page 428. 8 Feb 1832. Timothy **Davis**, adminr of Amos **Bird**, decd, to same. For the sum of $201, about 300 acres, more or less, on the river about five miles below the head of Bois Brule Bottom; part of a tract formerly belonging to James **McLane**, decd, purchased by Gustavus A. **Bird** for the benefit of the estate of Amos **Bird**, decd. Sold in 1829 on order of County Court issued Aug Term 1828 for sale of the land of sd decd to pay bills due by the estate. Signed Timothy **Davis**. Wit Frederick C. **Hase** (JP). Rec 11 Sep 1834.

476. Page 429. 10 Jun 1834. Nathan **Pusey** of Bois Brule Bottom to Timothy **Davis** of St. Marys Landing. For the sum of $200, 100 acres in Bois Brule Bottom; part of a tract of 640 acres confirmed to Solomon **Morgan**, and part of the same purchased by sd **Pusey** from the estate of Amos **Bird**, decd; beginning at the N corner of William **Flynn**'s land under ___ **Dutton**, and also bounded by **Millard** under **Crosley**, **Dunks**, and **Hickman**. Signed Nathan **Pusey**. Wit W. **Searcy** (JP). Rec 11 Sep 1834.

477. Page 430. 1 Sep 1834. John **Scott** and Harriet, his wife, to Timothy **Davis** of Ste. Genevieve Co., Mo. For the sum of $640, 640 acres, more or less, being an undivided moiety of a tract in Bois Brule Bottom; beginning on the survey line of M. **Brooks**; being Survey No. 1866 in Twp 36 & 37 N, Rng 11 E confirmed to Andrew **Dunks**, patented to sd **Scott** and Beverly **Allen**, and assigned to sd **Dunks** on 1 May 1826 in Certificate No. 720. Signed John **Scott**, Harriet J. **Scott** (RD). Wit Jos. D. **Grafton**, Clerk of Ste. Genevieve Co. Circuit Court. Rec 11 Sep 1834.

478. Page 431. 3 Mar 1820. Ezekiel **Fenwick** [and Isabel, his wife] to Thomas **Fenwick**, both of Ste. Genevieve Co., Mo. For the sum of $850, 500 arpens between Apple and Meat Creeks; being a 1/6 part of 3000 arpens confirmed to Joseph **Fenwick**, decd, and to which sd Ezekiel is entitled as one of the heirs of Joseph **Fenwick**, decd. Signed E. **Fenwick**, Isabel **Fenwick**. Wit James J. **Fenwick**, Leo **Fenwick**, Fenwick **Hamilton**, Elias **Barber** (JP). Rec 14 Oct 1834.

479. Page 432. 15 Jul 1823. Thomas **Allen** [and Sally, his wife] to Samuel **Allen** and William **Allen**. Deed of gift for 150 or 156 arpens, more or less, on the bank of the Mississippi River; bounded on the NE by Isaack **Meredith** and SW by James **Beasley**, and where Thomas **Allen** now resides; being their full portion of his real and personal estate, and excepting the improvement and house where they still reside, about 75 acres. It is to be understood that if Sally **Allen** lives longer than Thomas **Allen**, then she is to enjoy and house and 75 acres during her natural lifetime or widowhood, but that sd Samuel and William may dispose of the house and land should she remarry. Signed Thomas **Allen**, Sally (x) **Allen** (RD). Wit Nathaniel S. **Divine** (JP). Rec 14 Oct 1834.

480. Page 433. 18 Jul 1833. Samuel **Allen** [and Mahala, his wife] to William **Allen**. For the sum of $100, his half of 150 or 156 acres, more or less, on the bank of the Mississippi River; as described in the preceding deed (1:432) and subject to the same stipulations of the deed of gift from Thomas **Allen**. Signed Samuel (x) **Allen**, Mahala (x) **Allen** (RD). Wit Nathaniel S. **Divine** (JP). Rec 14 Oct 1834.

481. Page 434. 29 Sep 1834. Benedict **Hagan** to Bernard **Layton**. For the sum of $40, an improvement where sd **Hagan** now resides and the growing crop; and for the further sum of $40, one yoak of oxen, one bay mare, and one cow. Signed Benedict (x) **Hagan**. Wit R. S. **Dorsey** (JP). Rec 11 Oct 1834.

482. Page 435. 23 Sep 1834. Wm. **Cuningham** to F. J. **Hamilton**. For the sum of $38.50, mortgage on one black cow that sd **Cuningham** purchased from Wm. **Gill**, marked with two crops and two underbits; one red cow with the same mark; one white heifer with some black specks on her head and legs, marked with the frost when a calf; one black heifer with white on her flanks and tail, marked with a crop and an under and uper bit in each ear; two red yearlins marked in the same manner as the above black heifer, one with white in its face and the other with a white back; and five sheep. Sd **Cuningham** owes sd **Hamilton** the debt by 1 Sep 1835. Signed Wm. (x) **Cuningham**. Wit Elias **Barber** (JP). Rec 23 Oct 1834.

483. Page 436. 17 May 1828. Gustavus A. **Bird** and Hannah L., his wife, of St. Louis, Mo. to John **Logan**, now of Brownsville, Ill. In confirmation of a deed made 18 Nov 1823; in performance of a convenant in sd deed and for the sum of $500, undivided moiety of 450 arpens in the town of Cinque Hommes near the waters of Cape Cinque Hommes Creek and in Bois Brule Bottom; confirmed to Mary **Lockhard**, conveyed by her and William **Lockard** to David **Holly** and James **McLane**, and by them to sd **Bird**. Signed G. A. **Bird**, Hannah L. **Bird**. Wit R. E. **Vash**, Judge of Mo. Supreme Court. Rec 30 Oct 1834.

484. Page 436. 20 Nov 1833. Pierre **Menard** and Angelique, his wife, of Kaskaskia, Randolph Co., Ill. to John **Logan** of Jackson Co. Ill. For the sum of $200, 400 arpens, more or less, on the W side of the Mississippi River immediately above the mouth of Apple Creek; granted to sd **Menard** by the Spanish Government on 5 Nov 1798, and recorded in the Office of the Recorder of Land Titles, Book E, page 25; and which is now before the Board of Commissioners. Signed Pierre **Menard**, Angelique **Menard** (RD). Wit W. **Meane**, H. **Anderson**, James **Hughes**, Notary Public in Randolph Co., Ill., Savinien **St. Vrain**. Rec 30 Oct 1834.

485. Page 437. 29 Oct 1834. Joab **Cotten** to Henry **Little**. For the sum of $50, one horse, 14 hogs, one stear, 75 bushels of corn, more or less, a note on Fonzo **Abernathy** for $6, a note on Rene **Whitingberg** for $3.75, an account on Lewis **Painter** for $7, an account on James **Bernes** for $5.75, and an account on John **Quick**, Minister, for $5; all of Perry Co. except sd **Painter** is from Cape Girardeau Co., Mo. Sd **Cotten** is to retain the property for one year. Sd **Cotten** owes sd **Little** the debt payable in one year.

Signed Joab **Cotten**, Hry. **Little**. Test R. S. **Dorsey** (JP). Rec 30 Oct 1834.

486. Page 438. 16 Jun 1830. Tunis and Nancy **Quick** to H. **Tucker**, J. **Abernathy**, C. D. **Abernathy**, L. **Taylor**, and J. W. **Quick**, Trustees for the Methodist Episcopal Church. For the sum of $20, Lot No. 24 in Perryville, fronting on North St and Spring St. Signed Tunis **Quick**, Nancy **Quick** (RD). Wit Frederick C. **Hase** (JP). Rec 1 Nov 1834.

487. Page 439. 28 Jul 1833. Jones **Abernathy** to Alonzo **Abernathy**. For natural love and affection which he bears to his son and for his better maintenance, 80 acres, being the W 1/2, NW 1/4, Sec 35, Twp 35 N, Rng 11 E. The deed is not to take effect until the death of Jones **Abernathy**. Signed J. **Abernathy**. Test John W. **Quick**, Miles **Farrar**, James **Burns**, James **Rice** (JP). Rec 3 Nov 1834.

488. Page 440. 13 Jul 1833. State of Mo. by Henry **Shurlds**, Auditor of Public Accounts for Mo., to Frederick C. **Hase**. For the sum of $2.76 in back taxes and penalties, 640 acres, being Survey No. 2146 in Twp 36, Rng 10 & 11; originally claimed by Benjamin **Cox**. Sold on 1 Jul 1833 to pay sd taxes due on the tract for 1832, with interest assessed after 1 Dec 1832. Signed Henry **Shurlds**, Auditor of Public Accounts. Wit Frederick C. **Hase**, Clerk. Rec 4 Nov 1834.

End of Book 1

Perry County Land Record Book 2

489. Page 1. __ __ 1833. James **Caldwell** and James W. **Smith**, both of St. Francois Co., Mo., to William **Price**. For the sum of $206.25, 237 acres on the waters of Brazo Creek about five miles from the Mississippi River; being the W part of Theophilus **Williams'** settlement right of 640 acres. Signed James **Caldwell**, James W. **Smith**. May **Caldwell**, wife of James, RD. Wit William **Murphy**, JCC for St. Francois Co., Mo. Rec 20 Nov 1834.

490. Page 2. 10 Dec 1831. Bernard **Cissell** and Monica, his wife, to Joseph D. **Simpson**. For the sum of $125, 230 acres on a branch of the S fork of Saline Creek; part of 640 acres, beginning at a white oak marked 'L. E'. Signed Bernard **Cissell**, Monica (x) **Cissell** (RD). Wit Joseph **Cissell**, John **Layton** (JP). Rec 8 Dec 1834.

491. Page 3. 27 Sep 1834. Bernard **Layton** and Mary, his wife, to Hugh **Wells**. For the sum of $262.50, 80 acres, being the E 1/2, SW 1/4, Sec 22, Twp 34 N, Rng 12 E. Signed Bernard **Layton**, Mary (x) **Layton** (RD). Wit John **Layton** Senr (JP), Mark **Brewer**. Rec 8 Dec 1834.

492. Page 4. 17 Jul 1833. Clement **Cissell** and Ann, his wife, to Joseph D. **Simpson**. For the sum of $125, 230 acres, more or less, on a branch of the S fork of Saline Creek, part of 640 acres on which R. **Boyd** now lives, and to be taken off the upper end of sd tract; beginning at a white oak marked 'L. E.'. Signed Clement **Cissell**, Ann **Cissell** (RD). Wit William **Cissell**, Pious **Hagan**, John **Layton** Senr (JP). Rec 8 Dec 1834.

493. Page 5. 30 Nov 1825. Commissioners of Perryville to James **Logan**. For the sum of $19.50, Lot No. 16 in Perryville. Signed R. T. **Brown**, Thomas **Riney**, Joseph **Tucker** senr.,

Commissioners. Wit Cornelius M. **Slattery** (JP). Rec 11 Dec 1834.

494. Page 5. 11 Dec 1834. James **Logan** of Jackson Co., Ill. to Charles **Stuart**. For the sum of $50, Lot No. 16 in Perryville. Signed James **Logan**. Test R. S. **Dorsey** (JP). Rec 11 Dec 1834.

495. Page 6. 9 Sep 1834. Brice **Young** to Samuel **Mansker** of Ill. For the sum of $600 ($193.74 1/2 in hand and $406.25 1/2 payable in 12 months), four negroes: a woman **Binday** about 25 years old, and three children **Bill** about 6 years old, **Patsey** about 2 years 6 months old, and **Sam** about 1 year old. Signed Brice **Young**. Test A. H. **Puckett**, Elisha **Eggers**, Joab W. **Burgee** (JP). Rec 11 Dec 1834.

496. Page 6. 19 Dec 1833. Joseph de **St. Ledger** to John **Hoofman**. For the sum of $65.60, deed of trust on one hand organ with three cylinders; numerous books [titles specified in the deed]; kitchen furniture, consisting of one iron pott, two pair shovells & tongs, a skillit, two sauce pans, small do.., two pair andirons, and three kitchen ovens; bedding for two beds, consisting of five coverlids & quilts, 6 blankets, 6 pair sheets, 6 pillow cases & pillows, a buffalowrobe, skins, etc; paintings, consisting of two Flemish paintings representing a sea storm & the death of King Ludovericus, and a mermaid(?) taking from Shakespeare's tragedy; the busts of General Carrol, Coffee & Gain, Marshalls Monsey & Nay, each in a large quilt frame; busts of General Washington, Charlotte de Cande, Darno, Voltaire & Rouseau, St. Just Despair, Robespierre, Marah Molliere, Madison, & Monroe; three sets of window & bed curtens; a shot gun silver mounted; powder horn; & shot bag. The debt is due in year in a note with a seal (commonly called a single bill) of even date; with the property to be sold if not paid; and any surplus to go to sd **St. Legor**. Signed J. **St. Leger**. Wit Wm. C. **Moore**, John **Layton** (JP). Rec 5 Jan 1835.

497. Page 8. 13 Oct 1834. Isidore **Erstricher** and Gertrude, his wife, to Godfrey **Blackley**. For the sum of $165, 80 acres, being the N 1/2, NE 1/4, Sec 36, Twp 34 N, Rng 11 E; purchased by sd **Erstricher** of Clara **Welker** on 25 Apr 1833 (1:364). Signed Isidore **Erstreicher**, Gertrude **Erstreicher** (RD). Wit Jones **Abernathy** (JP). Rec 5 Jan 1835.

498. Page 9. 2 Jan 1835. Henry **Shurlds**, Auditor of Public Accounts for Mo., to Charles **Stewart**. For the sum of $0.56 in taxes and penalties, 1/2 of Lot No. 16 in Perryville, originally claimed by James **Logan** as per the tax list of 1833. Signed Henry **Shurlds**, Auditor of Public Accounts. Rec 5 Jan 1835.

499. Page 10. 11 Nov 1834. Commissioners to sell land of John Anson **McLane** and the legal heirs of John **Shoults**, decd, to John Anson **McLane**. For the sum of $1710, 103.48 acres, being Lot No. 7, NE 1/4, Sec 4, Twp 33, Rng 12 E. Sold on order of Circuit Court issued Nov Term 1834 on petition to partition land owned by sd **McLane** and the legal heirs of John **Shoults**, decd; that is, Francis **Shoults**, widow of sd **Shoults**, Sarah **Shoults**, Franklin **Shoults**, John Alfred **Shoults**, and Emely Jane **Shoults**, with John **Logan** appointed as guardian to the minor heirs. Signed Wm. A. **Bull**, Robert **Wilson**, Archibald **Mitchel**. Wit Robert **Mitchell**, Elias **Barber** (JP). Rec 27 Jan 1835.

500. Page 11. 29 Dec 1834. John **Johnson** to Priscilla **Johnson**. For the sum of $50, 40 acres on both sides of White Water, being the NW 1/4, NW 1/4, Sec 24, Twp 34 N, Rng 8 E; that John **Johnson** purchased from the U. S. A. on 7 Dec 1833. Signed John (x) **Johnson**. Wit John L. **Conrad**, Mary (x) **Tucker**, R. S. **Dorsey** (JP). Rec 31 Jan 1835.

501. Page 11. 17 Nov 1834. Henry **Welker** to Robert **Hinkle** and John **Welker**. For the sum of $50.25, mortgage on __ acres, being the SW 1/4, SW 1/4, Sec 31, Twp 34 N, Rng 12 E. Henry **Welker** borrowed the debt from the grantees on 17 Nov 1834, due one year from date with 10% interest per annum. Signed Henry (x) **Welker**. Wit R. S. **Dorsey** (JP). Rec 5 Jul 1835.

502. Page 12. 18 Jan 1834. Henry **Eddlemon** and Mary, his wife, to John **Welker**. For a valuable consideration, 25 acres adjoining sd **Welker**'s land; beginning at sd **Eddlemon**'s SE corner, which is part of the E 1/2, SW 1/4, Sec 22, Twp 34 N, Rng 11 E. Signed Henry **Eddlemon**, Mary (x) **Eddlemon** (RD). Wit James **Mattingly** (JP). Rec 5 Jul 1835.

503. Page 13. 4 Feb 1835. Lucretia **Reardon** to Charles **Gregoire**. For the sum of $40, __ acres on the S fork of Saline Creek adjoining sd **Gregoire**'s mill; being her dower right as widow of William **Reardon**, decd. Signed Lucretia (x) **Reardon**. Wit William **Searcy** (JP), Rosannah W. **Searsey**. Rec 13 Feb 1835.

504. Page 13. 7 Apr 1831. Bernard **Brown** and Ann, his wife, to William **Haydon**. For the sum of $13, Lot No. 5 in Perryville; deeded to sd **Brown** by the Commissioners on 30 Nov 1825. Signed Bernard (x) **Brown**, Ann (x) **Brown** (RD). Wit W. **Dickinson**, JCC. Rec 11 Feb 1835.

505. Page 14. 25 Jun 1834. Jonas **Winfield** and Eleoner, his wife, of Marion Co., Ken. to William **Winfield**. For the sum of $1, 80 acres, being the W 1/2, NW 1/4, Sec 20, Twp 34 N, Rng 11 E. Signed Jonas **Winfield**, Eleanor **Winfield** (RD). Wit Samuel **Spalding**, Clerk of Marion Co., Ken. Court, John **Ferguson**, JP in Marion Co., Ken. Rec 2 Mar 1835.

506. Page 16. 18 Dec 1832. William **Alexander** and Jane, his wife, of Bourbon Co., Ken. to William B. **Phillips** of Mason Co., Ken. For the sum of $1000, __ acres in Bois Brule Bottom on the Mississippi River; the upper half of 600 or 640 arpens granted to Alexander **McConnoehie** as a concession under the Spanish Government; sold by sd **McConnoehie** to Georg **Robinson**, and by sd **Robinson** to John H. **Sandees**, and by sd **Sandees** to N. P. **Robinson**, and by sd **Robinson** to sd **Alexander**; beginning at a stake, the lower corner on the Mississippi River. Signed William **Alexander**, Jane S. **Alexander**. Wit Wm. B. **Branham**, Presiding Justice of Bourbon Co., Ken. Court, Thomas P. **Smith**, Clerk of Bourbon Co., Ken. Court. Rec 26 Mar 1835.

507. Page 17. 28 Feb 1835. Alexander **Patterson** Jr. and Nancy, his wife, of St. Francois Co., Mo. to William **Patterson**. For the sum of $200, 100 acres in Bois Brule Bottom; being the NW 1/2 of 200 acres willed to Alexander **Patterson** Junr by his father Alexander **Patterson** Senr; part of 640 acres confirmed to Alexander **Patterson** Ser.; and bounded on the E by John **Patterson**'s part of the tract. Signed Alexander (x) **Patterson**, Nancy (x) **Paterson** (RD). Test David **Pinksten**, Thomas **Haile**, JCC in St. Francois Co., Mo. Rec 26 Mar 1835.

508. Page 18. 25 Dec 1834. Phineas **Block** and Delia, his wife, of Pike Co., Mo. to Joseph **Shoults**. For the sum of $100, Lot No. 57

in Perryville; conveyed to sd **Block** by the Commissioners on 24 Nov 1829. 25 Dec 1834. Signed Phineas **Block**, Delia **Block** (RD). Wit William **Stephenson**, JCC in Pike Co., Mo. Rec 26 Mar 1835.

509. Page 19. 2 Sep 1834. William Augustus **Keyte** and Ann, his wife, to John **Logan**. For the sum of $20, Lot No. 27 in Perryville on Main St., adjoining sd **Logan**'s tanyard. Signed Wm. A. **Keyte**. Greer W. **Davis**, Richard **Cogan**, and James **Evans** swear before R. S. **Dorsey**, JP, that the signature is that of sd **Keyte**. Rec 26 Mar 1835.

510. Page 20. 1 Jun 1831. U. S. A. to Benedicta **Fenwick** of Bethlehem Convent. Patent for 41.60 acres, being the NE fractional 1/4, Sec 14, Twp 35 N, Rng 10 E. Signed Andrew **Jackson**, President. Wit Elijah **Hayword**, Commissioner of the General Land Office. Rec in Vol. 2:390. Rec 16 Apr 1835.

511. Page 21. 13 Apr 1835. Juliana **Fenwick**, alias Sister Benedicta **Fenwick**, late Superior of Bethlehem Convent and now Superior of St. Michaels Convent, Madison Co., Mo., to Margaret **O'Bryan**, alias Sister Beatrix, Superior of Bethlehem Convent. For the sum of $500, six tracts; 37.64 acres, being SW fractional 1/4, Sec 13, Twp 35, Rng 10 E, as described in Patent No. 946 (Vol. 3, page 485 at the Land Office); 157.64 acres adjoining the first tract, being the NW fractional 1/4 of Sec 13, as described in Patent No. 116 (3:31 in the Land Office); 41 and sixteenths(?) acres, being the NE fractional 1/4, Sec 14, Twp 35, Rng 10 E, as described in Patent No. 970 (2:390 at the Land Office); 4.57 acres, conveyed to sd **Fenwick** by Zachariah **Layton** and Mary, his wife, on 21 Jan 1831 (1:282), on which sd convent is built; 80.33 acres, being the W 1/2, NW 1/4, Sec 31, Twp 34 N, Rng 12 E, as described in Patent No. 1007 (2:422 in the Land Office); and __ acres near Apple Creek adjoining the previous tract, conveyed to sd **Fenwick** by Joseph **Schnowbush**, and on which a log church, house, and other buildings of the Convent of St. Joseph was lately established. Signed J. Julia **Fenwick**, alias Sister Benedicta. Wit William M. **Newbery**, Circuit Clerk of Madison Co., Mo. Rec 16 Apr 1835.

512. Page 22. 15 Oct 1833. U. S. A. to Julia **Fenwick**, Superior of Bethlehem Convent. Patent No. 1116 for 157.64 acres, being the NW fractional 1/4, Sec 13, Twp 35 N, Rng 10 E. Signed Andrew **Jackson**, President. Wit Elijah **Hayword**, Commissioner of the General Land Office. Also recorded in 3:34 at the General Land Office. Rec 16 Apr 1835.

513. Page 22. 15 Oct 1833. Same to same. Patent No. 1007 for 80.33 acres, being the W 1/2, NW 1/4, Sec 31, Twp 34 N, Rng 12 E. Signed Andrew **Jackson**, President. Wit Elijah **Hayword**, Commissioner of the General Land Office. Also recorded in 2:423 in the General Land Office. Rec 16 Apr 1835.

514. Page 23. 1 Oct 1831. Joseph **Snowbush** and Elizabeth, his wife, to same. For love, for propagating the Roman Catholick Religion, and the sum of $1, 49.53 acres, part of the E 1/2, NW 1/4, Sec 31, Twp 34 N, Rng 12 E; beginning at the NW corner of sd tract; and part of the same patented to sd **Snowbush** by Certificate No. 814. Sd **Snowbush** reserves to himself and his wife the right of dwelling on sd property until their deaths. Signed Joseph (x) **Snorbush**, Elizabeth (x) **Snourbush** (RD). Wit J. **Timon**, Francis (x) **Snowbush**, James **Mattingly** (JP). Rec 16 Apr 1835.

515. Page 24. 2 Oct 1831. U. S. A. to same. Patent No. 946 for 37.64 acres, being the SW fractional 1/4, Sec 13, Twp 35 N, Rng 10 E. Signed Andrew **Jackson**, President. Wit Jno. M. **Moore**, Acting Commissioner of the General Land Office. Also recorded in 3:485 in the General Land Office. Rec 16 Apr 1835.

516. Page 25. 17 Apr 1835. James **Manning** Senr and Elizabeth, his wife, to Elizabeth **Warren**. For the sum of $100, 80 acres, beginning at a black oak on Peter **Holster** Sr.'s NE line. Signed James (x) **Manning**, Elizabeth (x) **Manning** (RD). Wit R. S. **Dorsey** (JP). Rec 16 Apr 1835.

517. Page 25. 25 Dec 1834. Francois **Clark** and Eveline, his wife, to John **Daugherty**. Deed of partition for an undivided moiety of 180.68 acres in Bois Brule Bottom, being the S 1/2, fractional Sec 35, Twp 37 N, Rng 10 E; to be divided equally by a line running N-S. Sd **Clark** and wife to receive the W 1/2, and sd **Daugherty** the E 1/2. Signed Francis **Clark**, Evaline **Clark** (RD), John **Daugherty**. Wit W. **Searcy** (JP). Rec 25 Apr 1835.

518. Page 27. 1 May 1835. William **Price** and Darcus, his wife, to Robert **Wilson**, James **Rosebrough**, and Daniel U. **Cline**, Trustees for the Presbyterian Church of Brazo. For the sum of $12.75, 10 acres, being the S end of the SW fractional 1/4, Sec 7, Twp 34 N, Rng 13 E. Signed William **Price**, Darcus **Price** (RD). Wit Elias **Barber** (JP). Rec 4 May 1835.

519. Page 28. 9 Sep 1834. Last will and testament of Andrew **McCasling**. To his brother-in-law Archibald **Thurmond**: all his horses and cattle, with the exception of one yearling colt, which he bequeaths to his brother Henry **McCaslin**, along with his work and wearing clothes and one saddle. To his sisters Elizabeth **Thurmond** and Sarah **Talbat** or their heirs of their bodies: equal parts of his land in Bois Brule Bottom. To his brother James **McCaslin** and brother-in-law William **Talbot** and their heirs: equal parts of a 4-acre lot in the vicinity of Albany, Floyd Co., Ind. James **McCaslin** and William **Talbot** are appointed executors. Signed Andrew **McCaslin**. Wit Austin **Hozard**, John **Belsha**, Fredk. C. **Hase**, Clerk. Rec 4 May 1835.

520. Page 28. 30 Mar 1835. William **Flynn** to the children of Mary **Burget**, wife of John E. **Burget**, when they reach age 21. For natural affection for his daughter Mary **Burget**, a negro girl **Maria**, in her 16th year, and her increase; sd girl to belong to sd Mary until her decease, then to her children. Signed William **Flynn**. Wit Timothy **Davis**, Jacob J. **Everts**, Joab W. **Burgee** (JP). Rec 4 May 1835.

521. Page 29. 30 Mar 1835. John E. **Burget** and Mary C., his wife, to William **Flynn**. For the sum of $100, 33.07 acres, more or less, on Horse Island in Bois Brule Twp, being the SW fractional 1/4, Sec 17, Twp 37 N, Rng 11 E. Signed John E. **Burgett**, Mary C. **Burgett** (RD). Wit Joab W. **Burgee** (JP). Rec 11 May 1835.

522. Page 30. 13 Nov 1826. David L. **Caldwell**, Collector of Perry Co., to Nancy **Burget**. For the sum of $10.35 in taxes and costs, 6 acres assessed to Amos **Bird**'s estate for 1825, to be run off a tract confirmed to Solomon **Morgan**; adjoined on the lower side by William **Flynn** and fronting on the Mississippi River. Signed D. L. **Caldwell**, Collector. Nancy **Burget** to her son John **Burget**. Quit claim to the tract dated 1 Oct 1833. Signed Nancy (x) **Burget**. Test Jacob J. **Everts**, Frederick C. **Hase**, Clerk. John

Logan and R. S. **Dorsey** swear to the signature of sd **Caldwell**. Rec 19 May 1835.

523. Page 31. 23 May 1835. William **Burns** and Martha Mulvine, his wife, to Benjamin **Allbright** and Elenore **Hund**. For the sum of $700, Lot No. 34 in Perryville; conveyed to sd Barnabas **Burns** by the Commissioners, and bequeathed to William **Burns** by Barnabas **Burns**. Signed William **Burns**, Martha M. (x) **Burns** (RD). Wit Fredk. C. **Hase**, J. **Abernathy** (JP). Rec 23 May 1835.

524. Page 32. 23 May 1835. Benjamin **Allbright** and Nancy, his wife, and Elenore **Hund** to William **Burns**. For the sum of $400, mortgage on Lot No. 34 in Perryville as described in the preceding deed (2:31). The debt is due in two payments: $200 due by 1 Oct 1835, and $200 due by 18 May 1836. Signed Benjamin **Allbright**, Nancy (x) **Allbright** (RD), Elenore (x) **Hund**. Wit Fredk. C. **Hase**, J. **Abernathy** (JP). Rec 23 May 1835.

525. Page 33. 3 Feb 1835. Auditor of Public Accounts to John **Logan**. For the sum of $4.27 in back taxes for 1832, penalties, and costs, 300 acres, being Survey No. 147 in Twp 37, Rng 11; possessed in the name of John F. **Henry** and originally claimed by Alexr. **McConohue**; and sold on 1 Jul 1833 to Francis **Clark**. Signed Henry **Shurlds**, Auditor of Public Accounts. Rec 8 Jun 1835.

526. Page 34. 28 Jul 1835. Francis **Scherer** to James **Michaels** Junr. For the sum of $325, 50 acres, more or less, the NE part of 640 acres confirmed to John **Layton**. Signed Francis **Sherarer**. Wit John **Layton** senr (JP), James F. **Tucker**. Rec 30 Jul 1835.

527. Page 35. 17 Nov 1834. James **Rice**, adminr de bonis non of Thomas **Moore**, decd, to William **Manning**. For the sum of $100, 70 acres, more or less, being an undivided right to a tract confirmed to James **Moore** Senior, decd, grandfather of Thomas **Moore**, as Survey No. 2137, in Twp 35 N, Rng 10 E. Sold on 16 Aug 1833 on order of County Court issued in 1833 to pay debts of the estate. Signed James **Rice**. Test R. S. **Dorsey** (JP). Rec 30 Jul 1835.

528. Page 36. 25 Jul 1835. Commissioners of Perryville to Martin L. **Moore**. For the sum of $9.75, Lot No. 41 in Perryville. Signed R. T. **Brown**, Thomas **Riney**, Commissioners. Wit John **Layton** (JP). Rec 10 Sep 1835.

529. Page 37. 6 Aug 1835. David **Crips** and Thereassa, his wife, to Thomas **Brown** and Wilford **Manning**. In consideration of $71.65 of the 3% fund borrowed from Perry Co., mortgage on 286 acres of Survey No. 2186 in Twp 36, Rng 10 & 11; confirmed to sd **Crips**. The debt is due with 10% interest per annum. Signed David (x) **Crips**, Threassa (x) **Crips** (RD). Wit James **Rice** (JP). Rec 6 Aug 1835.

530. Page 38. 10 Aug 1835. Commissioners to sell land of Samuel **Anderson**, decd, to Charles **Ingram**. For the sum of $900, two tracts; $300 for 224 acres, and $600 for 256 acres; part of 640 acres belonging to sd decd; beginning at a white oak on the S of Brazou Creek. Sold in Aug 1835 at order of Circuit Court issued Mar Term 1835 on petition to partition filed by Miles R. **Anderson**; Pinkney K. **Anderson**; Thomas W. **Anderson**; Margaret A. **Anderson**, widow of sd **Anderson** and now wife of Benjamin **Wilson**; and John **Logan**. All are heirs of sd **Anderson** except John **Logan**. Sd land is divided as follows: 160 acres to John **Logan** on the N end of the survey, beginning at a stake on James' line and also bounded by Theophilus **Williams**; and 480 acres to the heirs of sd **Anderson**, to be sold in two lots. Signed Robert **Wilson**, William **Price**, Archibald **Mitchel**, Commissioners. Wit Fredk. C. **Hase**, Clerk. Rec 10 Aug 1835.

531. Page 40. 25 Apr 1835. Delinquent tax list. Tax, penalties at the rate of 15% per annum, and 37 cents costs due by 7 Jul 1835, or the tracts will be sold.

In whose name Assessed	Original Claimant or Patentee	Quantity (acres/100ths)	Parts of Sec. or Survey No.	Twp	Rng	To whom sold
Coen, Elias	Elias **Coen**	40	89	36	10	Frederick C. **Hase**
Crips, James	David **Crips**	160	2186	36	10 & 11	Frederick C. **Hase**
Lawless, Virginia	Robert **Hinkston**	640	865	34	13	State
Donohue, John	Joseph **James** Sr.	Lot No. 29 in Perryville - North & Jackson St				Frederick C. **Hase**
Layton, Ignatius	Ignatius **Layton**	Lot No. 19 in Perryville - Spring St				Frederick C. **Hase**
Layton, Bernard	Bernard **Layton**	Lot No. 20 in Perryville - Spring St				Frederick C. **Hase**
Logan, James	James **Logan**	Lot No. 16 in Perryville - Spring St				Frederick C. **Hase**
Moore, James C.	James C. **Moore**	Lot No. 27 in Perryville - Main St				Frederick C. **Hase**
Ragland, Elias, estate	Thomas **Cody**	Lot No. 50 in Perryville - North St				Frederick C. **Hase**
Snearbush, Joseph	Joseph **Snearbush**	Lot No. 13 in Perryville - Spring St				Frederick C. **Hase**

Signed Peter G. **Glover**, Auditor of Public Accounts for Missouri. Wit Fredk. C. **Hase**, Clerk. Rec 10 Aug 1835.

532. Page 42. 10 Aug 1835. William A. **Keyte** by Sheriff Thomas J. **Tucker** to Richard **Cogan**. For the sum of $185, Lot Nos. 7, 8, & 27 in Perryville; Lot No. 8 includes a one-story brick house and other buildings. Sold on the second Monday of Aug 1835 on order of Circuit Court issued 1 Apr 1835 in favor of sd **Cogan** and against sd **Keyte** for $620.02 and $14 costs. Signed Thomas J. **Tucker**, Sheriff. Wit Fredk. C. **Hase**, Clerk. Rec 14 Aug 1835.

533. Page 43. 29 Mar 1834. John **Duvall** to Benjamin **Wilson** of Cape Girardeau Co., Mo. For the sum of $37.25, Lot Nos. 73 & 74 in Perryville, whereon Pious **Brewer** once resided. Signed John **Duvall**. Test R. S. **Dorsey** (JP). Rec 9 Sep 1835.

534. Page 44. 10 Sep 1835. Edward **McGinnis** to John **Brands**. For the sum of $100, mortgage on 80 acres, being the W 1/2, SE 1/4, Sec 26, Twp 35 N, Rng 10 E. The debt is due to sd **Brands** by 10 Sep 1836. Signed Edward **McGinnis**. Wit Joseph R. **Wiseman**, John **Conners**, John **Layton** (JP). Rec 10 Sep 1835.

535. Page 45. 19 Sep 1835. Joseph **Shoults** and Eliza, his wife, to Mathias **Barringer**. For the sum of $25, part of Lot No. 57 in Perryville; beginning 25 ft from the SW corner of the lot and fronting on St. Marys St.; and sold to Phinias **Block** by the Commissioners on 24 Nov 1829, and sold by sd **Block** and Delia, his wife, to sd **Shoults** on 25 Dec 1834. Signed Joseph **Shoults**, Eliza B. **Shoults** (RD). Test Fredk. C. **Hase**, Clerk. Rec 19 Sep 1835.

536. Page 46. 21 Sep 1835. Joseph B. **Mattingly** and Maria, his wife, to Joseph **Cissell**. For the sum of $1.13, mortgage on 113 acres, more or less, being the SW 1/4, Sec 19, Twp 34 N, Rng 11 E. The debt is due to sd **Cissell** in two years with 6% interest per annum. Signed Joseph **Mattingly**, Maria (x) **Mattingly** (RD). Wit James **Rice** (JP). Rec 21 Sep 1835. [Marginal note: Full satisfaction received on 19 Sep 1837. Signed Joseph **Cissell**. Wit Fredck. C. **Hase**, Clerk.]

537. Page 47. 25 Sep 1835. Walter **McClane** to Edward **McClane** of Ste. Genevieve Co., Mo. For the sum of $300, his half of the property of William **McClain** and wife, as deeded to them by sd William and wife. Signed Walter **McClane**. Wit James **Evans**, Frederick C. **Hase**, Clerk. Rec 25 Sep 1835.

538. Page 48. 8 Oct 1835. Landon **Reardin** to Charles **Gregoire**. For the sum of $200, undivided 1/3 of 550 arpens, more or less, on the S fork of Saline Creek; bounded on the E by the heirs of Francis **Valley**, decd, S by Henry **Tucker**, and W & N by public land; conveyed by Amos **Rowark** and Marthy, his wife, to Robert **Reardon** on 12 Aug 1818 (Ste. Genevieve Co. Book C:85). Signed Landon (x) **Reardon**. Wit Fredk. C. **Hase**, Clerk. Proved by George **McKnew** and William **Reardon**. Rec 8 Oct 1835.

539. Page 49. 24 Sep 1835. Augustin Zimerman **Hase** and Elizabeth, his wife, to Frederick C. **Hase**. For the sum of $250, 65.45 acres, being fractional Sec 19, Twp 35 N, Rng 11 E; and the same purchased from the U. S. A. by Christopher **Hines**, sold by sd **Hines** and Teresa, his wife, to Augustin Z. **Hase** on 7 Jul 1834 (1:415, 416). Signed Augustin Z. **Hase**, Elizabeth **Hase** (RD). Wit John **Layton** Senr (JP), Augustine **Layton**. Rec 24 Oct 1835.

540. Page 50. 22 Oct 1835. Charles **French** to Silas **French**. For the sum of $50, deed of trust on three cattle, three beds and bedding, six hogs, and all his household and kitchen furniture. Sd Charles owes a debt to sd Silas, and if it is not paid by 1 Oct 1836, sd Silas is to dispose of the property at public sale, with any excess to go to Charles **French**. Signed Charles (x) **French**, Silas (x) **French**. Wit Fredk. C. **Hase**, Clerk. Rec 22 Oct 1835.

541. Page 51. 16 Oct 1835. Daniel **Killian** to J. **Pratte** and P. R. **Pratte**. For the sum of $40, Lot No. 63 in Perryville on the SW corner of the public square, fronting on St. Joseph and Jackson Sts. Signed Daniel **Killian**. Wit James **Rice** (JP). Rec 31 Oct 1835.

542. Page 52. 19 Sep 1835. Ignatius **Layton** Senr to Mathias **Barringer**. For the sum of $40, Lot No. 31 in Perryville, fronting on Main St. Signed Ignatius **Layton**. Wit Jas. **Rice** (JP). Rec 31 Oct 1835.

543. Page 52. 25 May 1835. Last will and testament of Cornelius **Cobbs**. To his father, mother, and sisters Elizabeth L. & Sarah M. **Cobbs** for the support of his parents: all his property after debts and funeral costs are paid. To his sisters Elizabeth L. & Sarah M. **Cobbs**, and Ann **Hervey**, formerly Ann **Cobbs**: each to have 1/3 of his remaining personal and perishable property after the death of his parents. To his sisters Elizabeth L. & Sarah M. **Cobbs**: even division of his real estate by quantity and quality. John **Noell**, his uncle, is appointed executor. Signed Cornelius **Cobbs**. Wit J. **Abernathy**, Martin L. **Moore**, John W. **Noell**, J. A. C. **Hase**, Dep Clerk. Rec 3 Nov 1835.

544. Page 53. 9 Nov 1835. Abner **Baugh** to William **Tucker** and James **Hagan**. For the sake of securing to sd **Tucker** property valued at $24.56 1/4: one bay mare, one steer, one grubing hoe, and one shovel plow; deed of trust on one mill on Bois Brule Creek. Sd **Hagan** shall sell the mill if sd **Baugh** does not provide the property to sd **Tucker** on demand, with the residue to go to sd **Baugh** after the sale. Signed Abner **Baugh**, William **Tucker**, James **Hagan**. Test Fredk. C. **Hase**, Clerk. Rec 9 Nov 1835.

545. Page 54. 18 Sep 1834. Heirs of Zar **Sturdevant** Senr, decd-- Rachel **Sturdevant**, widow, Zar **Sturdevant** Junr, Homer **Sturdevant**, and Harriet **Sturdevant**--to Thomas **Kenedy**. For the sum of $325, an estimated 155 acres on the headwaters of St. Lorent Creek; the SW end of a tract purchased by Zar **Sturdevant**, decd, from Thomas **Donohue** and Mary, his wife, on 15 Aug 1818; and being the part not sold by sd **Sturdevant** during his lifetime and where he resided at the time of his death. Signed Rachel (x) **Sturdevant**, Zar **Sturdevant**, Homer **Sturdevant**, Harriet **Sturdevant**. Wit W. **Searcy** (JP). Rec 17 Nov 1835.

546. Page 55. 31 Oct 1835. Ignatius **Layton** to Joseph **Shoults**. For the sum of $110, 22 acres, more or less, beginning at a stake near a large white oak standing on the most SE line of a tract granted by the U. S. A. to John **Layton** senior, decd; bounded on the NE corner by John **Layton** Jr. Signed Ignatius **Layton** Senr. Wit John **Layton** senr (JP), Thos. J. **Tucker**. Rec 24 Nov 1835.

547. Page 56. 20 Apr 1835. Hilarion **Manning** and Mary, his wife, to Adison **Walker**. For the sum of $80, Lot No. 17 in Perryville; conveyed by George **Killian** to sd **Manning**; and on which is erected a dwelling house. Signed Hilarion **Manning**, Mary (x) **Manning** (RD). Wit John **Layton** senr (JP). Rec 26 Nov 1835.

548. Page 57. 26 Nov 1835. William Addison **Walker** and Mary, his wife, to Hyman **Block**. For the sum of $100, Lot No. 17 in Perryville as conveyed to sd **Walker** by Hilarion **Manning**, as described in the preceding deed (1:56). Signed Wm. A. **Walker**, Mary **Walker** (RD). Wit Frederick C. **Hase**, Clerk. Rec 26 Nov 1835.

549. Page 58. 4 Nov 1835. William **Winfield** and Helen, his wife, to the Commissioner of the 3% fund for Perry Co. For the sum of $146.81 1/4, mortgage on 50 acres in Bois Brule Twp in the SW fractional 1/4, Sec 16, Twp 36 N, Rng 12 E. The sum is due by 3 Nov 1836 with 10% interest per annum. Signed William **Winfield**, Helen **Winfield** (RD). Wit Nathaniel J. **Divine** (JP), Amyd. (x) **Chandler**. Rec 14 Dec 1835. [Marginal note: Full amount received on 27 Oct 1837. Signed P. R. **Pratte**, Comm.]

550. Page 59. 23 May 1835. John B. **Bossier** and Martha, his wife, of Madison Co., Mo., to Jean Bte. **Valle** of Ste. Genevieve Co., Mo. and Pierre **Menard** of Randolph Co., Ill. For the sum of $122, __ acres, being the undivided 1/2 of the NE 1/4, Sec 30,

Twp 35 N, Rng 10 E. Signed J. B. **Bossier**, Mthe. **Bossier** (RD). Wit William M. **Newberry**, Madison Co., Mo. Clerk. Rec 14 Dec 1835.

551. Page 60. 13 Dec 1835. Thomas **Brown** to Martin L. **Moore**. For serving as security for a bond obligatory, mortgage on one cow and calf red colour, three years old last spring, marked with a hole and crop in each ear; 50 bushels of corn lying in Hillary **Knott**'s house; six hogs red colour, one sow and five pigs about 5 weeks old; one feather bed and bedding; one cherry bureau which four drawers and brass mounted; and all the corn with he owns, about 30 bushels. Sd **Moore** has entered into a bond obligatory with sd **Brown** for costs in a suit in Circuit Court, wherein sd **Brown** appeals a judgment of John **Layton**, JP, and John **Bright** is appealee. Signed Thomas (x) **Brown**. Test James **Rice** (JP). Rec 17 Dec 1835.

552. Page 61. 7 Apr 1835. Elizabeth **Hall** to Abner H. **Hall**. For the good will, love, and affection she has for her beloved son; undivided 1/2 of 171.57 acres, more or less, in three parcels; 54.57 acres in the W end of lot No. 7, NW 1/4, Sec 5, Twp 33 N, Rng 12 E, lying parallel with the E-W line of sd Lot; 77 acres, more or less, in the E 1/2, SE 1/4, Sec 31, Twp 34 N, Rng 12 E, beginning at the SW corner of the tract and bounded in part by Seth **Hall**'s part of Lot No. 7 aforesaid; and 40 acres, more or less, in the W 1/2, SW 1/4, Sec 32, Twp 34 N, Rng 12 E, beginning at a stake 58 poles N of the SW corner. She reserves all rights and priveleges to the tracts during her lifetime. Signed Elizabeth **Hall**. Wit James **Dunlap**, George P. **Rosse**, Elias **Barber** (JP). Rec 28 Dec 1835.

553. Page 63. 7 Apr 1835. Elizabeth **Hall** to Seth **Hall**. For the sum of $200, 55 acres in two tracts; 52 acres of Lot No. 7, NW 1/4, Sec 5, Twp 33 N, Rng 12 E, lying in the E end of sd lot; and 3 acres, more or less, beginning at the NW corner of the first tract. Signed Elizabeth **Hall**. Wit James **Dunlap**, George P. **Ross**, Elias **Barber** (JP). Rec 28 Dec 1835.

554. Page 64. 7 Apr 1835. Seth **Hall** to Elizabeth **Hall**. For the sum of $200, 40 acres, more or less, in the W 1/2, SW 1/4, Sec 32, Twp 34 N, Rng 12 E, beginning at a stake 58 poles N of the SW corner of sd lot. Seth **Hall** reserves the right to use any quantity of water from the spring branch, and to make or keep up a dam on sd branch within eight poles of the upper end of the tanyard race, not exceeding eight inches high. Signed Seth **Hall**. Wit James **Dunlap**, George P. **Ross**, Elias **Barber** (JP). Rec 28 Dec 1835.

555. Page 65. 7 Apr 1835. Children and heirs of Abner **Hall**, decd, to Elizabeth **Hall**, late wife of sd Abner **Hall**. For the sum of $300, two tracts; 80 acres, being the E 1/2, SE 1/4, Sec 31, Twp 34 N, Rng 12 E; and 106.57 acres, being Lot No. 7, NW 1/4, Sec 5, Twp 33 N, Rng 12 E. Signed Seth **Hall**, George **Hall**, Phebe **Hall**, Harriet M. A. **Hall**, Abner H. **Hall**. Wit James **Dunlap**, George P. **Ross**, Elias **Barber** (JP). Rec 28 Dec 1835.

556. Page 66. 7 Apr 1835. Seth **Hall** to George **Hall**. For the sum of $20, 12 acres, more or less, in the W 1/2, SW 1/4, Sec 32, Twp 34 N, Rng 12 E; beginning at a stake on the E line of sd lot, on the S side of the spring branch. Also the right to make or keep up a dam eight inches high on sd branch, within eight poles of the upper end of the tanyard. Signed Seth **Hall**. Wit James **Dunlap**, George P. **Ross**, Elias **Barber** (JP). Rec 28 Dec 1835.

557. Page 67. 29 Dec 1835. James **Phillips** and Elizabeth, his wife, to George **Preston**. For the sum of $62, 44 acres, more or less, being an undivided moiety of fractional Sec 24, Twp 36 N, Rng 11 E; purchased from the U. S. A. by sd **Preston** and sd **Phillips** on 11 Mar 1834. Signed James (x) **Phillips**, Elizabeth (x) **Phillips** (RD). Wit James **Rice** (JP). Rec 29 Dec 1835.

558. Page 68. 1 Mar 1833. John **Juden** Jr. and Abbey, his wife, and William **McGuire** and Susan, his wife, all of Cape Girardeau Co., Mo., to John **Thompson**. For the sum of $28.43 3/4, 22.74 acres, being the SE fractional 1/4, Sec 16, Twp 36 N, Rng 12 E; purchased from the U. S. A. by sd **Juden** and sd **McGuire** on 15 Jul 1825. Signed John **Juden** Jr., Abbey **Juden** (RD), Wm. **McGuire**, Susan **McGuire** (RD). Wit George **Henderson**, JCC in Cape Girardeau Co., Mo., Andrew **Martin**, JCC in Cape Girardeau Co., Mo. Rec 31 Dec 1835.

559. Page 69. 27 Aug 1835. John **Thompson** and Mary, his wife, to Francis L. **Jones** of Fort Monroe, Vir. For the sum of $100, 22.74 acres as described in the preceding deed (2:68). Signed John (x) **Thompson**, Mary (x) **Thomson** (RD). Test J. W. **Burgee** (JP). Rec 31 Dec 1835.

560. Page 70. 17 Jul 1835. James **Taylor** and Rachel, his wife, to Perry **Evans**. For the sum of $200, 50 acres, more or less, in Bois Brule Bottom, being the upper 1/2 of a tract purchased by sd **Taylor** from William **Morris** on 23 Dec 1825; bounded in front by the river, on the upper side by sd **Evans**, back by land entered by Francis **Clark**, and on the lower side by the division line between sd **Evans** and the widow **Taylor**. Signed James **Taylor**, Rachel **Taylor** (RD). Wit W. **Searcy** (JP). Rec 9 Jan 1836.

561. Page 71. 17 Jul 1835. Charles **Maddin** of Ste. Genevieve Co., Mo. to same. For the sum of $325, 100 acres, more or less, in Bois Brule Bottom; bounded in front by the Mississippi River, on the upper side by the widow **Taylor**, lower side by Joe **Dixon**--a colored free man, and back by John **Daugherty**. Signed Chs. **Maddin**. Wit Timothy **Davis**, W. **Searcy** (JP). Rec 9 Jan 1836.

562. Page 72. 12 Jan 1836. John **Juden** Jr. and Abbey, his wife, of Cape Girardeau Co., Mo. to Thomas J. **Finch**. For the sum of $240, 100 acres in Bois Brule Bottom, part of a claim confirmed to William **Hickman**; beginning at the most S corner of sd **Hickman**'s survey. Signed John **Juden** Jr., Abbey **Juden** (RD). Wit John D. **Cook**, Judge of 4th Judicial Circuit. Rec 1 Feb 1836.

563. Page 73. 14 Jan 1836. Same and same to John P. **Finch**. For the sum of $440, 220 acres in Bois Brule Bottom, part of a claim confirmed to William **Hickman**, commencing at the most N corner of sd **Hickman**'s survey. Signed John **Juden** Jr., Abbey **Juden** (RD). Wit John D. **Cook**, Judge of 4th Judicial Circuit. Rec 1 Feb 1836.

564. Page 74. 30 Dec 1835. Joab W. **Burgee** and Elizabeth, his wife, to Joel **Kinnison**, all of Bois Brule Twp. For the sum of $210, 53 1/4 acres, more or less, in Bois Brule Twp, part of a tract confirmed to Archibald **Camster** senr; bounded on the N by George **Camster**, E by land confirmed to **Hickman**, S by Katharine **Bellsha**, and W by sd **Kinnison**. Signed Joab W. **Burgee**, Elizabeth **Burgee** (RD). Test John P. **Finch**, Nathaniel J. **Divine** (JP). Rec 1 Feb 1836.

565. Page 75. 12 Jul 1834. Bernard **Layton** and Mary, his wife, to David **Hellard**. For the sum of $50, 40 acres, being the NE 1/4, NE 1/4, Sec 27, Twp 34 N, Rng 12 E. Signed Bernard **Layton**, Mary (x) **Layton** (RD). Wit Jonas **Abernathy** (JP). Rec 1 Feb 1836.

566. Page 76. 16 Oct 1835. David **Hellard** and Mary, his wife, to Pinkney K. **Anderson**. For the sum of $210, two tracts on the waters of Indian Creek in Sec 27, Twp 34, Rng 12 E; 40 acres, being the NE 1/4, NE 1/4; and the NE 1/4, SE 1/4. Signed David **Hellard**, Mary **Hellard** (RD). Wit Elias **Barber** (JP). Rec 1 Feb 1836.

567. Page 77. 24 Jul 1832. Hilliard **Fowler** by Sheriff John **Logan** to Nathan **Pusey**. For the sum of $3, 100 arpents in Bois Brule Bottom that sd **Fowler** acquired in right of his wife; that Francis R. **Cissell** owned and where he resided at the time of his death. Sold on 25 Mar 1830 by former Sheriff David L. **Caldwell** on an execution issued 23 Jan 1830 by Circuit Court in favor of Johnson **Ranney** and against sd **Fowler** for $164.50 debt and $10.07 1/2 costs. Signed John **Logan**, Sheriff. Wit Fredk. C. **Hase**, Clerk. Rec 1 Feb 1836.

568. Page 79. 17 Nov 1834. John **Townsend** of Warren Co., Miss. to William **Shannon** of Ste. Genevieve Co., Mo. In release of a mortgage for $2000, four tracts in Bois Brule Bottom; 140 acres confirmed to Theophilus **Hickman** and patented to sd **Shannon** on 9 Dec 1822, known as the Round Pond Tract; 1/2 of a tract confirmed to John **Smith** Senr and William **Russell**, and conveyed by sd **Smith** to William **Searcy** and wife, who conveyed it to sd **Shannon** on 11 Dec 1822; 137.16 acres, being two fractional parts of Sec 28, Twp 37 N, Rng 11 E, one part patented to sd **Shannon**, the other patented to sd **Shannon** and Isaac **Flynn** on 31 May 1824; 1/2 of 300 arpens confirmed to Mark **Brooks**, sold by him to Thomas **Oliver** and William **Searcy**, and by them to sd **Shannon** on 21 Feb 1820. Sd **Shannon** mortgaged the tracts to sd **Townsend** on 11 Feb 1828 to secure payment of $2000. Signed John **Townsend**. Wit John M. **Henderson**, Clerk of Warren Co., Miss. Rec 1 Feb 1836.

569. Page 80. 14 Jul 1835. William **Shannon** and Susan, his wife, to Timothy **Davis**, all of Ste. Genevieve Co., Mo. For the sum of $900, 255.20 acres in Bois Brule Bottom; confirmed to Mark **Brooks** under John **O'Conner**, and patented to sd **Brooks** on 27 Mar 1826. Signed Wm. **Shannon**, Susan (x) **Shannon**. Wit John S. **Barrett**, JCC for Ste. Genevieve Co., Mo. Rec 1 Feb 1836.

570. Page 80. 9 Dec 1834. Joseph **Bogy** and Marie, his wife, to William **Shannon**, all of Ste. Genevieve Co., Mo. For the sum of $350, undivided 1/2 of 300 arpens, more or less, in Bois Brule Bottom in Brooks Prairie; that **Oliver** and **Searcy** purchased from Mark **Brooks** on 1 Oct 1819, and then conveyed to sd **Shannon** on 21 Feb 1820; bounded on the N by sd **Shannon** or **McKnight & Brady**, S by H. B. **Nusam**, E by Mrs. **Perrin**, late Mrs. **Meredith**, and claimed by **Shannon**. Signed Joseph **Bogy**, Marie **Bogy** (RD). Wit Jos. D. **Grafton**, Clerk of Ste. Genevieve Co., Mo. Rec 1 Feb 1836.

571. Page 82. 24 Jan 1836. Benjamin **Wilson** of Cape Girardeau Co., Mo. to Luther **Taylor**. For the sum of $166.32, 24 3/4 acres, more or less, beginning at the SE corner of Perryville, adjoining John **Logan**. Signed Ben. **Wilson**. Wit Frederick C. **Hase**, Clerk. Rec 2 Feb 1836.

572. Page 82. 9 Jan 1836. Perry **Evans** and Dianna, his wife, to Joseph **Pratte** and Peter R. **Pratte**. For the sum of $200, 20 acres, more or less, beginning at a stake at the second corner of Edward **McGinnis**' corner on the old line of John **Layton**, decd. Signed Perry **Evans**, Dianna (x) **Evans** (RD). Wit Robert **Abernathy**, Felix **Seems**, John **Layton** (JP). Rec 3 Feb 1836.

573. Page 83. 14 Jan 1836. John **Juden** Jr. and Abbey, his wife, of Cape Girardeau Co., Mo. to Austin **Hogard**. For the sum of $360, 120 acres in Bois Brule Twp, part of a survey confirmed to William **Hickman**, beginning at the most W corner of the piece of sd survey belonging to **McCausland**. Signed John **Juden** Jr., Abbey **Juden** (RD). Wit John D. **Cook**, Judge of 4th Judicial Circuit. Rec 13 Feb 1836.

574. Page 84. 15 Jan 1836. Clement **Cissell** and Nancy, his wife, Joseph **Cissell** and Mary, his wife, and Simon **Duvall**, widower of Mary **Duvall**, decd (formerly Mary **Cissell** and daughter and heir of Bernard **Cissell**, decd), to Lewis **Cissell**. For the sum of $73.50 1/4 to each, 177 3/4 acres in Survey No. 1131 in Twp 35 & 36, Rng 10 E; part of 640 acres confirmed to Bernard **Cissell** and his heirs in a patent dated 28 Jul 1835 and recorded in Vol 8:79 of the General Land Office; and their shares of 237 acres not heretofore disposed of by sd Bernard. Signed Clement **Cissell**, Nancy **Cissell** (RD), Joseph **Cissell**, Mary **Cissell** (RD), Simon **Duvall**. Wit John **Layton** (JP). Rec 15 Feb 1836.

575. Page 86. 12 Jan 1836. James **Rice**, Peter R. **Pratte**, and David **Burns**, commissioners to partition the real estate of Barnabas **Burns**, decd., to William **Burns**. For the sum of $250.50, Lot No. 35 in Perryville, whereon are erected a cotton gin, screw, etc., and all the improvements thereunto belonging. Sold on 6 May 1833 on order of Circuit Court issued Mar Term 1833 for sale of sd real estate. Signed Jas. **Rice**, P. R. **Pratte**, David **Burns**, Commissioners. Wit John **Layton** (JP). Rec 16 Feb 1836.

576. Page 88. 15 Mar 1834. Zenas N. **Ross** and Sada, his wife, to Samuel **Barber**. For the sum of $250, 40 acres, being the SW 1/4, NE 1/4, Sec 6, Twp 34 N, Rng 13 E. Signed Zenas N. **Ross**, Sadah **Ross** (RD). Test Elias **Barber** (JP). Rec 17 Feb 1836.

577. Page 89. 19 Feb 1836. Joseph **Shoults** and Eliza, his wife, to Matthias **Barringer**. For the sum of $100, Lot No. 57 in Perryville. Signed Joseph **Shoults**, Eliza K. **Shoults** (RD). Wit John **Layton** Senr (JP). Rec 19 Feb 1836.

578. Page 90. 22 Feb 1836. William **Burns** and Martha, his wife, to Hynman **Block**. For the sum of $250, Lot No. 35 in Perryville, sold by order of Circuit Court by Commissioners to partition real estate of the heirs of Barnabas **Burns**, decd, to William **Burns**. Signed William **Burns**, Martha (x) **Burns** (RD). Wit Jas. **Rice** (JP). Rec 22 Feb 1836.

579. Page 91. 2 Jan 1836. Benjamin **Allbright** and Nancy, his wife, to Peter **Faherty**. For the sum of $275, Lot No. 68 in Perryville. Signed B. **Allbright**, Nancy **Allbright** (RD). Wit Fredk. C. **Hase**, Clerk. Rec 26 Feb 1836.

580. Page 92. 4 Mar 1836. Fenwick J. **Hamilton** to Charles **Swan**. For the sum of $300, three lots laid out by the commissioners to partition real estate of George A. **Hamilton**, decd, and bounded on

the E by lands formerly owned by John **Manning**, and W by Robert **Hinkston**'s survey; 96 acres, more or less, being Lot No. 13 set out for Walter F. **Hamilton**, bounded on the S by Lot No. 14 for Josiah F. **Hamilton** and N by Lot No. 12 for Leo **Hamilton**; 109 acres, more or less, being Lot No. 12 drawn for Leo F. **Hamilton**, bounded on the S by Lot No. 13 for Walter F. **Hamilton** and N by Lot No. 11 for Matilda **Hamilton**; and 108 acres, more or less, being Lot No. 14, bounded on the S by Congress land and N by Lot No. 13. Signed Fenwick J. **Hamilton**. Wit Elias **Barber** (JP). Rec 7 Mar 1836.

581. Page 93. 15 Oct 1829. Robert **Wilson** and Rachel, his wife, to Richard **Swann**. For the sum of $8, 4 acres, 61 poles, part of Sec 36, Twp 35 N, Rng 12 E; beginning at the half mile corner on the W line. Signed Robert **Wilson**, Rachel **Wilson** (RD). Wit Elias **Barber** (JP). Rec 7 Mar 1836.

582. Page 94. 25 Oct 1829. Benjamin **Wilson** and Jane, his wife, of Cape Girardeau Co., Mo. to same. For the sum of $242, 160 acres, being the SW 1/4, Sec 36, Twp 35 N, Rng 12 E. Signed Benj. **Wilson**, Jane **Wilson** (RD). Wit Elias **Barber** (JP). Rec 7 Mar 1836.

583. Page 95. 7 Mar 1836. James **Michael** to Ferdinand **Rozier** Jr. For the sum of $200, mortgage on two or three barrels of whiskey, brandy, cloves, almonds, candy, cider, wines, bottles, glassware, and sundry other articles of groceries. The debt is due in two years, or the property is to be sold, with any excess going to sd **Michael**. Signed James **Michael**, Ferdinand **Rozier** Jr. Wit John **Layton** (JP). Rec 7 Mar 1836.

584. Page 96. 7 Mar 1836. Joseph **Shoults** and Eliza, his wife, to Ferdinand **Rozier**. For the sum of $65, part of Lot No. 57 in Perryville, beginning at the corner of land sold by sd **Shoults** to Mathias **Barringer**, next to the brick dwelling of sd **Shoults**. Signed Joseph **Shoults**, Eliza **Shoults** (RD). Wit James **Rice** (JP). Rec 7 Mar 1836.

585. Page 97. 7 Mar 1836. Mathew **Smoot** and Elizabeth, his wife, of Bois Brule, to Timothy **Davis**. For the sum of $45, __ acres in Bois Brule Bottom, which they hold as the interest of sd Elizabeth as one of the heirs of her father William **Morris**, decd, and as an heir of her sister Hannah **Morris**, decd; where William **Morris** resided at the time of his death; part of a tract confirmed to John **Morgan**, decd, and where James **Nichol** now resides. Signed Matthew (x) **Smoot**, Elizabeth (x) **Smoot**. Wit Fredk. C. **Hase**, Clerk. Rec 7 Mar 1836.

586. Page 98. 5 Mar 1836. Joseph **Shoults** and Eliza, his wife, to Mathias **Barringer**. For the sum of $25, part of Lot No. 57 in Perryville, beginning 20 feet from the SW corner of sd lot, fronting on St. Marys St. The same transaction is recorded in 2:45, but gave an incorrect point of beginning. The former deed is null and void. Signed Joseph **Shoults**, Eliza R. **Shoults** (RD). Wit James **Rice** (JP). Rec 9 Mar 1836.

587. Page 100. 3 Feb 1836. Samuel **Borrows** to Richard **Cogan**. For the sum of $75, mortgage on a chesnut sorrel mare 8 years old, blind and 14 hands high; a dutch clock worth $40, one cow with a motly face six years old and calf worth $10, and one wind mill. Signed Samuel **Borrows**. Wit Jas. **Rice** (JP). Rec 9 Mar 1836. [Marginal note: Full satisfaction received on 2 Oct 1837. Signed Richd. **Cogan**. Wit Fredk. C. **Hase**, Clerk.]

588. Page 100. 19 Mar 1836. Thomas **Maddin** of Washington Co., Mo. to Charles **Maddin** of Ste. Genevieve Co., Mo. For the sum of $1, three tracts; 306.24 acres surveyed to William **Flynn** on the Mississippi River, beginning at a walnut, and including the Gillard tract; 100 acres in Bois Brule Bottom, part of a tract formerly owned by Timothy **Kelly**, and where he resided in his lifetime, bounded on the NE by the Mississippi River, and on the upper side by land Timothy **Maddin** purchased from the heirs of sd **Flynn**, decd, and on the lower side by the widow **Campster** on Campster's Creek, part of a tract claimed by William **Dunn** as heir of sd **Kelly**, decd; and 10.22 acres as described in receiver's certificate #481 dated 26 Jan 1824. Signed Thomas **Maddin**. Wit J. C. **Brickey**, Clerk of Washington Co., Mo., John **Brickey**, Justice of Washington Co., Mo. Court. Rec 28 Mar 1836.

589. Page 102. 22 Mar 1836. John **Sipe** and Elizabeth, his wife, to Edward **Harter**. For the sum of $250, two tracts on on Apple Creek; 40 acres, being the NE 1/4, SW 1/4, Sec 34, Twp 34 N, Rng 11 E; and 40 acres, more or less, being the SE 1/4, NW 1/4, Sec 34, Twp 34 N, Rng 11 E. Signed John (x) **Sipe**, Elizabeth (x) **Sipe** (RD). Wit Mark **Brewer** (JP), H. **Block**. Rec 1 Apr 1836.

590. Page 103. 8 Apr 1836. Richard F. **Spalding** and Anne, his wife, to Jeffry **Power**. For the sum of $100 paid on 15 Feb last, 40 acres, being the W 1/2 of Lot No. 1, NE 1/4, Sec 2, Twp 34 N, Rng 10 E; reserving to the grantors 1 3/4 acres and 30 perches bounded on the E by a line running due N 32 pole chains from the S boundary line of the tract, and by Stephen **Dawlson**'s tract, and N & W by public lands. Signed Richard F. **Spalding**, Anne (x) **Spalding** (RD). Wit Fredk. C. **Hase**, Clerk. Rec 8 Apr 1836.

591. Page 104. 14 Apr 1836. Ignatius **Layton** to Jos. **Pratte** and Peter R. **Pratte**. For the sum of $250, 58 acres, more or less, part of the tract confirmed to John **Layton** Senior, decd; beginning at a post 44 rods from the corner of sd survey. Signed Ignatius **Layton**. Wit James **Rice** (JP). Rec 14 Apr 1836.

592. Page 105. 13 Apr 1836. Commissioners to partition land of Joseph **Bess**, decd, to Adam J. **Bollinger**. For the sum of $461, 80 acres, being the E 1/2, NW 1/4, Sec 29, Twp 34 N, Rng 9 E. Sold on 5 Mar 1836 at order of Circuit Court issued 15 Dec 1835 on petition to partition of Delila **Bess** by her guardian John **Bess**, Mary **Bess** by her guardian John L. **Conrad**, Ruey **Bess** by her guardian John **Bess**, and Joshua **Bess** by his guardian Lawson **Bess**, all heirs of Joseph **Bess**, decd. Signed Peter **Conrad**, Jacob **Conrad**, Simon **Duvall**. Wit Fredk. C. **Hase**, Clerk. Rec 14 Apr 1836.

593. Page 106. 13 Apr 1836. John **Logan** by Sheriff Thomas J. **Tucker** to Henry **Seibert**. For the sum of $126, 640 acres, more or less, in Brazeau Twp on which sd **Logan** formerly had a mill, known as Logan's Mill. Sold on 22 Nov 1825 by former sheriff Robert T. **Brown** on order of Circuit Court issued 22 Aug 1825 in favor of the State of Mo. and against sd **Logan**, Josiah F. **Hamilton**, and Thomas **Brady** for $200 debt, $15 damages, and $9.20 costs. A deed was not issued at that time, and this deed confirms the transaction. Signed Thos. J. **Tucker**, Shff. Wit Fredk. C. **Hase**, Clerk. Rec 14 Apr 1836.

594. Page 108. 11 May 1836. Alexander **Baily** and Margaret, his wife, to Joseph V. **Bovie** and Avarice **DeLassus** of Ste Genevieve Co., Mo. For the sum of $2400 ($400 in hand and the balance secured by mortgage and notes), two tracts whereon sd **Baily** now lives, known as Baily's Landing on the Mississippi River, and patented to sd **Baily**; 138.40 acres, being the NE fractional 1/4, Sec 10, Twp 35 N, Rng 12 E; and 33.68 acres, being the NW fractional 1/4, Sec 11, Twp 35 N, Rng 12 E. The deed is subject to the nature of Richd. **Cogan**'s tenure and right of possession. Signed Alexander **Baley**, Margaret **Baley** (RD). Wit Jas. **Rice** (JP). Rec 13 May 1836.

595. Page 110. 11 May 1836. Joseph V. **Bovie** of Ste. Genevieve Co., Mo. to Alexander **Baily**. For the sum of $2000, mortgage on the tracts described in the preceding deed (2:108). The debt is due by 11 May 1838. Signed Joseph V. **Beauvise**. Wit James **Rice** (JP). Rec 13 May 1836. [Marginal note: Full satisfaction received on 20 Dec 1839. Signed Alexander **Baley**. Test Fredk. C. **Hase**, Clerk.]

596. Page 110. 2 May 1836. John P. **Tucker** and Sarah, his wife, to William **Taylor**. For the sum of $350, 40 acres, being the NE 1/4, SW 1/4, Sec 36, Twp 35 N, Rng 10 E. The grantors will repay the price if anyone has a better claim to the land. Signed John P. **Tucker**, Sarah **Tucker** (RD). Test Thomas **Taylor**, Michael **Spalding**, Mark **Brewer** (JP). Rec 14 May 1836.

597. Page 111. 16 May 1836. James N. **Moore** and Sally, his wife, to Sylvester **Moore**. For love and affection they have for their son and for the sum of $100, 100 acres, more or less, part of a tract confirmed to James N. **Moore** by the U. S. A., beginning at the NW corner thereof. Signed James N. **Moore**, Sally (x) **Moore** (RD). Wit Jas. **Rice** (JP). Rec 20 May 1836.

598. Page 113. 22 Apr 1836. Ignatius **Layton** to Joseph **Layton**. For the sum of $35, 13 acres, more or less, on the W fork of Saline Creek, part of the land originally belonging to Michael **Tucker**, commencing on the E and W line of sd **Tucker**'s original line. Signed Ignatius **Layton** senr. Wit John **Layton** senr. (JP). Rec 21 May 1836.

599. Page 113. 4 May 1836. John **Layton**, adminr of Juliana **Wathen**, decd, to Beatrix **O'Brian**. For the sum of $125, 44.15 acres, beginning at a point where the NE boundary line of Joseph **Manning**'s land corners on Zachariah **Layton**'s land, etc. to a point where Zachariah **Layton**'s land corners on the seminary land. Sold on 3 Nov 1835 on order of County Court issued Aug Term 1835 for sale of the real estate of sd decd. Signed John **Layton**, adminr. Wit Fredk. C. **Hase**, Clerk. Rec 21 May 1836.

600. Page 115. 3 Jun 1836. Heirs of Clare **Hamilton**, decd, by Circuit Court in Chancery to Francis Xavier **Dahmer**, John M. **Odin**, and Joseph **Paquin**. Title decree for Lot No. 4, being an undivided 1/6 part of about 3000 arpens that sd Clare received as one of the heirs of Joseph **Fenwick**, decd; beginning 80 chs. 15 lks. from the NW corner N. B. line. The tract was ceded by Clare **Hamilton** to Lewis William **Dubourg**, and by sd **Dubourg** through his attorney in fact Joseph **Rosati** to the grantees. Executed on order of Circuit Court in Chancery issued Dec 1835 in case of sd **Dahmer**, sd **Odin**, and sd **Paquin**, complainants, vs. Josiah F. **Hamilton**, Fenwick J. **Hamilton**, Leo **Hamilton**, Walter **Hamilton**, George **Hamilton**, and Eulia **Hamilton**, defendants and heirs of Clare **Hamilton**, decd. Signed Frederick C. **Hase**, Clerk. Rec 3 Jun 1836.

601. Page 116. 4 Jun 1836. William A. **Keyte** and William H. **Keyte**, by his atty in fact James **Evans**, by Circuit Court in Chancery to Richard **Cogan**. Title decree for Lot No. 8 in Perryville; purchased by William A. **Keyte** of Anthony **Pares** for $120. Sd **Pares** did not have title and gave an order on Ignatius **Layton**, legal owner of sd lot, for a deed of conveyance to be made to sd **Keyte**. Sd **Keyte** occupied sd lot until he left the state, and became indebted to sd **Cogan** for about $600 in goods. Sd **Keyte** then presented the order to sd **Layton**, and transferred the lot to his 14-year-old son William H. **Keyte**, in an effort to defraud his creditors. Sd **Cogan** recovered part of the debt, but $375.02 is not recovered. This title decree recovers the debt. Executed on order of Circuit Court in Chancery issued 14 Apr 1836 in case of Richard **Cogan**, complainant, vs. William A. **Keyte** and William H. **Keyte** by his guardian James **Evans**, defendants. Signed Frederick C. **Hase**, Clerk. Rec 4 Jun 1836.

602. Page 118. 1 Apr 1836. Daniel U. **Cline** and Darcus H., his wife, to William **Price**. For the sum of $24, 19 acres, more or less, part of the NW fractional 1/4, Sec 7, Twp 34 N, Rng 13 E; beginning at a white oak on the W line of a tract confirmed to Theofiles **Williams**. Signed Daniel U. **Cline**, Dorcas H. **Cline** (RD). Wit Elias **Barber** (JP). Rec 7 Jun 1836.

603. Page 119. 25 Feb 1831. Moses **Farrar**, surviving partner of the firm of **Abernathy & Farrar**, and Francis, his wife, and the heirs of the estate of James F. **Abernathy**--Jones **Abernathy** and Elizabeth, his wife; James **Abernathy** and Francis, his wife; John **Farrar**, formerly the husband of Mary **Abernathy** or Mary **Farrar**, decd; Joshua **Abernathy** and Martha, his wife; George **Rutledge** and Sarah Ann, his wife; James **Burns** and Deza, his wife; Robert **Abernathy** and Arpa, his wife; and Alonzo **Abernathy** and Permealea, his wife; to Henry **Little**. For the sum of $920.85, three tracts in Sec 2, Twp 34 N, Rng 11 E; 152.06 acres, being the NE fractional 1/4, entered by Moses **Farrar** and James F. **Abernathy** as No. 791; 80 acres, being the E 1/2, SE 1/4, entered as No. 792; and 80 acres, more or less, being the W 1/2, SE 1/4, entered by Moses **Farrar** as No. 852. Signed Moses **Farrar**, Frances **Farrar** (RD), J. **Abernathy**, Elizabeth **Abernathy** (RD, James **Abernathy**, Franky **Abernathy** (RD), John **Farrar**, Joshua **Abernathy**, James **Burns**, Dizy **Burns** (RD), Robert **Abernathy**, Ann Arpy **Abernathy** (RD), George **Rutledge**, Sara Ann **Rutledge** (RD), Alonzo **Abernathy**, Permeely (x) **Abernathy** (RD), Martha **Abernathy** (RD). (Two of the signers, Jones **Abernathy** and Robert **Abernathy**, have deceased since they signed the deed, but their signatures are proved by William **Farrar** and Ransom **Little**.) Wit A. **Hogard**, Wm. **Farrar**, Ransom **Little**, Mark **Brewer** (JP). Rec 11 Jun 1836.

604. Page 121. 7 Mar 1836. Joseph **Pratte** and Mary, his wife, to Robert **Black** and Ansel **Ferrel**. For the sum of $400 with interest, 200 arpens, more or less, in Bois Brule Bottom, being an undivided interest in a tract confirmed to James **Moredock** and purchase by sd **Pratte** of John **Hawkins** etc. Signed Jh. **Pratte**, Mari Valle **Pratte** (RD). Wit W. **Searcy** (JP). Rec 11 Jun 1836.

605. Page 122. 20 Feb 1836. Thomas **Riney** and Sarah, his wife, to Zachariah **Layton**. For the sum of $1, Lot Nos. 76, 77, 78, 86, 96, & 97 in Perryville. Signed Thomas **Riney**, Sarah (x) **Riney** (RD). Wit M. L. **Moore**, John **Layton** senr. (JP). Rec 25 Jun 1836.

606. Page 123. 16 May 1836. Andrew Henry **Tucker** and Ellen, his wife, to William B. **Woodruff**. For the sum of $75, 320 acres on the S fork of Saline Creek, on which Henry **Tucker** resided in his lifetime, and formerly owned by Archibald **Huddleston**. Signed A. H. **Tucker**, Ellen (x) **Tucker** (RD). Wit Willis **Ellis**, Isaac **Hill**, John **Morris** (JP). Rec 27 Jun 1836.

607. Page 124. 7 May 1836. Samuel **Smith** and Jane, his wife, of Jackson Co., Ill. to William **Flynn**. For the sum of $96.40, undivided moiety of 96.48 acres, being the NE fractional 1/4, Sec 20 and SE fractional 1/4, Sec 17 of Twp 37 N, Rng 11 E; purchased from the U. S. A. by sd **Smith** and James L. **Lamb**. Signed Saml. **Smith**, Jane **Smith**. Wit Am. **Jenkins**, John M. **Hanson**, D. H. **Brush**, Dep Clerk of Jackson Co., Ill. Court. Rec 29 Jun 1836.

608. Page 125. 7 Jul 1836. Charles **Maddin** to John **Walsh** and Edward **Walsh** of St. Louis, Mo. and Thomas M. **Horine** of Washington Co., Mo. For the sum of $5000, four tracts, 1/3 of each to each grantee; 306.24 acres surveyed to William **Flynn**, beginning at a walnut, and including the Gillard Tract; 100 acres in Bois Brule Bottom, part of a tract formerly owned by Timothy **Kelly** and whereon he resided in his lifetime, bounded on the NE by the Mississippi River, on the upper side by land Timothy **Maddin** [Kelly] purchased from the heirs of William **Flynn**, decd, and on the lower side by the widow **Camster**, part of a tract claimed by William **Dunn** as heir of sd **Kelly**; 10.22 acres as described in Receivers' Certificate No. 481 to sd **Maddin**, dated 26 Jan 1824; and all lands adjoining the foregoing tracts, and that were conveyed to him by Timothy **Maddin** on 19 Mar 1836 (2:100). Signed Chs. **Maddin**. Wit Fredk. C. **Hase**, Clerk. Rec 7 Jul 1836.

609. Page 127. 8 Jun 1836. John **Finch** and Mary Ann, his wife, to Hester **Belsha**. For the sum of $300, 60 acres, part of a tract confirmed to William **Hickman**; beginning on the W boundary of sd claim. Signed John P. **Finch**, Mary Ann **Finch** (RD). Test John **Belsha**, Nathaniel J. **Divine** (JP). Rec 19 Jul 1836.

610. Page 128. 23 Jul 1836. Joseph **Miller** and Elizabeth, his wife, and Jacob **Conrad** and Sally, his wife, to Peter R. **Pratte**. For the sum of $35, Lot No. 22 in Perryville; bounded on the N by Joshuah **Abernathy**, W by Mathias **Barringer**, S by Peter R. **Pratte**, and E by Spring St; conveyed to the grantors by Bernard **Brown** and Ann, his wife, on 22 Nov 1831 (1:326). Signed Joseph **Miller**, Elizabeth (x) **Miller** (RD), Jacob **Conrad**, Sally (x) **Conrad** (RD). Wit Fredk. C. **Hase**, Clerk. Rec 23 Jul 1836.

611. Page 129. 2 Aug 1836. Richard **Cogan** to J. & E. **Walsh** of St. Louis, Mo. For the sum of $745.16, mortgage on Lot Nos. 7 & 8 in Perryville, with all dwellings and improvements, and Lot No. 27 in Perryville that sd **Cogan** recovered from Wm. A. **Keyte**. Sd **Cogan** owes a note dated 5 Sep 1835. Signed Richd. **Cogan**. Test R. P. **Dorsey**, Fredk. C. **Hase**, Clerk. Rec 2 Aug 1836.

612. Page 130. 16 May 1836. Isaac **Hill** and Elizabeth, his wife, of Ste. Genevieve Co., Mo. to William B. **Woodruff**. For the sum of $75, their undivided share of 320 acres, more or less, on the S fork of Saline Creek; on which Henry **Tucker** Senr. resided in his lifetime, and formerly owned by Archibald **Huddleston**. Signed Isaac **Hill**, Elizabeth (x) **Hill** (RD). Wit Willis **Ellis**, A. H. **Tucker**, John **Morris** (JP), Fredk. C. **Hase**, Clerk. Rec 3 Aug 1836.

613. Page 131. 16 May 1836. George **McNew** and Louisiana, his wife, to same. For the sum of $75, their undivided share of the land described in the preceding deed (2:130). Signed George (x) **McNew**, Louisiana (x) **McNew** (RD). Wit Willis **Ellis**, Isaac **Hill**, John **Morris** (JP), Fredk. C. **Hase**, Clerk. Rec 3 Aug 1836.

614. Page 132. 1 Mar 1836. Walter F. **Hamilton** to Fenwick J. **Hamilton**. For the sum of $75, 96 acres, more or less, being Lot No. 13 as drawn by the commissioners to partition real estate of George A. **Hamilton**, decd, for Walter F. **Hamilton**; bounded on the E by lands formerly owned by John **Manning**, S by Lot No. 14 for Josiah F. **Hamilton**, W by Robert **Hinkston**'s survey, and N by Lot No. 12. Signed Walter F. **Hamilton**. Wit Elias **Barber** (JP). Rec 3 Aug 1836.

615. Page 133. 20 Jul 1836. George **Camster** and Martha, his wife, of Cape Girardeau Co., Mo. to Pouncy **Duggin**. For the sum of $400, 150 arpens, more or less, in Bois Brule Bottom, fronting on the Mississippi River; the lower part of a tract confirmed to Archibald **Camster**'s representatives; bounded on the lower side by **Murdock**'s claim, and on the upper and back sides by the remainder of the confirmation. Signed George **Camster**, Martha **Camster**. Wit Wm. **Johnson**, Judge of Cape Girardeau Co. Court. Rec 3 Aug 1836.

616. Page 134. 11 May 1830. Leo F. **Hamilton** to Fenwick J. **Hamilton**. For the sum of $35, 109 acres, being Lot No. 12 as drawn for sd Leo F. **Hamilton** by the commissioners to partition real estate of George A. **Hamilton**, decd; bounded on the E by lands formerly owned by John **Manning**, S by Lot No. 13 for Walter J. **Hamilton**, W by Robt. **Hinkston**'s survey, and N by Lot No. 11 for Matilda **Hamilton**. Signed Leo F. **Hamilton**. Wit Robert **Greenwell**, James J. **Fenwick** (JP). Rec 3 Aug 1836.

617. Page 135. 12 Apr 1836. William **Burns** and Martha, his wife, to George **Vessels**. For the sum of $114, 57.35 acres, more or less, in Bois Brule Bottom, part of a tract confirmed to James **Burns**, decd, and sold by order of Circuit Court, at which sale Barnabas **Burns**, brother of sd James, was the purchaser; and which has since been divided among the heirs of sd Barnabas; beginning at the W corner of Lot No. 4. Signed Williams **Burns**, Martha (x) **Burns** (RD). Wit Joab W. **Burgee** (JP), Nancy (x) **Cummen**. Rec 5 Aug 1836.

618. Page 136. 4 May 1836. Robert **Woods** to Miles **Farrar**. For the sum of $100, 25.07 acres, being the NE fractional 1/4, SW fractional 1/4, Sec 21, Twp 35 N, Rng 13 E. Signed Robert (x) **Wood**. Wit Elias **Barber** (JP). Rec 8 Aug 1836.

619. Page 137. 15 Jun 1836. Henry **Seibert** and Catharine, his wife, to Charles **Ingram**. For the sum of $5000, 540 acres on Apple Creek; part of 640 acres, Survey No. 1845, in Twp 33 & 34 N, Rng 13 E; confirmed to Francis **Barthume**, except for 100 acres deeded to John **Logan** Senior in the SE corner of the survey. Signed Henry **Seibert**, Katharina **Seibert** [in German]. Wit Singleton H. **Kimmel**, JCC, George W. **Martin**. Rec 9 Aug 1836.

620. Page 138. 16 Jul 1836. Luther **Taylor** and Hannah, his wife, to Reuben **Shelby**. For the sum of $150, __ acres adjoining Perryville on the E side; beginning at John **Logan**'s corner. Signed Luther **Taylor**, Hannah **Taylor** (RD). Wit James **Rice** (JP). Rec 20 Aug 1836.

621. Page 140. 23 Oct 1834. James Stidman **Kelly** and Ann, his wife, to George **Cotner** of Cape Girardeau Co., Mo. For the sum of $63, 50.175 acres, being the W 1/2, Lot No. 7, NE 1/4, Sec 3, Twp 33 N, Rng 12 E; as appears in Receiver's Receipt dated 13 Aug 1833. Signed James S. **Kelly**, Ann **Kelly** (RD). Wit William **Manning** (JP). Rec 22 Aug 1836.

622. Page 141. 30 Jan 1836. Daniel **Cline** and Leah, his wife, to John B. **Farrar**. For the sum of $325, 80 acres, being the E 1/2, SW 1/4, Sec 2, Twp 34 N, Rng 12 E; purchased by sd **Cline** in 1831. Signed Daniel **Cline**, Leah (x) **Cline** (RD). Test James **Ferguson** (JP). Rec 27 Aug 1836.

623. Page 142. 20 Jul 1836. George **Camster** and Martha, his wife, of Cape Girardeau Co., Mo. to John **Carlisle**. For the sum of $1850, two tracts; 103.63 acres in Bois Brule Bottom, being fractional Sec 4, Twp 36 N, Rng 11 E; 153 acres, more or less, on the bank of the Mississippi River, part of a tract of 420 arpens confirmed to William **Fitzgiven**, 200 acres of which sd **Fitzgiven** sold to George **Sturdivant**, and which is bounded on the upper side by **McConniho** and lower side by Dr. **Pucket**. Signed George **Camster**, Martha **Camster**. Wit William **Johnson**, Judge of Cape Girardeau Co. Court. Rec 2 Sep 1836.

624. Page 143. 23 Aug 1836. John **Scudder** to Singleton H. **Kimmel** of St. Louis Co., Mo. and James **Taylor** of Perry Co., of the firm of Kimmel & Taylor. For the sum of $3500, mortgage on 102.98 acres on the bank of the Mississippi River above the mouth of Apple Creek, being the SW fractional 1/4, Lot No. 1, NW 1/4, Sec 5, Twp 33 N, Rng 14 E; deeded to sd **Scudder** by sd **Kimmel & Taylor**. Sd **Scudder** owes three notes for $875 each, payable with 6% interest in one, two, and three years from 1 Sep next. Signed John **Scudder**, Rebecca **Scudder**. Wit William H. **Scudder**, Isaac **Wade**, Jno. **Tuland**, Circuit Court Clerk of St. Louis Co., Mo. Rec 5 Sep 1836.

625. Page 144. 31 Dec 1835. Walter B. **Wilkinson** of Chester, Ill., late of Perry Co., Mo., to Robert M. C. **Stewart**. For the sum of $24.63, his interest in 19.71 acres, being fractional Sec 18, Twp 37 N, Rng 11 E; as per a receipt from the Receiver of Public Moneys at the Land Office in Jackson. Signed W. B. **Wilkinson**. Wit W. **Searcy** (JP). Rec 6 Sep 1836.

626. Page 145. 17 Aug 1836. Robert M. C. **Stewart** and Sally, his wife, to John **Burget**. For the sum of $450, two tracts in Twp 37 N, Rng 11 E; 19.71 acres on Horse Island, being fractional Sec 18; and 42.38 acres, being the NE fractional 1/4, Sec 19. Signed R. M. C. **Stewart**, Sally **Stewart** (RD). Wit W. **Searcy** (JP). Rec 6 Sep 1836.

627. Page 146. 8 Jun 1836. Ansel **Ferrel** and Esther, his wife, and Robert **Black** and Sarah, his wife, to Alfred **Parks**. For the sum of $500, 78 acres, more or less, in Bois Brule Bottom; beginning at the S corner of a tract confirmed to James **Moredook**; also bounded by **Kinnerson** and the Mississippi River. Signed Ansel (x) **Ferrel**, Esther (x) **Ferrel** (RD), Robert **Black**, Sarah (x) **Black** (RD). Wit James **Ferguson** (JP), Nathaniel J. **Divine** (JP). Rec 7 Sep 1836.

628. Page 147. 13 May 1836. William **Manning** and Martha, his wife, to Henry **Seibert**, all of Cape Girardeau Co., Mo. For the sum of $1050, 500 arpens on Indian Creek in Brazo Twp; the W part of land assigned to Ezekiel and Thomas **Fenwick** out of a tract of 3000 arpens originally confirmed to Joseph **Fenwick**; beginning on the W end of sd part. Signed William **Manning**, Martha M. J. **Manning** (RD). Wit S. H. **Kimmel**, JCC. Rec 17 Sep 1836.

629. Page 148. 15 Jun 1836. Charles **Ingram** and Mary, his wife, to Henry **Seibert**. For the sum of $3000, mortgage on 540 acres on the waters of Apple Creek in Twp 33 & 34 N, Rng 13 E; part of 640 acres confirmed to Francis **Berthume**, less 100 acres in the SE corner, having previously been sold to John **Logan** Senr. Sd **Ingram** owes sd **Seibert** as follows: $1000 by 1 Apr 1837, $1000 by 1 Apr 1838, and $1000 by 1 Apr 1839; due with interest, costs, and charges. Signed Charles **Ingram**, Mary (x) **Ingram** (RD). Wit Singleton H. **Kimmel**, JCC, George W. **Martin**. Rec 17 Sep 1836. [Marginal note: Full satisfaction received on 2 May 1842. Signed Henry **Seibert**. Wit J. W. **Noell**, Clerk.]

630. Page 150. 6 Sep 1836. Last will and testament of Mark **Manning**. To his wife Margaret during her lifetime: all his property after his debts are paid. She is to pay to each of his daughters Clare and Matilda, when they leave her, a horse creature, cow, bed, and necessaries as the other children have been helped to when they left. To his youngest son John after his mother's death: the land and plantation whereon he now lives. After the death of his wife, his slaves to be sold to the highest bidder among his heirs, and the personal property to be sold to the best advantage, and the proceeds to be divided among all his children. His sons Alexius and Cornelius are appointed execrs. Signed Mark (x) **Manning**. Wit Isidore **Moore**, Larkin **Abernathy**, Fredk. C. **Hase**, Clerk. Rec 15 Oct 1836.

631. Page 151. 3 Sep 1836. Martin **Butz** and Elizabeth, his wife, to Hugh **Wells**. For the sum of $150, 40 acres, being the NE 1/4, NW 1/4, Sec 27, Twp 34 N, Rng 12 E. Signed Matern **Butz**, Elizabeth (x) **Butz** (RD). Test James **Ferguson** (JP). Rec 17 Oct 1836.

632. Page 152. 20 Oct 1836. Maria **Loper** to Henry **Drury**. For the sum of $150, __ acres in Cinq Homme Twp, her dower right to the property of Charles **Vessels**, decd, during her lifetime. Signed Maria (x) **Loper**. Test Levi **Block**, Wm. J. **Hayes**, Frederick C. **Hase**, Clerk. Rec 20 Oct 1836.

633. Page 153. 15 Feb 1836. Robert M. C. **Stewart** and Sally, his wife, to David M. **Anderson**, all of Bois Brule Twp. For the sum of $300, 88 acres in Bois Brule Bottom whereon sd **Anderson** now lives; the E 1/2 of a tract purchased by sd **Stewart** from Robert **Middleton** and the E 1/2 of a tract purchased by sd **Stewart** of John **Morgan**. Signed R. M. C. **Stewart**, Sally **Stewart** (RD). Wit W. **Searcy** (JP). Rec 29 Oct 1836.

634. Page 154. 5 Nov 1836. Nancy **Bullitt** of Cape Girardeau Co., Mo. to Robert T. **Brown**. For the sum of 1000, two tracts; one undivided 1/7 part of 1000 arpens in Twp 36 N, Rng 9 E in Ste. Genevieve Co., Mo., confirmed to the representatives of Francis **Valli**; and an undivided 1/7 part of one league square in Twp 36, Rng 9 & 10 E on Saline Creek in Perry & Ste. Genevieve Cos., which was confirmed to the representatives of Francis **Valli**, decd. Sd 1/7 part is subject to the life estate of Beverly **Allen**, Esq., tenant by courtesy. Signed Nancy **Bullitt**. Wit Peter R. **Garrett**, Clerk of Cape Girardeau, Mo. County Court. Rec 8 Nov 1836.

635. Page 154. 4 Nov 1836. Amzi **Osborn** and Esther, his wife, to William **Manning**. For the sum of $870, mortgage on six tracts in Perry and Cape Girardeau Cos.; 40 acres, being the E 1/2, Lot No. 1, NW 1/4, Sec 6, Twp 33 N, Rng 14 E; 80 acres, being Lot No. 1, NE fractional Sec 3, Twp 33 N; 40 acres, being the NE 1/4, SE 1/4, Sec 7, Twp 33 N, Rng 14 E; 40 acres, being the NE 1/4, SE 1/4, Sec 3, Twp 33 N, Rng 13 E; 40 acres, being the SE 1/4, SE 1/4, Sec 1, Twp 33 N, Rng 13 E; and 40 acres, being the NW 1/4, SE 1/4, Sec 1, Twp 33 N, Rng 13 E. Sd **Osborn** owes a note dated 4 Nov next to sd **Manning**, payable in six months with 10% interest per annum. Signed Amzi **Osborn**, Esther H. **Osborn** (RD). Wit S. H. **Kimmel**, JCC, Thos. (x) **Ryne**. Rec 9 Nov 1836.

636. Page 155. 20 Jan 1835. William **Hancock** to Stephen **Tucker**. For the sum of $250, 320 acres with the exception of the mill and mill yard where sd **Hancock** now resides. Sd **Hancock** is to give possession by 1 March; with payment to be made in two installments of $100 yearly when the deed is made [?]. Signed William **Hancock**, Stephen **Tucker**. Test Evan **Scott**, John **Woolford**, Fredk. C. **Hase**, Clerk. Rec 23 Nov 1836.

637. Page 156. 9 Nov 1835. Heirs of George **Hall**, decd, to George A. **Ross**. For diverse good causes and the sum of $220, 12 acres, more or less, being a lot in the W 1/2, SW 1/4, Sec 32, Twp 34 N, Rng 12 E; beginning at a stake on the E line of sd lot on the S side of the spring branch; and conveyed to George **Hall** by Seth **Hall** on 7 Apr 1835. The grantors also convey the right of keeping up a dam 8 inches high on sd spring branch. Signed Elizabeth **Hall**, Seth **Hall**, Harriet M. A. **Hall**, Abner H. **Hall**. Wit James **Dunlap**, Elizabeth **Flak**, Elias **Barber** (JP). Rec 1 Dec 1836.

638. Page 157. 28 Nov 1836. James [Irenus] **Whittenburg** to John **Farrar**. For the sum of $100, 40 acres, being the SW 1/4, SE 1/4, Sec 26, Twp 35 N, Rng 11 E; entered by sd **Whittenburg** on 28 Oct 1833. Signed Irenus **Whittenburg**. Test Miles **Farrar**, Franklin **Farrar**, James **Ferguson** (JP). Rec 6 Dec 1836.

639. Page 158. 8 Dec 1836. Benjamin **Wilson** of Cape Girardeau Co., Mo. to William **Taylor** and Henry **Caho**. For the sum of $293.75, 58 3/4 acres; beginning on the S boundary of Perryville center of Jackson St. Signed Benjamin **Wilson**. Wit Fredk. C. **Hase**, Clerk. Rec 8 Dec 1836.

640. Page 159. 8 Dec 1836. Same to Charles **Stuart**. For the sum of $297.50, 59 1/2 acres; beginning on the S boundary of Perryville center of Main St. Signed Benjamin **Wilson**. Wit Fredk. C. **Hase**, Clerk. Rec 8 Dec 1836.

641. Page 159. 8 Dec 1836. Same to Reuben **Shelby**. For the sum of $205, 51 acres, more or less, beginning at the NW corner of Perryville. Signed Benjamin **Wilson**. Wit Fredk. C. **Hase**, Clerk. Rec 8 Dec 1836.

642. Page 160. 9 Dec 1836. Same to John **Logan**. For the sum of $224, 39 1/2 acres; being all the lands conveyed to him [by] Bernard **Layton** on 6 Apr 1824, lying N of the Jackson Rd; lands conveyed by him to Luther **Taylor** and E of Flynn's Ferry Rd; and lands sold by him to sd **Taylor** and not yet conveyed. Signed Benjamin **Wilson**. Wit Fredk. C. **Hase**, Clerk. Rec 9 Dec 1836.

643. Page 161. 23 Sep 1834. Roland **Boyd** and Julia, his wife, to Timothy **Davis** of Ste. Genevieve Co. For the sum of $300, 200 acres at the lower end of Bois Brule Bottom; part of 640 acres confirmed to Charles **Ellis** senr, decd, and conveyed by him to sd **Boyd**, out of which 440 acres has heretofore been sold to Joab **Waters** senr, decd. Signed Roland **Boyd**, Julia **Boyd** (RD). Wit R. T. **Brown**, F. C. **Merideth**, John **Morris** (JP). Rec 12 Dec 1836.

644. Page 162. 15 Feb 1836. Robert M. C. **Stewart** and Sarah, his wife, to same. For the sum of $260, 90 acres in Bois Brule; the W end of two tracts, one of which sd **Stewart** purchased from Robert **Middleton**, the other from John **Morgan**, part of a tract confirmed to sd **Morgan**, decd; and being the remainder of sd two tracts not sold by sd **Stewart** to David M. **Anderson**. Signed R. M. **Stewart**, Sarah **Stewart** (RD). Wit W. **Searcy** (JP). Rec 12 Dec 1836.

645. Page 163. 15 Mar 1834. Robert **Middleton** of St. Clair Co., Ill. to Robert M. C. **Stewart**. For the sum of $150, 98 2/3 acres in Bois Brulie Bottom, part of a Spanish grant owned by Archibald **Morgan** in his lifetime, and descended at his death to his daughter Lucretia **Sadler**, and sold by her and her husband [not named] to sd **Middleton**. Signed Robert **Middleton**. Test Aeson **Scott**, Smith **Crane**, John **Hay**, Clerk of St. Clair Co., Ill. Rec 12 Dec 1836.

646. Page 163. 20 Aug 1836. Singleton H. **Kimmel** and Sarah, his wife, and James **Taylor** to John **Scudder** of St. Louis Co., Mo. For the sum of $3500, 102.98 acres on the bank of the Mississippi River above the mouth of Apple Creek; being the SW fractional 1/4, and Lot No. 1, NW 1/4 of Sec 5, Twp 33 N, Rng 14 E. Signed Singleton H. **Kimmel**, Sarah G. **Kimmel**, James **Taylor**. Wit Augustus **Davis**, Benjamin **Davis** (JP). Rec 17 Dec 1836.

647. Page 165. 1 Oct 1836. John **Logan** and Elizabeth, his wife, of Jackson Co., Ill. to Amzi **Osborn** of St. Louis, Mo. For the sum of $1700 in notes and mortgage bearing equal date, 350 arpents, more or less, at the mouth of Apple Creek, now occupied and in the possession of sd **Osborn**; the balance of a confirmation (after taking off 100 arpents). Signed John **Logan**, Elizabeth **Logan** (RD). Wit Daniel H. **Brush**, Clerk of Jackson Co., Ill. Rec 17 Dec 1836.

648. Page 166. 4 Nov 1836. Singleton H. **Kimmel** to Amzi **Osborn**. For the sum of $250, two tracts; 40 acres, being the SE 1/4, SE 1/4, Sec 1, Twp 33 N, Rng 13 E; and 40 acres, being the NW 1/4, SE 1/4, Sec 1, Twp 33 N, Rng 13 E. Signed Singleton H. **Kimmel**. Wit J. R. **McLane**, JCC for Cape Girardeau Co., Mo. Rec 17 Dec 1836.

649. Page 166. 4 Nov 1836. William **Manning** and Martha, his wife, to same. For the sum of $500, three tracts; 40 acres, being the NE 1/4, SE 1/4, Sec 7, Twp 33 N, Rng 14 E; 40 acres, being the NE 1/4, SE 1/4, Sec 3, Twp 33 N, Rng 13 E; and 80 acres, being Lot No. 1, NE 1/4, fractional Sec 3, Twp 33 N, Rng 13 E. Signed William **Manning**, Martha M. S. **Manning** (RD). Wit S. H. **Kimmel**, J. R. **McLane**, JCC in Cape Girardeau Co., Mo. Rec 17 Dec 1836.

650. Page 167. 4 Nov 1836. James **Taylor** to same. For the sum of $120, 40 acres, being the E 1/2, Lot No. 1, NW 1/4, Sec 6, Twp 33 N, Rng 14 E. Signed James **Taylor**. Wit S. H. **Kimmel**, JCC, Wm. **Manning**. Rec 17 Dec 1836.

651. Page 168. 13 May 1836. Richard **Maddox** senr and Elizabeth, his wife, to John **Timon**. For the sum of $28, 12 1/2 acres, beginning on the E side of Saline Creek at the corner of the Seminary Mill Tract at a certain black oak; including a small improvement; and bounded in part by Nicholas **Moore**. Signed Richd. **Maddock**, Elizabeth (x) **Maddock** (RD). Wit John **Layton** senr. (JP). Rec 19 Dec 1836.

652. Page 169. 15 Jun 1836. James **Reddick** and Mary, his wife, to same. For the sum of $50, 8.3 acres, beginning at the NE corner of John **Moranville**'s land; also bounded by Joseph **Manning** and land sold by sd **Manning** to sd **Reddick**. Signed James **Reddick**, Mary **Reddick** (RD). Wit John **Layton** senr (JP). Rec 19 Dec 1836.

653. Page 170. 24 Aug 1836. Ignatius **Layton** to same. For the sum of $20, 20.24 acres, beginning at the corner of the Seminary Mill Tract on the W bank of Saline Creek at a red bud, elm, and sycamore; the boundaries to include 12 1/2 acres sold by sd **Layton** to George **Killian**, by sd **Killian** to Richard **Maddox**, and by sd **Maddox** to sd **Timon**; and to include 7.74 acres more. Signed Ignatius **Layton**. Wit John **Layton** senr (JP). Rec 19 Dec 1836.

654. Page 171. 28 Dec 1836. Peter **Tucker** senr and Elizabeth, his wife, to Benjamin **Reed**. For the sum of 43.75, 35 acres, part of 156.27 acres, the NE fractional 1/4, fractional Sec 35, Twp 36 N, Rng 10 E; beginning at the NW corner of sd fractional 1/4 Sec. Signed Peter **Tucker** senr, Elizabeth (x) **Tucker** (RD). Test Fredk. C. **Hase**, Clerk. Rec 28 Dec 1836.

655. Page 172. 7 Dec 1836. Irenius **Whittenburg** to Pouncey **Duggins**. For the sum of $230, 80 acres, being the E 1/2, NE 1/4, Sec 14, Twp 35 N, Rng 11 E. Signed Irenius **Whittenburg**. Wit Nathaniel J. **Divine** (JP). Rec 2 Jan 1836.

656. Page 172. 23 Dec 1836. Matthias **Barringer** and Eliza, his wife, to Ferdinand **Rozier** Jr. For the sum of $200, part of Lot No. 57 in Perryville, beginning at the SW corner of sd lot; purchased by sd **Barringer** of Joseph **Shoults** on 19 Feb 1836. Signed Maths. **Barringer**, Eliza (x) **Barringer** (RD). Wit James **Rice** (JP). Rec 10 Jan 1837.

657. Page 173. 20 Jan 1821. William **McLain** and Alley, his wife, to Susan M. **Evans**. For a valuable and good consideration in law, equal and undivided 1/2 of Lot No. 42 in Perryville, purchased by sd **McLain** and Wilford **Layton** of the commissioners; bounded on the N and fronted by St. Joseph St, S by Lot No. 41, E and fronted by Main St, and W by Lot No. 43. Signed William (x) **McLain**, Alley **McLain** (RD). Wit Alvan **Cook** (JP). Rec 13 Jan 1837.

658. Page 174. [no date] Benedict **Riley** and Ann, his wife, to George **Fenwick**. For the sum of $600, 266 acres, more or less, on the headwaters of Boisebruley Creek, lying in a tract of 640 acres confirmed to Clement **Hayden**, decd, held by an improvement made by Luke **Mattingly** prior to 25 Dec 1803. Signed Benedict **Riley**, Ann (x) **Riley**. Test Clement **Hayden**, Thomas **Riney**, Joab **Waters**, JCC, Benjamin **Davis**, JCC, James **Mattingly**, JCC. Rec 13 Jan 1837.

659. Page 175. 1 Aug 1825. Clement **Hayden** to same. For the sum of $350, 133 1/3 acres, more or less, on Bosprule Creek; lying in a tract of 640 acres as described in the preceding deed (2:174). Signed Clement **Hayden**. Test Thomas **Riney**, Zachariah **Layton**, John **Layton** (JP). Rec 13 Jan 1837.

660. Page 176. 27 Oct 1831. Bernard **Brown** and Nancy, his wife, to same. For the sum of $100, 55 1/2 acres, beginning at a stone and hickory marked "B"; part of a tract whereon sd **Brown** now resides, and the same on which James **Brown** now resides. Signed Bernard (x) **Brown**, Nancy (x) **Brown** (RD). Wit Fredk. C. **Hase** (JP). Rec 13 Jan 1837.

661. Page 177. 5 Nov 1826. Commissioners of Perryville to William **McLain**. For the sum of $39, Lot Nos. 38, 87, 88, 91, 92, & 93 in Perryville. Signed R. T. **Brown**, Thomas **Riney**, Joseph **Tucker** senr., Commissioners. Wit John **Layton** (JP). Rec 14 Jan 1837.

662. Page 178. 16 Apr 1827. Aquila **Hagan** and Mary, his wife, to their son James **Hagan**. For love and affection, 104 acres to be run off a tract originally owned by Thomas **Allen**; beginning at the SW corner of a tract now owned by George **Preston**, formerly sd **Allen**. Signed Aquila **Hagan**, Mary (x) **Hagan** (RD). Test F. J. **Hamilton**, John **Layton** (JP). Rec 14 Jan 1837.

663. Page 179. 23 Mar 1830. Commissioners of Perryville to James **Myers**. For the sum of $28.75, Lot Nos. 39, 80, 95, and 99 in Perryville. Signed R. T. **Brown**, Thomas **Riney**, Joseph **Tucker** senr., Commissioners. Wit W. **Wilkinson** (JP). Rec 14 Jan 1837.

664. Page 179. 12 Jan 1836. John **Juden** Jr. and Abbey, his wife, and William **McGuire** and Susan, his wife, all of Cape Girardeau Co., Mo., to William **Allen**. For the sum of $63, 75.09 acres, more or less, in Bois Brule Twp, in NW fractional 1/4, Sec 16, Twp 36 N, Rng 12 E. Signed John **Juden** Jr., Abbey **Juden** (RD), Wm. **McGuire**, Susan **McGuire** (RD). Wit John D. **Cook**, Judge of 4th Judicial Circuit, Wm. **Johnson**, JCC in Cape Girardeau Co., Mo. Rec 17 Jan 1837.

665. Page 180. 15 Aug 1836. Reuben **Shelby** to Henry **Swann**. For the sum of $75, __ acres, beginning at a post at John **Logan**'s corner. Signed Reuben **Shelby**. Wit Jas. **Rice** (JP). Rec 17 Jan 1837.

666. Page 181. 14 Dec 1836. William **Taylor** and Mary, his wife, to Joseph Francis **Doll**. For the sum of $410, 40 acres, more or less, being the NE 1/4, SW 1/4, Sec 36, Twp 35 N, Rng 10 E. Signed William **Taylor**, Mary (x) **Taylor** (RD). Wit Jas. **Rice** (JP). Rec 19 Jan 1837.

667. Page 182. 7 Jan 1837. John P. **Finch** and Mary Ann, his wife, to John **Hagard**. For the sum of $500, 60 acres in Bois Brule Bottom, part of a tract confirmed to William **Hickman** and sold to sd **Finch** by John **Juden** Jr.; commencing at the most N corner of sd **Hickman**'s survey; also bound by Hester **Belsha**, Austin **Hagard**, and Hemsted. Signed John P. **Finch**, Mary Ann **Finch** (RD). Wit Nathaniel J. **Divine** (JP). Rec 21 Jan 1837.

668. Page 183. 12 Jan 1837. Reuben **Shelby** and Sarah A., his wife, to Joseph **Shoults**. For the sum of $84, 13 3/4 acres adjoining Perryville on the W side; beginning at the NW corner of the town. Signed Reuben **Shelby**, Sarah A. **Shelby** (RD). Wit James **Rice** (JP), John **Tucker**. Rec 23 Jan 1837.

669. Page 184. 3 Feb 1837. Bede **Moore** and Berlinder, his wife, to James **Tucker** senior. For the sum of $1, equal undivided 1/4 of 640 acres, more or less, on the waters of Saline Creek, the original head right donation or settlement right of sd **Moore**, and confirmed to him by the commissioners on 9 Jul 1832 and 2 Mar 1833, and by an act of Congress on 4 Jul 1836; taken off the W end of the tract, with the division line run across the tract parallel with the interior boundary line. This conveyance fulfills a bond obligatory executed on 9 May 1833 from sd **Moore** to John **Scott** of Ste. Genevieve Co., Mo., to convey this share of the tract. Sd **Scott** was to prosecute the case for confirmation of sd tract, and has done so. He later assigned the bond to sd **Tucker** on 13 Dec 1836. Signed Bede **Moore**, Berlinder (x) **Moore** (RD). Wit James **Rice** (JP). Rec 3 Feb 1837.

670. Page 185. 25 Jan 1837. George **Scott** and Maria, his wife, of Ste. Genevieve Co., Mo. to Squire D. **Ensley**. For the sum of $165, 40 acres, being the SE 1/4, SW 1/4, fractional Sec 23, Twp 36 N, Rng 9 E. Signed George **Scott**, Maria Ann (x) **Scott** (RD). Test Fredk. C. **Hase**, Clerk. Rec 6 Feb 1837.

671. Page 186. 2 Jan 1837. Alfred **Sadler** to Robert **Manning**. For the sum of $131.45, two mares and colts, two cows, eight sheep, one sow and 16 shoats, and one clock. Signed Alfred **Sadler**. Wit John M. **Duvall**, Fredk. C. **Hase**, Clerk. Rec 7 Feb 1837.

672. Page 187. 12 Nov 1836. George Washington **Gill**, of Illinois but now of Marshall Co., Miss., to Garland **Laughlin** of Union Co., Ill. For the sum of $1000, all property, real, personal, and mixed, bequeathed to him by his late father James **Gill** of Jackson Co., Ill., in his last will and testament, as recorded in Jun 1827 in Brownsville, Jackson Co., Ill.; fractional Sec 23, and NW 1/4, Sec 24, Twp 10 S, R 4 W in Jackson Co., Ill., entered by James **Gill** at Kaskaskia on 29 Sep 1817; 151 acres, more or less, on the bank of the Mississippi River in Perry Co., formerly owned by James **Manning**, and opposite the first tract of land; and all his right to the negroes of his father's estate. Signed George Washington **Gill**. Wit L. J. **Church**, M. L. **Gill**, Samuel **Legate**, John **Whiteaker**, JP in Union Co., Ill., Winstead **Davie**, Clerk of Union Co., Ill. Rec 15 Feb 1837.

673. Page 188. [no date] Same and Mary, his wife, to same. For the sum of $1000, the property described in the preceding deed. Signed George W. **Gill**, Mary **Gill** (RD). Wit William H. **Bausland**, Clerk of Marshall Co., Miss. Probate Court, Hardy H. **Whitaker**, Judge of Marshall Co., Miss. Probate Court. Rec 15 Feb 1837.

674. Page 189. 28 Dec 1836. Peter **Tucker** senior and Elizabeth, his wife, to Peter J. **Tucker**. For the sum of $900, 366 acres, 2 chains, and 2 links on Saline Creek, beginning at the corner of the tract sold to Joseph **Cissel**. Signed Peter **Tucker** senr, Elizabeth (x) **Tucker** (RD). Wit Fredk. C. **Hase**, Clerk. Rec 18 Feb 1837.

675. Page 191. 4 Jul 1834. Clement **Knott** and Elizabeth, his wife, to John Babtist **Layton** Junior. For love and affection and other valuable considerations, 130 1/2 acres and 36 perches, more or less, beginning at Hilarion **Knott**'s most W corner; part of a tract obtained from the U. S. by virtue of settlement and cultivation prior to 20 Dec 1803. Signed Clement (x) **Knott**, Elizabeth (x) **Knott** (RD). Wit James **Rice** (JP). Rec 21 Feb 1837.

676. Page 192. 14 Nov 1829. Robert **Wimsett** and James **Wimsett** to James J. **Moore**. For the sum of $300, 127 1/2 acres, the corner of the lands belonging to Clement **Knott**, beginning at a black oak. Signed Robert **Wimsatt**, James **Wimsatt**. Wit Joab **Waters** (JP). Mary **Wimsatt** RD. Rec 28 Feb 1837.

677. Page 193. 18 Feb 1837. Ferdinand **Rozier** and Constance, his wife, of Ste. Genevieve Co., Mo. to Ferdinand **Rozier** Junior. For the sum of $10, two lots in Perryville; Lot No. 54, purchased from Joseph **Duvall** and wife on 20 Mar 1830 (1:409); and Lot No. 69 that sd **Rozier** purchased from Robert T. **Brown** and wife on 15 Mar 1834 (1:408). Signed Ferdinand **Rozier**, Constance **Rozier** (RD). Wit Jos. D. **Grafton**, Clerk of Ste. Genevieve Co., Mo. Rec 1 Mar 1837.

678. Page 194. 2 Dec 1833. Henry **Rudisel** and Elizabeth, his wife, to Daniel **Welker**. For a valuable consideration, 20 acres adjoining sd **Welker**'s land, beginning at his SE corner, which is the half mile corner of the original line between Secs 21 & 28; lying on the W side of the SE 1/4, Sec 21, Twp 34 N, Rng 11 E. Signed Henry **Rudisil**, Elizabeth **Rudisil** (RD). Wit James **Mattingly** (JP). Rec 1 Mar 1837.

679. Page 195. 18 Jan 1834. Same and same to same. For the sum of $1.25 per acre, 10 acres in Sec 28, Twp 34 N, Rng 11 E, beginning at the half mile corner of the line between Secs 21 & 28. Signed Henry **Rudisil**, Elizabeth **Rudisil** (RD). Wit James **Mattingly** (JP). Rec 1 Mar 1837.

680. Page 196. 1 Nov 1836. John **Layton** and Monica, his wife, to John **Timon**. For the sum of $200, 50 acres, beginning at the E corner of an offset of sd **Layton**'s land. Signed John **Layton**, Monica (x) **Layton** (RD). Wit Lewis **Moore**, James **Layton**, Mark **Brewer** (JP). Rec 2 Mar 1837.

681. Page 196. 7 Nov 1833. William **McLane** and Alley Louisa, his wife, to Alfred H. **Puckett**. For the sum of $15, Lot No. 38 in Perryville. Signed William (x) **McLane**, Alley Louisa **McLane** (RD). Wit James **Rice** (JP). Rec 4 Mar 1837.

682. Page 197. 6 Mar 1836. Alfred H. **Puckett** and Emily, his wife, to John **Robinson**. For the sum of $750, Lot No. 9 in Perryville, purchased from Isidore **Moore** and wife by sd **Puckett** on 22 Sep 1829 (1:253). Signed Alfred H. **Puckett**, Emily **Puckett** (RD). Wit Reuben **Shelby**, JCC, David **Burns**. Rec 6 Mar 1857.

683. Page 198. 7 Mar 1837. Reuben **Shelby** and Sarah A., his wife, to same. For the sum of $200, two tracts; 6 acres, more or less, beginning at Charles **Stuart**'s corner on the E line of Perryville; and 20 acres, more or less, beginning at the W line of Perryville at a stone, the corner of Joseph **Shoults**. Signed Reuben **Shelby**, Sarah A. **Shelby** (RD). Wit Fredk. C. **Hase**, Clerk. Rec 7 Mar 1837.

684. Page 199. 9 Mar 1837. William **Tucker** and Sary, his wife, to Wilford **Manning**. For the sum of $53, 40 acres that sd **Tucker** purchased from the U. S., being the SE 1/4, NE 1/4, Sec 22, Twp 36 N, Rng 10 E. Signed William **Tucker**, Sarah (x) **Tucker** (RD). Wit Frederick C. **Hase**, Clerk. Rec 9 Mar 1837.

685. Page 200. 13 Sep 1828. Same and same to George **Fenwick**. For the sum of $125, about 63 acres and 1/2, the W end of a tract which fell on a division to John **Hayden**, one of the heirs of Clement **Hayden**, decd, and was purchased by sd **Tucker**. Signed William **Tucker**, Sarah (x) **Tucker** (RD). Wit Marier **Vesells**, Ann (x) **Brown**, Fredk. C. **Hase**, Clerk. Rec 9 Mar 1837.

686. Page 201. 27 Jan 1837. Reuben **Shelby** and Sarah, his wife, to William **Taylor**. For the sum of $40, 7 acres, more or less, beginning at a stake on the W line of Perryville, and bounded in part by **Layton**. Signed Reuben **Shelby**, Sarah A. **Shelby** (RD). Wit James **Rice** (JP). Rec 9 Mar 1837.

687. Page 202. 15 Feb 1837. John **Scott** to Joseph **Duvall**, both of Ste. Genevieve Co., Mo. For the sum of $200, 400 arpents, more or less, on the waters of Boisbrule Creek; the original head right of John **Townsend**, and conveyed by sd **Townsend** to Ezekiel **Able**, and the right of sd **Able** conveyed to sd **Scott** by Sheriff Henry **Dodge** on 15 Jul 1809; bounded on the S by Thomas **Hawkins**, and N, E, & W by vacant land. Signed John **Scott**. Wit Jos. D. **Grafton**, Clerk of Ste. Genevieve Co., Mo. Rec 11 Mar 1837.

688. Page 203. 28 Jul 1828. Commissioners of Perryville to Joseph **Duvall**. For the sum of $9, Lot No. 54 in Perryville. Signed R. T. **Brown**, Joseph **Tucker** senr., Thomas **Riney**, Commissioners. Wit John **Layton** (JP). Rec 11 Mar 1837.

689. Page 204. 11 Mar 1837. Benjamin **Albright** and Nancy, his wife, and Eleanor **Hunt** to Reuben **Shelby**. For the sum of $900, Lot No. 34 in Perryville, bequeathed to William **Burns** by the last will and testament of Barnabas **Burns**, and conveyed by him to sd **Albright** & sd **Hunt** on 23 May 1835. Signed Benjamin **Allbright**, Nancy **Allbright** (RD), Eleonore (x) **Hunt**. Wit Fredk. C. **Hase**, Clerk. Rec 11 Mar 1837.

690. Page 205. 7 Sep 1836. Robert **Wilson** and Rachal, his wife, to Milus and John A. **Hughey**. For the sum of $387, 75 acres and 99 rods, being the W 1/2, NW 1/4, Sec 36, Twp 35 N, Rng 12 E. Signed Robert **Wilson**, Rachel **Wilson** (RD). Wit Thomas B. **Mitchel**, David W. **Morrison**, Elias **Barber** (JP). Rec 17 Mar 1837.

691. Page 206. 27 Sep 1823. John B. **Shery** and Clarissa, his wife (late Clarissa **Hamilton**), Josiah **Hamilton**, and Fenwick **Hamilton** to William **James** of Ste. Genevieve Co., Mo., in trust for the children of Ezekiel **Fenwick** and Isabella, his wife. For the sum of $1 and diverse good causes and considerations, deed of trust for 20 acres near the W margin of the Mississippi River, beginning at a marked corner at the SE corner of Ezekiel **Fenwick**'s field fence on the little creek running near his house, and including his house and improvement; also bounded by the N boundary of the survey of George A. **Hamilton**, decd; and surveyed so as to form an irregular oblong square. Ezekiel **Fenwick** and Isabella, his wife, are to have free use of the tract for their respective lives free of rent, but must pay taxes. At their deaths, the land shall descend to their children or to their children's heirs if any have married and died; these children being Ulila, Evaline, and Joseph Alexander. Signed Josiah F. **Hamilton**, Fenwick J. **Hamilton**, trustees for the heirs and legal representatives of Ezekiel **Fenwick**. Wit Saml. **Anderson**, James C. **Manning**, James J. **Fenwick** (JP). Rec 18 Mar 1837.

692. Page 208. 30 Jan 1837. Amzi **Osborn** and Esther, his wife, to John **Scudder**. For the sum of $365.25, five tracts; 40 acres, being the SE 1/4, SE 1/4, Sec 1, Twp 33 N, Rng 13 E; 40 acres, being the NW 1/4, SE 1/4, Sec 1, Twp 33 N, Rng 13 E; 40 acres, being the E 1/2, Lot No. 1, NW 1/4, Sec 6, Twp 33 N, Rng 14 E; 248.30 acres, being the E part, fractional Sec 32, Twp 34 N, Rng 14 E on an island called Big Sandy Twp; and 40 acres, being the N 1/2, Lot No. 2, NW 1/4, fractional Sec 5, Twp 33 N, Rng 14 E. Signed Amzi **Osborn**, Esther **Osborn** (RD). Wit W. H. **Scudder**, Benjamin **Davis** (JP). Rec 27 Mar 1837.

693. Page 209. 27 Mar 1837. Frederick C. **Hase** to John **Clodfelter** of Washington Co., Mo. For the sum of $2 in back taxes, Lot No. 19 in Perryville, purchased by sd **Hase** at Jefferson City on 31 Jul 1835. Signed Fredk. C. **Hase**. Wit M. **McLaughlin**, Joab W. **Burgee** (JP). Rec 27 Mar 1837.

694. Page 210. 15 Mar 1837. Thomas **Morris** of Bois Brule to Timothy **Davis** of St. Marys Landing. For the sum of $50, 80 acres in Bois Brule Bottom; purchased by William **Morris**, the father of sd Thomas from Joseph **Bland**, and part of a tract of 640 acres confirmed to John **Morgan**, decd. Signed Thomas **Morris**. Wit W. **Searcy** (JP). Rec 28 Mar 1837.

695. Page 211. 3 Dec 1836. Joseph **Murray** and Mary, his wife, to Thomas **Wilkinson** and John **Wilkinson**. For the sum of $175, 76.41 acres, being the E 1/2, SW 1/4, Sec 18, Twp 35 N, Rng 13 E. Signed Joseph **Murray**, Mary (x) **Murray** (RD). Wit Elias **Barber** (JP). Rec 1 Apr 1837.

696. Page 212. 27 Apr 1837. Commissioners to sell lands of Michael **Burns**, decd, to David **Crips**. For the sum of $105, 170.83 acres, being Survey No. 663 in Twp 36, Rng 11, confirmed to Michael **Burns**, decd; where Mrs. Mary **Burns**, decd, resided. Sold on 15 Dec 1835 on order of Circuit Court, issued at Aug 1835 term on petition to partition in case of Frederick C. **Hase**, guardian of Nancy and Margaret **Allen**; David **Burns** for himself and as guardian for William **Burns**; Jessee **Dickson** for himself and guardian of Elizabeth and Emily Ann **Burns**; William **Flynn**, guardian of Henry and Letitia **Burns**; John **McClanahan** and Lydia, his wife; George **Preston** and Mary, his wife; Jessee **Dicson**; Mary **Flynn**; Lydia **Burns**; Richard S. **Dorsey** and Louvice, his wife; James **Burns**; John E. **Burget** and Mary, his wife; Isaac **Meredith** and Sarah, his wife; Mary **Kennison**; William **Allen**; Jacob **Shoults** and Mary, his wife; and Alexander **Baley** and Margaret, his wife vs. _____ **Allcorn** and Lydia, his wife, late Lydia **Stewart**, late Lydia **Allen**; Elizabeth **Roberts**, late Elizabeth **Burns**; and Samuel **Allen**. Signed John **Logan**, P. R. **Pratt**, Jas. **Rice**, Joel **Kinnison**. Wit William **Flynn**, John **Layton** (JP). Rec 8 Apr 1837.

697. Page 214. 15 Mar 1837. Thomas **Morris** of Bois Brule to Timothy **Davis** of St. Marys Landing. For the sum of $50, his interest in 80 acres in Bois Brule Bottom, purchased by the father of sd **Morris** from Joseph **Bland**; part of 640 acres confirmed to John **Morgan**, decd.; and where the mother of sd **Morris** now resides. Sd **Morris** holds the interest in the tract as one of the heirs of his father William **Morris**, decd, and of his sister Hannah **Morris**, decd. Signed Thomas **Morris**. Wit W. **Searcy** (JP). Rec 28 Mar 1837.

698. Page 215. 28 Mar 1835. Valerio **Faina** and Matilda, his wife, to John **Clodfelter** of Washington Co., Mo. For the sum of $200, Lot No. 18 in Perryville. Signed Valerio **Faina**, Matilda **Faina** (RD). Test R. S. **Dorsey** (JP). Rec 18 Apr 1837.

699. Page 216. 1 Feb 1833. John **Smith** and Jane, his wife, to John **Clodfelter**, all of Cape Girardeau Co., Mo. For the sum of $40, Lot No. 19 in Perryville. Signed John **Smith**, Fanny **Smith** (RD). Wit John **Layton** (JP), Matilda **Layton**. Rec 28 Apr 1837.

700. Page 216. 1 Oct 1836. Amzi **Osborn** of St. Louis, Mo. to John **Logan** of Jackson Co., Ill. In consideration that he bought 350 arpents from sd **Logan** and the sum of $1, mortgage on 350 arpents at the mouth of Apple Creek. Sd **Osborn** owes sd **Logan** two notes of equal date totaling $1100, one for $550 due in nine months, and one for $550 due in 15 months from 1 Sep 1836. Signed Amzi **Osborn**. Wit W. **Garner**, Elizabeth **Logan**, Elias **Barber** (JP). Rec 1 May 1837. [Marginal note: Full satisfaction received 25 Mar 1840. Signed John **Logan**. Wit John F. **Hase**, Dep. Clerk.]

701. Page 217. 8 Apr 1837. James L. **Lamb** and Susan H., his wife, of Sangamon Co., Ill. to William **Flynn**. For the sum of $80, undivided moiety of 96.48 acres in two tracts in Twp 37 N, Rng 11 E; the NE fractional 1/4, Sec 20; and the SE fractional 1/4, Sec 17; purchased from the U. S. by Samuel **Smith** and sd **Lamb**. Signed James L. **Lamb**, Susan H. **Lamb** (RD). Wit V. R. **Mathery**, Clerk of Sangamon Co., Ill. Rec 1 May 1837.

702. Page 218. 28 Oct 1833. Irenius **Whittenburg** to Alonzo **Abernathy**. For the sum of $137, 40 acres, being the SE 1/4, NW 1/4, Sec 35, Twp 35 N, Rng 11 E. Signed James **Whittenburg**. Wit Miles **Farrar**, John **Farrar**, James **Ferguson** (JP). Rec 1 May 1837.

703. Page 219. 26 Nov 1836. George A. **Ross** and Phebe, his wife, to Edward J. **Morrill** and Abner H. **Hall**. For the sum of $270, their interest in 12 acres, more or less, in the W 1/2, SW 1/4, Sec 32, Twp 34 N, Rng 12 E; beginning at a stake on the E line of sd lot and S side of the spring branch; as conveyed by Seth **Hall** to George **Hall** on 7 Apr 1835, and then conveyed on 9 Nov 1835 by Elizabeth **Hall**, Seth **Hall**, Harriett M. A. **Hall**, and Abner H. **Hall**, heirs of George **Hall**, decd, to sd **Ross**, who intermarried with Phebe, the sister and one of the heirs of George **Hall**, decd. The grantors also convey the right to make a dame eight inches high and no higher on the spring branch, within 8 poles of the upper end of the tanyard run. Signed Geo. A. **Ross**, Phebe **Ross** (RD). Wit James **Dunlap**, William **Mattingly**, Elias **Barber** (JP), Frederick C. **Hase**, Clerk. Rec 1 May 1837.

704. Page 221. 16 Jan 1837. [Translated from German to English by Frederick C. **Hase**.] Anthony **Fleck** and Adolph **Rix** have paid for 80 acres described below, with sd **Fleck** taking the S 1/2, and sd **Rix** the N 1/2. Half of sd **Rix**'s 40 acres is to go to his wife Helena **Buts**, the other half to his children as designated below. Last will and testament of Adolph **Rix**. To his wife [Helena]: 1/2 of all his real and personal estate. To his "own" children: the other half of his real and personal estate. The real estate is the N 1/2 of 80 acres in E 1/2, NE 1/4, [Sec 30,] Rng 12 E, Twp 34 N. [Signed Adolph (x) **Rix**.] Test Anthony **Fleak**, Sebastian **Haas**. Wit Joseph **Branstetter**, Ignatius **Winkler**, Fredk. C. **Hase**, Clerk. Rec 1 May 1837.

705. Page 222. 10 Jan 1837. Columbus **Price** and Lydia, his wife, to Robert P. **Slaughter** of Cape Girardeau Co., Mo. For the sum of $800, two tracts in Twp 35 N, Rng 13 E; 39.78 acres, being the NE 1/4, NE 1/4, fractional Sec [27]; and 72.56 acres, being the NW fractional 1/4, fractional Sec 27. Signed Columbus **Price**, Lydia **Price** (RD). Wit Elias **Barber** (JP). Rec 11 May 1837.

706. Page 223. ___ Apr 1837. Robert P. **Slaughter** and Evaline M., his wife, to Alfred A. **McLane**. For the sum of $800, the two tracts described in the preceding deed (2:222). Signed Robert P. **Slaughter**, Evalina M. **Slaughter** (RD). Wit Elias **Barber** (JP). Rec 11 May 1837.

707. Page 224. 4 May 1837. James **Burns** to Alonzo **Abernathy**. For the sum of $50, 40 acres, being the SW 1/4, NW 1/4, Sec 12, Twp 34, Rng 11 E; purchased by sd **Burns** on 6 Feb 1837 at Benton, Scott Co., Mo. Signed James **Burns**, Dizy **Burns** (RD). Wit Jas. **Ferguson** (JP). Rec 20 May 1837.

708. Page 224. 29 Apr 1837. Benjamin **Wilson** of Cape Girardeau Co., Mo. to Luther **Taylor**. For the sum of $200, 35 acres, more or less, beginning on the boundary of Perryville near the center of Main St. Signed Ben. **Wilson**. Wit James **Rice** (JP). Rec 23 May 1837.

709. Page 225. 24 Aug 1831. Charles C. **Valle** and Milanie, his wife, of Ste. Genevieve Co., Mo. to Charles **Grigoir** Jr. For the sum of $500, 900 arpents, part of an undivided Spanish grant on Saline Creek, known as the grand glaise tract; so as to include the farm and improvements where sd **Valle** lately resided, and where sd **Grigoir** now resides. Signed Chs. C. **Valle**, Milanie **Valle** (RD). Wit Jos. D. **Grafton**, Clerk of Ste. Genevieve Co., Mo. Rec 5 Jun 1837.

710. Page 226. 29 Oct 1836. Joseph **Murray** and Mary, his wife, to Andrew **Morrison**. For the sum of $320, 80 acres on the waters of Indian Creek in Brauzau Twp, being the W 1/2, SE 1/4, Sec 15, Twp 34 N, Rng 12 E. Signed Joseph **Murray**, Mary (x) **Murray** (RD). Wit Elias **Barber** (JP). Rec 9 Jun 1837.

711. Page 227. 10 Jun 1837. Reuben **Shelby** and Sarah A. **Shelby** to John **Robinson**. For the sum of $1050, Lot No. 34 in Perryville; conveyed to Barnabus **Burns** by the commissioners on 9 Jun 1823, bequeathed by sd **Burns** to his son William, sold by sd William and wife to Benjamin **Allbright** and Elenor **Hunt**, and by them to sd **Shelby** on 11 Mar 1837. Signed Reuben **Shelby**, Sarah A. **Shelby** (RD). Wit Jas. **Rice** (JP). Rec 10 Jun 1837.

712. Page 228. 10 Jun 1837. John **Robinson** and Drusilla, his wife, to Peter R. **Pratte**, Commissioner of the Road and Canal Fund for Perry Co. For the sum of $400, mortgage on Lot No. 34 in Perryville. The debt is due with 10% interest per annum in 12 months. Signed John **Robinson**, Drusilla **Robinson** (RD). Wit James **Rice** (JP). Rec 10 Jun 1837.

713. Page 229. 3 Dec 1834. Joseph **Mattingly** and Maria, his wife, to Lewis **French**. For the sum of $130, 36 1/4 acres, more or less, on the N branch or fork of Apple Creek, beginning at the NW corner of sd French'es survey. Signed Joseph B. **Mattingly**, Maria (x) **Mattingly** (RD). Wit John **Layton** (JP). Rec 12 Jun 1837.

714. Page 229. 21 Jun 1837. Charles **Gregoire** and Eulalia, his wife, to Joseph **Pratte**. For the sum of $12,000, the mills and appurtenances on the S fork of Saline Creek, along with the land attached, in two tracts; 850 arpents, more or less, as sold to sd **Gregoire** by Charles **Valle** and Milanie, his wife, on 24 Aug 1831 (2:225); and 500 arpents, more or less, known as the Roark &

Reardin Tract, conveyed to sd **Gregoire** by William **Rex** and others. Signed Chs. **Gregoire**, Eulalia **Gregoire** (RD). Wit W. **Searcy** (JP). Rec 28 Jun 1837.

715. Page 230. 1 Nov 1830. Reddick **Eason** to his friend George **Killian**. Power of attorney to sell a lot in Perryville and pay taxes on the same. Sd **Eason** is about to leave the state. Signed Reddick **Eason**. Wit Joab **Waters** (JP), D. L. **Caldwell**. Rec 28 Jun 1837.

716. Page 231. 9 Apr 1832. Thomas **Madden** to Charles **Madden** and Philip **Madden**, all of Washington Co.; Mo. For the sum of $100, quit claim to two tracts; 406 arpens, French measure, (345.68 acres) on the Mississippi River, being Survey No. 87, beginning on the bank of the Mississippi River, as confirmed to Thomas **Donnehoe**; and 40 acres, part of 300 arpens or 255.20 acres confirmed to James **McLane**. Also for the sum of $100, Thomas **Madden** quits claim to Charles, Philip, & Malachi **Madden** for 215.20 acres, part of the second tract, beginning at a post. Signed Thoms. **Madden**. Wit John **Trimble**, JP in Washington Co., Mo., Israel **McGready**, Clerk of Washington Co., Mo. Rec 29 Jun 1837.

717. Page 232. 18 Jun 1837. Benjamin **Wilson** and Jane, his wife, of Cape Girardeau Co., Mo. to Luther **Taylor**. For the sum of $200, Lot Nos. 73 & 74 in Perryville. Signed Ben. **Wilson**, Jane **Wilson** (RD). Wit J. R. **McLane**, JP in Cape Girardeau Co., Mo. Rec 4 Jul 1837.

718. Page 233. 29 Apr 1837. William **Pinkerton** and Sarah, his wife; John **Pinkerton** and Dizah, his wife; Ellen **Pinkerton**; David **Pinkerton** and Margaret, his wife; Joseph **Murray** and Mary, his wife; Noble **Johnson** and Margaret, his wife; Henry **Pinkerton** and Elizabeth, his wife; Adam **Pinkerton** and Ann, his wife; and Robert **Cashion** and Cinthia, his wife, to Samuel **Borrows**. For the sum of $81, their undivided right to 80 acres, being the real estate of John **Pinkerton** Senior, decd, and the W 1/2, NW 1/4, Sec 25, Twp 35 N, Rng 11 E. The grantees reserve the dower rights of the widow of John **Pinkerton** during her natural life, but the rights to go to sd **Borrows** at her death. Signed Adam (x) **Pinkerton**, Ann (x) **Pinkerton** (RD), David (x) **Pinkerton**, Margaret (x) **Pinkerton** (RD), Henry (x) **Pinkerton**, Elizabeth (x) **Pinkerton** (RD), Robert (x) **Cashion**, Sinthy (x) **Cashion** (RD), Ellenor (x) **Pinkerton**, Joseph **Murray**, Mary (x) **Murry** (RD), Noble **Johnson**, Margaret (x) **Johnson** (RD), William **Pinkerton**, Sarah A. (x) **Pinkerton** (RD), John (x) **Pinkerton**, Dizy (x) **Pinkerton** (RD). Wit Adam M. **Martin**, William T. **Watts**, James **Ferguson** (JP), John **Hughey** (JP), Elisha **Eggers** (JP). Rec 13 Jul 1837.

719. Page 236. 20 Jan 1836. William **Allen** and Almira, his wife, of Perry Co. and Samuel **Allen** and Mahaly, his wife of Jackson Co., Ill. to David **Burns**. For the sum of $192, their interest in the real and personal property of Michael **Burns**, decd, and Mary **Burns**, decd, being the 1/7 part of a 1/8 distributive share to each. Signed Samuel (x) **Allen**, Mahala (x) **Allen** (RD), William **Allen**, Almira (x) **Allen** (RD). Wit A. **Burns**, Joab W. **Burgee** (JP), Mark **Miles**. Rec 25 Jul 1837.

720. Page 237. 7 Dec 1835. Hiram **Lee** and Elizabeth, his wife, of Jackson Co., Ill. to same. For the sum of $92.50, the 1/6 part of an eighth share of the real and personal property of Michael **Burns**, decd, and their interest in the estate of Mary **Burns**, decd. Signed Hiram **Lee**, Elizabeth (x) **Lee**. Sworn to in Jackson Co., Ill. County Court, J. **Manning**, Clerk. Rec 25 Jul 1837.

721. Page 238. 9 May 1835. James **Burns** and Lucinda, his wife, to same. For __, their interest in the real and personal property of Michael **Burns**, decd, and Mary **Burns**, decd. Signed James **Burns**, Lucinda (x) **Burns** (RD). Wit Joab W. **Burgee** (JP). Rec 25 Jul 1837.

722. Page 239. 20 Jan 1836. Michael **Roberts** and Elizabeth, his wife, James **Roberts** and Sophrona, his wife, and David **Roberts** and Catharine, his wife, all of Jackson Co., Ill. to same. For the sum of $90.50 to each party, their interest in the real and personal property of Michael **Burns**, decd, and Mary **Burns**, decd, being a 1/6 part of a 1/8 distributive share to each party. Signed Michael **Roberts**, Elizabeth (x) **Roberts** (RD), James **Roberts**, Sophrona **Roberts** (RD), David S. **Roberts**, Kathrine **Roberts** (RD). Test A. **Burns**, Joab W. **Burgee** (JP). Rec 25 Jul 1837.

723. Page 240. 30 Jan 1837. Martha **Roark**, John **Cox**, Lucinda **Roark**, and James **Roark** to Timothy **Davis**. For the sum of $150, their interest in 400 arpens on St. Lorent, confirmed to the Martha **Roark** and John **Cox**, and to Andrew **Cox** Jr. and William **Cox**, now decd; as Andrew **Cox**'s widow and legal representatives. Signed Marthy (x) **Roark**, John **Cox**, James **Roark**, Lucinda **Roark**. Wit W. **Searcy** (JP). Rec 26 Jul 1837.

724. Page 241. 25 Feb 1831. Jonas **Abernathy** and Elizabeth, his wife; James **Abernathy** and Francis, his wife; John **Farrar**, formerly the husband of Mary **Abernathy** or otherwise Mary **Farrar**, decd; Joshua **Abernathy** and Martha, his wife; Jas. **Burns** and Diza, his wife; Robert **Abernathy** and Arpa, his wife; and Alonzo **Abernathy** and Permalia, his wife; all heirs of James F. **Abernathy**, decd, to George **Rutledge**. For the sum of $21, 1/2 of Lot Nos. 61 & 62 in Perryville, sold by the Commissioners to James F. **Abernathy** and George **Rutledge**. Signed J. **Abernathy**, Elizabeth (x) **Abernathy** (RD), James **Abernathy**, Franky **Abernathy** (RD), John **Farrar**, Joshua **Abernathy**, Martha **Abernathy** (RD), Robert **Abernathy**, Ann Arpy **Abernathy** (RD), James **Burns**, Dizy **Burns** (RD), Alonzo **Abernathy**, Permely (x) **Abernathy** (RD). Wit A. **Hagard**, Wm. **Farrar**, Ransom A. **Little**, Mark **Brewer** (JP). (Jones and Robert **Abernathy** deceased since signing the deed, and their signatures are proved by Wm. **Farrar** and Ransom A. **Little**.) Rec 26 Jul 1837.

725. Page 243. 7 Jan 1837. Martin L. **Moore** to Robert L. **Glasscock**. For the sum of $12, Lot No. 41 in Perryville, purchased from the Commissioners on 25 Jul 1835 (2:36). Signed Martin L. **Moore**. Wit James **Rice** (JP). Rec 3 Aug 1837.

726. Page 244. 7 Aug 1837. Robert L. **Glasscock** and Elizabeth, his wife, to Isidore **Hagan**. For the sum of $20, Lot No. 41* in Perryville, as described in the preceding deed (2:243). Signed R. L. **Glasscock**, Elizabeth **Glasscock** (RD). Wit Fredk. C. **Hase**, Clerk. Rec 7 Aug 1837.

727. Page 245. 2 Aug 1837. James C. **Manning** to Daniel **Cline**. For the sum of $140, three tracts in Twp 34 N, Rng 13 E; 27 acres, being the NW fractional 1/4, Sec 32; 25.87 acres, being the SW fractional 1/4, Sec 29; and 27.67 acres, being the SW fractional 1/4 Sec 32. Signed James C. **Manning**. Wit Elias **Barber** (JP). Rec 7 Aug 1837.

728. Page 246. 8 Aug 1837. Commissioners of Perryville to Joshua **Abernathy**. For the sum of $10, Lot No. 23 in Perryville. Signed R. T. **Brown**, Thomas **Riney**, Joseph **Tucker** senr., Commissioners. Wit Jas. **Rice** (JP). Rec 8 Aug 1837.

729. Page 246. 8 Aug 1837. Commissioners of Perryville to Peter **Faherty**. For the sum of $20, Lot No. 75 in Perryville, adjoining a lot formerly sold to sd **Faherty**. Signed R. T. **Brown**, Thomas **Riney**, Joseph **Tucker** senr., Commissioners. Wit Jas. **Rice** (JP). Rec 8 Aug 1837.

730. Page 247. 31 Jan 1837. Walter **Wilkinson** of Chester, Ill. to Perry **Evans**. For the sum of $1850, 225 acres, more or less, in Bois Brule Bottom, lying between land sold by James **Taylor** to Joseph **Dixon** and land belonging to St. Marys Seminary; that he purchased from Charles **Maddin**, and part of a tract confirmed to Archibald **Morgan**. Signed Walter B. **Wilkinson**. Wit Timothy **Davis**, James N. **Pettit**, W. **Searcy** (JP). Rec 9 Aug 1837.

731. Page 248. 8 Aug 1837. James G. **Alldrige** and Louisa, his wife and formerly Louisa **Shaner**, to James **Strickland**. For the sum of $50, 160 acres on Braze Creek, the NW 1/4 of 640 acres confirmed in the name of Benjamin **Harrison** in Rng 13 E, Twp 34 N, Sec 16; and conveyed by Jacob **Sheaner** to John **Shaner**. James G. & Louisa **Alldrige** are heirs of John **Sheaner**, decd. Signed James G. (x) **Alldrige**, Louisa M. **Aldrige**. Sworn to in open court by Fenwick **Hamilton** and Leo **Fenwick**. Wit Fredk. C. **Hase**, Clerk. Rec 9 Aug 1837.

732. Page 249. 6 Jun 1837. Jonas A. **Rutledge** and Caroline, his wife, to George **Rutledge**. For the sum of $50, 38.53 acres, being the NW 1/4, NE 1/4, Sec 3, Twp 34 N, Rng 11 E; purchased at the land office by Jonas A. **Rutledge** on 6 Feb 1837 at Benton, Scott Co., Mo. Signed Jones A. **Rutledge**, Frances C. **Rutledge**. Wit John **Farrar**, Miles **Farrar**, Mark **Brewer** (JP). Rec 9 Aug 1837.

733. Page 250. 29 Jun 1835. Robert **Abernathy** and Ann Arpy, his wife, to same. In consideration of the exchange of lands herein mentioned, 10 acres in Aubrazeau Twp, part of the E 1/2, SW 1/4, Sec 34, Twp 35 N, Rng 11 E as entered by sd **Abernathy**; beginning at the half corner on the S line of sd Sec. Signed Robert **Abernathy**, Ann Arpy **Abernathy** (RD as widow of Robert), George **Rutledge**, Susanna **Rutledge** (RD). Wit Alonzo **Abernathy**, Mark **Brewer** (JP). Rec 9 Aug 1837.

734. Page 252. 29 Jun 1835. George **Rutledge** and Sarah Ann, his wife, to Robert **Abernathy**. In consideration of the exchange of lands herein mentioned, 10 acres in Aubrazeau Twp, part of the W 1/2, SW 1/4, Sec 34, Twp 35 N, Rng 11 E and part of the W 1/2, NW 1/4 of sd Sec; beginning 20 rods from the S line of sd Sec; part of the land entered by sd **Rutledge** at the land office. Signed George **Rutledge**, Susann **Rutledge** (RD), Robert **Abernathy**, Ann Arpy **Abernathy** (RD as widow of Robert). Wit Alonzo **Abernathy**, Mark **Brewer** (JP). Rec 9 Aug 1837.

735. Page 253. 27 Mar 1837. Commissioners to sell lands of Michael **Burns**, decd, to Joab W. **Burgee**. For the sum of $716, 424.29 acres, being Survey No. 118 in Twp 36 N, Rng 11 E, confirmed to Michael **Burns**. Sold on 15 Dec 1835 on order of Circuit Court, issued at Aug 1835 term on petition to partition in case of Frederick C. **Hase**, guardian of Nancy and Margaret **Allen**; David **Burns** for himself and as guardian for William **Burns**; Jessee **Dickson** for himself and guardian of Elizabeth and Emily Ann **Burns**; William **Flynn**, guardian of Henry and Letitia **Burns**; John **McClanahan** and Lydia, his wife; George **Preston** and Mary, his wife; Jessee **Dicson**; Mary **Flynn**; Lydia **Burns**; Richard S. **Dorsey** and Louvice, his wife; James **Burns**; John E. **Burget** and Mary, his wife; Isaac **Meredith** and Sarah, his wife; Mary **Kennison**; William **Allen**; Jacob **Shoults** and Mary, his wife; and Alexander **Baley** and Margaret, his wife vs. _____ **Allcorn** and Lydia, his wife, late Lydia **Stewart**, late Lydia **Allen**; Elizabeth **Roberts**, late Elizabeth **Burns**; and Samuel **Allen**. Signed John **Logan**, P. R. **Pratt**, J. **Rice**, Joel **Kinnison**. Wit William **Flynn**, John **Layton** (JP). Rec 10 Aug 1837.

736. Page 255. 10 Aug 1837. William **Burns** to Marshel **Dickson**. For the sum of $470, his undivided interest in two tracts patented to the legal representatives of William **Burns**, decd, and which he holds as an heir of sd William **Burns**, in Sec 20, Twp 35 N, Rng 13 E; 98.39 acres, being the NE fractional 1/4; and 79.93 acres, being the E side, NW fractional 1/4. Signed William **Burns**. Wit Frederick C. **Hase**, Clerk. Rec 14 Aug 1837.

737. Page 257. 16 Aug 1837. Isidore **Hagan** to Hyman **Block**. For the sum of $14, Lot No. 41 in Perryville, purchased from the Commissioners by Martin L. **Moore** on 25 Jul 1835 (2:36), conveyed by him to Robert L. **Glasscock** on 7 Jan 1837, and by him to sd **Hagan** on 7 Aug 1837. Signed Isidore (x) **Hagan**. Wit Fredk. C. **Hase**, Clerk. Rec 18 Aug 1837.

738. Page 257. 17 Feb 1837. James B. **Mattingly** and Mary, his wife, to the heirs of Charles **Vessels**, decd. For the sum of $100, 80 acres, more or less, being the W 1/2, NE 1/4, Sec 22, Twp 36 N, Rng 10 E. Signed James B. **Mattingly**, Mary **Mattingly** (RD). Wit John **Morris** (JP), Frederick C. **Hase**, Clerk. Rec 18 Aug 1837.

739. Page 259. 29 Sep 1830. Bernard **Layton** and Mary, his wife, to John **Smith** of Cape Girardeau Co., Mo. For the sum of $20, Lot No. 20 in Perryville, adjoining Lot No. 33 on which Levy **Block** now resides. Signed Bernard **Layton**, Mary (x) **Layton** (RD). Wit John **Layton** (JP), James **Layton**. Rec 30 Aug 1837.

740. Page 259. 14 Aug 1837. John **McLane** of Cape Girardeau Co., Mo. to Ignatius **Winkler**. For the sum of $100, 60 acres, more or less, being all the land on the N of Apple Creek in Lot No. 7, NW 1/4, Sec 3, Twp 33 N, Rng 12 E; bounded by the meanders of the creek. Signed John **McLane**. Test Eleazar **Cobb**, Elias **Barber** (JP). Rec 1 Sep 1837.

741. Page 260. 2 Sep 1837. Daniel **O'Meara** and Elizabeth, his wife, to Anne **Hagan**. For the sum of $6.25, 5 acres, in the SW corner of a lot of 40 acres, being the SW 1/4, SE 1/4, Sec 27, Twp 35 N, Rng 10 E; bounded on the S by Ann **Hagan**, W by the public, and N & E by sd **O'Meara**. Signed Danl. **O'Meara**, Elizabeth **O'Meara** (RD). Wit Fredk. C. **Hase**, Clerk. Rec 2 Sep 1837.

742. Page 261. 7 Sep 1837. William **Allen** to James R. **Beasly**. For the sum of $125, 75 acres, more or less, being the NW fractional 1/4, Sec 6, Twp 36 N, Rng 12 E; title being made from the U. S. A. to John **Juden** Junr. and Wm. **McGuire**, and from them to sd **Allen**. Signed William **Allen**, Almira (x) **Allen** (RD). Wit Alfred L. **Parks** (JP). Rec 8 Sep 1837.

743. Page 262. 4 Aug 1831. John **Juden** Junr and Abbey, his wife, and William **McGuire** and Susan, his wife, to same. For the sum of $55, 48.57 acres, being the NE fractional 1/4, Sec 17, Twp 36 N, Rng 12 E; purchased from the U. S. by sd **Juden** and sd **McGuire**, and patented on 15 Jul 1825. Signed John **Juden** Jr, Abbey **Juden** (RD), Wm. **McGuire**, Susan **McGuire** (RD). Wit George **Henderson**, JCC for Cape Girardeau Co., Mo., F. T. **Overfield**, JP in Cape Girardeau Co., Mo. Rec 8 Sep 1837.

744. Page 264. 21 Jun 1837. Joseph **James** and James **Michael**. Contract. Sd **James** bought from sd **Michael**, 1 pair of blacksmith's bellows, 1 anvill, 1 vice, 1 sledge hammer, 2 hand hammers, 1 sett of Shoeing tools, 8 pr tongs, 1 sett hammer and nail hammer, 1 Hardy, 2 screw plates, 4 heading tools, 8 punches, 1 pr Clamps, 1 large punche, 1 fuller(?) & punch, 2 Eye Wedges for oxes, 1 far mattick, 1 fire scraper, and 3 Cherers. Sd **James** agrees to pay $75 in ploughs cary to be laid with steel at $.25 pr pound, payable four ploughs pr. month to be done in workmanlike manner. The tools will remain in security for payment of the sum, and are to be delivered by 26 Jun. Signed Joseph **James**, James (x) **Michael**. Wit Levi **Block**, Frederick C. **Hase**, Clerk. Rec 12 Sep 1837.

745. Page 265. 12 Sep 1837. Squire D. **Ensley** and Olive, his wife, to William **Berry**. For the sum of $200, 40 acres, being the SE 1/4, SW 1/4, Sec 3, Twp 36 N, Rng 9 E. Signed Squire D. **Ensley**, Olive (x) **Ensley** (RD). Wit Fredk. C. **Hase**, Clerk. Rec 12 Sep 1837.

746. Page 266. 30 Sep 1837. Joseph B. **Mattingley** and Maria, his wife, to Robert S. **Manning**. For the sum of $130, 83 acres, more or less, purchased by sd **Mattingley** from Samuel **Bond**; beginning at the NW corner on the exterior boundary of sd tract. Signed Joseph B. **Mattingley**, Maria (x) **Mattingley** (RD). Wit James **Rice** (JP), Matilda **Mattingley**. Rec 30 Sep 1837.

747. Page 267. 30 Sep 1837. Same and same to Lewis **French**. For the sum of $70, 30 acres, more or less, part of fractional 1/4 Sec 19, Twp 34 N, Rng 11 E; the remainder of a tract of which part was sold to Robert S. **Manning** on this date (2:266); beginning on the exterior boundary of the tract where the creek intersects sd line. Signed Joseph B. **Mattingley**, Maria (x) **Mattingley** (RD). Wit James **Rice** (JP), Matilda **Mattingley**. Rec 30 Sep 1837.

748. Page 269. 4 Oct 1837. P. R. **Pratte**, Commissioner of the Road and Canal Fund for Perry Co., to John **Robinson** and Drusilla, his wife. For the consideration they made on 10 Jun 1837 in a deed to sd **Pratte** (2:228), Lot No. 34 in Perryville. Signed P. R. **Pratte**, Commissioner. Wit James **Rice** (JP). Rec 7 Oct 1837.

749. Page 270. 4 Oct 1837. John **Robinson** and Drusella, his wife, to Benjamin R. **Allbright**. For the sum of $550, the N 1/2 of Lot No. 34 in Perryville; with sd **Robinson** to retain the right to get water from a well on sd half lot. Signed John **Robinson**, Drusilla **Robinson** (RD). Wit James **Rice** (JP). Rec 7 Oct 1837.

750. Page 271. 9 Oct 1837. Benjamin R. **Allbright** [and Ann, his wife,] to Peter R. **Pratte**, Commissioner of the Road and Canal Fund. For the sum of $413.33 1/3, mortgage on the N 1/2 of Lot No. 34 in Perryville. Sd **Allbright** owes a note dated 7 Oct 1837 to sd **Pratte**, with Joshua J. **Old** as security, payable by 10 Jun 1838 with 10% interest per annum. Signed B. R. **Allbright**, Ann (x) **Allbright** (RD). Wit James **Rice** (JP). Rec 9 Oct 1837. [Marginal note: Full satisfaction received from Benjamin **Allbright** and Nancy, his wife, on 8 Mar 1839. Signed Levi **Block**, Treasurer and Commissioner.]

751. Page 273. 13 Oct 1837. John **Robinson** and Drusilla, his wife, to James **Rice**. For the sum of $125, 21 acres, more or less, a portion of a tract confirmed to Bernard **Layton**, on which is situated the town of Perryville; beginning on the W line of Perryville at a stone, the corner of Joseph **Shoults**. Signed John **Robinson**, Drusilla **Robinson** (RD). Wit Frederick C. **Hase**, Clerk. Rec 13 Oct 1837.

752. Page 275. 4 Oct 1837. William **Taylor** and Mary, his wife, to Reuben **Shelby**. For the sum of $500, 80 acres in two tracts in Sec 12, Twp 34 N, Rng 10 E; the NE 1/4, NW 1/4; and the NW 1/4, NE 1/4. Signed William **Taylor**, Mary (x) **Taylor** (RD). Wit James **Rice** (JP), Henry **Caho**. Rec [1]4 Oct 1837.

753. Page 276. 14 Oct 1837. James B. **May** and Maria, his wife, to Ignatius **Moore**. For the sum of $250, bond to make a deed on 490 acres, being Survey No. 2137 in Twp 35, Rng 10. Sd **May** has sold sd **Moore** the undivided share of sd Maria in the 490 acres devised by James **Moore** senr, decd, her grandfather, to her and other heirs. Signed James B. **May**, Maria (x) **May** (RD). Wit James **Rice** (JP). Rec 14 Oct 1837.

754. Page 277. 21 Oct 1837. John **Robinson** and Drusilla, his wife, to Hyman **Block**. For the sum of $550, the S 1/2 of Lot No. 34 in Perryville; conveyed by the commissioners to Barnabas **Burns** on 9 Jun 1823, bequeathed by sd **Burns** to his son William **Burns**, and by William **Burns** and wife to Benjamin **Allbright** and Eleanor **Hunt**, and sold to sd **Shelby** on 11 Mar 1837. Signed John **Robinson**, Drusilla **Robinson** (RD). Wit Levi **Block**, Fredk. C. **Hase**, Clerk. Rec 23 Oct 1837.

755. Page 279. 23 Oct 1837. John **Robinson** and Drusilla, his wife, to Joab W. **Burgee**. For the sum of $250, the N 1/2 of Lot No. 9 [in Perryville]; purchased from Isadore **Moore** and wife by Alfred H. **Puckett** on 22 Sep 1829 (1:253), and sold by sd **Puckett** to sd **Robinson** on 6 Mar 1837 (2:197). Signed John **Robinson**, Drusilla **Robinson** (RD), Wit Fredk. C. **Hase**, Clerk. Rec 23 Oct 1837.

756. Page 280. 23 Oct 1837. Joab W. **Burgee** and Elizabeth, his wife, to John **Robinson**. For the sum of $1000, 425.29 acres in Bois Brule Twp, being Survey No. 118 in Twp 36 N, Rng 11 E confirmed to Michael **Burns**. Signed Joab W. **Burgee**, Elizabeth **Burgee** (RD). Wit Elisha **Eggers** (JP), John **Waters**. Rec 23 Oct 1837.

757. Page 282. 24 Oct 1837. Luther **Taylor** and Hannah, his wife, to Charles **Roy**. For the sum of $40, Lot No. 73 in Perryville. Signed Luther **Taylor**, Hannah **Taylor** (RD). Wit Reuben **Shelby**, JCC. Rec 24 Oct 1837.

758. Page 283. 8 Sep 1837. William **Winfield** and Helen, his wife, and Lewis **Thorp** and Ann, his wife. Partition of 155.35 acres, being the SW fractional 1/4, Sec 16, Twp 36 N, Rng 12 E. Sd **Winfield** is to receive 100 acres on the N side of the tract, sd **Thorp** to receive 55.35 acres on the S side. Signed Lewis **Tharp**, Ann (x) **Tharp** (RD), William **Winfield**, Helen (x) **Winfield** (RD). Wit James **Rice** (JP), William **Cox**. Rec 8 Sep 1837.

759. Page 285. 28 Oct 1837. William **Winfield** and Helen, his wife, to Mark **Miles**. For the sum of $120, 50 acres, part of a tract purchased in copartnership by sd **Winfield** and Lewis **Thorp**, and divided between them on 8 Sep 1837; this portion set off by a N-S line from the part sold to Daniel **Meredith** on this day. Signed William **Winfield**, Helen (x) **Winfield** (RD). Test James **Rice** (JP). Rec 28 Oct 1837.

760. Page 286. 28 Oct 1837. Same and same to Daniel **Meredith**, son of Isaac **Meredith**. For the sum of $525, 50 acres, part of the N part of a tract partitioned between sd **Winfield** and Lewis **Thorp** on 8 Sep 1837; divided from a tract sold to Mark **Miles** on this day by a N-S line. Signed William **Winfield**, Helen (x) **Winfield** (RD). Wit James **Rice** (JP). Rec 28 Oct 1837.

761. Page 288. 3 May 1837. Elizabeth **Abernathy** to Alonzo **Abernathy**. For natural love and affection she bears unto her beloved son, a negro woman Hannah and a negro man Ransom. Signed Elizabeth (x) **Abernathy**. Test James S. **Abernathy**, Elijah B. **Abernathy**, Jas. **Ferguson** (JP). Rec 4 May 1837.

762. Page 289. 24 Apr 1837. Joseph D. **Burns** to Royal **Thompson** of Cape Girardeau Co., Mo. For the sum of $100, mortgage on all the goods, household stuff, implements, and furniture, and all other goods and chattels: one waggon, two large yoke of oxen, seven cattle, five sheep, nine hogs, two plows, one pair of gears, and household and kitchen furniture. The debt is due according to a bond to sd **Thompson** by 25 Dec 1840, and sd **Thompson** is to sell the property should the debt not be paid, with any overplus rendered to sd **Burns**. Signed Joseph **Burns**. Wit John A. **Thompson**, Elias **Barber** (JP). Rec 3 Nov 1837.

763. Page 291. 18 Mar 1837. Lewis **Cissell** and Ann M., his wife, to Simon **Duvall**. For the sum of $300, two parcels of land in Sec 14, Twp 34 N, Rng 9 E; 40 acres, being the SE 1/4, NW 1/4; and 40 acres adjoining the first, being the SW 1/4, NW 1/4. Signed Lewis **Cissell**, Ann M. **Cissell** (RD). Wit Clement **Cissell**, Ignatius **Layton**, John **Layton** (JP). Rec 18 Mar 1837.

764. Page 292. 24 Sep 1837. Simon **Duvall** to Joseph **Duvall** Junior. For the sum of $150, two 40 acre tracts as described in the preceding deed (2:291). Signed Simon **Duvall**. Wit James **Rice** (JP). Rec 24 Sep 1837.

765. Page 293. 5 Nov 1837. Joseph **Duvall** and Eveline, his wife, to Lewis **Cissell**. For the sum of $300, 200 arpens, more or less, on the head of an E branch of Cinque Hommes Creek, commonly called McClanahan's Creek; originally granted to William **Boyce** by concession settlement right; adjoined on the E by a tract granted to John **Duvall**, decd; and conveyed to Joseph **Duvall** by John **Duvall** on 13 Nov 1824 (1:110). Signed Joseph **Duvall**, Eveline (x) **Duvall** (RD). Wit James **Rice** (JP). Rec 5 Nov 1837.

766. Page 295. 30 Oct 1837. Irenus [James] **Whittenburg** to John **Farrar**. Power of attorney to lease, sell, or devise a tract in Bois Bruly Bottom. Signed Irenus **Whittenburg**. Wit Alonzo **Abernathy**, JCC. Rec 30 Oct 1837.

767. Page 296. 11 May 1830. Leo F. **Hamilton** to James J. **Fenwick**. For the sum of $50, his undivided 1/6 right to 76 acres in the Mississippi Bottom near the mouth of Brazaw Creek, being his late mother's dower, on which the mansion house, orchard, and farm stand; as designated by the commissioners appointed by the Circuit Court of Perry Co. to partition the lands of the heirs of George A. **Hamilton**, decd; and above lands granted to Mark **Manning**. Signed Leo F. **Hamilton**. Wit Elias **Barber** (JP). Rec 11 May 1830.

768. Page 297. 30 Dec 1829. Fenwick J. **Hamilton** [atty in fact for his sister Eulila **Hamilton**] to James J. **Fenwick**. For the sum of $25, 105 acres, a lot set aside for Eulila F. **Hamilton** by the commissioners appointed by Circuit Court to partition the real estate of George A. **Hamilton**, decd; bounded on the E by the tract where Mrs. Elenor **Manning** now lives, S by Lot No. __? drawn for Matilda **Hamilton**, W by Hinkson's survey, and N by Lot No. 9 drawn for Fenwick J. **Hamilton**. Signed Fenwick J. **Hamilton**. Wit Robert **Greenvoll**, Joseph **James**, Elias **Barber** (JP). Rec 6 Nov 1837.

769. Page 298. 23 Feb 1830. Josiah F. **Hamilton** of Scott Co., Mo.; Fenwick J. **Hamilton** for himself and as atty in fact for Eulila **Hamilton**; Leo F. **Hamilton**; and Leo A. **Fenwick**, guardian for Walter F. and George A. **Hamilton**; to same. For the sum of $30, __ acres, a lot designated for Matilda F. **Hamilton** by the commissioners appointed by Circuit Court to divide lands among the heirs of George A. **Hamilton**, decd. Signed Fenwick J. **Hamilton**, Fenwick J. **Hamilton**, atty in fact for Eulila **Hamilton**, Leo F. **Hamilton**, Josiah F. **Hamilton**. Test Leo F. **Hamilton**, Fenwick J. **Hamilton**, Elias **Barber** (JP). Rec 6 Nov 1837.

770. Page 300. 17 Apr 1837. Beverley **Allen** and Penelope, his wife, to Timothy **Davis**. For the sum of $400, 1/2 in 4 months and the residue in 12 months from 5 Mar last, the undivided moiety of 640 acres, known as the claim of John **Dunks**, and confirmed to sd **Dunks**' legal representatives; and conveyed to him by Henry **Clark** or sd **Davis**. Signed Beverley **Allen**, Penelope **Allen** (RD). Wit Henry **Chouteau**, Clerk of St. Louis Co. Rec 8 Nov 1837.

771. Page 301. 31 May 1837. Amzi **Osborn** and Esther, his wife, to John **Scudder**. For the sum of $850, 400 arpents, more or less, at the mouth of Apple Creek, being Block No. 10 on Front St in the town of Birmingham, Perry Co.; an undivided 1/2 of the tract bought by sd **Osburn** from John **Logan**; and excepting and reserving Block No. 11 in sd town, and so much of sd tract as may be included in SW fractional 1/4 sec and Lot No. 1 in the NW 1/4, Sec 5, Twp 33 N, Rng 14 E. Signed Amzi **Osbern**, Esther H. **Osburn**. Wit James **Haneld**, Benjamin **Davis** (JP). Rec 11 Nov 1837.

772. Page 303. 31 May 1837. Amzi **Osborn** and Esther, his wife, to Rebecca **Scudder**. For the sum of $2400, Block No. 11 on second street in Birmingham. Signed Amzi **Osborn**, Esther H. **Osborn**. Wit James **Haneld**, Benjamin **Davis** (JP). Rec 11 Nov 1837.

773. Page 304. 6 Nov 1837. Andrew **Doere** and Christina, his wife, to Frederick **Sutterr** [**Sudderer**]. For the sum of $17.50, 14.87 acres in the NW 1/4, NW 1/4, fractional Sec 20, Twp 35 N, Rng 11 E; the S part of 40 acres entered by sd **Doerr**. Signed Andreas **Doerr**, Christina **Doerr** (RD). Wit Fredk. C. **Hase**, Clerk. Rec 13 Nov 1837.

774. Page 305. 31 Oct 1837. Joseph **Pratte** and Mary, his wife, and Peter R. **Pratte** and Mary L., his wife, to William **Taylor**. For the sum of $80, Lot No. 63 in Perryville, fronting on Jackson St and St. Joseph St. Signed J. **Pratte**, Marie **Pratte** nee **Valle** (RD), P. R. **Pratte**, Marie Louise **Pratte** (RD). Wit Reuben **Shelby**, JCC. Rec 21 Nov 1837.

775. Page 307. 31 Oct 1837. Same, same, same, and same to Mathias **Barringer**. For the sum of $700, 78 acres, more or less, beginning at a stake at the corner of J. **Shoults**' land. Signed Joseph **Pratte**, Marie **Pratte** nee **Valle** (RD), P. R. **Pratte**, Marie Louise **Pratte** (RD). Wit Reuben **Shelby**, JCC. Rec 21 Nov 1837.

776. Page 308. 6 Nov 1837. Mark L. **Manning** and Mary, his wife, to James **Hagan**. For the sum of $51.56 1/4, mortgage on 40 acres in Cinque Hommes Twp, being the NW 1/4, NE 1/4, Sec 19, Twp 36 N, Rng 11 E. The debt with 10% interest per annum is due by 8 Feb 1837 [1838?]. Signed Mark L. **Manning**, Mary (x) **Manning** (RD). Wit Joab W. **Burgee** (JP). Rec 22 Nov 1837.

777. Page 309. 25 Oct 1837. Amzi **Osborn** to John **Scudder**, both of Birmingham. For the sum of $1 and in fulfillment of an agreement, undivided 1/2 two tracts; 400 arpents at the mouth of Apple Creek, acquired by sd **Osborn** of John **Logan**; and 248.30 acres on Sandy Island in Sec 32, Twp 34 N, Rng 14 E. An agreement was made on 10 Apr 1835 between sd **Osborn** and Esther **Perrine**, that in case a marriage should be solemnized between them, that sd **Osborn** should transfer property worth $8000 to her or her assigns during her natural life. Sd marriage has occurred, and this deed fulfills the agreement. Signed Amzi **Osborn**, John **Scudder**. Wit Augustus **Davis** (JP). Rec 23 Nov 1837.

778. Page 311. 25 Oct 1837. John **Scudder** and Robeca, his wife, to Esther **Osborn**, wife of Amzi **Osborn**, formerly Esther **Perrine**, all of Birmingham. In consideration of fulfilling an agreement as described in the preceding deed (2:309), transfer of the tracts described in the preceding deed, under the conditions described. Signed John **Scudder**, Rebecca **Scudder**. Wit Augustus **Davis** (JP). Rec 23 Nov 1837.

779. Page 313. 25 Nov 1837. Legal representatives of James D. **Abernathy**, decd, and Eligah B. **Abernathy**, decd, to Alonzo **Abernathy** and John H. **Abernathy**. Power of attorney to sell property of the decd and perform all other legal acts whatsoever. Signed Jere. **Abernathy**, Bernice **Abernathy**, John H. **Abernathy**, Patsy T. **Abernathy**, Susanna **Abernathy**, Jere. **Abernathy**, natural guardian for Joseph A. **Abernathy**, Perneely L. **Abernathy** by her husband Alonzo **Abernathy**. Wit James **Ferguson** (JP). Rec 27 Nov 1837.

780. Page 314. 28 Nov 1837. Commissioners to partition the estate of George **Keller**, decd, to William G. **Moore** and Singleton H. **Kimmel**. For the sums of $581, two parcels; 240 acres, being Lot Nos. 6, 7, & 8 in the NW 1/4, Sec 6, Twp 33 N, Rng 11 E; and 268.77 acres in three tracts; 148.77 acres, being Lot No. 6, NE 1/4, Sec 1, Twp 33 N, Rng 11 E; 80 acres, being Lot No. 5, NE 1/4, Sec [1], Twp 33 N, Rng 11 E; 40 acres, being the SE 1/4, SW 1/4, Sec 36, Twp 34 N, Rng 11 E. Sold on order of Circuit Court issued 14 Apr 1836 in case of William **Moore** and wife vs. Thomas **Keller** and others on petition to partition amongst the heirs of George **Keller**, decd. Signed Alfred **McLain**, John **Hofman**, James **Elmore**. Wit Fredk. C. **Hase**, Clerk. Rec 28 Nov 1837.

781. Page 317. 28 Nov 1837. Moses **Farrar** to Joseph Vitalle **Beauvais**. For the sum of $400, 105.59 acres, being the SE fractional 1/4, Sec 11, Twp 35 N, Rng 12 E; and entered by William **Pinkerton**. Signed Moses **Farrar**. Wit Greer W. **Davis**, James **Rice** (JP). Rec 28 Nov 1837.

782. Page 318. 29 Nov 1837. Nicholas P. **Tucker** and Sarah, his wife, to Joseph **Cissell**. For the sum of $40, mortgage on 40 acres, being the NE 1/4, SW 1/4, Sec 27, Twp 35 N, Rng 10 E. The debt is due with 10% interest per annum by 1 Jul next. Signed Nicholas P. **Tucker**, Sarah (x) **Tucker** (RD). Wit John **Layton** (JP). Rec 2 Dec 1837. [Marginal note: Full satisfaction received on 29 Aug 1840. Signed Joseph **Cissell**. Test Fredk. C. **Hase**, Clerk.]

783. Page 319. 18 Jul 1837. Henry **Caho** and Maria, his wife, to William **Taylor**. For the sum of $200, __ acres, beginning in the middle of Jackson St. on the S side of Perryville; bounded by __ **Duvall** and __ **Michael**. Signed Henry **Caho**, Maria **Caho** (RD). Wit Reuben **Shelby** (JP). Rec 4 Dec 1837.

784. Page 320. 8 Dec 1837. Amzi **Osborn** and Esther H., his wife, to David **Thomas** of Essex Co., N. Jer. For the sum of $296.42, three tracts; 40 acres, being the W 1/2 of Lot No. 3, NW 1/4, Sec 6, Twp 33 N, Rng 14 E; __ acres, being the undivided 1/2 of Lot No. 6, NW 1/4 and SE 1/4 of Lot No. 7, NW 1/4, Sec 6, Twp 39 N, Rng 14 E, and the same entered by **Scudder** and sd **Osborn** on 28 Jan 1837; and 40 acres, being the undivided 1/2, N 1/2, Lot No. 2, NW 1/4, fractional Sec 5, Twp 33 N, Rng 14 E (1/2 having previously been sold to John **Scudder**). Signed Amzi **Osborn**, Esther H. **Osborn**. Wit Augustus **Davis** (JP). Rec 8 Dec 1837.

785. Page 321. 8 Dec 1837. Same and same to John **Scudder**. For the sum of $1, mortgage on two tracts; __ acres, being 1/2 of the E part, fractional Sec 32, Twp 34 N, Rng 14 E (the other 1/2 being previously sold to sd **Scudder** on 30 Jan 1837); and the undivided interest to 350 arpens or more at the mouth of Apple Creek, purchased by sd **Osborn** from John **Logan** and wife on 1 Oct 1836. Also the following personal property: one yoke of oxen of red and white color; three cows of red and white color; three calves of the same color; one steer two years old of same color; three steers one year old, two red and white and one black with a white face; one yearling heiffer of red and white color; one sorrel mare supposed to be about eight years old; one brown mare supposed to be 11 years old; two horse colts, one brown and the other a cream or dun color; one lot of hogs containing 19 shoats and five sows; 12 goates; one steem boiler or boiler for steame ingine now lying on the bank of Apple Creek; ten plate stove; one corn sheller; one pair of smith's bellaces; one anvill; one vice; one hammer; one tongs; one sledge; one pair of patent scales and beam; one old Gig and harness; six chairs; one bedstead and bedding; one rocking chair; one large looking glass; one Shellbed temple or mantle ornament; two frame paintings; one piano; one round Table; and one dressing table. The debt is owed on two drafts dated 5 Sep 1837 drawn by sd **Osborn** in favor of David **Thomas** with sd **Scudder** as security, one for $2467 payable two years after date, the other for $2168 payable three years after date. The property is to be applied to the debts if they are not paid. Signed Amzi **Osborn**, Esther H. **Osborn**. Wit Augustus **Davis** (JP). Rec 8 Dec 1837. [Marginal note: Full satisfaction received on 9 Oct 1843. Signed John **Scudder**. Test John W. **Noell**, Clerk.]

786. Page 323. 15 Jul 1837. Amzi **Osborn** to same. For $900 in a promissory note due six months from date, one negro woman slave **Hinney** [**Pinney**?]. Signed Amzi **Osborn**. Wit Augustus **Davis** (JP). Rec 8 Dec 1837.

787. Page 324. 1 Jul 1837. Odile **Valle** nee **Delassus**, widow of Louis **Valle** of Ste. Genevieve, Mo. to her sister Louisa **Delassus**, wife of Peter R. **Pratte**; Cerant **Delassus**; and Leon **Delassus**. For the sum of $1 and natural love and affection to her family, all her interest in the lands and estate as an heir of Camille **Delassus**. Also to Cereant **Delassus**, Leon **Delassus**, and to the present children of her sister Louisa **Delassus**, real estate in the city of St. Louis, being conveyed to her by J. B. **Valle** (St. Louis Book X:164), but possession is not to be given until 1 Jan 1843. Signed Odile **Valle** nee **Delassus**. Wit Felix **Valle**, Jos. D. **Grafton**, Clerk of Ste. Genevieve Co., Mo. Rec 9 Dec 1837.

788. Page 325. 27 Jul 1837. Andrew H. **Tucker** and Ellen, his wife, in trust to Samuel A. **Coale** & Co. of St. Louis, Mo. for the benefit of James T. **Severingen**, and Edward **Bredell** (Sweringen & Bredell) of St. Louis, Mo. In consideration of a debt and trust, and for the sum of $1, deed of trust on 100 acres in Bois Brule Bottom, acquired by sd **Tucker** of William **Flynn** and wife, Josephus **Tucker** and wife, Isaac **Hill** and wife, and George **McNew** and wife on 3 Aug 1836. Sd **Tucker** has executed a promissory note dated 26 Jul 1837 for $1360 to Sweringen & Bredell, payable 60 days after date. If the debt is not paid, sd **Coale** is to sell the land to pay it. Signed A. H. **Tucker**, Ellen (x) **Tucker**. Wit L. L. **Chambers**, Elijah **Boyd**, William G. **Boyd**, JP in Saline Twp, Ste. Genevieve Co., Mo., Fredk. C. **Hase**, Clerk. Rec 11 Dec 1837.

789. Page 327. 13 Sep 1837. David **Crips** and Terecy, his wife, to Hillary **Vessels**. For the sum of $174.37 1/2, 160 acres, more or less, the SW part of 640 acres confirmed to sd **Crips**. Signed David **Crips**, Terecy (x) **Crips** (RD). Wit Joab W. **Burgee** (JP). Rec 27 Dec 1837.

790. Page 328. 5 Dec 1837. Hillary **Vessels** and Monica, his wife, to P. R. **Pratte**, Commissioner of the Road and Canal Fund for Perry Co. For the sum of $70, 160 acres, the SW part of 640 acres confirmed to David **Crips** and sold to sd **Vessels** on 13 Sep 1837. Sd **Vessels** owes a debt of equal date, due with 10% interest per annum to sd **Pratte**. Signed Henry **Vessels**, Monica (x) **Vessels** (RD). Wit James **Rice** (JP). Rec 3 Jan 1838. [Marginal note: Full satisfaction received on 6 Apr 1852. Bernard **Cissell**, Treasurer of Perry Co.]

791. Page 330. 29 Jun 1832. Joseph **Hagan** by Elias **Barcroft**, Auditor of Public Accounts for Mo., to Michael **Hagan**. For the sum of $0.75 in taxes, penalties, and costs; 83 acres, being Survey No. 852 in Twps 35 & 36, Rng 10. Sold on 18 Jun 1832 at the Auditor's Office for delinquent taxes, penalties, and costs for 1831, due by 1 Dec 1831 with 5% interest per month. Signed E. **Barcroft**, Auditor of Public Accts. Rec 5 Jan 1838.

792. Page 331. 19 Oct 1827. U. S. A. to Joseph **Tucker**. Grant for 640 acres, beginning at a post on the line of Aquila **Hagan**'s survey, and designated as No. 855; as Certificate No. 1056. Signed John Q. **Adams**, President. Wit Geo. **Graham**, Commissioner of the General Land Office. Rec 5 Jan 1838.

793. Page 333. 12 Mar 1830. Joseph **Tucker** senr and Elener, his wife, to Guy **Elder**. In consideration of the love and kindness they bear to their children, namely sd **Elder** and Elizabeth, his wife, Lot Nos. 35 & 36 in Perryville. Signed Joseph **Tucker**, Elener **Tucker** (RD). Wit W. **Wilkinson** (JP). Rec 5 Jan 1838.

794. Page 334. 7 Jan 1833. Nicholas **Tucker** and Mary, his wife, to same. For the sum of $300, 250 arpens or 212.65 acres, part of 640 acres confirmed to Joseph **Tucker**; beginning at a w. oak marked "N. T." on the SE boundary of sd survey. Signed Nicholas **Tucker**, Mary (x) **Tucker** (RD). Wit John **Layton** (JP). Rec 5 Jan 1838.

795. Page 336. 13 Mar 1835. Apolnerius **Tucker** of St. Louis Co., Mo., Valerio **Fania** and Matilda, his wife, to same. For the sum of $312.50, 240 acres, more or less, in Survey No. 855 in Twp 35 N, Rng 10 E; confirmed to Joseph **Tucker** Senior, and the same conveyed by the heirs of Joseph **Tucker**, decd, to Apolnerius **Tucker** and Valerio **Fainia** on 8 Aug 1833 (1:372). Signed Apos. **Tucker**, Valerio **Fainia**, Madilta **Fania** (RD). Wit R. S. **Dorsey** (JP). Rec 5 Jan 1838.

796. Page 338. 24 Jan 1838. Daniel U. **Cline** and Dorcas, his wife, to Samuel **Barber**. For the sum of $50, 20 acres, being the N end of the SW 1/4, SE 1/4, Sec 6, Twp 34 N, Rng 13 E. Signed Daniel U. **Cline**, Dorcas H. **Cline** (RD). Wit Elias **Barber** (JP). Rec 6 Jan 1838.

797. Page 339. 7 Jan 1837. John **Payton** and Samuel **Payton** to Jacob **Shaner**. For the sum of $250.50, mortgage on four tracts; 40 acres, being the S 1/2, Lot No. 2, NW fractional 1/4, Sec 5, Twp 33 N, Rng 14 E; 40.08 acres, being the SW fractional 1/4, fractional Sec 32, Twp 34 N, Rng 14 E; 139.18 acres, being the SW fractional 1/4, Sec 30, Twp 34 N, Rng 14 E; and 40 acres, being the NE 1/4, NW 1/4, Sec 26, Twp 38, Rng 6 E. Sd **Shaner** holds two notes on John & Samuel **Payton** dated 20 Dec 1836, payable one day from date with 10% interest; one for $175; and one for $75.50. The notes must be paid by 20 Dec 1839. Signed John **Payton**, Samuel **Payton**. Wit Elias **Barber** (JP). Rec 8 Jan 1838.

798. Page 341. 9 Sep 1837. Ferdinand **Rozier** and Harriet, his wife, to Joseph **Shoults**. For the sum of $310, Lot No. 57 in Perryville; purchased by sd **Rozier** from Mathias **Barringer** and wife on 23 Dec 18[36] (2:172). Signed Ferdinand **Rozier**, Harriet **Rozier** (RD). Wit James **Rice** (JP). Rec 9 Jan 1838.

799. Page 342. 6 Jan 1838. David **Crips** and Terecy, his wife, to Joab W. **Burgee**. For the sum of $50, 40.17 acres, part of a tract purchased by sd **Crips** of James **Rice**, John **Logan**, Peter R. **Pratte**, and Joel **Kinnison**, commissioners to partition and sell the real estate of Michael **Burns**, decd; beginning at the SW corner of sd survey. Signed David (x) **Crips**, Trecy (x) **Crips** (RD). Wit Elisha **Eggers** (JP). Rec 13 Jan 1838.

800. Page 344. 26 May 1834. Henry **McAtee** senr to Peter P. **Tucker**. For the sum of $200, 160 acres, more or less, the NW part of 324 acres granted to David **Crips** and surveyed by Isidore **Moore**. Signed Henry **McAtee** Senr. Wit John **Layton** (JP). Rec 23 Jan 1838.

801. Page 345. 23 Jan 1838. Charles **Steward** and Mary Jane, his wife, to Luther **Taylor** and Valario **Frainna**. For the sum of $10, 1 acre, more or less, beginning at a stake in the center of Jackson St on the S side of Perryville. Signed Charles **Steward**, Mary Jane (x) **Steward** (RD). Wit Reuben **Shelby**, JCC. Rec 23 Jan 1838.

802. Page 346. 23 Jan 1838. William **Taylor** and Mary, his wife, to same and same. For the sum of $200, 14 acres, more or less, beginning on the S side of Perryville in the center of Jackson St; bounded in part by Charles **Steward**. Signed Wm. **Taylor**, Mary (x) **Taylor** (RD). Wit Reuben **Shelby**, JCC. Rec 23 Jan 1838.

803. Page 347. 15 Dec 1837. John **Thompson** and Mary, his wife, to Ferdenand **Belsha**. For the sum of $500, 80 acres in Boisbrule Bottom in two entries in Sec 24, Twp 36 N, Rng 11 E; 40 acres, being the NE 1/4, SE 1/4; and 40 acres, being the NW 1/4, SE 1/4. Signed John (x) **Thompson**, Mary (x) **Thompson** (RD). Wit Alfred L. **Parks** (JP). Rec 24 Jan 1838.

804. Page 348. 2 Jan 1838. John P. **Finch** and Mary Ann, his wife, to William P. **Belsha**. For the sum of $100, 50 acres in Boisbrule Bottom, part of a claim confirmed to William **Hickman**; beginning on his SW boundary at the corner of John **Belsha**, and also bounded by ___ **Haggard**. Should anyone produce a better title to the land, then sd **Finch** shall pay the value of the land back to William **Belsha**. Signed John P. **Finch**, Mary Ann **Finch** (RD). Wit Elisha **Eggers** (JP). Rec 2 Jan 1838.

805. Page 350. 2 Jan 1838. Same and same to John **Bellsha**. For the sum of $100, 50 acres in Boisbrule Bottom; beginning at the most W corner of William **Hickman**, and part of the same. Should anyone produce a better title to the land, then sd **Finch** shall pay the value of the land back to sd **Belsha**. Signed John P. **Finch**, Mary Ann **Finch** (RD). Wit Elisha **Eggers** (JP). Rec 2 Jan 1838.

806. Page 351. 29 Jan 1838. James J. **Moore** and Cecelia, his wife, to John **Manning**. For the sum of $100, 80 acres, the undivided moiety of sd **Moore** in Survey No. 868 in Twp 35 N, Rng 11 E, confirmed to James **Moore** (son of James) and father of sd James J. **Moore**. Signed James J. **Moore**, Cecelia (x) **Moore** (RD). Wit James **Rice** (JP). Rec 29 Jan 1838.

807. Page 352. 27 Jan 1838. Thomas **Taylor** and Balbina, his wife, to Peter R. **Pratte**, commissioner of the Road and Canal Fund for Perry Co. For the sum of $79.40, mortgage on 46.96 acres, being the E 1/2, Lot No. 2, NW 1/4, Sec 1, Twp 34 N, Rng 10 E. Sd **Taylor** owes the debt with 10% interest per annum from this date, and due by 22 Jan 1839. Signed Thomas **Taylor**, Belbina (x) **Taylor** (RD). Wit James **Rice** (JP). Rec 30 Jan 1838. [Marginal note: Full satisfaction received on 5 Apr 1839. Signed Levi **Block**, Treasurer and Commissioner.]

808. Page 354. 23 Jan 1838. Luther **Taylor** and Hannah, his wife, and Valario **Fainia** and Matilda, his wife, to Hyman **Block**. For the sum of $150, two lots; Lot No. 1 in the addition to Perryville laid out by sd **Taylor** and **Fainia**, fronting on Jackson St and adjoining sd town on the S; and 7 acres, more or less, beginning at a stake on the SW corner of the addition to Perryville, bounded in part by Charles **Steward**. Signed Luther **Taylor**, Hannah **Taylor** (RD), Valerio **Faina**, Matilda **Faina** (RD). Wit Reuben **Shelby**, JCC. Rec 23 Jan 1838.

809. Page 355. 16 Jan 1838. Jonas A. **Rutledge** and Francis C., his wife, to Charles C. **Rutledge**. For the sum of $200, 80 acres in two parcels; 40 acres, being the NW 1/4, NW 1/4, Sec 12, Twp 34 N, Rng 11 E; and 40 acres, being the SW 1/4, SW 1/4, Sec 1, Twp 34 N, Rng 11 E. Signed Jonas A. **Rutledge**, Francis C. **Rutledge** (RD). Wit Mark **Brewer** (JP). Rec 3 Feb 1838.

810. Page 357. 17 Jun 1837. H. C. C. **Tate** of Pike Co., Mo. to John W. **Noell**. Power of attorney to act in his name and settle any claims that he may incur as an heir of John **Noell**. Signed H. C. C. **Tate**. Wit Timothy **Ford**, JP in Pike Co., Mo., Michael J. **Noyes**, Clerk of Pike Co., Mo., William **Stephenson**, Presiding Judge of Pike Co., Mo. Rec 5 Feb 1838.

811. Page 358. 5 Feb 1838. Joseph **Rhodes** and Bernice, his wife, to Timothy **Davis**. For the sum of $50, all the interest to 80 acres in Bois Brule Bottom that sd Bernice inherited; purchased by her father William **Morris**, decd, from Joseph **Bland**, decd; and which sd Bernice inherited as one of the heirs of William **Morris**, and of her sister Hannah **Morris**, decd. Signed Joseph (x) **Rhodes**, Bernice (x) **Rhodes**. Wit Joab W. **Burgee**, Alonzo **Abernathy**, Fredk. C. **Hase**, Clerk. Rec 6 Feb 1838.

812. Page 360. 10 Apr 1835. Amzi **Osborn** of New Orleans, La. to Esther **Perrine** of St. Louis, Mo. Marriage contract. In case the marriage should be performed, and in consideration of the affection and esteem which he entertains for Miss **Perrine**, $8000 of property to be taken from his lands New Orleans, the state of Miss., or personal property during her natural life. Signed Amzi **Osborn**, Esther H. **Perrine**. Wit James M. **DeBow**, Peter **Lott**, John **Scudder**, Daniel **Hough**, Notary Public in St. Louis, Mo., Augustus **Davis** (JP). Rec 14 Feb 1838.

813. Page 361. 3 Mar 1838. Thomas **Riney** and Sarah, his wife, to J. W. **Noell**. For the sum of $150, Lot No. 66 in Perryville, fronting on St. Marys St and Jackson St. Signed Thomas **Riney**, Sarah (x) **Riney** (RD). Wit Reuben **Shelby**, JCC. Rec 5 Mar 1838.

814. Page 362. 6 Mar 1838. Elisha **Eggers** to John **Logan**. For securing a note and the sum of $1, mortgage on one black mare about four years old next spring. Sd **Eggers** owes sd **Logan** in a note for $60.50 payable in three months, with sd **Eggers** to retain the mare until then. Signed Elisha **Eggers**. Wit Fredk. C. **Hase**, Clerk. Rec 6 Mar 1838.

815. Page 363. 26 Jan 1838. William R. **Dickerson** to Jacob J. **Everets**. For the sum of $100, on Bois Brule Creek, the undivided 1/5 part of 443 acres, more or less, owned by his father Henry **Dickerson**, decd, and where his father lived at the time of his death; bounded on the N by Francis **Clark**, E by the heirs of David L. **Caldwell**, decd, W by the heirs of Amos **Roark**, and S by public land. Signed William R. **Dickerson**. Wit Robert **Trotter** (JP). Rec 9 Mar 1838.

816. Page 364. 5 Mar 1838. Charles F. **Brazeau** of Chester, Ill. to Roseman **Pratte** of Perry Co. and Charles **Dumont** of St. Louis, Mo. For securing a debt and the sum of $1, deed of trust on the undivided 1/3 part of 255 acres, more or less, on Brul's Bottom on the Mississippi River nearly opposite Horse Island, which he holds in right of his wife Caroline, late Caroline **Ellis**; that Charles **Ellis**, father of Caroline, died seized of. Sd **Brazeau** owes sd **Dumont** $1200 by 23 May next; or the land can be sold at the request of sd **Dumont** to pay it. Signed Charles F. **Brazeau**, C. **Dumont** by M. P. **Laffeirre**. Wit Henry **Chouteau**, Clerk of St. Louis Co., Mo. Rec 16 Mar 1838.

817. Page 366. 9 Mar 1837. Anthony **Fleck** and Elizabeth, his wife, to Pertelus **Wilson**. For the sum of $100, 3 acres, more or less, part of a 40 acre lot conveyed by John **Ross** to sd **Fleck** in the

NE 1/4, SW 1/4, Sec 28, Twp 34 N, Rng 12 E; beginning at the building where sd Wilson now lives. Signed Anthony **Fleck**, Elizabeth **Fleck** (RD). Wit James **Ferguson** (JP). Rec 17 Mar 1838.

818. Page 367. 7 Mar 1837. John **Ross** and Hanah W., his wife, to Anthony **Fleck**. For the sum of $75, 40 acres, being the NE 1/4, SW 1/4, Sec 28, Twp 34 N, Rng 12 E. Signed John **Ross**, Hanah W. **Ross** (RD). Wit Elias **Barber** (JP). Rec 19 Mar 1838.

819. Page 368. 20 Jul 1837. Moses **Farrar** to Francis Leak **Jones** of the U. S. Army. For the sum of $60, the 1/3 part of two tracts; 138.22 acres, more or less, on Cape Cinque Hommes Island in the Mississippi River, being the SE fractional 1/4, Sec 22, Twp 36 N, Rng 12 E; and 5.22 acres, being the fractional Sec 23, Twp 36 N, Rng 12 E; conveyed by Samuel **Allen** and wife to sd **Farrar** on 12 Aug 1833 (1:381). Signed Moses **Farrar**. Wit James **Rice** (JP), Nelson **Jones**. Rec 19 Mar 1838.

820. Page 369. 1 Mar 1837. Adam M. **Martin** and Elizabeth, his wife, to James **Lappin**, merchant of Cape Girardeau, Mo. For the sum of $400, 87 acres, more or less, in Twp 35 N, Rng 13 E, Sec 18; bounded on the E by **Mays**' tract, N by the Mississippi River, W by **Wilkinson**, and S by Congress land. Signed Adam M. **Martin**, Elizabeth **Martin** (RD). Wit Ja. **Ferguson** (JP), Julius E. **Parks**. Rec 20 Mar 1838.

821. Page 371. 7 Dec 1837. M. P. **Cassilly** and Sophia, his wife, of Cincinnati, Ohio to Joseph Vital **Beauvois**. For the sum of $500, 80 acres, being the W 1/2, NE 1/4, Sec 19, Twp 36 N, Rng 13 E. Signed M. P. **Cassilly**, Sophia **Cassilly** (RD). Wit William Henry **Harrison**, Clerk of the Hamilton Co., Ohio Court of Pleas and Quarter Sessions. Rec 20 Mar 1838.

822. Page 372. 21 Feb 1838. Michael P. **Cassilly**, admr of the estate of James **Lappin**, decd, late of Cape Girardeau Co., Mo. to same. For the sum of $650, 87 acres in Perry Co.; bounded on the E by the Mays Tract, N by the Mississippi River, W by **Wilkinson**'s Tract, and S by Congress land. Executed on order of Cape Girardeau Co. Circuit Court in Chancery for $600 with interest from 8 Aug 1837, being the balance after deduction for former payments, and $100 allowed sd **Cassilly** for quieting the title. Signed M. P. **Cassilly**, admr. of James **Lappin**, decd. Wit Hy. **Sanford**, Circuit Clerk of Cape Girardeau Co., Mo. Rec 20 Mar 1838.

823. Page 375. 12 Mar 1838. Anthony **Fleck** and Elizabeth, his wife, to Francis **Dossenbach**. For the sum of $155, one equal half of 80 acres, more or less, being the E 1/2, NE 1/4, Sec 30, Twp 34 N, Rng 12 E; purchased by sd **Fleck** and Adolph **Rix** as tenants in common. Signed Anton **Fleck**, Elizabeth **Fleck** (RD). Wit James **Ferguson** (JP). Rec 26 Mar 1838.

824. Page 376. 6 Jan 1837. George **Campster** and Martha, his wife, to Frank J. **Allen**, all of Cape Girardeau Co., Mo. For the sum of $500, 106.12 acres in Bois Brule Bottom near the Mississippi River; being the NW fractional 1/4, Sec 23, Twp 36 N, Rng 11 E; purchased by sd **Campster** of the U. S. Signed George **Camster**, Martha **Camster** (RD). Wit Peter R. **Garrett**, County Clerk of Cape Girardeau Co., Mo. Rec 26 Mar 1838.

825. Page 377. 12 Mar 1838. Alfred A. **McLain** and Sarah, his wife, and Samuel F. **McLain** to William H. **McLain** of Cape Girardeau Co., Mo. For the sum of $200, 31.88 acres, being the NW fractional 1/4, SE 1/4, Sec 27, Twp 35 N, Rng 13 E. Signed Samuel **McLain**, Alfred A. **McLain**, Sarah **McLain**. Wit Elias **Barber** (JP). Rec 26 Mar 1838.

826. Page 378. 12 Mar 1838. Alfred A. **McLain** and Sarah, his wife, to same. For the sum of $1000, two lots in Twp 35 N, Rng 13 E; 39.78 acres, being the NE 1/4, NE 1/4, fractional Sec [27]; and 72.56 acres, being the NW fractional 1/4, fractional Sec 27. Signed Alfred A. **McLain**, Sarah **McLain** (RD). Wit Elias **Barber** (JP). Rec 26 Mar 1838.

827. Page 379. 17 Aug 1837. William **Dickey** to Columbus **Price** of Cape Girardeau Co., Mo. For the sum of $350, 39.84 acres, being the NW 1/4, Sec 6, Twp 34 N, Rng 13 E. Signed Wm. **Dickey**. Wit John **Hughes** (JP). Rec 27 Mar 1838.

828. Page 380. 23 Feb 1836. Charles **Madden** to James **Taylor**. For the sum of $172.50, 115 acres, more or less, in Bois Brule Botton; commencing on the river bank and bounded in part by Atticus **Tucker**. Signed Chs. **Madden**. Wit Erastus **Davis**, Wm. **Searcy** (JP). Rec 27 Mar 1838.

829. Page 381. 4 Apr 1831. Robert T. **Brown** and Catharine, his wife, to Charles C. **Valle**. For the sum of $500, 700 arpents on Saline Creek, part of an undivided Spanish Grant and known as the Grand Glaise Tract. Signed R. T. **Brown**, Catharine **Brown** (RD). Wit W. **Wilkinson**, JCC. Rec 27 Mar 1838.

830. Page 382. 18 May 1837. Garland **Laughlin** of Jackson Co., Ill. to John **Hurst** of Union Co., Ill. For the sum of $1200, all the real and personal property bequeathed to George Washington **Gile**, son and heir of James **Gile**, decd, by his last will and testament, proven in Brownsville, Jackson Co., Ill. in Jun or Jul 1827. The same was purchased by sd **Laughlin** of George Washington **Gile** on 12 Nov 1836, and recorded in Jackson Co., Ill. The property includes fractional Sec 23 and NW 1/4 Sec 24, Twp 10 S, Rng 4 W in Jackson Co., Ill., entered by James **Gile** on 29 Sep 1817; 151 acres, more or less, formerly owned by James **Manning** in Perry Co. on the bank of the Mississippi River opposite the first tract; negroes; and every kind of property mentioned in the will. Signed Garland **Laughlin**, Jane (x) **Laughlin** (RD). Wit Benningsen **Boon**, JP in Jackson Co., Ill., Augustus **Davis** (JP). Rec 27 Mar 1838.

831. Page 384. 1 Aug 1831. Timothy **Davis**, admr de bonis non of the estate of Amos **Bird**, decd, to David L. **Caldwell**. For the sum of $200, 500 acres, more or less, in Bois Brule Bottom near **Logan**'s tanyard below; commonly known as the Sweat House Spring Tract; the greater part thereof is bottomland heavily and well timbered and not convenient to the river. Sold in Mar 1829 at order of County Court issued at Aug 1828 Term to sell sd lands to pay debts of the estate. Signed Timothy **Davis**. Wit James **Rice** (JP). Rec 29 Mar 1838.

832. Page 386. 28 Mar 1838. James **Nicholas** and Mary Ann, his wife, to Timothy **Davis**. For the sum of $105, 1/3 part of 80 acres, more or less, in Bois Brule Bottom, the life estate of sd Mary Ann which she has as tenant in dower as an heir of her child Hannah; purchased by the former husband of Mary Ann--William **Morris**, now decd, from Joseph **Bland**, decd.; where sd **Morris** resided at the time of his death. Signed James **Nicholas**, Mary Ann (x)

Nicholas. Wit John **Logan**, Nelson **Jones**, Fredk. C. **Hase**, Clerk. Rec 29 Mar 1838.

833. Page 387. 20 Apr 1831. Joseph **Manning** and Mary, his wife, to James **Reddick**. For the sum of $310, 94 acres, more or less, part of a 640 acre survey confirmed to sd **Manning**, Survey No. 840; beginning at the NW corner of 180 acres sold to John B. **Moranville** out of the same survey. Signed Joseph **Manning**, Mary (x) **Manning** (RD). Wit John **Layton** (JP). Rec 31 Mar 1838.

834. Page 388. 1 Dec 1832. James **Wimsatt** and Elenor, his wife, and Robert **Wimsatt** and Susanna, his wife, to Austin **Layton**. For the sum of $150, 127 1/2 acres, more or less, beginning on the SE corner adjoining Bede **Moore**, and also adjoined by James J. **Moore**, Clement **Knott**, Henry **McAtee**, Elisha **Belsha**, and John **Duvall**. Signed James **Wimsatt**, Elenor (x) **Wimsatt** (RD), Robert **Wimsatt**, Susanna (x) **Wimsatt** (RD). Wit John **Layton** (JP), James **Layton**. Rec 3 Apr 1838.

835. Page 390. 2 Apr 1838. John **Daugherty** to John **Logan**. For securing a debt and the sum of $1, mortgage on 90.03 acres in Bois Brule Bottom, being the E 1/2, S 1/2, fractional Sec 35, Twp 37 N, Rng 10 E. Sd **Daugherty** owes sd **Logan** a note for $300 payable in six months with legal interest. Signed John **Daugherty**. Wit W. **Searcy** (JP). Rec 5 Apr 1838.

836. Page 391. 3 Apr 1838. Jacob **Clodfelter** senr and Elizabeth, his wife, of Cape Girardeau Co. to John **Clodfelter** of Union Co., Ill. For the sum of $260, 160 acres in Sec 32, Twp 34 N, Rng 12 E; being the W 1/2, SE 1/4, and E 1/2, SW 1/4. Signed Jacob **Clodfelter**, Elizabeth **Clodfelter** (RD). Wit Jas. **Taylor**, J. R. **McLane**, JCC in Cape Girardeau Co., Mo. Rec 6 Apr 1838.

837. Page 392. 6 Aug 1828. Commissioners of Perryville to John **Duvall**. For the sum of $ 41.50, Lot Nos. 45, 73, 74, & 83 in Perryville. Signed Robert T. **Brown**, Thomas **Riney**, Joseph **Tucker** senr., Commissioners. Wit John **Layton** (JP). Rec 7 Apr 1838.

838. Page 393. 12 Oct 1831. John **Duvall** to Gabriel **Duvall**. For the sum of $25, Lot No. 45 in Perryville. Signed John **Duvall**. Wit John **Layton** (JP). Rec 7 Apr 1838.

839. Page 393. 5 Apr 1838. Joseph **Duvall** and Ann Arpy **Abernathy** to Gabriel M. **Duvall**. For the sum of $1, all their claim to 200 arpents intended to be an advancement to sd Gabriel, valued at $500; part of the original head right granted to John **Duvall**, decd; bounded on the N by Johnathan **Preston**, E by a tract confirmed to sd John **Duvall** under William **Boyce**, S by land confirmed to Charles **Lee** and James **Moore** son of James, and W by a portion of the same tract formerly conveyed to Robert **Abernathy** by way of advancement and valued at $500 by John **Duvall**, decd. Signed Joseph **Duvall**, Ann Arpy **Abernathy**. Wit James **Rice** (JP). Rec 7 Apr 1838.

840. Page 394. 5 Apr 1838. Joseph **Duvall**, Gabriel M. **Duvall**, and Ann Arpy **Abernathy**, heirs and legal representatives of John **Duvall**, decd. Deed of partition of their share of the slaves belonging to the estate of sd decd. Joseph **Duvall** is to receive **Sarah**, a woman, and her youngest child **Elizabeth**, appraised at $700; **Sam**, a boy, appraised at $700; and **Penelope**, a girl, appraised at $300. Gabriel M. **Duvall** is to receive **Melinda**, a girl, appraised at $700; **David**, a boy, appraised at $500; **Phoebe**, a girl, appraised at $400; and **Celeste**, a child, valued at $100. Ann Arpy **Abernathy** is to receive **Juliann**, a woman, appraised at $700; **Francis**, a boy, appraised at $550; **Minerva**, a girl, appraised at $300; and **Lucretia**, a young child, valued at $100. Sd Joseph and Gabriel M. are also to pay sd Ann Arpy $50 to make her share equal. Signed Joseph **Duvall**, Gabriel M. **Duvall**, Ann Arpy **Abernathy**. Wit Jas. **Rice** (JP), Simon **Duvall**. Rec 7 Apr 1838.

841. Page 396. 7 Apr 1838. Samuel **Burows** to Peter R. **Pratte**, commissioner of the Road and Canal Fund for Perry Co. For the sum of $1 and for securing a debt, mortgage on 80 acres, being the W 1/2, NW 1/4, Sec 25, Twp 35 N, Rng 11 E. Sd **Burows** owes a debt to the fund of $150 due in 12 months with 10% interest. Signed Samuel **Borrows**. Wit James **Rice** (JP). Rec 7 Apr 1838.

842. Page 397. 16 Mar 1838. Luther **Taylor** and Hanah, his wife, and Valario **Fania** and Matilda, his wife, to Hyman **Block**. For the sum of $40, two lots in the addition to Perryville laid out by the grantors; Lot No. 2 fronting on High St and Jackson St; and Lot No. 3 fronting on High St. Signed Luther **Taylor**, Hannah **Taylor** (RD), Valario **Fainia**, Matilda **Faina** (RD). Wit Reuben **Shelby**, JCC. Rec 9 Apr 1838.

843. Page 398. 16 Apr 1838. Edward **McLain** and Ellen, his wife, of Ste. Genevieve Co., Mo. to Charles **Stewart**. For the sum of $25, 2 1/2 acres, beginning at a stake on the S corner of sd **Stewart**'s land, as purchased from Luther **Taylor**. Signed Edward (x) **McLain**, Ellen (x) **McLain** (RD). Wit Jos. D. **Grafton**, Clerk of Ste. Genevieve Co., Mo. Rec 21 Apr 1838.

844. Page 399. 14 Apr 1838. Samuel **McDaniel** to Elizabeth **Lockart**. For the sum of $100, mortgage on 540 acres in Cape Cinque Hommes Twp, confirmed to Elizabeth **Carns**, except 100 acres in the SE part of sd confirmation deeded to Elizabeth **Morris**. Sd **McDaniel** owes sd **Lockart** the debt by 25 Dec 1839. Signed Samuel C. **McDaniel**. Test A. L. **Parks** (JP). Rec 23 Apr 1838.

845. Page 400. 19 Mar 1838. Thomas **Long** and Margaret, his wife, to John **Stearns** of Randolph Co., Ill. For the sum of $166, mortgage 50 acres in Bois Brule Bottom, the E 1/2 of 100 acres deeded to sd **Long** and Newton **Long** by Alexander **Patterson**. The debt is due with 10% interest. Signed Thomas **Long**, Margaret (x) **Long** (RD). Wit A. L. **Parks** (JP). Rec 24 Apr 1838.

846. Page 401. 14 Apr 1838. Elizabeth **Lockart** and Elisha **Eggers** and Elizabeth, his wife, to Samuel **McDaniel**. For the sum of $300, 540 acres in Cape Cinque Hommes Twp; confirmed to Elizabeth **Carns**, except 100 acres in the SE part deeded to Elizabeth **Morris**. Signed Elizabeth (x) **Lockart**, Elisha **Eggers**, Elizabeth (x) **Eggers** (RD). Test A. L. **Parks** (JP). Rec 25 Apr 1838.

847. Page 402. 2 Apr 1838. Elizabeth **Hogard** of Livingston Co., Ken. to Thomas J. **Finch**. For the sum of $950, 60 acres in Bois Brule Twp, that her late husband John **Hogard** bought from John P. **Finch**, and conveyed to her by the last will and testament of John **Hogard**, decd, now on record in Livingston Co., Ken.; beginning at the N corner of a survey confirmed to William **Hickman**. Signed Elizabeth (x) **Hogard**. Wit A. **Hogard**, John M. **Wilson**, Wm. **Hogard**, James **Dallam**, Clerk of Livingston Co.,

Ken. Court, Ths. Willis, JP in Livingston Co., Ken. Rec 28 Apr 1838.

848. Page 404. 30 Dec 1835. U. S. A. to Stephen **Dolson**. Patent for 88.97 acres, being the E 1/2, Lot Nos. 1 & 2, E 1/4, Sec 2, Twp 34 N, Rng 10 E. Signed A. **Donelson** for President Andrew **Jackson**. Wit Ethan A. **Brown**, Commissioner of the General Land Office. Rec 28 Apr 1838.

849. Page 404. 25 Apr 1838. Timothy **Davis** and Nancy, his wife, to William B. **Burget**. For the sum of $450, 400 arpens on St. Lorent Creek; adjoining the tract on which Nancy **Burget** resided at the time of her death, and confirmed to the widow and legal representatives of Andrew **Coxe** Senior, decd. Signed Timothy **Davis**, Nancy **Davis** (RD). Wit James **Rice** (JP). Rec 28 Apr 1838.

850. Page 406. 28 Apr 1838. Clement **Knott** and Elizabeth, his wife, to James **McCowley**. For the sum of $1 and other diverse good causes, 150 acres, more or less, beginning at the S corner of a small tract laid off to William **McCowley** in the original tract confirmed to sd **Knott**. Signed Clement (x) **Knott**, Elizabeth (x) **Knott** (RD). Wit James **Rice** (JP). Rec 28 Apr 1838.

851. Page 407. 3 Apr 1838. Amzi **Osborn** and John **Scudder** to Robert **Manning** as trustee. For the sum of $1200 received from James **Taylor** and sd **Manning**, deed of trust on about 400 arpens on both sides of Apple Creek near its mouth; on which sd **Osborn** and sd **Scudder** have a steem saw mill and other buildings; and which sd **Osborn** purchased from John **Logan**. Sd **Taylor**, in the name of William **Manning**, as plaintiff for the use of James **Taylor**, has obtained a judgment in Circuit Court last Mar against sd **Osborn** for $870 debt, $121.44 damages, and costs received; also an execution has been issued by Circuit Court in favor of William **Manning** for the use of sd **Taylor** on sd judgment for $991.44 debt, $8 damages, and $15.88 costs. This mortgage is granted to allow sd **Osborn** and sd **Scudder** to raise more money and give collateral for the payment. The property is to be sold by sd **Manning** if the debts with 10% interest per annum are not paid by 1 Apr next. Signed Amzi **Osborn**, John **Scudder**. Wit Hugh **Wells**, Mary Philip **Ledue**, JCC in St. Louis Co., Mo. Rec 2 May 1838. [Marginal note: John **Scudder** having purchased the judgment from him, this deed is declared null and void on 25 Mar 1839. Signed James **Taylor**]

852. Page 410. 27 Apr 1838. Amzi **Osborn** to John **Scudder**. For the sum of $175, quit claim to his interest in the undivided half of eight tracts; about 400 arpens at the mouth of Apple Creek in Cape Girardeau and Perry counties; a tract acquired by sd **Osborn** from John **Logan**; 248.30 acres on Sandy Island in Sec 32, Twp 34 N, Rng 14 E; 40 acres, being the E 1/2, Lot No. 1, NW 1/4, Sec 6, Twp 33 N, Rng 14 E; 80 acres, being Lot No. 1, NE 1/4, fractional Sec 3, Twp 33 N, Rng 13 E; 40 acres, being the NE 1/4, SE 1/4, Sec 7, Twp 33 N, Rng 14 E; 40 acres, being the NE 1/4, SE 1/4, Sec 3, Twp 33 N, Rng 13 E; 40 acres, being the SE 1/4, SE 1/4, Sec 1, Twp 33 N, Rng 13 E; and 40 acres, being the NW 1/4, SE 1/4, Sec 1, Twp 33 N, Rng 13 E. Signed Amzi **Osborn**. Wit M. P. **Ledue**, JCC in St. Louis Co., Mo. Rec 5 May 1838.

853. Page 411. 21 Apr 1838. John **Daugherty** to Joseph **Pratt**. For securing a debt and the sum of $1, mortgage on 90.34 acres in Bois Brule Bottom, being the E 1/2, S 1/2, fractional Sec 35, Twp 37 N, Rng 10 E. Sd **Daugherty** owes sd **Pratt** a note of this date for $115, payable in six months with legal interest. Signed John **Daugherty**. Wit W. **Searcy** (JP). Rec 5 May 1838.

854. Page 412. 17 Mar 1838. Nelson **Grissom** to John **Belsha**. For the sum of $51.93 1/4, mortgage on two bay mares. Sd **Grissom** is to have the use of sd horses for making his crop until the debt is paid. Signed Nelson (x) **Grissom**. Test A. L. **Parks** (JP). Rec 7 May 1838.

855. Page 412. 12 Apr 1838. Mosses S. **Harris** and Mary A. K., his wife, of Marion Co., Mo. to John W. **Quick**. For the sum of $1000, three tracts that are part of the Seminary land; 40 acres, being the SW 1/4, NE 1/4, Sec 12, Twp 34, Rng 11; 160 acres, being the W 1/2, SE 1/4 and the E 1/2, SW 1/4, Sec 12, Twp 34, Rng 11 E; and 40 acres, being the SE 1/4, NW 1/4, Sec 12, Twp 34, Rng 11 E; all recorded in the Auditor's Office on 22 May 1835. Signed Mosses S. **Harris**, Mary A. K. **Harris** (RD). Wit Jordan J. **Montgomery**, Clerk of Marion Co., Mo. Rec 9 May 1838.

856. Page 414. 20 Jul 1837. Singleton H. **Kimmel** and Sarah, his wife, to Benjamin **Davis**. For the sum of $100, 80 acres, being Lot No. 1, NE 1/4, Sec 2, Twp 33 N, Rng 13; purchased by sd **Kimmel** from the U. S. A. on 6 Sep 1836. Signed Singleton H. **Kimmel**, Sarah G. **Kimmel**. Wit Elias **Barber** (JP). Rec 10 May 1838.

857. Page 415. 30 Apr 1838. Benjamin **Davis** to John W. **Noell**. For the sum of $50, Lot No. 67 in Perryville. Signed Benjamin **Davis**, Jane (x) **Davis** (RD). Wit Joseph **Morgan**, Washington **Davis**, Augustus **Davis** (JP). Rec 11 May 1838.

858. Page 416. 12 Apr 1838. Pater **Faherty** and Matilda, his wife, to Addison **Walker**. For the sum of $110, the S side of Lot No. 68 in Perryville; bounded on the E by Jackson St., S by John W. **Noell**, W by sd **Faherty**, and N by North St. Signed Peter **Faherty**, Matilda **Faherty** (RD). Wit James **Rice** (JP). Rec 19 May 1838.

859. Page 417. 25 Feb 1838. John W. **Tucker** and Christina, his wife, to James **Cameron**. For the sum of $155, 40 acres, more or less, in Cinque Hommes Twp, being the SW 1/4, SW fractional 1/4, Sec 29, Twp 36 N, Rng 10 E; purchased by sd **Tucker** from the U. S. A. Signed John W. **Tucker**, Christana **Tucker**. Wit Robert **Trotter** (JP). Rec 26 May 1838.

860. Page 418. 12 Mar 1838. Robert **Black** and Sarah, his wife, to Daniel **Cline** Senr. For the sum of $500, mortgage on 40 acres, being the NE 1/4, SE 1/4, Sec 5, Twp 34 N, Rng 12 E; 40 acres, being the NE 1/4, NW 1/4, Sec 8, Twp 34 N, Rng 12 E; and a negro man named **Dick**. Sd **Cline** holds notes on sd **Black**. Signed Robert **Black**, Sarah (x) **Black**. Wit James **Ferguson** (JP). Rec 28 May 1838. [Marginal note: Full satisfaction received on 3 May 1841. Signed Daniel **Cline**. Test Fredk. C. **Hase**, Clerk.]

861. Page 419. 21 May 1838. Hannah **Harris**, formerly of Cape Girardeau Co., Mo. but now of Perry Co., to Alonzo **Abernathy** and John H. **Abernathy**. For diverse causes and considerations, power of attorney to take charge of her real and personal property in both counties and make contracts in her name. Signed Hannah **Harris**. Wit James **Ferguson** (JP). Rec 29 May 1838.

862. Page 420. 2 Jun 1838. William H. **White** and Mary, his wife, to Felix **Sims**. For the sum of $31.61, 25.29 acres, being the NW fractional 1/4, Sec 23, Twp 35 N, Rng 10 E; purchased by William Henry **White** from the U. S. A. Signed William H. **White**, Mary (x) **White** (RD). Wit Fredk. C. **Hase**, Clerk. Rec 2 Jun 1838.

863. Page 422. 2 Jun 1838. Felix **Sims** and Ann, his wife, to William Henry **White**. For the sum of $27.50, 22 acres, being the SW fractional 1/4, Sec 23, Twp 35 N, Rng 10 E; being purchased by sd **Sims** from the U. S. A. Signed Felix **Sims**, Ann (x) **Sims** (RD). Wit Frederick C. **Hase**, Clerk Rec 2 Jun 1838.

864. Page 423. 12 May 1838. Johnathan **Shaw** and Malinda, his wife, to John **Woolford**. For the sum of $200, 40 acres, being the NE 1/4, SW 1/4, Sec 29, Twp 35 N, Rng 9 E. Signed Jonathan **Shaw**, Malinda (x) **Shaw** (RD). Wit Robert **Trotter** (JP). Rec 4 Jun 1838.

865. Page 424. 28 Jul 1837. William **Flynn** and Nancy, his wife, to David M. **Anderson**, all of Bois Brule. For the sum of $200, 80 acres, the 1/8 part of 640 acres confirmed to John **Morgan** senr, decd, purchased by sd **Flynn** from Solomon **Morgan**. Signed William **Flynn**, Nancy (x) **Flynn** (RD). Wit Joab W. **Burgee** (JP), Martin J. **Moore**. Rec 5 Jun 1838.

866. Page 425. 3 Aug 1837. George **Rutledge** and Saraann, his wife, to Reuben **Shelby**. For the sum of $100, Lot Nos. 61 & 62 in Perryville. Signed George **Rutledge**, Saraann **Rutledge** (RD). Wit Alonzo **Abernathy**, JCC. Rec 5 Jun 1838.

867. Page 426. 12 Jun 1838. Reuben **Shelby** to Thomas **McAtee**. For the sum of $1000, 160 acres in Sec 12, Twp 34 N, Rng 10 E; being the W 1/2, NW 1/4; NE 1/4, NW 1/4; and NW 1/4, NE 1/4. Signed Reuben **Shelby**. Wit James **Rice** (JP). Rec 26 Jun 1838.

868. Page 427. 6 Jun 1838. John **Manning** to Pious **Manning**. For the sum of $200, bond to make a deed for 22 acres adjoining the land whereon sd Pious now lives; part of a tract of 640 acres confirmed to Joseph **Manning** Senior by the Board of Commissioners. Sd Pious has paid $60 for the land. Signed John **Manning**. Wit Lewis **Moore**, John **Layton** (JP). Rec 29 Jun 1838.

869. Page 428. 27 Dec 1837. Joseph **Shoults** and Eliza, his wife, to Michael **Muhlfelt**. For the sum of $265, part of Lot No. 10 in Perryville, fronting on Spring St and St. Joseph St. Signed Joseph **Shoults**, Eliza R. **Shoults** (RD). Wit Reuben **Shelby**, JCC. Rec 6 Jul 1838.

870. Page 429. 24 Jul 1837. John **Venable** to Charles **Venable**. For the sum of $50, 40 acres, being the NE 1/4, SW 1/4, Sec 21, Twp 35 N, Rng 12 E. Signed John **Venable**. Wit Jas. **Rice** (JP), Thomas J. **Finch**, Levi **Block**. Rec 18 Jul 1838.

871. Page 430. 8 Feb 1837. Robert Nathan **Cochran** and Mary O., his wife, to John **Stephenson**. For the sum of $325, 155.15 acres, being the NE fractional 1/4, Sec 9, Twp 34 N, Rng 13 E, as patented on 15 Oct 1833. Signed Robert N. **Cochran**, Mary O. (x) **Cochran** (RD). Wit Elias **Barber** (JP). Rec 24 Jul 1838.

872. Page 432. 19 Jan 1836. Beverley **Allen** and Penelope, his wife, of St. Louis Co., Mo. to Timothy **Davis** of Ste. Genevieve Co., Mo. For the sum of $450, undivided moiety of 640 acres, more or less, granted by the U. S. A. to John **Scott** and sd **Allen** as assignees of Andrew **Dunks** by patent dated 1 May 1836. Signed Beverley **Allen**, Penelope **Allen** (RD). Wit Henry **Chouteau**, Clerk of St. Louis Co., Mo. Rec 24 Jul 1838.

873. Page 433. 14 May 1838. David M. **Anderson** and Margaret, his wife, to Timothy **Davis**. For the sum of $100, 1/2 of 80 acres in Bois Brule Bottom purchased by sd **Anderson** from William **Flynn** on 28 Jul 1837, which sd **Flynn** purchased from Solomon **Morgan**, and which sd **Morgan** inherited as one of the heirs of John **Morgan** Senr, decd; being the W end of 640 acres confirmed to the heirs of John **Morgan** Senr, decd. Signed David M. **Anderson**, Margaret A. **Anderson** (RD). Wit W. **Searcy** (JP). Rec 24 Jul 1838.

874. Page 434. 20 Aug 1836. Abraham **Roberts** and Nancy, his wife, to Timothy **Davis** of Ste. Genevieve Co., Mo. For the sum of $50, two tracts in Bois Brule Bottom in Twp 36 N, Rng 11 E; 10.42 acres, being the NW fractional 1/4, fractional Sec 10; and 19 acres, being fractional Sec 3. Signed Abraham **Roberts**. Wit Robert C. **Powell**, W. **Searcy** (JP). Rec 24 Jul 1838.

875. Page 435. 18 May 1838. Joab W. **Burgee** and Elizabeth, his wife, to William **Kirkpatrick**. For the sum of $250, the N 1/2 of Lot No. 9, purchased from Isadore **Moore** and wife by Alfred H. **Puckett** on 22 Sep 1829 (1:253), purchased from sd **Puckett** and wife by John **Robinson** on 6 Mar 1837 (2:197), and purchased from sd **Robinson** and wife by sd **Burgee** on 23 Oct 1837 (2:279). Signed Joab W. **Burgee**, Elizabeth **Burgee** (RD). Wit Elisha **Eggers** (JP). Rec 28 Jul 1838.

876. Page 436. 25 Aug 1837. Elizabeth **Newsom** to William B. **Burget**. For the sum of $500, all her right to the lands and real estate which she inherits as one of the heirs of her father John **Burget**, decd, and also as one of the heirs of her mother Nancy **Burget**, decd. Signed Elizabeth **Newsom**. Wit W. **Searcy** (JP). Rec 8 Aug 1838.

877. Page 437. 28 Jul 1838. John **Manning** and Ann, his wife, to Adam **Klob** and George **Bergman**. For the sum of $300, 80 acres, part of a tract patented to James **Moore**, son of James, on 27 Mar 1826; beginning at a stake at the SE corner of the survey. Signed John **Manning**, Ann **Manning** (RD). Wit Reuben **Shelby**, JCC. Rec 30 Jul 1838.

878. Page 439. 30 May 1831. John **Hahn** and Elizabeth, his wife, of Cape Girardeau Co., Mo. to Richard **Maddock**. For the sum of $110, 80 acres, being the W 1/2, SW 1/4, Sec 36, Twp 35 N, Rng 9 E. Signed John (x) **Hahn**, Elizabeth (x) **Hahn** (RD) Wit John **Layton** (JP), Francis J. **Zeigler**. Rec 7 Aug 1838.

879. Page 440. 17 May 1838. James N. **Pettit** and Rachel A., his wife, to Timothy **Davis** of St. Marys Landing. For the sum of $375, two tracts in Bois Brule Bottom; 116.42 acres, an undivided moiety of the NE fractional 1/4, Sec 33, Twp 37 N, Rng 11 E; and 33.60 acres, an undivided moiety of the SW fractional 1/4, Sec 28, Twp 37 N, Rng 11 E. Signed Jas. N. **Pettit**, Rachel A. **Pettit** (RD). Wit W. **Searcy** (JP). Rec 7 Aug 1838.

880. Page 441. 2 Sep 1837. William **Winfield** and Helen, his wife, to John B. **Cissell**. For the sum of $250, 80 acres, being the W 1/2, NW 1/4, Sec 20, Twp 34 N, Rng 11 E. Signed William **Winfield**, Helen (x) **Winfield** (RD). Wit Alfred L. **Clark** (JP). Rec 8 Aug 1838.

881. Page 442. 13 Apr 1838. Last will and testament of Precilla **Johnson**. To her son John **Johnson**: two tracts in Sec 24, Twp 34 N, Rng 8 E -- the SW 1/4, NE 1/4, and SE 1/4, NW 1/4, purchased by her from the U. S. A. on both sides of Whitewater, and where she now resides; also the NW 1/4, NW 1/4, Sec 24, Twp 34 N, Rng 8 E, that she purchased from sd John on 29 Dec 1834; also two yoke of oxen, one sorrel filly three years old, one white cow, one bedstead, bed, and furniture. To her daughters Saley, Mary, and Jane: $5 each. To Clotilda, Pricilla, and Lucinda **Johnson**, heirs of her son Joseph **Johnson**, decd: $5 to be equally divided amongst them. The sums of money are to be paid within six months after her decease, and the remainder of her estate is to be divided equally among all her legatees. Signed Precilla (x) **Johnson**. Wit Henry **Johnson**, John L. **Conrad**, James **Rice** (JP), Fredk. C. **Hase**, Clerk. Rec 9 Aug 1838.

882. Page 444. 4 Dec 1837. Mary **McArthur** of Ioway County, Wisc. Terr., to Jacob **Tatum**. For the sum of $70 and from motives of benevolence and humanity, manumission of sd **Tatum**, her negro man aged about 58. Signed Mary Ann **McArthur**. Wit R. S. **Black**, Edward **McSherry**, JP in Iowa Co., Wisc. For the sum of $200, release of sd Jacob **Tatum** from services he was to render to Chs. **Gregoire** in remuneration of sd **Gregoire** having emancipated him whilst in the State of Mo. Signed Chs. **Gregoire**. Wit Henry **Messersmith**, Registrar, Iowa Co., Wisc. Rec 13 Aug 1838.

883. Page 445. 24 Jun 1837. Robert C. **Stewart** and Sarah, his wife, to Timothy **Davis** of St. Marys Landing. For the sum of $120, one undivided 1/8 part, less 40 acres, which Nancy **Burget**, mother of sd Sarah, had to 400 arpents on St. Laurent Creek confirmed to Andrew **Cox**'s widow and representatives; adjoining sd **Davis**. Signed Robt. M. C. **Stewart**, Sarah **Stewart**. Wit Fredk. C. **Hase**, Clerk, Wm. **Searcy** (JP). Rec 17 Aug 1838.

884. Page 446. 7 Apr 1836. James **Taylor** and Rachel, his wife, to Joseph **Dixon**, a free man of color, all of Bois Brule Bottom. For the sum of $450, __ acres in Bois Brule Bottom, commencing on the river bank; adjoining Atticus **Tucker**'s survey, and also bounded by sd **Dixon** and John **Daugherty**. Signed James **Taylor**, Rachal **Taylor** (RD). Wit Wm. **Searcy** (JP). Rec 17 Aug 1838.

885. Page 447. 15 Aug 1838. Joseph **Dixon**, a free man of color of Bois Brule Bottom, to John **Logan** of Perryville. For the sum of $1288.99, deed of trust on __ acres in Bois Brule Bottom where sd **Dixon** resides, as described in the preceding deed (2:446); all his stock of cattle; his negro woman **Abelina** which he bought from Joseph **Laveille** and with whom he is living as wife; and her two children living here. Sd **Dixon** is indebted in three notes due 1 Jan next; one to T. **Davis** & Co. for $686.99 by a note with 10% interest, to William **Redford** for $100 for wood cut on his land, and to sd **Logan** for $152 for the hire of a negro man **Nathan**. He also owes a note to sd **Laveille** for $350 due Oct next, with Timothy **Davis** as security. Sd **Logan** is to sell the property if the debts are not being paid. Signed Joseph (x) **Dixkson**, John **Logan**. Wit Perry **Evans** (JP). Rec 17 Aug 1838.

886. Page 449. 30 Jan 1838. Henry **McAtee** and Maria, his wife, to Thomas **McAtee**. For the sum of $120, 93.36 acres, being the SE fractional 1/4, fractional Sec 12, Twp 35 N, Rng 10 E; and the same purchased by Henry **McAtee** on 12 Dec 1835, per receipt No. 2535. Signed Henry **McAtee**, Mariah (x) **McAtee** (RD). Wit Reuben **Shelby**, JCC. Rec 17 Aug 1838.

887. Page 450. 30 Jun 1838. Thomas **McAtee** and Mary, his wife, to William **Taylor**. For the sum of $1000, 320 acres, being all the tract where sd **Taylor** now resides, and fractional Sec 12, Twp 35 N, Rng 10 E; 277 acres of which was entered by sd **McAtee** and 93 acres by Henry **McAtee** and sold to sd Thomas on 30 Jan 1838. Signed Thomas **McAtee**, Mary (x) **McAtee** (RD). Wit Reuben **Shelby**, JCC. Rec 17 Aug 1838.

888. Page 451. 19 May 1838. Redick **Eason** and Nancy, his wife, of Pulaski Co., Ark. to Joseph **Shoults**. For the sum of $200, Lot No. 58 in Perryville, in Block No. 6 fronting on St. Marys St, and running back with Jackson St. Signed Redick **Eason**, Nancy **Eason**. Wit Mark **Brewer** (JP). Rec 17 Aug 1838.

889. Page 452. 8 Mar 1838. John **Daugherty** to Timothy **Davis**. For the sum of $1200, 250 acres in Bois Brule Bottom; that sd **Daugherty** purchased from Lawrence **Clark**, and on which is situated the ___? and distillery of sd **Daugherty**. Signed John **Daugherty**. Wit W. **Searcy** (JP). Rec 17 Aug 1838.

890. Page 453. 7 Jul 1838. John **Robinson** and Drucilla, his wife, to Edward M. **Holden**. For the sum of $900, two tracts; the S 1/2 of Lot No. 9 in Perryville, purchased from Isidore **Moore** and wife by Alfred **Puckett**, and from sd **Puckett** and wife by sd **Robinson**, including the brick building; and 6 acres, more or less, adjoining the E boundary of Perryville, beginning at Charles **Stewart**'s corner. Signed John **Robinson**, Drucilla **Robinson** (RD). Wit James **Rice** (JP). Rec 27 Aug 1838.

891. Page 455. 29 Aug 1838. Edward M. **Holden** to Levi **Block**, Commissioner of the Road and Canal Fund. For the sum of $320 with 10% interest, mortgage on the two tracts described in the preceding deed (2:453). Sd **Holden** is indebted with James **Rice** as security. Signed Edward M. **Holden**. Wit Fredk. C. **Hase**, Clerk. Rec 29 Aug 1838.

892. Page 457. 1 Aug 1838. Gabriel M. **Duvall**, late of the state of La. but now of Perry Co., to Joseph **Duvall**. For the sum of $500, his undivided right to 20 acres, more or less, on the Mississippi River at or near the head of Bois Brule Bottom, formerly owned by John **Duvall**, decd; between land now owned by Rebecca **Write** and fronting on the river; that John **Duvall** acquired by right of his first wife as heir of Joseph **Donohowe**, and purchased from Thomas **Donohowe** and wife on 17 Nov 1821. Signed Gabriel M. **Duvall**. Wit James **Rice** (JP). Rec 4 Sep 1838.

893. Page 458. 2 Sep 1837. William **Winfield** and Helen, his wife, to John B. **Cissell**. For the sum of $250, 80 acres, being the W 1/2, NW 1/4, Sec 20, Twp 34 N, Rng 11 E. Signed William **Winfield**, Helen (x) **Winfield** (RD). Wit Fredk. C. **Hase**, Clerk. Rec 8 Sep 1838.

894. Page 459. 10 Sep 1838. Felix **Sims** and Anna, his wife, to John Baptist **Layton**. For the sum of $50, 40 acres, being the NE 1/4, NW 1/4, Sec 34, Twp 35 N, Rng 10 E; purchased by sd **Sims** from the U. S. A. Signed Felix **Sims**, Anna (x) **Sims** (RD). Wit Fredk. C. **Hase**, Clerk. Rec 10 Sep 1838.

895. Page 461. 18 Sep 1838. William C. **Kirkpatrick** and Charlott, his wife, to Robert T. **Brown** Jr. For the sum of $250, the N 1/2 of Lot No. 9 in Perryville, fronting on Spring St.; purchased by Alfred H. **Puckett** from Isadore **Moore** and wife, and by John **Robinson** from sd **Puckett** and wife, by Joab W. **Burgee** from sd **Robinson** and wife, and by sd **Kirkpatrick** from sd **Burgee** and wife. Signed William C. **Kirkpatrick**, Charlott T. (x) **Kirkpatrick** (RD). Wit Fredk. C. **Hase**, Clerk. Rec 25 Sep 1838.

896. Page 462. 8 Mar 1828. John **Welker** to William **Welker**. For the sum of $550, three tracts in Twp 34 N, Rng 11 E; 40 acres, being the SW 1/4, SW 1/4, Sec 36, transferred by David **Welker** and Mary, his wife, to sd John **Welker**; 40 acres, being the NE 1/4, SW 1/4, Sec 36; and 40 acres, being the NE 1/4, SE 1/4, Sec 35. Signed John **Welker**. Test Alonzo **Abernathy**, JCC. Rec 29 Apr 1838.

897. Page 463. 5 Aug 1837. Joseph B. **Mattingly** and Maria, his wife, to Thomas **Stewart**. For the sum of $80, 16.36 acres in Bois Brule Twp, being fractional Sec 32, Twp 37 N, Rng 11 E. Signed Joseph B. **Mattingly**, Mariah (x) **Mattingly** (RD). Wit Joab W. **Burgee** (JP). Rec 1 Oct 1838.

898. Page 464. 26 Jun 1838. Charles **Stewart** and Mary Jane, his wife, to same. For the sum of $20, Lot No. 16 in Perryville on Spring St. Signed Charles **Stewart**, Mary Jane (x) **Stewart** (RD). Wit Reuben **Shelby**, JCC. Rec 1 Oct 1838.

899. Page 465. 10 Oct 1838. Thomas **Stewart** and Isabell T., his wife, to James F. **Tucker**. For the sum of $200, 40 acres, being the NW 1/4, SW 1/4, Sec 22, Twp 36 N, Rng 11 E; entered by sd **Stewart** on 26 Oct 1837. Signed Thomas **Stewart**, Isabella T. **Stewart** (RD). Wit Reuben **Shelby**, JCC. Rec 11 Oct 1838.

900. Page 466. 19 Oct 1838. James F. **Tucker** and Mary Ann, his wife, to Henry **Caho**. For the sum of $175, 40 acres as described in the preceding deed (2:465). Signed James F. **Tucker**, Mary Ann (x) **Tucker** (RD). Wit James **Rice** (JP). Rec 20 Oct 1838.

901. Page 467. 23 Oct 1838. Tunis **Quick** and Nancy, his wife, to John P. **Finch**. For the sum of $1 and diverse other causes and considerations, about 200 acres, more or less, being the land confirmed to sd **Quick** that has not already been disposed of and where sd **Quick** now lives with his family; after deducting the portions sold to Clement **Knott** and John W. **Quick**. Signed Tunis **Quick**, Nancy (x) **Quick** (RD). Wit James **Rice** (JP). Rec 23 Oct 1838.

902. Page 468. 5 Nov 1838. David **Burns**, admr of John W. **Quick**, decd, to Peter R. **Pratte**. For the sum of $350, 200 acres, more or less, part of the survey on which Tunis **Quick** now resides; and part of the land confirmed to Tunis **Quick** and conveyed to John W. **Quick**, decd. Sold on March 25 1837 at order of County Court issued 3 Nov 1836 on petition for sale of slaves and real estate to pay the debts of the estate. Signed David **Burns**, admr of the estate of John W. **Quick**, decd. Wit James **Rice** (JP), John **Farrer**. Rec 5 Nov 1838.

903. Page 470. 20 Aug 1836. John **McLane**, execr of James G. C. **Morton**, to William A. **Bull**. For the sum of $550, 80 acres, being Lot No. 3, NE 1/4, Sec 2, Twp 33 N, Rng 12 E in Cape Girardeau Co., Mo. Signed John **McLane**, execr of the last will and testament of James G. C. **Morton**, decd, Robert **McBride**, E. **Cobbs**. Wit Royal **Thompson**, JP in Cape Girardeau Co., Mo. Rec 6 Nov 1838.

904. Page 471. 6 Nov 1838. Peter R. **Pratte** and Mary Louisa, his wife, to William **Winfield**. For the sum of $375, 200 acres, more or less, in the survey confirmed to Tunis **Quick**, sold by sd **Quick** to his son John W. **Quick**, and sold by order of County Court by the admr of John W. **Quick** to sd **Pratte** on 5 Nov 1838. Signed P. R. **Pratte**, M. L. **Pratte** (RD). Wit James **Rice** (JP), Reuben **Shelby**. Rec 7 Nov 1838.

905. Page 472. 5 Nov 1838. Henry **Caho** and Maria, his wife, to Thomas **Stewart**. For the sum of $110, 40 acres, being the NW 1/4, SW 1/4, Sec 21, Twp 36 N, Rng 11 E; entered by sd **Stewart** on 26 Oct 1837, sold by him to James F. **Tucker**, and by sd **Tucker** to sd **Caho**. Signed Henry **Caho**, Maria **Caho** (RD). Wit Reuben **Shelby**, JCC. Rec 9 Nov 1838.

906. Page 473. 27 Aug 1836. Andrew H. **Tucker** and Ellen, his wife, to John **Daugherty**. For the sum of $275, 100 acres on the waters of Louret Creek, to be run off the SE end of a tract purchased by Zar **Sturdivant** of Thomas **Donnohoe**, and sold by him to Atticus **Tucker**, decd. Signed Andrew H. **Tucker**, Ellen (x) **Tucker**. Test Hugh F. **McKenelly**, W. B. **Woodruff**, John **Morris** (JP). Rec 11 Nov 1838.

907. Page 474. 16 Oct 1838. Austin **Hogard** and Mary, his wife, to Thomas J. **Finch**. For the sum of $60, 21.17 acres in Bois Brule Twp, part of a survey confirmed to William **Hickman**; beginning on a corner on **McCasland**'s line. Signed Austin **Hogard**, Mary (x) **Hogard** (RD). Wit John **Patterson**, Alfred L. **Parks** (JP). Rec 11 Nov 1838.

908. Page 475. 4 Jul 1838. William **Taylor** and Mary, his wife, to Reuben **Shelby**. For the sum of $1000, two tracts of land; Lot No. 63 in Perryville, fronting on Jackson St and St. Joseph St; and 53 acres, more or less, beginning 17 rods W of Perryville on James **Rice**'s line, also bounded by **Layton**, and part of the land originally granted to Barnard **Layton**. Signed William **Taylor**, Mary (x) **Taylor** (RD). Wit Mark **Brewer** (JP). Rec 24 Nov 1838.

909. Page 476. 6 Nov 1838. Thomas **Stewart** and Isabell T., his wife, to Peter J. **Tucker**. For the sum of $90, mortgage on 40 acres, being the NW 1/4, SW 1/4, Sec 21, Twp 36 N, Rng 11 W[sic]; entered by sd **Stewart** at the Land Office in Jackson on 26 Oct 1837. Sd **Stewart** owes a note to Henry **Caho** for $90 with interest by 3 Oct 1839, for which sd **Tucker** is bound to sd **Caho**. Signed Thomas **Stewart**, Isabell T. **Stewart** (RD). Wit Reuben **Shelby**, JCC. Rec 24 Nov 1838.

910. Page 477. 24 Nov 1838. Reuben **Shelby** to Jesse R. **Walker**. For the sum of $200, the S 1/2 of Lot No. 63 in Perryville, fronting on St. Joseph St and Jackson St, where sd **Walker** now lives. Signed Reuben **Shelby**. Wit Frederick C. **Hase**, Clerk. Rec 24 Nov 1838.

911. Page 477. 7 Nov 1838. John **Scott** of Ste. Genevieve Co., Mo. to Pierre **Menard** of Randolph Co., Ill. and John Bte. **Vallie** of Ste. Genevieve Co., Mo. For the sum of $640, 320 acres in Bois Brule Bottom; an equal and undivided half of a tract of 640 acres confirmed to John **Dunks** and patented to him by the U. S., then sold by sd **Dunks** to Henry **Clark**, by the Sheriff of Perry Co. to Timothy **Davis**, by sd **Davis** and wife to **Scott** & **Allen**, and also

by deed of release from sd **Clark**. Signed John **Scott**. Wit Conrad C. **Zeigler**, Jos. D. **Grafton**, Clerk of Ste. Genevieve Co., Mo. Rec 26 Nov 1838.

912. Page 478. 15 Aug 1838. John E. **Burgett** and Mary, his wife, to William **Burgett**. For the sum of $200, one undivided share, a 1/7 part, of three tracts; 640 arpens confirmed to John **Burgett** or his heirs, where John **Burgett**, decd, last resided; 165 acres adjoining the first tract on the S or SW side, known as the Donnohoe or old mill tract confirmed to Thomas **Donnohoe**, assignee of **Barnhart**; and the interest that John **Burgett**, decd, had in 400 arpens confirmed to the widow and legal representatives of Andrew **Cox**, decd, joining the John **Burgett** confirmation on the NW. John E. **Burgett** received or is entitled to the tracts by heirship as an heir of his father John **Burget**, decd. Signed J. E. **Burget**, Mary **Burget** (RD). Wit W. **Searcy** (JP). Rec 26 Nov 1838.

913. Page 479. 14 Jun 1837. John E. **Burgett** and Mary, his wife, of Bois Brule Bottom, to Timothy **Davis** of St. Marys Landing. For the sum of $120, on undivided 1/8 part of the interest of Nancy **Burget**, decd, mother of sd John E., in 400 arpens confirmed to the widow and legal representatives of Andrew **Cox**, decd, adjoining the tract where sd **Davis** now resides; and which sd John E. inherited as an heir of his mother. Signed J. E. **Burgett**, Mary **Burgett** (RD). Wit W. **Searcy** (JP). Rec 26 Nov 1838.

914. Page 480. 26 Nov 1838. Thomas J. **Finch** and Elizabeth, his wife, to Jesse **Dickson**. For the sum of $500, their undivided interest, being a 1/4 part, in two tracts in Sec 20, Twp 35 N, Rng 13 E; 98.39 acres, being the NE fractional 1/4; and 79.93 acres, being the E side of the NW fractional 1/4, and the same confirmed by patent on 31 May 1824 to the legal representatives of William **Burns**, decd. Sd Elizabeth is one of the legal representatives of sd decd. Signed Thomas J. **Finch**, Elizabeth **Finch**. Wit Fredk. C. **Hase**, Clerk. Rec 26 Nov 1838.

End of Book 2.

Deed Book 3

915. Page 1. 27 Nov 1838. Commissioners to partition lands of John **Stevenson**, decd, to James **Bell**. For the sum of $551.50, about 155.15 acres on the waters of Brazeau Creek about 16 miles SE of Perryville in Sec 9, Twp 34 N, Rng 13 E; where John **Stevenson** resided with his family at the time of his death. Sold on 27 Nov 1838 at order of Circuit Court issued Jul 1838 on petition to partition of the heirs and representatives of sd **Stevenson**, decd; being James **Bell** and Mary, his wife, Margaret A. **Stevenson**, Elizabeth **Stevenson**, James M. **Stevenson**, John L. **Stevenson**, and Sarah Ann **Stevenson**, infants by David **Luckey**, their guardian. Signed Samuel A. **Campbell**, Solomon **Cline**, Robert N. **Cochran**, Commissioners. Wit Frederick C. **Hase**, Clerk. Rec 27 Nov 1838.

916. Page 2. 31 Oct 1836. Michael **Burns** and Rebecca, his wife, to Alexander **Bailey**. For the sum of $60, 40.64 acres, more or less, being Lot No. 2 as set apart for sd **Burns** by Commissioners appointed by the Circuit Court; beginning at the most S corner of Lot No. 1. Signed Michael **Burns**, Rebeca **Burns** (RD). Wit Joab W. **Burgee** (JP). Rec 29 Nov 1838.

917. Page 3. 1 Dec 1838. James **Craig** to John **Thompson**. For the sum of $1 and in consideration of sd **Thompson** providing bail, deed of trust on one sorrel horse, two cows, four beds, two tables, and all furniture now in his dwelling. Sd **Thompson** has provided bail of $100 to guarantee that sd **Craig** shall appear at the next Circuit Court to answer a recognizance. Signed James **Craig**. Wit James **Rice** (JP). Rec 1 Dec 1838. [Marginal note: Satisfaction received on 26 Mar 1841. Signed John **Thompson**. Test Fredk. C. **Hase**, Clerk.]

918. Page 4. 4 Jun 1838. John **Grass** and Matilda, his wife, to Joseph **Grass**. For the sum of $125, all their right and interest to 640 acres adjoining Lewis **Cissel** on the S; a tract confirmed to his father Henry **Grass**. Signed John (x) **Grass**, Matilda (x) **Grass** (RD). Wit Joab W. **Burgee** (JP). Rec 4 Dec 1838.

919. Page 5. 27 Dec 1831. Simon **Duval** and Maryann, his wife, to George W. **Hudson**. For the sum of $300, 640 acres on the S fork of Saline Creek; being the land surveyed to sd **Duval** under Joseph **Tucker** senr., [Survey] 956 surveyed by Henry **Eliott** 6 & 7 Jan 1818; except 1/2 of the ore and mineral that may be discovered on the land is reserved for the use of Thomas **Riney**. Signed Simon **Duval**, Maryann **Duval**. Test Joseph **Duval**, Tresia **Duval** [now Treasia **Layton**] Wit James **Rice** (JP). Rec 7 Dec 1838. [A copy of the survey is included on p. 6 of the deed book.]

920. Page 7. 3 Mar 1838. James **McCauley** and Rosanna, his wife, to Colonel **Buckanan**. For the sum of $110, 80 acres, being the E 1/2, NW 1/4, Sec 23, Twp 35 N, Rng 11 E. Signed James **McCauley**, Rosanna **McCauley**. Wit Reuben **Shelby**, JCC, Wm. **Rutledge**. Rec 8 Dec 1838.

921. Page 7. [no date] David **Crips** to the **County of Perry**. For the sum of $60.50, mortgage on 130.66 acres in Bois Brule Twp, part of Survey No. 663 in Twp 36, Rng 11; purchased by sd **Crips** from the commissioners to partition the estate of Michael **Burns**, decd. Sd **Crips** borrowed the money form the County Road and Canal Fund, and it is due by 5 Aug 1839 with 10% interest per annum. Signed David (x) **Crips**. Test J. W. **Burgee**, Alfred L. **Parks** (JP). Rec 8 Dec 1838.

922. Page 8. 16 Nov 1838. William **Shaw** and Jane, his wife, to James **Cameron**. For the sum of $400, 79.89 acres, more or less, in Cinque Hommes Twp in two tracts in Sec 32, Twp 36 N, Rng 10 E; being the NW 1/4, NW 1/4, and NE 1/4, NW fractional 1/4; and purchased from the U. S. A. 24 Apr 1837. Signed William (x) **Shaw**, Jane (x) **Shaw** (RD). Wit Joseph P. **Wilkinson**, Frances V. **Brown**, Robert **Trotter** (JP). Rec 24 Dec 1838.

923. Page 9. 13 Dec 1838. Robert T. **Brown** and Catharine, his wife, to Joseph H. **Massey**. For the sum of $200, 160 acres, more or less, beginning at a white oak standing on the bank of Rock Spring Branch at the junction of a small branch. Signed R. T. **Brown**, Catharine (x) **Brown**. Wit Robert **Trotter** (JP). Rec 27 Dec 1838.

924. Page 10. 2 Jan 1839. Daniel **Omeara** to William **Mattingly**. For the sum of $1 and securing execution of a judgment, mortgage on one white and red pied muley cow and her calf, one red and white heiffer three years old, one bull two years old, and one clock. Sd **OMeara** will hold sd **Mattingly** harmless as security for a judgment in a suit instituted by Joel W. **Noel** and heard before James **Rice**, JP in Cinque Hommes Twp on 10 Nov 1838, for

$34.86 debt, and $.81 costs; with the obligation dated 13 Nov 1838 for the purpose of staying the execution. Signed Daniel **OMeara**. Wit Frederick C. **Hase**, Clerk. Rec 2 Jan 1839.

925. Page 11. 2 Jan 1839. John **Thompson** to John **Logan**. For the sum of $1 and in consideration of securing a note, mortgage on one red and white cow about five years old next spring; two red and white steers and two red heiffers, all two years old next spring and summer; and six sheep. Sd **Thompson** owes sd **Logan** a note for $36.97 due six months after date with interest. Signed John **Thompson**. Wit Fredk. C. **Hase**, Clerk. Rec 2 Jan 1839.

926. Page 12. 2 Jan 1839. Alfred F. **Sadler** to Robert S. **Manning**. For the sum of $1 and holding sd **Manning** harmless for a security, mortgage on one black mare and her colt, one stud colt with a bald face and white legs, one roan filley about three years old, four cows and three yearlings, two sows and ten pigs, three sheep, and one clock. Sd **Sadler** owes a judgment in favor of J. Pratte & Son heard before James **Rice**, JP, for $80.10 debt and costs, for which sd **Manning** is security; and sd **Sadler** also owes sd **Manning** $29.72. Signed Alfred F. **Sadler**. Wit Frederick C. **Hase**, Clerk. Rec 2 Jan 1839.

927. Page 13. 17 Dec 1838. Last will and testament of Charles **Stewart**. To his six oldest children William, Thomas, Charles, Mary, Sarah Ann, and James: $5 each in addition to what he has already given them. To his wife Mary Ann Jane: the balance of his estate after debts are paid, and at her death, to go to his children Sipreon, Elizabeth, Christeen, Margaret, Josiphean, and Rosamore. Wife Mary Ann Jane is appointed executrix. Signed Charles **Stewart**. Wit John **Logan**, Elizabeth (x) **McCauley**, Bennett **McCauley**, Frederick C. **Hase**, Clerk. Rec 14 Jan 1839.

928. Page 14. 9 Jan 1839. William **Guitar** to Charles **Miles**. For the sum of $150, mortgage on 80 acres in two tracts in Sec 30, Twp 36 N, Rng 12 E; 40 acres, being the SW 1/4, NW 1/4; and 40 acres, being the NW 1/4, NW 1/4. Sd **Guitar** owes sd **Miles** a note of even date to be paid in Jan 1840. Signed William (x) **Guitar**. Wit Joseph **Dufner**, Alfred L. **Parks** (JP). Rec 12 Jan 1839.

929. Page 15. 20 Jun 1836. Levi **Hagan** and Ann, his wife, to Michael **Hagan**. For the sum of $15, 40 acres, more or less, part of a survey of 640 acres originally granted and confirmed by the commissioners to Joseph **Hagan**, decd. Signed Levi (x) **Hagan**, Ann (x) **Hagan** (RD). Wit John **Layton** Senr. (JP). Rec 12 Jan 1839.

930. Page 16. 21 Jan 1839. John **Bright** to Ferdinand **Rozier**. For securing a note and the sum of $1, mortgage on one sorrel mare supposed to be nine years old; two heiffers, one two years old next spring, the other three years old next spring; and 15 hogs. Sd **Bright** owes sd **Rozier** a note for $75 bearing even date, with interest. Signed John **Bright**. Wit Fredk. C. **Hase**, Clerk. Rec 21 Jan 1839.

931. Page 17. 21 Jan 1839. Same to Joseph **French**. For securing a debt and the sum of $1, mortgage on seven sheep, two bulls one year old each, one cupboard, one beauro, one man's saddle, one ladies saddle, and one bay colt with white face. Sd **Bright** owes a debt of $63 to sd **French**, due in 12 months. Signed John **Bright**. Wit Fredk. C. **Hase**, Clerk. Rec 21 Jan 1839.

932. Page 18. 21 Jan 1839. Thomas **Stewart** and Isabelle, his wife, to Thomas **Riney**. For the sum of $150, Lot No. 16 in Perryville, fronting on Spring St; conveyed by Charles **Stewart** to sd Thomas **Stewart**. Signed Thomas **Stewart**, Isabelle **Stewart** (RD). Wit Fredk. C. **Hase**, Clerk. Rec 21 Jan 1839.

933. Page 19. 8 Jan 1839. Joseph **Duffner** and Anna, his wife, to William **Belsha**. For the sum of $211, 80 acres, being the E 1/2, NW 1/4, Sec 30, Twp 36 N, Rng 12 E. Signed Joseph (x) **Duffner**, Anna **Duffner** (RD). Wit H. D. **McCaslin**, Charles **Miles**, Alfred L. **Parks** (JP). Rec 22 Jan 1839.

934. Page 20. 16 Oct 1838. Thomas J. **Finch** and Elizabeth, his wife, to Elisha **Belsha**. For the sum of $350, 50 acres in Bois Brule Twp, part of a survey confirmed to William **Hickman**; beginning at a corner in George **Preston**'s line. Signed Thomas J. **Finch**, Elizabeth **Finch** (RD). Test John **Patterson**, Alfred L. **Parks** (JP). Rec 22 Jan 1839.

935. Page 21. 12 Dec 1838. Henry **Little** to Ransom A. **Little**. For love and affection, 152.06 acres, being the NE fractional 1/4, Sec 2, Twp 34 N, Rng 11 E; purchased by James F. **Abernathy** on 7 Apr 1829, and sold to Henry **Little** by the legal representatives of sd **Abernathy** on 25 Feb 1831. Signed Henry **Little**. Wit Alonzo **Abernathy**, JCC. Rec 26 Jan 1839.

936. Page 22. 17 Jun 1836. Last will and testament of Ignatius **Layton**. To his son Bede: $25. To his daughter Rosana and his son Vincent de Andre: $60 each. To his two youngest daughters Matilda and Ann Elizabeth: $75 each. He owns 335 acres and improvements at the place where he now lives, and that is to stay as a place of residence and home for his children until the youngest reaches age 18 or marries, and the land is then to be sold to the highest bidder. All the stock, farming utensils, and household furniture needed to enable his children who stay at home to live are to be sold at the same time. His negro man **Peter** is to be sold to some Roman Catholic in the neighborhood and as near the residence of his wife as practicable, or may be hired out by the year as his executors see fit. To his children John Baptist, Hillry, Joseph, Cecily, Mary Austin, Bede, Rosana, Severious, Vincent de Andre, Matilda, and Ann Elizabeth: the remainder of his estate, including a debt of $35 due from his son Joseph, to be equally divided. His eldest sons John Baptiste and Hillarey are named executors. Signed Ignatius **Layton**. Wit Isidore **Moore**, Eulila **Moore**, Elizabeth **Moore**, Frederick C. **Hase**, Clerk. Rec 26 Jan 1839.

937. Page 23. 12 Oct 1836. John **Layton** and Monica, his wife, to Joseph **Cissell**. For the sum of $200, Lot No. 59 in Perryville, adjoining on the E a lot occupied by William A. **Keyte**. Signed John **Layton**, Monica **Layton** (RD). Wit James **Rice** (JP). Rec 1 Feb 1839.

938. Page 24. 23 Nov 1833. Isac **Johnson** and Priscilla, his wife, to same. For the sum of $400, 400 acres, more or less, on a branch of the S fork of Saline Creek where sd **Johnson** now resides; joined on the S by Bernard & Clement **Cissell**, part of the same tract, and N by Rowland **Boiyd**. The rights to any lead mineral that may be discovered on the tract are reserved by Roland **Boyd** and wife to Joseph **Shoults**, by a deed dated 6 Dec 1825, and by deed from sd **Shoults** and wife to sd **Johnson** on 27 Jan 1830. Signed Isac (x) **Johnson**, Priscilla (x) **Johnson** (RD). Wit John **Layton** Senr (JP), Joseph D. **Simpson**. Rec 4 Feb 1839.

939. Page 26. 17 Dec 1838. Timothy **Davis**, admr of the estate of Nathan **Pusey**, decd, by Frederick C. **Hase**, County Court Clerk, to Timothy **Davis**. For the sum of $860, about 300 acres, of which 20 are improved, about five miles below the head of Bois Brule Bottom, fronting on the slough running between Horse Island and the main shore of the river; being the farm on which sd **Pusey** resided at the time of his death; adjoined above by the farm of William **Flynn**; and containing two log cabins. The tract was part of a tract formerly belonging to James **McLean**, decd, and purchased by Gustavus A. **Bird** for the use of the estate of Amos **Bird**, decd, and purchased by sd **Pusey** from Timothy **Davis**, admr of Amos **Bird**, decd, on 8 Feb 1832. Sd **Pusey** sold 100 acres off the back end to sd **Davis**, and the tract includes a moiety of 100 arpens on the upper side, fronting on the river, that was sold by James **McLean**, decd, to Francis **Cissell**, decd, then sold to sd **Pusey** by Lewis **Greeny** and Winifried, his wife, on 4 Feb 1833. Sold on 12 Mar 1836 at order of County Court issued Feb 1836 on a petition to sell the real estate of sd decd to pay debts of the estate. Signed Fredk. C. **Hase**, Clerk. Wit James **Rice** (JP). Rec 5 Feb 1839.

940. Page 28. 9 Jan 1839. Charles **Miles** to William **Guitar**. For the sum of $150, two tracts in Sec 20, Twp 36 N, Rng 12 E; 40 acres, being the SW 1/4, NW 1/4; and 40 acres, being the NW 1/4, NW 1/4. Signed Charles (x) **Miles**. Wit Joseph **Duffner**, Alfred L. **Parks** (JP). Rec 6 Feb 1839.

941. Page 29. 13 Aug 1838. Robert **Wilson** to Jacob **Shaner**. For the sum of $198, mortgage on 80 acres, being the W 1/2, SW 1/4, Sec 5, Twp 34 N, Rng 13 E. Sd **Wilson** owes sd **Shaner** a debt with 10% interest to be paid within two years. Signed Robert **Wilson**. Wit Elias **Barber** (JP). Rec 6 Feb 1839.

942. Page 31. 6 Dec 1838. James **Stricklin** and Margaret, his wife, to same. For the sum of $34, all the interest that James P. **Aldridge** and Louisa, his wife, formerly Louisa **Shaner**, have in 160 acres on Brazeau Creek, the NW 1/4 of 640 acres surveyed and confirmed to Benjamin **Harrison**; being Rng 13 E, Twp 34 N, Sec 16; conveyed by Jacob **Shaner** to John **Shaner**. Signed James **Strickland**, Margaret (x) **Strickland** (RD). Wit Elias **Barber** (JP). Rec 6 Feb 1839.

943. Page 32. 8 Feb 1839. George **Fenwick** and Margaret, his wife, to Adam **Kline**. For the sum of $400, 55 acres, beginning at a stone and hickory marked B. Signed George (x) **Fenwick**, Margaret (x) **Fenwick** (RD). Wit Fredk. C. **Hase**, Clerk. Rec 8 Feb 1839.

944. Page 33. 11 Feb 1839. Protest of the Steam Boat *Pawnee*. Deposition before James **Ferguson** (JP) outlining the loss of the steamboat, which left St. Louis on 27 Jan 1839 bound for New Orleans. The *Pawnee* ran aground on a gravel bar near Baleys Landing in the Mississippi River, and eventually struck an object and took on too much water to save. Signed James **Ferguson** (JP), John **Carlisle**, Master, John C. **Watson**, Pilot, H. B. **Curtis**, 1st Engineer, Joseph **Retherford**, Carpenter, John **Williame**. Test [illegible], James **Walter**. Rec 13 Feb 1839.

945. Page 36. 16 Feb 1839. Thomas **Stewart** to John W. **Noell**. For the sum of $32.13, two horse creatures, one a brown bay mare formerly owned by P. R. **Pratte** of Perryville about 12 or 13 years of age and about 14 hands high and named Hit, the other a sorrel mare formerly owned by John **Bright** and supposed to be aged about nine years. Sd **Stewart** owes sd **Noell** the debt with interest at 10% per annum, payable by 1 Apr 1839. Signed Thomas **Stewart**. Test James **Rice** (JP). Rec 16 Feb 1839.

946. Page 37. 10 May 1838. Pierre **Menard** and Angelique, his wife, of Kaskaskia, Ill. to Erastus **Davis**. For the sum of $690, 250 acres, more or less, near the head of Bois Brule Bottom; confirmed to Thomas **Donohoo** under Jesse **Evans**, and sold by Timothy **Davis**, admr of the estate of Amos **Bird**, decd, to sd **Menard**; commonly known as the Alfred Bird Place. Signed Pierre **Menard**, Angelique **Menard** (RD). Wit James **Hughes**, JP in Randolph Co., Ill. Rec 19 Feb 1839.

947. Page 38. 26 Aug 1837. Pouncy **Duggins** and Elizabeth, his wife, to Irenus **Whittenburg**. For the sum of $500, 150 arpens, more or less, in Bois Brule Bottom; that George **Campster** conveyed on 20 Jul 1836, and that was part of a piece confirmed to Archibald **Camster**'s representatives, formerly on the Mississippi River; bounded on the upper and back side by sd confirmation, and on the lower side by **Mordock**'s claim. Signed Pouncey **Duggens**, Elizabeth **Duggens** (RD). Wit Alonzo **Abernathy**, JCC. Rec 20 Feb 1839.

948. Page 39. 8 Oct 1838. Jacob **Shoults** of Cape Girardeau Co., Mo. to Alfred H. **Puckett**. For the sum of $1200, bond to guarantee a good title to the land described below. Sd **Puckett** has delivered a like obligation of William **Burns**, Jr. to sd **Shoults**, and sd **Burns** has purchased 255 acres, more or less, in Bois Brule Bottom, where sd **Burns** now lives; part of a tract confirmed to James **Burns**. Signed Jacob (x) **Shoults**. Wit Elisha **Eggers** (JP). Rec 21 Feb 1839.

949. Page 39. 9 Oct 1838. Mathias **Barringer** to William and Mathias M. **Barringer**, his sons. For natural love and affection and the sum of $1, about 80 acres, being the plantation on which he now lives a little N of Perryville, purchased from J. **Pratte** and P. R. **Pratte** on 31 Oct 1837; reserving control of the plantation to himself and to his wife Eliza **Barringer** after his death, so long as she remains unmarried. Signed Mathias **Barringer**. Wit Reuben **Shelby**, JCC. Rec 22 Feb 1839.

950. Page 40. 26 Feb 1839. Lewis **French** and Mary, his wife, to Peter J. **Tucker**. For the sum of $900, four tracts; __ acres, part of fractional 1/4 Sec 19, Twp 34, Rng 11 E, the remaining part of a tract, part of which had been conveyed to Robert S. **Manning** by Joseph B. **Mattingley** and Maria, his wife, on 30 Sep 1837 and the remainder to sd **French** by sd **Mattingley** and wife on 30 Sep 1837; 6 3/4 acres, more or less, on the N bank of Apple Creek in Sec 19, Twp 34, Rng 11, conveyed to sd **French** by Jones **Winfield** on 1 Sep 1830; 36 acres, more or less, conveyed to sd **French** by sd **Mattingley** and Maria, his wife, on 3 Dec 1834; and 80 acres, being the W 1/2, SE 1/4, Sec 19, Twp 34 N, Rng 11 E, patented by sd **French** on 1 Jun 1829. Signed Lewis **French**, Mary (x) **French** (RD). Wit Fredk. C. **Hase**, Clerk. Rec 26 Feb 1839.

951. Page 42. 26 Feb 1839. Peter J. **Tucker** and Mary, his wife, to Lewis **French**. For the sum of $900, 366 acres, 2 chains and links on Salien Crek, beginning at the corner of the tract sold to Joseph **Cissell**. Signed Peter J. **Tucker**, Mary Ann (x) **Tucker** (RD). Wit Fredk. C. **Hase**, Clerk. Rec 26 Feb 1839.

952. Page 43. 11 Mar 1839. Benjamin R. **Albright** and Nancey, his wife, to Morris **Block**. For the sum of $450, the N 1/2 of the N 1/2, Lot No. 34 in Perryville; beginning at the NW corner of the lot; but reserving the right to sd **Albright** to get water out of the well on the lot. Signed Benjamin R. **Albright**, Nancey **Albright** (RD). Wit Fredk. C. **Hase**, Clerk. Rec 11 Mar 1839.

953. Page 44. 24 Apr 1838. Francis Joseph **Doll** and Mary, his wife, to Roland **Rease** of New Orleans, La. For the sum of $150, 40 acres, being the NE 1/4, SW 1/4, Sec 36, Twp 35 N, Rng 10 E, and the same formerly conveyed by William Taylor and wife to sd **Dolle** on 14 Dec 1836 (2:181); also the undivided half of his claim in the grist mill purchased from sd **Taylor**, situated on 39.86 acres on the NW 1/4, SE 1/4, Sec 36, Twp 35 N, Rng 10 E, but only during the natural life of sd **Dolle** and no longer. Signed Francis Joseph **Dolle**, Mary (x) **Dolle** (RD). Wit James **Rice** (JP). Rec 15 Mar 1839.

954. Page 45. 29 Nov 1838. Mark **Miles** to Francis Leak **Jones** of the U. S. Army. For the sum of $600, 50 acres, more or less, a portion of a tract purchased in partnership by William **Winfield** and Lewis **Thorp**, and since partitioned by them on 8 Sep 1839; divided by a line running at about N and S from the part of the tract formerly sold to Daniel **Meridith** Jr. on 28 Oct 1837. Signed Mark **Miles**. Wit James **Rice** (JP), Thomas **Stewart**. Rec 19 Mar 1839.

955. Page 46. 26 Jan 1839. George Anthony **Ross** and Febby, his wife, to John **Ross**. For the sum of $250, mortgage on 40 acres, being the SW 1/4, NE 1/4, Sec 30, Twp 35 N, Rng 13 E. George **Ross** owes John **Ross** $150 [sic] with 10% interest from this date. Signed George A. **Ross**, Pheby **Ross** (RD). Wit James **Ferguson** (JP). Rec 23 Mar 1839.

956. Page 47. 20 Mar 1839. Alexander M. **Cobs** and Catharine, his wife, to Mathias **Barringer**. For securing a note for $100, mortgage on a lot in Perryville, beginning 20 feet E of the SW corner of Lot No. 57, purchased by sd **Cobbs** from sd **Barringer** on this date. Sd **Cobbs** is to pay sd **Barringer** a note for $100 with due in 12 months with 10% interest. Signed Alexander M. **Cobbs**, Catharine **Cobbs** (RD). Wit Reuben **Shelby**, JCC. Rec 23 Mar 1839.

957. Page 48. 11 Feb 1839. John **Scudder** and Rebeca, his wife, to William H. **Scudder**. For the sum of $1000, Block No. 25 in Birmingham. Signed John **Scudder**, Rebeca **Scudder**. Wit Augustus **Davis** (JP), John A. **Jones**. Rec 25 Mar 1839.

958. Page 49. 11 Feb 1839. Same and same to Arthur M. **Bliss**. For the sum of $200, Lot Nos. 13 & 14, Block No. 24 in Birmingham. Signed John **Scudder**, Rebeca **Scudder**. Wit Augustus **Davis** (JP), John A. **Jones**. Rec 25 Mar 1839.

959. Page 51. 25 Feb 1839. Same and same to William M. **Perrine**. For the sum of $300, Lot Nos. 1 & 2, Block No. 8 in Birmingham. Signed John **Scudder**, Rebeca **Scudder**. Wit A. M. **Bliss**, Michael **Anstadt**, Augustus **Davis** (JP). Rec 26 Mar 1839.

960. Page 52. 11 Feb 1839. Same and same to John **Cochran**. For the sum of $50, Lot No. 17, Block No. 12 in Birmingham. Signed John **Scudder**, Rebeca **Scudder**. Wit Augustus **Davis** (JP), John A. **Jones**. Rec 26 Mar 1839.

961. Page 53. 11 Feb 1839. Same and same to John A. **Jones**. For the sum of $100, Lot Nos. 15 & 16, Block No. 12 in Birmingham. Signed John **Scudder**, Rebeca **Scudder**. Wit Augustus **Davis** (JP), Michael **Anstadt**. Rec 26 Mar 1839.

962. Page 54. 25 Oct 1838. Henry S. **Osborne**, formerly of Perry Co., to Joseph C. **Lindsley** of St. Louis, Mo. For the sum of $350, 40 acres, being the W 1/2, Lot No. 4, NW 1/4, Sec 6, Twp 33 N, Rng 14 E. Signed Henry S. **Osborne**. Wit John **Scudder**, William H. **Scudder**, Augustus **Davis** (JP). Rec 26 Mar 1839.

963. Page 55. 11 Feb 1839. John A. **Jones** to John **Scudder**. For the sum of $150, mortgage on Lot Nos. 15 & 16, Block No. 12 in Birmingham. Sd **Jones** owes two notes with legal interest from this date, one for $75 due in six months, the other for $75 due in 12 months. Signed John A. **Jones**. Wit Augustus **Davis** (JP), Esther H. **Osborne**. Rec 26 Mar 1839.

964. Page 56. 25 Mar 1839. Alexander **Bailey** and Margaret, his wife, to Samuel **Allen**. For the sum of $400, two tracts; 40.50 acres, being Lot No. 1 assigned by the commissioners to partition among the heirs of Barnabas **Burns** to sd **Bailey** and wife, beginning at the line of Hezekiah P. **Harris**; and 40.64 acres, being Lot No. 2 assigned to Michael **Burns**, beginning at the most S corner of Lot No. 1. Signed Alexander **Bailey**, Margaret **Bailey**. Test Greer W. **Davis**, Fredk. C. **Hase**, Clerk. Proved by Jesse **Dickson** and Thomas J. **Finch**. Rec 25 Mar 1839.

965. Page 57. 25 Mar 1839. James **Cammeron** and Elizabeth, his wife, to Clement **Cissell**. For the sum of $400, __ acres on the S fork of Saline Creek, part of the survey of Henry **Grass**, decd; beginning at the E corner of sd survey, and bounded in part by Bernard **Cissell**. Signed James (x) **Cambron**, Elizabeth (x) **Cambron**. Wit Michael **Tucker**, Joseph D. **Simpson**, Fredk. C. **Hase**, Clerk. Rec 26 Mar 1839.

966. Page 58. 12 Mar 1839. John T. **Tucker** and Mary, his wife, to Thomas **McAtee**. For the sum of $300, 40 acres, being the SW 1/4, SW 1/4, Sec 12, Twp 34 N, Rng 10 E; entered by sd **Tucker** on 9 Feb 1837 in the land office at Jackson. Signed John T. (x) **Tucker**, Mary (x) **Tucker** (RD). Wit Reuben **Shelby**, JCC. Rec 26 Mar 1839.

967. Page 59. 26 Mar 1839. John P. **Finch** and Mary Ann, his wife, to Alexander **Bailey**. For the sum of $254, two tracts; 40 acres, more or less, being the NE 1/4, NE 1/4, Sec 19, Twp 35 N, Rng 12 E; and 40 acres, more or less, being the SE 1/4, SE 1/4, Sec 18, Twp 35 N, Rng 12 E. Signed John P. **Finch**, Mary Ann **Finch** (RD). Wit James **Rice** (JP). Rec 26 Mar 1839.

968. Page 61. 20 Oct 1838. James **McCauley** and Rosanna, his wife, to David **Pinkerton**. For the sum of $55, 40 acres, being the NE 1/4, SW 1/4, Sec 23, Twp 35 N, Rng 11 E; entered by sd **McCauley** at Jackson on 11 Mar 1837, No. 5179. Signed James **McCauley**, Rosanna **McCauley** (RD). Wit Reuben **Shelby**, JCC. Rec 1 Apr 1839.

969. Page 62. 14 Feb 1839. Mark **Brooks** of Pointe Coupee Parish, La. to John **Kinnison**. For the sum of $400, cancellation of a previous deed for 62 or 63 acres, more or less, in Bois Brule Bottom, part of a tract confirmed to Jones **Newsom**, father of Sinai **Kinnison**, wife of sd John, and where sd **Newsom** lived and died. Sd **Brooks** purchased the tract from sd **Kinnison** and wife in 1823 or 1824. Sd **Kinnison** could not produce a good and legal title, in consequence of failure to get a signature on a written agreement by Jones **Newsom** Junior, decd, another heir of John **Newsom** Senior. Signed Mark **Brooks**. Wit John B. **Brooks**, Samuel **Stewart**, Alexander **Ardery**, JP in Pointe Coupee Parish, La., Valery **Ledoux**, Dep. Clerk of Pointe Coupee Parish, La. Rec 2 Apr 1839.

970. Page 63. 5 Feb 1839. Richard **Cogan** by Sheriff Hugh **Wells** to Walter B. **Wilkinson** and Bernard **Pratte**. For the sum of $37, Lot No. 7 on St Marys St in Perryville. Sold on 26 Nov 1838 on a writ of fieri facias issued by Circuit Court 21 Aug 1838 on a petition for foreclosure filed 2 Mar 1838 by John **Walsh** and Edward **Walsh** against sd **Cogan**. Signed Hugh **Wells**, Sheriff. Wit Fredk. C. **Hase**, Clerk. Rec 3 Apr 1839.

971. Page 65. 26 Nov 1838. Same by Sheriff Hugh **Wells** to John and Edward **Walsh** of St. Louis Co., Mo. For the sum of $360, Lot No. 8 in Perryville on Main St and Spring St, and on which there is a brick house and outhouse. Sold on 26 Nov 1838 on a writ of fieri facias issued by Circuit Court 26 Jul 1838 on a petition for foreclosure filed 2 Aug 1838 by John and Edward **Walsh** against sd **Cogan**, for $745.16 debt and $128.28 costs. Signed Hugh **Wells**, Sheriff. Wit Fredk. C. **Hase**, Clerk. Rec 3 Apr 1839.

972. Page 67. 14 Nov 1837. U. S. A. to Thomas **Taylor**. Patent No. 4873 for 46.96 acres, being the E 1/2, Lot No. 2, NW 1/4, Sec 1, Twp 34 N, Rng 10 E. Signed Martin **Van Buren** by A. **Van Buren**, Secretary. Wit Jos. S. **Wilson**, Acting Recorder of the General Land Office. Rec in Vol. 9, page 426. Rec 5 Apr 1839.

973. Page 67. 2 Apr 1839. Thomas **Taylor** and Balbina, his wife, to John **Wilhelm**. For the sum of $180, 40.96 acres, being the E 1/2, Lot No. 2, NW 1/4, Sec 1, Twp 34 N, Rng 10 E. Signed Thomas **Taylor**, Balbina (x) **Taylor** (RD). Wit Mark **Brewer** (JP). Rec 5 Apr 1839.

974. Page 68. 6 Apr 1839. Edward **McLain** and Ellen, his wife, to Benjamin **Albright** and Isaac **Whitworth**. For the sum of $37 1/2, Lot Nos. 87 & 88 in Perryville. Signed Edward **McLain**, Elenor **McLain** (RD). Wit Fredk. C. **Hase**, Clerk. Rec 6 Apr 1839.

975. Page 70. 6 Apr 1839. Same and same to John G. **Basher**. For the sum of $22, Lot No. 93 in Perryville, fronting on West St and running back with St. Mary St to a street on the W boundary of Perryville. Signed Edward **McLain**, Elenor **McLain** (RD). Wit Fredk. C. **Hase**, Clerk. Rec 6 Apr 1839.

976. Page 71. 6 Apr 1838. Same and same to Casper H. **Fonderheider**. For the sum of $16, Lot No. 92 in Perryville, fronting on West St and running back to a street on the W boundary of Perryville. Signed Edward **McLain**, Elenor **McLain** (RD). Wit Fredk. C. **Hase**, Clerk. Rec 6 Apr 1839.

977. Page 72. 9 Apr 1839. William **Mattingley** to Robert **Manning**. For securing a debt and the sum of $1, mortgage on one four wheeled wagon and geer, one sorrel horse called Charley, and one brown mare called Blaze. Sd **Manning** is security for a debt owed by sd **Mattingley** to Joseph **Pratte** & Son for a judgment [amount not given] obtained on 5 Apr 1839 before James **Rice**, JP for Cinque Hommes Twp. Signed William **Mattingley**. Wit Fredk. C. **Hase**, Clerk. Rec 9 Apr 1839.

978. Page 74. 3 Jan 1839. Luther **Taylor** and Hannah, his wife, and Valerio **Faina** and Matilda, his wife, to Ruffus **Walker**. For the sum of $40, Lot No. 4 adjoining Perryville on the S, fronting on West St and High St; bounded on the E by Himan **Block** and N by **Murphey**. Signed Luther **Taylor**, Hannah **Taylor** (RD), Valerio **Faina**, Matilda **Faina** (RD). Wit James **Rice** (JP). Rec 11 Apr 1839.

979. Page 75. 20 Mar 1839. Mathias **Barringer** and Eliza, his wife, to Alexander M. **Cobbs**. For the sum of $100, part of a lot in Perryville, beginning 20 feet E of the SW corner of Lot No. 57; purchased from Joseph **Shoults** and wife by sd **Barringer**. Signed Mathias **Barringer**, Eliza **Barringer** (RD). Wit Reuben **Shelby**, JCC. Rec 12 Apr 1839.

980. Page 76. 15 Apr 1839. Rufus **Walker** to Hyman **Block**. For the sum of $35, Lot No. 4 adjoining Perryville on the S, fronting on West St and High St; bounded on the E by sd **Block** and N by B. **Murphey**. Signed Rufus **Walker**. Wit Frederick C. **Hase**, Clerk. Rec 15 Apr 1839.

981. Page 77. 25 Jul 1838. James **Farquher** of Washington Co., Mo. to John **Tucker** Senior. For the sum of $176.93, the undivided 1/2 of 680.55 acres confirmed to the representatives of James **Samuels**, decd; the same that sd **Tucker** purchased from Benjamine C. **Amareaux**, admr of George **Jackson**, decd for $.52 per acre ($353.86) on 25 Jul 1838; and of which sd **Farquher** was joint proprietor with sd **Jackson**. Signed James **Farquher**. Wit James **Rice** (JP), Ferdinand **Rozier** Jr. Rec 18 Apr 1839.

982. Page 78. 25 Jul 1838. Benjamine **Amoreaux**, admr of the estate of George E. **Jackson**, decd, to same. For the sum of $176.93 ($.52 per acre), undivided 1/2 of 680.55 acres, being Survey No. 958 in Twp 35 & 36 N, Rng 11 E confirmed to the representatives of James **Samuels**; about five miles NE of Perryville on the waters of Cinque Hommes Creek; beginning at a post. Sold on 24 Jul 1838 at order of Ste. Genevieve Co., Mo. Court issued May 1838 to sell sd land. Signed Benjamin C. **Amoreux**, admr of George E. **Jackson**, decd. Wit James **Rice** (JP), Ferdinand **Rozier** Jr. Rec 18 Apr 1839.

983. Page 81. 13 Apr 1839. William **Dean** and Teresa, his wife, to William **Taylor**. For the sum of $212.50, 40 acres, being the NW 1/4, NE 1/4, Sec 14, Twp 34 N, Rng 10 E. Signed William (x) **Dean**, Terressa (x) **Dean** (RD). Wit James **Rice** (JP). Rec 20 Apr 1839.

984. Page 82. 18 Mar 1835. James C. **Moore** and Rebeca, his wife, to John **Logan**. For the sum of $250, 255 acres, more or less, on the waters of Cinque Hommes Creek; conveyed to sd **Moore** by Isadore **Moore** and wife on 1 Jul 1830. Signed James C. **Moore**, Rebeca **Moore** (RD). Wit R. S. **Dorsey** (JP). Rec 3 May 1839.

985. Page 83. 6 May 1839. Joseph **Pratte** and Marie, his wife, Robert T. **Brown** and Catharine, his wife, Emilie **Wilkinson**, and Francois **Valle** Junr. Deed of partition for 7056 arpents on Saline Creek in Ste. Genevieve and Perry counties granted to Francois **Valle** senr, decd, and confirmed to him or his legal representatives on 4 Jul 1836. His heirs are Francois **Valle** Jnr., Charles C. **Valle**, Catharine **Valle** intermarried with Robert T. **Brown**, Emilie **Valle** intermarried with Walter **Wilkinson**, Celeste **Valle** intermarried with George **Bullitt**, Julia **Valle** intermarried with Walter **Fenwick**, and Mary **Valle** intermarried with Joseph **Pratte**. Julia **Fenwick**, by her last will and testament, bequeathed her share to Catharine **Brown**, wife of Robert T. **Brown**. Sd **Brown** also purchased a 1/7 share from Nancy **Bullitt**, devisee of George **Bullitt**, heir at law of Celeste M. **Allen**, formerly Celeste **Bullitt**. Charles C. **Valle** sold 900 arpents of his 1/7 part to Charles **Gregoire**, leaving him 180 arpents; but is to receive his share, by mutual agreement, out of the portion of Robert T. **Brown**, the above named 900 arpents and the 180, totaling 1080 arpents as the share of sd Charles C. Sd **Pratte** has since purchased the interest of Charles **Gregoire**. Robert T. **Brown** and Catharine, his wife, get Lot Nos. 2 & 6, containing 3397.21 acres; Joseph **Pratte** and Marie, his wife, as purchasers from sd **Gregoire** and heirs of Francois **Valle**, decd, get Lot Nos. 4 & 5, containing 1756.69 acres; Emily **Wilkinson**, formerly Emily **Valle**, gets Lot No. 1, containing 847.72 acres; and Francois **Valle** gets Lot No. 3, containing 650.74 acres. Signed Robert T. **Brown**, Catharine **Brown**, Fracois **Valle**, Joseph **Pratte**, Marie **Pratte**, Emilie **Wilkinson**. Wit John F. **Hase**, Dep Clerk. Rec 6 May 1839.

986. Page 86. 27 Mar 1839. John **Hager** and Cyntha, his wife, and Hugh M. **Saddler** to William **Harrington**. For the sum of $20, 2/9 of an undivided tract of 80 acres, the NE 1/4, SE 1/4 and NW 1/4, NE 1/4 in Sec 8, Twp 35 N, Rng 12 E; entered by Zachariah **Saddler**, decd; and which passed to them by heirship. Signed John **Hager**, Cyntha (x) **Hager**, Hugh M. (x) **Saddler**. Wit James **Rice** (JP), John C. **Hase**, Dep Clerk. Rec 6 May 1839.

987. Page 87. 13 Feb 1839. Hugh M. **Saddler** and John **Hager** to same. For the sum of $100, their undivided interest in slaves **Milley**, **Susan**, **Haner**, and **Wiiliam**; belonging to the heirs of Zachariah **Saddler**, decd. Signed Hugh M. (x) **Saddler**. John **Hager**. Wit James **Rice** (JP). Rec 6 May 1839.

988. Page 88. 2 Apr 1833. Isidore **Moore** and Lear, his wife, to Richard **Maddock**. For the sum of $100, their undivided 1/3 part of about 239 acres, more or less, on the S fork of Saline Creek in Sec 15, Twp 35 N, Rng 10 E; being 159.83 acres, the NW fractional 1/4 and 39.13 acres, the SW fractional 1/4; owned and occupied by the late Nicholas **Moore**, father of sd Isidore, and purchased by him from Ignatius **Layton** and Nicholas **Miles** on 31 Jul 1821. Signed Isidore **Moore**, Leah (x) **Moore** (RD). Wit Eulalia **Moore**, Cecily **Moore**, Elizabeth **Moore**, John **Layton** (JP). Rec 7 May 1839.

989. Page 89. 21 Mar 1839. Edward **McLain** and Walter **McLain** to Jacob **Shaner**. For the sum of $87.50, mortgage on 160 acres, the SE corner of Survey No. 2129 confirmed to Bernard **Layton**, in Twp 35 N, Rng 11 E. A note of even date is payable 12 months after date. Signed Edward **McLain**, Walter **McLain**. Wit Elias **Barber** (JP). Rec 7 May 1839. [Marginal note: Full satisfaction received on 2 Feb 1841. Signed Jacob **Shaner**. Test Fredk. C. **Hase**, Clerk.]

990. Page 90. 23 Oct 1833. Aristides **Anduze** of Iberville Parish, La. to John **Timon** of St. Marys Seminary. Power of attorney to convey an undivided 1/2 of 640 acres, more or less, on the waters of Brazeau Creek (see 3:91). Signed A. **Anduze**. Wit J. F. **Scott**, Celestia **Roth**, Louis **Petit**, Notary Public in Iberville Parish, La., A. B. **Roman**, Governor of La., by George **Enstis**, Sec. of State of La., as to sd **Petit**. Rec 8 May 1839.

991. Page 91. 8 May 1839. Same by his atty in fact Revd. John **Timon**, and Thomas H. **Benton** by his atty in fact Revd. John **Timon** to Johann George **Gube**. For the sum of $3200, quit claim to 640 acres, more or less, as described in the preceding deed. The tract was granted and confirmed to Robert **Hinkston** under settlement right, and afterward conveyed by the Sheriff of Ste. Genevieve Co. to Reuben **Smith** on 16 Aug 1815 (Ste. Genevieve Co. Book B:33), conveyed by sd Smith to Luke Edward **Lawless** on 14 Dec 1819, by the Sheriff of Perry Co. to sd **Anduze** under decree of foreclosure on 19 Nov 1822 (1:51), then 1/2 was conveyed by sd **Anduze** by his atty in fact Edmund **Sulnier** to sd **Benton** and Thomas **Biddle** for the benefit of Virginia **Lawless**, wife of sd Luke Edward on 27 May 1826 (1:147, 148), and sd **Biddle** is now dead. Signed John **Timon**, atty in fact for Aristides **Anduze**, Thomas H. **Benton** by his atty in fact John **Layton** senr. Wit J. **Hammilton**, John **Layton** senr. (JP). Rec 8 May 1839.

992. Page 93. 10 May 1839. John **Scott** of Ste. Genevieve Co., Mo. to Luke E. **Lawless** of St. Louis Co., Mo. For the sum of $100, quit claim to 640 acres on Brazeau Creek as described in the preceding deed (3:91). Signed John **Scott**. Wit Adolphus **Rozier**, Joseph D. **Grafton**, Clerk of Ste. Genevieve Co., Mo. Rec 8 May 1839.

993. Page 94. 1 May 1839. Luke Edward **Lawless** of St. Louis, Mo. to Johann George **Gube**. For the sum of $1, all his interest in the preceding deed and the land herein described (3:91, 93). Signed L. E. **Lawless**. Wit John **Ruland**, Circuit Clerk of St. Louis Co., Mo. Rec 8 May 1839.

994. Page 95. 11 Nov 1831. Thomas H. **Benton**, surviving trustee of Virginia **Lawless**, to Revd. John **Timon**. Power of attorney to convey the moiety of the tract described in the preceding deeds (3:91, 93, 94). Signed Thomas H. **Benton**. Wit Archibald **Gamble**, County Clerk of St. Louis Co., Mo. Rec 8 May 1839.

995. Page 96. 1 Aug 1838. U. S. A. to Henry **Kunze**. Patent No. 5775 for 40 acres, being the NW 1/4, SE 1/4, Sec 6, Twp 34 N, Rng 11 E. Signed Martin **Van Buren** by [illegible], Secretary. Wit Joseph S. **Wilson**, Acting Recorder of the General Land Office. Rec in Vol. 11:444. Rec 14 May 1839.

996. Page 97. 14 Apr 1838. Henry **Kunz** to John B. **Taylor**. For the sum of $100, 40 acres as described in the preceding deed (3:96). Signed Henry **Kunz**. Wit Mark **Brewer** (JP). Rec 14 May 1839.

997. Page 97. 8 May 1839. John B. **Taylor** to Pricilla **Taylor**. For natural love and affection for his wife and for her future support, 40 acres as described in the preceding deeds (3:96, 97), one yoak of oxen, one cow with her yearling, one horse, and all his hogs and household furniture. Signed John B. **Taylor**. Wit James **Evans**, Thomas **Thompson**, Frederick C. **Hase**, Clerk. Rec 14 May 1839.

998. Page 98. 22 Apr 1839. Last will and testament of John **Ross**, decd. To his wife Hannah: his Indian Creek farm and his negro man **Georg** as long as she remains a widow, with the benefit of his horses, cows, sheep, hogs, and poultry with farming utensils and plantation wagon for her and his family that live with her; and if she marries only what the law allows her. To his daughter Peggy: $100. To his son Zenas N.: $5. To his daughter Jane L.: $100. His son Robert is to sell his Brazeau tract, with 1/2 to go to his

daughter Peggy, the other 1/2 equally divided between Jenny and Ibby **Ross**. To his daughter Lidia **Barber**: $15. To his daughter Betsey **Barber**: $5. To Rachel R. **Ross**: $10. To his daughter Ibby: $100 and a horse worth $65 or $70. To his son George A.: $25. None of the above legacies will be demanded during the life or widowhood of his wife Hannah. When his family is dissolved and at the death or marriage of his widow, the land not mentioned to divided equally between his two younger sons Robert H. and John E. His rifle gun is to remain on the farm as long as his family lives there. Should any minerals or mines be discovered on the Indian Creek farm, his sons Zeno N. and Robert will management the same, and divide the profits among the rest of the family. His wife Hannah and son Robert H. are appointed executors. Signed John **Ross**. Wit James **Ferguson**, Joseph **Underhiner**, Moses **Martin**, Fredk. C. **Hase**, Clerk. Rec 16 May 1839.

999. Page 100. 20 May 1839. John M. **Odin** to Joseph **Underiner**. For the sum of $52.50, 40 acres, being the NW 1/4, SE 1/4, Sec 27, Twp 34 N, Rng 12 E; as described in Patent No. 6001 received 23 Jan 1838. Signed John M. **Odin**. Wit Joseph V. **Wiseman**, John **Layton** (JP). Rec 16 May 1839.

1000. Page 101. 11 Jun 1839. Clement **Vessels** and Catharine, his wife, and Hillary **Vessells** and Monica, his wife, to Henry **Drewry**. For the sum of $32, their undivided interest in two tracts that they hold as heirs of Charles **Vessels**, decd, father of sd Clement; 150.27 acres, being the SE fractional 1/4, Sec 22, Twp 36 N, Rng 10 E; and 26 acres, more or less, in Twp 36, Rng 10 E. Signed Clement (x) **Vessells**, Catharin (x) **Vessells** (RD), Hillary (x) **Vessells**, Monica (x) **Vessells** (RD). Wit James **Rice** (JP). Rec 11 Jun 1839.

1001. Page 102. 11 Jun 1839. Robert S. **Manning** and Nancey, his wife, to Peter J. **Tucker**. In consideration of a contract between Lewis **French** and sd **Tucker**, and for the sum of $1, 50 1/2 acres, more or less, part of a fractional 1/4 Sec 19, Twp 34 N, Rng 11 E; bounded on the N & W by the township line. Signed Robert S. **Manning**, Nancey (x) **Manning** (RD). Wit James **Evans**, Fredk. C. **Hase**, Clerk. Rec 11 Jun 1839.

1002. Page 103. 10 Apr 1839. Moses S. **Harris** and Mary A., his wife, of Marion Co., Mo. to Johann Gorge **Gube** of St. Louis Co., Mo. For the sum of $1000, 341 acres, beginning at the upper corner of James **Manning**'s survey on the Mississippi River, and also bounded by G. A. **Hamilton** and Brazeau Creek, as described in a deed by Robert S. **Manning** and others to sd **Harris**. Signed Moses S. **Harris**, Mary A. **Harris** (RD). Wit Jordan J. **Montgomery**, Clerk of Marion Co., Mo. Rec 11 Jun 1839.

1003. Page 105. 23 Apr 1839. George W. **Martin** and Catharine, his wife, to same. For the sum of $1000, 80 acres, more or less, being the W 1/2, NE 1/4, Sec 34, Twp 34 N, Rng 13 E as described in Patent No. 1406. Signed George W. **Martin**, Catharine **Martin** (RD). Wit J. F. **Hamilton**, C. Ch. W. **Miller**, Augustus **Davis** (JP). Rec 11 Jun 1839.

1004. Page 106. 11 Jun 1839. Robert S. **Manning** and Anna, his wife, to same. For the sum of $372.50, 298.98 acres, more or less, beginning at the NW corner of James **Manning**'s Survey No. 2130, bounded in part by George A. **Hamilton**'s survey; part of a tract of 640 acres confirmed to John **Manning** on 30 Mar 1826, and bequeathed by him to his sons John **Manning** and Robert S. **Manning** in his last will and testament dated 27 Dec 1813 (Ste. Genevieve Co. Will Records). Signed Robert S. **Manning**, Anna (x) **Manning** (RD). Wit Fredk. C. **Hase**, Clerk. Rec 11 Jun 1839.

1005. Page 108. 11 Jun 1839. Gabriel **Duvall** to Hyman **Block**. For the sum of $27, Lot No. 45 in Perryville, fronting on Jackson St and South St. Signed Gabriel **Duvall**. Wit Reuben **Shelby**, JCC. Rec 11 Jun 1839.

1006. Page 108. 7 May 1839. Luther **Taylor** and Hannah, his wife, to Peter R. **Pratte**. For the sum of $265, Lot No. 74 and a certain house in Perryville, latterly in the possession of James **Saddler** and formerly possessed and occupied by Pius **Brewer**. Signed Luther **Taylor**, Hannah **Taylor** (RD). Wit James **Rice** (JP). Rec 11 Jun 1839.

1007. Page 109. 20 Apr 1838. Isaac **Greeniwalt**, William **Greeniwalt**, Frederick **Greeniwalt**, Polly **Estes**, Catharine **Estes**, Reuben **Estes** and Betsey, his wife, and David **Morgan** and Susan, his wife, all heirs of John **Greeniwalt**, decd, to John **Logan**. For the sum of $100, 640 acres in Bois Brule Bottom on Bois Brule Creek, confirmed to John **Greeniwalt** Jur. by the Commissioners; on the E side of James **Newsom**'s survey. Signed Isaac (x) **Greenewalt**, Polly (x) **Esters**, William (x) **Greenewalt**, Catharine (x) **Estes**, Frederick (x) **Greenewalt**, Elizabeth (x) **Greenewalt** (RD) [wife of William], Susannah (x) **Morgan** (RD), Matilda (x) **Greenewalt** (RD) [wife of Isaac], David (x) **Morgan**, Reuben (x) **Estes**, Elizabeth (x) **Estes**. Wit W. **Searcy** (JP), Elisha **Eggers** (JP), Frederick C. **Hase**, Clerk, Margaret **Dickson**, George **Preston**, John F. **Hase**, Dep Clerk. Rec 6 May 1839.

1008. Page 112. 13 Mar 1837. Richard **Cogan** and Elizabeth, his wife, to John **Oshea**. For the sum of $240, 40 acres, on the waters of Meete River; being the NE 1/4, SW 1/4, Sec 14, Twp 35 N, Rng 12 E. Signed Richard **Cogan**, Elizabeth **Cogan** (RD). Wit R. T. **Brown**, Fredk. C. **Hase**, Clerk. Rec 12 Jun 1839.

1009. Page 113. 15 Jun 1839. William **Guitar** to Charles **Miles**. For the sum of $150, 80 acres in two tracts in Sec 30, Twp 36 N, Rng 12 E; 40 acres, being the SW 1/4, NW 1/4; and 40 acres, being the NW 1/4, NW 1/4. Signed William **Guitar**. Wit A. L. **Parks** (JP). Rec 20 Jun 1839.

1010. Page 114. 22 Jun 1839. Edward **McLane** and Ellen, his wife, to James P. **Cogan**. For the sum of $36.50, Lot No. 91 in Perryville. Signed Edward (x) **McLane**, Ellen (x) **McLane** (RD). Wit James **Rice** (JP). Rec 22 Jun 1839.

1011. Page 115. 16 Aug 1838. William **Taylor** and Mary, his wife, to Henry **Caho**. For the sum of $300, 100 acres, more or less, beginning where the section line between Sec 13 & Sec 12 of Twp 35 N, Rng 10 E; intersects **Moore**'s line; about 90 acres of which was entered by Henry **McAtee**, and the balance by Thomas **McAtee**. Signed William **Taylor**, Mary (x) **Taylor** (RD). Wit Reuben **Shelby**, JCC. Rec 28 Jun 1839.

1012. Page 116. 3 Jul 1839. Benjamine R. **Allbright** to John W. **Noell** and Henry C. C. **Tate**. For securing debts and the sum of $1, mortgage on part of Lot No. 34 in Perryville, fronting on Main St and situated between Hyman **Block** on the S and Morris **Block** on the N. Sd **Allbright** owes two notes of even date with 10% interest after due date to sd **Noell** and **Tate**; one for $100 payable by 25 Dec next; and one for $300 payable 12 months. Signed B. R. **Allbright**. Wit Fredk. C. **Hase**, Clerk. Rec 3 Jul 1839.

[Marginal note: Full satisfaction received on 2 Nov 1846. Signed John W. **Noell**, surviving partner of Noell & Tate. Test J. W. **Noell**, Recorder.]

1013. Page 117. 12 Mar 1839. Samuel **Merry** and Catharine M., his wife, of St. Louis, Mo. to John **Scudder**. For the sum of $400, two tracts on Township Island; 55.90 acres, being the NE part of fractional Sec 5, Twp 33 N, Rng 14 E; and 101.55 acres, being fractional Sec 33, Twp 34 N, Rng 14 E. Signed Samuel **Merry**, C. M. **Merry** (RD). Test M. P. **Ledue**, JCC in St. Louis Co., Mo. Rec 6 Jul 1839.

1014. Page 119. 27 Jun 1839. William **Taylor** and Mary, his wife, to Ferdinand **Rozier** Junier. For the sum of $500, 230 acres, more or less, in Sec 12, Twp 35 N, Rng 10 E; beginning at the corner of Henry **Caho**'s land purchased from sd **Taylor**, on the section line between Sec 12 & Sec 13; bounded in part by James **Moore**'s confirmation. land sold by sd **Taylor** to Michael **Spalding**, and land sold by sd **Taylor** to sd **Caho**; entered by Thomas **McAtee** and sold to sd **Taylor**. Signed William **Taylor**, Mary (x) **Taylor** (RD). Wit Reuben **Shelby**, JCC. Rec 8 Jul 1839.

1015. Page 120. 1 Jun 1839. William C. **Moore** and Mary, his wife, to Singleton H. **Kimmel**. For the sum of $400, the undivided 1/2 of 508.77 acres on Apple Creek; sold on 28 Nov 1837 by Alfred A. **McLane**, John **Hofman**, and James **Elmore**, commissioners to make partition of the land amongst the heirs of George **Keller**, decd, on order of Circuit Court to sd **Moore** and sd **Kimmel**. Signed William C. **Moore**, Mary T. **Moore** (RD). Wit Fr. **Flack**, Dep. Clerk of Cape Girardeau Co., Mo. Rec 22 Jul 1839.

1016. Page 122. 12 Jun 1839. Johann George **Gube** to Johann Gottlieb **Palisch**. For the sum of $1000, 80 acres, being the W 1/2, NE 1/4, Sec 34, Twp 34 N, Rng 13 E; patented to George Washington **Martin** on 15 Oct 1833 as No. 1406 (General Land Office Book 3:315). Signed Johann George **Gube**. Test Benjamine **Davis**, Christian Gottfried **Schlimpert**, Augustus **Davis** (JP). Rec 23 Jul 1839.

1017. Page 123. 12 Jul 1839. Same to Christian Gottfried **Schlimpert**. For the sum of $350, 80 acres, being the NW 1/4, SW 1/4 and SE 1/4, SW 1/4, Sec 3, Twp 34 N, Rng 13 E; patented on 14 May 1839 as No. 6856. Signed Johann George **Gube**. Test Benjamine **Davis**, Johann Gottlieb **Palisch**, Augustus **Davis** (JP). Rec 23 Jul 1839.

1018. Page 124. 25 Jul 1839. Richard **Cogan** by Sheriff Hugh **Wells** to John **Logan**. For the sum of $1, Lot No. 27 in Perryville. Sold on 26 Nov 1838 on a writ of fieri facias issued by Circuit at Jul Term 1838 on petition of John **Walsh** and Edward **Walsh** for foreclosure of mortgage against sd **Cogan** for debt, interest, and costs. Signed Hugh **Wells**, Sheriff. Wit Fredk. C. **Hase**, Clerk. Rec 25 Jul 1839.

1019. Page 125. 25 Jul 1839. Amzi **Osborn** by Sheriff Hugh **Wells** to John **Scudder**. For the sum of $13, 80 acres, being Lot No. 3, NE 1/4, Sec 2, Twp 33 N, Rng 12 E. Sold at order of Circuit Court issued at Mar 1839 Term on a judgment against sd **Osburn** and in favor of J. B. **Bailey** for an action of debt for $481, and $86.53 damages and costs. Signed Hugh **Wells**, Sheriff. Wit Fredk. C. **Hase**, Clerk. Rec 25 Jul 1839.

1020. Page 127. 28 Mar 1839. William Bowie **Cowan** of Washington Co., Mo. to Rensselaer N. **Haven** of Pittsburgh, Pa. For the sum of $200, one undivided 1/3 part of six parcels entered by sd **Cowan**, John Epee **Cowan**, and E. H. **Eastman** in partnership; being the E 1/2, NE 1/4, Sec 16, Twp 35 N, Rng 10 E; the W 1/2, SE 1/4, Sec 28, Twp 35 N, Rng 10 E; the N 1/2, SW 1/4, Sec 35, Twp 34 N, Rng 10 E; the E 1/2, SW 1/4, Sec 11, Twp 34 N, Rng 9 E; the W 1/2, NW 1/4, Sec 33, Twp 35 N, Rng 10 E; and the NE 1/4, NE 1/4, Sec 35, Twp 35 N, Rng 9 E. Signed William Bowie **Cowan**. Wit M. B. **Lowrie**, Alderman in Pittsburgh, Pa. [No rec date.]

1021. Page 128. 1 Aug 1839. John W. **Noell** and Mary A., his wife, to Henry C. C. **Tate**. For the sum of $25, undivided 1/2 of the SE 1/4, NW fractional 1/4, Sec 32, Twp 35 N, Rng 11 E. Signed John W. **Noell**, Mary **Noell** (RD). Wit Reuben **Shelby**, JCC. Rec 1 Aug 1839.

1022. Page 129. 16 Oct 1838. Thomas J. **Finch** and Elizabeth, his wife, to John **Patterson** Junior. For the sum of $350, 50 acres in Bois Brule Twp, part of a survey confirmed to William **Hickman**; beginning at a corner in **McCasland**'s line. Signed Thomas J. **Finch**, Elizabeth **Finch**. Wit A. **Hogard**, Alfred L. **Parks** (JP). Rec 1 Aug 1839.

1023. Page 130. 13 Aug 1838. Christian **Hahn** and Elizabeth, his wife, to John **Hahn**. For the sum of $13.06, 10.45 acres, beginning at the S end of the NE 1/4, SE fraction, Sec 33, Twp 34 N, Rng 9 E. Signed Christian (x) **Hahn**, Elizabeth (x) **Hahn** (RD). Wit John **Layton** Senr (JP), Maria **Layton**. Rec 5 Aug 1839.

1024. Page 131. 12 Apr 1839. George A. **Hamilton** to James **Fenwick** and Chloe **Fenwick**, heirs of James J. **Fenwick**, decd. For the sum of $150, 44 acres, more or less, bounded on the N and W by the dower lands of the decd mother of sd **Hamilton**, S by the heirs of Harrison **Young**, decd. and E by the Mississippi River. Signed George A. **Hamilton**. Wit Leo **Fenwick**, Robert P. **Slaughter**, Elias **Barber** (JP). Rec 7 Aug 1839.

1025. Page 132. 1 May 1839. Richard **Maddock** Senr and Elizabeth, his wife, assignee of Isadore **Moore**; Bede **Moore** and Verlinger, his wife; and James N. **Moore** and Sally, his wife; all heirs of Nicholas **Moore**, decd. Deed of partition for 239 acres in three tracts; 39.13 acres, part of a tract granted to Michael **Tucker**, as per a deed from Ignatius **Layton**, Nicholas **Miles**, and their wives on 31 Jul 1821; 159.83 acres adjoining the first tract and lying N and NE of it, being the fractional 1/4, Sec 15, Twp 35 N, Rng 10 E; and 40.05 acres lying between the first two tracts, being a wedge-shaped parcel, the SW fractional 1/4, Sec 15, Twp 35 N, Rng 10 E as patented on 31 May 1824. To Bede **Moore**: 93 1/2 acres, more or less, beginning on the westernmost line of the NW fractional 1/4, near the N bank of the S fork of Saline Creek at two sycamores, one marked BM and the other JM. To James **Moore**: 78 1/4 acres, beginning at the two sycamores, and bounded in part by Michael **Tucker**. To Richard **Maddock**: 67 1/4 acres, beginning at a stone near a hickory and two white oaks, bounded in part by sd **Tucker**, Ignatius **Layton**, and Nicholas **Miles**, and including the improvements of sd decd. Signed Richard **Maddock**, Bede **Moore**, James N. **Moore**, Sally (x) **Moore** (RD). Wit James **Rice** (JP), William **Moore**. Rec 15 Aug 1839.

1026. Page 135. 12 Aug 1839. Edward **McLain** and Lemanow [**Allen**], his wife, to John **Schmidt**. For the sum of $200, 40 acres, more or less, being the SE 1/4, SE 1/4, fractional Sec 15, Twp 34 N, Rng 13 E, and No. 6867. Signed Edward **McLain**, Allen (x) **McLain** (RD). Wit Henry C. **Bimpage**, Jacob **Shaner**. Elias **Barber** (JP). Rec 20 Aug 1839.

The transactions following are numbered in the Deed Book, starting with No. 808.

1027. Page 136. 7 Apr 1838. Joseph **Duvall**, Gabriel M. **Duvall**, and Ann Arpy **Abernathy**, heirs of John **Duvall**, decd, to Bartholimew **Murphey**. For a valuable consideration paid to sd decd, Lot No. 83 in Perryville. Signed Joseph **Duvall**, Gabl. M. **Duvall**, Ann Arpy **Abernathy**. Wit James **Rice** (JP). Rec 26 Aug 1839. [No. 808]

1028. Page 137. 26 Aug 1839. Leo **Mattingley**, admr de bonis non of the estate of James **Mattingley**, decd, to Gabriel M. **Duvall**. For the sum of $50, Lot No. 81 in Perryville, fronting on St. Joseph St; purchased by James **Mattingley** from the commissioners in his lifetime. Sold on 27 Mar 1838 at order of County Court issued Nov [1837] to pay debts of sd estate. Signed Leo **Mattingley**, admr de bonis non of the estate of James **Mattingley**, decd. Wit James **Rice** (JP), Peter R. **Pratte**. Rec 26 Aug 1839. [No. 809]

1029. Page 138. 30 Aug 1839. Ferdinand **Belsha** to James R. **Beasly**. For the sum of $525, two tracts in Sec 24, Twp 36 N, Rng 11 E originally purchased by John **Thompson** on 15 Dec 1837; 40 acres, being the NE 1/4, SE 1/4, Sec 24, Twp 36 N, Rng 11 E; and 40 acres, being the NW 1/4, S[E] 1/4, Sec 24, Twp 36 N, Rng 11 E. Signed Ferdinand **Belsha**. Wit Lewis **Dickinson**, Fredk. C. **Hase**, Clerk. Rec 30 Aug 1839. [No. 810]

1030. Page 139. 26 Aug 1839. Gabriel M. **Duvall** to Walter B. **Wilkinson**. For the sum of $50, Lot No. 81 in Perryville, fronting on St. Joseph St; that sd **Duvall** purchased from Leo **Mattingley**, admr de bonis non of the estate of James **Mattingley**, decd. Signed G. M. **Duvall**. Wit Reuben **Shelby**, JCC. Rec 3 Sep 1839. [No. 811]

1031. Page 140. 4 Sep 1839. Joseph D. **Burns** to Royal **Thompson** of Cape Girardeau Co., Mo. For the sum of $102, mortgage on two tracts in Sec 26, Twp 35 N, Rng 11 E; 40 acres, being the SE 1/4, SW 1/4; and 40 acres, being the NE 1/4, SE 1/4. Sd **Burns** owes sd **Thompson** a note of even date. Signed Joseph D. **Burns**. Wit Alonzo **Abernathy**, JCC. Rec 5 Sep 1839. [Marginal note: Full satisfaction received on 13 Feb 1840. Signed Royal **Thompson**.] [No. 812]

1032. Page 141. 11 Apr 1829. Nelson B. **Jones** of Lauderdale Co., Ala., to Alphonso C. and Francis L. **Jones**. For the sum of $2308, 15 slaves; a mulatto wench **Harriet** age 36 years, a mulatto wench **Kate** age 17, **Tenet** age 10, **Henry** age 7, **Romulus** age 5, **Qually** age 3, **James** age 1, **Rose** age 6, **Isaac** age 3, **Georges** age 1, **Emaly** age 6, **Cortase** age 5, **Mary** age 1, **Orange** age 7, and **Lucey** age 4. Signed Nelson P. **Jones**, Francis L. **Jones**, Alphonso C. **Jones**. Wit L. **Farrot**, Parish Judge in West Baton Rouge Parish, La., William **Joyce**, Albert **Duplantier**. Rec 12 Sep 1839. [No. 813]

1033. Page 142. 23 Apr 1830. Nelson P. **Jones** of Missouri to Francis L. **Jones** of East Baton Rouge Parish, La. For the sum of $3000, 80 acres in Saline Co., Mo. known as Edward Reaves Salt Licks; mettle for salt works and all the implements belonging thereunto, and the stock of horses, hogs, and black cattle belonging; slaves, including a negro man **John** aged 25 years, **Henry** 26, **Willis** 17, **Joe** 32, a wench named **Fillis** aged 42, **Jack** 10, and **Sonter** 12; household furniture and cooking utensils in use on the plantation described above. Signed Nelson P. **Jones**, F. L. **Jones**. Wit John **Maillard** Senr., John **Maillard** Jur., Ch. W. **Crawford**, Notary Public in East Baton Rouge Parish, La. Rec 12 Sep 1839. [No. 814]

1034. Page 143. 18 Nov 1830. Nelson P. **Jones** by Valmont **Hebert**, Sheriff of West Baton Rouge Parish, La., to James **McCalop**. For the sum of $100, the following slaves: **Phillis** a negro woman aged about 35 years, **Harriet** a mulato woman aged about 30, **Kitty** a molato woman aged about 19, **Joe** a negro man aged about 30, **John** a negro man aged about 28, **Harry** a negro man aged about 25, **Willis** a negro boy about 15, **Tinna** a negro girl aged about 10, and **Henry** a negro boy about 7. Sold on order of La. 4th District Court on a judgment against sd **Jones** and for William H. **Ragsdale**. Signed James **McCalop**, Valmont **Hebert**, Sheriff. Wit August **Lirique**, Thomas **Williams**. James **McCalop** sells the slaves to Francis L. **Jones** of East Baton Rouge Parish, La. on 10 May 1832 for the sum of $100. Signed James **McCalop**, F. L. **Jones**. Wit W. **Joyce**. Rec 12 Sep 1839. [No. 815]

1035. Page 144. 20 Aug 1839. Alexander M. **Cobbs** and Catharine, his wife, to Ferdinand **Rozier** Jur. For the sum of $135, part of Lot No. 57 in Perryville, beginning 20 feet E of the SW corner of sd lot, and bounded in part by sd **Rozier**; purchased by sd **Cobbs** from M. **Barringer**. Signed Alexander M. **Cobbs**, Catharine **Cobbs** (RD). Wit Reuben **Shelby**, JCC. Rec 17 Sep 1839. [No. 816]

1036. Page 145. 12 Apr 1839. Richmond **Penny** and Olly, his wife, to Mark **Adler**. For the sum of $50, 40 acres, more or less, being the SE 1/4, SE 1/4, Sec 35, Twp 35 N, Rng 11 E. Signed Richmond (x) **Penny**, Olly **Penny** (RD). Wit James **Ferguson** (JP). Rec 21 Sep 1839. [No. 817]

1037. Page 146. 17 Sep 1839. Joseph **Bland** Jur and Nancy, his wife, of Perry Co., Ill. to Henry **Burns**. For the sum of $80, their interest in 25 acres, bounded on the N by the Mississippi River, E by Francis **Cissell**'s heirs, S by Perry **Evans**' land purchased from Timothy **Davis**, and W by Thomas **Horine**; formerly owned by Joseph **Bland** Senior, and descended from him to his heirs Joseph **Bland** Jur., John **Bland**, and Harriet **Bland** to be divided equally. Signed Joseph (x) **Bland** Jur., Nancey (x) **Bland** (RD). Wit Matt **Jones**, John D. **Burklow**, County Clerk of Perry Co., Ill. Rec 25 Sep 1839. [No. 818]

1038. Page 148. 25 Sep 1839. James **Rice**, admr of Thomas **Moore**, decd, by Clerk Frederick C. **Hase** to James **Rice**. For the sum of $50.25, a 1/8 interest in 80 acres, more or less, being Survey No. 868 in Twp 35 N, Rng 11 E, as confirmed to James **Moore**, son of James, and father of sd Thomas. Sold on 16 Aug 1833 to pay debts of the estate at order of County Court issued May Term 1833 on petition of sd **Rice** for sale of sd land and good cause why Thomas **Hayden**, former admr, could not comply with a former order of sale. Signed Fredk. C. **Hase**, Clerk. Wit John **Layton** (JP). Rec 25 Sep 1839. [No. 819]

1039. Page 151. 25 Sep 1839. Deposition of John **Kinnison** regarding a deed. The tract is 420 arpents, in Bois Brule Bottom on the Mississippi River about two and a half miles below the lower end of Horse Island; confirmed to Cornelius (alias Neal, alias Noel) **Hornbeck**, decd.; and bounded on the S & W by land confirmed to William **Fitz Gibbons**, N by land confirmed to John **Smith** Senr. Given before James **Rice** and John **Layton** in a case filed Jul Term 1839 in Circuit Court, David **Steuger**, Judge of 9th Judicial Circuit, presiding, on petition of Timothy **Phelps** by his atty Philip **Cole**, who purchased the tract from Clarity **Gaty**, admr of William **Gaty**, decd. In about 1801, sd **Hornbeck** sold the land to sd **Gaty**, and executed a deed in 1810, which has been lost and is not recorded. Sd **Gaty** died in 1825, and his heirs sold the tract to sd **Phelps**; and this can be proved by the testimony of sd **Kinnison** of Perry Co., and John **Holly**, David **Holly**, and John **McClanahan** of Ste. Genevieve Co. Sd **Kinnison** deposes he knew sd **Hornbeck** as early as 1799 in Ken., and that they came to Upper La. in Nov 1799 to Mississippi Salien, or Dodge's Salt Works, and resided together for most of the winter 1799-1800 at the house of the deponent's uncle. Sd **Hornbeck** returned to Ken. in spring 1800, and sd **Kinnison** next saw him in New Orleans in Jan 1810 in company with sd **Gaty**, commonly called William **Girty**, who was also at the salt works in 1799; and sd **Hornbeck** and sd **Gaty** were negotiating conveyance of the land for either $100 in salt or 100 bushels of salt, which he can't recall. Sd **Kinnison** accompanied them to the Governor's House in New Orleans to get the deed legally authenticated. Sd **Gaty** later told sd **Kinnison** he had lost the deed from his provender bag on his way back from New Orleans to Upper La., supposing his horse had eaten it. He had a notion to take sd **Kinnison**'s deposition, along with John **Greenewalt**, James **Burns**, and William **Burns**, who were present when the deed was executed, to establish title; but was advised by Maj. **Waters** to let the land go for taxes and buy it back. Sd **Gaty** raised corn on the tract from 1801 until he moved to Scott Co. in 1820. Signed John **Kinnison**. Wit James **Rice** (JP), John **Layton** (JP), Fredk. C. **Hase**, Clerk. Rec 25 Sep 1839. [No. 820]

1040. Page 156. 20 Jan 1837. U. S. A. to Thomas **McAtee**. Patent for 86.49 acres, being the NE fractional 1/4, fractional Sec 12, Twp 35 N, Rng 10 E, in Certificate No. 2536. Signed Andrew **Jackson** by A. **Jackson** Jr., Secretary. Wit Hudson M. **Garland**, Recorder of the General Land Office. Rec in Vol. 5:212 of the General Land Office. Rec 27 Sep 1839. [No. 821]

1041. Page 156. 14 Nov 1837. Same to same. Patent for 40 acres, being the SE 1/4, NW 1/4, fractional Sec 12, Twp [35] N, Rng 10 E, in Certificate No. 4815. Signed Martin **Van Buren** by Martin **Van Buren**, Secretary. Wit Jos. S. **Wilson**, Acting Recorder of the General Land Office. Rec in Vol. 9:370 of the General Land Office. Rec 27 Sep 1839. [No. 822]

1042. Page 157. 14 Nov 1837. Same to same. Patent for 119.95 acres, being the NW 1/4, SW 1/4, fractional Sec 12, Twp 35 N, Rng 10 E, in Certificate No. 4814. Signed Martin **Van Buren** by M. **Van Buren**, Secretary. Wit Jos. S. **Wilson**, Acting Recorder of the General Land Office. Rec in Vol. 9:369 of the General Land Office. Rec 27 Sep 1839. [No. 823]

1043. Page 158. 14 Nov 1837. Same to same. Patent for 30.34 acres, being the NE 1/4, NW 1/4, fractional Sec 12, Twp 35 N, Rng 10 E, in Certificate No. 4841. Signed Martin **Van Buren** by M. **Van Buren**, Secretary. Wit Jos. S. **Wilson**, Acting Recorder of the General Land Office. Rec in Vol. 9:395 of the General Land Office. Rec 27 Sep 1839. [No. 824]

1044. Page 159. 13 Nov 1837. Elias E. **Bruner** and Ann, his wife, to William B. **Burgett**. For the sum of $400, their right to any land or real estate which they inherited as heirs of their father John **Burget**, decd, and as heirs of Nancey **Burget**, decd. Signed Elias E. **Bruner**, Ann Bruner. Wit R. Jno. **Gurhz**, JP in Warren Co., Miss., Edward B. **Scarborough**, Clerk of Probate Court in Warren Co., Miss. Rec 28 Sep 1839. [No. 825]

1045. Page 160. 13 Nov 1837. Peter L. **Burget** to same. For the sum of $400, his right to any land or real estate which he inherited as an heir of his father John **Burget**, decd, and as heir of his mother Nancey **Burget**, decd. Signed Peter **Burgett**. Wit E. H. **Maxey**, JP in Warren Co., Miss., Edward B. **Scarborough**, Clerk of Probate Court in Warren Co., Miss. Rec 28 Sep 1839. [No. 826]

1046. Page 161. 6 Apr 1839. Last will and testament of Zachariah **Layton**, decd. To his wife Mary: 1/3 of all his personal estate and real estate during her lifetime. To his son John: 139 acres entered by Clement **Hayden**, also for services rendered since he became of age: one bald horse of a sorrel colour, one cow and calf. To his two sons Nerius and Felix: 230 acres where he now lives, provided that these sons will support their mother during her lifetime and widowhood, and also support their brother Marcell during his life. To Thomas **Layton**: $50 when he comes of age, paid equally by Nerius and Felix. To the balance of his children, Martin, John, Leo, Sarah, Mary, Andrew, and Christeen: an equal share of the remainder of his estate, with the following deductions--from Martin $57, from Leo $114.58, from Peter **Brown** $53, from William **Manning** and Sarah, his wife, $100, from John $173, and from Andrew $100. To all his children: Lot Nos. 78, 77, 86, 76, 97, and 96 in Perryville; which are to be sold by his executors and the proceeds equally divided. Martin **Layton** and Nerius **Layton** are appointed executors. Signed Zachariah **Layton**. Wit John **Layton** Sinor, James **Layton**, Fredk. C. **Hase**, Clerk. Rec 10 Oct 1839. [No. 827]

1047. Page 162. 2 Oct 1839. William **Belsha** to Isaac **Meredith**. For the sum of $250, 80 acres, being the E 1/2, NW 1/4, Sec 30, Twp 36 N, Rng 12 E. Signed William **Belsha**. Wit Mark **Miles**, Alfred L. **Parks** (JP). Rec 12 Oct 1839. [No. 828]

1048. Page 163. 2 Oct 1839. Charles **Miles** to same. For the sum of $125.75, two 40 acre lots in Sec 30, Twp 36 N, Rng 12 E; the SW 1/4, NW 1/4 and NW 1/4, NW 1/4. Signed Charles (x) **Miles**. Wit David **Hardon**, Allen Burns **Richardson**, Alfred L. **Parks** (JP). Rec 12 Oct 1839. [No. 829]

1049. Page 164. 14 Nov 1837. U. S. A. to John P. **Finch**. Patent for 40 acres, being the SE 1/4, SE 1/4, Sec 18, Twp 35 N, Rng 12 E, in Certificate No. 5091. Signed Martin **Van Buren** by M. **Van Buren**, Secretary. Wit Jos. S. **Wilson**, Acting Recorder of the General Land Office. Rec in Vol 10:144 of the General Land Office. Rec 21 Oct 1839. [No. 830]

1050. Page 165. 14 Nov 1837. Same to same. Patent for 40 acres, being the NE 1/4, NE 1/4, Sec 19, Twp 35 N, Rng 12 E, in Certificate No. 5092. Signed Martin **Van Buren** by M. **Van Buren**, Secretary. Wit Jos. S. **Wilson**, Acting Recorder of the General Land Office. Rec in Vol 10:145 of the General Land Office. Rec 21 Oct 1839. [No. 831]

1051. Page 166. 7 Oct 1839. Alexander **Bailey** and Margaret, his wife, to Leon **Delassus**. For the sum of $400, two tracts in Twp 35 N, Rng 12 E; 40 acres, more or less, being the NE 1/4, NE 1/4, Sec 19; and 40 acres, more or less, being the SE 1/4, SE 1/4, Sec 18. Signed Alexander **Bailey**, Margaret **Bailey** (RD). Wit Reuben **Shelby**, JCC. Rec 21 Oct 1839. [No. 832]

1052. Page 167. 18 May 1839. Robert P. **Slaughter** to Elias **Barber** and Hugh **Wells**. For the sum of $750, mortgage on __ acres in the Mississippi Bottom, the dower land of Clara **Hamilton**, and sold by the commissioners to partition sd lands between the heirs of George A. **Hamilton**, decd to Sarah **Young**, and sold by her to sd **Slaughter**. Sd **Barber** and sd **Wells** are security for sd **Slaughter** on a note payable to Leo **Fenwick**, admr of Cloe **Fenwick**, decd, payable 12 months after 18 May 1839. Signed Robert P. **Slaughter**. Wit John **Hughey** (JP). Rec 24 Oct 1839. [No. 833]

1053. Page 168. 5 Oct 1839. Last will and testament of Nicholas **Tucker**, decd. To his wife Mary: the home plantation, a negro girl **Mary**, and 1/3 of the rest of his property during her lifetime, and then to descend to my heirs or legal representatives. To his children Leander, Stephen, and Joana: $75 apiece when they come of age. To his children Lewis, Henry, Hillrey, Elizabeth, Michael, John, Charles, Leander, Stephen, and Joana: the remainder of his estate to be equally divided between them, or to their legal representatives if they are dead at the time of distribution. His sons Henry and Michael are appointed executors. He requests that his executors deed to his son John 43.44 acres, being the SW fractional 1/4, Sec 6, Twp 35 N, Rng 11 E, provided that John pay the estate $84.30. Signed Nicholas (x) **Tucker** Senr. Wit Peter **Tucker** Senr, Joseph **Cissell** Jur., Elizabeth (x) **Tucker**, Fredk. C. **Hase**, Clerk. Rec 2 Oct 1839.

1054. Page 169. 4 Nov 1839. Simon **Duvall** and Mary, his wife, formerly Mary **Miles**, daughter of Henry **Miles**, decd, to Leo **Miles**. For the sum of $100, their undivided share of 185 acres, more or less, which belonged to Henry **Miles**, decd; part of a tract confirmed to Joseph **Miles**, decd. Signed Simon **Duvall**, Mary **Duvall**. Wit John F. **Hase**, Dep Clerk. Rec 4 Nov 1839. [No. 834]

1055. Page 171. 6 Nov 1839. David **Flynn** and Elizabeth, his wife and formerly Isabella **Vessels**, and Thomas B. **Brown** and Precilla, his wife and formerly Precilla **Vessels**, to Henry **Drewrey**. For the sum of $64, all their interest in two tracts that they have as heirs of Charles **Vessels**, decd, father of sd Isabella and Precilla; 150.27 acres, being the SE fractional 1/4, Sec 22, Twp 36 N, Rng 10 E; and 26 acres, more or less, in Twp 36 N, Rng 10 E. Signed David **Flynn**, Elizabeth (x) **Flynn**, Thomas **Brown**, Precilla (x) **Brown**. Wit John F. **Hase**, Dep Clerk. Rec 9 Nov 1839. [No. 835]

1056. Page 172. 20 Nov 1839. Edward **McGinnis** and Margert, his wife, to Reubin **Shelby**. For the sum of $550, two tracts; 80 acres, being the W 1/2, SE 1/4, Sec 26, Twp 35 N, Rng 10 E, patented to sd **McGinnis** on 15 Oct 1833; and 40 acres, being the NW 1/4, NE 1/4, Sec 35, Twp 35 N, Rng 10 E, purchased by sd **McGinnis** as school land in Nov 1838. Signed Edward **McGinnis**, Margaret **McGinnis** (RD). Wit John M. **Odin**, John **Layton** Senr (JP). Rec 20 Nov 1839. [No. 836]

1057. Page 174. 18 Nov 1839. John **Clotfelter** and Sarah, his wife, of Jackson Co., Ill. to Seth **Hall**. For the sum of $800, 160 acres, being the W 1/2, SE 1/4 and E 1/2, SW 1/4 of Sec 32, Twp 34 N, Rng 12 E. Signed John **Clotfelter**, Sara (x) **Clotfelter**. Wit Robt. **Manning**, Augustus **Davis** (JP). Rec 21 Nov 1839. [No. 837]

1058. Page 175. 16 May 1839. Edward M. **Holden** to John **Holden** of Adams Co., Miss. For the sum of $1250, three tracts; 20 acres, more or less, adjoining the W line of Perryville, beginning at a stone at the corner of Joseph **Shoults**' land, and also bounded by James **Layton**; 6 acres, more or less, adjoining the first tract, beginning at the NW corner of **Stewart**'s line on the E line of Perryville, offered by Edward M. **Holden** as security for payment of $320 to the commissioners of the internal improvements fund; and the S 1/2, Lot No. 9 in Perryville, fronting on Spring St and St. Josephs St. Signed Edward M. **Holden**. Wit Douglas C. **Dunlap**, Judge of Probate Court in Adams Co., Miss., Ralph **North**, Clerk of Probate Court in Adams Co., Miss., Fredk. C. **Hase**, Clerk. Rec 22 Nov 1839. [No. 838]

1059. Page 176. 27 Jul 1837. George **Preston** and Mary, his wife, to James **Preston**, their son. For love and affection and the sum of $1, two tracts and personal property; 120 acres on McClanahan's Creek purchased by George **Preston** from Ansel **Ferrel** and Esther, his wife, on 9 Sep 1826, being the SE corner of 640 acres confirmed to Thomas **Allen**, and adjoining 200 acres formerly sold by sd **Allen** to Acquila **Hagan**; 150.18 acres, being the NE fractional 1/4, Sec 24, Twp 36 N, Rng 11 E, purchased by George **Preston** from James **Philips** on 11 Mar 1834; two negro slaves that George **Preston** purchased from the estate of Michael **Burns**, decd, a boy **Jack** aged about 15 years, and a girl **Sally** about 11, but the use of sd **Sally** is reserved to Mary **Burns** during her lifetime; four horse creatures, a grey mare six years old last spring and her yearling sorrel colt, a bay horse colt about three months old, and the old bald mare's colt; and two cows and calves, the choice of his stock of cattle. Signed George **Preston**, Mary (x) **Preston** (RD). Wit James **Rice** (JP). Rec 22 Nov 1839. [No. 839]

1060. Page 178. 5 Oct 1839. Samuel A. **Coale** to Conrad C. **Ziegler**. For securing a note and the sum of $1, deed of trust on 100 acres in Bois Brule Bottom, conveyed by Andrew H. **Tucker** and wife in trust to sd **Coale** on 27 Jul 1837. Sd **Tucker** owes a note for $1360 payable in 60 days after 26 Jul 1837 to Sweringer & Bredell, which sd **Coale** had secured, and which sd **Ziegler** now is empowered to sell. Signed Samuel A. **Coale**. Wit Lewis V. **Bogy**, John **Ruland**, Clerk of St. Louis Co. Rec 26 Nov 1839. [No. 840]

1061. Page 179. 20 Nov 1839. Seth **Hall** to Singleton H. **Kimmel**. For the sum of $800, mortgage on five tracts on Apple Creek; 160 acres, being the W 1/2, SE 1/4, and E 1/2, SW 1/4, Sec 32, Twp 34 N, Rng 12 E, and deeded to sd **Hall** by John **Clotfelter** and wife; 52 acres, being the E end of Lot No. 7, NW 1/4, Sec 5, Twp 33 N, Rng 12 E; 3 acres, more or less, beginning at the NW corner of the 52 acre lot; 35 acres, being as much of Lot No. 7 in the NE 1/4, Sec 5, Twp 33 N, Rng 12 E, beginning at the NE corner of Sec 5, Twp 33 N, Rng 12 E; and 28 acres in the S part of the W 1/2, SW 1/4, Sec 32, Twp 34, Rng 12 E. Sd **Hall** owes a note of equal date to sd **Kimmel**, payable in five years with 6% interest per annum. Signed Seth **Hall**. Wit C. J. **Ladd**, William **Manning**, Elias **Barber** (JP). Rec 26 Nov 1839. [No. 841]

1062. Page 181. 12 Nov 1839. William **Burns** to Samuel **Allen**. In consideration of securing a note, mortgage on two mares, one bay and the other a sorrel; one red cow and calf; one pied cow; one beauro; cupboard; and a table. Sd **Burns** owes Swanwick & Homes a note dated 5 Oct 1839 for $75, with sd **Allen** as security, with interest from 5 Apr 1840. Signed William **Burns**. Wit Ferdinand **Belsha**, Alfred L. **Parks** (JP). Rec 26 Nov 1839. [No. 842]

1063. Page 182. 12 Apr 1839. George A. **Hamilton** to Leo **Fenwick**. For the sum of $55.70, 7 acres and some poles, more or less, drawn for Matilda **Hamilton** by the commissioners to partition lands of George A. **Hamilton**, decd; bounded on the N by Lot No. 3 owned by the heirs of Harrison **Young**, decd, and where his widow now resides, W by the dower lands of the late Clara **Hamilton**, decd, S by Lot No. 5 where sd **Fenwick** now lives, and E by the Mississippi River. Signed George A. **Hamilton**. Wit Joseph C. **Fenwick**, Robert P. **Slaughter**. Elias **Barber** (JP). Rec 26 Nov 1839. [No. 843]

1064. Page 183. 27 Nov 1839. Robert T. **Brown** Senr to Joseph **Pratte** & Emanual **Pratte**. "Whereas from the precipitant rush of my creditors upon me at this time and from the hard times and the preasure of the Country for raising available funds, it is out of the question at this time to rais the money sufficient to meet the demands that now imediately oppress me...", for the sum of $5000, mortgage on negroes: **Henry** a man about 43 years of age; **Piere**, a man 45; **Polette**, a man 45; **Aron**, a man 36; **Alexander**, a boy about 8; **Paul**, a boy 2; **Peter**, a boy 7; **Lucile**, a woman about 40; **Tharesa**, a girl age 4; **Nathan**, a boy about 15; **Chaney**, a woman about 22 and her child infant; **Caroline**, a girl about 9; and **James**, a boy about 7. The debt is due by 27 Nov 1840. Signed Robert T. **Brown**. Wit James **Evans**, Francis H. **Wilkinson**, James **Rice** (JP). Rec 27 Nov 1839. [No. 844]

1065. Page 184. 20 Jul 1839. Johann George **Gube** to Henry C. **Bimpage**. For services rendered to a number of Germans in the Evangelical Lutheran Congregation settled on or near the mouth of Brazeau Creek and the sum of $5, 6 acres, more or less, on the Mississippi River, beginning at the SE corner of Survey No. 2173 for 640 acres in the name of John **Manning** in Twp 34 N, Rng 14 E. Signed Johann George **Gube**. Wit Johann Gottlieb **Palisch**, Manervia A. **Davis**, Augustus **Davis** (JP). Rec 29 Nov 1839. [No. 845]

1066. Page 185. 23 Mar 1830. Commissioners of Perryville to Thomas **Allen**. For the sum of $19, Lot Nos. 82 & 85 in Perryville. Signed R. T. **Brown**, Thomas **Riney**, Joseph **Tucker**, Commissioners. Wit Walter **Wilkinson** (JP). Rec 30 Nov 1839. [No. 846]

1067. Page 186. 9 Nov 1839. Thomas **Allen** to Levi **Block**. For the sum of $19, Lot Nos. 82 & 85 in Perryville. Signed Thomas **Allen**. Wit Thomas **Long**, Alfred L. **Parks** (JP). Rec 30 Nov 1839. [No. 847]

1068. Page 187. 23 Nov 1839. Reuben **Shelby** and Mary, his wife, to Leon **Delassus**. For the sum of $200, two tracts entered by Mary **Shelby** on 21 Sep 1839; 39.26 acres, being the SE 1/4, SW 1/4, Sec 18, Twp 35 N, Rng 12 E; and 120 acres, being the W 1/2, NE 1/4 and the SE 1/4, NE 1/4, Sec 19, Twp 35 N, Rng 12 E. Signed Reuben **Shelby**, Mary E. **Shelby** (RD). Wit James **Rice** (JP). Rec 2 Dec 1839. [No. 848]

1069. Page 188. 14 Oct 1837. James J. **Moore** and Cecelia, his wife, James **Rice** and Sabina, his wife, William **Moore**, and Ignatius **Moore** to James B. **May**. For the sum of $40, their undivided shares of 100 acres in Survey No. 2137 in Twp 35 N, Rng 10 E confirmed to James **Moore** Senior, decd; the portion bequeathed by the will of James **Moore** Senior to his daughter Barbara or her oldest son, on the condition that they would support his other daughter Elizabeth, provided they take possession of the land within seven years, or it was to descend to his grandchildren, children of his son James **Moore**, decd; beginning at the end of the lane that runs through the farm. Signed James J. **Moore**, Cecelia (x) **Moore** (RD), James **Rice**, Sabina (x) **Rice** (RD), William **Moore**, Ignatius **Moore**. Wit Mark **Brewer** (JP). Rec 3 Dec 1839. [No. 849]

1070. Page 189. 12 May 1838. Henry J. **Rhodes** to James B. **May**. For the sum of $10, an undivided interest in 100 acres as described in the preceding deed (3:188). Signed Henry J. (x) **Rhodes**. Wit James **Rice** (JP), Francis **Rice**. Rec 3 Dec 1839. [No. 850]

1071. Page 190. 2 Dec 1839. Levi **Block** and Susan, his wife, to Walter B. **Wilkinson**, all of Perryville. For the sum of $40, Lot No. 85 in Perryville. Signed Levi **Block**, Susan **Block** (RD). Wit Fredk. C. **Hase**, Clerk. Rec 5 Dec 1839. [No. 851]

1072. Page 191. 29 Nov 1839. John **Daugherty** to Mathias **Barringer**. For the sum of $400, his interest in an undivided 100 acres on the waters of St. Laurant Creek, to be taken off the SE end of the tract; purchased by Zar **Sturdivant** from Thomas **Donohoe**, and by Atticus **Tucker**, decd, from sd **Sturdivant**. Signed John **Daugherty**. Wit John F. **Hase**, Dep Clerk. Rec 29 Nov 1839. [No. 852]

1073. Page 192. 10 Dec 1839. Edward M. **Holden** to Reuben **Shelby**. For securing a debt and the sum of $1, deed of trust on one sorrel horse and one bay horse now in his possession in Perryville; one white and red pied cow; one white cow; one two-year-old steer with black sides and white back; six sheep; two yearling calves with white faces, one a red brindle and the other black; one waggon purchased by him at the sale of Martin **Wagner**, decd. Sd **Holden** owes John **Logan** a note for $130 of even date, payable in six months with 10% interest per annum from this date, and the property is to be sold by sd **Shelby** if the debt is not paid. Signed Edward M. **Holden**. Wit Fredk. C. **Hase**, Clerk. Rec 10 Dec 1839. [No. 853]

1074. Page 194. 9 Nov 1839. Robert **Farrar** and Susan, his wife, formerly of St. Clair Co., Ill. to Marx **Adler**. For love and affection that they bear toward their son-in-law, quit claim to two tracts in Sec 25, Twp 35 N, Rng 11 E; 40 acres, being the SW 1/4, SE 1/4, patented by sd **Farrar** on 1 Aug 1838; and 1 acre off the NE end of the SE 1/4, SW 1/4, beginning on the E side by the E boundary line. Signed Robert **Farrar**, Susan (x) **Farrar** (RD). Wit Alonzo **Abernathy**, JCC. Rec 19 Dec 1839. [No. 854]

1075. Page 195. 18 Sep 1839. 18 Sep 1839. Joseph **Miles** Jr. and Rosana, his wife, to Silus **French**. For the sum of $115, 40 acres, being the E 1/2, Lot No. 1, NE 1.4, Sec 5, Twp 34 N, Rng 10 E. Signed Joseph **Miles**, Rosana **Miles** (RD). Wit John **Layton** senior (JP), Augustin **Layton**. Rec 21 Dec 1839. [No. 855]

1076. Page 196. 27 Dec 1839. Joseph B. **Mattingley** and Maria, his wife, to Joab W. **Burgee**. For the sum of $212.50, 40 acres, being the NE 1/4, NE 1/4, Sec 19, Twp 36 N, Rng 11 E; patented by sd **Mattingley** on 14 Jun 1837. Signed Joseph B. **Mattingley**, Maria (x) **Mattingley** (RD). Wit Reuben **Shelby**, JCC. Rec 27 Dec 1839. [No. 856]

1077. Page 197. 13 Dec 1839. Thomas **Blaylock** and Elizabeth, his wife, to James **Sadler**. For the sum of $50, 37.56 acres, being the NE 1/4, NE 1/4, Sec 6, Twp 34 N, Rng 11 E; entered at the Land Office by sd **Blaylock** on 15 Oct 1839. Signed Thomas **Blaylock**, Elizabeth (x) **Blaylock** (RD). Wit R. **Shelby**, JCC. Rec 30 Dec 1839. [No. 857]

1078. Page 198. 9 Nov 1839. Allen R. **Smith** and Jane, his wife, of Avoyelles Parish, La. to David **Flynn**. For the sum of $100, 34.56 acres in Bois Brule Twp in Sec 19, Twp 37 N, Rng 11 E, the undivided part of a tract entered by sd **Flynn** and sd **Smith** in 1836. Signed Allen R. (x) **Smith**, Jane (x) **Smith**, David **Flynn**. Wit Wm. C. **Howard**, T. **Wilson**, James E. **Howard**, Notary Public in Avoyelles Parish, La. Rec 2 Jan 1840. [No. 858]

1079. Page 199. 6 Jan 1840. Isidore **Moore** Jur. and Mary, his wife, to James **Hagan**. For the sum of $55, 40 acres, being the SE 1/4, SE 1/4, Sec 29, Twp 36 N, Rng 11 E, purchased from the U. S. A. on 11 Nov 1837. Signed Isidore **Moore** Jr., Mary (x) **Moore** (RD). Wit James **Rice** (JP). Rec 6 Jan 1840. [No. 859]

1080. Page 200. 9 Jan 1840. George M. **Vessels** and Mary, his wife, to Samuel **Cline**. For the sum of $300, three tracts in Twp 36 N, Rng 10 E: 40 acres, more or less, being the NW 1/4, NW 1/4, Sec 26; and his share in two tracts to which he is entitled as an heir of his father Charles **Vessels**, decd; 150.27 acres, being the SE fractional 1/4, Sec 22; and 26 acres, more or less. Signed George **Vessels**, Mary (x) **Vessels** (RD). Wit James **Rice** (JP). Rec 9 Jan 1840. [No. 860]

1081. Page 201. 18 Oct 1839. Joseph V. **Beauvais** and Matilda V., his wife, to Leon **Delassus**. For the sum of $100, 80 acres in Sec 17, Twp 35 N, Rng 12 E, being the SW 1/4, SW 1/4, and the NW 1/4, SE 1/4. Signed Joseph V. **Beauvais**, Matilda V. **Bauvais** (RD). Wit Reuben **Shelby**, JCC. Rec 15 Jan 1840. [No. 861]

1082. Page 203. 1 Jan 1840. Edward M. **Holden** to Reuben **Shelby**. For securing a note and the sum of $1, deed of trust on one beauro; one side bord or press; one large falling leaf table; one small work table; six windsor chairs, two turned; bed steads, beds, and bedding; and one gigg and harness. Walter **Wilkinson** is security for sd **Holden** for a note of even date for $72 to John **Burgett** for the hire of a negro woman, payable twelve months after date; and sd **Shelby** is to sell the property to sell as much of the property as is needed to pay the debt. Signed Edward M. **Holden**. Wit John F. **Hase**, Dep Clerk. Rec 16 Jan 1840. [No. 862]

1083. Page 204. 19 Oct 1839. Henry **Caho** and Maria, his wife, to William **Taylor**. For the sum of $300, 100 acres, more or less, beginning where the section line between Sec 12 & Sec 13 of Twp 35 N, Rng 10 E intersects James **Moore**'s line. Signed Henry **Caho**, Maria **Caho** (RD). Wit Reuben **Shelby**, JCC. Rec 17 Jan 1840. [No. 863]

1084. Page 205. 7 Jan 1840. Reuben **Shelby** and Mary E., his wife, to Alexander M. **Cobbs**. For the sum of $250, the N 1/2 of Lot No. 63 in Perryville, fronting on Jackson St. Signed Reuben **Shelby**, Mary E. **Shelby** (RD). Wit John **Layton** Senr (JP). Rec 17 Jan 1840. [No. 864]

1085. Page 206. 7 Jan 1840. Alexander M. **Cobbs** to Perry County for the benefit of the inhabitants of Twp 35 N, Rng 10 E. For the sum of $170, mortgage on the N 1/2 of Lot No. 63 in Perryville, fronting on Jackson St. For the note he has executed a bond with Martin L. **Moore** and William B. **Burns** as securities, bearing this date with 10% interest per annum, due by 7 Jan 1841. Signed Alexander M. **Cobbs**. Wit Reuben **Shelby**, JCC. Rec 17 Jan 1840. [No. 865]

1086. Page 207. 3 Dec 1839. Thomas **Stewart** and Isabela, his wife, to Peter J. **Tucker**. For the sum of $100, two tracts; 16.36 acres in Bois Brule Twp, being the fractional Sec 32, Twp 37 N, Rng 11 E; and 40 acres, being the NW 1/4, SW 1/4, Sec 21, Twp 36 N, Rng 11 E. Signed Thomas **Stewart**, Isabella (x) **Stewart** (RD). Test Mark **Brewer** (JP). Rec 18 Jan 1840. [No. 866]

1087. Page 208. 20 Jan 1840. John N. **Tucker** to James **Rice**. For diverse good causes and considerations and the sum of $1, mortgage on his undivided share of any property to which he is entitled as an heir of his father Nicholas **Tucker**, decd; one grey mare about four years old this ensuing spring and about 14 hands high; and 20 hogs. Sd **Tucker** owes two notes totaling $65.50, due on demand, to Henry and Michael **Tucker**, exec of sd Nicholas **Tucker**. Signed John N. **Tucker**. Wit Reuben **Shelby**, JCC. Rec 20 Jan 1840. [No. 867]

1088. Page 209. 17 Jan 1840. William **Taylor** and Mary, his wife, to Reuben **Shelby**. For the sum of $600, 140 acres, more or less, beginning where the section line between Sec 12 & Sec 13, Twp 35 N, Rng 10 E intersects James **Moore**'s survey. Signed William **Taylor**, Mary (x) **Taylor** (RD). Wit John **Layton** Senr (JP). Rec 29 Jan 1840. [No. 868]

1089. Page 210. 28 Jan 1840. Reuben **Shelby** and Mary, his wife, to Ferdinand **Rozier**. For the sum of $600, 140 acres, more or less, as described in the preceding deed (3:209). Signed Reuben **Shelby**, Mary **Shelby** (RD). Wit James **Rice** (JP). Rec 29 Jan 1840. [No. 869]

1090. Page 212. 16 Aug 1839. Ezekiel **Foster**, admr of the estate of Baley **Fleming**, decd, to Charles **Venable**. For the sum of $300, 80 acres, more or less, being the E 1/2, SW 1/4, Sec 22, Twp 35 N, Rng 12 E. Sold in Jul 1839 at order of County Court issued May Term 1839 to sell sd lands to pay debts of the estate. Signed Ezekiel **Foster**, admr of the estate of Baley **Fleming**, decd. Wit Fredk. C. **Hase**, John F. **Hase**, Dep Clerk. Rec 3 Feb 1840. [No. 870]

1091. Page 213. 15 Oct 1836. John **Hager** and Lucey, his wife, to James **Clifton**. For the sum of $200, 80 acres, being the E 1/2, SE 1/4, Sec 30, Twp 35 N, Rng 12 E. Signed John **Hager**, Lucy (x) **Hager**. Wit Jesse **Dickson**, John **Hughey** (JP). Rec 3 Feb 1840. [No. 871]

1092. Page 214. 13 Jul 1839. James **Clifton** to Rebeca **Watts**, wife of William **Watts**, formerly Rebeca **Clifton**. For natural love and affection for his daughter and for her better maintenance, 80 acres, being the E 1/2, SE 1/4, Sec 30, Twp 35 N, Rng 12 E; entered by John **Hager**, and deeded to sd **Clifton** on 15 Oct 1836. Signed James **Clifton**. Wit Alonzo **Abernathy**, JCC. Rec 3 Feb 1840. [No. 872]

1093. Page 215. 9 Mar 1835. Haleyburton **Parks** and Jane, his wife, to William **Black**. For the sum of $300, 39.53 acres, being the NW 1/4, SW 1/4, Sec 7, Twp 34 N, Rng 12 E. Signed Haleyburton **Parks**, Jane **Parks** (RD). Wit Jones **Abernathy** (JP). Rec 3 Feb 1840. [No. 873]

1094. Page 216. 14 Jan 1840. Joseph **Fultz** and Helanna B., his wife, to John G. **Hemmann**. For the sum of $1500, two tracts in Sec 28, Twp 34 N, Rng 12 E; 80 acres, being the E 1/2, NE 1/4; and 40 acres, being the SW 1/4, NE 1/4. Signed Joseph **Volz**, Helena **Behrle** (RD). Wit Elias **Barber** (JP). Rec 4 Feb 1840. [No. 874]

1095. Page 217. 14 Jan 1840. Edward **Harter** and Mary F., his wife, to Joseph **Fultz**. For the sum of $750, two tracts in Sec 34, Twp 34 N, Rng 11 E; 40 acres, being the SE 1/4, NW 1/4; and 40 acres, being the NE 1/4, SW 1/4. Signed Edward **Harter**, Mariana **Fischer** (RD). Wit Elias **Barber** (JP). Rec 4 Feb 1840. [No. 875]

1096. Page 218. 21 Jun 1837. James **Starr** to Samuel Lewis **Moore**. For the sum of $150, 40 acres, more or less, being the NE 1/4, NE 1/4, Sec 23, Twp 34 N, Rng 11 E; patented by sd **Starr** in Feb 1836. Signed Jas. **Starr**. Wit John **Welker**, Mark **Brewer** (JP). Rec 4 Feb 1840. [No. 876]

1097. Page 219. 3 Feb 1840. Alexander M. **Cobbs** to Samuel M. **Cobbs**. For the sum of $1600, mortgage on the N 1/2, Lot No. 63 in Perryville, fronting on Jackson St; subject to another mortgage executed by sd **Cobbs** on 7 Jan last in favor of Perry Co.; also one safe; three beds and bedding thereunto attached; 14 windsor chairs; one rocking chair; three bedsteads; one certain bedstead; one Yankee clock; and five trunks. A note is due in two years from date with lawful interest. Signed Alexander M. **Cobbs**. Test James **Rice** (JP). Rec 4 Feb 1840. [No. 877]

1098. Page 221. 9 Nov 1839. Robert **Farrar** and Susan, his wife, formerly of St. Clair Co., Ill. to Nelson **Yarborough**. For love and affection for their son-in-law and other considerations, 40 acres, being the NE 1/4, SW 1/4, Sec 25, Twp 35 N, Rng 11 E; entered by sd **Farrar** on 15 Oct 1833. Signed Robert **Farar**, Susan V. **Farrar** (RD). Wit Alonzo **Abernathy**, JCC. Rec 8 Feb 1840. [No. 878]

1099. Page 222. 6 Feb 1840. William A. **Walker** and Maryann, his wife, to Hyman **Block**. For the sum of $200, the S side of Lot No. 68 in Perryville; bounded on the E by Jackson St, S by John W. **Noell**, W by Peter **Faharty**, and N by North St. Signed Wm. A. **Walker**, Mary Ann **Walker** (RD). Wit Reuben **Shelby**. JCC. Rec 10 Feb 1840. [No. 879]

1100. Page 223. 14 Jan 1840. Perletus **Wilson** and Elizabeth, his wife, to John G. **Hemmann**. For the sum of $180, 3 acres, more or less, in the NE 1/4, SW 1/4, Sec 28, Twp 34 N, Rng 12 E; being where sd **Wilson**'s buildings stand on the N line of sd tract. Signed Perletus **Wilson**, Elizabeth **Wilson** (RD). Wit Elias **Barber** (JP). Rec 12 Feb 1840. [No. 880]

1101. Page 224. 4 Feb 1830. Robert **Hinkston** and Mary, his wife, of Washington Co., Mo. to Miles R. **Anderson** and Pinkney K. **Anderson**. For the sum of $132.50, equal undivided 1/6 part of __ acres in Brazeau Twp; bounded on the E by Joseph **James**, S by public land or land entered by William **Garner** and Elias **Barber**, W by land formerly owned by Theopilus **Williams**, and N by public land; on which Samuel **Anderson** resided in his lifetime. Signed Robert **Hinkston**, Mary **Hinkston** (RD). Wit Thos. **Fenwick**, Leo **Fenwick**, Charles **Springer**, JP in Washington Co., Mo., James J. **Fenwick** (JP), Israel **McGready**, Clerk of Washington Co., Mo. Rec 12 Feb 1840. [No. 881]

1102. Page 225. 13 Feb 1840. Joseph **Burns** and Alvira, his wife, to Conrad **Ox**. For the sum of $300, 40 acres, being the SE 1/4, SW 1/4, Sec 6, Twp 35 N, Rng 11 E; with about 30 acres under fence, 12 acres in cultivation, a dwelling house, stables, corncrib, and other outhouses. Signed Joseph **Burns**, (x) Alvira **Burns** (RD). Wit James **Rice** (JP), Royal **Thompson**. Rec 13 Feb 1840. [No. 882]

1103. Page 226. 6 Nov 1839. Zeno **Layton** to Christina **Layton**. For the sum of $100, bond to make a deed on 40 acres, being the NW 1/4, NW 1/4, Sec 35, Twp 35 N, Rng 10 E; for which Christina **Layton** has paid the sum of $55. Signed Zeno **Layton**. Wit John **Layton** senr (JP), Amatus **Layton**. Rec 14 Feb 1840. [No. 883]

1104. Page 227. 15 Feb 1840. Conrad C. **Ziegler** of Ste. Genevieve Co., Mo. to James T. **Sweringen**. In fulfillment of a deed of trust and for the sum of $800, 100 acres in Bois Brule Bottom, acquired by Andrew H. **Tucker** and wife from William **Flynn** and wife, Josephus **Tucker** and wife, Isaac **Hill** and wife, and George **McNew** and wife on 3 Aug 1836. Andrew H. **Tucker** and Ellen, his wife, executed a deed of trust dated 27 Jul 1837 to Samuel A. **Coale** to secure sd **Sweringen** and Edward **Breedwell** for payment of a promissory note for $1360 dated 26 Jul 1837 and due in six months. Sd **Coale** conveyed the trust to sd **Ziegler** on 5 Oct 1839, and sd **Tucker** has failed to pay the note. Signed Conrad C. **Ziegler**. Wit Fredk. C. **Hase**, Clerk. Rec 15 Feb 1840. [No. 884]

1105. Page 229. 11 Aug 1837. Last will and testament of George **Preston**, decd. To his wife Mary and son James: all his real and personal property except that which he and his wife have conveyed to his son James on 21 Jul 1837. All debts and demands due him, and the proceeds of the sale of such personal property as is not needed for the maintenance of his wife and son, are to be collected by his execr, and the proceeds are to apply to the maintenance of his wife and son James. To his wife Mary: his old bald faced breeding mare; and any increase of colts to his son James. Lewis **Tharp** of Bois Brule Twp is appointed execr. Signed George **Preston**. Wit James **Rice**, William **Moore**, Fredk. C. **Hase**, Clerk. Rec 17 Feb 1840. [No. 885]

1106. Page 230. 1 Oct 1839. Commissioners to partition lands of the heirs of Thomas **Cochran** to Lewis **French**. For the sum of $51, 150 acres, in the river hills near Bois Brule Bottom, part of a tract confirmed to James **Thompson**, and formerly owned by sd **Cochran**. Sold in Jul 1838 at order of Circuit Court issued Mar Term 1838 on petition to partition of George **Preston** and Mary, his wife, and James **Preston**, by his guardian Thomas **Cochran**; in which the widow of Thomas **Cochran**, now Mary **Preston**, also receives 1/3 of the proceeds of the sale. Signed John **Logan**,

Francis **Clark**, James **Rice**, commissioners. Wit Reuben **Shelby**, JCC. Rec 17 Feb 1840. [No. 886]

1107. Page 233. 29 Aug 1818. Archabald **Morgan** of Ste. Genevieve Co., Mo. to Jackson **Taylor**. For the sum of $600, 100 acres in Bois Brule (Bob Ruley), the upper side of 640 acres granted to sd **Morgan** by the government as a settlement right; beginning on the Mississippi River. Signed Archabald **Morgan**. Wit A. **Bird**, JP in Ste. Genevieve Co., Mo., Jno. **Morris**. Rec 18 Feb 1840. [No. 887]

1108. Page 233. 12 Oct 1818. Jackson **Taylor** of Ste. Genevieve Co., Mo. to Charles **Ellis**. For the sum of $680, 100 acres in Bois Brule Bottom, part of 640 acres granted to Archabald **Morgan**, and sold by him to sd **Taylor** on 29 Aug 1818; beginning on the Mississippi River. Signed Jackson **Taylor**. Wit Guy **Gaylard**, William **Flynn**, Fredk. C. **Hase**, Clerk. Rec 18 Feb 1840. [No. 888]

1109. Page 234. 23 Dec 1825. William **Morris** to James **Taylor**. For the sum of $500, 100 acres in Bois Brule Bottom, conveyed by Archabald **Morgan** to Jackson **Taylor** on 29 Aug 1818. Signed William (x) **Morris**. Wit James **Wilcox**, John **Logan**, Fredk. C. **Hase**, Clerk. Rec 18 Feb 1840. [No. 889]

1110. Page 235. 15 Oct 1833. U. S. A. to James **Clifton**. Patent for 80 acres, being the E 1/2, NE 1/4, Sec 28, Twp 35 N, Rng 12 E; in Certificate No. 1463. Signed Andrew **Jackson** by A. J. **Donelson**, Secy. Wit Elijah **Hayward**, Commissioner of the General Land Office. Rec in Vol. 3:79 of the General Land Office. Rec 18 Feb 1840. [No. 890]

1111. Page 236. 28 Jan 1840. John **Scudder** and Rebecca, his wife, of Birmingham to Henry S. **Osborn** of New Orleans, La. For the sum of $100, Lot Nos. 9, 10, & 11, Block No. 12 in Birmingham. Signed John **Scudder**, Rebecca **Scudder** (RD). Wit A. M. **Bliss**, Augustus **Davis** (JP). Rec 18 Feb 1840. [No. 891]

1112. Page 237. 3 Feb 1840. Same and same to Elianor **Rice** of Monmouth Co., N. Jer. For the sum of $100, Lot No. 24, Block No. 12 in Birmingham. Signed John **Scudder**, Rebecca **Scudder** (RD). Wit A. M. **Bliss**, Augustus **Davis** (JP). Rec 18 Feb 1840. [No. 892]

1113. Page 238. 28 Jan 1840. Same and same to Michael **Olmstedt**. For the sum of $200, Lot No. 18, Block No. 8 in Birmingham. Signed John **Scudder**, Rebecca **Scudder**. Wit A. M. **Bliss**, Augustus **Davis** (JP). Rec 18 Feb 1840. [No. 893]

1114. Page 239. 11 Feb 1840. Hugh McFail **Saddler** to John **Hager**. For the sum of $41, 40 acres, being the SW 1/4, SE 1/4, Sec 5, Twp 35 N, Rng 12 E; patented to sd **Saddler** on 24 Jan 1837. Signed Hugh McFail (x) **Saddler**. Wit John F. **Hase**, Dep Clerk. Rec 25 Feb 1840. [No. 894]

1115. Page 240. 3 Aug 1836. William **Flynn** and Nancey, his wife, Josephus **Tucker** [and Nancey, his wife], Isaac **Hill** and Elizabeth, his wife, and George **McNew** and Louisiana, his wife, to Andrew H. **Tucker**. For the sum of $330, two tracts; 100 acres in Bois Brule Bottom, purchased by Atticus **Tucker**, decd, from Charles **Ellis**, decd, part of a tract of 350 acres purchased by sd **Ellis** from William **Dunn**; and 100 acres, being purchased by Atticus **Tucker** from Zar **Sturdivant**, decd, and part of a larger tract. Signed William **Flynn**, Nancey (x) **Flynn**, George (x) **McNew**, Elizabeth (x) **Hill**, Isaac **Hill**, Louisiana (x) **McNew**, Josephus (x) **Tucker**, Nancey (x) **Tucker** (RD). Wit John **Morris** (JP). Rec 25 Feb 1840. [No. 895]

1116. Page 241. 15 Oct 1833. U. S. A. to James **Clifton**. Patent for 80 acres, being the W 1/2, SE 1/4, Sec 20, Twp 35 N, Rng 12 E; in Certificate No. 1162. Signed Andrew **Jackson** by A. J. **Donelson**, Secy. Wit Elijah **Haywood**, Commissioner of the General Land Office. Rec in Vol. 3:78 of the General Land Office. Rec 27 Feb 1840. [No. 896]

1117. Page 242. 15 Oct 1833. U. S. A. to James **Clifton**. Patent for 40 acres, being the NE 1/4, NE 1/4, Sec 29, Twp 35 N, Rng 12 E; in Certificate No. 1164. Signed Andrew **Jackson** by A. J. **Donelson**, Secy. Wit Elijah **Haywood**, Commissioner of the General Land Office. Rec in Vol. 3:80 of the General Land Office. Rec 27 Feb 1840. Rec 27 Feb 1840. [No. 897]

1118. Page 243. 15 Oct 1833. U. S. A. to James **Clifton**. Patent for 40 acres, being the NE 1/4, SE 1/4, Sec 15, Twp 35 N, Rng 12 E; in Certificate No. 1166. Signed Andrew **Jackson** by A. J. **Donelson**, Secy. Wit Elijah **Haywood**, Commissioner of the General Land Office. Rec in Vol. 3:82 of the General Land Office. Rec 27 Feb 1840. Rec 27 Feb 1840. [No. 898]

1119. Page 244. 15 Oct 1833. U. S. A. to Eli **Clifton**. Patent for 40 acres, being the SE 1/4, NW 1/4, Sec 14, Twp 35 N, Rng 12 E; in Certificate No. 1238. Signed Andrew **Jackson** by A. J. **Donelson**, Secy. Wit Elijah **Haywood**, Commissioner of the General Land Office. Rec in Vol. 3:150 of the General Land Office. Rec 27 Feb 1840. Rec 27 Feb 1840. [No. 899]

1120. Page 245. 15 Oct 1833. U. S. A. to Eli **Clifton**. Patent for 40 acres, being the SW 1/4, NW 1/4, Sec 14, Twp 35 N, Rng 12 E; in Certificate No. 1239. Signed Andrew **Jackson** by A. J. **Donelson**, Secy. Wit Elijah **Haywood**, Commissioner of the General Land Office. Rec in Vol. 3:151 of the General Land Office. Rec 27 Feb 1840. Rec 27 Feb 1840. [No. 900]

1121. Page 245. 13 Jul 1839. James **Clifton** to Milton **Clifton**. For natural love and affection and for the better maintenance of his son, 120 acres in two tracts in Sec 20, Twp 35 N, Rng 12 E; the W 1/2, SE 1/4 and the NE 1/4, NE 1/4; patented to James **Clifton**. Signed James **Clifton**. Wit Alonzo **Abernathy**, JCC. Rec 27 Feb 1840. [No. 901]

1122. Page 246. 13 Jul 1839. Same to Wiley **Clifton**. For natural love and affection and for the better maintenance of his son, three tracts in Twp 35 N, Rng 12 E; 40 acres, being the NE 1/4, SE 1/4, Sec 15, patented to James **Clifton** on 15 Oct 1839; 40 acres, being the SE 1/4, NW 1/4, Sec 14; and 40 acres, being the SW 1/4, NW 1/4, Sec 14, patented to Eli **Clifton** on 15 Oct 1833 and deeded to James **Clifton** by Eli **Clifton** and Isabela, his wife, on 15 Jan 1836. Signed James **Clifton**. Wit Alonzo **Abernathy**, JCC. Rec 27 Feb 1840. [No. 902]

1123. Page 248. 15 Jan 1836. Eli **Clifton** and Isabella, his wife, to James **Clifton**. For the sum of $100, 80 acres in Sec 14, Twp 34 [35?] N, Rng 12 E, being the SE 1/4, NW 1/4 and the SW 1/4, NW 1/4. Signed Eli **Clifton**, Isabella (x) **Clifton** (RD). Wit James **Ferguson** (JP). Rec 27 Feb 1840. [No. 903]

1124. Page 249. 14 Jan 1840. Joseph **Boss** and Lieot, his wife, to Gotlieb **Vonderlick**. For the sum of $700, two tracts in Sec 28, Twp 34 N, Rng 12 E; 40 acres, being the SE 1/4, NW 1/4; and 40 acres, being the NW 1/4, SE 1/4. Signed Joseph **Boss**, Lugarts **Boss** (RD). Wit Elias **Barber** (JP). Rec 28 Feb 1840. [No. 904]

1125. Page 250. 11 Jan 1840. Thomas S. **McKee** and Rhoda, his wife, to Isaac **Hill**. For the sum of $150, 80 acres, more or less, in two tracts in Cinque Hommes Twp in Twp 35 N, Rng 9 E; 40 acres, being the SE 1/4, SW 1/4, Sec 14; and 40 acres, being the NW 1/4, NE 1/4, Sec 23. Signed Thomas S. **McKee**, Rhoda **McKee** (RD). Wit Robert **Trotter** (JP). Rec 29 Feb 1840. [No. 905]

1126. Page 251. 4 Jan 1840. Elisha **Belsha** to John **Moore**. For the sum of $100, 62 1/2 acres, being 1/2 of the undivided plantation on which Elisha **Belsha**, decd, lived, and which he willed to Elisha **Belsha**, son of James **Belsha**, and Jeramiah **Belsha**, son of Jerry **Belsha**. Signed Elisha **Belsha**. Wit John **Layton** Senr (JP). Test Mark **Brewer**. Rec 2 Mar 1840. [No. 906]

1127. Page 252. 26 Feb 1840. Peter R. **Pratte**, admr of the estate of Joseph **Greenawalt**, decd, to John **Logan**. For the sum of $10, 640 acres on Bois Brule Creek in Bois Brule Bottom on the E side of Jones **Nusom**'s survey; a confirmation granted to John **Greenawalt** Jr., decd, on 4 Jul 1836, and which John **Greenawalt** Senr, decd, owned as heir and legal representative of John **Greenawalt** Jr., decd. Sold in Nov 1839 at order of County Court issued Aug Term 1839 for sale of sd lands to pay debts of the estate. Signed P. R. **Pratte**, admr. Wit Fredk. C. **Hase**, Clerk. Rec 2 Mar 1840. [No. 907]

1128. Page 253. 10 Mar 1838. George **Cotner** and Sarah, his wife, of Cape Girardeau Co., Mo. to Stephen **Winkler**. For the sum of $70, 50.175 acres, more or less, being the W 1/2, Lot No. 7, NE 1/4, Sec 3, Twp 33 N, Rng 12 E. Signed George (x) **Cotner**, Sarah (x) **Cotner** (RD). Wit Elias **Barber** (JP). Rec 2 Mar 1840. [No. 908]

1129. Page 254. 4 Nov 1826. Commissioners of Perryville to James **Hutchins**. For the sum of $13.37 1/2, Lot Nos. 72 & 89 in Perryville. Signed R. T. **Brown**, Thomas **Riney**, Joseph **Tucker** senr., Commissioners. Wit John **Layton** (JP). Rec 3 Mar 1840. [No. 909]

1130. Page 255. 12 Jul 1830. James **Hutchins** and Barbara, his wife, to Joseph J. **James**. For the sum of $30, Lot Nos. 72 & 89 in Perryville. Signed James (x) **Hutchins**, Barbara (x) **Hutchins** (RD). Wit Thomas **Coty**, John **Layton** (JP). Rec 3 Mar 1840. [No. 910]

1131. Page 256. 27 Apr 1839. Joseph J. **James** and Mary Elizabeth, his wife, to Benjamine R. **Allbright** and Isaac G. **Whitworth**. For the sum of $20, Lot No. 89 in Perryville. Signed Joseph J. **James**, Mary Elizabeth (x) **James** (RD). Wit Fredk. C. **Hase**, Clerk. Rec 3 Mar 1840. [No. 911]

1132. Page 257. 13 Aug 1838. John **Hagar** to Charles **Cource**. For the sum of $1000, 98.24 acres, being the NE fractional 1/4, fractional Sec 13, Twp 35 N, Rng 12 E. Signed John **Hagar**. Wit James **Ferguson** (JP). Rec 4 Mar 1840. [No. 912]

1133. Page 258. 21 Jan 1840. Robert T. **Brown** Jur to Eli **Clifton**. For securing a debt and the sum of $1, mortgage on one black mare with bald face; her black mare colt two years old next spring; one small bay horse with a sway back; one black cow; one white and red pied cow; two dun coloured cows; one brindle heifer with white back and belly; four calves; one yoke of red muley oxen; one ox cart; on beauro; six windsor chairs; one large falling leaf table; one high post bed stead; and 50 stock hogs, including sows, pigs, and shotes. Sd **Brown** owes a note of even date to sd **Clifton** for $267 with 10% interest per annum until paid. Signed Robert T. **Brown** Jur. Wit John **Hughey** (JP). Rec 4 Mar 1840. [No. 913]

1134. Page 259. 21 Jan 1840. Same to John **Holden** of Adams Co., Miss. For the sum of $285, $5 in hand and the rest to be paid to John **Logan**; the N 1/2 of Lot No. 9 in Perryville, fronting on Spring St; purchased by sd **Brown** from William C. **Kirkpatrick**. Sd **Brown** owes sd **Logan** a note with sd **Holden** as security, and this secures the debt. Signed Robert T. **Brown** Jur. Wit John **Hughey** (JP). Rec 4 Mar 1840. [No. 914]

1135. Page 260. 14 Nov 1837. U. S. A. to Michael **Tucker**. Patent for 26.05 acres, being the NE 1/4, NE 1/4, fractional Sec 6, Twp 35 N, Rng 11 E; in Certificate No. 5065. Signed Martin **Van Buren** by A. **Van Buren**, Secy. Wit Joseph B. **Watson**, Acting Recorder of the General Land Office. Rec in Vol. 10:118 of the General Land Office. Rec 27 Feb 1840. Rec 4 Mar 1840. [No. 915]

1136. Page 261. 4 Sep 1839. Nicholas **Tucker** Senr and Mary, his wife, to Michael **Tucker**. For the sum of $77.75, 62.24 acres, beginning at the SE corner. Signed Nicholas (x) **Tucker**, Mary (x) **Tucker** (RD). Wit James **Rice** (JP), John N. **Tucker**. Rec 4 Mar 1840. [No. 916]

1137. Page 262. 7 Mar 1840. Mark L. **Manning** to John **Logan**. To secure a debt and for the sum of $1, mortgage on one bay mule three years old this spring, one red cow and calf, one red and white cow and calf, 15 sheep, and 23 hogs. Sd **Manning** owes sd **Logan** $46 with interest. Signed Mark L. **Manning**. Wit Fredk. C. **Hase**, Clerk. Rec 7 Mar 1840. [No. 917]

1138. Page 263. 9 Mar 1840. Robert T. **Brown** Senior and Robert T. **Brown** Junior to James **Rice**. For securing several notes and the sum of $1, deed of trust on the goods invoiced by F. **Wilkinson** and F. **Gregoire** for sd **Browns**. Sd **Browns** owe notes as follows: for $330.37 dated 18 Nov 1839 to J. S. **Pease** & Co. of St. Louis; $900 or more with interest to J. & E. **Walsh** & Co.; $300 or more to **Shaw** & **Larkin**; and $150.23 with interest dated 18 Sep 1839 to James W. **Doughty**. Sd **Rice** is to sell the property to pay these debts on 23 Mar 1840 if the **Browns** default. Signed Robert T. **Brown** Senr, Robert T. **Brown** Jur. Wit Fredk. C. **Hase**, Clerk, Robert **Trotter** (JP). Rec 11 Mar 1840. [No. 918]

1139. Page 265. 15 Mar 1837. U. S. A. to Michael **Tucker**. Patent for 21 acres, being the SE fractional 1/4, fractional Sec 26, Twp 35 N, Rng 13 E; in Certificate No. 3492. Signed Martin **Van Buren** by A. **Van Buren**, Secy. Wit H. M. **Garland**, Recorder of the General Land Office. Rec in Vol. 7:21 of the General Land Office. Rec 12 Mar 1840. [No. 919]

1140. Page 265. 15 May 1839. Sarah **Young** to Robert P. **Slaughter**. For the sum of $600, 76.21 acres in the Mississippi Bottom, assigned to Clara **Hamilton**, relict of George A.

Hamilton, decd, as dower land. Signed Sarah **Young**. Wit Elias **Barber** (JP). Rec 12 Mar 1840. [No. 920]

1141. Page 266. 9 Mar 1840. Mathias **Barringer** to Robert **Manning**. For the sum of $437, two tracts; 70 acres, more or less, part of a tract confirmed to John **Layton** Senior, and the same conveyed to Mathias **Barringer** by J. **Pratte** and wife and Peter R. **Pratte** and wife on 21 Oct 1837 (3:39), then conveyed by sd **Barringer** to William **Barringer** and Mathias M. **Barringer** with certain restrictions on 22 Feb 1839, beginning at a stake at the corner of Joseph **Shoults**; and Lot No. 31 in Perryville, fronting on Main St. Signed Mathias **Barringer**. Wit Fredk. C. **Hase**, Clerk. Rec 12 Mar 1840. [No. 921]

1142. Page 268. 20 Dec 1839. Henry Cristoper **Bimpage**, admr of the estate of Johann George **Gube**, decd, to Henry C. **Bimpage**, Frederick Wilh. **Barthels**, and Christian Friedk. **Muller**, and all their survivors. For diverse good causes and considerations, 640 acres, more or less, on Brazeau Creek and the Mississippi River, being Survey No. 2173 in Twp 34 N, Rng 14 E; originally granted to John **Manning**, and lately bought from Moses S. **Harris** and Robert S. **Manning** by sd **Gube**; beginning at a post on Henrey **Riley**'s survey; less 6 acres previously sold to sd **Bimpage** on 12 Jan 1839. The grantees will lay out a town to be called Wittenberg on the land. Sold on a decree issued on 29 Nov 1839 by Circuit Court in Chancery. Signed Henry C. **Bimpage**, admr of Johann G. **Gube**. Wit Gustav **Pfau**, F. **Gottschelk**, Fredk. C. **Hase**, Clerk. Rec 13 Mar 1840. [No. 922]

1143. Page 270. 1 Jan 1840. James **Evans** to William **James** of Ste. Genevieve Co., trustee for Susan M. **Evans**. For natural love and affection for his wife and "...wishing to secure...certain property for her future support against the hungrey grasp of a cold and uncharitable world in the event of any accident happening to me...," one negro named woman named **Flora** aged about 56 years, one negro girl **Mary Annah** aged about 15, one eight day clock, all the beds and furniture belonging to the same. Signed James **Evans**. Wit Fredk. C. **Hase**, Clerk, John F. **Hase**. Rec 16 Mar 1840. [No. 923]

1144. Page 271. 12 Mar 1840. Robert P. **Slaughter** and Evaline, his wife, to Gottfried **Jaeger**. For the sum of $2000, two tracts; 76.21 acres, more or less, in the Mississippi Bottom, assigned to Clare **Hamilton**, relict of George A. **Hamilton**, decd as dower land; joined to the E by the Mississippi River and N fractional Sec 6, Twp 34 N, Rng 14 E; part of the land confirmed to George A. **Hamilton**, and sold by Sarah **Young** to sd **Slaughter** on 15 May 1839; and an undivided 1/6 part of 457 acres in the NW corner of a tract originally granted to George A. **Hamilton**, decd, which was allotted to the widow as a portion of her dower, commonly called the Hill Tract, sold to sd **Slaughter** by George A. **Hamilton** on 23 Sep 1839. Signed Robert P. **Slaughter**, Evaline M. **Slaughter** (RD). Wit Elias **Barber** (JP). Rec 17 Mar 1840. [No. 924]

1145. Page 272. 2 Mar 1840. Alexander **Kinnison** and Nicey Jane, his wife, to John **Kinnison**. For the sum of $1, 85.06 acres, more or less, beginning at the most S corner of Alexander **McConnohoe**'s survey near a lake; conveyed to sd Alexander by his father John **Kinnison**. Signed A. S. **Kinnison**, Nicy Jane **Kinnison** (RD). Wit Alfred L. **Parks** (JP). Rec 18 Mar 1840. [No. 925]

1146. Page 273. 17 Mar 1840. John **Kinnison** and Sinia, his wife, to William H. **Diggs** and George **McKinistry** Junr. For the sum of $1000, 85.06 acres fronting on the Mississippi River, a portion of a tract confirmed to Alexander **McConnohoe**, decd, and conveyed by him to sd **Kinnison**, and by sd **Kinnison** to his son Alexander **Kinnison**, and reconveyed by Alexander **Kinnison** and wife to John **Kinnison** on 2 Mar 1840; as described in the preceding deed (3:272). Signed John **Kinnison**, Sinia **Kinnison** (RD). Wit James **Rice** (JP). Rec 18 Mar 1840. [No. 926]

1147. Page 275. 23 Mar 1840. Timothy **Phelps** by Sheriff Hugh **Wells** to James G. **Evans**. For the sum of $181, 238.19 acres in Twp 36 & 37 N, Rng 11 E, being Survey No. 377 confirmed to Noel **Hornbeck**. Sold on 23 Mar 1840 on a writ of fieri facias issued 16 Nov 1839 by Circuit Court of Washington Co., Mo. in favor of Austin **Hawkins** and against sd Phelps for $150 damages plus costs. Signed Hugh **Wells**, Sheriff. Wit Fredk. C. **Hase**, Clerk. Rec 25 Mar 1840. [No. 927]

1148. Page 276. 23 Mar 1840. Thomas E. **Johnson** to John **Logan**. For the sum of $741, mortgage on three tracts; 160 acres on Apple Creek in Perry and Cape Girardeau Cos., being Lot Nos. 4 & 5, Sec 2, Twp 33 N, Rng 12 E, and a New Madrid Certificate located by Stephen **Bird** and John **Primm**, originally confirmed to Joseph **Generdeaux**; purchased from the estate of Robert N. **Cochran**; 80 acres adjoining the first tract on the E down sd creek, that was purchased from Nathan **Vanhorne**; and 40 acres about two miles from the mouth of Apple Creek, which was purchased from Thomas **Rhyne**. Sd **Logan** is security for sd Johnson in a note to Alexander H. **Stephenson**, admr of the estate of Robert N. **Cochrin**, decd, for payment of $741 due 12 months after date, and which was the consideration for the first tract. Signed Thos. E. **Johnson**. Wit Fredk. C. **Hase**, Clerk. Rec 24 Mar 1840. [No. 928]

1149. Page 278. 17 Apr 1839. Washington **Dorsey** of Yazoo Co., Miss. to Richard S. **Dorsey**. For the sum of $50, 16.63 acres, being the SW fractional 1/4, Sec 29, Twp 35 N, Rng 11 E. Signed W. **Dorsey**. Wit George **Crockett**, Clerk of Yazoo Co., Miss. Probate Court, Thomas P. **Slader**, Clerk of Yazoo Co., Miss. Circuit Court. Rec 24 Mar 1840. [No. 929]

1150. Page 279. 1 Dec 1838. Charles **Gregoire** and Eulila, his wife, to Joseph **Pratte**. For the sum of $100, 50 acres, the remainder of a tract conveyed to sd **Pratte** by sd **Gregoire** on 21 Jun 1837 (2:229). Signed Charles **Gregoire**, Eulalie **Gregoire**. Wit W. **Searcy** (JP). Rec 25 Mar 1840. [No. 930]

1151. Page 279. 4 Nov 1839. John **Carlisle** and Joanah, his wife, to Moses H. **Diggs** and George **McKinstry** of Vicksburg, Miss. For the sum of $2200, 256.63 acres in two parcels; 153 acres in Bois Brule Bottom on the bank of the Mississippi River, part of 420 arpents confirmed to William **Fitzgibon**; 200 acres of which was purchased from George **Sturdivant** by A. H. **Puckett**; and 103.63 acres, being fractional Sec 4, Twp 36 N, Rng 11 E, entered by George **Camster** and conveyed to sd **Carlisle**. Signed John **Carlisle**, Joanna M. **Carlisle** (RD). Wit W. C. **Simpleton**, John **Ruland**, Clerk of 3rd Judicial Dist Superior Court. Rec 25 Mar 1840. [No. 931]

1152. Page 281. 12 Mar 1840. Robert T. **Brown** Junior to James **Rice**. For the sum of $400, two tracts; the undivided 1/2 of 80 acres, being the N 1/2, NW 1/4, Sec 14, Twp 35 N, Rng 12 E, patented to sd **Brown** and William **Brown**; and 38.70 acres, being the NW 1/4, SW fractional 1/4, Sec 31, Twp 36 N, Rng 10 E, patented to Robert T. **Brown** Jur. Signed Robert T. **Brown** Jur. Wit Reubin **Shelby**, JCC. Rec 25 Mar 1840. [No. 932]

1153. Page 282. 14 Jan 1840. Mathias **Rix** and Barbara, his wife, to Joseph **Boss**. For the sum of $740, 40 acres, being the SE 1/4, SE 1/4, Sec 19, Twp 34 N, Rng 12 E. Signed Mathias **Rix**, Barbara **Rix** (RD). Wit Elias **Barber** (JP). Rec 26 Mar 1840. [No. 933]

1154. Page 283. 21 Mar 1840. William **McLain** and Alley, his wife, to Ezra **Shelby**. For the sum of $400, 160 acres purchased from Bernard **Layton** and wife on 21 Feb 1820; the SE corner of a tract confirmed to sd **Layton**, and part of the tract on which Perryville is located. Signed William (x) **McLain**, Alley **McLain** (RD). Wit Reuben **Shelby**, JCC. Rec 26 Mar 1840. [No. 934]

1155. Page 284. 21 Mar 1840. Edward **McLain** and Ellin, his wife, to same. For the sum of $1000, 157 1/2 acres, beginning at a stake standing in a cluster of white oaks in the most S corner of a tract confirmed to Bernard **Layton**, except for 2 1/2 acres sold to Charles **Stewart** on 16 Apr 1838; part of the tract on which Perryville is located. Signed Edward **McLain**, Ellin (x) **McLain** (RD). Wit Reuben **Shelby**, JCC. Rec 26 Mar 1840. [No. 935]

1156. Page 285. 26 Mar 1840. Amzi **Osborn** by Sheriff Hugh **Wells** to John **Scudder**. For the sum of $30, six tracts in Perry and Cape Girardeau Cos.; 40 acres, being the E 1/2, Lot No. 1, NW 1/4, Sec 6, Twp 33 N, Rng 14 E; 80 acres, being Lot No. 1, NE 1/4, fractional Sec 3, Twp 33 N, Rng 13 E; 40 acres, being the NE 1/4, SE 1/4, Sec 7, Twp 33 N, Rng 14 E; 40 acres, being the NE 1/4, SE 1/4, Sec 3, Twp 33 N, Rng 13 E; 40 acres, being the SE 1/4, SE 1/4, Sec 1, Twp 33 N, Rng 13 E; and 40 acres, being the NW 1/4, SE 1/4, Sec 1, Twp 33 N, Rng 13 E. Sold on 23 Mar 1840 on two writs of fieri facias issued on 16 Jan 1840 by Circuit Court; one in favor of William **Manning** for the use of James **Taylor** and against sd **Osborn** for $870 debt, $121.43 damages, and $14.95 1/4 costs; the other in favor of William A. **Bull** and against sd **Osborn** for $575.08 damages and $16.85 costs. Signed Hugh **Wells**, Sheriff. Wit James **Evans**, Fredk. C. **Hase**, Clerk. Rec 27 Mar 1840. [No. 936]

1157. Page 287. 25 Jul 1837. Commissioners to partition land of Harrison **Young**, decd, to Sarah **Young**. For the sum of $560, 76.21 acres in Brazeau Bottom on the Mississippi River, being the dower assigned to the widow Clara **Hamilton**, decd, from a large tract confirmed to George A. **Hamilton**. Sold in Jul 1837 at order of Circuit Court issued Mar Term 1837 in case of Sarah **Young**, widow, and the minor heirs of Harrison **Young**, decd, vs. Leo **Fenwick**, Rebeca **Fenwick**, and others in a petition to partition sd lands. Signed Jeffrey **Power**, Charles **Swan**, Jacob **Shaner**. Wit James **Rice** (JP). Rec 27 Mar 1840. [No. 937]

1158. Page 290. 14 Aug 1839. Benedict **Riley** and Anna, his wife, Cornelius **Rhodes** and Mary, his wife, William **Manning** and Sarah, his wife, and Elizabeth **Manning**, widow of James **Manning**, decd, all heirs of Henry **Riley**, decd, to Rezin L. **Bishop**. For the sum of $100, 107 acres, more or less, on the bank of the Mississippi River near the Grand Tower, adjoining Mrs. **Gill**; confirmed to Henry **Riley**, decd. Signed Benedict **Riley**, Anna **Riley** (RD), Cornelious **Rhodes**, Mary (x) **Rhodes** (RD), Elizabeth **Manning** (RD), William **Manning**, Sarah **Manning** (RD). Wit James **Rice** (JP). Rec 27 Mar 1840. [No. 938]

1159. Page 291. 1 Feb 1840. Henry C. **Bimpage** to Fenwick J. **Hamilton**, guardian of James and Chloe **Fenwick**. For the sums of $94.56 1/4 and $200, mortgage on two tracts; 6 acres, more or less, from his tract in Wittenberg; beginning at the SE corner of Survey No. 2173 for 600 acres in the name of John **Manning** in Twp 34 N, Rng 14 E, and bounded by the Mississippi River in part; as described in a deed of J. G. **Gube** to sd **Bimpage** dated 29 Nov 1839; and 120 acres, being the undivided 1/2 of the W 1/2, NW 1/4 and NE 1/4 NW 1/4, Sec 24, Twp 34 N, Rng 13 E, entered in the names of sd **Hamilton** and sd **Bimpage** in Certificate No. 6964. Sd **Bimpage** owes sd **Hamilton** the two sums with interest in two years. Signed Henry C. **Bimpage**. Wit F. C. **Hase**, Clerk. Rec 27 Mar 1840. [No. 939]

1160. Page 292. 27 Mar 1840. Elizabeth J. **Swan**, admr of Henry **Swan**, decd, to John **Logan** by his agent Joseph **Pratte**. For the sum of $81, about 6 acres adjoining Perryville on the E and sd **Logan**; beginning at a post at the corner of sd **Logan**'s land; purchased by Henry **Swan**, decd, from Reuben **Shelby** (2:180). Sold on 26 Mar 1839 at order of County Court issued Feb Term 1839 on petition for sale of sd real estate to pay debts of the estate. Signed Elizabeth J. **Swan**, admr. Wit James **Rice** (JP). Rec 29 Mar 1840. [No. 940]

1161. Page 294. 4 Mar 1840. Edward M. **Holden** to James **McGillycuddy** of Vicksburg, Miss. To secure a debt and for the sum of $1, mortgage on one sorrel horse; one bay horse; three cows and calves; one two-horse waggon; six sheep and their future increase; two sows and a lot of other hogs; one gigg and harness; one beauro; one side board or press; six windsor chairs; one rocking chair; bedsteads beds and bedding; one clock; one large falling leaf table; one small table; one work stand; one man saddle; one ladie saddle; two year-old steers; two one-year-old steers; and several law and other books [enumerated in the deed]. Sd **Holden** is indebted to sd **McGillycuddy** by a note for $800 due on demand; the property to go to sd **McGillycuddy** after the payment of two debts, one to John **Logan** and one to John A. **Burget**, for which part of the property is pledged. Signed Edward M. **Holden**. Wit Fredk. C. **Hase**, Clerk. Rec 20 Mar 1840. [No. 941]

1162. Page 296. 3 Apr 1840. George **Propst** and Hanna, his wife, of Cape Girardeau Co., Mo. to Michael **Renner**. For the sum of $400, 40 acres, being the E 1/2, Lot No. 3, NE 1/4, Sec 4, Twp 33 N, Rng 11 E; patented to sd **Propst** on 15 Oct 1833. Signed George (x) **Propst**, Hannah (x) **Propst** (RD). Wit Hyman **Block**, Reuben **Shelby**, JCC. Rec 3 Apr 1840. [No. 942]

1163. Page 297. 27 May 1839. John G. **Gube** to William F. **Cook**. For the sum of $50, __ acres, being the SE 1/4, SW 1/4, Sec 14, Twp 34 N, Rng 13 E. Signed John George **Gube**. Wit Augustus **Davis** (JP), Manerva A. **Davis**. Rec 4 Apr 1840. [No. 943]

1164. Page 298. 26 Jun 1839. Samuel **Merry**, Jacob **Hawkins**, and David **Goodspeed** by their atty in fact John Epes **Cowan** to Michael M. **Clark** and John P. **Cunningham**, all of St. Louis Co., Mo. For the sum of $1000, their 1/2 interest in four tracts entered by sd **Merry**, sd **Cowan**, sd **Goodspeed**, William **Houston**, sd **Hawkins**, and Jno. W. **Lott**; 160 acres, being the W 1/2, SW 1/4, and W 1/2, NW 1/4, Sec 33, Twp 35 N, Rng 10 E; 80 acres, being the W 1/2, SE 1/4, Sec 28, Twp 35 N, Rng 10 E; 80 acres, being the W 1/2, NE 1/4, Sec 7, Twp 34 N, Rng 10 E; and 80 acres, being the E 1/2, SW 1/4, Sec 11, Twp 34 N, Rng 9 E. Signed Samuel **Merry**, Jacob **Hawkins**, David **Goodspeed** by their atty in fact J. Epes **Cowan**. Test John W. **Speer**, John **Ruland**, Clerk of St. Louis Co Circuit Court. Rec 9 Apr 1840. [No. 944]

1165. Page 299. 19 Jan 1836. John **Layton** and Monica, his wife, to Francis J. **Ziegler**. For the sum of $1, 50 acres, more or less, beginning on the line of St. Marys Seminary within a few rods of the dwelling house of sd **Ziegler**. Signed John **Layton**, Monica **Layton** (RD). Wit James **Rice** (JP). Rec 10 Apr 1840. [No. 945]

1166. Page 300. 4 Feb 1840. Mark **Brewer**, admr of the estate of Patrick **McBride**, decd, to John **Odin**. For the sum of $101, 40 acres, being the NE 1/4, SW 1/4, Sec 35, Twp 35 N, Rng 10 E. Sold on order of County Court issued Nov 1839 Term. Signed Mark **Brewer**, admr. Wit Reuben **Shelby**, JCC. Rec 20 Apr 1840. [No. 946]

1167. Page 301. 12 Mar 1839. John **Logan** to William **Cox**. For the sum of $250, 150 acres, more or less, on Thompson's Fork of McClanahan's Creek, the lower part of a tract confirmed to James **Thompson**; also bounded by **Long**'s old improvement. Signed John **Logan**. Wit W. **Searcy** (JP). [Includes plat showing portion of the original confirmation that belongs to Lewis **French** No. 1, 150 acres; sd **Cox** No. 2; and Elizabeth **Warthen** No. 3, 40 acres.] Rec 6 May 1840. [No. 947]

1168. Page 302. 18 Apr 1840. Henry **McAtee** and Mari, his wife, to James **McCauley**. For the sum of $325, two tracts in Sec 31, Twp 36 N, Rng 11 E; 65.17 acres, more or less, being the SE fractional 1/4; and 30 acres, more or less, being the S part of the NE fractional 1/4, purchased by sd **McAtee** from Jona **Windfield** and wife on 18 Oct 1830; bounded by J. **Preston**, ___ **Duvall**. Signed Henry **McAtee**, Maria (x) **McAtee** (RD). Wit Reuben **Shelby**, JCC, Jeffrey **Power**, County Surveyor, John C. **Hase**, Dep Clerk. Rec 4 May 1840. [No. 948]

1169. Page 304. 4 May 1840. Jacob **Shoults** and Mary, his wife, to Ferdinand **Belsha**. For the sum of $600, 57 acres, more or less, in Bois Brule Bottom; part of a tract confirmed to James **Burns** and on which sd **Shoults** resided. Signed Jacob (x) **Shoults**, Mary **Shoults**. Wit Fredk. C. **Hase**, Clerk. Rec 4 May 1840. [No. 949]

1170. Page 305. 15 Nov 1837. William **Hancock** and Nelly, his wife, to Stephen **Tucker** and William **Keyton**. For ___, 320 acres on Cedar Fork of Saline Creek in Twp 35 N, Rng 9 E; being the upper 1/2 of 640 acres, settled by Henry **Tucker** and deeded from James **Henderson** to Francis **Keener** and William **Handcock**; less 4 acres containing the mill and mill yard contracted to sd **Tucker** and sd **Keyton**. Signed William **Handcock**, Nelly (x) **Handcock** (RD). Wit James F. **Keener**, L. C. **Handcock**, Robert **Trotter** (JP). Rec 4 May 1840. [No. 950]

1171. Page 306. 4 May 1840. Frederick **Rix** to Mathias **Rix**. For the sum of $60, 40 acres, more or less, being the SE 1/4, SE 1/4, Sec 19, Twp 34 N, Rng 12 E. Signed Frederick (x) **Rix**. Wit James **Rice** (JP), James B. **May**. Rec 4 May 1840. [No. 951]

1172. Page 306. 9 Oct 1839. Richard **Maddock** Seniar to Richard **Maddock** Junior. For the sum of $50, 40 acres, being the SE 1/4, NW 1/4, Sec 35, Twp 35 N, Rng 9 E; entered by Richard **Maddock** Senr. Signed Richard **Maddock** Senr. Test Mark **Brewer** (JP). Rec 6 May 1840. [No. 952]

1173. Page 307. 10 Feb 1840. Marschal **Dickson** to Jesse **Dickson**. For the sum of $500, the undivided 1/4 part of two tracts; 98.39 acres, being the NE fractional 1/4, Sec 20, Twp 35 N, Rng 13 E; and 79.93 acres, being the E 1/2, NW fractional 1/4, Sec 20, Twp 35 N, Rng 13 E, patented to the heirs of Wm. **Burns**, decd, on 31 May 1824, and sold by William **Burns**, one of the heirs, to Marschal **Dickson** on 14 Aug 1837. Signed Marshal **Dickson**. Wit Robert T. **Brown**, JCC. Rec 7 May 1840. [No. 953]

1174. Page 308. 13 Apr 1827. Aquila **Hagan** and Mary, his wife, to Martin J. **Moore**. For the sum of $80, 80 acres, part of 640 acres originally owned by Thomas **Allen**; beginning at the NE corner of the original survey. Signed Aquilla **Hagan**, Mary (x) **Hagan** (RD). Test F. J. **Hamilton**, John **Layton** (JP). Rec 11 May 1840. [No. 954]

1175. Page 310. 24 Jul 1822. Heirs and assigns of Clemment **Hayden**, decd, to Thomas **Riney**. For the sum of $0.50, quit claim to a tract sold by sd **Riney** to sd **Hayden** on 8 Feb 1809 (Ste. Genevieve Co. Book B:32). Signed Susana **Hayden**, William **Tucker**, Benedict **Riley**, George (x) **Fenwick**, Clement **Hayden**, Sarah (x) **Tucker** [wife of William], Margaret (x) **Fenwick** [wife of George], Ann (x) **Riley** [wife of Benedict]. Wit Joab **Waters**, Benjamine **Davis**, Cornelius M. **Slattery** (JP). Rec 11 May 1840. [No. 955]

1176. Page 311. 1 Aug 1825. George **Fenwick** and Margaret, his wife, to same. For the sum of $250, 150 acres on the head waters of Bois Brule Creek; part of 250 acres left to Margaret by Clement **Hayden**, decd; and beginning at a point on Bernard **Brown**'s W line, and surveyed so as to include Barnard **Smith**'s present improvement lying in sd **Riney**'s 640 acre improvement right grant. Signed George **Fenwick**, Margaret (x) **Fenwick**. Wit Joab **Waters**, Benjamin **Davis**, James **Mattingley**, all JCC. Rec 11 May 1840. [No. 956]

1177. Page 312. 17 Jan 1832. Barnard **Brown** and Ann, his wife, to same. For the sum of $450, 184 1/4 acres, the S part of a tract sold by sd **Riney** to sd **Brown** on 24 Jul 1822, and where sd **Brown** now resides. Signed Bernard (x) **Brown**, Ann (x) **Brown**. Wit R. T. **Brown**, JCC. Rec 11 May 1840. [No. 957]

1178. Page 313. 20 Feb 1836. Zachariah **Layton** and Mary, his wife, to same. For the sum of $1, Lot Nos. 14 &66 in Perryville, on the W side of the courthouse. Signed Zachariah **Layton**, Mary (x) **Layton** (RD). Wit John **Layton** Senr (JP). Rec 11 May 1840. [No. 958]

1179. Page 314. 24 Feb 1840. Martin J. **Moore** and Nancey, his wife, to same. For the sum of $200, 80 acres, part of 640 acres originally owned by Thomas **Allen**; beginning at the NE corner of the original survey; and deeded to sd **Moore** by Aquila **Hagan** and Mary, his wife. Signed Martin (x) **Moore**, Nancey (x) **Moore** (RD). Rec Robert **Trotter** (JP). Wit 11 May 1840. [No. 959]

1180. Page 315. 24 Apr 1840. Michael **Tucker** to Mary **Holster**. For the sum of $91.25, one horse of a brown or bay colour, purchased by sd **Tucker** at the estate sale of Peter **Holster**, decd. Signed Michael (x) **Tucker**. Signed Elisha **Eggers** (JP). Rec 12 May 1840. [No. 960]

1181. Page 315. 27 Dec 1839 [on "...the third Holy Christmas day in the year 1839, in after noon one quarter of an hour before four of the clock..."]. Noncuperative last will and testament of Christian August **Heilmann**. To John David **Loesch** as universal heir: all his real and personal property, to be distributed as directed as sd **Heilmann**'s death. Sd **Loesch** is to deliver 20 acres in Frohna from the Rev. Mr. **Heyle** that sd **Heilmann** has paid for. To Johanna Sophie **Heyenigen**, wife of John Gottfied **Heinigan**, weaver, residing in Saxony, sister of sd **Heilmann**: $30 after seven years. To Johanna **Heyenigin**, daughter of Johanna Sophie **Heyenigin**: $20 dollars after seven years. To the Church at Frohna in America: $15 in six months to be paid to Ferdinand Willhelm **Schnebert** as church warden of sd church. To John Frederick **Binger** for the use of the Lutheran College: $5 after six months. To the Fund for the Poor at Frohna: $5 in six months. Debts to be paid after eight weeks: John Henrich **Weindhalf** $9.50, Gottleib **Helling** $10, August **Uhlig** $1, Gottlieb **Helbig** $3.75, **Heinig** $1.25, **Landgraf** $2, **Brightson** $1, **Burkharett** $2.18 3/4, Gottlob **Groeste** $3.50, and **Naumann** $2.50. Wit John Frederick (x) **Bunger**, Willhelm Adolph **Bergt**, Christian Adolph **Bertt**, Christian Frederick **Landgraf**, Johann Gottfried **Heinig**, Frederick August **Ahlich**. Fredk. C. **Hase**, Clerk and translator from German to English. Rec 12 May 1840. [No. 961]

1182. Page 317. 4 Apr 1835. Wm. **McGuire** and Susan, his wife, and John **Juden** Jr. and Abby, his wife, to William **Burns** and Andrew **Burns**. For the sum of $115, two tracts; 50.47 acres, more or less, being the W fractional 1/2, Sec 26, Twp 36 N, Rng 12 E; and 41.84 acres, more or less, being the N fractional 1/2, Sec 22, Twp 36 N, Rng 12 E. Signed Wm. **McGuire**, Susan **McGuire** (RD), John **Juden**, Abbey **Juden** (RD). Wit Hy. **Sanford**, Clerk of Cape Girardeau Co., John D. **Cook**, Judge of 10th Judicial Circuit. Rec 17 May 1840. [No. 962]

1183. Page 318. 12 May 1840. Andrew **Burns** and Elizabeth, his wife, of Perry Co. and William **Burns**, son of sd Andrew, and Getty, his wife, of Jackson Co., Ill. to Francis L. **Jones**. For the sum of $366, 48 acres, more or less, on Cape Cinque Hommes Island on the Mississippi River; being the W fractional 1/2, Sec 26, Twp 36 N, Rng 12 E; purchased from Wm. **McGuire** and wife and John **Juden** and wife on 4 Apr 1835. Signed A. **Burns**, Elizabeth (x) **Burns** (RD), W. **Burns**, Getty (x) **Burns** (RD). Wit James **Rice** (JP), Perletus **Wilson**. Rec 15 May 1840. [No. 963]

1184. Page 320. 1 May 1840. 21 May 1840. William H. **Diggs** to George **McKinstry** Jur. For the sum of $4500, his undivided moiety in three tracts; two on the Mississippi River in Bois Brulle Bottom, purchased by sd **Diggs** and sd **McKinstry** in co-partnership from John **Carlisle** and Joanna M., his wife, on 4 Nov 1839 (3:279), one being 153 acres, more or less, part of 420 arpens confirmed to William **Fitz Gibbon**, of which 200 acres was purchased from George **Sturdivant** by Alfred H. **Puckett**, and 103.63 acres, more or less, being fractional Sec 4, Twp 36 N, Rng 11 E, entered by George **Campster**; and 85.06 acres, purchased by sd **Diggs** and sd **McKinstrey** from John **Kinnison** and Sina, his wife, on 17 Mar 1840 (3:273), part of a tract confirmed to Alexander **McConohoe**, who conveyed it to sd **Kinnison**, who conveyed to his son Alexander **Kinnison**, who reconveyed it to John **Kinnison** on 2 Mar 1840, beginning at the most S corner of the confirmation. Signed Wm. H. **Diggs**. Wit James **Rice** (JP). Rec 25 May 1840. [No. 964]

1185. Page 322. 23 Oct 1833. Perry **Evans** and Dianna, his wife, to John **Logan**. For the sum of $200, 150 acres, more or less, on Thompson's Fork of McClanahan's Creek, the lower part of a tract confirmed to James **Thompson** near **Long**'s old improvement, running up sd creek to two hollows. Signed Perry **Evans**, Dianna (x) **Evans** (RD). Wit W. **Searcy** (JP). Rec 27 May 1840. [No. 965]

1186. Page 323. 14 Jan 1840. Anthony **Fleck** and Elizabeth, his wife, to Christian Gotlieb **Frenzil**. For the sum of $350, 40 acres, being the NE 1/4, SW 1/4, Sec 28, Twp 34 N, Rng 12 E; except a lot previously sold to Perletus **Wilson** on the N line of the tract. Signed Anthony **Fleck**, Elizabeth **Fleck** (RD). Wit Elias **Barber** (JP). Rec 29 May 1840. [No. 966]

1187. Page 324. 29 [May] 1840. John J. **Johnson** to Ferdinand **Rozier** Jur. For securing a note and the sum of $1, mortgage on two tracts in Sec 24, Twp 34 N, Rng 8 E; __ acres, being the SW 1/4, NE 1/4; and __ acres, being the SE 1/4, NW 1/4. Sd **Johnson** owes a note dated 28 May 1840 for $99.26 with legal interest to sd **Rozier**. Signed John J. (x) **Johnson**. Wit Fredk. C. **Hase**, Clerk. Rec 29 May 1840. [No. 967]

1188. Page 325. 25 Apr 1840. Moses **Rody** and Hetty, his wife, to Ferdinand **Rozier**. For the sum of $71.56, 40 acres, being the E 1/2, Lot No. 1, NE 1/4, Sec 3, Twp 34 N, Rng 10 E. Signed Moses **Rody**, Hetty (x) **Rody**. Wit B. R. **Albright**, Reuben **Shelby**, JCC. Rec 30 May 1840. [No. 968]

1189. Page 326. 10 Jun 1840. George **McKinstry** Jur. to Charles **McKinstry**. For the sum of $4500, one equal 1/2 of three tracts as described in 3:320. Signed G. **McKinstry**. Wit James **Rice** (JP). Rec 11 Jun 1840. [No. 969]

1190. Page 328. 10 Jun 1840. Charles **McKinstry** to George **McKinstry** Jur. For securing a debt and the sum of $1, mortgage on the land described in 3:320. Charles **McKinstry** owes George **McKinstry** Junior a note of even date for $4500, 1/2 payable in 18 months, the other 1/2 payable in 36 months. Signed C. **McKinstry**. Wit James **Rice** (JP). Rec 11 Jun 1840. [No. 970]

1191. Page 329. 22 May 1840. Barnard **Brown** by Hiram H. **Baber**, Auditor of Mo. to Frederick C. **Hase**. For the sum of $0.36 in taxes and penalties due the state for 1835, Lot No. 5 in Perryville. Signed Hiram H. **Baber**, Auditor of Public Accounts. Wit John F. **Hase**, Dep. Clerk. Rec 11 Jun 1840. [No. 971]

1192. Page 330. 25 Mar 1839. Nicholas **Tucker** Senr and Mary, his wife, to Peter **Brown**. For the sum of $39.50, 31.92 acres, part of the N part of the SW fractional 1/4, fractional Sec 1, Twp 35 N, Rng 10 E. Signed Nicholas **Tucker**, Mary (x) **Tucker** (RD). Wit James **Rice** (JP). Rec 13 Jun 1840. [No. 972]

1193. Page 331. 2 Jun 1840. Christiane **Voelker** to Henry **Voelker**. For the sum of $50, 40 acres, more or less, in Cinque Hommes Twp, being the SW 1/4, SE 1/4, fractional Sec 9, Twp 36 N, Rng 10 E. Signed Christiane (x) **Voelker**. Wit Robert **Trotter** (JP). Rec 16 Jun 1840. [No. 973]

1194. Page 332. 18 Jun 1840. John **Johnson** to William C. **Moore** of Cape Girardeau Co. For the sum of $52.82, mortgage on 40 acres, being the NE 1/4, NE 1/4, Sec 23, Twp 34 N, Rng 8 E. Sd **Johnson** owes sd **Moore** a debt with 10% interest within six months. Signed John (x) **Johnson**. Wit John **Layton** (JP). Rec 19 Jun 1840. [Marginal note: Full satisfaction received. No date. Signed William H. **McLaine**, assignee of William C. **Moore**. Wit John W. **Noell**, Clerk.] [No. 974]

1195. Page 332. 19 Jun 1840. George **McKinstry** Junior to Alfred H. **Puckett**. For securing debts and for the sum of $1, mortgage on 1/2 of three tracts as described in 3:320. Sd **McKinstry** owes several sums of money to sd **Puckett**, being an unascertained balance of an unsettled account for which sd **Puckett** is security; all debts of George **McKinstry** Jur in A. H. **Puckett** & Co. and William H. **Diggs** & Co. totaling $3580, due by 1 Jan 1841; and after the amount due to sd **Puckett** is deducted, the money due to John **Kinnison** as security by 1 Nov 1840, amounting to $670. Signed G. **McKinstry** Jur. Wit James **Rice** (JP). Rec 22 Jun 1840. [No. 975]

1196. Page 336. 24 Mar 1840. Jacob **Gross** and Sarah, his wife, to Gottlob F. **Gross**. For the sum of $250, 40 acres, being the NE 1/4, NE 1/4, Sec 6, Twp 34 N, Rng 13 E. Signed Jacob (x) **Gross**, Sary (x) **Gross**. Wit Augustus **Davis** (JP). Rec 25 Jun 1840. [No. 976]

1197. Page 336. 2 Jun 1840. Gottlob F. **Grosse** and Henrietta, his wife, to Johann Gottfried **Hemmann**. For the sum of $233, mortgage on 40 acres, being the NE 1/4, NE 1/4, Sec 26, Twp 34 N, Rng 13 E, described in Receiver's Certificate No. 7177. Sd **Grosse** owes sd **Hemmann** the debt with 8% interest per annum, due in two years. Signed Gottlob Frederick **Grosse**, Henrietta **Grosse** (RD). Test Frederick S___. Wit Augustus **Davis** (JP). Rec 25 Jun 1840. [Marginal note: Full satisfaction received on 31 May 1844. Signed Johann G. **Hemmann**. Wit John W. **Noell**, Clerk.] [No. 977]

1198. Page 337. 10 May 1832. James **McCalop** of West Baton Rouge Parish, La. to Francis L. **Jones**. For the sum of $100, assignment of negros purchased by him at Sheriff's sale on 4 Oct 1830; including **Phillis**, a woman aged about 35; **Harriett**, a molatto woman about 35; **Kitty**, a molatto woman aged about 19; **Joe**, a man aged about 30; **John**, a man aged about 28; **Harry**, a man aged about 25; **Willis**, a boy age about 15; **Tenna**, a girl aged about 10; and **Henry**, a boy aged about 7. Signed James **McCalop**, F. L. **Jones**, Wm. **Joice**, Allen **Shaw**, Phillip **Thirth**(?), M. **White**. Wit John **Reid**, Notary Public. Rec 26 Jun 1840. [No. 978]

1199. Page 339. 26 Oct 1839. Samuel **Burrows** to Cornelius **Manning**. For the sum of $90, mortgage on 40 acres, being the NE 1/4, NW 1/4, Sec 25, Twp 35 N, Rng 11 E. Sd **Burrows** owes a debt to sd **Manning**, and this deed serves as security for the debt. Signed Samuel **Burrows**. Wit Henry **Horrell**, Alonzo **Abernathy**, JCC. Rec 27 Jun 1840. [No. 979]

1200. Page 340. 10 Feb 1840. Joseph **Duvall** and Evaline, his wife, of Ste. Genevieve Co., Mo. to John B. **Moore**. For the sum of $200, 113 acres, more or less, on the waters of Bois Brulle Creek, part of 400 arpents confirmed to Ezekiel **Able** under John **Townsend**; beginning at the SW corner of the survey. Signed Joseph **Duvall**, Evaline **Duvall** (RD). Wit W. **Searcy** (JP). Rec 29 Jun 1840. [No. 980]

1201. Page 341. 11 May 1840. Henry C. **Hardin** to Nathaniel J. **Divine**. For the sum of $200, mortgage on 41.84 acres, being the N fractional 1/2, Sec 22, Twp 36 N, Rng 12 E; purchased from William **McGuire** by Andrew **Burns**, and by sd **Hardin** from sd **Burns**, a portion of which, estimated at 9.80 acres, more or less, has fallen into the river; two horses, one brown, the other bay; and two cows and calves. Sd **Hardin** owes sd **Divine** $200 with interest. Signed Henry C. **Hardin**. Wit Alfred J. **Parks** (JP). Rec 9 Jul 1840. [No. 981]

1202. Page 342. 7 Mar 1836. Luther **Taylor** and Hannah, his wife, to Charles **Stewart**. For the sum of $212.50, 11 1/4 acres, more or less, beginning at the SE corner of Lot No. 12 in Perryville, and bounded in part by Elanor **Hunt** and sd **Stewart**. Signed Luther **Taylor**, Hannah **Taylor** (RD). Wit James **Rice** (JP). Rec 13 Jul 1840. [No. 982]

1203. Page 343. 2 Nov 1835. Benjamin **Wilson** and Jane, his wife, of Cape Girardeau Co., Mo. to same. For the sum of $65, 10 3/4 acres, beginning at the SE corner of Perryville, bounded in part by Main St and ___ **McLain**. Signed Benjamin **Wilson**, Jane **Wilson** (RD). Wit Wm. **Johnson**, Presiding Judge of Cape Girardeau Co., Mo. Rec 13 Jul 1840. [No. 983]

1204. Page 343. 11 Mar 1840. James **McCauley** and Rossanna, his wife, to Charles **Stewart** Senior. For the sum of $300, 150 acres, more or less, beginning at the S corner of a small tract laid off to William **McCauley** in the original survey of land confirmed to Clement **Knott**; also bounded by Isadore **Moore**. Signed James **McCauley**, Rosana **McCauley** (RD). Test Mark **Brewer** (JP). Rec 13 Jul 1840. [No. 984]

1205. Page 345. 22 May 1840. Joseph **Cissell** and Mary, his wife, to Elanor **Hunt**. For the sum of $300, 100 acres, more or less, beginning at the NE corner of a tract confirmed to Bernard **Layton**, and part of the same tract where Perryville is located; bounded in part by William **McLain**. Signed Joseph **Cissel**, Mary (x(**Cissell** (RD). Wit Reuben **Shelby**, JCC. Rec 13 Jul 1840. [No. 985]

1206. Page 346. 27 Sep 1839. Joseph **Tucker** and Sarahann, his wife, to Moses **Rhody**. For the sum of $60, 40 acres, being the E 1/2, Lot No. 1, NE 1/4, Sec 3, Twp 34 N, Rng 10 E. Signed Joseph (x) **Tucker**, Sarah (x) **Tucker** (RD). Wit Reuben **Shelby**, JCC. Rec 22 Jul 1840. [No. 986]

1207. Page 346. 20 Jul 1840. Thomas **Stewart** and Isabella, his wife, and Charles **Stewart** to Peter J. **Tucker**. For the sum of $132, the SW corner of Lot No. 58 in Perryville, fronting on St. Marys St and Jackson St. Signed Thomas **Stewart**, Isabella **Stewart** (RD), Charles **Stewart**. Test Mark **Brewer** (JP). Rec 22 Jul 1840. [No. 987]

1208. Page 348. 2 Jul 1840. Charles **Hayden**, admr with the will annexed of the estate of Charles **Stewart**, decd, to Henry **Caho**. For the sum of $250 paid to sd **Stewart** in his lifetime, two tracts; 40 acres purchased by sd **Stewart** from James & Bennett **McCauley**, purchased by them from Rezin L. **Bishop**; beginning at a stake at the NW corner of sd tract; and ___ acres, being the NE fractional 1/4, Sec 13, Twp 35 N, Rng 10 E, purchased by sd **Stewart** from William **McCauley**. Executed on order of Circuit Court in Chancery in the case of sd **Caho** vs. sd **Hayden** for conveyance of sd tracts; sd **Stewart** having sold them in his lifetime to sd **Caho**. Signed Charles **Hayden**, admr. Wit John F. **Hase**, Dep Clerk. Rec 27 Jul 1840. [No. 988]

1209. Page 349. 28 Jul 1840. John Livingston **van Dorin** by Sheriff Hugh **Wells** to Mason **Frippell**. For the sum of $10, 102 acres on the Mississippi River near the mouth of Apple Creek, being Lot No. 1, NW 1/4 and SW fractional 1/4, Sec 5, Twp 33 N, Rng 14 E. Sold on 27 Jul 1840 on a pluveis execution issued by St. Francois Co., Mo. Circuit Court on 26 Mar 1838 in favor of John D. **Haynes** and against sd **van Dorin** for $1500 debt, $93.75 damages, and costs. Signed Hugh **Wells**, Sheriff. Wit John F. **Hase**, Dep Clerk. Rec 28 Jul 1840. [No. 989]

1210. Page 351. 10 Aug 1839. John **Shufford** to Lot **Abernathy**. For the sum of $100, mortgage on a negro girl named **Margaret**, aged about 4 years. Sd **Shufford** owes a debt with 10% interest, due 1 Jan 1840. Signed John **Shufford**. Wit Alonzo **Abernathy**, JCC. Rec 27 Jul 1840. [No. 990]

1211. Page 352. 6 Apr 1839. John **Logan** to Francis **Clark**. For the sum of $50, 5 acres, more or less, part of a tract confirmed to Henry **Clark**, son of Francis, beginning at the NE corner of the survey; bounded in part by Francis **Clark**'s survey. Signed John **Logan**. Wit W. **Searcy** (JP). Rec 28 Jul 1840. [No. 991

1212. Page 353. 22 May 1840. George **Camster** and Simeon **English**, admr of the estate of Abner **Kinnison**, decd, to Elizabeth **Waters**, David C. **Waters**, Joseph **Holston** and Rosana, his wife, James L. **Watters**, Robert **Watters**, Margaret **Waters**, Theodore **Watters**, and Richard J. **Waters**; all heirs of Joab **Waters**, decd. For the sum of $200, 100 arpens in Bois Brulle Bottom on the Mississippi River, part of a survey owned by Presley **Kinnison**, and occupied by Abner **Kinnison** during his lifetime. Sold on 23 Nov 1829 at order of County Court issued Aug Term 1829; in which a negro man **George** was reserved from sale, and the real estate was sold to pay debts of the estate. A deed was not made before the decease of sd **Waters**, who left his relict Elizabeth and the other heirs. The land is to go to Elizabeth **Waters** during her natural life, then to the heirs at law of sd **Waters**. Signed George **Camster**, Simeon **English**, admr. Wit Peter R. **Garrett**. Cape Girardeau County Clerk. Rec 28 Jul 1840. [No. 992]

1213. Page 354. 28 Jul 1840. Richard **Maddock** Senior and Elizabeth, his wife, to Marcella **Layton**. For the sum of $1200, mortgage on land and personal property; 79 acres, more or less, being the NW fractional 1/4, Sec 15, Twp 35 N, Rng 10 E, and the same purchased from Isadore **Moore** and Leah, his wife, by sd **Maddock**, being the undivided 1/3 of his father's land, and since divided by a deed of partition among sd **Maddock** and the other heirs, James and Bede **Moore**; one gray mare eight years old; one carriage; two cows and calves; two yearlings; one ten plate stove; one walnut beauro; one cherry desk and buffet; one walnutpress(?); one dressing glass; one eight day clock; one cherry folding table; one walnut table; six windsor chairs; two long bed steads with feather beds and bedding; one ox cart; one wool carding machine 13 inches in the card; 2000 feet of oak scantling(?), 500 feet of oak plank, 200 pounds of wool, 200 pounds of wool rolls, one pair of mill stones and irons with the necessary material of repairing the mill and carding machine; and 1/3 of a crop of corn of one field. Sd **Maddock** owes Marcella **Layton** $130 by 1 Feb next, and $1070 by 1 Feb 1844. Signed Richard **Maddock** Senr, Elizabeth (x) **Maddock** (RD). Wit John **Layton** Sr. (JP), Maria **Layton**. Rec 29 Jul 1840. [Marginal note: Full satisfaction received on 28 Apr 1845. Signed George **Nurse**, who intermarried with Marcella **Layton**. Test John W. **Noell**, Clerk.] [No. 993]

1214. Page 356. 30 May 1840. Arthur M. **Bliss** and Nancey, his wife, to John **Scudder**. For the sum of $108, Lot Nos. 13 & 14, Block No. 24 in Birmingham. Signed A. M. **Bliss**. Wit Henry S. **Osburn**, Benjamin **Davis**, Augustus **Davis** (JP). Rec 29 Jul 1840. [No. 994]

1215. Page 357. 16 Mar 1840. John **Hirst** and Cynthia, his wife, of Union Co., Ill. to Napoleon B. **Gill**. For the sum of $1333.33 1/2, all their interest in real and personal property bequeathed to George Washington **Gill** by his father James **Gill**, decd, formerly of Jackson Co., Ill.; conveyed to Garland **Laughlin**, and by him to sd **Hirst**; including __ acres on the E bank of the Mississippi River, being fractional Sec 23 and the NW 1/4 of Sec 24, Twp 10 S, Rng 4 W; and 151 acres, more or less, on the W bank of the Mississippi River opposite the first tract, on which Mrs. Sarah **Gill** lives. Signed John **Hirst**, Cynthia **Hirst** (RD). Wit Daniel H. **Brush**, Commissioners Court Clerk of Jackson Co., Ill. Rec 29 Jul 1840. [No. 995]

1216. Page 358. 9 May 1840. Nathaniel B. **Smith** and Eliza Elvira, his wife, late of Ill. and now of Hempsted Co., Ark., to same. For the sum of $200, their interest in __ acres, on the E bank of the Mississippi in Jackson Co., Ill., being fractional Sec 23 and the NW 1/4 of Sec 24, Twp 10 S, Rng 4 W; entered by James **Gill** at Kaskaskia; and to all the negroes and other property belonging to the estate and willed to sd Eliza Elvira by her decd father James **Gill**. Signed Nathaniel B. (x) **Smith**, Eliza Elvira **Smith**. Wit Chant. **Etter**, S. S. **Sanders**, Clerk of Hempstead Co., Ark. Rec 29 Jul 1840. [No. 996]

1217. Page 359. 29 Jul 1840. Robert T. **Brown** by Sheriff Hugh **Wells** to John Y. **Brown**. For the sum of $10, __ acres confirmed to Francois **Valle**, decd, on which sd **Brown** now lives and which he holds by virtue of his marriage with his wife Catharine, formerly Catharine **Valle**. Sold on 28 Jul 1840 at order of Circuit Court issued 26 Nov 1839 in favor of Pierre **Menard** and John Bate. **Valle** and against sd **Brown** for $4405.31 1/2 debt, damages, and costs. Signed Hugh **Wells**, Sheriff. Wit John F. **Hase**, Dep Clerk. Rec 29 Jul 1840. [No. 997]

1218. Page 360. 24 Mar 1840. John **Daugherty** by same to Joseph **Pratte**. For the sum of $55, 100 acres on St. Laurant Creek, to be run off the S end of a tract purchased by Zar **Sturdivant** from Thomas **Donohoe**, and purchased by Atticus **Tucker**, decd, from sd **Sturdivant**. Sold on 24 Mar 1840 on a writ of fieri facias issued by Circuit Court issued 17 Jun 1840 in favor of sd **Pratte** and against sd **Daugherty** for $115.65 debt, $8.66 damages, and $6 costs. Signed Hugh **Wells**, Sheriff. Wit John F. **Hase**, Dep Clerk. Rec 29 Jul 1840. [No. 998]

1219. Page 362. 30 Jul 1840. Alexander M. **Cobbs** by same to Michael **Daley**. For the sum of $78.50, the N 1/2, Lot No. 63 in Perryville. Sold on 24 Mar 1840 at order of Circuit Court issued 28 Feb 1840 in favor of Ferdinand **Rozier** Jur for the use of Reuben **Shelby** and against Alexander M. **Cobbs**, on a case heard before Mark **Brewer**, JP in Cinque Hommes Twp. Signed Hugh **Wells**, Sheriff. Wit John F. **Hase**, Dep Clerk. Rec 30 Jul 1840. [No. 999]

1220. Page 363. 30 Jul 1840. Nelson P. **Jones** by same to Francis L. **Jones**. For the sum of $5, 40 acres, being the NW 1/4, SW 1/4, Sec 36, Twp 36 N, Rng 11 E. Sold on 24 Mar 1840 at order of Circuit Court issued 10 Feb 1840 in favor of Wm. H. **Ragsdale** for the use of Francis L. **Jones** against Nelson P. **Jones** for $6361.81 debt and damages, and $1.75 costs. Signed Hugh **Wells**, Sheriff. Wit John F. **Hase**, Dep Clerk. Rec 30 Jul 1840. [No. 1000]

1221. Page 365. 24 Nov 1839. John **Dougherty** by same to John **Logan**. For the sum of $300, 90.34 acres in Bois Brule Bottom, being the E 1/2, S 1/2, fractional Sec 35, Twp 37 N, Rng 10 E. Sold on 25 Nov 1839 on a writ of fieri facias issued by Circuit Court on 24 Jul 1839 on petition for foreclosure of mortgage against sd **Daugherty** for $300 debt, $23.25 damages, and $6.51 costs. Signed Hugh **Wells**, Sheriff. Wit John F. **Hase**, Dep Clerk. Rec 30 Jul 1840. [No. 1001]

1222. Page 367. __ Jul 1840. James **Evans** by same to Morris **Block**. For the sum of $76, Lot Nos. 42, 43, & 46 in Perryville. Sold on 30 Jul 1840 on an execution from Circuit Court issued 25 Jun 1840 in favor of James S. **McCuslian**(?) and against sd **Evans**. Signed Hugh **Wells**, Sheriff. Wit John F. **Hase**, Dep Clerk. Rec 30 Jul 1840. [No. 1002]

1223. Page 368. 30 Jul 1840. William H. **Martin** by same to John **Garner**. For the sum of $50, 40 acres, being the SW 1/4, SE 1/4, Sec 27, Twp 34 N, Rng 13 E. Sold on 28 Mar 1840 at order of Circuit Court on a judgment for sd **Garner** and against sd **Martin**, heard before Elias **Barber**, JP, on 14 Dec 1839 for $54.02 1/2 debt, $2 damages, and $2.50 costs. Signed Hugh **Wells**, Sheriff. Wit John F. **Hase**, Dep Clerk. Rec 30 Jul 1840. [No. 1003]

1224. Page 370. 30 Jul 1840. Edward M **Holden** by same to Conrad C. **Ziegler** and John S. **Brickey**. For the sums of $1 and $5, two tracts; 6 acres, more or less, beginning at the NW corner of **Stewart**'s line on the E side of Perryville; and the S 1/2, Lot No. 9 in Perryville fronting on Spring St, and adjoining the first tract. Sold on 6 Jul 1840 on three executions issued in Apr 1840 by Circuit Court against sd **Holden**; one in favor of Joseph **Hagan** on 8 Apr 1840, one in favor of John and Edward **Walsh** on 25 Mar 1840, and one in favor of James **Jackson** on 21 Mar 1840. Signed Hugh **Wells**, Sheriff. Wit John F. **Hase**, Dep Clerk. Rec 30 Jul 1840. [No. 1004]

1225. Page 372. 29 Jul 1839. Pinkney H. **Anderson** and Jane F., his wife, to Michael **Boak** Senr, Michael **Boak** Junior, and Gottlob **Fechler**, son-in-law. For the sum of $350, two tracts in Sec 27, Twp 34, Rng 12 E; 40 acres, being the NE 1/4, NE 1/4; and 40 acres, being the NE 1/4, SE 1/4. Signed Pinkney H. **Anderson**, Jane F. **Anderson** (RD). Wit Elias **Barber** (JP). Rec 30 Jul 1840. [No. 1005]

1226. Page 373. 20 Jul 1840. Peter J. **Tucker** and Mary, his wife, to Anthony **Pairs**. For the sum of $200, 40 acres, being the NW 1/4, SW 1/4, Sec 21, Twp 36 N, Rng 11 E; entered by Thomas **Stewart** on 26 Oct 1837, sold by him to James F. **Tucker**, by sd **Tucker** to Henry **Caho**, by sd **Caho** to sd **Stewart**, and by sd **Stewart** to Peter J. **Tucker**. Signed Peter J. **Tucker**, Mary (x) **Tucker** (RD). Test Ferdinand **Rozier** Junior, Reuben **Shelby**, JCC. Rec 1 Aug 1840. [No. 1006]

1227. Page 374. 1 Aug 1840. John B. **Taylor** and Druscilla, his wife, to Henry **Kunze**. For the sum of $270, mortgage on 40 acres, being the NW 1/4, SE 1/4, Sec 6, Twp 34 N, Rng 11 E. Sd **Taylor** owes the debt with interest by 1 Jan 1843. Signed John B. **Taylor**, Drusilla (x) **Taylor** (RD). Test Mark **Brewer** (JP). Rec 3 Aug 1840. [No. 1007]

1228. Page 375. 13 Oct 1835. Peter **Tucker** and Elizabeth, his wife, to Ignatius **Layton** Senior. For the sum of $17, 17 acres, being the NE part of a section on Saline Creek; beginning at the NE corner. Signed Peter **Tucker** Senr, Elizabeth **Tucker** (RD). Wit John **Layton** (JP), Lewis **Layton**. Rec 5 Aug 1840. [No. 1008]

1229. Page 376. 14 Jul 1840. Solomon **Huffman** [and Polly, his wife] to William **Hayden**. For the sum of $130, 40 acres, being the NW 1/4, SW 1/4, Sec 28, Twp 34 N, Rng 11 E. Signed Solomon **Huffman**, Polly (x) **Huffman** (RD). Wit Reuben **Shelby**, JCC. Rec 6 Aug 1840. [No. 1009]

1230. Page 377. 14 Sep 1833. Elias **Barber** and Elizabeth H., his wife, to James G. **Myers**. For the sum of $15, 9 acres and 143 1/2 rods on the waters of Brazeau Creek, beginning on the creek bank at a white oak on the E line of a sd **Barber**'s tract, confirmed to Charles **Dunkaster**. Signed Elias **Barber**, Elizabeth H. **Barber** (RD). Wit Benjamine **Davis** (JP). Rec 6 Aug 1840. [No. 1010]

1231. Page 378. 22 Feb 1839. William **Garner** and Louisa V., his wife, of Union Co., Ill. to same. For the sum of $335, 94.31 acres, more or less, on the bank of the Mississippi River, being the NE fractional 1/4, Sec 36, Twp 35 N, Rng 13 E. Signed W. **Garner**, Louisa **Garner** (RD). Wit Samuel M. **Myers**, William M. **Myers**, Augustus **Davis** (JP). Rec 6 Aug 1840. [No. 1011]

1232. Page 379. 12 Mar 1840. Robert P. **Slaughter** and Evaline M, his wife, to same. For the sum of $50, 21 acres, being the SE fractional 1/4, fractional Sec 26, Twp 35 N, Rng 13 E; as described in Patent No. 3942. Signed Robert P. **Slaughter**, Evaline M. **Slaughter**. Wit Elias **Barber** (JP). Rec 6 Aug 1840. [No. 1012]

1233. Page 380. 3 Aug 1840. Samuel Miller **Myers**, William Marion **Myers**, and Elijah Asbury **Myers** to James Garner **Myers**. For the sum of $800, three tracts; 40 acres, being the NW 1/4, NE 1/4, Sec 35, Twp 35 N, Rng 13 E, entered by Elija A. **Myers** on 24 Jun 1836; 76.64 acres, being the W 1/2, NW fractional 1/4, fractional Sec 36, Twp 35 N, Rng 13 E, entered by William **Myers** on 16 Jun 1836; and 63.65 acres, being the E 1/2, NW 1/4, fractional Sec 36, Twp 35 N, Rng 13 E, entered by Samuel Miller **Myers** on 24 Jun 1836. Signed Samuel M. **Myers**, William M. **Myers**, Elijah A. **Myers**. Wit Elias **Barber** (JP). Rec 6 Aug 1840. [No. 1013]

1234. Page 381. 1 May 1840. Michael **Daly** to Joseph **Paquin**. For the sum of $50, 36.43 acres, being the SW 1/4, fractional Sec 12, Twp 35 N, Rng 10 E. Signed Michael **Daly**. Wit Reuben **Shelby**, JCC. Rec 17 Aug 1840. [No. 1014]

1235. Page 382. 1 Jun 1836. Sister Beatrix, alias Margaret **O'Bryan**, Superior of Bethlehem Convent, to Joseph **Paquin**. For the sum of $2000, seven tracts, the first five being contiguous and where Bethlehem Convent is located; 37.64 acres, being the SW fractional 1/4, Sec 13, Twp 35, Rng 10 E; 157.64 acres, the NW fractional 1/4, Sec 13, Twp 35, Rng 10 E, adjoining the first tract; 41.6 acres, being the NE fractional 1/4 of Sec 14, Twp 35 N, Rng 10 E; 44.15 acres conveyed to her by John **Layton**, admr of Juliana **Warthen** (2:113); 4.57 acres (1:281, 2:21); 80.33 acres, being the W 1/2, NW 1/4, Sec 31, Twp 34 N, Rng 12 E, described in Patent No. 1007; and __ acres conveyed by Joseph **Schnerebush** to Julia **Fenwick** on which is the log church of St. Josephs. Signed Margaret **O'Bryan**. Wit John **Layton** (JP). Rec 17 Aug 1840. [No. 1015]

1236. Page 383. 10 Aug 1840. David **Burns** and Margaret J., his wife, to Perry Co. for the use of the inhabitants of Twp 36 N, Rng 12 E. For the sum of $600, mortgage on 465 acres, more or less, originally confirmed by the U. S. to John R. **McLaughlin** as Survey No. 142, Twp 36 N, Rng 11 E; where sd **Burns** now resides, and purchased by him from the commissioners to partition the estate of James **Burns**, decd, father of sd David (1:393). David **Burns** owes the sum with interest with James **Rice** and William **Burns** senr as securities, due in 12 months. Signed David **Burns**, Margaret J. **Burns** (RD). Wit James **Rice** (JP). Rec 17 Aug 1840. [No. 1016]

1237. Page 384. 11 May 1839. Josephus **Tucker** and Nancey, his wife, to Willis **Ellis**. For the sum of $70, 40 acres, more or less, in Cinque Hommes Twp, being the SW 1/4, SE 1/4, Sec 11, Twp 35 N, Rng 9 E. Signed Josephus (x) **Tucker**, Nancey (x) **Tucker** (RD). Wit Robert **Trotter** (JP). Rec 18 Aug 1840. [No. 1017]

1238. Page 385. 18 Apr 1840. Commissioners' report. Partition of 502 arpens (427 acres) in Bois Brule Bottom on both sides of Bois Brule Creek, being Survey No. 447, granted to James **Newsom** Junior. To Robert **Caldwell**, Lot No. 1 containing 292.61 acres on the W side. To John **Kinnison** and Sina, his wife, Lot No. 2 containing 107.76 acres. To the unknown heirs of Henry B. **Newsom**, Lot No. 3 containing 26.63 acres. Made at order of Circuit Court issued Mar Term 1840 in case of Robert **Caldwell** vs. John **Kinnison** and Sina, his wife, and unknown heirs of Henry B. **Newsom**, decd. Signed Francis **Clark**, A. H. **Puckett**, commissioners. Wit Fredk. C. **Hase**, Clerk. Rec 23 Aug 1840. [No. 1018]

1239. Page 386. 24 Aug 1840. John B. **Cissell** and Susan, his wife, to Jacob **Shoults**. For the sum of $280, 80 acres, more or less, being the W1/2, NW 1/4, Sec 20, Twp 34 N, Rng 11 E; purchased from William **Winfield** and Helen, his wife, on 2 Sep 1837 (2:458); and the crop now growing on sd land. Signed John B. (x) **Cissell**, Susan (x) **Cissell** (RD). Wit James **Rice** (JP), Valario **Faina**. Rec 24 Aug 1840. [No. 1019]

1240. Page 388. 6 Jan 1838. Benjamin **Williams** to Guy **Elder**. For the sum of $200, about 100 acres, beginning at a white oak on Peter J. **Tucker**'s N line marked with the "J T"; also bounded by James **Moore** Senr and Nicholas **Tucker**, and the house wherein Joseph **Tucker** Senior decd. Signed Benjamin **Williams**. Wit Robert **Trotter** (JP). Rec 31 Aug 1840. [No. 1020]

1241. Page 388. 6 Apr 1839. William **Bell** and Ann, his wife, to Charles **Stewart**. For the sum of $80, 40 acres, being the NW 1/4, SW 1/4, Sec 34, Twp 35 N, Rng 10 E. Signed William (x) **Bell**, Ann (x) **Bell** (RD). Wit John **Layton** (JP), Maria **Layton**. Rec 4 Sep 1840. [No. 1021]

1242. Page 389. 18 Jul 1840. Joseph **Shoults** and Elizabeth R., his wife, of Perryville to Thomas **Stewart** and Charles **Stewart**. For the sum of $100, the SW corner of Lot No. 58 in Perryville, fronting on St. Marys St and Jackson St. This deed is to affirm an earlier conveyance that was lost. Signed Joseph **Shoults**, Eliza R. **Shoults** (RD). Wit James **Rice** (JP). Rec 4 Sep 1840. [No. 1022]

1243. Page 391. 28 Aug 1840. John B. **Taylor** to Henry **Kunze**. For the sum of $50, mortgage on a young mare two years old, a dark chestnut sorrel colour, branded with a cross on the near shoulder; and two black and white pied heiffers, one two years old, the other three years old. Sd **Taylor** owes sd **Kunze** a debt with interest due by 1 Jan 1843. Signed John B. **Taylor**. Test Mark **Brewer** (JP). Rec 5 Sep 1840. [No. 1023]

1244. Page 391. 2 Aug 1840. Martin **Stephens** to Singleton H. **Kimmel**. For the sum of $150, two tracts; 40 acres, being the SW 1/4, NE 1/4, Sec 23, Twp 34 N, Rng 13 E, entered by sd **Stephens** on 2 May 1839; and 80 acres, being the E 1/2, SW 1/4, Sec 22, Twp 34, Rng 13 E. The latter entry has been changed from the name of sd **Stephens** to that of Johann George **Gube**, and has been done without sd **Stephens**' permission. Signed Martin **Stephans**. Wit A. J. **Dickinson**, W. M. **Guthrie**, Circuit Court Clerk of Randolph Co., Ill., Sidney **Breese**, Presiding Judge of Randolph Co., Ill. Rec 11 Sep 1840. [No. 1024]

[Pages 392 and 393 skipped in the original.]

1245. Page 394. 23 Apr 1840. Etienne **Govereau** Junior; Louis **Pepin** and Mary, his wife and formerly Mary **Govereau**, daughter of Etienne **Govereau**, decd; Antonio **Cortise** and Susan, his wife and formerly Susan **Govereau**, daughter of Etienne **Govereau**, decd; to Willis **Ellis**. For the sum of $50, 800 arpens on a branch of the S fork of Saline Creek; beginning at the mouth of sd branch; granted by Zeno **Trudeau**, Lt. Gov. of Upper La., to Etinne **Parent** and Etienne **Govereau** on 1 Feb 1798, and confirmed to them on 4 Jul 1836. Signed Antone (x) **Cortois**, Susan (x) **Courtois**, Louis (x) **Pepin**, Mary Louisa (x) **Pepin**, Etienne (x) **Govereau**. Wit Joseph D. **Grafton**, Clerk of Ste. Genevieve Co., Mo. Court. Rec 14 Sep 1840. [No. 1025]

1246. Page 396. 12 Sep 1840. James N. **Moore** and Sally, his wife, to Luther **Taylor**. For the sum of $15, Lot No. 28 in Perryville, on the E side of Main St; purchased by sd **Moore** of the commissioners. Signed James N. **Moore**, Sally (x) **Moore** (RD). Wit James **Rice** (JP). Rec 17 Sep 1840. [No. 1026]

1247. Page 397. 7 Sep 1840. Bede **Moore** and Verlinder, his wife, to Hillary **Layton**. For the sum of $1, 100 acres, more or less, a portion of a tract confirmed to sd **Moore** by the Commissioners; beginning at the SE corner of the tract given by sd **Moore** to his son-in-law Hoyle **Manning**; also bounded by Joseph **Tucker**. The tract was given by sd **Moore** to his granddaughter Clotildia **Manning**, daughter of Ann **Moore** and Joseph **Manning** Jr. Clotildia has since intermarried with Vincent **Layton**, who sold the tract to his brother Hillary **Layton**. Signed Bede **Moore**, Verlinder (x) **Moore** (RD). Wit James **Rice** (JP). Rec 17 Sep 1840. [No. 1027]

1248. Page 398. 17 Sep 1840. Hillary **Layton** to John **Moore**. For the sum of $100, mortgage on the tract described in the preceding deed (3:397). Sd **Layton** owes a debt to sd **Moore**, due in 12 months with 10% interest per annum. Signed Hillary **Layton**. Wit

James **Rice** (JP). Rec 17 Sep 1840. [Marginal note: 30 acres sold by the mortgagee are hereby released from the lien on 3 May 1847. Full satisfaction received on 6 Sep 1854. Signed John **Moore**.] [No. 1028]

1249. Page 399. 1 Aug 1839. John W. **Noell** and Mary A., his wife, to John **Hacher**. For the sum of $100, Lot No. 67 in Perryville. Signed John W. **Noell**, Mary **Noell** (RD). Wit Reuben **Shelby**, JCC. Rec 24 Sep 1840. [No. 1029]

1250. Page 400. 8 Aug 1840. Joseph **Duvall** Jur. and Rosanna, his wife, daughter and heir of Ignatius **Layton**, decd, to Reuben **Shelby**. For the sum of $60, 335 acres, part of 640 acres confirmed to Michael **Tucker**; part of which was sold to sd **Layton** by sd **Tucker** and Nicholas **Miles**, and part sold to sd **Layton** by Peter **Tucker** Senr. Signed Joseph **Duvall**, Rosanna (x) **Duvall**. Test Alonzo **Abernathy**, JCC. Rec John F. **Hase**, Dep Clerk. Rec 26 Sep 1840. [No. 1030]

1251. Page 402. 15 Mar 1837. U. S. A. to Christian **Oser**. Patent for 40 acres, being the NW 1/4, SE fractional 1/4, fractional Sec 20, Twp 35 N, Rng 11 E; in Certificate No. 3471. Signed Martin **Van Buren** by A. **Van Buren**, Secy. Wit H. M. **Garland**, Acting Recorder of the General Land Office. Rec in Vol. 7:1 of the General Land Office. Rec 29 Sep 1840. [No. 1031]

1252. Page 402. 22 Aug 1840. Henry S. **Osborn** of New Orleans, La. to Wm. H. **Scudder**. For the sum of $200, Lot No. 17, Block No. 12 in Birmingham. Signed Henry S. **Osborn**. Wit Augustus **Davis** (JP), Fredrich **Sproede**. Rec 29 Sep 1840. [No. 1032]

1253. Page 403. 9 Jul 1840. John **Cochran** and Jane, his wife, of Union Co., Ill. to James **Cox** and Arthur M. **Bliss**. For the sum of $110, Lot No. 17, Block No. 12 in Birmingham. Signed James H. **Cochran**, Jane **Cochran** (RD). Wit G. A. **Lemley**, James H. **Cochran**, JP in Union Co., Ill., Wiley **Willis**, Winstead **Davie**, Clerk of Union Co., Ill. Court. Rec 29 Sep 1840. [No. 1033]

1254. Page 404. 1 Aug 1840. Arthur M. **Bliss** and James **Cox** and Mary, his wife, to Henry S. **Osborn** of New Orleans, La. For the sum of $135, Lot No. 17, Block No. 12 in Birmingham. Signed Arthur M. **Bliss**, James (x) **Cox**, Mary **Cox** (RD). Wit John A. **Hart**, Augustus **Davis** (JP). Rec 29 Sep 1840. [No. 1034]

1255. Page 405. 30 Aug 1839. Rezin L. **Bishop** and Rebeca, his wife, to Samuel T. **Donalds**. For the sum of $200, 7 acres on the Mississippi River, beginning at a post on the SE corner of Henry **Riley**'s Survey No. 364; part of 107.55 acres in sd **Riley**'s survey. For diverse considerations and the sum of $1, free use of a spring in the survey of sd **Riley**. Signed Rezin L. **Bishop**, Rebecca (x) **Bishop**. Wit Augustus **Davis** (JP), Sophia **Hueschel**. Rec 12 Oct 1840. [No. 1035]

1256. Page 407. 21 Oct 1840. Gabriel M. **Duvall** to John **Moore**. For the sum of $150, 200 arpens, more or less, part of the original head right of John **Duvall**, decd; bounded on the N by Johnathan **Preston**, E by land confirmed to John **Duvall** under William **Boyce**, S by land confirmed to Charles **Lee** and James **Moore**, son of James, and W by a portion of the original head right; and being a portion of sd head right conveyed to Robert **Abernathy** by way of advancement. Signed G. M. **Duvall**. Wit John **Layton** senr (JP). Rec 21 Oct 1840. [No. 1036]

1257. Page 408. 24 Oct 1840. William R. **Hayden** to Lawrence **Keizer**. For the sum of $200, 40 acres, being the NW 1/4, SW 1/4, Sec 28, Twp 34 N, Rng 11 E; bounded on all sides by public lands. Signed William R. **Hayden**. Wit Reuben **Shelby**, JCC. Rec 24 Oct 1840. [No. 1037]

1258. Page 408. 2 Mar 1840. Charles **Stewart** to Henry **Caho**. For the sum of $150, 80 acres, being the NW 1/4, SW 1/4, Sec 34, Twp 35 N, Rng 10 E. Signed Charles **Stewart**. Wit Reuben **Shelby**, JCC. Rec 27 Oct 1840. [No. 1038]

1259. Page 409. 20 Jan 1840. David **Flynn** and Isabella, his wife, to Joseph **Rhodes**. For the sum of $200, 34.56 acres, being a small island at the head of Horse Island in Twp 37 N, Rng 11 E, balance of Sec 19. Signed David **Flynn**, Isabella (x) **Flynn** (RD). Wit W. **Searcy** (JP). Rec 29 Oct 1840. [No. 1039]

1260. Page 410. 14 Aug 1840. Joseph **Paquin** to John **Piet** of Jefferson Co., Vir. For the sum of $1416, 202.40 acres in three tracts in Twp 35 N, Rng 10 E; 35.43 acres, being the SW fractional 1/4, SW 1/4, fractional Sec 12; 30.85 acres in the NE fractional 1/4, Sec 14; and 136.12 acres in the NE fractional 1/4, Sec 13; the latter two tracts beginning at the SW corner of the first lot, bounded by Joseph **Miles**, land ceded by Juliana **Warthen** to Joseph **Manning**. Signed Joseph **Paquin**. Wit John **Timon**, Reuben **Shelby**, JCC. Rec 31 Oct 1840. [No. 1040]

1261. Page 411. 27 Oct 1840. Richmond **Penny** to Charmic L. **Cox**. For securing notes and the sum of $1, mortgage on three cows and three calves, one white and two pied; one Yankee clock; three beds, bedsteads, and bedding; one lot of about 20 hogs; and one ladies side saddle. Sd **Penny** owes sd **Cox** $62.50 in two notes; one for $30 given by sd **Penny** to John **Hagar** for corn purchased at public sale, signed by William **Farrar** as security, and traded by sd **Hagar** to sd **Cox**; and one to sd **Cox** for $22.50 executed in 1840, being the balance due for a mule. Signed Richmond **Penny**. Wit William **Farrar** (JP). Rec 2 Nov 1840. [No. 1041]

1262. Page 413. 20 Aug 1840. Henry C. **Bimpage**, admr of the estate of Johann George **Gube**, decd, to Heinrich Aug. **Dorderlein**. For the sum of $__, 63 acres, being the SW part of the NW 1/4, Sec 23, Twp 34 N, Rng 13 E; commencing at the SW corner of Sec 23. Sold on decree of Circuit Court in Chancery issued Nov 1839. Signed Henry C. **Bimpage**, admr. Wit Fred. Wilh. **Barthel**, Augustus **Davis** (JP). Rec 2 Nov 1840. [No. 1042]

1263. Page 414. 20 Aug 1840. Same to Sophia **Schnider**. For the sum of $__, two tracts; 44.52 acres, more or less, the W part of the SE fractional 1/4, Sec 14, Twp 34 N, Rng 13 E; commencing at the SW corner of sd section, bounded in part by Survey No. 865 originally granted to Robert **Hinkston**; and 91 acres, more or less, being the N part of the NW 1/4, Sec 23, Twp 34 N, Rng 13 E, beginning at the NW corner of sd section. Sold on decree of Circuit Court in Chancery issued Nov 1839. Signed Henry C. **Bimpage**, admr. Wit Fredr. Wilh. **Barthel**, Augustus **Davis** (JP). Rec 2 Nov 1840. [No. 1043]

1264. Page 415. 24 Aug 1838. Charles **Hayden** to Joseph **Moll**. For the sum of $600, 80 acres in Brazeau Twp, being the NE 1/2, NE 1/4, Sec 19, Twp 34 N, Rng 12 E; bounded on the N by Alexander **Hinkle**, E by Joseph **Brunstrater**, S by James **Nolson**, and W by public land. Signed Charles **Hayden**. Test W. G. **Watts**, James **Ferguson** (JP). Rec 2 Nov 1840. [No. 1044]

1265. Page 416. 11 Jul 1840. Last will and testament of John Bernhard **Schmidt**, formerly of Cahla, decd. Being single and without relation, he leaves to the three children of the Revd. Mr. **Loeber**, Henry, Martha, and Gotthilf **Loeber**, and the three children of Mrs. **von Wurmb**, widow, Maria, Theobald, and Sarah: 160 acres, more or less, in Altenburg, less 40 acres sold to **Grother** and **Goethe**, cart wright; and all his cash on hand, about $200; provided Mr. **Loeber** serve as executor, demand money due, see to his burial, and pay the bill of Dr. **Bunger**, reward Mr. **Otts** and Risina **Block** for their attendance during his sickness, and give his Godson Gothwirth **Schmidt** of Louisdore(?) that he has received of him at St. Louis. He also wishes that any money due him from the Treasury go to pay the following debts: $19.75 to Mr. **Richter** of Desden for items purchased at the auction of **Gube**, decd, about $15 to Mr. **Bochlau** for store goods. To the following heirs: about $500 Rthlr. Prussian currency (RPC) due to him in Cahla; 10 RPC to his Godson **Thieme** of Kleinentrsdorf(?), $6.15 to his Godson **Huepe** of Eicherberg, D15 to his Godson **Deaumee** ibid, d 10 RPC to his cousin **Birntrie** of Cahla, shoemaker (releasing him from a debt), 10 RBC to Dr. **Schmidt** of Cahla, F 40 to such deserving and wanting poor of Cahla as Dr. **Schmidt** thinks proper, and the balance to his cousins Christian **Schmidt**, butcher, and Carl **Schmidt** of Cahla. To Rev. Mr. **Gruber** of Paitzdorf, Perry Co.: $30 due to him as an advancement to build a parish house in a note of 12 Nov 1839. To be spent on the education of a well qualified boy: $50 advanced for the congregation here. To the Church Warden and Trustees of the Congregation here: $300 RPC deposited at St. Louis in the Treasury for building of a church. To the families of Mrs. **Lober** and Mrs. **von Wurmb**: all his linen, beds, books, men's clothing, vessels, chests, tools, stove, and carriage, which they may equally divide or cast lots for. To be divided among Frederick Henning **Koeppel**, shoemaker, **Wunderlich** (to get his old cloak for garments for his two boys), **Otto** and sister, and **Mylius**: all his worn clothing, boots, etc. To **Wentes**, school master: his watch and relief from a debt owed to him. Signed John Barnhard **Schmidt**. Wit Gottfred **Schmidt**, Gottlog **Kranner**, Henry C. **Bimpage**, translator from German, Fredk. C. **Hase**, Clerk. Rec 3 Nov 1840. [No. 1045]

1266. Page 419. 14 Nov 1837. U. S. A. to Frederick C. **Hase**. Patent for 14.18 acres, being the NE fractional 1/4, Sec 18, Twp 35 N, Rng 11 E; in Certificate No. 5196. Signed Martin **Van Buren** by A. **Van Buren**, Secy. Wit Joseph S. **Wilson**, Acting Recorder of the General Land Office. Rec in Vol. 10:243 of the General Land Office. Rec 9 Nov 1840. [No. 1046]

1267. Page 419. 12 Oct 1840. William **Flynn** and Nancey, his wife, to John E. **Burgett**. For the sum of $500, 75 acres, more or less, on Horse Island, beginning at the upper corner on the Mississippi River on a entry made by sd **Burgett**, and purchased by sd **Flynn**; being a corner between an entry of Walter B. **Wilkinson** and sd **Burgett**. Signed William **Flynn**, Nancey (x) **Flynn** (RD). Wit W. **Searcy** (JP). Rec 9 Nov 1840. [No. 1047]

1268. Page 421. 14 Nov 1837. U. S. A. to Henry **McAtee**. Patent for 80 acres, being the E 1/2, NW 1/4, Sec 9, Twp 34 N, Rng 11 E; in Certificate No. 4859. Signed Martin **Van Buren** by A. **Van Buren**, Secy. Wit James S. **Wilson**, Acting Recorder of the General Land Office. Rec in Vol. 9:413 of the General Land Office. Rec 9 Nov 1840. [No. 1048]

1269. Page 422. 14 Nov 1837. U. S. A. to Henry **McAtee**. Patent for 80 acres, being the W 1/2, SE 1/4, Sec 9, Twp 34 N, Rng 11 E; in Certificate No. 5099. Signed Martin **Van Buren** by A. **Van Buren**, Secy. Wit Joseph S. **Wilson**, Acting Recorder of the General Land Office. Rec in Vol. 10:152 of the General Land Office. Rec 9 Nov 1840. [No. 1049]

1270. Page 422. 10 Nov 1840. Henry **Caho** and Maria, his wife, to Etienne **Turine**. For the sum of $250, 80 acres, being the N 1/2, SW 1/4, Sec 34, Twp 35 N, Rng 10 E. Signed Henry **Caho**, Maria **Caho** (RD). Wit Reuben **Shelby**, JCC. Rec 11 Nov 1840. [No. 1050]

1271. Page 423. 28 Aug 1840. Joanna **Myers**, admr of the estate of James **Myers**, decd, to Moses **Rody**. For the sum of $32, Lot No. 99 in Perryville. Sold at order of County Court issued May Term 1839 to sell sd lands to pay debts of the estate. Signed Joanna (x) **Myers**. Wit Elias **Barber** (JP). Rec 11 Nov 1840. [No. 1051]

1272. Page 425. 2 Nov 1840. Moses **Roady** and Hetty, his wife, to Hyman **Block**. For the sum of $32, Lot No. 99 in Perryville. Signed Moses **Roady**, Hetty (x) **Roady** (RD). Wit James **Rice** (JP). Rec 9 Nov 1840. [No. 1052]

1273. Page 427. 4 May 1840. Martin **Layton** and Nerius **Layton**, execrs of the last will and testament of Zachariah **Layton**, decd, to same. For the sum of $9, Lot No. 96 in Perryville. Signed Martin **Layton**, Nerius **Layton**. Wit Reuben **Shelby**, JCC. Rec 9 Nov 1840. [No. 1053]

1274. Page 427. 4 Nov 1840. Alonzo **Abernathy**, execr of James **Clifton**, decd, to William **Farrar**. For the sum of $98, 78.34 acres, being the W 1/2, SW 1/4, Sec 6, Twp 34, Rng 12 E; entered by sd **Clifton** in his life time. Executed at order of County Court issued Nov Term 1840. Sd **Clifton** sold the tract to sd **Farrar** on 4 Apr 1837, but did not execute a deed. Signed Alonzo **Abernathy**, execr. Wit Fredk. C. **Hase**, Clerk. Rec 11 Nov 1840. [No. 1054]

1275. Page 429. 5 Nov 1840. Henry **McAtee** and Maria, his wife, to Thomas **McAtee**. For the sum of $500, three tracts in Twp 34 N, Rng 10 E; __ acres, being the E 1/2, NE 1/4, Sec 12; about 35 acres in the NW 1/4, NE 1/4, Sec 12; and __ acres, being the SW 1/4, SE 1/4, Sec 1. Signed Henry **McAtee**, Maria (x) **McAtee**. Sit Fredk. C. **Hase**, Clerk. Rec 11 Nov 1840. [No. 1055]

1276. Page 430. 28 Aug 1840. Joanna **Myers**, admr of the estate of James **Myers**, decd, to James G. **Myers**. For the sum of $10.50, Lot No. 95 in Perryville. Sold at order of County Court issued May Term 1839 to sell sd lands to pay debts of the estate. Signed Joanna (x) **Myers**. Wit Elias **Barber** (JP). Rec 11 Nov 1840. [No. 1056]

1277. Page 432. 3 Jan 1833. Robert **Abernathy** and Ann Arpy, his wife, to Nicholas **Tucker** Senr. For the sum of $237 1/2, 200 arpens, the equal 1/2 of a tract originally granted to John **Duvall**; beginning at the SW corner of the original survey; conveyed to sd **Abernathy** by sd **Duvall** on 13 Nov 1824. Signed Robert **Abernathy**, Arpy Ann **Abernathy** (RD). Wit J. **Abernathy** (JP). Rec 14 Nov 1840. [No. 1057]

1278. Page 433. 1 Jan 1831. U. S. A. to George **Rutledge**. Patent for 80 acres, being the W 1/2, NE 1/4, Sec 9, Twp 34 N, Rng 11 E; in Certificate No. 874. Signed Andrew **Jackson**. Wit Elijah **Hayward**, Commissioner of the General Land Office. Rec in Vol. 2:295 of the General Land Office. Rec 17 Nov 1840. [No. 1058]

1279. Page 434. 30 Jun 1835. George **Rutledge** [and Susana, his wife] to Alexander **Little**. For the sum of $100, 80 acres, being the W 1/2, NE 1/4, Sec 9, Twp 34 N, Rng 11 E. Signed George **Rutledge**, Susana **Rutledge** (RD). Wit Alonzo **Abernathy**, JCC. Rec 17 Nov 1840. [No. 1059]

1280. Page 435. 19 Feb 1839. Alexander **Little** and Fanny, his wife, to Henry **McAtee**. For the sum of $300, 80 acres as described in the preceding deed, being patented to George **Rutledge** on 1 Jan 1831, and sold by him to sd **Little** on 30 Jun 1835. Signed Alexander **Little**, Fanny **Little** (RD). Wit Alonzo **Abernathy**, JCC. Rec 17 Nov 1840. [No. 1060]

1281. Page 437. 22 Oct 1840. James **Cashion** and Anna, his wife, to Ferdnand **Bergmon**. For the sum of $200, 40 acres, being the NW 1/4, NE 1/4, Sec 28, Twp 35 N, Rng 11 E. Signed James **Cashion**, Anna (x) **Cashion** (RD). Wit Reuben **Shelby**, JCC. Rec 17 Nov 1840. [No. 1061]

1282. Page 438. 12 Jul 1834. Wilford **Layton** and Susanna, his wife, to Anselm **Layton**. For the sum of $275, 320 acres, more or less, the SE part of James **Thompson**'s survey; confirmed to Josephus **Tucker**; to be surveyed agreeable to a line marked by sd **Tucker** and Wilford **Layton**. Signed Wilford **Layton**, Susanna (x) **Layton** (RD). Wit John **Layton** (JP), Maria **Layton**. Rec 18 Nov 1840. [No. 1062]

1283. Page 439. 23 Nov 1840. Richard S. **Dorsey** of Hickman Co., Ken. to James **Evans** of Perry Co. in trust for Charles **Dorsey** of Hickman Co., Ken. For natural love and affection to Charles **Dorsey**, 16.63 acres, being the SW fractional 1/4, Sec 29, Twp 35 N, Rng 11 E; conveyed by Washington **Dorsey** to Richard S. **Dorsey**. Signed Richard S. **Dorsey**. Wit John F. **Hase**, Dep Clerk. Rec 26 Nov 1840. [No. 1063]

1284. Page 440. 25 Nov 1840. William H. **White** and Mary, his wife, to Anthony **Hunt**. For the sum of $160, 22 acres, being the SW fractional 1/4, Sec 23, Twp 35 N, Rng 10 E. Signed William H. **White**, Mary (x) **White** (RD). Test Mark **Brewer** (JP). Rec 29 Nov 1840. [No. 1064]

1285. Page 441. 9 Jun 1839. Henry **McAtee** and Maria, his wife, to Thomas **McAtee**. For the sum of $50, 40 acres, being the SE 1/4, SW 1/4, Sec 12, Twp 34 N, Rng 10 E. Henry **McAtee**, Maria (x) **McAtee** (RD). Wit Reuben **Shelby**, JCC. Rec 29 Nov 1840. [No. 1065]

1286. Page 442. 4 Nov 1840. Richmond **Peney** to William **Penny**. For securing $40 by account and the sum of $1, mortgage on all the corn now standing in the field or on the premises where he resides and 16 sheep. The debt is due by 1 Nov 1841. Signed Richmond (x) **Peney**. Wit Mark **Brewer** (JP). Rec 30 Nov 1840. [No. 1066]

1287. Page 442. 4 Mar 1837. Nicholas **Miles** and Ignatius **Layton**. Deed of partition for 640 acres, more or less, in Cinque Hommes Twp, part of the claim of Michael **Tucker**. The portion to sd **Miles** is two parcels, one of 40 acres begins on the W bank of Saline Creek on a line between Peter **Tucker** and Michael **Tucker**; the other of 160 acres, being the most S corner of the 640 acres, and beginning at the same point. The portion to sd **Layton** is [440 acres] the remainder of sd tract. Signed Ignatius **Layton**, Nicholas **Miles**. Wit John **Layton** (JP), Augustin **Layton**. Rec 30 Nov 1840. [No. 1067]

1288. Page 444. 27 Mar 1840. Martin **Layton** and Nerius **Layton**, execrs of the last will and testament of Zachariah **Layton**, decd, to Anthony **Parres**. For the sum of $11.25, Lot No. 78 in Perryville. Signed Martin **Layton**, Nerius **Layton**. Wit John T. **Daly**, Reuben **Shelby**, JCC. Rec 5 Dec 1840. [No. 1068]

1289. Page 444. 11 May 1840. Anthony **Parres** and Mary, his wife, to Martin **Borne**. For the sum of $20, Lot No. 78 in Perryville. Signed Anthony **Parres**, Mary (x) **Parres** (RD). Wit Reuben **Shelby**, JCC. Rec 5 Dec 1840. [No. 1069]

1290. Page 445. 20 Sep 1839. Jesse R. **Walker** and Elizabeth, his wife, to Reuben **Shelby**. For the sum of $225, the S 1/2, Lot No. 63 in Perryville, fronting on St. Joseph St and Jackson St. Signed Jesse R. **Walker**, Elizabeth **Walker** (RD). Wit James **Rice** (JP). Rec 5 Dec 1840. [No. 1070]

1291. Page 446. 28 Jan 1840. Reuben **Shelby** and Mary, his wife, to William **Taylor**. For the sum of $250, part of Lot No. 63, beginning at the corner of Jackson St and St. Joseph St. Signed Reuben **Shelby**, Mary **Shelby** (RD). Wit James **Rice** (JP). Rec 28 Jan 1840. [No. 1071]

1292. Page 447. 6 Dec 1840. Martin **Born** and Elizabeth, his wife, of Cape Girardeau Co., Mo. to Andrew **Deer**. For the sum of $45, Lot No. 78 in Perryville. Signed Martin **Born**, Elizabeth **Born** (RD). Wit Bennet A. **Reeves**, JP in Cape Girardeau Co., Mo., Fredk. C. **Hase**, Clerk. Rec 14 Dec 1840. [No. 1072]

1293. Page 449. 24 Jan 1837. U. S. A. to James **Cashion**. Patent for 40 acres, being the NW 1/4, NE 1/4, Sec 28, Twp 35 N, Rng 11 E; in Certificate No. 3295. Signed Andrew **Jackson** by A. **Jackson**, Secy. Wit Hudson M. **Garland**, Recorder of the General Land Office. Rec in Vol. 6:364 of the General Land Office. Rec 7 Dec 1840. [No. 1073]

1294. Page 449. 7 Nov 1840. Robert S. **Manning** and Nancey, his wife, to George **Hooss**. For the sum of $125, Lot No. 31 in Perryville, fronting on Main St; purchased from Mathias **Barringer** and wife on 9 Mar 1840 (3:266). Signed Robert S. (x) **Manning**, Nancey (x) **Manning**. Wit James **Rice** (JP). Rec 14 Dec 1840. [No. 1074]

1295. Page 451. 7 Dec 1840. George **McKinstrey** to Joseph S. **Pease**, Lewis G. **Irving**, and Henry L. **Pease**, trading as J. S. Pease & Co. For securing a note and the sum of $1, assignment of mortgage on several tracts mortgaged to George **McKinstry** by Charles **McKinstry** on 10 Jun 1840. George **McKinstry** owes a note dated 10 Jun 1840 and payable in 18 months to J. S. Pease & Co. Once this note is paid, the deed is assigned to pay another note for $2250 dated 10 Jun 1840 held by Wm. J. **Hungerford** and Richard M. **Livingston**. Signed Geo. **McKinstry**. Wit James **Rice** (JP). Rec 16 Dec 1840. [No. 1075]

1296. Page 452. 9 Nov 1840. Adam Gothelf **Schnider** to John Gotfrey **Hemmann**. For the sum of $50, mortgage on 40 acres, being the SW 1/4, SE 1/4, Sec 21, Twp 34 N, Rng 12 E. Sd **Schnider** owes sd **Hemmann** a debt due in 12 months with 8% interest. Signed Adam Gotthelf **Schnider**. Wit Elias **Barber** (JP). Rec 17 Dec 1840. [No. 1076]

1297. Page 453. 2 Mar 1840. Jesse **Dickson** and Barbara Rebeca, his wife, to Marshal **Dickson**. For the sum of $500, the 1/7 part of three tracts in Bois Brule Bottom in Twp 36 N, Rng 12 E. being all their interest in the estate of Lewis **Dickson**, decd; 320 arpens, bounded on the E by the Mississippi River, N by **Fisher**, and S & W by Lewis **Dickson**'s heirs, purchased from J. B. **Bosier** and Henry **Eliott** by Lewis **Dickson** in his lifetime on 21 Jan 1820; 640 acres, more or less, bounded on the E by the Mississippi River, N by the first tract, W by one other tract belonging to the estate, and S by **Russell**, confirmed to Lewis **Dickson** by the U. S. in his lifetime; and 640 acres, bounded on the E by the second tract and **Fisher**, N by **Smith**, S by unknown lands, confirmed to Abraham **Armstrong** by the U. S. A., and purchased by Lewis **Dickson** in his lifetime on 9 Jul 1819. Signed Jesse **Dickson**, Barbara R. **Dickson** (RD). Wit Robert T. **Brown**, JCC. Rec 22 Dec 1840. [No. 1077]

[No. 1078 skipped in original]

1298. Page 454. 23 Dec 1840. Protest of the steamboat *Little Red* by Stephen **Price**, master, Andrew **Williams**, engineer, Thomas **Linn**, mate, Wm. **Motherley** and Wm. **Thompson**, pilots before Robert T. **Brown**, Jr. Sd steamboat left St. Louis on 20 Dec at about 1/2 past 11 o'clock in the forenoon, bound for N. Orleans. On Tuesday night, 22 Dec, the boat landed at Vitals Woodyard, and proceeded the next morning. It hit a gravelly bar about 1/2 mile below the landing, and took on water. Three pumps were used to pump water, and with the aid of the steamboat *Jatan*, was put afloat and gotten off the bar. All the crew were on duty and at their posts, and protest against all damages and expenses. Signed Stephen **Price**, Thomas M. **Lynn**, mate, Wm. **Motherley**, William **Thompson**, A. **Vollant**, R. T. **Brown** Jr. (JP). Rec 1 Jan 1841. [No. 1079]

1299. Page 455. 10 Sep 1840. William B. **Phillips** and Mary, his wife, of Louisville, Jefferson Co., Ken. to John C. **Land**, trustee for Julia **Montfort**. For the sum of $2000, 300 arpens, more or less, in Bois Brule Bottom, part of 600 arpens patented to Alexander **McConohoe** by the Spanish Government; beginning at a stake on the Mississippi River at the lower corner. Signed Wm. B. **Phillips**, Mary **Phillips**. Wit Edward P. **Pope**, Clerk of Jefferson Co., Ken. Circuit Court, John J. **Marshall**, Judge of Jefferson Co., Ken. Circuit Court. Rec 1 Jan 1841. [No. 1080]

1300. Page 457. 1 Aug 1838. Joseph **Duvall** and Evaline, his wife, to Gabriel M. **Duvall**. For the sum of $700, three undivided shares, being 100 acres out of 300 acres, part of a tract of 1920 acres formerly belonging to John **Donohoe**, the 300 acres being purchased from sd **Donohoe** by John **Duvall** on 13 Dec 1815 (Ste. Genevieve Co. Book C:93). Signed Joseph **Duvall**, Evaline (x) **Duvall** (RD). Wit James **Rice** (JP). Rec 1 Jan 1841. [No. 1081]

1301. Page 458. 1 Aug 1838. Same and same to same. For the sum of $500, quit claim to part of two tracts in Twp 35 & 36, Rng 10 & 11 E, to which they are entitled as heirs of John **Duvall**, decd, and not formerly conveyed by them to Gabriel M. **Duvall**; 640 acres formerly confirmed to Benjamine **Cox** Senior as Survey No. 2147; and 640 acres, confirmed to Benjamine **Cox** Junior as Survey No. 2146. The tracts were conveyed to John **Duvall**, decd, by Timothy **Davis** and Nancey, his wife, on 19 Mar 1825. Signed Joseph **Duvall**, Evaline (x) **Duvall** (RD). Test James **Rice** (JP). Rec 1 Jan 1841. [No. 1082]

1302. Page 459. 1 Jan 1841. Gabriel M. **Duvall** to Moses **Farrar**. For the sum of $600, the undivided 1/2 of a child's part of three tracts belonging to the heirs of John **Duvall**, decd, as described in the preceding two deeds (3:457, 458). Signed G. M. **Duvall**. Test W. B. **Wilkinson**, James **Rice** (JP). Rec 1 Jan 1841. [No. 1083]

1303. Page 461. 4 Jan 1841. Ferdinand **Rozier** and Harriet, his wife, to Daniel **Callier**. For the sum of $70, 40 acres, being the E 1/2, Lot No. 1, NE 1/4, Sec 3, Twp 34 N, Rng 10 E. Signed Ferdinand **Rozier** Jur., Harriet **Rozier**. Wit Reuben **Shelby**, JCC. Rec 4 Jan 1841. [No. 1084]

1304. Page 462. 16 Dec 1840. Robert S. **Manning** [and Nancey, his wife] to Peter J. **Tucker**. For the sum of $1, 50.50 acres on Apple Creek, being a part of the NW fractional 1/4, Sec 19, Twp 34 N, Rng 11 E; beginning at the SE corner of the NW 1/4 at a stake. Signed Robert S. (x) **Manning**, Nancey (x) **Manning** (RD). Wit Mark **Brewer** (JP). Rec 4 Jan 1841. [No. 1085]

1305. Page 463. 16 Dec 1840. Peter J. **Tucker** [and Mary Ann, his wife] to Robert S. **Manning**. For the sum of $1 and in pursuance of a previous agreement, 50 1/2 acres, part of fractional 1/4, Sec 19, Twp 34 N, Rng 11 E; bounded on the N & W by the township line; deeded to sd **Tucker** by sd **Manning** on 11 Jun 1839. Signed Peter J. **Tucker**, Mary Ann (x) **Tucker** (RD). Test Mark **Brewer** (JP). Rec 4 Jan 1841. [No. 1086]

1306. Page 464. 5 Jan 1841. Luther **Taylor** and Hannah, his wife, to Ciril **Besan**. For the sum of $275, two tracts in Sec 36, Twp 35 N, Rng 10 E; 76 acres, being the E 1/2, SE fractional 1/4; and 20 acres, being the E 1/2, NW 1/4, SE 1/4. Signed Luther **Taylor**, Hannah **Taylor** (RD). Wit James **Rice** (JP). Rec 5 Jan 1841. [No. 1087]

1307. Page 465. 4 May 1840. James B. **May** to Joseph **Cissell**. For the sum of $200, mortgage on his undivided interest in 100 acres in Survey No. 2137 in Twp 35 N, Rng 10 E confirmed to James **Moore** Senior, decd; beginning at the end of the lane which runs through the farm on which sd **Moore** lived in his lifetime. Sd **May** owes sd **Cissell** a debt with 10% interest by 13 Apr 1841. Signed James B. **May**. Wit James **Rice** (JP). Rec 14 Jan 1841. [Marginal note: Full satisfaction received on 22 Aug 1849. Signed Joseph **Cissell**. Wit J. W. **Noell**, Recorder.] [No. 1088]

1308. Page 466. 5 Dec 1840. Peter **Conrad** and Sarah, his wife, to William **Conrad**. For the sum of $50, 40 acres, being the SW 1/4, SW 1/4, Sec 21, Twp 34 N, Rng 10 E; entered by sd **Conrad** on 15 Oct 1833. Signed Peter **Conrad**, Sarah (x) **Conrad** (RD). Wit Alonzo **Abernathy**, JCC. Rec 16 Jan 1841. [No. 1089]

1309. Page 467. 1 Dec 1839. William **McCauley** to Charles Stewart Senior. For the sum of $100, 54.76 acres, being the NE fractional 1/4, Sec 13, Twp 35 N, Rng 10 E. This deed replaces one executed in 1834 and lost or misplaced. Signed Wm. **McCauley**. Wit James **Rice** (JP). Rec 21 Jan 1841. [No. 1090]

1310. Page 468. 1 Dec 1837. Bennett **McCauley** and Charlotte, his wife, and James **McCauley** and Rosanna, his wife to same. For the sum of $225, 40 acres, part of a tract conveyed by Joseph **Manning** and Mary, his wife, to Rezin L. **Bishop** and originally claimed by John **Layton**, decd; then conveyed by sd **Bishop** and Rebecca, his wife, to sd **McCauleys** in 1826; and beginning at a stake at the NW corner of sd tract. This deed replaces one executed in 1834 and lost or misplaced. Signed Bennett **McCauley**, Charlotte (x) **McCauley** (RD), James **McCauley**, Rosanna (x) **McCauley** (RD). Wit James **Rice** (JP). Rec 21 Jan 1841. [No. 1091]

1311. Page 469. 11 Jan 1841. John **Martin** and Susanna, his wife, to the Pleasant Grove Baptist Church. For the sum of $2, 1 1/2 acres in Brazeau Twp; part of the NW 1/4, SW 1/4, Sec 30, Twp 35 N, Rng 12 E; commencing at a certain marked post oak. The church is also to have free access to the spring on sd 40-acre tract. John (x) **Martin**, Susan (x) **Martin** (RD). Test William **Farrar** (JP). Rec 25 Jan 1841. [No. 1092]

1312. Page 470. 20 Jan 1841. William **Shaw** and Jane, his wife, to John **Johnson**. For the sum of $200, 40 acres, more or less, being the NW 1/4, NE 1/4, Sec 24, Twp 34 N, Rng 8 E; entered by Jane **Shaw** on 20 Jul 1839. Signed William (x) **Shaw**, Jane (x) **Shaw**. Wit James **Rice** (JP). Rec 26 Jan 1841. [No. 1093]

1313. Page 471. 25 Jan 1841. William H. **White** to Felix **Miles**. For securing two notes and the sum of $1, mortgage on one old sorrel mare, one roan colt two years old next Jul, one red bull one year old last spring, one cuppoard, one clock, one lot of hogs, one lot of corn, and one lot of carpenter's tools. Sd **White** owes two notes; one of even date to sd **Miles** for $55, due in 12 months; and one to Reuben **Shelby** for $33 with interest payable in four months, for which sd **Miles** is security. Signed William H. **White**. Wit Reuben **Shelby**, JCC. Rec 26 Jan 1841. [No. 1094]

1314. Page 472. 24 Sep 1840. John **Hasher** to Griswold W. **Wheeler**. For the sum of $70, the N 1/2, Lot No. 67 in Perryville, lying between Hyman **Block** on the N and the present dwelling house of sd **Hasher** on the remainder of sd lot on the S. Signed John **Hasher**. Wit James **Rice** (JP). Rec 29 Jan 1841. [No. 1095]

1315. Page 473. 11 Feb 1840. William **Black** and Elizabeth, his wife, to Ransom A. **Little**. For the sum of $50, 40 acres, being the NE 1/4, SW 1/4, Sec 1, Twp 34 N, Rng 11 E; entered by sd **Black** in Feb 1837. Signed William (x) **Black**, Elizabeth (x) **Black** (RD). Wit Alonzo **Abernathy**, JCC. Rec 29 Jan 1841. [No. 1096]

1316. Page 474. 26 Jan 1841. Ransom A. **Little** and Polly, his wife, to H. Jacob **Adler**. For the sum of $250, two tracts in Sec 1, Twp 34 N, Rng 11 E; 40 acres, being the NE 1/4, SW 1/4, entered by William **Black** in Feb 1837, and sold by him and Elizabeth, his wife, to sd **Little** on 11 Feb 1840; and 40 acres, being the NW 1/4, SW 1/4, patented to sd **Little** on 14 Nov 1837. Signed Ransom A. **Little**, Polly (x) **Little**. Wit Alonzo **Abernathy**, JCC. Rec 29 Jan 1841. [No. 1097]

1317. Page 475. 27 Jan 1841. Isaac **Meredith** and William **Patterson**. For the sum of $1 each, deed of partition for 150.41 acres, more or less, being the SE fractional 1/4, Sec 17, Twp 36 N, Rng 12 E. Sd **Patterson** is to receive 75.20 acres, beginning at the corner of Secs 16, 17, 20 & 21, running N; and sd **Meredith** is to receive 75.20 acres, beginning at the corner of the 1/4 section on the E-W line between Secs 16 & 17, thence S. Signed Isaac **Meredith**, Sarah (x) **Meredith** (RD), William (x) **Patterson**, Rachel (x) **Patterson** (RD). Test Wm. **Allen**, A. L. **Barks** (JP). Rec 1 Feb 1841. [No. 1098]

1318. Page 477. 2 Feb 1841. Thomas **Stewart** of Perryville to Peter J. **Tucker**. For the sum of $382, all his stock of liquors now on hand in his grocery in Perryville, consisting of wines and cordials and all the liquor in the grocery and in the cellar; and 30 sacks of salt now at Watters Landing on the bank of the Mississippi River. Sd **Stewart** owes three notes to sd **Tucker**; two for $125 each, one for $132. Signed Thomas **Stewart**. Wit James **Evans**, Fredk. C. **Hase**, Clerk. Rec 2 Feb 1841. [No. 1099]

1319. Page 478. 23 Sep 1839. George A. **Hamilton** to Robert P. **Slaughter**. For the sum of $70, the undivided 1/6 part of a tract of 457 acres in the NE corner of a tract originally granted to George A. **Hamilton**, decd; allotted to the widow as a portion of her dower, commonly called the Hill tract; and in the rear of Lot Nos. 1, 2, 3, 4, 5, 6, and 7. Signed George A. **Hamilton**. Wit F. J. **Hamilton**, Leo **Fenwick**, Fredk. C. **Hase**, Clerk. Rec 3 Feb 1841. [No. 1100]

1320. Page 479. 10 Feb 1841. James N. **Moore** and Sally, his wife, to Joseph J. **Layton**. For the sum of $125, 75.25 acres, more or less, on Saline Creek, the undivided moiety of sd **Moore** in the real estate which descended to him from his father Nicholas **Moore**, decd; as further described in a deed of partition dated 1 May 1839 (3:132). Signed James N. **Moore**, Sally (x) **Moore** (RD). Wit James **Rice** (JP). Rec 10 Feb 1841. [No. 1101]

1321. Page 480. 18 Feb 1841. Felix **Holster** to Mary **Holster**. For securing a debt and the sum of $1, mortgage on one iron grey horse, one gray mare, one cow and calf, one heifer one year old, and 30 hogs. Sd Felix owes sd Mary $122 by 1 Mar 1843. Signed Felix **Holster**. Wit Henry **Drewry** (JP). Rec 19 Feb 1841. [No. 1102]

1322. Page 480. 20 Feb 1841. Adam **Klop** to James **Rice**. For the sum of $174.56, mortgage on two tracts; the undivided moiety of 80 acres, more or less, purchased by sd **Klop** and George **Bergeman** in copartnership from John **Manning** and Nancey, his wife, on 28 Jul 1838 (2:437); and 37.27 acres, being the NW 1/4, SW 1/4, fractional Sec 17, Twp 35 N, Rng 11 E. Sd **Klop** owes sd **Rice** two notes of even date, as specified in the notes. Signed Adam **Klob**. Wit Reuben **Shelby**, JCC. Rec 20 Feb 1841. [Marginal note: Full satisfaction received on 26 Apr 1848. Signed James **Rice**. Test Jno. W. **Noell**, Recorder.] [No. 1103]

1323. Page 481. 20 Feb 1841. James **Wimsatt** to Joseph B. **Holmes** and Francis **Swanwick** of Randolph Co., Ill. For the sum of $442.94, one gray mare about eight years old, one strawberry roan mare about five years old, one strawberry rone horse about four years old, one brown colt about two years old, one iron gray filley about three years old, five cows and calves, one pair of work oxen, two steers about four years old, one cart, four steers about two years old, two heifers about three years old, nine sheep and three lambs, 50 hoggs, 150 bushels of corn, 500 pounds of bacon, one clock, one cupboard, one mans saddle, one womans saddle, two other cattle about one year old, and two bee gums. Signed James **Wimsatt**. Wit J. E. **Burgett**, John **Gener**(?), Fredk. C. **Hase**, Clerk. Rec 20 Feb 1841. [No. 1104]

1324. Page 482. 17 Jul 1838. Joseph V. **Beauvais** and Matildia, his wife, to Anthony **Vallars**. For the sum of $1140, two tracts; 87.64 acres, being the SE fractional 1/4, Sec 18, Twp 35 N. Rng 13 E, entered by Adam Moore **Martin** on 1 Feb 1836, Certificate No. 2709, sold by sd **Martin** to James **Lappin** on 31 Mar 1837, and conveyed by Michael P. **Casley**, admr of sd **Lappin**, by order of Cape Girardeau Co. Circuit Court to sd **Beauvais** on 21 Feb 1838; and 80 acres, being the W 1/2, NE 1/4, Sec 19, Twp 36 N, Rng 13 E, entered by Michael P. **Casley** on 10 Nov 1837, Certificate No. 5835, and conveyed to sd **Beauvais** on 21 Feb 1838. Signed Joseph V. **Beauvais**, Matilda **Beauvais** (RD). Wit Reuben **Shelby**, JCC. Rec 20 Feb 1841. [No. 1105]

1325. Page 484. 8 Oct 1840. Last will and testament of Sophia **Bertramm**, born **Miller**. To her husband Ludwig Ernst Edward **Bertramm**: $37 cash (to be used in part to pay the doctor and funeral expenses), about $60 due to her out of the credit fund, 7 acres in the Bottom of Altenberg, and beds and sundry wearing apparel. She has no children. Signed Sophia **Bertramm** born **Miller**, at Altenburg. Wit Gottfried **Schmidt**, Johannes **Leible**, Fredk. C. **Hase**, Clerk. Rec 6 Mar 1841. [No. 1106]

1326. Page 485. 15 Oct 1833. U. S. A. to Jacob **Clifton**. Patent for 40 acres, being the NW 1/4, SE 1/4, Sec 17, Twp 34 N, Rng 12 E; in Certificate No. 1495. Signed Andrew **Jackson** by A. J. **Donelson**, Secretary Wit Elijah **Haywood**, Commissioner of the General Land Office. Rec in Vol. 3:404 of the General Land Office. Rec 8 Mar 1841. [No. 1107]

1327. Page 485. 26 Apr 1838. Jacob **Clifton** and Catharine, his wife, to Jacob **Stemmer**. For the sum of $250, 40 acres as described in the preceding deed (3:485). Signed Jacob **Clifton**, Catharine (x) **Clifton** (RD). Wit James **Ferguson** (JP). Rec 8 Mar 1841. [No. 1108]

1328. Page 486. 12 Feb 1841. John **Patterson** to William P. **Belsha**. For the sum of $350, 50 acres in Bois Brule Twp, part of a survey confirmed to William **Hickman**; beginning at a corner in **McCasland**'s line. Signed John **Patterson**. Wit A. L. **Parks** (JP). Rec 8 Mar 1841. [No. 1109]

1329. Page 487. 13 Jul 1839. James **Clifton** to James **Clifton**. For natural love and affection for his son and for his better maintenance. 80 acres, being the E 1/2, NE 1/4, Sec 28, Twp 35 N, Rng 12 E; entered by James **Clifton** on 15 Oct 1833. Signed James **Clifton**. Wit Alonzo **Abernathy**, JCC. Rec 8 Mar 1841. [No. 1110]

1330. Page 487. 15 Mar 1841. Ignatius **Hutchings** to Barbara **Hutchings**. For the sum of $110, mortgage on 40 acres, being the SE 1/4, NE 1/4, Sec 34, Twp 35 N, Rng 10 E; 30 acres, being the NE 1/4, NE 1/4, Sec 34, Twp 35 N, Rng 10 E; one yoak of oxen; five sheep; and three sows and pigs. Ignatius **Hutchings** owes Barbara **Hutchings** the debt by 15 Mar 1846. Signed Ignatius (x) **Hutchings**. Test John **Layton** Senr (JP). Rec 18 Mar 1841. [Marginal note: Full satisfaction received on 8 Nov 1841. Signed Barbara (x) **Hutchings**. Wit John F. **Hase**, Dep Clerk.] [No. 1111]

1331. Page 488. 19 Mar 1841. Joseph D. **Burns** to Royal **Thompson** of Cape Girardeau Co., Mo. For the sum of $250, mortgage on 40 acres, being the NE 1/4, SE 1/4, Sec 26, Twp 35 N, Rng 11 E; one waggon; two yoke of oxen; one cow and calf; two yearling steers; three sheep; and ten hogs. Sd **Burns** owes a note of even date to sd **Thompson** in 12 months with interest. Signed Joseph D. **Burns**. Wit Louson **Thompson**, James B. **Reid**, William **Farrar** (JP). Rec 20 Mar 1841. [No. 1112]

1332. Page 489. 22 Mar 1841. Guy **Elder** to Leonard **Fath**. For the sum of $50, Lot No. 36 in Perryville. Signed Guy **Elder**. Wit James **Rice** (JP), Chas. **Avery**. Rec 22 Mar 1841. [No. 1113]

1333. Page 490. 20 Mar 1841. John **Hughey** to George **Seibert**. For the sum of $72.90, mortgage on 40 acres, being the SW 1/4, SW 1/4, Sec 1, Twp 34 N, Rng 12 E. Sd **Hughey** owes sd **Seibert** an obligation of even date by 20 Sep next with 10% interest. Signed John **Hughey**. Wit Augustus **Davis** (JP). Rec 24 Mar 1841. [Marginal note: Full satisfaction received on 12 Mar 1842. Signed George **Seibert**. Wit John W. **Noell**, Clerk.] [No. 1114]

1334. Page 491. 12 Apr 1839. Marx **Adler** and Elizabeth, his wife, to Richmond **Penny**. For the sum of $50, 40 acres, being the NE 1/4, SE 1/4, Sec 25, Twp 35 N, Rng 11 E. Signed Marx **Adler**, Elizabeth **Adler** (RD). Wit James **Ferguson** (JP). Rec 30 Mar 1841. [No. 1115]

1335. Page 491. 16 Oct 1840. Richmond **Penny** and Olive, his wife, to John **Martin** Senr. For the sum of $150, two tracts; 40 acres, being the NE 1/4, SE 1/4, Sec 25, Twp 35 N, Rng 11 E, conveyed by Marx **Adler** and wife to sd **Penny** after sd **Adler** entered it at the land office; and 39.36 acres, being the NW 1/4, SW 1/4, Sec 30, Twp 35 N, Rng 12 E, entered by sd **Penny** on 6 Mar 1839. Signed Richmond (x) **Penny**, Olly **Penny** (RD). Wit William **Farrar** (JP) Rec 30 Mar 1841. [No. 1116]

1336. Page 493. 26 Mar 1841. John **Hughey** to James **Starr**. For the sum of $36.90, mortgage on one year-old horse colt this spring, one cow that carries the bell and calf, one red stripped cow and spotted heifer year old past, 12 sheep, two sows and 13 pigs, and one bee-stand, cutting knife, and box. Sd **Hughey** owes sd **Starr** two notes, one for $18.45 and one for $18.45, due in nine months with interest. Signed John **Hughey**. Wit Fredk. C. **Hase**, Clerk. Rec 30 Mar 1841. [Marginal note: Full satisfaction received on 1 Feb 1847. Signed Jas. **Starr**.] [No. 1117]

1337. Page 493. 3 Apr 1841. Martin **Layton** and Nerius **Layton**, execrs of the last will and testament of Zachariah **Layton**, decd, to Peter J. **Tucker**. For the sum of $7, Lot No. 77 in Perryville on West and St Marys St. This deed replaces one to Thomas **Stewart** that is supposed lost or mislaid, and sd **Tucker** purchases this lot at his risks. Signed Martin **Layton**, Nerius **Layton**. Wit James **Rice** (JP). Rec 3 Apr 1841. [No. 1118]

1338. Page 494. 7 Apr 1841. Hosea **Cox** to William **Cox**. For the sum of $20, mortgage on four cattle (two yearlings, one steer, and one bull); a cow four years old with a crop off the left ear and a swallow fork in the right ear with her young calf; a feather bed, bedstead, and bed clothes; and 10 hogs, 6 small shotes, 3 yearlings, and one old sow with a swallow fork in the left ear and a crop off the right ear. Hosea **Cox** owes William **Cox** a note of even date for $25, due by 7 Apr 1844. Signed Hosea (x) **Cox**. Wit James **Rice** (JP). Rec 8 Apr 1841. [No. 1119]

1339. Page 495. 14 Jan 1841. Thomas **Riney** and Sarah, his wife, to Anthony **Parres**. For the sum of $75, Lot No. 16 in Perryville, fronting on Spring St. Signed Thomas **Riney**, Sarah (x) **Riney** (RD). Wit Reuben **Shelby**, JCC, M. **Daly**. Rec 15 Apr 1841. [No. 1120]

1340. Page 496. 5 Nov 1840. State of Missouri to Henry **McAtee**. For the sum of $50, patent for school land, being 40 acres, the NW 1/4, NE 1/4, Sec 16, Twp 34, Rng 11. Signed Lilburn W. **Boggs**, Governor. Wit Hiram H. **Baber**, Auditor. Rec 24 Apr 1841.

1341. Page 497. 28 Apr 1840. Edward M. **Holden** to Charles **Hayden**, Luther **Taylor**, and Walter B. **Wilkinson**. For securing two notes and the sum of $1, mortgage on one iron gray horse which he purchased from James **Keener**; one bay pony horse purchased in Ste. Genevieve Co.; one cow and calf purchased from John **Tucker**; one cart and one book press or cupboard that he purchased from Stephen **Tucker**'s property; and one desk purchased at the sale of Wm. **Flynn**'s property. Sd **Holden**, with sd **Hayden** and sd **Taylor** as securities, owes a note for $100 with 10% interest dated 25 Aug 1840 and payable in 12 months; and sd **Holden**, with sd **Hayden**, sd **Taylor**, and sd **Wilkinson** as securities, owes another for $84 with 10% interest. Signed Edward M. **Holden**. Wit Fredk. C. **Hase**, Clerk. Rec 1 May 1841. [No. 1122]

1342. Page 498. 28 Aug 1840. Thomas **Brown**, admr of the estate of Charles **Vessels**, decd, to Wilford **Manning**. For the sum of $122.50, 80 acres in Sec 22, Twp 36 N, Rng 10 E; purchased by sd **Vessels** and conveyed to his heirs by James B. **Mattingley**. Sold on 26 Mar 1839 at order of County Court issued Feb 1839 Term on petition for sale of sd real estate to pay debts of the estate. Signed Thomas **Brown**, admr of Charles **Vessels**, decd. Wit James **Rice** (JP). Rec 1 May 1841. [No. 1123]

1343. Page 499. 19 Feb 1841. John **Whitledge** and Francis, his wife, to Lyna Harrison **Whitledge**. For the sum of $50, 20 acres, being the N 1/2, E 1/2, Lot No. 6, NW 1/4, Sec 1, Twp 33 N, Rng 12 E. Signed John **Whitledge**, Francis **Whitledge** (RD). Wit Elias **Barber** (JP). Rec 3 May 1841. [No. 1124]

1344. Page 500. 5 Sep 1837. George **Rutledge** and Saraann, his wife, to Jeramiah **Abernathy**, William **Farrar**, George **Rutledge**, Lot **Abernathy**, John H. **Abernathy**, James **Burns**, and Alonzo **Abernathy**, trustees for the Methodist Episcopal Church. For the sum of $50, 40 acres, being the NW 1/4, SW 1/4, Sec 2, Twp 34 N, Rng 11 E; entered by sd **Rutledge** on 2 Aug 1837; for the use of the Methodist Episcopal Church to build a house of worship. The church is to use the property as specified in the deed. Signed George **Rutledge**, Saraann **Rutledge** (RD). Wit Batte **Abernathy**, Ezekiel **Foster**, Mark **Brewer** (JP). Rec 3 May 1841. [No. 1125]

1345. Page 502. 16 Sep 1837. Ezekiel **Foster** to same. For the sum of $5, 4 acres and 50 rods, more or less, beginning at the SW corner of the NE 1/4, SW 1/4, Sec 2, Twp 34 N, Rng 11 E. Signed Ezekiel **Foster**. Wit Mark **Brewer** (JP). Rec 3 May 1841. [No. 1126]

1346. Page 504. 20 Jun 1840. Francis **Clark** and Evaline, his wife, to Frederick A. **Kent**, Jerome **Merrit**, and E. W. **Geer** of Ste. Genevieve Co., Mo. For the sum of $300, two tracts purchased by sd **Clark** at the General Land Office; 25.91 acres, being the SW fractional 1/4, Sec 10, Twp 36 N, Rng 10 E; and 53.95 acres, being the NE fractional 1/4 and N 1/2, SE fractional 1/4, Sec 9, Twp 36 N, Rng 10 E. Signed Francis **Clark**, Evaline **Clark** (RD). Wit George P. **Clark**, William **Searcy** (JP). Rec 4 May 1841. [No. 1127]

1347. Page 505. 1 Sep 1839. John M. M. **Powell** and Harriot, his wife, to same, same, and E. Woodbridge **Geer** of Ste. Genevieve Co., Mo. For the sum of $600, 156.92 acres, being the NW fractional 1/4, fractional Sec 10, Twp 36 N, Rng 10 E; patented on 16 Jun 1836. Signed J. M. M. **Powell**, Harriet **Powell** (RD). Wit Wm. **Searcy** (JP). Rec 4 May 1841. [No. 1128]

1348. Page 506. 5 Mar 1841. Charles **Brewer** and Mary, his wife and daughter and heir of Ignatius **Layton**, decd; and Austin **Layton**, son of Ignatius **Layton**, decd, and Tresa, his wife, to Reuben **Shelby**. For the sum of $120, their portion of 320 acres that Ignatius **Layton** possessed, part of 640 acres confirmed by the U. S. A. to Michael **Tucker**, part purchased by Ignatius **Layton** from Nicholas **Miles** and Michael **Tucker**, and part from Peter **Tucker** Senr. Signed Charles **Brewer**, Mary (x) **Brewer**. Wit Fredk. C. **Hase**, Clerk. Rec 5 May 1841. [No. 1129]

1349. Page 508. 5 May 1841. Robert M. C. **Stewart**, now of Miss., to Edward M. **Holden**. Power of attorney to obtain his share of the estate of John **Boyce**, decd; his having intermarried with Sarah **Boyce**, daughter and heir of sd **Boyce**. Signed R. M. C. **Stewart**. Wit Fredk. C. **Hase**, Clerk. Rec 6 May 1841. [No. 1130]

1350. Page 509. 10 Feb 1841. Walter **Wilkinson** to the County of Perry. For the sum of $1000, mortgage on Lot Nos. 81 & 85 in Perryville. Sd **Wilkinson** has borrowed the money from the Road and Canal Fund, to be repaid with 10% interest per annum. Signed W. B. **Wilkinson**. Wit Reuben **Shelby**, JCC. Rec 11 May 1841. [No. 1131]

1351. Page 509. 3 Jun 1841. Michael **Daly** and Rose, his wife, to Samuel M. **Cobbs**. For the sum of $100, the N 1/2, Lot No. 63 in Perryville; purchased by sd **Daly** on 24 Mar 1840 at Sheriff's sale as the property of Alexander M. **Cobbs**. Signed Michael **Daly**, Rose (x) **Daly** (RD). Wit Fredk. C. **Hase**, Clerk. Rec 4 Jun 1841. [No. 1132]

1352. Page 510. 2 Jun 1841. Anthony **Swank** and Tresey, his wife, to Sebastian **Dropp**. For the sum of $100, mortgage on 80 acres, being the NW 1/4, SW 1/4 and the SW 1/4, NW 1/4, Sec 27, Twp 34 N, Rng 12 E. Sd **Swank** owes David **Evans** a note, with sd **Dropp** as security, due by 1 Jun 1841 with interest. Signed Anton **Swank**, Tresy **Swank** (RD). Wit A. M. **McPhearson** (JP). Rec 11 Jun 1841. [Marginal note: Full satisfaction received on 7 Apr 1856. Signed Joseph **Meyer**, admr of Sebastian **Dropp**, decd. Test C. C. **Ellis**, Clerk.] [No. 1133]

1353. Page 511. 5 Feb 1840. David **Burns**, admr of the estate of John W. **Quick**, decd, to Julia **Quick**. For the sum of $900, three tracts in Sec 12, Twp 34 N, Rng 11 E; 40 acres, being the SW 1/4, NE 1/4; 160 acres, being the W 1/2, SE 1/4 and E 1/2, SW 1/4; and 40 acres, being the SE 1/4, NW 1/4. Sold on 6 Nov 1838 at order of County Court issued Aug Term 1838 on petition for sale of sd lands to pay debts by William **Burns**, agent for David **Burns**. Signed David **Burns**, admr of the estate of John W. **Quick**, decd. Wit James **Rice** (JP), J. W. **Noell**. Rec 14 Jun 1841. [No. 1134]

1354. Page 513. 29 Sep 1840. John **Scudder** and Rebeca, his wife, to Nicholas Noel **Destrihan** of Jefferson Parish, La. For the sum of $5000, deed of trust on 955 acres in six tracts on which they now reside in Perry and Cape Girardeau Cos.; 400 arpens at the mouth of Apple Creek, known as Pierre **Menard**'s claim, confirmed to sd **Menard**, conveyed by him to John **Logan** of Ill., by sd **Logan** to Nancey **Osborn**, and by her to sd **Scudder**; 405.75 acres, being Town Isle in Twp 33 & 34 N, Rng 14 E; 40 acres, being Lot No. 2, NW 1/4, fractional Sec 5, Twp 33 N, Rng 14 E; 40 acres, being the E 1/2, Lot No. 1, NW 1/4, Sec 6, Twp 33 N, Rng 14 E; 80 acres, being Lot No. 1, NE 1/4, fractional Sec 3, Twp 33 N, Rng 13 E; and 40 acres, being NE 1/4, SE 1/4, Sec __, Twp 33 N, Rng 14 E. The following lots are excepted: Block No. 25; Lot Nos. 1, 2, & 18 in Block No. 8; Lot Nos. 9, 10, 11, 15, 16, & 17 in Block No. 12; and Lot Nos. 7 & 8, Block No. 4. Sd **Scudder** is about to lease the Planters Hotel in New Orleans from Oct or Nov next for one year from ___ **Paulding**, and expects to pay about $8000 for the use of sd house, and this secures the rent, on which sd **Destrihan** is security. Sd **Destrihan** is to sell the property if sd **Scudder** fails in payment of the rent. Signed John **Scudder**, Rebeca **Scudder**. Wit Augustus **Davis** (JP), Henry S. **Osborn**. Rec 24 Jun 1841. [No. 1135]

1355. Page 515. 15 Mar 1841. Nicy Jane **Kinnison**, widow of Alexander S. **Kinnison**, decd, to John **Kinnison**. For the sum of $340, 100 arpens on the Mississippi River in Bois Brule Bottom; part of a tract confirmed to Alexander **McConoho**, and where Alexander **Kinnison** lived at the time of his death; bounded on the lower side by land sold by John **Kinnison** to William **Diggs** and George **McKinstry**, upper side by land sold by John **Kinnison** to Thomas **Sanders**, back by land sold by John **Carlisle** to sd **Diggs** and **McKinstry**, and front by the Mississippi River. Signed Nicy Jane **Kinnison**. Wit Hy. **Sandford**, Circuit Clerk of Cape Girardeau Co., Mo. Rec 15 Jun 1841. [No. 1136]

1356. Page 516. 15 Mar 1841. John **Kinnison** to Nicy Jane **Kinnison** of Cape Girardeau Co., Mo. For the sum of $290, mortgage on 50 arpens in Bois Brule Bottom, part of 100 arpens conveyed by Nicy Jane **Kinnison** to John **Kinnison** on this day. John **Kinnison** owes a note to Nicy Jane **Kinnison** by 1 Nov 1841. Signed John **Kinnison**. Wit Hy. **Sandford**, Circuit Clerk of Cape Girardeau Co., Mo. Rec 15 Jun 1841. [No. 1137]

1357. Page 517. 22 Dec 1840. Joseph **Manning** to Pius **Manning**. For the sum of $1000, bond to make a deed for 74 1/2 acres, commencing at the W corner of James **Reddick**'s tract, also bounded by Joseph **Miles**' confirmation. Sd Joseph has, for natural love and affection for his son and the sum of $50 paid to John **Manning** for his interest, conveyed his real estate to sd Pius. Sd Pius has also paid the further consideration of $75 in a note due two years after date to sd Joseph, with the deed to be executed when the note is paid. Signed Joseph **Manning**. Wit John **Layton** (JP). Rec 15 Jun 1841. [No. 1138]

1358. Page 518. 15 Jun 1841. John W. **Cox** to Francis L. **Jones**. For the sum of $120, mortgage on 94.44 acres, more or less, being the E fractional 1/2, fractional Sec 33, Twp 36 N, Rng 11 E. Sd **Cox** owes a note dated 6 Mar 1841 to sd **Jones** by 6 Mar 1844 with interest of 6% per annum. Signed John W. **Cox**. Test James **Rice** (JP). Rec 15 Jun 1841. [Marginal note: Full satisfaction received on 13 Feb 1844. Signed F. L. **Jones**. Test Jno. W. **Noell**, Clerk.] [No. 1139]

1359. Page 518. 15 Jun 1841. J. Livingston **Van Dorin** by Sheriff Joseph D. **Simpson** to John **Scudder**. For the sum of $10.50, 102 acres, more or less, being the SW fractional 1/2, Lot No. 1, NW 1/4, Sec 5, Twp 33 N, Rng 14 E. Sold on 14 Jun 1841 on a writ of fieri facias issued at Mar 1838 Term of Circuit Court of St. Francis Co., Mo. in favor of John D. **Haynes** and against sd **Van Dorin** for $1593.75 damages plus costs. Signed Joseph D. **Simpson**, Sheriff. Wit John F. **Hase**, Dep Clerk. Rec 15 Jun 1841. [No. 1140]

1360. Page 520. 20 Dec 1839. Henry Christoph **Bimpage**, admr of the goods and estate of Johann George **Gube**, decd, to Henry C. **Bimpage**, Friederich Wilh. **Barthels**, and Christian Fred. **Muller**. In pursuance of previous contracts, 640 acres, more or less, on Brazeau Creek and the Mississippi River; being Survey No. 2173 in Twp 34 N, Rng 14 E, originally granted to John **Manning** and lately bought from Moses S. **Harris** and Robert S. **Manning** by sd **Gube**, then sold to sd **Bimpage** on 12 Jan 1839; beginning at a post on the line of Henry **Riley**. Sold on decree of Circuit Court in Chancery issued 29 Nov 1839. Bought to lay out the town of Wittenberg. Signed Henry C. **Bimpage**, admr. Wit Gustave **Pfau**, F. **Gottschelk**, Fredk. C. **Hase**, Clerk. Rec 15 Jun 1841. [No. 1140 repeated]

1361. Page 522. 15 Jun 1841. Same to Johann Gottlieb **Palisch**, George **Kleugle** Sr. and Aug. Henr. **Doederlien**. In pursuance of previous contracts, 102.92 acres, being fractional Sec 13, Twp 34 N, Rng 13 E and 40.50 acres out of the E part, SE 1/4, fractional Sec 14, Twp 34 N, Rng 13 E. Sold on the conditions in 3:520. Conveyed for the benefit of those who were members of the German Lutheran Settlement on Brazeau Creek on 22 June 1839. Signed Henry C. **Bimpage**, admr. Wit Fredk. C. **Hase**, Clerk. Rec 15 Jun 1841. [No. 1142]

1362. Page 523. 15 Jun 1841. Same to same, same, and same. In pursuance of previous contracts, 40 acres, being the SW 1/4, NE 1/4, Sec 23, Twp 34, Rng 13 E. Sold on the conditions in 3:520. Conveyed for the erection of a house of worship for the use and members of the Lutheran Church for the inhabitants of Wittenberg, Selitz, Dresden, Altenberg, and Neideifrohne; with two members from each settlement to be elected to a Board of Trustees to function as designated in the deed. Signed Henry C. **Bimpage**, admr. Wit Fredk. C. **Hase**, Clerk. Rec 15 Jun 1841. [No. 1143]

1363. Page 524. 20 Aug 1840. Same to Sophia **Schnider**. For money sd **Schnider** gave to sd **Gube** to enter land, two tracts; 44.50 acres, more or less, being the W part, SE fractional 1/4, Sec 14, Twp 34 N, Rng 13 E, beginning at the SW corner of sd Sec; and bounded in part by Robert **Hinkson**'s Survey No. 865; and 91 acres, more or less, N part, NW 1/4, Sec 23, Twp 34 N, Rng 13 E, commencing at the NW corner of sd Sec. Sold on the conditions in 3:520. Signed Henry C. **Bimpage**, admr. Wit Fred. Wilh. **Barthels**, Augustus **Davis** (JP). Rec 15 Jun 1841. [No. 1144]

1364. Page 526. 20 Aug 1840. Same to Henrich Aug. **Doederlein**. For money sd **Doederlein** paid to sd **Gube** to enter land, 63 acres, more or less, being the SW part, NW 1/4, Sec 23, Twp 34 N, Rng 13 E, beginning at the SW corner of sd section. Sold on the conditions in 3:520. Signed Henry C. **Bimpage**, admr. Wit Fredk. Wilh. **Barthel**, Augustus **Davis** (JP). Rec 15 Jun 1841. [No. 1145]

1365. Page 527. 10 Nov 1840. Same to Johann Christ. **Graefe**. For money sd **Graefe** paid to sd **Gube** to enter land, 6 acres, being the E part, S 1/2, NW 1/4, Sec 23, Twp 34 N, Rng 13 E, beginning at the center of Sec 23. Sold on the conditions in 3:520. Signed Henry C. **Bimpage**. Wit Fredk. C. **Hase**, Clerk. Rec 25 Jun 1841. [No. 1146]

1366. Page 528. 13 Nov 1840. Same to Samuel Gottleib **Kaempfe**. For money sd **Kaempfe** paid to sd **Gube** to enter land, 105 acres, commencing at the NW corner of the SW 1/4, Sec 23, Twp 34 N, Rgn 13 E. Sold on the conditions in 3:520. Signed Henry C. **Bimpage**. Wit Fredk. C. **Hase**, Clerk. Rec 15 Jun 1841. [No. 1147]

1367. Page 529. 15 Nov 1840. Same to Friederich **Bunger**. For money sd **Bunger** paid to sd **Gube** to enter land, 6 acres, commencing 8.50 links E of the SW corner, SW 1/4, Sec 23, Twp 34 N, Rng 13 E. Sold on the conditions in 3:520. Signed Henry C. **Bimpage**. Wit Fredk. C. **Hase**, Clerk. Rec 15 Jun 1841. [No. 1148]

1368. Page 530. 15 Jun 1841. Same to Samuel G. **Kaempfe** and Johann Gottleib **Palisch**. For money sd **Kaempfe** and **Palisch** paid to sd **Gube** to enter land, two tracts; 4 acres in the SW 1/4, Sec 23, Twp 34 N, Rng 13 E; and 20 acres, being the E 1/2, SW 1/4, NW 1/4, Sec 26, Twp 34 N, Rng 13 E. Sold on the conditions in 3:520, for the construction of a house of worship, a school house and other necessary buildings to perpetuate the Lutheran creed in the colony of Dresden, under conditions specified in the deed. Signed Henry C. **Bimpage**, admr. Wit Fredk. C. **Hase**, Clerk. Rec 15 Jun 1841. [No. 1149]

1369. Page 531. 16 Nov 1840. Same to Andreas **Estel**. For money sd **Estel** paid to sd **Gube** to enter land, 5 acres, beginning at the SW corner of the SE 1/4, SW 1/4, Sec 23, Twp 34 N, Rgn 13 E. Sold on the conditions in 3:520. Signed Henry C. **Bimpage**. Wit Fredk. C. **Hase**, Clerk. Rec 15 Jun 1841. [No. 1150]

1370. Page 532. 17 Nov 1840. Same to Frederick **Sproede**. For money sd **Sproede** paid to sd **Gube** to enter land, 92 acres in two tracts; 80 acres, being the W 1/2, NE 1/4, Sec 26, Twp 34 N, Rng 13 E; and 12 acres, being the W part, SW 1/4, SE 1/4, Sec 23, Twp 34 N, Rng 13 E, beginning at the SW corner, SE 1/4, Sec 23. Sold on the conditions in 3:520. Signed Henry C. **Bimpage**. Wit Fredk. C. **Hase**, Clerk. Rec 15 Jun 1841. [No. 1151]

1371. Page 533. 17 Nov 1840. Same to Johann Gottleib **Palisch** and Carl Gottleib **Zeibig**. For money sd **Palisch** and sd **Zeibig** paid to sd **Gube** to enter land, 108 acres in Sec 23, Twp 34 N, Rng 13 E in two tracts; 80 acres, being the E 1/2, SE 1/4, Sec 23, Twp 34 N, Rng 13 E; and 28 acres, being the E part, SW 1/4, SE 1/4, beginning at the SW corner of the E 1/2, SE 1/4. Sd **Zeibig** is entitled to 34 acres, and sd **Palisch** to 74 acres. Sold on the conditions in 3:520. Signed Henry C. **Bimpage**. Wit Fredk. C. **Hase**, Clerk. Rec 15 Jun 1841. [No. 1152]

1372. Page 534. 17 Nov 1840. Same to August Frederick **Hacker**. For money sd **Hacker** paid to sd **Gube** to enter land, 30 acres, beginning at the NE corner, NW 1/4, Sec 26, Twp 34 N, Rng 13 E. Sold on the conditions in 3:520. Signed Henry C. **Bimpage**. Wit Fredk. C. **Hase**, Clerk. Rec 15 Jun 1841. [No. 1153]

1373. Page 535. 17 Nov 1840. Same to Natalie **Geier**. For money sd **Geier** paid to sd **Gube** to enter land, 5 acres, beginning at the NE corner, NW 1/4, NW 1/4, Sec 26, Twp 34 N, Rng 13 E. Sold on the conditions in 3:520. Signed Henry C. **Bimpage**. Wit Fredk. C. **Hase**, Clerk. Rec 15 Jun 1841. [No. 1154]

1374. Page 536. 18 Nov 1840. Same to Christeni **Bunger**, widow. For money sd **Bunger** paid to sd **Gube** to enter land, 11 acres, beginning at the NW corner, NW 1/4, Sec 26, Twp 34 N, Rng 13 E. Sold on the conditions in 3:520. Signed Henry C. **Bimpage**. Wit Fredk. C. **Hase**, Clerk. Rec 15 Jun 1841. [No. 1155]

1375. Page 537. 18 Nov 1840. Same to Gustave **Pfau**. For money sd **Pfau** paid to sd **Gube** to enter land, 24 acres, beginning at the SW corner, NW 1/4, NW 1/4, Sec 26, Twp 34 N, Rng 13 E. Sold on the conditions in 3:520. Signed Henry C. **Bimpage**. Wit Fredk. C. **Hase**, Clerk. Rec 15 Jun 1841. [No. 1156]

1376. Page 538. 11 Jun 1841. Same to Johann Gottfried **Deichmann** and Johann Gottleib **Palisch**. For money sd **Deichmann** and sd **Palisch** paid to sd **Gube** to enter land, 3 acres out of the SW corner, NE 1/4, NW 1/4, Sec 26, Twp 34 N, Rng 13 E. Sold on the conditions in 3:520. Signed Henry C. **Bimpage**, admr. Wit Fredk. C. **Hase**, Clerk. Rec 15 Jun 1841. [No. 1157]

1377. Page 539. 18 Nov 1840. Same to Johann Christ. **Richter**. For money sd **Richter** paid to sd **Gube** to enter land, 27 acres in two tracts in Sec 26, Twp 34 N, Rng 13 E; 7 acres, beginning at the SE corner, NE 1/4, NW 1/4; and 20 acres, being the W 1/2, SW 1/4, NW 1/4, beginning at the SW corner of the NW 1/4. Sold on the conditions in 3:520. Signed Henry C. **Bimpage**. Wit Fredk. C. **Hase**, Clerk. Rec 15 Jun 1841. [No. 1158]

1378. Page 540. 19 Nov 1840. Same to Louise **Marbach**, wife of Francis Adolph **Marbach**. For money Francis Adolph **Marbach** paid to sd **Gube** to enter land, 40 acres, being the SE 1/4, NW 1/4, Sec 26, Twp 34 N, Rng 13 E. Sold on the conditions in 3:520. Signed Henry C. **Bimpage**, admr. Wit Fredk. C. **Hase**, Clerk. Rec 15 Jun 1841. [No. 1159]

1379. Page 541. 19 Nov 1840. Same to Johann August **Steizle**. For money sd **Steizle** paid to sd **Gube** to enter land, two tracts; 80 acres, being the N 1/2, SW 1/4, Sec 26, Twp 34 N, Rng 13 E; and 16 acres, being the S part, W 1/2, NW 1/4, Sec 35, Twp 34 N, Rng 13 E, beginning at the SW corner of the NW 1/4. Sold on the conditions in 3:520. Signed Henry C. **Bimpage**. Wit Fredk. C. **Hase**, Clerk. Rec 15 Jun 1841. [No. 1160]

1380. Page 542. 20 Aug 1840. Same to Johann Gottleib **Palisch**. For money sd **Palisch** paid to sd **Gube** to enter land, two tracts; 40 acres, being the SE 1/4, SW 1/4, Sec 26, Twp 34 N, Rng 13 E; and 50.14 acres, being the W fractional 1/2, SE 1/4, Sec 34, Twp 34 N, Rng 13 E. Sold on the conditions in 3:520. Signed Henry C. **Bimpage**. Wit Frederick Wilh. **Barthel**, Augustus **Davis** (JP). Rec 15 Jun 1841. [No. 1161]

1381. Page 543. 19 Nov 1840. Same to Johann Gottleib **Hochne** and his brother Johann Carl Aug. **Hochne**. For money sd **Hochne** brothers paid to sd **Gube** to enter land, 64 acres, being the N part, W 1/2, NW 1/4, Sec 35, Twp 34 N, Rng 13 E, beginning at the NW corner of the NW 1/4; 43 acres to John Gottleib **Hochne**, and 21 acres to John Carl Aug. **Hoechne**. Sold on the conditions in 3:520. Signed Henry C. **Bimpage**. Wit Fredk. C. **Hase**, Clerk. Rec 15 Jun 1841. [No. 1162]

1382. Page 544. 2 Jun 1841. Same to Ernst Moritz **Burger**. For money sd **Burger** paid to sd **Gube** to enter land, 15 acres, more or less, being Lot No. 1 out of Claim No. 865, Twp 34 N, Rgn 13 E, originally granted to Robert **Hinkston**; beginning at the center of originally granted to Robert **Hinkston**; beginning at the center of Claim No. 865. Sold on the conditions in 3:520. Signed Henry C. **Bimpage**, admr. Wit Fredk. C. **Hase**, Clerk. Rec 15 Jun 1841. [No. 1163]

1383. Page 545. 16 Jan 1841. Same to Johann Christian **Hinklemann** and Johann Christian **Poppits**. For money sd **Hinklemann** and sd **Poppits** paid to sd **Gube** to enter land, 7.5 acres, being Lot No. 2 in Claim No. 865, Twp 34 N, Rng 13 E originally granted to Robert **Hinkston**; for the construction of a school house for the use of members of the Lutheran Church as specified in the deed. Sold on the conditions in 3:520. Signed Henry C. **Bimpage**, admr. Wit Fredk. C. **Hase**, Clerk. Rec 15 Jun 1841. [No. 1164]

1384. Page 547. 10 Jun 1841. Same to Johanne Sophia **Shlimpert**. For money sd **Shlimpert** paid to sd **Gube** to enter land, 56.50 acres in Claim No. 865, Twp 34 N, Rng 13 E, originally granted to Robert **Hinkston**; 13.5 acres in Lot No. 3, and 43 acres in either Lot Nos. 26, 27, or 32. Sold on the conditions in 3:520. Signed Henry C. **Bimpage**. Wit Fredk. C. **Hase**, Clerk. Rec 15 Jun 1841. [No. 1165]

1385. Page 548. 10 Jun 1841. Same to Christian Gottfried **Schlimpert**. For money sd **Schlimpert** paid to sd **Gube** to enter land, 197 acres, more or less, out of Claim No. 865, Twp 34 N, Rng 13 E, originally granted to Robert **Hinkston**; being 3.30 acres in Lot No. 4, 3 acres in Lot No. 10, 81.70 acres in Lot No. 24, 31 acres in Lot No. 29, and 78 acres in either Lot No. 25, 28 or 30. Sold on the conditions in 3:520. Signed Henry C. **Bimpage**, admr. Wit Fredk. C. **Hase**, Clerk. Rec 15 Jun 1841. [No. 1166]

1386. Page 549. 10 Jun 1841. Same to Johann Christian **Kunhert**, Johanne Sophia **Storlin**, and Johann Gottfried **Schubert**. For money sd **Kunhert**, **Storlin**, and **Schubert** paid to sd **Gube** to enter land, four tracts out of Claim No. 865, Twp 34 N, Rng 13 E, originally granted to Robert **Hinkston**; 4.20 acres, Lot No. 5. to sd **Kunhert**; 3 acres, Lot No. 6, and 6.5 acres, Lot No. 19 to sd **Storlin**; and 7.35 acres, Lot No. 7, to sd **Shubert**. Sold on the conditions in 3:520. Signed Henry C. **Bimpage**, admr. Wit Fredk. C. **Hase**, Clerk. Rec 15 Jun 1841. [No. 1167]

1387. Page 550. 10 Jun 1841. Same to Gottlieb **Richter**, Christian **Richter**, and Johann Christian **Hinklemann**. For money the **Richter**s and sd **Hinklemann** paid to sd **Gube** to enter land, four tracts out of Claim No. 865, Twp 34 N, Rng 13 E, originally granted to Robert **Hinkston**; 3 acres, Lot No. 8, to Gottlieb **Richter**; 3 acres, Lot No. 22, to Christian **Richter**; and 6 acres, Lot No. 9, and 20 acres out of either Lot Nos. 26, 27, or 32 to sd **Hinklemann**. Sold on the conditions in 3:520. Signed Henry C. **Bimpage**, admr. Wit Fredk. C. **Hase**, Clerk. Rec 15 Jun 1841. [No. 1168]

1388. Page 551. 10 Jun 1841. Same to Traugott **Schlimpert**, Christian Gottfried **Muller**, and Johann Adam **Kuhn**. For money sd **Schlimpert**, sd **Muller**, and sd **Kuhn** paid to sd **Gube** to enter land, five tracts; 3.15 acres, Lot No. 11 to sd **Schlimpert**; 3.15 acres, Lot No. 12 and 23 acres out of either Lot Nos. 26, 27, or 32 to sd **Muller**, and 9 acres, Lot No. 13 and 7 acres, Lot No. 28 to sd **Kuhn**. Sold on the conditions in 3:520. Signed Henry C. **Bimpage**, admr. Wit Fredk. C. **Hase**, Clerk. Rec 15 Jun 1841. [No. 1169]

1389. Page 552. 10 Jan 1841. Same to Maria Theresia **Benedictine**, Johanne Rosina **Saupin**, Johann Gottleib **Dade**, and Gottleib **Augustin**. For money sd **Benedictine**, sd **Saupin**, sd **Dade**, and sd **Augustin** paid to sd **Gube** to enter land, four tracts out of Claim No. 865, Twp 34 N, Rng 13 E originally granted to Robert **Hinkston**; 3 acres, Lot No. 14 to sd **Benedictine**; 2.5 acres, Lot No. 15 to sd **Saupin**; 3.15 acres, Lot No. 16 to sd **Dade**; and 3 acres, Lot No. 17 to sd **Augustin**. Sold on the conditions in 3:520. Signed Henry C. **Bimpage**. Wit Fredk. C. **Hase**, Clerk. Rec 15 Jun 1841. [No. 1170]

1390. Page 553. 11 Jun 1841. Same to Gottfred **Lorenz**, Gotchold **Darnstedt**, Frederick **Engest**, and Christian Frederick **Uhlig**. For money sd **Lorenz**, sd **Darnstedt**, sd **Engest**, and sd **Uhlig** paid to sd **Gube** to enter land, four tracts out of Claim No. 865, Twp 34 N, Rng 13 E originally granted to Robert **Hinkston**; 2 acres, Lot No. 18 to sd **Lorenz**; 7 acres, Lot No. 20 to sd **Darnstedt**; 1.5 acres, Lot No. 21, to sd **Engerst**; and 34 acres from either Lot Nos. 26, 27, or 32 to sd **Uhlig**. Sold on the conditions in 3:520. Signed Henry C. **Bimpage**, admr. Wit Fredk. C. **Hase**, Clerk. Rec 15 Jun 1841. [No. 1171]

1391. Page 554. 10 Jun 1841. Same to Johann Christian **Poppitz**. For money sd **Popits** paid to sd **Gube** to enter land, five tracts out of Claim No. 865, Twp 34 N, Rng 13 E originally granted to Robert **Hinkston**; 54.80 acres, being Lot No. 23; 40 acres, Being Lot No. 31; 80 acres, being Lot Nos. 33 & 34; 35 acres out of Lot Nos. 25 or 30; and 138.60 acres, being the NE fractional 1/4, Sec 10, Two 34 N, Rng 13 E. Sold on the conditions in 3:520. Signed Henry C. **Bimpage**, admr. Wit Fredk. C. **Hase**, Clerk. Rec 15 Jun 1841. [No. 1172]

1392. Page 555. 15 Jun 1841. Same to George **Klugle** Sr and Johann **Schmit**. For money sd **Klugle** and sd **Schmit** paid to sd **Gube** to enter land, 8 acres, more or less, being 4 acres in each of Lot Nos. 11 & 12 in the Borough Altenberg; for the purpose of erecting a house of worship for the use of the Lutheran Church, as specified in the deed. Sold on the conditions in 3:520. Signed Henry C. **Bimpage**. Wit Fredk. C. **Hase**, Clerk. Rec 15 Jun 1841. [No. 1173]

1393. Page 556. 9 Jan 1841. Same to Johann **Schmidt**. For money sd **Schmidt** paid to sd **Gube** to enter land, five tracts in Twp 34 N, Rng 13 E totaling 267.75 acres; 45.50 acres, being the SE fractional 1/4, Sec 10; 16.70 acres, being the SW 1/4, fractional Sec 11; 21.76 acres, being the NE fractional Sec 14; 120 acres, being the N 1/2, SW 1/4 and SW 1/4, SW 1/4, Sec 14; and 63.48 acres, being the W fractional 1/2, SE 1/4, Sec 15. Sold on the conditions in 3:520. Signed Henry C. **Bimpage**. Wit Fredk. C. **Hase**, Clerk. Rec 15 Jun 1841. [No. 1174]

1394. Page 557. 21 Jan 1841. Same to same. For money sd **Schmidt** paid to sd **Gube** to enter land, 4 acres, being Lot No. 27 in Borough Altenberg. Sold on the conditions in 3:520. Signed Henry C. **Bimpage**, admr. Wit Fredk. C. **Hase**, Clerk. Rec 15 Jun 1841. [No. 1175]

1395. Page 558. 9 Jan 1841. Same to Barnhard **Schmidt**. For money sd **Schmidt** paid to sd **Gube** to enter land, five tracts in Twp 34 N, Rng 13 E; 80 acres, being the NW 1/4, SW 1/4 and the SW 1/4, SW 1/4, Sec 22; 8.08 acres, being the E fractional 1/4, NW 1/4, Sec 22; 40 acres, being the SE 1/4, SE 1/4, Sec 21; 20 acres, being the N part of E 1/2, NE 1/4, Sec 28; and 2 acres, being Lot Nos. 37 & 38 in Borough Altenberg. Sold on the conditions in 3:520. Signed Henry C. **Bimpage**. Wit Fredk. C. **Hase**, Clerk. Rec 15 Jun 1841. [No. 1176]

1396. Page 559. 9 Jan 1841. Same to Jŏhann Gottfried **Otto**. For money sd **Otto** paid to sd **Gube** to enter land, two tracts; 10 acres in the NW 1/4, NW 1/4, Sec 27, Twp 34 N, Rng 13 E, commencing at the NE corner of sd 1/4 section; and 2 acres. being the S 1/2, Lot No. 36(?) in Borough Altenberg. Sold on the conditions in 3:520. Signed Henry C. **Bimpage**. Wit Fredk. C. **Hase**, Clerk. Rec 15 Jun 1841. [No. 1177]

1397. Page 560. 9 Jan 1841. Same to Johann Gottlieb **Goethe**. For money sd **Goethe** paid to sd **Gube** to enter land, two tracts in Twp 34 N, Rng 13 E; 7.5 acres, being the W fractional 1/2, NW 1/4, Sec 22; and 32.40 acres, being the NW 1/4, SW 1/4, Sec 22, beginning at the NE corner. Sold on the conditions in 3:520. Signed Henry C. **Bimpage**. Wit Fredk. C. **Hase**, Clerk. Rec 15 Jun 1841. [No. 1178]

1398. Page 561. 9 Jan 1841. Same to Lutze **Grother**. For money sd **Grother** paid to sd **Gube** to enter land, two tracts in Twp 34 N, Rng 13 E; 40 acres, being the NE 1/4, SE 1/4, Sec 21; and 7.50 acres in the NW 1/4, SE 1/4, Sec 22, commencing at the NW corner. Sold on the conditions in 3:520. Signed Henry C. **Bimpage**. Wit Fredk. C. **Hase**, Clerk. Rec 15 Jun 1841. [No. 1179]

1399. Page 562. 9 Jan 1841. Same to Johann **Holschen**. For money sd **Holschen** paid to sd **Gube** to enter land, 37.35 acres, being the NE fractional 1/4, Sec 21, Twp 34 N, Rng 13 E. Sold on the conditions in 3:520. Signed Henry C. **Bimpage**. Wit Fredk. C. **Hase**, Clerk. Rec 15 Jun 1841. [No. 1180]

End of Volume 3rd John F. Hase

1400. Page 1. 9 Jan 1841. Same to Johanne **Bochman**. For money sd **Bochman** paid to sd **Gube** to enter land, 10 acres out of the NW 1/4, NW 1/4, Sec 27, Twp 34 N, Rng 13 E, commencing at the SE corner. Sold on the conditions in 3:520. Signed Henry C. **Bimpage**. Wit Fredk. C. **Hase**, Clerk. Rec 15 Jun 1841. [No. 1181]

1401. Page 2. 14 Jan 1841. Same to Frederick **Niemann**, Michael **Nitzschker**, and Sophia **Mullerin**. For money sd **Niemann**, sd **Nitzschker**, and sd **Mullerin** paid to sd **Gube** to enter land, 20 acres, being the W 1/2, NW 1/4, NW 1/4, Sec 27, Twp 34 N, Rng 13 E; 5 acres of the S end to sd **Niemann**, 8 acres joining sd **Niemann** to sd **Nitzschker**, and 7 acres on the N end to sd **Mullerin**. Sold on the conditions in 3:520. Signed Henry C. **Bimpage**. Wit Fredk. C. **Hase**, Clerk. Rec 15 Jun 1841. [No. 1182]

1402. Page 3. 20 Aug 1840. Same to George **Kleugle** Senr. For money sd **Kleugle** paid to sd **Gube** to enter land, four tracts in Twp 34 N, Rng 13 E; 80 acres, being the W 1/2, NW 1/4, Sec 27; 80 acres, being the N 1/2, SW 1/4, Sec 27; 60 acres out of the S end, E 1/2, NE 1/4, Sec 28; and 20 acres out of the N part, E 1/2, SE 1/4, Sec 28. Sold on the conditions in 3:520. Signed Henry C. **Bimpage**. Wit Fredk. C. **Hase**, Clerk. Rec 15 Jun 1841. [No. 1183]

1403. Page 4. 21 Jan 1841. Same to same. For money sd **Kleugle** paid to sd **Gube** to enter land, Lot Nos. 29 (4 acres), 39 (2 acres), & 40 (2 acres) in Borough Altenbergh. Sold on the conditions in 3:520. Signed Henry C. **Bimpage**. Wit Fredk. C. **Hase**, Clerk. Rec 15 Jun 1841. [No. 1184]

1404. Page 5. 14 Jan 1841. Same to Gottfried **Nonning** Sr. and Gottfried **Nonning** Jr. For money sd **Nonnings** paid to sd **Gube** to enter land, two tracts in Twp 34 N, Rng 13 E; 60 acres out of the S end, E 1/2, NE 1/4, Sec 28; and 40 acres, being the NE 1/4, NE 1/4, Sec 33. Sold on the conditions in 3:520. Signed Henry C. **Bimpage**. Wit Fredk. C. **Hase**, Clerk. Rec 15 Jun 1841. [No. 1185]

1405. Page 6. 15 Jan 1841. Same to Maria D. **Weber**. For money sd **Weber** paid to sd **Gube** to enter land, 340 acres in Sec 27, Twp 34 N, Rng 13 E; being the S 1/2, SW 1/4; N 1/2, SE 1/4; and S 1/2, NE 1/4. Sold on the conditions in 3:520. Signed Henry C. **Bimpage**. Wit Fredk. C. **Hase**, Clerk. Rec 15 Jun 1841. [No. 1186]

1406. Page 7. 21 Jan 1841. Same to Gottfried **Cranner** and Gottlob **Schmidt**, for him and his brothers. For money sd **Cranner** and sd **Schmidt** paid to sd **Gube** to enter land, five parcels; 40 acres, being the NE 1/4. NE 1/4, Sec 27, Twp 34 N, Rng 13 E; and 4 acres each in Lot Nos. 2, 3, 16, & 28 in Borough Altenberg. Sold on the conditions in 3:520. Signed Henry C. **Bimpage**. Wit Fredk. C. **Hase**, Clerk. Rec 15 Jun 1841. [No. 1187]

1407. Page 8. 15 Jun 1841. Same to Johann Carl **Wonderlich**. For money sd **Wonderlich** paid to sd **Gube** to enter land, 20 acres, being the W 1/2, SE 1/4, SE 1/4, Sec 22, Twp 34 N, Rng 13 E. Sold on the conditions in 3:520. Signed Henry C. **Bimpage**. Wit Fredk. C. **Hase**, Clerk. Rec 15 Jun 1841. [No. 1188]

1408. Page 9. 15 Jan 1841. Same to Christian **Lober** and George Jochinn **Schmidt**. For money sd **Lober** and sd **Schmidt** paid to sd **Gube** to enter land, 20 acres, being the E 1/2, SE 1/4, SE 1/4, Sec 22, Twp 34 N, Rng 13 E; sd **Lober** to receive 10 acres on the S end and sd **Schmidt** 10 acres on the N end. Sold on the conditions in 3:520. Signed Henry C. **Bimpage**. Wit Fredk. C. **Hase**, Clerk. Rec 15 Jun 1841. [No. 1189]

1409. Page 10. 19 Jan 1841. Same to Gottlieb **Barthel** and Johanne Rosine **Hoffman**. For money sd **Barthel** and sd **Hoffman** paid to sd **Gube** to enter land, 40 acres, being the NE 1/4, SE 1/4, fractional Sec 22, Twp 34 N, Rng 13 E; sd **Barthel** is to receive 15.75 acres, and sd **Hoffman** 24.25 acres. Sold on the conditions in 3:520. Signed Henry C. **Bimpage**, admr. Wit Fredk. C. **Hase**, Clerk. Rec 15 Jun 1841. [No. 1190]

1410. Page 11. 21 Jan 1841. Same to Gottfried **Schmidt** and Gottfried **Jahn**. For money sd **Schmidt** and sd **Jahn** paid to sd **Gube** to enter land, 4 acres, more or less, being Lot No. 9 in Borough Altenberg. Sold on the conditions in 3:520. Signed Henry C. **Bimpage**, admr. Wit Fredk. C. **Hase**, Clerk. Rec 15 Jun 1841. [No. 1191]

1411. Page 12. 21 Jan 1841. Same to Johann Christ. **Richte**. For money sd **Richte** paid to sd **Gube** to enter land, 4 acres, being Lot No. 31 in Borough Altenberg. Sold on the conditions in 3:520.

Signed Henry C. **Bimpage**, admr. Wit Fredk. C. **Hase**, Clerk. Rec 15 Jun 1841. [No. 1192]

1412. Page 13. 21 Jan 1841. Same to Heinrich Gottfred Christian **Marksworth**. For money sd **Marksworth** paid to sd **Gube** to enter land, 4 acres, being Lot No. 33 in Borough Altenberg. Sold on the conditions in 3:520. Signed Henry C. **Bimpage**, admr. Wit Fredk. C. **Hase**, Clerk. Rec 15 Jun 1841. [No. 1193]

1413. Page 13. 2 Jun 1841. Same to Christian Fredk. **Muller**. For money sd **Muller** paid to sd **Gube** to enter land, 4 acres, being Lot No. 32 in Borough Altenberg. Sold on the conditions in 3:520. Signed Henry C. **Bimpage**, admr. Wit Fredk. C. **Hase**, Clerk. Rec 15 Jun 1841. [No. 1194]

1414. Page 14. 2 Jun 1841. Same to Wilhelm Frederick **Buck**, Michael Sigmund **Walter**, and George **Ilgin**. For money sd **Buck**, sd **Walter**, and sd **Ilgen** paid to sd **Gube** to enter land, 4 acres each in Lot Nos. 34 & 35 in Borough Altenberg; Lot No. 34 to sd **Ilgen**, and Lot No. 35 to sd **Buck** and sd **Walter**. Sold on the conditions in 3:520. Signed Henry C. **Bimpage**, admr. Wit Fredk. C. **Hase**, Clerk. Rec 15 Jun 1841. [No. 1195]

1415. Page 15. 7 Jun 1841. Same to John **Seible**, Conrad **Theiz**, Jacob **Seible**, Rozina **Block**, and Johann Frederick **Kopple**. For money sd **Seibles**, sd **Theiz**, sd **Block**, and sd **Kopple** paid to sd **Gube** to enter land, 4 acres in each of three lots in Borough Altenberg; Lot No. 6 to sd **Kopple**; Lot No. 7 to Jacob **Seible** and Rozina **Block**; and Lot No. 8 to Johann **Seible** and sd **Theiz**. Sold on the conditions in 3:520. Signed Henry C. **Bimpage**, admr. Wit Fredk. C. **Hase**, Clerk. Rec 15 Jun 1841. [No. 1196]

1416. Page 16. 5 Jan 1841. Same to Conrad **Geisel**, Jacob **Fisher**, and Johann Fredk. **Fisher**. For money sd **Geisel** and sd **Fishers** paid to sd **Gube** to enter land, 4 acres each in three lots in Borough Altenberg; Lot No. 5 to sd **Geisel**, Lot No. 13 to Jacob **Fisher**, and Lot No. 14 to Johann Fredk. **Fisher**. Sold on the conditions in 3:520. Signed Henry C. **Bimpage**. Wit Fredk. C. **Hase**, Clerk. Rec 15 Jun 1841. [No. 1197]

1417. Page 17. 2 Jun 1841. Same to Frederick **Heinig**, Hartmann **Graibing**, and Frederick **Richter**. For money sd **Heinig**, sd **Graibing**, and sd **Richter** paid to sd **Gube** to enter land, 4 acres each in three lots in Borough Altenberg; Lot No. 15 to sd **Heinig**, Lot No. 16 to sd **Graibing**, and Lot No. 21 to sd **Richter**. Sold on the conditions in 3:520. Signed Henry C. **Bimpage**, admr. Wit Fredk. C. **Hase**, Clerk. Rec 15 Jun 1841. [No. 1198]

1418. Page 18. 2 Jun 1841. Same to George **Burger**, Johann Christ. **Daumer**, and Rosina **Goehring**. For money sd **Burger**, sd **Daumer**, and sd **Goehring** paid to sd **Gube** to enter land, 4 acres each, more or less, in two lots in Borough Altenberg; Lot No. 17 to sd **Burger** and sd **Daumer**, and Lot No. 19 to sd **Goehring**. Sold on the conditions in 3:520. Signed Henry C. **Bimpage**, admr. Wit Fredk. C. **Hase**, Clerk. Rec 15 Jun 1841. [No. 1199]

[No. 1200 not used]

1419. Page 19. 2 Jun 1841. Same to Gottfried **Jahn**. For money sd **Jahn** paid to sd **Gube** to enter land, 4 acres, being Lot No. 20 in Borough Altenberg. Sold on the conditions in 3:520. Signed Henry C. **Bimpage**, admr. Wit Fredk. C. **Hase**, Clerk. Rec 15 Jun 1841. [No. 1201]

1420. Page 20. 2 Jun 1841. Same to Barnhart **Eisenschmidt**. For money sd **Eisenschmidt** paid to sd **Gube** to enter land, 4 acres, more or less, being Lot No. 23 in Borough Altenberg. Sold on the conditions in 3:520. Signed Henry C. **Bimpage**, admr. Wit Fredk. C. **Hase**, Clerk. Rec 15 Jun 1841. [No. 1202]

1421. Page 21. 15 Jun 1841. Same to George **Kluegle** Jr. and Johann **Schmidt**. For money sd **Kluegle** and sd **Schmidt** paid to sd **Gube** to enter land, 4 acres each in Lot Nos. 4, 22, 24, 25, 26, & 36; and the N 1/2, Lot No. 30; all in Borough Altenberg. Sd **Kluegle** and sd **Schmidt** are to sell the lots and divide the proceeds equally among all the original settlers of Altenberg. Sold on the conditions in 3:520. Signed Henry C. **Bimpage**, admr. Wit Fredk. C. **Hase**, Clerk. Rec 15 Jun 1841. [No. 1203]

1422. Page 22. 21 Jan 1841. Same to Ernst Gerard Wilhelm **Keyle**. For money sd **Keyle** paid to sd **Gube** to enter land, two tracts in Sec 20, Twp 34 N, Rng 13 E; 160 acres, being the SE 1/4; and 120 acres, being the NE 1/4, NE 1/4. Sold on the conditions in 3:520. Signed Henry C. **Bimpage**, admr. Wit Fredk. C. **Hase**, Clerk. Rec 15 Jun 1841. [No. 1204]

1423. Page 23. 21 Jan 1840. Same to Gottfried **Heining** and Louise **Voelker**. For money sd **Heining** and sd **Voelker** paid to sd **Gube** to enter land, 40 acres, being the SE 1/4, NE 1/4, Sec 20, Twp 34 N, Rng 13 E. Sold on the conditions in 3:520. Signed Henry C. **Bimpage**, admr. Wit Fredk. C. **Hase**, Clerk. Rec 15 Jun 1841. [No. 1205]

1424. Page 24. 24 Jul 1840. Washington **Dorsey** by Sheriff Hugh **Wells** to Moritz **Behrley**. For the sum of $6, 16.36 acres, more or less, being the SW fractional 1/4, Sec 29, Twp 35 N, Rng 11 E. Sold on a writ of fieri facias issued by Circuit Court on 10 Apr 1840 in a judgment in favor of Frederick C. **Hase**, H. **Wells**, and others against sd **Dorsey** for $26.96 debt plus costs. Signed Hugh **Wells**, Sheriff. Wit Fredk. C. **Hase**, Clerk. Rec 16 Jun 1841. [No. 1206]

1425. Page 26. 21 Jun 1841. Augustin **Layton** to Lewis **Layton**. For securing two notes and the sum of $1, mortgage on a black mare about nine years old and her colt, one rone filley about one year old, one brown pied cow, one muley cow and calf, one red steer and one blue dun steer each about one year old, one red heifer about two years old, one sow and 14 shotes, 11 sheep, one mans saddle, one buro, and a growing crop of wheat and corn. Sd Augustin is indebted to sd Lewis for $148.87 1/2 in two notes dated 11 Jun 1841; one for $64.87 1/2 payable in 12 months, and one for $84 payable in two years. Signed Augustin **Layton**. Wit Fredk. C. **Hase**, Clerk. Rec 21 Jun 1841. [Marginal note: Full satisfaction received on 9 Dec 1842. Signed Lewis **Layton**. Wit J. W. **Noell**, Clerk.] [No. 1207]

1426. Page 27. 1 Aug 1840. John **Scudder** and Rebeca, his wife, to Thomas **Robinson**, all of Birmingham. For the sum of $50, Lot Nos. 7 & 8, Block No. 4 in Birmingham. Signed John **Scudder**, Rebecka **Scudder** (RD). Test A. M. **Bliss**, Wm. H. **Scudder**, Augustus **Davis** (JP). Rec 22 Jun 1841. [No. 1208]

1427. Page 27. 12 Jul 1841. Peter R. **Pratte** to Joseph **Coffman** of Ste. Genevieve Co., Mo. For securing a debt, mortgage on five slaves; **Leah** or **Emily** and her child **Sophia**, **Sophia** and her child, and **Susan**. Sd **Pratte** owes sd **Coffman** a note for $1000, payable by 12 Jan 1842 with 10% interest per annum. Signed P. R. **Pratte**. Wit Fredk. C. **Hase**, Clerk. Rec 12 Jul 1841. [No. 1209]

1428. Page 28. 10 Jul 1841. Gabriel M. **Duvall** and Matilda, his wife, to Ezra **Shelby**. For the sum of $500, 640 acres, Survey No. 2146 confirmed to Benjamin **Cox**, Jr. in Twp 35 N, Rng 10 & 11 E. Signed Gabriel M. **Duvall**, Matilda **Duvall** (RD). Wit Reuben **Shelby**, JCC. Rec 14 Jul 1841. [No. 1210]

1429. Page 29. 10 Jul 1841. Same and same to same. For the sum of $1200, undivided 1/2 of 300 acres in Twp 35 N, Rng 10 & 11 E, taken out of 1920 acres formerly belonging to John **Donohoe**; purchased from sd **Donohoe** by John **Duvall**, decd, on 13 Dec 1815 (Ste. Genevieve Co. Book C:93). The 1920 acres was confirmed to Benjamin **Cox** Sr., Benjamin **Cox** Jr., and William **Middleton**. Signed Gabriel M. **Duvall**, Matilda **Duvall** (RD). Wit Reuben **Shelby**, JCC. Rec 14 Jul 1841. [No. 1211]

1430. Page 30. 18 Aug 1840. Henry C. **Bimpage**, Fredk. Wilh. **Barthel**, and Christian Fredk. **Muller**, trustees for the town of Wittenberg, to Henry C. **Bimpage**. For services rendered and in pursuance of agreements among the different settlers of the German Lutheran Congregation settled on Brazeau Creek, Lot No. 51 in Wittenberg, fronting on Water St and joined by Lot Nos. 50 & 52. Signed Henry C. **Bimpage**, Fredk. Wilh. **Barthel**. C. F. **Muller**, trustees. Wit August Henry **Doederlein**, Augustus **Davis** (JP). Rec 14 Jul 1841. [No. 1212]

1431. Page 31. 20 Jul 1841. William J. **McCombs** to George **Baldock** of Barren Co., Ken. For securing a debt and the sum of $1, mortgage on one sorrell horse, one black mare, one bay horse, one cow and calf, 1500 gallons of stone ware, a 16-acre field of corn, and 11 hogs. Sd **McCombs** is indebted to sd **Baldock** for $150.56 with 6% interest from 10 Feb 1838, due by 1 Sep 1841. Signed William J. **McCombs**. Wit Fredk. C. **Hase**, Clerk. Rec 20 Jul 1841. [No. 1213]

1432. Page 32. 30 Jul 1841. John **Logan** to Robert C. **Powell**. For the sum of $550, 90.34 acres in Bois Brule Bottom, being the E 1/2, S 1/2, fractional Sec 35, Twp 37 N, Rng 10 E. Signed John **Logan**. Test Robert L. **Phillips**, Fredk. C. **Hase**, Clerk. Rec 30 Jul 1841. [No. 1214]

1433. Page 33. 2 Aug 1840. Wm. H. **Scudder** to Henry S. **Osborn** of New Orleans, La. For the sum of $160, 80 acres, being the E 1/2, Lot Nos. 3 & 4, NE 1/4, Sec 3, Twp 33 N, Rng 13 E. Signed Wm. H. **Scudder**. Wit Augustus **Davis** (JP), Fredk. **Sproede**. Rec 31 Jul 1841. [No. 1215]

1434. Page 33. 16 Sep 1833. Last will and testament of Thomas **Newbery** Senior, decd. To his wife Sarah: all his property, which has been chiefly acquired by their joint industry, and thinking it necessary to enable her to live with convenience and comfort. Signed Thos. **Newberry**. Wit Fredk. C. **Hase**, Clerk, Levi **Block**, Hyman **Block**. Rec 3 Aug 1841. [No. 1216]

1435. Page 35. 26 May 1841. Robert **Slaughter** to Jacob **Shaner**. For the sum of $250, mortgage on two lots in Wittenberg; Lot No. 46, fronting on first second street and Ferry St, joining Lot No. 45; and Lot No. 42, fronting on first street. Sd **Slaughter** owes a note to sd **Shaner**, dated 26 May 1841, [due] 20 May 1842 with 10% interest. Signed Robert P. **Slaughter**. Wit Augustus **Davis** (JP). Rec 3 Aug 1841. [Marginal note: Full satisfaction received on 1 Feb 1847. Signed Jacob **Shaner**. Test J. W. **Noell**, Clerk. [No. 1217]

1436. Page 35. 7 Aug 1841. Charles **Brewer** Junior to James S. **Brown** of Ste. Genevieve Co., Mo. For the sum of $75, 40 acres, being the SE 1/4, SW 1/4, Sec 28, Twp 35 N, Rng 9 E. Signed Charles **Brewer** Jr. Wit W. B. **Wilkinson**, Reuben **Shelby**, JCC. Rec 7 Aug 1841. [No. 1218]

1437. Page 36. 14 Jul 1841. Ezra **Shelby** to Gabriel M. **Duvall**. For securing a debt, mortgage on the undivided 1/2 of 300 acres, part of 1920 acres formerly belonging to John **Donohoe**, sold by him to John **Duvall** on 13 Dec 1815, and purchased by sd **Shelby** of Gabriel M. **Duvall** on 10 Jul 1841. Sd **Shelby** owes sd **Duvall** $900 without interest, due six years from this date. Signed Ezra **Shelby**. Wit Reuben **Shelby**, JCC. Rec 14 Jul 1841. [Marginal note: Full satisfaction received on 24 Dec 1845. Signed Moses **Farrar**, admr of the estate of Gabriel M. **Duvall**. Wit Jno. W. **Noell**, Recorder.] [No. 1219]

1438. Page 37. 18 Aug 1840. Trustees of Wittenberg to Frederick Wilh. **Barthel**. For services rendered to the German Lutheran Congregation settled on Brazeau Creek, Lot No. 39 in Wittenberg, fronting on First St and Pleasant St. Signed Henry C. **Bimpage**, Frederick Wilhelm **Barthel**, Christian Frederick **Muller**, trustees. Wit August Henry **Doederlein**, Augustus **Davis** (JP). Rec 14 Aug 1841. [No. 1220]

1439. Page 38. 9 Aug 1841. Seth **Hall** to William **Manning** of Cape Girardeau Co., Mo. in trust for Singleton H. **Kimmell** of Philadelphia. For securing a debt and the sum of $1, deed of trust for five tracts on Apple Creek in Perry and Cape Girardeau Counties; 160 acres, being the W 1/2, SE 1/4 and E 1/2, SW 1/4, Sec 32, Twp 34 N, Rng 12 E; 52 acres, the E end of Lot No. 7, NW 1/4, Sec 5, Twp 33 N, Rng 12 E; 3 acres, more or less, beginning at the NW corner of the second tract; 35 acres in Lot No. 7, Sec 5, Twp 33 N, Rng 12 E, beginning at the NE corner; and 28 acres, being the S part, W 1/2, SW 1/4, Sec 32, Twp 34 N, Rng 12 E. Sd **Hall** owes sd **Kimmel** $1762.22 in a note with Abner **Hall** dated 9 Aug 1841, payable four and 1/2 months after date, with 10% interest per annum. The property is to be sold by sd **Manning** to pay sd **Kimmel** if the debt is not paid by 9 Aug 1843. Signed Seth **Hall**, Wm. **Manning**, Singleton H. **Kimmell**. Wit A. M. **McPhearson** (JP), Robert **McPhearson**. Rec 17 Aug 1841. [No. 1221]

1440. Page 40. 11 Feb 1840. Joseph **Parks** to Jesse **Dickson**. For the sum of $300, mortgage on a negro boy about 12 years old named **Morrough**. Sd **Parks** owes sd **Dickson** the debt, for which the boy is to work for sd **Dickson** to pay the interest during the lifetime of sd **Parks**. At the death of sd **Parks**, his heirs are to pay the debt, or the boy is to become the property of sd **Dickson**. Signed Joseph **Parks**. Wit Elias **Barber** (JP). Rec 27 Aug 1841. [No. 1222]

1441. Page 40. 6 Aug 1840. William **Taylor** and Mary, his wife, to Luther **Taylor**. For the sum of $200, 40 acres, being the SE 1/4, SE 1/4, Sec 36, Twp 35 N, Rng 10 E. Signed William **Taylor**, Mary (x) **Taylor**. Wit Reuben **Shelby**, Fredk. C. **Hase**, Clerk. Rec 1 Sep 1841. [No. 1223]

1442. Page 41. 9 Aug 1841. Thomas **McAtee** and Mary Magdalen, his wife, to Robert S. **Manning**. For securing several bonds and a debt to sd **Manning** and the sum of $1, mortgage on four tracts in Twp 34 N, Rng 10 E; __ acres, being the E 1/2, NE 1/4, Sec 1 and about 35 acres in the NW 1/4, NE 1/4, Sec 1; __ acres, being the SE 1/4, Sec 1; the preceding three tracts were purchased by Thomas **McAtee** from Henry **McAtee** on 11 Nov 1840 (3:429); and __ acres, being the SW 1/4, Sec 12, purchased by Thomas **McAtee** of John T. **Tucker**. Sd **Manning** is security for sd **McAtee** in three bonds dated 23 Dec 1839, payable to Henry **McAtee** for $150 each; one due in 12 months, one due in two years, and one due in three years. Sd **Manning** is also security for Thomas **McAtee** in a bond payable to John E. **Burgett**, guardian of Burgett **Everetts**, for $68, dated 1 Jan 1841 and due in 12 months; and owes another joint debt to sd **Manning** for $259.36 by note of even date, payable in two years with 10% interest. Signed Thomas **McAtee**, Mary Magdalen (x) **McAtee** (RD). Wit Mark **Brewer** (JP). Rec 1 Sep 1841. [Marginal note: All interest in the mortgage is relinquished to Thomas **McAtee** on 24 Jan 1842. Signed Robt. S. **Manning**.] [No. 1224]

1443. Page 43. 4 Sep 1841. Thomas **McAtee** to same. For securing debts and the sum of $1, mortgage on four cows and their calves; one black steer with white face; one red steer with white face; one red heifer; one young yoke of steers one year old last spring; one heiffer and one yearling steer; three grey horses; one sorrel horse; one bay horse; two sorel mares; one bay filly; four suckling colts; 12 sheep; two lots of 31 and 18 hogs; one four horse waggon and geer; two stills and all the apurtenances belonging to them; the crop of corn, oats, etc. on his plantation; one press; and one beauro. Executed to secure the debts described in the preceding deed (4:41). Signed Thomas **McAtee**. Wit Fredk. C. **Hase**, Clerk. Rec 4 Sep 1841. [Marginal note: All interest in the mortgage is relinquished to Thomas **McAtee** on 24 Jan 1842. Signed Robt. S. **Manning**.] [No. 1225]

1444. Page 44. 14 Jul 1841. John **Scudder**, assignee of Amzi **Osborn**, to John **Logan** of Jackson Co., Ill. Release from a bond to make a deed on __ acres on the W bank of the Mississippi River, known as the Menard Claim. Sd **Scudder** has purchased the tract from sd **Osborn**, who purchased it from sd **Logan**; sd **Logan** executed a bond to sd **Osborn** to convey the same; and the bond had never been released. Signed John **Scudder**. Test Augustus **Davis** (JP), W. **Garner**. Rec 11 Sep 1841. [No. 1226]

1445. Page 45. 13 Feb 1841. Leander **Marechal** and Rose, his wife, to Ferdinand **Rozier** Junior. For the sum of $46, 40 acres, being the NW 1/4, SE 1/4, Sec 34, Twp 35 N, Rng 10 E. Signed Leander **Merechal**, Rose (x) **Marechal**. Wit Reuben **Shelby**, JCC. Rec 23 Sep 1841. [No. 1227]

1446. Page 46. 23 Sep 1841. Ferdinand **Rozier** and Harriet, his wife, to Pierre Theodore **Boeuf** and Francois Flavier **Boeuf**. For the sum of $50, 40 acres, being the NW 1/4, SE 1/4, Sec 34, Twp 35 N, Rng 10 E. Signed Ferdinand **Rozier**, Harriet **Rozier** (RD). Wit Reuben **Shelby**, JCC. Rec 23 Sep 1841. [No. 1228]

1447. Page 47. 22 Jun 1839. Hiram H. **Baber**, Auditor of Public Accounts, to Frederick C. **Hase**. For the sums of $0.72 and $1.22 in back taxes for 1834 and penalties, two tracts; 40 acres, part of Survey 89 in Twp 36, Rng 10, originally owned by and assessed to Elias **Coen**; and 160 acres, part of Survey 2186 in Twp 36 N, Rng 10 & 11 E, originally owned by David **Crips** and assessed to James **Crips**. Sold on 7 Jul 1835. Signed Hiram H. **Baber**, Auditor. Rec 24 Sep 1841. [No. 1229]

1448. Page 48. 22 Jun 1839. Same to same. For the sums of $0.46, $0.46, $0.48, and $0.43 in back taxes and penalties, four lots in Perryville; Lot No. 29 on North St and Jackson St, originally owned by Joseph **James** Senr and assessed to John **Donohoe**; Lot No. 19 on Spring St, originally owned and assessed to Ignatius **Layton**; Lot No. 20 on Spring St, originally owned and assessed to Bernard **Layton**; and Lot No. 13 on Spring St, originally owned and assessed to Joseph **Snearbush**. Sold on 7 Jul 1835. Signed Hiram H. **Baber**, Auditor. Rec 24 Sep 1841. [No. 1230]

1449. Page 50. 27 Aug 1841. Peter **Carpenter** to Giles **Pease** of Ste. Genevieve Co., Mo. For the sum of $26, all his crop of about 9 acres of corn now in the field near his house; sd house being the property of Thomas **Donohoe** and mortgaged to Timothy **Davis**; and reserving 10 bushels per acre rent. Signed Peter **Carpenter**. Wit Henry F. **Clark**, Perry **Evans** (JP). Rec 27 Sep 1841. [No. 1231]

1450. Page 50. 30 Dec 1835. U. S. A. to Richard Fenwick **Spalding**. Patent for 40 acres, being the W 1/2, Lot No. 1, NE 1/4, Sec 2, Twp 34 N, Rng 10 E; in Certificate No. 1636. Signed Martin **Van Buren** by Andrew **Jackson** by A. J. **Donelson**, Secy. Wit Ethan A. **Brown**, Commissioner of the General Land Office. Rec in Vol. 4:45 of the General Land Office. Rec 27 Sep 1841. [No. 1232]

1451. Page 51. 1 Aug 1838. U. S. A. to Jeffrey **Powers**. Patent for 48.97 acres, being the W 1/2, Lot No. 2, NE 1/4, Sec 2, Twp 34 N, Rng 10 E; in Certificate No. 5659. Signed Martin **Van Buren** by A. **Van Buren**, Secy. Wit Joseph B. **Watson**, Acting Recorder of the General Land Office. Rec in Vol. 11:333 of the General Land Office. Rec 27 Sep 1841. [No. 1233]

1452. Page 52. 25 Sep 1841. Jeffery **Powers** and Elizabeth, his wife, to Jean Antonie **Prost**. For the sum of $500, two tracts in the NE 1/4, Sec 2, Twp 34 N, Rng 10 E; 40 acres, being the W 1/2, Lot No. 1; and 48.97 acres, being the W 1/2, Lot No. 2. Signed Jeffrey **Power**, Elizabeth (x) **Power** (RD). Wit Fredk. C. **Hase**, Clerk. Rec 27 Sep 1841. [No. 1234]

1453. Page 53. 25 Sep 1841. Perry **Evans** and Dianna, his wife, to John E. **Burgett**. For the sum of $1 and diverse other causes and considerations, quit claim to 2.55 acres, more or less, on the Mississippi River, part of a tract confirmed to Solomon **Morgan**; claimed by sd **Burgett** by virtue of a tax title from David L. **Caldwell**, Collector of Perry Co., to Mrs. Nancy **Burgett**, and from her to John E. **Burgett** on 1 Oct 1833 (2:30); and beginning at the upper corner of William **Flynn**'s survey. Signed Perry **Evans**, Diana **Evans** (RD). Wit James **Rice** (JP). Rec 28 Sep 1841. [No. 1235]

1454. Page 54. 27 Sep 1841. John E. **Burgett** and Mary, his wife, to Perry **Evans**. For the sum of $1 and diverse other considerations, quit claim to 3.45 acres, part of 6 acres of a tract confirmed to Solomon **Morgan**, adjoining William **Flynn** and fronting on the Mississippi River, where sd **Evans** now resides; part of a tract sold by David L. **Caldwell**, Collector of Perry Co., to Mrs. Nancy **Burgett**, decd, as part of the land of Amos **Bird**, decd, for back taxes for 1825, and conveyed by her to John E. **Burgett** on 1 Oct 1833; beginning at the upper corner of William

Flynn's survey. Signed John E. **Burgett**, Mary C. **Burgett** (RD). Wit James **Rice** (JP). Rec 28 Sep 1841. [No. 1236]

1455. Page 56. 21 Aug 1841. Lewis **Smaltz** to Philip **Smaltz**. For the sum of $150, one ox cart, one wheat fan, one roan gray colt about two years old last May, and one roan coloured mare six or seven years old. Signed Lewis **Smaltz**. Wit James **Rice** (JP). Rec 2 Oct 1841. [No. 1237]

1456. Page 56. 2 Oct 1841. Leo **Layton** and Mary Magdalen, his wife, to Henry **Dean**. For the sum of $5, 2 1/2 acres, more or less, in Cinque Hommes Twp, purchased by sd **Layton** of the U. S. A.; commencing at the SE corner, NE 1/4, Sec 25, Twp 36 N, Rng 11 E. Sd **Layton** also covenants him or his heirs to pay back the money if sd **Dean** is evicted or another party has a better title to the land. Signed Leo **Layton**, Mary Magdalen (x) **Layton** (RD). Wit Fredk. C. **Hase**, Clerk. Rec 2 Oct 1841. [No. 1238]

1457. Page 57. 3 Sep 1841. William J. **McCombs** to Daniel **Seibert**. For the sum of $50, mortgage on 40 acres, being the NE 1/4, SW 1/4, fractional Sec 13, Twp 34 N, Rng 12 E; and one yoke of steers five years old. Sd **McCombs** owes sd **Seibert** the debt with 10% interest in 12 months. Signed William J. **McCombs**. Wit Fredk. C. **Hase**, Clerk. Rec 2 Oct 1841. [No. 1239]

1458. Page 58. 27 Sep 1841. Thomas J. **Tucker** and Sally, his wife, to John E. **Burgett**. For the sum of $500, 50 acres on the Mississippi River, part of a tract confirmed to Josiah **Millard** under Elisha **Crosby**; beginning at a post on the line between the survey and Robert **McMahann** under Michael **McKay** or **McCoy**. Signed Thomas J. **Tucker**, Sarah W. **Tucker** (RD). Wit James **Rice** (JP). Rec 4 Oct 1841. [No. 1240]

1459. Page 59. 6 Oct 1841. Clement **Knott** and Elizabeth, his wife, to Francis J. **Zeigler**. For the sum of $100, Lot No. 64 in Perryville. Signed Clement (x) **Knott**, Elizabeth (x) **Knott** (RD). Wit James **Rice** (JP). Rec 6 Oct 1841. [No. 1241]

1460. Page 60. 15 Oct 1841. Hugh **Wells** by Sheriff Joseph D. **Simpson** to Frederick C. **Hase**. For the sum of $635, three tracts in Twp 34 N, Rng 12 E; 80 acres, being the E 1/2, SW 1/4, Sec 22, originally claimed by Bernard **Layton**; 40 acres, being the NE 1/4, SE 1/4, Sec 27, Martern **Butz**, original claimant; and 40 acres in Sec 22. Sold on 16 Jun 1841 on three orders against sd **Wells**; two from Circuit Court issued Jul Term 1840 on a judgment for sd **Hase**, and on 4 Feb 1841 for sd **Hase** for $1021.42 1/2 damages and $1 costs; and another issued by County Court in favor of Perry Co. for $1329.89 debt and $130.98 damages, and $0.70 costs. Signed Joseph D. **Simpson**, Sheriff. Wit Fredk. C. **Hase**, Clerk. Rec 15 Oct 1841. [No. 1242]

1461. Page 62. 14 Oct 1841. Commissioners to sell land of Adolph **Rix**, decd, to Mathias **Rix**. For the sum of $125, 40 acres [location not specified]. Sold on 27 Jul 1841 on order of Circuit Court for sale of sd lands. Signed Martin **Layton**, Leo **Moore**, Austin **Moore**, Commissioners. Wit James **Evans**, Fredk. C. **Hase**, Clerk. Rec 15 Oct 1841. [No. 1243]

1462. Page 63. 16 Jun 1841. Thomas **Cochran** by Sheriff Joseph D. **Simpson** to Austin **Hogard**. For the sum of $101, 255 acres, more or less, in Bois Brule Bottom in Twp 36 N, Rng 11 E; granted to Thomas **Cochran** under David **Clark** as Survey No. 117. Sold on 15 Jun 1841 on a writ of fieri facias issued by Circuit Court on 16 Jan 1841 in favor of John & Edward **Walsh** & Co. against sd **Cochran** for $461.15 debt and costs. Signed Joseph D. **Simpson**, Sheriff. Wit Fredk. C. **Hase**, Clerk. Rec 15 Oct 1841. [No. 1244]

1463. Page 65. 15 Oct 1841. Jones A. **Rutledge** by same to Edward B. **Cassley** of Cape Girardeau Co., Mo. For the sum of $21, two tracts in Twp 34 N, Rng 11 E; 40 acres, being the NW 1/4, NW 1/4, Sec 12; and 40 acres, more or less, being the SW 1/4, SW 1/4, Sec 1. Sold on 14 Jun 1841 on a writ of execution issued by Circuit Court on 10 Apr 1841, in favor of sd **Cassley** and against sd **Rutledge** for $330.20 debt, $13.31 damages, and costs. Signed Joseph D. **Simpson**, Sheriff. Wit Fredk. C. **Hase**, Clerk. Rec 15 Oct 1841. [No. 1245]

1464. Page 66. 15 Oct 1841. Daniel **Omeara** by same to Joseph **Cissell**. For the sum of $90, 35 acres, being the SW 1/4, SE 1/4, Sec 27, Twp 35 N, Rng 10 E. Sold on 16 Jun 1841 at order of Circuit Court, issued on a judgment heard before James **Rice**, JP, in favor or Richard **Maddock** Sr. and against sd **Omeara** for $74.75 damages and $1.31 costs. Signed Joseph D. **Simpson**, Sheriff. Wit Fredk. C. **Hase**, Clerk. Rec 15 Oct 1841. [No. 1246]

1465. Page 68. 15 Oct 1841. James **Saddler** by same to Reuben **Shelby**. For the sum of $36.37, 37.56 acres, more or less, being the NE 1/4, NE 1/4, Sec 6, Twp 34 N, Rng 11 E. Sold on 14 Jun 1841 on an execution issued by Circuit Court on 17 Mar 1840, on a judgment heard before James **Rice**, JP, in favor of Anthony **Parrs** and against sd **Saddler** for $70.40 debt, $2.11 costs. Signed Joseph D. **Simpson**, Sheriff. Wit Fredk. C. **Hase**, Clerk. Rec 15 Oct 1841. [No. 1247]

1466. Page 69. 16 Oct 1841. Roland **Boyd** Senr and Roland **Boyd** Jur by same to Joseph **Cissell**. For the sum of $402, 170 acres, more or less, on the S fork of Saline Creek, adjoining the survey originally granted to Roland **Boyd**; and granted to Archibald **Huddleston** as Survey No. 830, in Twp 36 N, Rng 9 E. Sold on 13 Oct 1841 on an execution issued by Circuit Court on 29 Jul 1840 in favor of Timothy **Davis** & Co. and against sd **Boyds**. Signed Joseph D. **Simpson**, Sheriff. Wit Fredk. C. **Hase**, Clerk. Rec 16 Oct 1841. [No. 1248]

1467. Page 71. 8 Sep 1841. Frederick **Sproede** and H. C. Bertha, his wife, to Elias **Barber**. For the sum of $75, mortgage on two tracts in Twp 34 N, Rng 13 E and personal property; 80 acres, being the W 1/2, NE 1/4, Sec 26; 12 acres, being the W part, SW 1/4, SE 1/4, Lot No. 23, beginning at the SW corner; one horse; 4 cattle; 12 hogs; 2 guns; one clock; one watch; and the rest of his property. Sd **Sproede** owes sd **Barber** a note for $50 drawing 10% interest, dated 17 Jul 1841 and due one day after date, and also $3 for recording fees. Signed Frederick **Sproede**, H. C. Bertha **Sproede** (RD). Wit Augustus **Davis** (JP). Rec 16 Oct 1841. [Marginal note: Full satisfaction received on 3 Aug 1842. Signed Elias **Barber**. Test John W. **Noell**, Recorder.] [No. 1249]

1468. Page 72. 26 Aug 1822. Barnard **Layton** and Mary, his wife, to Ignatius **Layton**. For the sum of $168.50, 75 acres and 36 poles near Cape Cinque Hommes Creek, beginning at the most SW corner of the survey at John **Layton**'s corner, so as to meet the entire part which Barnard **Layton** received from John **Layton**, decd. Signed Barnard **Layton**, Mary (x) **Layton**. Test Peter **Tucker**, John **Layton** (JP). Rec 22 Oct 1841. [No. 1250]

1469. Page 73. 14 Oct 1841. Partition of the land of James **Moore**, decd, by commissioners. The land is 640 acres, being Claim No. 2137 in Twp 35 N, Rng 10 E; plat surveyed by Jeffrey **Power**, Surveyor. Partitioned on 20 Jul 1841 as follows: 100 acres off the NW corner to the heirs of Elizabeth **Moore**, decd, as willed to her by James **Moore** (Lot No. 2); 50 acres in a square from the corner next to Henry **Miles** to Matilda **Moore**, who married Henry J. **Rhodes**, and her children, as per a codicil to the will (Lot No. 5); 164.37 acres (3/7) to William **Manning** (Lot No. 7); 86.25 acres (1/7) to Ignatius **Moore** (Lot No. 3); 1/7 to John **May** (Lot No. 6); 1/7 to Johanna **Hayden**, Margaret **Hayden**, William **Hayden**, Mary Ann **Hayden**, Elizabeth **Hayden**, James **Hayden**, Thomas **Hayden**, and John **Hayden** (Lot No. 4); 1/7 to Cessilia **May**, John **May**, Elizabeth **May**, Hellen **May**, and Martha Ann **May** (Lot No. 1). Executed on petition to partition filed in 10th Judicial Circuit Court on 16 Jun 1841, No. 443, William **Manning**, Ignatius **Moore**, and the heirs of Thomas **Hayden**, decd, by Bridget **Hayden**, their mother and guardian vs. the heirs of James **Moore**, Senior, decd. Signed John **Logan**, Peter R. **Pratte**, Francis **Clark**, Commissioners. Wit Fredk. C. **Hase**, Clerk. Rec 25 Oct 1841. [No. 1251]

1470. Page 75. 26 Oct 1841. John Baptist **Layton** and Elizabeth, his wife, to Richard F. **Spalding**. For the sum of $70, 40 acres, being the NE 1/4, NW 1/4, Sec 34, Twp 35 N, Rng 10 E; purchased by sd **Layton** from Felix **Simms** in 1838. Signed John Baptist **Layton**, Elizabeth (x) **Layton** (RD). Wit Fredk. C. **Hase**, Clerk. Rec 26 Oct 1841. [No. 1252]

1471. Page 76. 8 May 1841. David W. **Morrison** and Eliner J., his wife, to Joseph **Murry**. For the sum of $75, 40 acres, being the NW 1/4, SE 1/4, Sec 15, Twp 34 N, Rng 12 E. Signed David W. **Morrison**, Elinor J. **Morrison** (RD). Wit William **Farrar** (JP). Rec __ Oct 1841. [No. 1253]

1472. Page 77. 22 Feb 1841. Cecile **Goverot**, Jean Bt. **Duval** and Carroline, his wife and formerly Caroline **Goverots**, to Charles F. **Notrebe**, all of Arkansas Co., Ark. For the sum of $120, quit claim to 800 arpents on the River Saline; being granted by the Spanish Government and confirmed to Etienne **Parent** and Etienne **Goverot**, Claim No. 196. Signed Cicile (x) **Goverot**, Jean Bte. (x) **Duval**, Caroline (x) **Duval**. Wit William **Price**, William H. **Doharty**, George W. **Stokes**, Clerk of Arkansas Co., Ark. Rec 1 Nov 1841. [No. 1254]

1473. Page 79. 11 Jul 1834. Robert T. **Brown** and Catharine, his wife, to the children of Clayton D. **Abernathy**: Nancy F. **Abernathy**, Starling G. **Abernathy**, Calidonia **Abernathy**, Sufphronia **Abernathy**, and Albartus O. **Abernathy**. For the sum of $50, Lot No. 65 in Perryville, purchased by sd **Brown** of the Commissioners. Signed R. T. **Brown**, Catharine **Brown** (RD). Wit R. S. **Dorsey** (JP). Rec 4 Nov 1841. [No. 1255]

1474. Page 79. 14 Nov 1837. U. S. A. to James **Dunn**. Patent for 40.77 acres, being the N 1/2, Lot No. 2, NW 1/4, Sec 18, Twp 34 N, Rng 11 E; in Certificate No. 4825. Signed Martin **Van Buren** by M. **Van Buren**, Secy. Wit Jos. S. **Wilson**, Acting Recorder of the General Land Office. Rec in Vol. 9:379 of the General Land Office. Rec 5 Nov 1841. [No. 1256]

1475. Page 80. 4 Nov 1841. James **Dunn** and Mary, his wife, to Ferdinand **Rozier** Jr. For the sum of $1000, two tracts; 40.77 acres, being the N 1/2, Lot No. 2, NW 1/4, Sec 18, Twp 34 N, Rng 11 E; and 80 acres, being the E 1/2, NE 1/4, Sec 13, Twp 34 N, Rng 10 E. Signed James **Dunn**, Mary (x) **Dunn**. Wit Reuben **Shelby**, JCC. Rec 5 Nov 1841. [No. 1257]

1476. Page 81. 28 Jun 1841. John W. **Brown** and Rachiel, his wife, and Rachiel **Smith**, alias Rachiel **Allaire**, to John J. **Bowie**, all of Ark. For the sum of $3000, 640 acres in Bois Brule Bottom, confirmed to Joseph **Allaire** or his legal representatives. Sd Rachiel **Brown** is the daughter and only heir, and sd Rachiel **Smith** is the relict of Joseph **Allaire**, decd. Signed John W. **Brown**, Rachiel (x) **Brown** (RD), Rachael (x) **Smith**. Wit Henry J. **Clark**, JP in Ste. Genevieve Co., Mo., Thomas **Donohoe**. Proved by John **Logan**, Walter B. **Wilkinson**. Rec __ Nov 1841. [No. 1258]

1477. Page 83. 16 Apr 1841. William Bowie **Cowan** to Martin L. **Eastman** of New Orleans, La. For the sum of $500, 80 acres, being the E 1/2, NE 1/4, Sec 16, Twp 35 N, Rng 10 E; entered by sd **Cowan** on 26 Nov 1838. Signed Wm. Bowie **Cowan**. Wit Amzi **Osborn**, Joseph W. **Schaumburg**, Duncan N. **Hermen**, Judge of 9th La. Judicial Circuit. Rec 5 Nov 1841. [No. 1259]

1478. Page 83. 8 Nov 1841. Ignatius **Hutchings** and Charlette, his wife, to Claude Joseph **Mauche**. For the sum of $250, two tracts in Sec 34, Twp 35 N, Rng 10 E; 40 acres, being the SE 1/4, NE 1/4; and 30 acres, part of the NE 1/4, NE 1/4. Signed Ignatius (x) **Hutchings**, Charlotte (x) **Hutchings** (RD). Wit W. B. **Wilkinson**, Fredk. C. **Hase**, Clerk. Rec 8 Nov 1841. [No. 1260]

1479. Page 84. 3 Nov 1841. Felix **Bey** to Paul Peter **Panier**. For the sum of $100, 80 acres, being the SW 1/4, NW 1/4 and NW 1/4, SW 1/4, Sec 36, Twp 35 N, Rng 10 E; entered by sd **Bey** on 9 Aug 1841. Signed Felix **Bey**. Wit Reuben **Shelby**, JCC. Rec 13 Nov 1841. [No. 1261]

1480. Page 85. 8 Nov 1841. Thomas **Taylor** and Balbina, his wife, to Antoin Joseph **Catlamy**. For the sum of $225, 40 acres, more or less, being the NE 1/4, SE 1/4, Sec 34, Twp 35 N, Rng 10 E. Signed Thomas **Taylor**, Balbina **Taylor** (RD). Wit Reuben **Shelby**, JCC. Rec 8 Nov 1841. [No. 1262]

1481. Page 86. 15 Sep 1841. Bernard S. **Pratte** and Jane, his wife, and Walter B. **Wilkinson** and Emaly, his wife, to Martin L. **Moore** and Isaac G. **Whitworth**. For the sum of $50, Lot No. 7 in Perryville. Signed B. S. **Pratte**, Sarah Jane **Pratte** (RD), Walter B. **Wilkinson**, Emily L. **Wilkinson** (RD). Wit Reuben **Shelby**, JCC, Celeste **Pratte**. [No rec date.] [No. 1263]

1482. Page 87. 8 Nov 1841. Mark L. **Manning** to Pius **Manning**. For securing two notes and the sum of $1, mortgage on one black horse purchased from Marcus **Block** and a growing crop of corn on the farm where he resides. Sd Pius is security for sd Mark L. in a note to Reuben **Shelby**, assigned to Gabriel M. **Duvall**, for $28.75, on a judgment before John **Layton**, JP; and sd Mark also owes a note to sd Pius, assigned to Leander **Tucker**, for $10.25. Signed Mark L. **Manning**. Wit Reuben **Shelby**, JCC. Rec 15 Nov 1841. [No. 1264]

1483. Page 88. 13 Nov 1841. William **Windfield** and Helen, his wife, to Clement **Knott**. For the sum of $200, deed of trust on 200 acres, more or less, of a survey confirmed to Tunis **Quick**, sold by sd **Quick** to his son John W. **Quick**, decd, and sold by Circuit

Court order to Peter R. **Pratte** on 5 Nov 1838; where sd **Windfield** now resides. Sd **Windfield** owes a writing obligatory to sd **Knott** for $200 by 13 Nov 1842 with 10% interest per annum, or sd **Knott** is to sell the land to pay the debt. Signed William **Windfield**, Helen (x) **Windfield** (RD). Wit James **Rice** (JP). Rec 15 Nov 1841. [No. 1265]

1484. Page 90. 10 Jun 1841. John **Hoffman** [and Anne, his wife,] to Charles **Jaeger**. For the sum of $600, two tracts in Cape Girardeau and Perry Cos. in Sec 1, Twp 33 N, Rng 11 E; 139.60 acres, being Lot No. 6, NW 1/4, Sec 1, Twp 33 N, Rng 11 E, patented in Certificate No. 324; and 80 acres, being Lot No. 5, NW 1/4, Sec 1, Twp 33 N, Rng 11 E, patented in Certificate No. 440; except for about 3 acres deeded to Joel **Rhyne**, Emanuel **Kastner** and others as trustees for the Lutheran Church, and 1/2 of the proceeds of any minerals which may be found to remain sd **Hoffman**'s during his lifetime. The mill dam can be raised eight feet high from the main rock of the creek. Signed John **Hoffman**, Anne (x) **Hoffman** (RD). Wit Joseph **Miller**, JP in Apple Creek Twp, Cape Girardeau Co., Mo. Rec 17 Nov 1841. [No. 1266]

1485. Page 91. 17 Nov 1841. Bede **Moore** and Verlinder, his wife, to Joseph **Paquin**. For the sum of $125, 50 acres, beginning at the SW corner of a tract sold by Hilary **Layton** and wife to sd **Paquin** on 16 Nov 1841, and also bounded by James **Tucker**. Signed Bede **Moore**, Verlinder (x) **Moore** (RD). Wit Reuben **Shelby**, JCC. Rec 22 Nov 1841. [No. 1267]

1486. Page 92. 16 Nov 1841. Hillary **Layton** and Elizabeth, his wife, to Joseph **Paquin**. For the sum of $75, 30 acres, beginning at the SW corner of a tract sold by Bede **Moore** to sd **Layton** on 7 Sep 1840. Signed Hilary **Layton**, Elizabeth (x) **Layton** (RD). Wit Reuben **Shelby**, JCC. Rec 22 Nov 1841. [No. 1268]

1487. Page 93. 27 Nov 1841. Hyman **Block** of Perryville to Levi **Block** of St. Charles, Mo. For the sum of $3070, five lots in **Taylor** and **Faina**'s addition to Perryville, joining on the S line of the town; Lot No. 1, fronting on Jackson St and High St, with a two-story new frame house, kitchen, and plank fence enclosed; 7 acres, more or less, beginning at a stake at the SW corner of the same addition, and bounded by Charles **Stewart**'s line, as per a deed from **Taylor & Faina** and wives (2:354); Lot Nos. 2 & 3 on High St, Jackson St, and West St, as per a deed from **Taylor & Faina** and wives (2:397); a lot fronting on West St and High St, E by the previous lots, and N by Bartholomew **Murphy**, as per a deed from Rufus **Walker** (3:76). Also seven lots in Perryville; the S 1/2, Lot No. 34 on the public square, as per a deed from John **Robinson** (2:277); Lot No. 17 in Perryville with a dwelling house, as per a deed from Wm. A. **Walker** and wife (2:57); part of Lot No. 68 in Perryville with a dwelling house, kitchen, etc, bounded E by Jackson St, S by J. W. **Noell**, W by Peter **Faherty**, and N by North St, as per a deed from Wm. A. **Walker** and wife (3:222); Lot No. 41 as per deed from Isadore **Hagan** (2:257); Lot No. 96 as per deed from Martin & Nerius **Layton**, execr of Zachariah **Layton**, decd (3:427); a lot that fronts on Jackson St and South St, as per a deed from Gabriel **Duval** (3:108); and Lot No. 99, as per a deed from Moses **Roady** and Hetty, his wife (3:425). Signed Hyman **Block**. Wit James **Rice** (JP). [No rec date.] [No. 1269]

1488. Page 95. 6 Dec 1841. James N. **Moore** and Sarah, his wife, to Martin Lindsay **Moore**. In consideration of 100 acres and labor done on that land to the value of $1500, 150 acres, more or less, part of a tract confirmed to James N. **Moore**; beginning at the SE corner of sd tract (58 acres as a deed of gift, 92 acres in consideration of the place sold). Signed James N. **Moore**, Sarah (x) **Moore** (RD). Wit Mark **Brewer** (JP). Rec 6 Dec 1841. [No. 1270]

1489. Page 96. 10 Nov 1841. J. M. M. **Powell** and Harriet, his wife, R. C. **Powell** and Sarinda, his wife, and James S. **Powell** and Juliann, his wife, to James B. **Lavielle**. For the sum of $637, their undivided 3/7 share of 210 arpens in Bois Brule Bottom, confirmed to Francis **Clark**, and transferred by D. L. **Caldwell** to Wm. **Powell**, decd. Signed J. M. M. **Powell**, Harriet **Powell** (RD), Robert C. **Powell**, Sarinda A. (x) **Powell** (RD), James S. **Powell**, Juliann **Powell** (RD). Wit Rebeca **Wright**, George **Vessels** (JP). Rec 11 Dec 1841. [No. 1271]

1490. Page 97. 7 Apr 1829. U. S. A. to Joseph **Best**. Patent for 80 acres, being the E 1/2, NW 1/4, Sec 29, Twp 34 N, Rng 9 E; in Certificate No. 1272. Signed Andrew **Jackson**. Wit Geo. **Graham**, Commissioner of the General Land Office. Rec in Vol. 2:215 of the General Land Office. Rec 14 Dec 1841. [No. 1272]

1491. Page 98. 18 Nov 1841. Michael **Muhlfelt** and Susannah, his wife, to John Claude **Besand**. For the sum of $261, two tracts in Lot No. 2, NE 1/4, Sec 1, Twp 34 N, Rng 10 E; 41.57 acres, being the E 1/2; and 29.57 acres, being the W 1/2, except for 12 acres sold to John **Wilhelm** on 15 Nov 1841. Signed Michael **Muhlfelt**, Susannah (x) **Muhlfelt** (RD). Wit Reuben **Shelby**, JCC. Rec 18 Dec 1841. [No. 1273]

1492. Page 99. 30 Nov 1841. Thomas **Stewart** and Isabella T., his wife, to Charles **Hayden**. For the sum of $5, all their claim to any estate of Charles **Stewart** Senr, decd. Signed Thomas **Stewart**, Isabella T. **Stewart** (RD). Wit Fredk. C. **Hase**, Clerk. Rec 21 Dec 1841. [No. 1274]

1493. Page 100. 5 Aug 1841. Certification of John W. **Noell** as duly elected Circuit Court Clerk of Perry Co., his having been elected. Signed Reuben **Shelby**, Presiding JCC. John W. **Noell** takes the oath of office. Signed John W. **Noell**. Wit Reuben **Shelby**, Presiding JCC. Rec 23 Dec 1841. [No. 1275]

1494. Page 100. 5 Aug 1841. Certification of James **Rice** as duly elected County Court Clerk of Perry Co., his having been elected. Signed Reuben **Shelby**, Presiding JCC. James **Rice** takes the oath of office. Signed James **Rice**. Wit Reuben **Shelby**, JCC. Rec 23 Dec 1841. [No. 1276]

1495. Page 101. 24 Jul 1839. Charles C. **Rutledge** and Mary Ann, his wife, to Thomas C. **Cobb** of Campbell Co., Tenn. For the sum of $302, two tracts; 40 acres, being the NW 1/4, NW 1/4, Sec 12, Twp 34 N, Rng 12 E; and 40 acres, being the SW 1/4, SW 1/4, Sec 1, Twp 34 N, Rng 11 E. Signed Charles C. **Rutledge**, Mary Ann (x) **Rutledge** (RD). Wit Alonzo **Abernathy**, JCC. Rec 1 Jan 1842. [No. 1277]

1496. Page 102. 11 Dec 1841. Lucretia **Reardon** to Burwell **Johnson** of Ste. Genevieve Co., Mo. For the sum of $200, undivided 1/7 part of 100 acres in Bois Brule Bottom, purchased by Atticus **Tucker**, now decd, from Charles **Ellis**, now decd, on 1 Aug 1819; part of 350 acres purchased by sd **Ellis** from William **Dunn**. Signed Lucinda (x) **Reardon**. Wit R. B. **Griffith**, JP in Ste. Genevieve Co., Mo. Rec 1 Jan 1842. [No. 1278]

1497. Page 103. 14 Mar 1840. Reuben **Shelby** and Mary E., his wife, to Catharine **Lukefahr**. For the sum of $500, 120 acres in two tracts in Twp 35 N, Rng 10 E; the W 1/2, SE 1/4, Sec 26 and the NW 1/4, NE 1/4, Sec 35; purchased from Edward **McGinnis** in 1839. Signed Reuben **Shelby**, Mary E. **Shelby** (RD). Wit Mark **Brewer** (JP). Rec 1 Jan 1842. [No. 1279]

1498. Page 104. 15 Feb 1840. Francis Victor **Courtois** and Jane Mary Felisete, his wife, to same. For the sum of $40, 31 acres, more or less, part of the E 1/2, SE 1/4, Sec 26, Twp 35 N, Rng 10 E; beginning at a post oak 20 inches in diameter on John **Layton**'s line. Signed F. V. **Courtois**, J. M. Felicite **Courtois** (RD). Wit Reuben **Shelby**, JCC, J. M. **Odin**. Rec 1 Jan 1842. [No. 1280]

1499. Page 105. 22 Jul 1841. Commissioners to partition land of Charles **Ellis**, decd, to Thomas J. **Tucker**. For the sum of $2950, 255.20 acres originally confirmed to Elisha **Crosby** as No. 1007 in Twp 37 N, Rng 11 E. Sold in Mar 1839 on order of Circuit Court issued 28 Nov 1838 in case of Thomas J. **Tucker** and Sarah, his wife and formerly Sarah **Ellis**, Charles G. **Ellis** by his guardian Thomas J. **Tucker**, Charles F. **Brazeau** and Caroline, his wife and formerly Caroline **Ellis**, and Catharine **Everett** by her guardian Jacob J. **Everett**, all heirs of Charles **Ellis**, decd, on partition to partition sd land. Signed Jh. [Joseph] **Pratte**. John **Logan**. Wit John W. **Noell**, Clerk. Rec 1 Jan 1842. [No. 1281]

1500. Page 107. 3 Dec 1841. George **McKinstry** to Joseph S. **Pease**. For serving as security for a debt and the sum of $1, deed of trust on personal property now at Port Perry at the mill of the late Charles **McKinstry**; three yokes of oxen, three cows, one heffer, one yoke steers; five sows; 13 shoats; two horses; one cart and three other carts of different value; farming tools; blacksmith's tools; carpenter's tools; household furniture; 100 cords of cord wood; 800 bushels of corn; one large bell; one boat; and all the lumber and shingles on the place. If a debt to Warburton & King for $640.93 is not paid, then sd **Pease** is to sell the property and give any overplus to sd **McKinstry**. Signed G. **McKinstry** Jr. Wit Louis T. **Labeaume**, JP in St. Louis Co., Mo. Rec 1 Jan 1842. [No. 1282]

1501. Page 108. 4 Jan 1842. Stephen **Melton** and Rebecca, his wife, and Helen **Hagan** to James **Dunn**. For the sum of $25 to each, their interest in 80 acres, being the W 1/2, NE 1/4, Sec 34, Twp 35 N, Rng 10 E; which was the land of Levi **Hagan**, decd, and to which they are entitled as heirs of sd **Hagan**. Signed Stephen (x) **Melton**, Rebecca (x) **Melton** (RD), Helen (x) **Hagan**. Wit Mark **Brewer** (JP). Rec 10 Jan 1842. [No. 1283]

1502. Page 109. 4 Jan 1842. Anne **Hagan** to same. For the sum of $15, 5 acres in the SW corner, SW 1/4, SE 1/4, Sec 27, Twp 35 N, Rng 10 E. Signed Anne (x) **Hagan**. Wit Mark **Brewer** (JP). Rec 10 Jan 1842. [No. 1284]

1503. Page 110. 14 Oct 1841. Henry C. **Bimpage** and Mary Jane, his wife, to Robert **Manning**. For the sum of $330.89, mortgage on their undivided interest in the estate of Dr. Leo **Fenwick**, decd, of which sd **Manning** is execr. Sd **Bimpage** owes sd **Manning** a note dated 5 Oct 1841 within one year. Signed Henry C. **Bimpage**, Mary Jane **Bimpage**. Wit J. C. **Fenwick**, Reuben **Shelby**, JCC. Rec 14 Jan 1842. [No. 1285]

1504. Page 111. 18 Jan 1842. Isaac **Hill** to Thomas J. **Tucker** and William B. **Burns**, admrs of the estate of David **Burns**, decd. For securing a bond and the sum of $1, mortgage on three parcels and personal property; 40 acres, being the SE 1/4, SW 1/4, Sec 14, Twp 35 N, Rng 9 E; 40 acres, being the NW 1/4, NE 1/4, Sec 23, Twp 35 N, Rng 9 E; the undivided 1/4 part of Lot No. 40 in Perryville; one bay mare 7 or 8 years old; one sorrel filly and one bay filly; one cart and oxen; one sorrel mare; and two feather beds. Sd **Hill** is bound with sd **Tucker** and sd **Burns** to the State of Mo. in a bond dated 8 Aug 1837 to discharge the duties of guardian of Louisa Ann **Hill** and Thomas W. **Hill**, his minor children and heirs at law of Isaac **Hill**, their grandfather, decd, (Probate Book 1:73); and this mortgage guarantees that he will provide just accounts for sd guardianship. Signed Isaac **Hill**. Wit James **Rice** (JP). Rec 18 Jan 1842. [Marginal note: Full satisfaction received on 4 Dec 1851. Signed Thos. J. **Tucker**. Test Charles C. **Ellis**, Clerk.] [No. 1286]

1505. Page 113. 18 Jan 1842. Same to Phoebe **Tucker**. For securing a debt and the sum of $1, mortgage on 40 acres, being the SE 1/4, NW 1/4, Sec 14, Twp 35 N, Rng 9 E, entered by sd **Hill** on 1 Sep 1837 as No. 5707; one blue plush seated side saddle; seven sheep, being one wether, one ram, and five ewes; one blue or dun colored cow with her calf; one speckled cow 14 or 15 years old with her yearling calf; one cherry bureau; and one wooden clock. Sd **Hill** owes sd **Tucker** a note of even date for $137 with interest. Signed Isaac **Hill**. Wit James **Rice** (JP). Rec 18 Jan 1842. [Marginal note: Full satisfaction received. Signed George (x) **McNew**. Wit Jno. W. **Noell**, Clerk.] [No. 1287]

1506. Page 114. 15 Jan 1842. Clement **Vessels** [and Catharine, his wife,] to Charles **Miles**. For securing a debt and the sum of $1, mortgage on __ acres, being the SW 1/4, SE 1/4, fractional Sec 14, Twp 36 N, Rng 10 E; one sorrel mare with blaze face; one iron grey horse; one sorrel filly; one sorrel colt and one black colt with ball faces; two cows and calves; a three-year-old heifer; seven sheep; and 14 hogs. Sd **Vessels** owes sd **Miles** a note for $125 dated 13 Jan 1842, payable in 18 months with 10% interest. Signed Clement **Vessels**. Wit John W. **Noell**, Clerk. Rec 18 Jan 1842. [No. 1288]

1507. Page 116. 7 Dec 1841. Conrad C. **Zeigler** and Elvina, his wife, of Ste. Genevieve Co., Mo. to Ferdinand **Rozier** Senior. For the sum of $1500, 150 acres, more or less, at the mouth of River Au Mete, being purchased at marshall's sale in Jun 1841, formerly owned by Robert T. **Brown** Senior. Signed Conrad C. **Zeigler**, Elvina C. **Zeigler**. Wit Jesse B. **Robins**, Clerk of Ste. Genevieve Co. Court. Rec 20 Jan 1842. [No. 1289]

1508. Page 117. 15 Jan 1842. Andrew **Derr** and Christeen, his wife, to Anthony **Parres**. For the sum of $50, Lot No. 78 in Perryville. Signed Andrew **Derr**, Christeen **Derr** (RD). Wit Reuben **Shelby**, JCC. Rec 20 Jan 1842. [No. 1290]

1509. Page 118. 24 Nov 1841. Joseph **Shoults** and Eliza R., his wife, to Luther **Taylor**. For the sum of $400, part of Lot Nos. 57 & 58 in Perryville, beginning on St. Marys St. Signed Joseph **Shoults**, Eliza R. **Shoults** (RD). Wit Reuben **Shelby**, JCC. Rec 24 Jan 1842. [No. 1291]

1510. Page 119. 25 Jan 1842. Guy **Elder** to Reuben **Shelby**. For the sum of $800, 250 arpents, part of a claim of 640 acres confirmed to Joseph **Tucker**; beginning at a white oak marked N. T. on the SE boundary of sd **Tucker**'s survey; and purchased by sd Elder of Nicholas **Tucker** on 7 Jan 1833. Signed Guy **Elder**. Test James **Rice** (JP). Rec 25 Jan 1843. [No. 1292]

1511. Page 120. 25 Jan 1842. Michael **Mihlfeld** to Joseph **Soutre**. For the sum of $110, part of Lot No. 10 in Perryville, fronting on Spring St and St Joseph St; conveyed by Joseph **Shoults** and wife to sd **Mihlfeld** on 7 Dec 1837 (2:428). Signed Michael **Mihlfeld**. Wit John W. **Noell**, Clerk. Rec 25 Jan 1842. [No. 1293]

1512. Page 121. 24 Jan 1842. James **Dunn** and Mary, his wife, to Ferdinand **Rozier** Junr. For the sum of $25, 20.37 acres, being the N 1/2, S 1/2, Lot No. 2, NW 1/4, Sec 18, Twp 34 N, Rng 11 E. Signed James **Dunn**, Mary (x) **Dunn** (RD). Wit Reuben **Shelby**, JCC. Rec 26 Jan 1842. [No. 1294]

1513. Page 122. 1 Jan 1842. Felix **Layton** and Feliciann, his wife, to Peter **Brown**. For the sum of $400, their undivided interest in 230 acres willed by Zechariah **Layton**, decd, to sd Felix and Nerius **Layton** on 6 Apr 1839. Signed Felix **Layton**, Feliciann **Layton** (RD). Wit Reuben **Shelby**, JCC. Rec 28 Jan 1842. [No. 1295]

1514. Page 123. 30 Dec 1841. William M. **Myers** to Jacob **Shaner**. For the sum of $150, 80.90 acres on the waters of Brazeau Creek; part of 100.90 acres, the W fractional 1/2, NE 1/4 and SE 1/4, NE 1/4, Sec 22, Twp 34 N, Rng 13 E; entered by sd **Myers** on 20 Feb 1840, less 20 acres sold by sd **Myers** to Lorenzo D. **Myers** on 24 Aug 1840. Signed William M. **Myers**. Wit A. M. **McPherson** (JP). Rec 29 Jan 1842. [No. 1296]

1515. Page 124. 29 Dec 1841. Catharine **Lukefahr** to Claude Francois **Guyot**, Fernal Francois **Guyot**, and Francois Xavier **Guyot**. For the sum of $1000, two tracts; 120 acres, being the W 1/2, SE 1/4, Sec 26 and NW 1/4, NE 1/4, Sec 35, Twp 34 N, Rng 10 E, purchased by sd **Lukefahr** from Reuben **Shelby** on 4 Mar 1840; and 31 acres, more or less, being a portion of the E 1/2, SE 1/4, Sec 26, Twp 34 N, Rng 10 E, beginning at a post oak 20 inches in diameter on John **Layton**'s land, part of a tract entered by Francis V. **Courtois**, and sold by him to sd **Lukefahr** on 15 Feb 1841. Signed Catharine (x) **Lukefahr**. Test Frederick C. **Hase**, Clerk. Rec 31 Jan 1842. [No. 1297]

1516. Page 125. 8 Jan 1842. Reuben **Shelby** and Mary E., his wife, to Aaron **Hager**. For the sum of $50, 37.56 acres, being the NE 1/4, 1/4 Sec 6, Twp 34 N, Rng 11 E. Signed Reuben **Shelby**, Mary E. **Shelby** (RD). Wit James **Rice** (JP). Rec 1 Feb 1842. [No. 1298]

1517. Page 126. 26 Aug 1840. John **Logan** to Luther **Taylor**. For the sum of $25, Lot No. 27 in Perryville. Signed John **Logan**. Wit Mark **Brewer** (JP). Rec 3 Feb 1842. [No. 1299]

1518. Page 127. 5 Jan 1842. John **Walsh** and Edward **Walsh** and Isabelle, his wife, of St. Louis, Mo. to John W. **Noell**. For the sum of $400, Lot No. 8 in Perryville. Signed John **Walsh**, Edward **Walsh**, Isabelle **Walsh**. Wit Julius **de Munn**, Clerk of St. Louis Co., Mo. Rec 3 Feb 1842. [No. 1300]

1519. Page 128. 1 Feb 1842. Charles **Roy** and Mary M, his wife, to M. L. **Moore** and Isaac G. **Whitworth**. For the sum of $50, Lot No. 73 in Perryville, deeded to sd **Roy** by Luther **Taylor** on 8 Sep 1837. Signed Charles **Roy**, Mary M. **Roy** (RD). Wit Reuben **Shelby**, JCC. Rec 3 Feb 1842. [No. 1301]

1520. Page 129. 24 Aug 1840. William Marrion **Myers** to Lorenzo Dow **Myers**. For the sum of $25, 20 acres, part of the SE 1/4, NE 1/4, Sec 22, Twp 34 N, Rng 13 E; beginning 160 rods S of the NE corner sd section; bounded in part by sd Lorenzo's 40-acre entry; and part of a tract entered by William M. **Myers**. Signed William M. **Myers**. Wit W. **Garner**, Henry L. **Leggett**, Elias **Barber** (JP). Rec 7 Feb 1842. [No. 1302]

1521. Page 130. 10 Jan 1842. Micajah **Shoults** and Berthena, his wife, to Dolinda **Clifton**. For the sum of $25, 20 acres, being the W 1/2, SE 1/4, SE 1/4, Sec 32, Twp 35 N, Rng 12 E; but sd **Shoults** is to have full possession of a spring now occupied by him. Signed Micajah **Shoults**, Berthena (x) **Shoults** (RD). Wit William **Farrar** (JP). Rec 7 Feb 1842. [No. 1303]

1522. Page 131. 14 Sep 1841. William P. **Belsha** and America, his wife, to Miles **Farrar** Senr. For the sum of $25, the 1/6 part of 1/2 of two tracts entered by James **Belsha** in his lifetime on 15 Oct 1833, in Sec 21, Twp 35 N, Rng 13 E, Certificate Nos. 1289 & 1290; 9.55 acres, being the NW fractional 1/4, fractional; and 39.76 acres, being the NW fractional 1/4, SW fractional 1/4. Signed Wm. P. (x) **Belsha**, America (x) **Belsha** (RD). Wit D. C. **Waters**, Alfred L. **Parks** (JP). Rec 7 Feb 1842. [No. 1304]

1523. Page 133. 1 Mar 1841. Catharine **Belsha** Senr to same. For the sum of $25, a 1/6 of 1/2 part of the two tracts described in the preceding deed (4:131). Signed Sarah [sic] (x) **Belsha**. Test Geo. **Huff**, William **Farrar** (JP). Rec 7 Feb 1842. [No. 1305]

1524. Page 134. 23 Feb 1841. Elisha **Belsha** to same. For the sum of $25, a 1/6 of 1/2 part of the two tracts described in 4:131. Signed Elisha **Belsha**. Test Alphonzo **Farrar**, William **Farrar** (JP). Rec 7 Feb 1842. [No. 1306]

1525. Page 135. 20 Feb 1841. James B. **Martin** and Sarah, his wife and formerly the wife of James **Belsha**, decd, to same. For the sum of $150, 1/2 of two tracts described in 4:131; being a widow's half of the tracts. Signed James B. **Martin**, Sarah (x) **Martin** (RD). Wit William **Farrar** (JP). Rec 7 Feb 1842. [No. 1307]

1526. Page 137. 23 Feb 1841. Micajah **Shoults** and Berthena, his wife, to same. For the sum of $25, 1/6 part of 1/2 of the two tracts described in 4:131. Signed Micajah **Shoults**, Berthena **Shoults** (RD). Test Alphonzo **Farrar**, William **Farrar** (JP). Rec 7 Feb 1842. [No. 1308]

1527. Page 138. 25 Oct 1841. Eli **Welker** to same. For the sum of $50, 40 acres, being the NW 1/4, NW 1/4, Sec 36, Twp 34 N, Rng 11 E. Signed Eli (x) **Welker**. Test Alphonzo **Farrar**, William **Farrar** (JP). Rec 7 Feb 1842. [No. 1309]

1528. Page 139. 25 Oct 1841. Benjamin **Carrico** and Mary, his wife, to same. For the sum of $50, 40 acres, being the NE 1/4, NW 1/4, Sec 36, Twp 34 N, Rng 11 E. Signed Benjamin **Carrico**, Mary (x) **Carrico** (RD). Test Alphonzo **Farrar**, William **Farrar** (JP). Rec 7 Feb 1842. [No. 1310]

1529. Page 140. 7 Feb 1842. William **Cox** and Margaret, his wife, to Francis L. **Jones**. For the sum of $295.54, mortgage on 145.41 acres, more or less, being the SW fractional 1/4, fractional Sec 18, Twp 36 N, Rng 12 E. Sd **Cox** owes sd **Jones** a note dated 16 Nov

1841 and due by 16 Nov 1843 with 10% interest per annum. Signed William **Cox**, Margaret (x) **Cox** (RD). Wit Alfred L. **Parks** (JP). Rec 7 Feb 1842. [Marginal note: Full satisfaction received on 1 Jan 1847. Signed F. L. **Jones**. Wit John W. **Noell**, Clerk.] [No. 1311]

1530. Page 141. 24 Jan 1842. Thomas **McAtee** and Mary, his wife, to Robert S. **Manning**. For securing several debts and the sum of $1, mortgage on four tracts and personal property; 160 acres, being the W 1/2 of the NW 1/4, the NE 1/4, NW 1/4, and the NW 1/4, NE 1/4 of Sec 12, Twp 34 N, Rng 10 E, conveyed by Reuben **Shelby** to sd **McAtee** on 12 Jun 1838; 40 acres, being the SW 1/4, SW 1/4, Sec 12, Twp 34 N, Rng 10 E, conveyed by John P. **Tucker** and wife to sd **McAtee** on 12 Mar 1839; __ acres, being the E 1/2, NE 1/4 and about 35 acres of the NW 1/4, NE 1/4, Sec 12, and the SW 1/4, SE 1/4, Sec 1, Twp 34 N, Rng 10 E, conveyed by Henry **McAtee** to Thomas **McAtee**; __ acres, being the SE 1/4, SW 1/4, Sec 12, Twp 34 N, Rng 10 E; five cows; two steers, one with red sides and white back, and one black with white face; two heifer calves with white back and belly; one pied heifer; one yellow pied steer calf; one yearling bull of brown color; one red heifer; one young yoke of steers, one year old last spring; one yearling heifer; one yearling steer; one gray mare; one black horse colt one year old; one sorrel ditto; three sorrel mare colts; one bay ditto; one gray horse; one sorrel horse; one bay horse; two sorrel mares; one bay filly; 12 sheep; 38 hogs; one four-horse waggon and gear; two copper stills and all the apparatus thereunto belonging; one press; and one bureau. Sd **Manning** is security for sd **McAtee** in two notes; one dated 1 Jan 1842, payable to George **Rutledge**, guardian of the minor heirs of Robert **Abernathy**, for $450, and due one year after date with 10% interest; and one payable to John E. **Burgett**, guardian of Burgett **Everett**, for $68, due 1 Jan 1842. Sd **McAtee** also owes a note for $259.36, dated 9 Aug 1841, payable in two years with 10% interest. Signed Thomas **McAtee**, Mary (x) **McAtee** (RD). Wit Reuben **Shelby**, JCC. Rec 7 Feb 1842. [No. 1312]

1531. Page 143. 8 Feb 1842. Peter R. **Pratte** and Mary Louise, his wife, to Martin L. **Moore** and Isaac G. **Whitworth**. For the sum of $200, part of Lot No. 32 in Perryville, beginning at the SE corner of sd **Pratte**'s store house. Signed P. R. **Pratte**, Marie L. **Pratte** (RD). Wit Reuben **Shelby**, JCC. Rec 9 Feb 1842. [No. 1313]

1532. Page 144. 13 Dec 1841. John **Logan** to Francis **Clark**. For the sum of $100, 71 acres, more or less, in Bois Brule Bottom, part of the confirmation of John **Greenwault** Jr or his legal representatives; beginning at the NE corner of Jones **Newsom**'s survey, and also bounded by John **Morgan** Senr and William T. **Laville**. Signed John **Logan**. Wit W. **Searcy** (JP). Rec 9 Feb 1842. [No. 1314]

1533. Page 146. About 24 Jan 1836. Plat of division between A. H. **Puckett** and George **Camster**. Signed C. H. **Perrin**, surveyor. Chain carriers Wm. B. **Marshall**, Thos. J. **Finch**. Rec 11 Feb 1842. [No. 1315]

1534. Page 146. 14 Feb 1842. Henry C. **Bimpage** and Mary Jane, his wife, to Morris **Block** and Charles **Avery**, trading as Block & Avery in Perryville. For securing debts and the sum of $1, all their interest in the real estate of Leo **Fenwick**, decd; 150 acres, more or less, in Brazeau Bottom fronting on the Mississippi River; and 327.47 acres known as the Hill Tract. Also their undivided interest in the slaves of sd **Fenwick**; one roan horse; two bay horses; one black mare and colt; one yoke of pied oxen; two brown cows; one spotted cow; 25 hogs; one ox cart; and four ploughs. The property is also subject to a mortgage dated 14 Oct 1841 to Robert **Manning** (4:110). Sd **Bimpage** owes Block & Avery $168.79 in two notes at 10% interest per annum; one dated 21 Apr 1841 payable one day after date for $95.04; one dated 19 Nov 1842 for $73.75. Signed Henry C. **Bimpage**, Mary Jane **Bimpage** (RD). Wit Reuben **Shelby**, JCC. Rec 15 Feb 1842. [No. 1316]

1535. Page 148. 14 Feb 1842. Same and same to Morris **Block**. For securing a debt and the sum of $1, mortgage to all the property described in the previous deed (4:146), subject to the other mortgages described. Sd **Bimpage** owes sd **Block** $124.98 in two notes at 10% interest per annum, payable one day after date; one dated 6 Apr 1841 for $75; and one dated 7 Jul 1841 for $7.11. Signed Henry C. **Bimpage**, Mary Jane **Bimpage** (RD). Wit Reuben **Shelby**, JCC. Rec 15 Feb 1842. [No. 1317]

1536. Page 150. 17 Feb 1842. John C. **Bacher** and Nancy, his wife, to Joseph D. **Simpson**, admr of the estate of Henry Casper **Vonderheide**, decd. For the sum of $30.20, mortgage on Lot No. 93 in Perryville. Sd **Bacher** owes sd **Simpson** the debt with 10% interest per annum by 1 Aug 1842. Signed John C. **Bacher**, Nancy **Bacher** (RD). Wit James **Rice** (JP). Rec 17 Feb 1842. [No. 1318]

1537. Page 151. 11 Jan 1842. Burwell **Johnson** of Ste. Genevieve Co., Mo. to James T. **Swearingen** of St. Louis Co., Mo. For the sum of $150, one undivided 1/7 part of 100 acres in Bois Brule Bottom, purchased by Atticus **Tucker**, decd, from Charles **Ellis** on 1 Aug 1819; part of 350 acres purchased by **Ellis** from William **Dunn**. Signed Burwell **Johnson**. Wit Jesse B. **Robins**, Clerk of Ste. Genevieve Co., Mo. Rec 18 Feb 1842. [No. 1319]

1538. Page 152. 18 Feb 1841. Christina **Layton** to John Claude Cassimere **Bey** and Augustin Melchior **Prevalet**. For the sum of 300 franks, 30 acres, part of the NW 1/4, NW 1/4, Sec 35, Twp 35 N, Rng 10 E. Signed Christina (x) **Layton**. Test John **Layton** Senr (JP). Rec 21 Feb 1842. [No. 1320]

1539. Page 153. 21 Feb 1842. Pierre T. **Boeuf** and Melanie, his wife, to same, same, Constant **L'homme**, and Victor **L'homme**. For the sum of 2000 franks ($372)--500 franks from sd **Bey**, 500 franks from sd **Prevalet**, 600 franks from Constant **L'homme**, and 400 franks from Victor **L'homme**; 80 acres, being the S 1/2, SE 1/4, Sec 34, Twp 35 N, Rng 10 E, in proportion to the amounts paid by each. Signed P. T. **Boeuf**, Melanie Cecille **Boeuf** (RD). Wit Reuben **Shelby**, JCC. Rec 21 Feb 1842. [No. 1321]

1540. Page 154. 31 Jan 1842. Lewis **Smalts** to Philip **Smalts**. For securing a note and the sum of $1, mortgage on two tracts; 40 acres, being the NW 1/4, SE 1/4, Sec 14, Twp 34 N, Rng 10 E; and 40 acres, being the SE 1/4, NE 1/4, Sec 14, Twp 34 N, Rng 10 E. Sd Lewis owes sd Philip $150, due three years from date, with 6% interest per annum. Signed Lewis **Smalts**. Test James **Rice** (JP). Rec 22 Feb 1842. [No. 1322]

1541. Page 155. 24 Feb 1842. Joab **Burgee**, admr of the estate of David **Crips**, decd, to Michael **Daly**. For the sum of $60.50 in a mortgage by sd **Crips** to Perry Co., and the additional sum of $23.12 1/2; 130.66 acres, partly in Bois Brule Bottom, and seven miles from the Mississippi River; purchased by sd **Crips** at the sale of Michael **Burns**, decd. There is a comfortable log dwelling, other out houses, 10-12 acres under cultivation in the bottom.

Sold at order of County Court issued 5 Nov 1841 to sell sd land to pay debts of the estate. Signed Joab W. **Burgee**, admr of the estate of David **Crips**, decd. Wit James **Rice** (JP). Rec 24 Feb 1842. [No. 1323]

1542. Page 157. 3 Nov 1841. Fenwick J. **Hamilton**, admr of the estate of Resin L. **Bishop**, decd, to Rebecca **Bishop**. For the sum of $480, 107.55 acres on the Mississippi River, being Claim No. 364 in Twp 34 N, Rng 14 E, originally granted to Henry **Riley**; less 7 acres sold to **Donald** in the lifetime of sd **Bishop**. There are a dwelling house, stable, other outhouses, and about 20 acres under cultivation. Sold on 3 Nov 1841 on order of County Court issued Aug Term [1841] to sell land to pay debts of sd estate. Signed Fenwick J. **Hamilton**, admr of R. L. **Bishop**. Test Fredk. C. **Hase**, Clerk. Rec 26 Feb 1842. [No. 1324]

1543. Page 159. 21 Feb 1842. Thomas **Swan** and George **Swan** to Jacob **Shaner**. For the sum of $307.82, mortgage on four tracts in Twp 34 N, Rng 13 E; 40 acres, being the NE 1/4, SW 1/4, Sec 24; 40 acres, being the NW 1/4, NW 1/4, Sec 25; 20 acres, more or less, being the S 1/2, SW 1/4, NW 1/4, fractional Sec 24; and 120 acres, being the E 1/2, NE 1/4 and NW 1/4, SE 1/4, Sec 23. Sd **Swans** owe sd **Shaner** a note payable one day after date and dated 21 Feb 1842, with 10% interest, due by 21 Feb 1844. Signed Thomas S. **Swan**, George **Swan**. Test Wm. F. **Cook**, Augustus **Davis** (JP). Rec 26 Feb 1842. [No. 1325]

1544. Page 160. 26 Feb 1842. Joseph A. **Massey** to James **Rice**. For securing a debt and the sum of $1, mortgage on 160 acres, more or less, beginning at a white oak standing on the bank of Rock Spring Branch. Sd **Massey** owes sd **Rice** $33.75 with interest. Signed Joseph A. **Massey**. Wit John W. **Noell**, Clerk. Rec 26 Feb 1842. [No. 1326]

1545. Page 162. 28 Jan 1842. Martin **Andrews** and Elizabeth, his wife, of Ste. Genevieve Co., Mo. to George **Bergmann**. For the sum of $63.50, 40 acres, being the NW 1/4, SW 1/4, Sec 28, Twp 35 N, Rng 11 E, purchased by sd **Andrews** from the U. S. on 28 Apr 1841. Signed Martin **Intres**, Elisabeth **Intres** (RD). Wit Jesse B. **Robbins**, Clerk of Ste. Genevieve Co. Circuit Court. Rec 6 Mar 1842. [No. 1327]

1546. Page 163. 7 Mar 1842. Michael **Mihlfeld** to Joseph **Suterer**. For the sum of $40, 81.84 acres, being Lot No. 2, NW 1/4, Sec 31, Twp 35 N, Rng 11 E; entered by sd **Suterer** on 22 Apr 1839 in the name of Susannah **Suterer**, late wife of sd **Mihlfeld**, now decd. Signed Michael **Mihlfeld**. Wit James **Rice** (JP). Rec 8 Mar 1842. [No. 1328]

1547. Page 164. 11 Mar 1842. Edward M. **Holden** to Thomas B. **English** of Cape Girardeau Co., Mo. For securing a note and the sum of $1, mortgage on one sorrel mare with a large starr in her forehead, now about eight years old. Sd **English** is security for sd **Holden** in a note to Milton **Harris**, given for two negro girls, dated 1 Jan 1842 and payable in 12 months. Signed Edward M. **Holden**. Wit John W. **Noell**, Clerk. Rec 12 Mar 1842. [No. 1329]

1548. Page 165. 11 Mar 1842. Julius H. **Smith**, admr of the estate of John **Smith** Jr., decd, to Peter R. **Pratte**. For the sum of $520, Lot No. 20 in Perryville, with a brick building on the same. Sold in Feb 1840 at order of County Court issued 20 Nov 1839. Signed Julius H. **Smith**, admr of John **Smith** Jr., decd. Wit Mark **Brewer** (JP). Rec 14 Mar 1842. [No. 1330]

1549. Page 166. 14 Mar 1842. Hyacinthus A. **Layton** to Walter **Layton**. For securing a note and the sum of $1, mortgage on 61.11 acres, being the NW fractional 1/4, fractional Sec 29, Twp 35 N, Rng 10 E, entered on 10 Nov 1841; one grey horse about six years old; one saddle and bridle; two beds, bedsteads, and bedding; one set of network curtains; one table; one stove and pipe; and one chest of mining tools, viz. two picks, two drills, one pick, and one hammer. Sd Hyacinthus owes sd Walter a note of even date for $500, due in two years. Signed Hyacinthus A. **Layton**. Wit John W. **Noell**, Clerk. Rec 14 Mar 1842. [No. 1331]

1550. Page 167. 5 May 1841. Joseph **Pratt** to David **Sepaugh**. For the sum of $154.22, __ acres, purchased by sd **Pratt** at Sheriff's sale from Hugh **Wells** on 4 Mar 1840 (3:360). Signed Jh. **Pratte**. Wit Perry **Evans** (JP). Rec 21 Mar 1842. [No. 1332]

1551. Page 168. 2 Nov 1841. Bede **Moore** and Verlinder, his wife, to Hillary **Layton**. For the sum of $1 and the consideration they bear unto their son-in-law, 130 acres, more or less, beginning at the most N corner of a survey confirmed to sd **Moore** by Congress; bounded in part by Joseph **Miles** and Joseph **Tucker**. Signed Bede **Moore**, Verlinder (x) **Moore** (RD). Wit James **Rice** (JP). Rec 21 Mar 1842. [No. 1333]

1552. Page 169. 12 Feb 1842. Trustees of Wittenburg to Robert P. **Slaughter**. For the sum of $50, Lot No. 46 in Wittenburg, fronting on front street and Perry St., and joined on the S by Lot No. 45. Signed Henry C. **Bimpage**, Fred. Wilh. **Barthell**, Christian Frederick **Muller**. Test Theod. F. L. **Hache**, Augustus **Davis** (JP). Rec 26 Mar 1842. [No. 1334]

1553. Page 170. 12 Feb 1842. Same to same. For the sum of $15, Lot No. 30 in Wittenburg, fronting on second street and Perry St, and bounded on the S by Lot No. 31. Signed Henry C. **Bimpage**, Fred. Wilh. **Barthell**, Christ. Fredr. **Muller**. Test Theod. F. L. **Hache**, Augustus **Davis** (JP). Rec 26 Mar 1842. [No. 1335]

1554. Page 171. 12 Feb 1842. Same to same. For the sum of $19, Lot No. 42 in Wittenberg, fronting on first street and second street, between Lot Nos. 41 & 43. Signed Henry C. **Bimpage**, Friedr. Wilh. **Barthel**, Christian Friedr. **Muller**. Test Theod. F. L. **Hache**, Augustus **Davis** (JP). Rec 26 Mar 1842. [No. 1336]

1555. Page 172. 29 Sep 1841. Thomas J. **Bishop**, John M. **Bishop**, and Redman **Philips** and Elizabeth, his wife and daughter of Resin L. **Bishop**, decd, all of Jackson Co., Ill. to same. For the sum of $90, all their right to the real and personal property of Resin L. **Bishop**, decd, late of Brazeau Twp. Signed Thomas J. **Bishop**, John **Bishop**, Redman **Philips**, Elizabeth (x) **Philips**. Test Robert **Manning**, John W. **Gray**, Augustus **Davis** (JP). Rec 26 Mar 1842. [No. 1337]

1556. Page 173. 14 Mar 1842. Peter R. **Pratte** and Mary Louise, his wife, to Valerio **Faina**. For the sum of $260, 1/2 of their right to Lot No. 20 in Perryville; conveyed by Julius C. **Smith**, admr of John **Smith**, decd, on 11 Mar 1842. Signed P. R. **Pratte**, Mary L. **Pratte** (RD). Wit John W. **Noell**, Clerk. Rec 29 Mar 1842. [No. 1338]

1557. Page 174. 3 Dec 1841. Henry **Vistler** and Mary, his wife, to Antoine Legis Gaspard **Collier** and Clotilda Virguire **Faivre**, his wife. For the sum of 175 francs, 20 acres, being the N 1/2, NE 1/4,

SW 1/4, Sec 2, Twp 34 N, Rng 10 E; and half of 40 acres divided by mutual consent of both parties. Signed Henry **Weistler**, Mary (x) **Vistler** (RD). Wit Reuben **Shelby**, JCC. Rec 30 Mar 1842. [No. 1339]

1558. Page 175. 24 Aug 1841. State of Missouri to Michael **McGinnis**. For the sum of $70, 40 acres, being the NW 1/4, SW 1/4, Sec 35. Twp 35 N, Rng 10 E; and part of the Township School Lands. Signed Th. **Reynolds**, Governor. Wit Jas. L. **Minor**, Sec of State. Rec 30 Mar 1842. [No. 1340]

1559. Page 176. 21 Mar 1842. Joseph **Pratte** to Pierre **Menard** of Randolph Co., Ill. and John Bte. **Vallee** of Ste. Genevieve Co., Mo., trading as Menard & Valle. For securing a note and the sum of $1, mortgage on two tracts; 850 arpens, more or less, purchased by Charles **Gregoire** from Charles C. **Valle** and wife, and sold by him to sd **Pratte** on 21 Jun 1837, part of a league confirmed to the heirs and representatives of Francis **Valle**, decd; and 500 to 550 arpens, more or less, known as the Roark and Reardon Tract, conveyed to sd **Pratte** by sd **Gregoire** and wife on 21 Jun 1837. Sd **Pratte** owes Menard & Valle a note for $8608.78 payable in one year with 7% interest per annum. Signed Jh. **Pratte**. Test Geo. **Pettit**, Henry **Drury** (JP). Rec 30 Mar 1842. [No. 1341]

1560. Page 178. 4 Apr 1842. Michael **Daly** and Rose, his wife, to Pierre Theodore **Boeuff**. For the sum of 2000 francs, 130.66 acres, a portion of a tract purchased by David **Crips** in his lifetime from the commissioners appointed by Circuit Court to partition the real estate of the heirs of Michael **Burns**, decd, and purchased by sd **Daly** from Joab W. **Burgee**, admr of sd **Crips**, on 5 Nov 1841. Signed Michael **Daly**, Rose **Daly** (RD). Wit John T. **Daly**, Reuben **Shelby**, JCC. Rec 4 Apr 1842. [No. 1342]

1561. Page 179. 4 Apr 1842. Jesse **Dixon** and Barbara Rebecca, his wife, to Francis L. **Jones**. For the sum of $1600 payable as $933.33 today, $333.33 by 13 Jun 1842, and $333.33 four months thereafter; four tracts in Rush Bottom, Brazeau Twp, fronting on the Mississippi River, in Sec 20, Twp 35 N, Rng 13 E; 40 acres, being the NW 1/4, SE 1/4, fractional Sec 20 in Certificate No. 3542; 79.93 acres, being three children's portions of the real estate of the legal representatives of William **Burns**, decd, and the E side, NW fractional 1/4 in Certificate No. 469; and 98.39 acres, being the NE fractional 1/4 in Certificate No. 470. The latter two tracts were entered by the representatives of William **Burns**, decd, and are the succession of Thomas J. **Finch** and Elizabeth **Finch**, formerly **Burns**, conveyed to sd **Dixon** (2:480); William **Burns** conveyed to Marshal **Dixon** (2:255), and by him to sd Jesse (3:307). Also the NE 1/4, SE 1/4, being entered by John Phillip **Edinger**, and conveyed to him by sd **Edinger** and Mary, his wife and formerly Mary **Burns**; also the succession of sd **Edinger** and wife, being 1/4 of the real estate of William **Burns**, decd, as conveyed to Jesse **Dixon** (1:421). The succession of William D. **Harrington** and Emily Ann **Burns**, now Emily Ann **Harrington**, is not included. Signed Jesse **Dixon**, Barbary **Dixon** (RD). Wit William **Farrar** Jun. (JP). Rec 4 Apr 1842. [No. 1343]

1562. Page 182. 31 Jan 1842. Merrit C. **Wilson** and Elizabeth, his wife, to James **Swan**. For the sum of $200, two tracts; 40 acres, more or less, being the SW 1/4, NW 1/4, fractional Sec 24. Twp 34 N, Rng 13 E; and 40 acres, more or less, being the SE 1/4, NW 1/4, Sec 24, Twp 34 N, Rng 13 E. Signed Merrit C. **Wilson**, Elizabeth J. **Wilson** (RD). Wit Augustus **Davis** (JP), Manerva A. **Davis**. Rec 5 Apr 1842. [No. 1344]

1563. Page 183. 7 Apr 1842. Archibald L. **Hager** to William D. **Cashion**. For the sum of $50, a 1/4 part of 120 acres, being all the real estate entered by William **Hager**, decd, and where Sally **Hager**, widow of William **Hager**, and sd **Cashion** now live; that descended to sd Archibald L. as one of the heirs of William **Hager**; subject to a life estate of Sally **Hager**. Signed Archibald L. **Hager**. Wit John W. **Noell**, Clerk. Rec 7 Apr 1842. [No. 1345]

1564. Page 184. 4 Aug 1841. Philip **Smalts** to Henry **Lukefahr**. For the sum of $160, 80 acres, being the N 1/2, NW 1/4, Sec No. 13, Twp 34 N, Rng 10 E. Signed Philip **Smalts**. Wit Mark **Brewer** (JP). Rec 12 Apr 1842. [No. 1346]

1565. Page 185. 13 Apr 1842. Thomas A. **Brown** to Nathaniel J. **Divine**. For the sum of $1, mortgage on one yoke of oxen five years old, black and white; and one bay mare nine or ten years old this spring. Sd **Brown** owes sd **Divine** $50, payable in a note as 200 bushels of corn and $4.56 due for bacon, by 15 Nov 1842. Signed Thomas A. (x) **Brown**. Wit James **Rice** (JP). Rec 13 Apr 1842. [No. 1347]

1566. Page 186. 25 Sep 1841. Robert C. **Powell** and Serinda, his wife, to Erastus **Davis**. For the sum of $400, 90.34 acres in Bois Brule Bottom, being the E 1/2, S 1/2, fractional Sec 35, Twp 37 N, Rng 10 E; conveyed to sd **Powell** by John **Logan**. Signed Robert C. **Powell**, Serinda (x) **Powell** (RD). Wit Perry **Evans** (JP). Rec 19 Apr 1842. [No. 1348]

1567. Page 187. 27 Mar 1833. Ann **Moore** to James **Rice**. For the sum of $50, 80 acres, more or less, in Survey No. 868 in Twp 35 N, Rng 11 E; being the undivided moiety of Ann **Moore** to a section of land confirmed to James **Moore** Junior, decd, her father. Signed Ann **Moore**. Wit A. H. **Puckett**, JCC. Rec 21 Apr 1842. [No. 1349]

1568. Page 187. 5 May 1834. William **Moore** to same. For the sum of $65, his undivided interest in 80 acres, more or less, being Survey No. 868 confirmed to his father, James **Moore**, son of James. Signed William **Moore**. Wit Joab W. **Burgee** (JP). Rec 21 Apr 1842. [No. 1350]

1569. Page 188. 18 Mar 1842. James F. **Swan** and Nancy, his wife, to Hallyburton **Parks**. For the sum of $500, two tracts in Sec 35, Twp 35 N, Rng 12 E; 80 acres, being the W 1/2, NE 1/4, in Certificate No. 1391, entered by Cullen **Penny** on 15 Oct 1833, and transferred by him to Thomas **Hellard**, and by him to sd **Swan** on 23 Apr 1838; and also see duplicate No. 6443 for 40 acres, the NE 1/4, SE 1/4, entered by sd **Swan** on 14 Nov 1838; less 3 acres, 3 roods, and 37 poles in the NE corner sold to Richard **Swan** on 30 Nov 1841. Signed James **Swan**, Nancy **Swan** (RD). Wit M. M. **McPherson** (JP). Rec 27 Apr 1842. [No. 1351]

1570. Page 190. 30 Apr 1842. Caleb **Hattan** to Richard **Maddock** senr. For the sum of $38, mortgage on two feather beds, clothing, and bedsteads; two bureaus; half dozen windsor chairs; and one eight day clock. Sd **Hattan** owes the debt to sd **Maddock** with 10% interest by 1 Nov next. Signed Caleb **Hatten**. Wit James **Evans**, Geo. **Vessels** (JP). Rec 30 Apr 1842. [No. 1352] [Marginal note: Full satisfaction received on 4 Jan 1844. Signed Richd. **Maddock** senor. Test Jno. W. **Noell**, Clerk.]

1571. Page 190. 29 Apr 1842. Mark **Brewer** and Mary, his wife, to James **Dunn**. For the sum of $250, 39.97 acres, being the SE 1/4, NW 1/4, Sec 27, Twp 35 N, Rng 10 E. Signed Mark **Brewer**, Mary (x) **Brewer** (RD). Wit James **Rice** (JP). Rec 30 Apr 1842. [No. 1353]

1572. Page 192. 3 Aug 1837. Daniel **O'Meara** to Ann **Hagan**. Plat of 5 acres in the SW corner of 40 acres, being the SW 1/4, SE 1/4, Sec 27, Twp 35 N, Rng 10 E; bounded on the S by sd **Hagan**, W by the public, and N & E by sd **O'Meara**. Signed Jeffrey **Power**. Rec 30 Apr 1842. [No. 1354]

1573. Page 192. 30 Apr 1842. Vincent **Hagan** to James **Dunn**. For the sum of $25, all his right to 80 acres, being the W 1/2, NE 1/4, Sec 34, Twp 35 N, Rng 10 E; that belonged to Levi **Hagan** at the time of his death. Signed Vincent (x) **Hagan**. Wit J. W. **Noell**, Clerk. Rec 30 Apr 1842. [No. 1355]

1574. Page 193. 28 Feb 1840. John **Logan** to William T. **Laville**. For the sum of $100, 100 acres in Bois Brule Bottom, part of a tract of 640 acres confirmed to John **Greenwault** Jr. by the commissioners, and where sd **Laveille** now resides; beginning on the N boundary of Jonas **Newsom**, and also bounded by Donohue under **Graham** and John **Morgan** Senr. Signed John **Logan**. Wit W. **Searcy** (JP). Rec 2 May 1842. [No. 1356]

1575. Page 194. 2 May 1842. Edward M. **Holden** to James **Rice**. For securing a note and the sum of $1, mortgage on one log chain that formerly belonged to Edward A. **Ketchum** of Ste. Genevieve Co.; two cows with young calves, one which sd **Holden** got from Willis **Ellis**, and the other from William **Perry**. Sd **Rice** is security for sd **Holden** in a note dated 29 Aug 1838 for $320, with 10% interest, and payable to Levi **Block**, Commissioner of the Road and Canal Fund. Signed Edward M. **Holden**. Wit John W. **Noell**, Clerk. Rec 2 May 1842. [No. 1357]

1576. Page 195. 12 Mar 1842. John **Hughy** and Elenor, his wife, to James A. **Woods** of Cape Girardeau Co., Mo. For the sum of $155, 40 acres, being the SW 1/4, SW 1/4, Sec 1, Twp 34 N, Rng 12 E; purchased by sd **Hughy** at the land office. Signed John **Hughy**, Elenor (x) **Hughey** (RD). Wit A. M. **McPierson** (JP). Rec 2 May 1842. [No. 1358]

1577. Page 196. 12 Apr 1840. J. M. **Odin** to Michael **McGinnis**. For the sum of $8/acre, bond to make a deed on a small portion of cultivated land on the improvement which he bought from Mr. **McBride**. Signed J. M. **Odin**. Wit O. **Claudet**. Rec 3 May 1842. [No. 1359]

1578. Page 196. 2 May 1842. Rebecca **Bishop** to Samuel T. **Donald**. For the sum of $650, 100.55 acres on the Mississippi River, being Claim No. 364 in Twp 34 N, Rng 14 E originally confirmed to Henry **Riley**, excepting 7 acres in the SE corner deeded by Resin L. **Bishop** in his lifetime; conveyed to Rebecca **Bishop** by F. J. **Hamilton**, admr of the estate of Resin L. **Bishop**, decd, on 3 Nov 1841 (4:158). Signed Rebecca (x) **Bishop**. Wit John W. **Noell**, Clerk. Rec 3 May 1842. [No. 1360]

1579. Page 197. 3 Jun 1841. Lemuel H. **Powell** of Dubuque, Ioway Terr., to James B. **Laville**. For the sum of $212, 1/7 undivided part of 202 arpens in Bois Brule Bottom, confirmed to Francis **Clark** and transferred by D. L. **Caldwell** to William **Powell**. Signed L. H. **Powell**. Wit J. M. M. **Powell**, Jas. **Griffeth**, John W. **Noell**, Clerk. Rec 3 May 1842. [No. 1361]

1580. Page 198. 3 May 1842. Hyacinthus A. **Layton** to Lewis W. **Layton**. For securing a note and the sum of $1, mortgage on one set of blacksmith's tools, one gray mare about eight years old, one falling leaf table, one set of windsor chairs, three sets of silver spoons, one clock, one cow and calf, one bedstead and bedding, and two saddles and bridles. Sd Hyacinthus owes a note for $300 to sd Lewis W. Signed Hyacinthus A. **Layton**. Test J. W. **Noell**, Clerk. Rec 3 May 1842. [No. 1362]

1581. Page 199. 10 Mar 1841. Daniel **Cline** and Leah, his wife, to Moses **Cline**. For the sum of $1251, four tracts that sd **Cline** purchased from James C. **Manning**: 420 acres on the E side of Survey No. 1243 confirmed to Joseph **Fenwick**, known as the Poplar Flat in Twp 33 & 34 N, Rng 12 & 13 E, being 1/6 of the survey, purchased by Robert S. **Manning** at Sheriff's sale, and the remainder not sold by sd **Manning** to William **Manning**; and three tracts entered by James C. **Manning** on 15 Oct 1833 in Twp 34 N, Rng 13 E; 27 acres, being the NW fractional 1/4, Sec 32, Duplicate No. 1336; 25.87 acres, being the SW fractional 1/4, Sec 29, Duplicate No. 1335; and 27.67 acres, being the SW fractional 1/4, Sec 32, Duplicate No. 1337. Signed Daniel **Cline**, Leah (x) **Cline** (RD). Wit A. M. **McPherson** (JP) Rec 4 May 1842. [No. 1363]

1582. Page 201. 22 Nov 1841. Ezra **Shelby** to Moses **Farrar**. For the sum of $1000, 370 acres, more or less, on Cinque Hommes Creek purchased by sd **Shelby** from Gabriel M. **Duvall**, late of Perry Co.; beginning at a stone standing on the line of a tract confirmed to Bernard **Layton**, and bounded in part by Benjamin **Cox** Junior. Signed Ezra **Shelby**. Wit Reuben **Shelby**, JCC. Rec 6 May 1842. [No. 1364]

1583. Page 202. 16 Oct 1841. Heirs of Jonathan **Preston**, decd, to Clement **Knott**. On decree of Circuit Court in Chancery and as per a title bond executed by sd **Preston** in his lifetime, 160 acres as described in the case of Clement **Knott** vs. Lewis **Thorp** and wife, Sarah (Sally) **Massey**, James **Preston**, Amzi **Chandler**, and Samuel **Partlet** and wife. Signed John W. **Noell**, Clerk. Rec 11 May 1842. [No. 1365]

1584. Page 203. 12 May 1842. William D. **Harrington** and Emily Ann, his wife, of St. Louis, Mo. to Francis L. **Jones**. For the sum of $450, 1/4 part of lands entered by the representatives of William **Burns**, decd, as described in a deed from Jesse **Dixon** and Barbary, his wife, to sd **Jones** on 4 Apr 1842 (4:180). Signed William D. **Harrington**, Emily A. **Harrington** (RD). Wit Christopher **Garvey** (JP). Rec 16 May 1842. [No. 1366]

1585. Page 204. 21 Jun 1832. Wilfred **Layton** and Susanna, his wife, John Baptist **Layton** Senr and Elizabeth, his wife, Ignatius **Layton** Jr and Cecilia, his wife, Ignatius **Layton** Senr and Elizabeth, his wife, Michael **Hagan** and Jane, his wife, and John **Layton** Senr, atty for Mary **Layton** and Elizabeth **Goodman**, late Elizabeth **Layton**, to Valerio **Faina**. For the sum of $123, 96 acres on the waters of Cinque Hommes Creek in The Barrens; being the most N part of 640 acres originally belonging to John **Layton** senr, decd, known as the Orphan Tract; joining Joseph **Manning**'s part of the original survey on the S between the division line and the parallel of Zechariah **Layton**. Signed Wilfred **Layton**, Susannah (x) **Layton** (RD), Ignatius **Layton**, Elizabeth (x)

Layton (RD). [John **Layton**, Elizabeth **Layton** (RD)], Michael (x) **Hagan**, Jane (x) **Hagan** (RD), Ignatius **Layton**. Wit John **Layton** (JP), James **Rice** (JP). Rec 20 May 1842. [No. 1367]

1586. Page 205. 25 May 1842. John J. **Johnson** to Reuben **Shelby**. For the sum of $269.83, deed of trust on six tracts in Twp 34 N, Rng 8 E; 40 acres, being the SW 1/4, NE 1/4, Sec 24; 40 acres, being the SE 1/4, NW 1/4, Sec 24; 40 acres, being the NW 1/4, NW 1/4, Sec 24; 40 acres, being the NW 1/4, NE 1/4, Sec 24; 40 acres, being the NE 1/4, NE 1/4, Sec 23; and 40 acres, being the NW 1/4, SE 1/4, Sec 24. Sd **Johnson** owes sd **Shelby** a bond by 25 Sep 1842, or the property is to be sold. Signed John J. (x) **Johnson**. Wit J. W. **Noell**, Clerk. Rec 25 May 1842. [No. 1368] [Marginal note: Conditions are fully satisfied on 8 Oct 1842. Signed Reuben **Shelby**, trustee. Wit John W. **Noell**, Clerk.]

1587. Page 207. 26 May 1842. John P. **Finch** to Ferdinand **Rozier** Junr, Commissioner of the Road and Canal Fund for Perry Co. For securing a debt and the sum of $1, mortgage on part of 237 acres, a tract confirmed to Tunis **Quick**, and deeded by sd **Quick** to sd **Finch** on 23 Oct 1838 (2:467); less portions sold to Clement **Knott** and John W. **Quick**. Sd **Finch** owes the fund $100 in a bond, payable in 12 months with 10% interest per annum. Signed John P. **Finch**. Wit John W. **Noell**, Clerk. Rec 26 May 1842. [No. 1369]

1588. Page 209. 28 May 1842. Joseph A. **Massey** to William L. **Kline**. For the sum of $95.24, mortgage on 160 acres, more or less, beginning at a white oak standing on the bank of the Rock Spring Branch. Sd **Massey** owes a note to sd **Kline**, due with 10% interest per annum by 25 May 1845, and dated 25 May 1842. The tract is also subject to a mortgage to James **Rice** executed on 26 Feb 1842 to secure payment of a note for $33.75 due 1 Jan 1843 with 10% interest per annum. Signed Joseph A. **Massey**. Wit James **Rice** (JP). Rec 28 May 1842. [No. 1370]

1589. Page 210. 7 Jan 1842. Henry **McAtee** Junr and Maria, his wife, to Josiah **Miles**. For the sum of $250, 50 acres, more or less, in two tracts; 28 acres, part of a tract confirmed to Jonathan **Preston**, bounded on the N by Joseph **Philips**, E by Clement **Knott**, S by Joseph Z. **Wimsett**, and W by Congress lands; and 22 acres adjoining the first tract, beginning at a stone set in the ground near two white oaks, bounded in part by Elisha **Belsha**. Signed Henry **McAtee** Jr, Maria (x) **McAtee** (RD). Test Mark **Brewer** (JP). Rec 7 Jun 1842. [No. 1371]

1590. Page 211. 13 Jun 1842. John R. **Layton** to Nereus **Layton**. For the sum of $500, 52 acres, being the NW fractional 1/4, Sec 22, Twp 36 N, Rng 10 E. Signed John R. **Layton**. Wit James **Rice** (JP). Rec 13 Jun 1842. [No. 1372]

1591. Page 212. 1 May 1842. Peter R. **Pratte** and Mary L., his wife, to Joseph **Pratte**. For the sum of $4000, five lots in Perryville; Lot No. 21 fronting on St. Marys St and Spring St; Lot No. 22 N of the first lot; Lot No. 74 fronting on North St and West St; Lot No. 32, fronting on St Marys St and Main St, except for the part sold to Martin L. **Moore** and Isaac G. **Whitworth**; and the undivided 1/2 of Lot No. 20 fronting on St Marys St and Spring St. Signed P. R. **Pratte**, Mary L. **Pratte** (RD). Wit Reuben **Shelby**, JCC. Rec 14 Jun 1842. [No. 1373]

1592. Page 213. 14 Jun 1842. John P. **Cunningham** by Sheriff Joseph D. **Simpson** to John Epse **Cowan**. For the sum of $125, 400 acres in four tracts; 160 acres, being the W 1/2, SW 1/4 and W 1/2, NW 1/4, Sec 33, Twp 35 N, Rng 10 E; 80 acres, being the W 1/2, SE 1/4, Sec 28, Twp 35 N, Rng 10 E; 80 acres, being the W 1/2, NE 1/4, Sec 7, Twp 34 N, Rng 10 E; and 80 acres, being the E 1/2, SW 1/4, Sec 11, Twp 34 N, Rng 9 E. Sold on 14 Feb 1842 on an execution issued by Circuit Court at Feb 1842 Term, on a judgment issued 9 Dec 1841 in favor of sd **Cowan** and against sd **Cunningham**. Signed Joseph D. **Simpson**, Sheriff. Wit John W. **Noell**, Clerk. Rec 14 Jun 1842. [No. 1374]

1593. Page 215. 20 Feb 1842. John Epse **Cowan** of Shannon Co., Mo. to John **Hinton** of St. Louis, Mo. For the sum of $125, the four tracts described in the preceding deed (4:213). Signed J. Epse **Cowan**. Wit Robert **Brown**, Circuit Clerk of Cape Girardeau Co., Mo. Rec 14 Jun 1842. [No. 1375]

1594. Page 216. 16 Jun 1842. William **Shannon**, decd, by Sheriff Joseph D. **Simpson** to Francis **Rice**. For the sum of $2189.33, four tracts; 640 acres in Bois Brule Bottom confirmed to sd **Shannon**, assignee of Theophilus **Hickman**, and patented to sd **Shannon** on 9 Dec 1822; 315 acres, part of Survey No. 1886 in Twp 36 N, Rng 11 E confirmed to John **Smith**; 159.66 acres, the undivided 1/2 of the SE fractional 1/4, Sec 28, Twp 37 N, Rng 11 E, patented to sd **Shannon** and Isaac **Flynn** as tenants in common on 31 May 1824; and 57 acres, being the NE fractional 1/4, Sec 28, Twp 37 N, Rng 11 E, patented to sd **Shannon** on 1 May 1824. Sold on 15 Jun 1841 on order of Circuit Court issued 15 May 1842 in case of George A. **Shannon** vs. William **Shannon**'s heirs, on petition to partition. Signed Joseph D. **Simpson**, Sheriff. Wit John W. **Noell**, Clerk. Rec 16 Jun 1842. [No. 1376]

1595. Page 220. 18 Jun 1842. Stephen **Tucker** by Sheriff Joseph D. **Simpson** to Henry **Tucker** and Richard **Maddock**. For the sum of $101, 1/2 of __ acres on Cedar Fork of Saline Creek in Sec 10, Twp 32 N, Rng 9 E, deeded by William **Hancock** and wife, to Stephen **Tucker** and ___ **Keyton**. Sold on 14 Oct 1841 on order of Circuit Court issued 15 Sep 1841, on a judgment heard before Mark **Brewer**, JP, for Henry **Tucker** and against Stephen **Tucker** for $88.50 debt and $1.62 1/2 costs. Signed Joseph D. **Simpson**, Sheriff. Wit John W. **Noell**, Clerk. Rec 18 Jun 1842. [No. 1377]

1596. Page 221. 17 Jun 1842. Archibald **Thurman** and Elizabeth, his wife, by Sheriff Joseph D. **Simpson** to John W. **Noell**. For the sum of $46, 200 acres, more or less, confirmed to William **Hickman**, Survey No. 1868 in Twp 36 N, Rng 11 & 12 E, being the interest of sd **Thurman** and Elizabeth, his wife and formerly Elizabeth **McCasland**, as willed to them by Andrew **McCasland**, decd. Sold on 15 Jun 1842 on two orders of Circuit Court issued 19 Apr 1842 and 21 Mar 1842 on two judgments; one issued 29 Jul 1840 for William **Talbot** and against sd **Thurman** for $32.35 costs; and one issued 18 Feb 1842 for sd **Talbot**, Hezekiah P. **Harris**, and Austin **Hoggard** and against sd **Thurman** and wife for $9.29 costs. Signed Joseph D. **Simpson**, Sheriff. Wit John W. **Noell**, Clerk. Rec 18 Jun 1842. [No. 1378]

1597. Page 223. 17 Jun 1842. William H. **Scudder** by Sheriff Joseph D. **Simpson** to John **Scudder**. For the sum of $10, Block No. 25, Lot No. 17, and Block No. 12 in Birmingham. Sold on 15 Jun 1842 on order of Circuit Court issued 28 Jan 1842 in favor of John **Scudder**, and against William H. **Scudder** for $81 debt, and $1.50 costs, on a judgment heard before Augustus **Davis**, JP. Signed Joseph D. **Simpson**, Sheriff. Wit John W. **Noell**, Clerk. Rec 18 Jun 1842. [No. 1379]

1598. Page 224. 17 Jun 1842. John **Dougherty** by Sheriff Joseph D. **Simpson** to Emanuel **Pratte**. For the sum of $56, 100 acres in Twp 36 N, Rng 10 E, part of Survey No. 86 confirmed to Thomas **Donohoe** under Christopher **Barnhart**. Sold on 16 Jun 1842 on order of Circuit Court issued 19 Mar 1842 in favor of John **Logan** and against sd **Dougherty** for $300 debt, and $23.25 damages, with costs. Signed Joseph D. **Simpson**, Sheriff. Wit John W. **Noell**, Clerk. Rec 18 Jun 1842. [No. 1380]

1599. Page 226. 18 Jun 1842. Joseph **Burns** by Sheriff Joseph D. **Simpson** to James A. **Beal** of Jefferson Co., Mo. For the sum of $3.25, three tracts in Sec 26, Twp 35 N, Rng 11 E; 40 acres, being the NE 1/4, SE 1/4, entered by sd **Burns**; __ acres, being the NW 1/4, SE 1/4, entered by James T. **Burns**; and __ acres, being the SE 1/4, NW 1/4, entered by Andrew R. **Burns**. Sold on 15 Jun 1842 on an execution issued by Circuit Court on 17 [Apr?] 1842 on a judgment in favor of Conrad **Ocks** and against sd **Burns** for $0.01 damages and $17.27 1/2 costs. Signed Joseph D. **Simpson**, Sheriff. Wit John W. **Noell**, Clerk. Rec 18 Jun 1842. [No. 1381]

1600. Page 228. 17 Jun 1842. James **Layton** by Sheriff Joseph D. **Simpson** to Francis J. **Zeigler**. For the sum of $19, Lot No. 64 in Perryville. Sold on 15 Jun 1842 on an execution issued by Circuit Court on 16 Mar 1842 on a judgment in favor of the State of Mo. and against sd **Layton** for $35.31 costs. Signed Joseph D. **Simpson**, Sheriff. Wit John W. **Noell**, Clerk. Rec 18 Jun 1842. [No. 1382]

1601. Page 229. 25 May 1841. Victor **Javaux** and Catharine, his wife, to John **Greener**. For the sum of $200, 40 acres, more or less, being the SW 1/4, SE 1/4, Sec 22, Twp 35 N, Rng 11 E. Signed Victor **Javaux**, Catharine **Javaux** (RD). Test Mark **Brewer** (JP), Aran **Nasslien**. Rec 20 Jun 1842. [No. 1383]

1602. Page 230. 20 Jun 1842. John **Grinner** to Kunegunda **Grinner** of St. Louis, Mo. For the sum of $200, mortgage on 40 acres, being the SW 1/4, SE 1/4, fractional Sec 22, Twp 35 N, Rng 11 E. Sd John owes sd Kunegunda $200 with legal interest by 20 Jun 1843. Signed John **Grinner**. Wit Fredek. C. **Hase**, John W. **Noell**, Clerk. Rec 20 Jun 1842. [No. 1384]

1603. Page 231. [Page 234 is used twice in the original] 22 Jan 1842. Last will and testament of Isidore **Moore** Senior, decd [was age 70 on 15 Nov last]. To his first three sons, James C., John, and Martin J., all the farm land and property they received at their respective marriages. "When I married my present wife, in 1799, we began very poor, and labored under great disadvantage, being opposed by friends on both sides. I determined to live under the frowns of no one. In the fall of 1800 we migrated for Missouri, then Upper Louisiana and settled under the Spanish government; where we obtained 510 acres of land by our settling thereon, being the first Roman Catholick family who settled in the Barrens. there being but seven other families, of any kind, then in the Barrens, except Indians. Whatever property I now possess has been acquired and preserved under the fostering hand of Providence; and through the joint exertions, care, and economy of us both, and often at great risk. My present wife, being the mother of sixteen children, thirteen of whom are alive and grown; and as I own but six slaves and three of them under thirteen years old, I think my wife should have considerable more than a child's part in the general distribution." To his son Samuel Lewis: $100 in specie to buy 80 acres where he now lives. To his daughter Sarah **Layton**: 75 acres on which she holds an unacknowledged conveyance, being the W 1/2, SE 1/4, Sec 13, Twp 34 N, Rng 11 E patented by him on 7 Apr 1829 in Certificate No. 794, except 5 acres of the S end that includes the spring and buildings of his son Stephen Theodore, which is to go to him. To his son Stephen Theodore: 77 1/2 acres of 160 acres patented to him in Certificate No. 2727 on 7 Mar 1827, as claimed under John P. **Chartier**, being the W 1/2, NE 1/4 and E 1/2, SW 1/4, Sec 24, Twp 34 N, Rng 11 E. To his daughter Martina: the remainder of this tract, being 82 1/2 acres. To his son Leo: 80 acres, being the W 1/2, NW 1/4, Sec 24, patented by him in Certificate No. 806 on 7 Apr 1829. A tract of 439 1/2 acres, the remainder of 640 acres in Twp 35 N, Rng 10 & 11 E, patented to him as assignee of Josephus **Tucker** as Survey No. 2170, Certificate No. 1014 on 30 Mar 1826; 200 1/2 acres having been sold to the heirs of Nicholas **Tucker**, decd, has been divided into 4 pieces, and any two legatees may request a resurvey. Of this tract, the NE 1/4, just under 110 acres, including a pond, spring, and plantation where she now lives is to go to his daughter Elizabeth **Cissell**; the NW 1/4 to his son Isidore; the SW 1/4 to his daughter Mary **Manning**; and the SE 1/4 to his daughter Ann **Manning**. To his single daughter Eulalia, the N 1/2 of 240 acres, including 160 acres, a preemption patented in Certificate No. 783 on 7 Apr 1829, being the SE 1/4, Sec 16, Twp 34 N, Rng 11 E; and 80 acres of the Fenwick claim adjoining from E to W and S of the Sec line. To his single daughter Christina: the S 1/2 of the preceding tract. To his single son Lewis William: 240 acres, including the spring, orchard, and buildings where he now lives; including 80 acres, being the W 1/2. SW 1/4, Sec 15, Twp 34 N, Rng 11 E in Certificate No. 795; 40 acres adjoining from E to W and S of the Sec line; and 120 acres that is part of the Fenwick claim, along with the E 1/2, SW 1/4 and SW 1/4, SE 1/4, Sec 15 patented on 10 Aug 1841; provided he live on the farm and care for his parents and see that they are not misused by the slaves. To his son Austin: 105 acres in the SE corner of the Fenwick claim, including where sd Austin now lives, being the E 1/2, NW 1/4, Sec 22, Twp 34 N, Rng 11 E; and part of 425 acres confirmed to sd Isidore as assignee of Thomas **Fenwick**. There is 120 acres, more or less, remaining from the Fenwick tract, being the SW 1/4, NW 1/4, Sec 22 and S 1/2, NE 1/4, Sec 21 on the S boundary. This is to be sold, and the money divided as follows so that they get portions nearly equal to Austin: 29 acres price to his daughter Sarah, 24 acres price to his sons Samuel L. and Leo, 21 1/2 acres price to his son Stephen Theodore, 21 1/2 acres price to his daughter Martina. To all his children by his present wife: the proceeds of the sale of the SE 1/2 of 510.42 acres on Cinque Hommes Creek, in Certificate No. 1001 dated 5 Nov 1824; the other 1/2 having been previously sold. To his wife Leah: his negro woman **Lucinda**, about 36 years old, to be sold at the death of his wife to one of his heirs or another Roman Catholick, with the proceeds to be equally divided among his children of his present wife except the single females; his pleasure carriage and the apparatus and horse, also to be sold at her death on the same terms; her side saddle; loom and gears; one table; one bedstead, bed, and bedding of her choice; her armed chair; all the poultry, turkeys and geese and Dunghill fowls, as much of the grain on hand or growing, hay and fodder, meat or hogs, coffee, sugar, and salt for one year's provision for the family; the money she claims as her own; $100 work of property selected by her after appraisement, including household and kitchen furniture, livestock, farming utensils, or other implements of industry. To his daughter Eulalia: his negro girl **Margaret** born on 15 Aug 1832, one horse creature, cow and calf, couple of sheep, sow and pigs, and $100 of appraised articles. To his daughters Christina and

Martina: his two mulatto slaves, a woman named **Lucy** 19 years old on 14 Nov last, hard of hearing and speaks with much difficulty, and a female child names **Agnes** born on 17 Jan 1841. If **Linda** should die before her mistress, then **Lucy** and **Margaret** are to wait on her. To his daughters Christina and Martina: $100 each in property, with each to have beds as other daughters have been, Martina is to have a good side saddle, bridle, and martingale worth about $22. His negro man **Josiah** 39 years old, and his boy **Henry** about 13 years old are to be sold, but not out of the county on account of his wife, with the proceeds to be divided among his children except the single females, with his sons James C., John, and Martin J. getting 1/2 shares; and if John dies without children, then his part is to be divided among James C. and Martin J. for the education of their children. The remainder of his property to be parceled in equal shares among his wife and all her children, or sold for their benefit. All his books are to be equally divided among his children. His wife is to have sole possession of the lower room on the E end of the dwelling house, and the girls the upper room which they now occupy so long as they remain single. Of the money on hand, $50 is to be paid for church services, one high mass, and distributed among the clergy for private services. "My children are numerous, some have rendered more service than others; some have been more expense and occasioned more trouble, of body and mind than others; Therefore I have bequeathed my property to suit my own inclinations, and if any of the heirs should be dissatisfied, take Counsel of a lawyer, and try to destroy the will, or any part thereof, such person, or persons, shall forfeit all interest therein." Alexius **Manning**, Martin **Layton**, and his son Lewis William are appointed executors. Signed Isidore **Moore**. Wit John W. **Noell**, Ferdinand **Rozier** Jr., James **Rice**, County Court Clerk. Rec 20 Jun 1842. [No. 1385]

1604. Page 237. 21 Jun 1842. James **Woods**, William T. **Christy**, and James **Christy**, trading as Woods Christy & Co., to Hyman **Block**. Power of attorney to sell all the goods, wares, and merchandise now in the store formerly kept by sd **Block** as per a bill of sale from sd **Block** dated 19 Jun 1842; one negro woman **Diueha**(?); three cows and two calves; two mares and one horse; six sheep; and two hogs. Sd **Block** is to receive 15 % of the amount of sale, and is to pay the monies received to Moses **Block** and **Avery**. Signed Woods Christy & Co. per Robert **Woods**, Hyman **Block**. Wit John W. **Noell**, Clerk. Rec 21 Jun 1842. [No. 1386]

1605. Page 238. 21 Jun 1842. Joseph **Sadler** and Elvrittia, his wife, to James **Philips**. For the sum of $74.48, 59.58 acres, part of the E 1/2, NW 1/4, Sec 7, Twp 35 N, Rng 12 E, and the N part of a tract entered by sd **Sadler** in Certificate No. 7509. Signed Joseph **Sadler**, Elvrittia **Sadler** (RD). Test F. A. **Abernathy**, Robert A. **Farrar**, William **Farrar** (JP). Rec 22 Jun 1842. [No. 1387]

1606. Page 239. 20 Jun 1842. Same and same to John **Sadler**. For the sum of $25, 20 acres off the S end of the E 1/2, NW 1/4, Sec 7, Twp 35 N, Rng 12 E; part of a tract of 79.58 acres entered by Joseph **Sadler** as Certificate No. 7509. Signed Joseph **Sadler**, Elvrittia **Sadler** (RD). Test F. A. **Abernathy**, Robert A. **Farrar**, William **Farrar** (JP). Rec 22 Jun 1842. [No. 1388]

1607. Page 241. 1 Jun 1842. William Y. K. **Warren** and Elizabeth, his wife, to Ceron E. **Delassues**. For the sum of $132, mortgage on 80 acres in Twp 35 N, Rng 11 E; being the SE 1/4, SW 1/4, Sec 12 and NW 1/4, NE 1/4, Sec 13; purchased by sd **Warren** in the land office on 23 May last. Sd **Warren** owes a note of even date, due in 12 months with 10% interest per annum. Signed William Y. K. (x) **Warren**, Elizabeth (x) **Warren** (RD). Wit Reuben **Shelby**, JCC. Rec 27 Jun 1842. [Inserted receipt: Full satisfaction received on 29 May 1849. Signed C. E. **Delassus**. Wit J. W. **Noell**, Clerk.] [No. 1389]

1608. Page 242. 14 Apr 1842. Peter **Ryne** and Elizabeth, his wife, to Emanuel **Costner**. For the sum of $12, 5 3/4 acres, more or less, being the SE corner, SW 1/4, NE 1/4, Sec 34, Twp 34 N, Rng 11 E; beginning at a post oak 18 inches in diameter. Signed Peter **Rhyne**, Elizabeth (x) **Rhyne** (RD). Wit Reuben **Shelby**, JCC. Rec 4 Jul 1842. [No. 1390]

1609. Page 243. 25 Jun 1842. John J. **Johnson** to Robert S. **Manning**. For the sum of $257, mortgage on five tracts in Sec 24, Twp 34 N, Rng 8 E; 40 acres, being the SW 1/4, NE 1/4; 40 acres, being the SE 1/4, NW 1/4; 40 acres, being the NW 1/4, NW 1/4; 40 acres, being the NW 1/4, NE 1/4; and 40 acres, being the NE 1/4, NE 1/4; subject to the lieu of a deed of trust by sd **Johnson** to Reuben **Shelby** dated 25 May 1842 (4:205). Sd **Johnson** owes a note of even date, with interest, by 25 Jun 1842. Signed John J. (x) **Johnson**. Wit James **Rice** (JP). Rec 4 Jul 1842. [No. 1391]

1610. Page 244. 15 Jun 1842. William **Burns**, admr of David **Burns**, decd, to James T. **Hamilton**. For the sum of $1360, 465 acres in the edge of Bois Brule Bottom, being Survey No. 142, Twp 36 N, Rng 11 E originally confirmed to John R. **McLaughlin**, and conveyed by him to James **Burns**, father of David **Burns**, decd. The tract is "one of the most valuable stock farms in Perry Co." and includes a double log dwelling house, kitchen, stable, cribs, apple orchard, and about 75 acres in cultivation, meadow, etc. Sold in Aug 1841 on order of County Court issued 3 May 1841 on petition for sale of sd real estate to pay debts of the estate. Signed William B. **Burns**, admr of David **Burns**, decd. Wit James **Rice** (JP). Rec 5 Jul 1842. [No. 1392]

1611. Page 246. 15 Jun 1842. James T. **Hamilton** and Margret, his wife, to Perry Co. for the benefit of the inhabitants of Twp 36 N, Rng 12 E. For the sum of $700, mortgage on 465 acres as described in the preceding deed. Sd **Hamilton** owes a note, with William **Manning** and Robert **Manning**, with interest, due in 12 months with 10% interest per annum. Signed James T. **Hamilton**, Margaret M. **Hamilton** (RD). Wit Reuben **Shelby**, JCC. Rec 5 Jul 1842. [No. 1393]

1612. Page 248. 5 Jul 1842. Augustine A. **Layton** to Ferdinand **Rozier** Junr. For the sum of $41.27, mortgage on 3 1/2 acres of tobacco and 6 acres of corn growing in the improvement of John B. **Layton** Senior on the waters of Saline Creek. Augustine **Layton** owes a note dated 23 Sep 1841, due on 25 Dec 1842, with 10% interest per annum from 24 Sep 1841. Signed Augustine A. **Layton**. Wit James **Rice** (JP). Rec 5 Jul 1842. [Marginal note: Full satisfaction received on 9 Sep 1843. Signed Ferdinand **Rozier** Jr. Test Jno. W. **Noell**, Clerk.] [No. 1394]

1613. Page 249. 25 Jun 1842. John W. **Noell** and Mary, his wife, to Jacob L. **Burrows**. For the sum of $186, Lot No. 66 in Perryville. Signed John W. **Noell**, Mary A. **Noell** (RD). Wit Reuben **Shelby**, JCC. Rec 5 Jul 1842. [No. 1395]

1614. Page 250. 9 May 1842. Peter J. **Tucker** and Mary, his wife, to Alfred H. **Puckett**. For the sum of $1, 16.36 acres, more or less, being the fractional Sec 32, Twp 37 N, Rng 11 E. Signed Peter J. **Tucker**, Mary (x) **Tucker** (RD). Wit James **Rice** (JP). Rec 5 Jul 1842. [No. 1396]

1615. Page 251. 6 Jul 1842. John **Wilhelm** and Catharine, his wife, to John C. **Rabold**. For the sum of $54, 40 acres, being the SW 1/4, SE 1/4, Sec 35, Twp 34 N, Rng 12 E. Signed John **Wilhelm**, Catharine (x) **Wilhelm** (RD). Wit John W. **Noell**. Clerk. Rec 6 Jul 1842. [No. 1397]

1616. Page 252. 6 Jul 1842. Henry **McAtee** and Maria, his wife, to Ferdinand **Rozier** Junr. For the sum of $15, 10 acres off the S end, W 1/2, SW 1/4, Sec 7, Twp 34 N, Rng 11 E. Signed Henry **McAtee**, Mariah (x) **McAtee** (RD). Wit John W. **Noell**, Clerk. Rec 6 Jul 1842. [No. 1398]

1617. Page 253. __ ___ 1841. William **Tucker**, guardian of Rosella **Vessels**, to Samuel **Kline**. For the sum of $40, the undivided interest of sd Rosella in the estate of her father Charles **Vessels**, decd, including two tracts; 150.27 acres, being the SE fractional 1/4, Sec 22, Twp 36 N, Rng 10 E; and 26 acres, more or less, in Twp 36 N, Rng 10 E. Signed William **Tucker**. Wit Henry **Drury** (JP). Rec 8 Jul 1842. [No. 1399]

1618. Page 254. 8 Jul 1842. Joseph **Pratte** to George **Collier** of St. Louis, Mo. and James **Fassett**, Theodore L. **Fassett**, and Alfred **Fassett**, trading as James Fassett & Co. in Philadelphia, Pa. For the sum of $1 to sd Collier, deed of trust on eight parcels; 600 acres, more or less, known as Pratte's Landing, where sd **Pratte** now resides, bounded on the N by St. Lero Creek, E by the Mississippi River, and S & W by John **Burgett** and lands formerly owned by Joseph **Donohue**, purchased by sd **Pratte** of Amos **Bird** on 3 Aug 1830; 500 arpents, more or less, being Lot No. 17 in the old mine concession in Washington Co., Mo., granted to Antoine **Govero** and now owned by sd **Pratte**; 990 arpents, being Lot No. 4 in Perry and Ste. Genevieve Co., part of one league square granted to Francis **Valle** and confirmed to his heirs on 4 Jul 1836, bounded on the S by Lot No. 5 owned by sd **Pratte**, E by Lot Nos. 3 & 6 belonging to Robert T. **Brown** and Francis **Valle**, W by Bernard **Pratte**, and N by unknown; Lot Nos. 21, 22, 74, 32 (except the part sold to Martin L. **Moore** and Isaac G. **Whitworth**), and the undivided 1/2 of No. 20 in Perryville, as deeded by Peter **Pratte** and wife to Joseph **Pratte** on 1 May 1842. Joseph **Pratte** and Emanuel **Pratte**, trading as Joseph **Pratte** & Son, owe three notes of even date to James **Fassett** & Co. for $3701.99, one payable in six months, one in 12 months, and one in 18 months from this date with 10% interest per annum; to be paid or sd **Collier** will sell the lands to pay them. Signed Joseph **Pratte**. Test Jno. W. **Noell**, Clerk. Rec 9 Jul 1842. [No. 1400]

1619. Page 256. 16 Jul 1842. George **Bergman** to John Conrad **Ockes**. For the sum of $66, 40 acres, being the SW 1/4, SW 1/4, Sec 28, Twp 35 N, Rng 11 E; purchased by sd **Bergman** of Martin **Intres** and wife on 28 Jan 1842 (4:162). Signed George **Bergmann**. Wit John W. **Noell**, Clerk. Rec 16 Jul 1842. [No. 1401]

1620. Page 257. 18 Jul 1842. William **Winfield** to John **Logan**. For the sum of $1 and securing a note, mortgage on 200 acres originally confirmed to Tunis **Quick**, conveyed by him to John W. **Quick**, sold by the admr of John W. **Quick** to Peter R. **Pratte**, and sold by sd **Pratte** and wife to sd **Winfield**. Sd **Winfield** owes sd **Logan** $90 in a note of even date payable on 1 Nov next with interest. The tract is also subject to a mortgage to Clement **Knott** dated 13 Nov 1841 (4:88). Signed William **Winfield**. Wit John W. **Noell**, Clerk. Rec 18 Jul 1842. [No. 1402]

1621. Page 259. 19 Jul 1842. James **Reddick** to Ferdinand **Rozier** Jr. For the sum of $300, deed of trust on 86 acres, more or less, out of 640 acres confirmed to Joseph **Manning** as Survey No. 840; beginning at the NW corner of 180 acres sold to John B. **Moranville** out of the same survey; and bounded by a piece sold by sd **Reddick** to John **Timon**. Sd **Reddick** owes a bond of even date to sd **Rozier**, due by 19 Jul 1843 with interest; and the property is to be sold by sd **Rozier** if the debt of interest is not paid, with any overplus to go to sd **Reddick**. Signed James **Reddick**. Wit Firman Andrew **Rozier**, Reuben **Shelby**, JCC. Rec 19 Jul 1842. [Marginal note: full satisfaction received on 28 Jan 1848. Signed Ferdinand **Rozier** Jur. Test J. W. **Noell**, Recorder.] [No. 1403]

1622. Page 260. 7 Sep 1840. Thomas **Anselm** and Teriece, his wife, formerly Tereice **Kelly**, to Jacob **Shoults**. For the sum of $150, mortgage on 40 acres, being the NW 1/4, NW 1/4, Sec 32, Twp 34 N, Rng 12 E; entered by Terrice **Kelle** on 12 May 1840 as No. 7727. Sd **Anselm** owes sd **Shoults** a note, due two years after date with 6% interest from this date. Signed Thomas **Anselm**, Terrice **Anselm** (RD). Test Alonzo **Abernathy**, JCC. Rec 19 Jul 1842. [No. 1404]

1623. Page 262. 16 Oct 1841. John B. **Pelletier** and Sally, his wife, to Ferdinand **Rozier** Jr. For securing a debt and the sum of $1, deed of trust on 71.56 acres, more or less, being the NE fractional 1/4, Sec 2, Twp 35 N, Rng 10 E. Sd **Pelletier** owes sd **Rozier** a note of even date for $100, and sd **Rozier** is to sell the land if sd **Pelletier** does not pay it. Signed John B. (x) **Pelletier** Sen. Sally (x) **Pelletier** (RD). Wit James **Rice** (JP). Rec 19 Jul 1842. [Marginal note: Full satisfaction received on 31 Jan 1844. Signed Ferdinand **Rozier** Jr. Wit J. W. **Noell**, Clerk.] [No. 1405]

1624. Page 264. 21 Jul 1842. Jacob **Shults** to James **Elmore**. Power of attorney to rent and manage 80 acres, being the W 1/2, NW 1/4, Sec 20, Twp 3[4] N, Rng 11 E; deeded by John B. **Cissell** and wife to sd **Shults** on 24 Aug 1840 (3:386). Sd Shults is going to absent himself from Perry Co. for a time. Signed Jacob **Shults**. Wit John W. **Noell**, Clerk. Rec 21 Jul 1842. [No. 1406]

1625. Page 265. 1 Jul 1842. George **Bergman** to Leonard **Fate**. For the sum of $250, five tracts in Sec 17, Twp 35 N, Rng 11 E and the crops now on the tracts; 40 acres, being the NE 1/4, SW fractional 1/4; 40 acres, being the NW 1/4, SE 1/4; 33.64 acres, being the NW fractional 1/4; and the undivided 1/2 of 80 acres, part of a tract granted to James **Moore**, son of James **Moore**, conveyed by John **Manning** and Ann, his wife, to Adam **Klobe** and sd **Bergman** on 28 Jul 1838. Signed George **Bergmann**. Wit James **Evans**, George **Hooss**, John. W. **Noell**, Clerk. Rec 22 Jul 1842. [No. 1407]

1626. Page 266. 1 Jul 1842. Same to same. For the sum of $91, one black mare about 10 years old ($40), two cows and calves ($20), two steers ($10), one heifer at $4.50, about 20 hogs ($15), one bee gum ($1.50). Signed George **Bergman**. Wit James **Evans**, George **Hooss**, John W. **Noell**, Clerk. Rec 22 Jul 1842. [No. 1408]

1627. Page 267. 19 May 1836. Joseph J. **James** and Mary Elizabeth, his wife, to Ferdinand **Rozier**. For the sum of $10, Lot

No. 72 in Perryville. Signed Joseph J. **James**, Mary Elizabeth (x) **James** (RD). Test Benjamin **Davis** (JP), Peter **Tucker** Senr. Rec 26 Jul 1842. [No. 1409]

1628. Page 268. 26 Jul 1842. Joseph **Cissell** and Elizabeth, his wife, to Joseph D. **Simpson**. For the sum of $880, just under 110 acres, the NE corner of a tract confirmed to Josephus **Tucker** as Survey No. 2170 in Twp 35 N, Rng 10 & 11 E; as devised by Isidore **Moore** Sr., decd, to his daughter Elizabeth **Cissell** (4:231); including the pond spring and plantation where sd **Cissell** now resides; and bounded in part by Michael **Tucker**. Signed Joseph **Cissell** Jr., Elizabeth **Cissell**. Wit James **Rice**, County Court Clerk. Rec 26 Jul 1842. [No. 1410]

1629. Page 269. 26 Jul 1842. John **Greener** and Kunnigunda, his wife, to Kunnigunda **Greener**. For the sum of $200, two tracts in Sec 22, Twp 35 N, Rng 11 E; 40 acres, being the SW 1/4, SE 1/4; and 40 acres, being the SE 1/4, SE 1/4. Signed John **Greener**, Kunnigunda **Greener** (RD). Test John W. **Noell**, Clerk. Rec 27 Jul 1842. [No. 1411]

1630. Page 271. 28 Jul 1842. Anthony **Schmoele** to Adolph **Yaeger**. For securing a debt and the sum of $1, mortgage on two cows and calves, 14 hogs, crop of wheat and 10 or 12 loads of straw, 3000 bundles of oats, 10 acres of corn growing in the field, one copper kettle, one cast kettle, and one large plow; all now in the possession of sd **Schmoele** on the farm of sd **Yaeger** purchased from John **Hoffman**. Sd **Schmoele** owes sd **Yaeger** $60 in a note dated 24 May 1842, payable one day after date with interest. Signed Anthony **Schmoele**. Wit John W. **Noell**, Clerk. Rec 28 Jul 1842. [No. 1412]

1631. Page 272. 17 Jun 1842. John P. **Cunningham** by Sheriff Joseph D. **Simpson** to Richard B. **Lee**. For the sum of $96, 200 acres in three tracts; 80 acres, being the W 1/2, NE 1/4, Sec 7, Twp 34 N, Rng 10 E; 40 acres, being the NE 1/4, NE 1/4, Sec 35, Twp 35 N, Rng 9 E; and 80 acres, being the W 1/2, SE 1/4, Sec 28, Twp 35 N, Rng 10 E. Sold on 15 Jun 1842 on an execution issued 4 Mar 1842 by Circuit Court on a judgment in favor of sd **Lee** and against sd **Cunningham** for $393.10 with costs. Signed Joseph D. **Simpson**, Sheriff. Wit John W. **Noell**, Clerk. Rec 30 Jul 1842. [No. 1413]

1632. Page 274. 17 Jun 1842. Same by same to same. For the sum of $1, 80 acres, being the E 1/2, S_ 1/4, Sec 11, Twp 34 N, Rng 9 E. Sold on 15 Jun 1842 on an execution issued 4 Mar 1842 by Circuit Court on a judgment in favor of sd **Lee** and against sd **Cunningham** for $393.10 with costs. Signed Joseph D. **Simpson**, Sheriff. Wit John W. **Noell**, Clerk. Rec 30 Jul 1842. [No. 1414]

1633. Page 275. 25 Jul 1842. Thomas **Anselm** and Terice, his wife, to Jacob **Sults**. For the sum of $150, 40 acres, being the NW 1/4, NW 1/4, Sec 32, Twp 34 N, Rng 12 E; and the same entered on 12 May 1840 as No. 7727. Signed Thomas **Anselm**, Lerice **Anselm** (RD). Wit Alonzo **Farrar**, Robert A. **Farrar**, William **Farrar** (JP). Rec 1 Aug 1842. [No. 1415]

1634. Page 276. 26 May 1840. Singleton H. **Kimmel** and Sarah, his wife, of Philadelphia, Pa. to John Hermon **Dolle**. For the sum of $1300, 508.77 acres in four tracts; 140 acres, being Lot Nos. 6, 7, & 8, NW 1/4, Sec 6, Twp 33 N, Rng 12 E; 148.77 acres, being Lot No. 6, NE 1/4, Sec 1, Twp 33 N, Rng 11 E; 80 acres, being Lot No. 5, NE 1/4, Sec 33, Twp 33 N, Rng 11 E; and 40 acres, being the SE 1/4, SW 1/4, Sec 36, Twp 34 N, Rng 11 E. Signed Singleton H. **Kimmel**, Sarah G. **Kimmel**. Wit Jno. **Swift**, Mayor of Philadelphia, Jno. B. **Kenney**. Rec 1 Aug 1842. [No. 1416]

1635. Page 278. 23 Jun 1842. Joseph **Cowan** and George W. **Cowan** to Elias **Barber**. For the sum of $180, mortgage on three parcels in Twp 34 N, Rng 13 E; 72.78 acres, being the SW 1/4, NW 1/4, Sec 4 and the SE 1/4, NE 1/4, Sec 5; 36.69 acres, being the NW 1/4, NW 1/4, Sec 4; and 36.15 acres, being the NE 1/4, NE 1/4, Sec 5. Sd **Cowans** owe a note to sd **Barber**, payable one day after date and drawing 10% interest, due in two years. Signed Joseph **Cowan**, George W. **Cowan**. Wit A. M. **McPherson** (JP). Rec 3 Aug 1842. [Marginal note: Full satisfaction received on 7 May 1849. Signed Elias **Barber**. Wit J. W. **Noell**, Recorder.] [No. 1417]

1636. Page 279. 5 Feb 1842. Report of the Commissioners to partition land of William **Flynn**, decd. Divided on order of Circuit Court issued 15 Oct 1841 in Case No. 641, John E. **Burgett** and Mary C., his wife, formerly Mary **Flynn**, vs. the other heirs of William **Flynn**, decd, on petition to partition; Sarah C. **Flynn** and Malissa **Flynn**, minor daughters of William **Flynn**, decd, represented by their guardian James **Rice**. Mary C. **Burgett**, formerly Mary C. **Flynn**, Sarah C. **Flynn**, and Malissa **Flynn** each get 1/3 each of two tracts. The first tract is 211.67 acres, being Survey No. 1310 patented to William **Flynn**; Lot No. 1 to Mary C. **Burgett**, 64.37 acres, beginning at the lower corner on the bank of the river; Lot No. 2 to Sarah C. **Flynn**, 68.53 acres, beginning on the bank of the river at the upper corner of Lot No. 1; and Lot No. 3 to Malissa **Flynn**, 78.87 acres, beginning at the upper corner of Lot No. 2. The second is 78.30 acres, being the NE fractional 1/4, Sec 20 and SE fractional 1/4, Sec 17, Twp 37 N, Rng 11 E and the undivided 1/2 of 27.77 acres, being the SW fractional 1/4, Sec 17, Twp 37 N, Rng 11 E. (John and Mary C. **Burgett** are entitled to the other 1/2 of the latter tract.); Lot No. 4 to John and Mary C. **Burgett**, 38.03 acres (13.88 acres of the last tract and 24.15 being the 1/3 part of the second tract), beginning at the corner of Secs 17, 18, 19, & 20; Lot No. 5 to Sarah C. **Flynn**, 30.28 acres, beginning at the lower corner of Lot No. 4 on the main river; and Lot No. 6 to Malissa **Flynn**, 37.70 acres, beginning at the lowest point on the Island on the main river. Signed Francis **Clark**, Caleb H. **Perrin**. Wit John W. **Noell**, Clerk. Rec 5 Aug 1842. [No. 1418]

1637. Page 283. 8 Aug 1842. Edward **Harter** and Mary, his wife, to Jacob **Shoults**, late of New Orleans, La. For the sum of $200, 80 acres, more or less, being the SE 1/4, SW 1/4, and the SW 1/4, SE 1/4, Sec 25, Twp 34 N, Rng 10 E. Signed Edward **Harter**, Mary **Harter** (RD). Wit James **Rice** (JP). Rec 8 Aug 1842. [No. 1419]

1638. Page 284. 9 Aug 1842. Gustavus **Pfau** to Johann A. G. **Estel**. For the sum of $30, 24 acres, beginning at the SW corner, NW 1/4, NW 1/4, Sec 26, Twp 34 N, Rng 13 E; deeded by Henry C. **Bimpage** to sd **Pfau** on 18 Nov 1840. Signed Gustav **Pfau**. Wit John W. **Noell**, Clerk. Rec 9 Aug 1842. [No. 1420]

1639. Page 285. 12 Aug 1842. Isidore **Hagan** of Ste. Genevieve Co., Mo. to James **Dunn**. For the sum of $25, all his right and interest to lands that Levi **Hagan** possessed at the time of his death; being 80 acres, the W 1/2, NE 1/4, Sec 34, Twp 35 N, Rng 10 E. Signed Isidore **Hagan**. Test J. W. **Noell**, Clerk. Rec 12 Aug 1842. [No. 1421]

1640. Page 286. 13 Aug 1842. Joseph D. **Simpson** and Mary, his wife, to Joseph **Cissell** Jr. For the sum of $900, just under 110 acres, more or less, the NE corner of Survey No. 2170 confirmed to Josephus **Tucker** in Twp 35 N, Rng 10 & 11 E; extending along the E boundary S to Nicholas **Tucker**'s line. Signed Joseph D. **Simpson**, Mary **Simpson** (RD). Wit James **Rice** (JP). Rec 13 Aug 1842. [No. 1422]

1641. Page 287. 22 Aug 1842. James **Philips** and Elizabeth, his wife, and Joseph **Sadler** and Elvrette, his wife, to Reuben **Shelby**. For the sum of $100, 79.585 acres, being the E 1/2, NW 1/4, Sec 7, Twp 35 N, Rng 12 E; except for the portion conveyed by Joseph **Sadler** to John **Sadler** on 20 Jun 1842 (4:239). Elizabeth (x) **Philips** (RD), Joseph **Sadler**, Elvirittia **Sadler** (RD). Wit John W. **Noell**, Clerk. Rec 22 Aug 1842. [No. 1423]

1642. Page 288. 22 Aug 1842. Joseph **Sadler** and Elvrittia, his wife, to John **Sadler**. For the sum of $25, 20 acres off the S end, E 1/2, NW 1/4, Sec 7, Twp 35 N, Rng 12 E; running by a due E & W line. Signed Joseph **Sadler**, Elvrittia **Sadler** (RD). Wit John W. **Noell**, Clerk. Rec 22 Aug 1842. [No. 1424]

1643. Page 289. 23 Aug 1842. Alonzo **Abernathy**, execr of the last will and testament of Henry C. C. **Tate**, decd, to John W. **Noell**. For the sum of $206, 120 acres, being the undivided half of the E 1/2, SE 1/4, and SE 1/4, NW 1/4, Sec 32, Twp 35 N, Rng 11 E. There is a new grist mill on the 40-acre tract known as Noell's and Tate's Mill. Sold on 14 Jun 1842 on order of County Court issued 2 May 1842 for sale of sd land to pay debts of the estate. Signed Alonzo **Abernathy**, execr of the last will and testament of H. C. C. **Tate**, decd. Wit James **Rice** (JP). Rec 23 Aug 1842. [No. 1425]

1644. Page 291. 2 Aug 1842. James T. **Sweringen** and Martha Jane, his wife, of St. Louis Co. to James **Steel** of Crawford Co., Mo. For the sum of $800, 100 acres in Bois Brule Bottom; acquired by Andrew H. **Tucker** and wife of William **Flynn** and wife, Josephus **Tucker** and wife, Isaac **Hill** and wife, and George **McNew** and wife on 3 Aug 1836 (3:240); sold by sd **Tucker** and wife to S. A. **Coale**, trustee, by him to C. C. **Zeigler** (3:178), and by him to sd **Sweringen** (3:227). Signed J. T. **Sweringen**, Martha J. **Sweringen** (RD). Wit Jas. H. **Milburn**, Dep Clerk of St. Louis Co., Mo. Rec 24 Aug 1842. [No. 1426]

1645. Page 293. 26 Aug 1842. Vincent **Hagan**, Benjamin **Cambron** and Adela, his wife, John W. **Tucker** and Christina, his wife, Pius **Hagan** and Mary, his wife, George W. **Hagan** and Nancy, his wife, and Agnes **Hagan** to Lewis **Cissell**. For the sum of $325, three tracts in Sec 8, Twp 35 N, Rng 10 E, all patented by Wilfred **Hagan**; 14.38 acres, being the SW fractional 1/4, patented on 15 Jul 1825; 40 acres, being the NW 1/4, SE 1/4, patented on 5 Dec 1836 in Receipt No. 4527; and 40 acres, being the NE 1/4, SE 1/4, entered on 31 Jan 1838 in Receipt No. 6022. Signed Vincent **Hagan**, Benjamin (x) **Cambron**, Adela (x) **Cambron** (RD), John W. **Tucker**, Christina (x) **Tucker** (RD), Pius (x) **Hagan**, Mary (x) **Hagan** (RD), G. W. **Hagan**, Nancy (x) **Hagan** (RD), Agnes (x) **Hagan**. Wit John W. **Noell**, Clerk. Rec 26 Aug 1842. [No. 1427]

1646. Page 295. 11 Jun 1842. Thomas **McAtee** and Mary, his wife, to Joseph **Souter**. For the sum of $29, 22.36 acres, beginning 10 chains N of the half mile corner between Secs 1 & 12, Twp 34 N, Rng 10 E. Signed Thomas **McAtee**, Mary **McAtee** (RD). Wit R. **Shelby**, JCC, Leonard **Fath**. Rec 29 Aug 1842. [No. 1428]

1647. Page 296. 22 Aug 1842. Joseph S. **Pease**, Lewis G. **Irving**, and Henry L. **Pease**, trading as Joseph S. Pease & Co. in St. Louis, Mo., to William **Paulding** of New York, N. Y. For the sum of $2250, their right to a mortgage from Charles **McKinstry** to George **McKinstry**, executed on 10 Jun 1840; and assigned to Joseph S. Pease & Co. by George **McKinstry** (3:328, 3:451). Signed Lewis G. **Irving**, Joseph S. **Pease**, Henry L. **Pease**. Wit Jas. B. **Walsh**, Dep. Clerk of St. Louis Co. Rec 29 Aug 1842. [No. 1429]

1648. Page 297. 29 Aug 1842. John **Hutchings** and Elizabeth **Horrell**. Marriage contract. Sd **Horrell** wishes to retain all rights to her real and personal property and to any property she obtains after the marriage. This includes 40 acres, being the SW 1/4, SW 1/4, Sec 16, Twp 34 N, Rng 11 E: and her dower right in the estate of her late husband, Henry **Horrel**, decd, including 40 acres, being the SE 1/4, SE 1/4, Sec 17, Twp 34 N, Rng 11 E, two horses, nine cattle, seven sheep, hogs, five beds and bedding, one beauro, two tables, one Yankey clock, and 1/3 of 20 acres of corn growing on the farm. They are both liable for any of their own debts. Sd **Hutchings** is also liable for any waste, destruction, or decay which may happen to her property during their marriage. Should sd **Horrell** survive sd **Hutchings**, she is entitled to 1/3 of his estate acquired during their marriage; but should he survive her, then she can dispose of 1/3 of their joint estate by last will and testament. Signed John B. (x) **Hutchings**, Elizabeth (x) **Horrell**. Wit John W. **Noell**, Clerk. Rec 30 Aug 1842. [No. 1430]

1649. Page 299. 30 Aug 1842. James **Riddick** to Reuben **Shelby**. For the sum of $100, mortgage on 86 acres purchased from Joseph **Manning** and wife on 20 Apr 1831; where sd **Riddick** now lives and mortgaged to F. **Rozier** Jr. Sd **Riddick** owes sd **Shelby** a note of even date due in 12 months with 10% interest per annum. Signed James **Riddick**. Wit James **Rice** (JP). Rec 30 Aug 1842. [Full satisfaction received on 24 Sep 1847. Signed Reuben **Shelby**. Test John W. **Noell**, Clerk.] [No. 1431]

1650. Page 300. 1 Jan 1842. Joseph **Cissell** and Mary, his wife, to Luther **Taylor**. For the sum of $300, 40 acres, beginning at a stone standing at the corner of 160 acres sold by Bernard **Layton** and wife to William **McLain**. Signed Joseph **Cissell** Sr., Mary (x) **Cissell** (RD). Wit Reuben **Shelby**, JCC. Rec 1 Sep 1842. [No. 1432]

1651. Page 301. 1 Apr 1840. Lewis **Cissell** and Maria, his wife, to Isidore **Moore** Jr. For the sum of $2 per acre, 40 1/2 acres and 29 perches of the confirmed claim of William **Boyce**, beginning at a post at the NW corner of the survey. Signed Lewis **Cissell**, Anne **Cissell** (RD). Wit James **Rice** (JP). Rec 3 Sep 1842. [No. 1433]

1652. Page 302. 14 Feb 1839. Mark **Brooks** of Point Coupee Parish, La. to John **Kinnison**. For the sum of $450, 62 or 63 acres, more or less, in Bois Brule Bottom, which he purchased from sd **Kinnison** and Sinai, his wife, in 1823 or 1824; part of a tract confirmed to Jones **Newsom**, father of Sinai **Kinnison**; and which sd **Kinnison** and wife had legal title in consequence of the death of Jones **Newsom** Jr., one of the heirs of Jones **Newsom** Sr. This deed cancels the previous conveyance. Signed Mark **Brooks**. Wit John T. **Brooks**, Samuel **Stua_te**, Alexander **Ardrey**, JP in Point

Coupee Parish, La., Valery **Ledoux**, Dep Clerk of Point Coupee Parish, La., James **Rice** (JP). Rec 3 Sep 1842. [No. 1434]

1653. Page 304. 9 Aug 1839. Thomas **Long** and Margaret, his wife, to Newton **Long**. For the sum of $182, 1/2 of 100 acres in Bois Brule Bottom, deeded to Thomas and Newton **Long** by Alexander **Patterson** and Nancy, his wife, of St. Francis Co., Mo. Signed Thomas **Long**, Margaret **Long** (RD). Test William **Burns**, Elisha **Eggers** (JP). Rec 5 Sep 1842. [No. 1435]

1654. Page 305. 18 Aug 1840. Newton **Long** and Fanny, his wife, to William **Patterson**. For the sum of $400, 1/2 of 200 acres willed to Alexander **Patterson** by his father Alexander **Patterson** Sr., and deeded to Thomas and Newton **Long** by Alexander **Patterson** Jr.; being the S corner of the tract and bounded on the NE by Daniel **Meredith**'s confirmation. Signed Newton **Long**, Fanny **Long** (RD). Wit A. L. **Parks** (JP). Rec 5 Sep 1842. [No. 1436]

1655. Page 306. 4 Apr 1842. Henry **McNeil** and James **Gillespie**, admrs of the estate of John **Sternes**, decd, of Randolph Co., Ill. to Thomas **Long**. Acknowledgment that a mortgage by sd **Long** to sd **Sternes** has been satisfied (2:400). Signed Henry **McNeil**, James **Gillespie**. Wit Harvey **Clendennin**, James **Thompson**, Probate Justice of the Peace in Randolph Co., Ill. Rec 5 Sep 1842. [No. 1437]

1656. Page 306. 7 Sep 1842. John W. **Noell** and Mary Ann, his wife, to Pouncy **Duggins**. For the sum of $250, 40 acres, being the SE 1/4, NW 1/4, Sec 32, Twp 35 N, Rng 11 E. Signed John W. **Noell**, Mary A. **Noell** (RD). Wit Mark **Brewer** (JP). Rec 10 Sep 1842. [No. 1438]

1657. Page 307. 7 Sep 1842. Same and same to George **Hunsucker**. For the sum of $250, 80 acres, being the E 1/2, SE 1/4, Sec 32, Twp 35 N, Rng 11 E; entered by sd **Noell** and Henry C. C. **Tate**, decd, and the undivided part conveyed to sd **Noell** by Alonzo **Abernathy**, execr of the last will and testament of sd **Tate** (4:289). Signed John W. **Noell**, Mary A. **Noell** (RD). Wit Mark **Brewer** (JP). Rec 10 Sep 1842. [No. 1439]

1658. Page 308. 3 Sep 1842. Guy **Elder** to his son Joseph **Elder** in trust for his brothers and sisters. For natural love and affection for his children and for his and their future maintenance, deed of trust for 247 acres, more or less, being Survey No. 855 confirmed by the U. S. to Joseph **Tucker** Sr., and where sd Guy now lives; five head of horses; one yoke of oxen; 13 cattle; his stock of hogs and sheep; crop of wheat and oats gathered and corn now growing on sd farm; two beds, bedsteads, and bedding; and all the household and kitchen furniture including a clock. The property is to be equally divided among all his children, and the heirs of any who are dead, when the youngest reaches age 21; with sd Joseph as trustee. His other children are George **Elder**, James G. **Elder**, Emily **Elder**, Mary M. **Elder**, and John **Elder**. Signed Guy **Elder**, Joseph **Elder** (signs to secure the indenture). Wit Mark **Brewer** (JP). Rec 10 Sep 1842. [No. 1440]

1659. Page 310. 13 Sep 1842. Leonard **Scollay** of St. Louis, Mo. to John **Piet** for the use of Sarah S. **Hickey**. For natural love and affection for his sister, wife of John J. **Hickey**, deed of trust on one negro girl called **Frances**, a mulatto by color and between 13 and 14 years old. Sd Sarah is to have the use of the girl and her offspring without the influence of her husband, and her children shall have the same in the event of her death. Signed Leonard **Scollay**, John **Piet** as trustee. Wit John W. **Noell**, Clerk. Rec 13 Sep 1842. [No. 1441]

1660. Page 311. 13 Sep 1842. Joseph H. **Massey** to John C. **Whybark** of Cape Girardeau Co., Mo. For securing a debt and the sum of $1, mortgage on one sorrel mare seven years old and branded with a "J" on the left shoulder and hip; a bay colt foaled about 1 May last; one red cow marked with a crop off the left ear and swallow fork and an upper bit in the right, about 5 years old with a black calf calved last spring; one white cow with a red head and some red spots on her sides, marked with a crop in her left ear and a swallow fork in the right ear, with a calf with white back calved last spring; one heifer with red sides and white back, marked with a crop in the left ear and a swallow fork in the right ear; one other red heifer with a little white on her back, marked in the same manner; two improvements on public land, adjoining John **Johnson**, one on Farmington Road, the other between the two roads after they divide in that neighborhood; and 30 hogs. Sd **Massey** owes a note to sd **Whybark** for $32.75 with 10% interest per annum from 10 Sep 1842. Signed Joseph H. (x) **Massey**. Wit John W. **Noell**, Clerk. Rec 13 Sep 1842. [No. 1442]

1661. Page 312. 31 Dec 1841. Luther **Taylor** and Hannah, his wife, to Joseph **Cissell**. For the sum of $300, part of Lot Nos. 57 & 58 in Perryville on St. Marys St. Signed Luther **Taylor**, Hannah **Taylor** (RD). Wit Reuben **Shelby**, JCC. Rec 15 Sep 1842. [No. 1443]

1662. Page 313. 6 Nov 1841. William **Berry** and Eliza, his wife, to Joseph **Cissell** Sr. For the sum of $132.96, mortgage on two tracts in Twp 36 N, Rng 9 E; 40 acres, being the SE 1/4, SW 1/4, fractional Sec 23; and 24.75 acres, being the NE fractional 1/4, NW fractional 1/4, Sec 26. Sd **Berry** owes a note to sd **Cissell** of even date, due by 6 May next with interest. Signed William **Berry**, Eliza Teresa **Berry** (RD). Wit James **Rice** (JP). Rec 15 Sep 1842. [Marginal note: Full satisfaction received on 12 Nov 1849. Signed Joseph **Cissell** Sen.] [No. 1444]

1663. Page 315. 1 Jun 1837. John **Scudder** and Rebecca, his wife, to Esther H. **Osborn**. For the sum of $2400, Block No. 10 in Birmingham, on Front St. Signed John **Scudder**, Rebecca **Scudder**. Wit James **Hanela**, Benjamin **Davis** (JP). Rec 15 Sep 1842. [No. 1445]

1664. Page 316. 17 Sep 1842. Cornelius **Manning** and Ann, his wife, to Bennet **McCauley**. For the sum of $600, 110 acres, the 1/4 part of 439 1/2 acres in the NW corner of Survey No. 2170 in Twp 35 N, Rng 10 & 11 E, devised to them by the last will and testament of Isidore **Moore** Sr, decd; bounded in part by land given to Mary **Manning**. Signed Cornelius **Manning**, Ann **Manning** (RD). Wit James **Rice**, County Court Clerk. Rec 17 Sep 1842. [No. 1446]

1665. Page 317. 17 Sep 1842. Michael **Spaulding** and Louisa, his wife, to John **Logan**, admr of the estate of George **Fenwick**, decd. For the sum of $90, mortgage on 49.37 acres, being the W 1/2 of Lot No. 2, NE 1/4, Sec 3, Twp 34 N, Rng 10 E. Sd **Spaulding** owes a note of even date to sd **Logan** as admr of George **Fenwick**, decd, due by 23 Jul next with interest and costs. Signed Michael **Spalding**. Test J. W. **Noell**, Clerk. Rec 17 Sep 1842. [No. 1447]

1666. Page 318. 6 Oct 1842. Pius **Manning** to Henry **Caho**. For securing two notes and the sum of $1, mortgage on 74 1/2 acres, commencing at the N corner of James **Reddick**'s tract and joining land formerly belonging to Joseph **Manning**, John **Piett**, and Joseph **Miles**; his interest in the estate of his father Joseph **Manning**; one ox; 13 hogs; one wheat fan; 1000 bundles of oats; five stacks fodder; one wooden clock; and 20 bushels wheat. Sd **Manning** owes sd **Caho** two notes, one for $230 payable in 12 months, and one for $234.37 1/2 due in two years for $464.37 1/2. Signed Pius **Manning**. Wit John W. **Noell**, Clerk. Rec 6 Oct 1842. [Marginal note: Full satisfaction received on 30 Nov 1843. Signed Henry **Caho**. Test Jno. W. **Noell**, Clerk.] [No. 1448]

1667. Page 319. 3 Oct 1842. Robert P. **Slaughter** and Evalina M., his wife, to Ernest Moritz **Tenz**. For the sum of $100, Lot No. 30 in Wittenburg, fronting on Second and Perry Sts. Signed Robert P. **Slaughter**, Evalina M. **Slaughter** (RD). Test Fred W. **Barthel**, August H. **Doederlein**, A. M. **McPherson** (JP). Rec 6 Oct 1842. [No. 1449]

1668. Page 320. 8 Oct 1842. John J. **Johnson** to Ferdinand **Rozier** Junr in trust for Robert S. **Manning**. For the sum of $550 paid by sd **Manning** and $1 paid by sd **Rozier**, deed of trust on six tracts in Twp 34 N, Rng 8 E; 40 acres, being the SW 1/4, NE 1/4, Sec 24; 40 acres, being the SE 1/4, NW 1/4, Sec 24; 40 acres, being the NW 1/4, NW 1/4, Sec 24; 40 acres, being the NW 1/4, NE 1/4, Sec 24; 40 acres, being the NE 1/4, NE 1/4, Sec 23; and 40 acres, being the NW 1/4, SE 1/4, Sec 24. Sd **Johnson** owes sd **Manning** a note bearing 10% interest per annum from this date, and if sd **Johnson** cannot pay the note by 25 Jun 1843, then the land is to be sold by sd **Rozier**. Signed John J. (x) **Johnson**. Wit James **Rice** (JP). Rec 8 Oct 1842. [No. 1450]

1669. Page 322. 3 Oct 1842. Henry **Knott** to Clement **Knott**. For the sum of $85, mortgage on two bay mares, one sorrel horse, one bay colt, one red and white pied cow, one red brindle cow, one red and white pied steer, and one crop of corn supposed to be about 300 bushels. Sd Henry owes sd Clement the debt by 1 Oct 1844 with legal interest from this date. Signed Henry (x) **Knott**. Test Mark **Brewer** (JP). Rec 10 Oct 1842. [No. 1451]

1670. Page 323. 12 Feb 1842. Trustees of Wittenburg to Ernest Morritz **Tenz**. For the sum of $15, Lot No. 43 in Wittenburg, on First St and Second St. Signed Henry C. **Bimpage**, Friedr. Wilh. **Barthel**, Christian Friedrich **Muller**. Test Theod. F. L. **Hacke**, Augustus **Davis** (JP). Rec 10 Oct 1842. [No. 1452]

1671. Page 324. 11 Oct 1842. Emanuel **Pratte** to Ernst William **Zacher**. For the sum of $210, 100 acres, part Survey No. 86 granted to Thomas **Donohue** under Christopher **Barnhart**, in Twp 34, Rng 10 E; and purchased by sd **Pratte** at Sheriff's sale on 17 Jun 1842 (4:224). Signed Emanuel **Pratte**. Wit W. B. **Wilkinson**, John F. **Hase** (JP). Rec 11 Oct 1842. [No. 1452, repeated]

1672. Page 325. 3 Oct 1842. Ernst Moritz **Tenz** and Friedericke Eleonore, his wife, to Robert P. **Slaughter**. For the sum of $100, Lot No. 43 in Wittenburg, fronting on First and Second Sts. Signed Ernst Moritz **Tenz**, Friedericke Eleonore **Tenz**. Test Fred. W. **Barthel**, August H. **Doederlein**, A. M. **McPherson** (JP). Rec 10 Oct 1842. [No. 1453]

1673. Page 326. 11 Oct 1842. William **Garner** by Sheriff Henry **Caho** to John W. **Noell**. For the sum of $25, 80 acres, being the E 1/2, NE 1/4, Sec 34, Twp 35 N, Rng 13 E. Sold on 11 Oct 1842 on an execution issued 31 Aug 1842 by Circuit Court on a judgment in favor of James **Evans** and against sd **Garner** for $7.50 debt. Signed Henry **Caho**, Sheriff. Wit John W. **Noell**, Clerk. Rec 11 Oct 1842. [No. 1454]

1674. Page 327. 12 Oct 1842. George **McKinstry** Junr by Sheriff Henry **Caho** to Alfred H. **Puckett**. For the sum of $145, three tracts in Bois Brule Bottom on the Mississippi River; 200 acres, the lower part of a tract confirmed to William **Fitzgibbons**, in Twp 36 N, Rng 11 E, sold to William H. **Digges** and sd **McKinstry** by John Carlisle and wife on 4 Nov 1839, and to sd **McKinstry** by sd **Digges** on 21 May 1840; 85.06 acres, part of the lands confirmed to Alexander **McConahoe**, sold by John **Kinnison** to William H. **Digges** and sd **McKinstry** on 17 Mar 1840; and 103.63 acres, more or less, being fractional Sec 4, Twp 36 N, Rng 11 E entered by George **Camster**, and mortgaged by sd **McKinstry** to Alfred H. **Puckett** on 19 Jun 1840. Sold on 11 Oct 1842 on an execution form Circuit Court issued 6 Jul 1842 in favor of John **Kinnison** and against sd **McKinstry** and sd **Puckett** (impleaded with William **Digges**) for $482.12 debt, $60.18 damages, and $16.22 1/2 costs. Signed Henry **Caho**, Sheriff. Wit John W. **Noell**, Clerk. Rec 15 Oct 1842. [No. 1455]

1675. Page 330. 12 Oct 1842. Nicholas **Schrimp** by Sheriff Henry **Caho** to Morritz **Behrle**. For the sum of $31, 40 acres, being the W 1/2, Lot No. 3, NE 1/4, Sec 4, Twp 33 N, Rng 11 E. Sold on 12 Oct 1842 on an execution issued 5 Jul 1842 on a judgment issued by Mark **Brewer**, JP, in favor of James **Elmore** and against Sd **Schrimp** for $30.50 with costs. Signed Henry **Caho**, Sheriff. Wit John W. **Noell**, Clerk. Rec 15 Oct 1842. [No. 1456]

1676. Page 332. 15 Oct 1842. James B. **Mattingly** and Mary, his wife, to John **Duvall** Junior. For the sum of $116, 40 acres, more or less, being the SW 1/4, NW 1/4, Sec 12, Twp 34 N, Rng 9 E, entered by Mary **Mattingly** on 7 Oct 1839, Certificate No. 7235. Signed James B. **Mattingly**, Mary (x) **Mattingly**. Wit John F. **Hase** (JP). Rec 15 Oct 1842. [No. 1457]

1677. Page 333. 15 Oct 1842. Peter J. **Tucker** and Mary, his wife, to Jacob L. **Burrows**. For the sum of $30, Lot No. 77 [in Perryville]. Signed Peter J. **Tucker**, Mary (x) **Tucker** (RD). Wit James **Rice** (JP). Rec 17 Oct 1842. [No. 1458]

1678. Page 334. 14 Oct 1842. William **Taylor** and Mary, his wife, to Reuben **Shelby**. For the sum of $800, part of Lot No. 63 in Perryville, beginning at the SE corner and facing on Jackson St. and St. Joseph St., and adjoining the brick house of sd **Shelby**. Signed William **Taylor**, Mary (x) **Taylor** (RD). Wit James **Rice** (JP). Rec 18 Oct 1842. [No. 1459]

1679. Page 335. 26 Oct 1841. James B. **May** to Joseph **Cissell** Sen. For sd **Cissell** acting as security in a note and the sum of $1, mortgage on 100 acres, being all his right to part of Survey No. 2137 confirmed to James **Moore** Senior, decd, in Twp 35 N, Rng 10 E; beginning at the end of a lane running to the farm of sd **Moore**; being the portion of the survey set apart for the maintenance of Elizabeth **Moore**, daughter of sd James; and also subject to a mortgage by sd May to sd **Cissell** executed 4 May 1840 (3:465). Sd **Cissell** is security for sd **May** in a note to Ignatius **Moore** dated 15 Oct 1841 for $155, due by 10 Feb 1842 with 6% interest per annum until due, and then 10% interest per annum until paid. Signed James B. **May**. Wit James **Rice** (JP).

Rec 20 Oct 1842. [Marginal note: Full satisfaction received on 22 Aug 1849. Signed Joseph **Cissell** Sen.] [No. 1460]

1680. Page 338. 28 Sep 1841. John **Kinnison** and Sinai, his wife, to John **Carlisle**. For the sum of $1000, 85.06 acres beginning on the Mississippi River at the upper corner of a tract sold by sd **Kinnison** to William H. **Digges** and George **McKinstry** Junr; also bounded by Thomas **Sanders** and Alexander **McConnohue**'s survey; part of a tract confirmed to sd **McConnohue** and sold to sd **Kinnison**. Signed John **Kinnison**, Sinai **Kinnison** (RD). Wit Alfred L. **Parks** (JP). Rec 21 Oct 1842. [No. 1461]

1681. Page 339. 14 Nov 1837. U. S. A. to John P. **Tucker**. Patent for 80 acres, being the W 1/2, NE 1/4, Sec 27, Twp 35 N, Rng 10 E; Certificate No. 4515. Signed Martin **Van Buren** by A. **Van Buren**. Wit Jos. S. **Wilson**, Acting Recorder, General Land Office. Rec in Vol. 9:90 of the General Land Office. Rec 22 Oct 1842. [No. 1462]

1682. Page 340. 21 Oct 1842. John P. **Tucker** and Sarah, his wife, to John **Ell**. For the sum of $400, 80 acres, being the tract described in the preceding deed (4:339). Signed John P. **Tucker**, Sarh **Tucker** (RD). Wit Philip **Fry**, Loranz **Endras**, John F. **Hase** (JP). Rec 22 Oct 1842. [No. 1463]

1683. Page 341. 22 Oct 1842. Mark L. **Manning** to Lewis **French**. For the sum of $16.31 1/4, mortgage on one yoke of oxen two years old next spring, both of a red color, and one ox cart. Sd **Manning** owes a note to sd **French**, due with interest. Signed Mark L. **Manning**. Wit John W. **Noell**, Clerk. Rec 22 Oct 1842. [Marginal note: Full satisfaction received on 4 Apr 1844. Signed Lewis **French**. Test J. W. **Noell**, Clerk.] [No. 1464]

1684. Page 342. 13 Jun 1842. Nereus **Layton** and Elizabeth, his wife, to John R. **Layton**. For the sum of $500, quit claim to 230 acres, their undivided interest in a tract willed to them and Felix **Layton** by Zechariah **Layton**, decd, on 6 Apr 1839. Signed Nereus **Layton**, Elizabeth (x) **Layton** (RD). Wit John **Layton** Senr (JP), Maria **Layton**. Rec 24 Oct 1842. [No. 1465]

1685. Page 343. 26 Oct 1842. John J. **Johnson** to John **Mutlins** [**Mullins**?] of Madison Co., Mo. For the sum of $1750, six tracts in Twp 34 N, Rng 8 E; the NE 1/4, NE 1/4, Sec 23; NW 1/4, SE 1/4, Sec 24; NW 1/4, NE 1/4, Sec 24; SE 1/4, NW 1/4, Sec 24; SW 1/4, NE 1/4, Sec 24; and NW 1/4, NW 1/4, Sec 24; as per Patent Nos. 7034, 2372, 1690, 1205, 1204, & 1691. Signed John J. (x) **Johnson**. Test J. W. **Noell**, Clerk, John G. **Johnson**. Rec 26 Oct 1842. [No. 1466]

1686. Page 344. 13 Oct 1842. John **Layton** Senr and Monica, his wife, to Joseph **Shoults**. For the sum of $130, 11 acres and 13 roods, the E part of a tract confirmed to John **Layton** Senr, decd; beginning at a set stone on a line made and laid off to sd **Shoults**, which was sold to him by Ignatius **Layton** Senr; and also bounded by Bernard **Layton**'s survey. Signed John **Layton**, Monica (x) **Layton** (RD). Wit Amatus **Layton**, Maria **Layton**, John F. **Hase** (JP). Rec 28 Oct 1842. [No. 1467]

1687. Page 345. 2 Nov 1842. Nelson **Yarber** and Sally, his wife, to Robert **Farrar**. For the sum of $48, mortgage on two tracts in Sec 25, Twp 35 N, Rng 11 E; 40 acres, being the NW 1/4, SE 1/4, entered by sd **Yarber** at the land office on 2 Mar 1839, Receipt No. 6582; and 40 acres, being the NE 1/4, SW 1/4, patented to sd **Farrar** on 15 Oct 1833 and sold by him and Susan, his wife, to sd **Yarber** on 9 Nov 1839 (3:221). Sd **Yarber** owes sd **Farrar** a note with interest by 2 Nov 1843. Signed Nelson (x) **Yarber**, Sarah (x) **Yarber**. Wit W. **Walker** (JP). Rec 7 Nov 1842. [Marginal note: Full satisfaction received on 18 May 1847. Signed Robert **Farrar**. Wit John W. **Noell**, Clerk.] [No. 1468]

1688. Page 347. 3 Nov 1842. Thomas **Rine** to Peter **Starnes**. For the sum of $13, mortgage on five horse beasts, four mares and one colt; one yoke of oxen; four cows and three calves; four yearlings; one waggon, fifteen sheep; 20 hogs; one wheat fan, about 40 bushels of wheat in the straw, more or less; 200 bushels of corn, more or less; two plows; two pair of geers; two mens saddles; one beauru; and one clock. Sd **Rine** has the right of the property as long as sd **Starnes** lives with him. Sd **Rine** owes sd **Starnes** a note with interest within 12 months. Signed Thomas (x) **Rine**. Test John F. **Hase**, John W. **Noell**, Clerk Rec 8 Nov 1842. [No. 1469]

1689. Page 348. 10 Nov 1842. Pierre T. **Boeuf** and Malina, his wife, to Francois Flavier **Boeuf**. For the sum of $50, undivided 1/2 of 40 acres, being the NW 1/4, SE 1/4, Sec 34, Twp 35 N, Rng 10 E. Signed Pierre Th. **Boeuf**, Malanie **Boeuf** (RD). Wit John W. **Noell**, Clerk. Rec 10 Nov 1842. [No. 1470]

1690. Page 349. 24 Oct 1842. John **Kinnison** and Sinia, his wife, of Perry Co. and Hiram **Kinnison** and Elizabeth, his wife, of Scott Co., Mo. to John **Moore**. For the sum of $200 each to sd John and sd Hiram, their 1/8 shares of 640 acres (80 acres each) in Bois Brule Bottom, a tract confirmed to the heirs and legal representatives of Absolem **Kinnison**, decd; bounded on the N by land confirmed to John **Smith** and to James **Burns**, E & S by land confirmed to John Roff **McLaughlin** and to Michael **Burns**, and W by land confirmed to **Dunks**. Signed John **Kinnison**, Sinai **Kinnison** (RD), Hiram **Kinnison**, Elizabeth (x) **Kinnison** (RD). Test Marcella **Neal**. Wit James **Rice** (JP), John P. **Hunt**, JP in Cape Girardeau Co., Mo., Caleb P. **Fulenwider**, Cape Girardeau Co. Clerk, as to sd **Hunt**. Rec 14 Nov 1842. [No. 1471]

1691. Page 351. 7 Nov 1842. Dalinder **Clifton** to Lewis **Dickson**. For the sum of $458, her 1/7 share of 3 tracts, part of the estate of Lewis **Dickson**, decd; 640 acres on the Mississippi River confirmed to Lewis **Dickson** during his lifetime as Survey No. 1846; 320 arpens on the Mississippi River, purchased by Lewis **Dickson** during his lifetime from J. P. **Bosia** and Henry **Elliott** on 21 Jan 1820, as Survey No. 1275; and 640 acres in Survey No. 2155 confirmed to Abraham **Armstrong** and purchased by Lewis **Dickson** during his lifetime at Ste. Genevieve Co. Sheriff's sale. Signed Dalinder (x) **Clifton**. Wit Solomon (x) **Mitchell**, Osbirn W. **Walker** (JP). Rec 15 Nov 1842. [No. 1472]

1692. Page 351. 4 Nov 1842. Ansel **Ferrell** and Esther, his wife, to John E. **Burgett**. For the sum of $1059.30, mortgage on 78 acres in Bois Brule Bottom on the Mississippi River, joining Alfred L. **Parks** below the Hempstead tract above; part of a tract confirmed to James **Moredock**; one negro boy **Josiah**; and one negro girl **Lucinda**. Sd **Ferrell** owes sd **Burget** a note of even date with interest, due 1 Jan 1844. Signed Ansel (x) **Ferrel**, Esther (x) **Ferrel** (RD). Wit Alfred L. **Parks** (JP). Rec 15 Nov 1842. [Marginal note: Full satisfaction received on 9 Apr 1845. Signed J. E. **Burgett**.] [No. 1473]

1693. Page 353. 15 Jan 1842. J. Frederick **Buenger** to Mrs. Johanne **von Wurmb**. For the sum of $4, 2 acres, more or less, commencing at the SE corner of 6 acres laid off in the SW 1/4, SW 1/4, Sec 23, Twp 34 N, Rng 13 E; purchased by sd **Buenger** from Henry C. **Bimpage**, admr of the estate of John George **Gube**, decd. Signed J. Frederick **Buenger**. Wit John J. **Newmiller**, William **Worth**, Jno. **Ruland**, Clerk of St. Louis Co., Mo. Rec 15 Nov 1842. [No. 1474]

1694. Page 354. 2 Sep 1842. Samuel Gottlieb **Kaempfe** and Juliann Christiane, his wife, to Johann Gottlieb **Palisch**. For the sum of $175, two tracts in Sec 23, Twp 34 N, Rng 13 E purchased by sd Kaempfe from Henry C. **Bimpage**, admr of the estate of John George **Gube**, decd; 80 acres, being the N 1/2, SW 1/4; and 14 acres of the SW 1/4, SW 1/4, commencing at the SW corner of Sec 23. Signed Gottlieb **Kaempfe**, Juliann Christiane **Kaempfe** (RD). Wit Johann Gottlieb **Hohne**, Carl Gottlieb **Zeibig**, Augustus **Davis** (JP). Rec 15 Nov 1842. [No. 1475]

1695. Page 355. 16 Nov 1842. Michael **Muhlfeld** and Matilda, his wife, to Philip **Rug**. For the sum of $160, 80 acres, being the E 1/2, NW 1/4, Sec 11, Twp 34 N, Rng 10 E, as per certificate issued 24 Nov 1841 from the Receiver's Office. Signed Michael **Muhlfeld**, Matilda (x) **Mihlfeld**. Wit John F. **Hase** (JP). Rec 16 Nov 1842. [No. 1476]

1696. Page 356. 19 Nov 1842. Seburn **Wadsworth** and Rebecca, his wife, to George **Bearkeman** [Bergmann]. For the sum of $125, 40 acres, being the NW 1/4, NE 1/4, Sec 25, Twp 35 N, Rng 11 E. Signed Seburn **Wadsworth**, Rebecca (x) **Wadsworth** (RD). Test Osbirn W. **Walker** (JP), James **Wadsworth**. Rec 22 Nov 1842. [No. 1477]

1697. Page 357. 22 Nov 1841. Moses **Farrar** and Ann Arpy, his wife and daughter of John **Duvall**, decd, and widow of Robert **Abernathy**, decd, to Ezra **Shelby**. For the sum of $1000, 300 acres, more or less, on Cape Cinque Hommes Creek that they hold as heirs at law of sd **Duvall**; beginning at the W corner of a survey confirmed to Benjamin **Cox** Junior, and also bounded by Bernard **Layton**'s survey. Signed Moses **Farrar**, Ann Arpy **Farar** (RD). Wit Reuben **Shelby**, JCC. Rec 23 Nov 1842. [No. 1478]

1698. Page 358. 26 Nov 1842. Anthony **Parres** and Mary Ann, his wife, to Morris **Block** and Charles **Avery**, trading as Block & Avery. For the sum of $75, Lot No. 16 in Perryville. Signed Anthony **Parres**, Mary Ann (x) **Parres** (RD). Wit John F. **Hase** (JP). Rec 26 Nov 1842. [No. 1479]

1699. Page 359. 26 Nov 1842. Michael **Spaulding** to John **Logan**. For the trusts mentioned, deed of trust on one black mare that he purchased from George **Fenwick** in his lifetime, and one waggon and gear purchased from Henry **Caho**. Sd **Spaulding** is indebted to the estate of George **Fenwick** in a note dated 7 Mar 1842, due 1 Jan 1843, for $28 at 10% interest per annum; and to Moses **Farrar**, admr of the estate of Gabriel M. **Duvall** by a note for about $22 or $23, with Stephen **Dolson** as security. The debts are due by 1 May next, or sd **Logan** is to sell the property. Signed Michael **Spalding**. Wit John W. **Noell**, Clerk. Rec 26 Nov 1842. [No. 1480]

1700. Page 361. 15 Aug 1842. Martin **Layton** and Narus **Layton**, execr of Zechariah **Layton**, decd, to John **Richardson** and John **Bridgeman**. For the sum of $12, Lot No. 86 in Perryville, fronting on West St and South St. Signed Martin **Layton**, Nereus **Layton**. Wit John W. **Noell**, Clerk. Rec 26 Nov 1842. [No. 1481]

1701. Page 362. 5 Sep 1842. Luther **Taylor** and Hannah, his wife, to Marcus **Block**. For the sum of $125, part of a lot in Perryville, beginning 2 1/2 ft W of the corner between Lot Nos. 57 & 58 on St. Marys St. Signed Luther **Taylor**, Hannah **Taylor** (RD). Wit James **Rice** (JP). Rec 28 Nov 1842. [No. 1482]

1702. Page 363. 2 Sep 1833. Thomas **Cody** and Elizabeth, his wife, to William W. **Taylor**. For the sum of $25, Lot No. 50 in Perryville. Signed Thomas **Cody**, Elizabeth **Cody** (RD). Wit John **Layton** senr (JP), John **Layton** Jr. Rec 30 Nov 1842. [No. 1483]

1703. Page 363. 11 Mar 1839. Perry **Evans** and Diana, his wife, to James **Taylor**. For the sum of $400, 40 acres, being the NW fractional 1/4, Sec 35, Twp 37 N, Rng 10 E. Signed Perry **Evans**, Diana **Evans** (RD). Wit W. **Searcy** (JP). Rec 30 Nov 1842. [No. 1484]

1704. Page 365. 10 Mar 1839. Same and same to same. For the sum of $200, 50 acres, more or less, in Bois Brule Bottom, the upper half of a tract purchased by sd **Taylor** from William **Morris** on 23 Dec 1825, and conveyed to sd **Evans** on 9 Jan 1834 (2:70); fronting on the Mississippi River, and bounded on the upper side by sd **Evans**, back by land entered [by] Francis **Clark**, and lower side by the division fence between sd **Evans** and the widow **Taylor**. Signed Perry **Evans**, Diana **Evans** (RD). Wit W. **Searcy** (JP). Rec 30 Nov 1842. [No. 1485]

1705. Page 366. 1 Sep 1842. Luther **Taylor** to Eli **Taylor**. For the sum of $500 and an agreement to support Luther **Taylor** and wife, and their minor children William W. **Taylor**, Joseph W. **Taylor**, and Levinia **Taylor** for six years; Lot Nos. 50 & 51 in Perryville, and 16.38 acres, being the SW fractional 1/4, Sec 18, Twp 35 N, Rng 11 E. Signed Luther **Taylor**. Wit Mark **Brewer** (JP). Rec 30 Nov 1842. [No. 1486]

1706. Page 367. 29 Aug 1842. Same to same. For $25 cash and two notes (one due on 1 Aug 1843, the other on 15 Jul 1844), negro slaves--**Luke**, a black man about 22 years old, **Paulina**, a woman about 27 years old, and her child **Catharine** about 3 years old. Signed Luther **Taylor**. Wit Edward M. **Holden**, John **Layton** (JP). Rec 30 Nov 1842. [No. 1487]

1707. Page 367. 30 Nov 1842. Same and Hannah, his wife, to John **Logan**. For securing debts, trusts herein mentioned, and the sum of $1; deed of trust on six parcels: Lot Nos. 52, 28, 7, & 27 in Perryville; 40 acres purchased from Joseph **Cissell** and wife by sd **Taylor** on 1 Jan 1842, beginning at a stake standing in the 160 acres sold by Bernard **Layton** and wife to William **McLane**; 35 acres, more or less, beginning on the N boundary line of Perryville near the center of Main St, bounded by Bernard **Layton**'s confirmation. Sd **Taylor** owes sd **Logan** a note of even date for $121; a note dated 1 Jan 1842 to George **Rutledge** as guardian of the minor heirs of Robert **Abernathy**, decd, for $196 with 10% interest per annum, with John W. **Noell** as security; a note to James **Rice** dated 1 Jan 1842 for $110 with 10% interest per annum; and two notes to Benjamin **Wilson**, one for $300 and one for $80. Sd **Logan** is to sell the land if sd **Taylor** does not pay the debts by 1 Dec 1844, or does not hold sd **Noell** harmless. Signed Luther **Taylor**, Hannah **Taylor** (RD). Test John F. **Hase** (JP), John W. **Noell**, Clerk. Rec 1 Dec 1842. [Marginal note: Full satisfaction of his interest in this deed of trust received on 26 Jul 1845. Signed George **Rutledge**. Test Jno. W. **Noell**, Clerk.] [No. 1488]

1708. Page 370. 1 Jun 1842. Same and same to Reuben **Shelby**. For the sum of $30, their undivided interest in Lot Nos. 7, 8, & 9 in Perryville and quit claim to Lot Nos. 5 & 6 in **Taylor** and **Faina**'s addition to Perryville adjoining the SW corner of town. Signed Luther **Taylor**, Hannah **Taylor** (RD). Wit John W. **Noell**, Clerk. Rec 1 Dec 1842. [No. 1489]

1709. Page 371. 30 Nov 1842. Luther **Taylor** to Alfred H. **Puckett**. For the sum of $120, two tracts; 11 1/2 acres, more or less, beginning at the SE corner of Lot No. 12 in Perryville and bounded in part by Elenor **Hunt** and Charles **Stewart**, and conveyed to sd **Taylor** by sd **Stewart** on 7 Mar 1836; and 10 3/4 acres, beginning at the SE corner of Perryville, bounded in part by ___ **McLain**; and conveyed to sd **Taylor** by sd **Stewart** and Benjamin **Wilson** on 2 Nov 1835. Signed Luther **Taylor**. Wit John W. **Noell**, Clerk. Rec 1 Dec 1842. [No. 1490]

1710. Page 372. 26 Nov 1842. Felix **Miles** and Caroline, his wife, to Gabriel Gagne **Pain**. For the sum of $223, 40 acres, being the SW 1/4, SE fractional 1/4, fractional Sec 22, Twp 35 N, Rng 10 E. Signed Felix **Miles**, Caroline (x) **Miles** (RD). Wit R. **Shelby**. John W. **Noell**, Clerk. Rec 1 Dec 1842. [No. 1491]

1711. Page 373. 2 Dec 1842. Luther **Taylor** to Eli **Taylor**. For the sum of $868.25 in two notes dated 29 Aug 1842 (one for delivery of 6000 bricks within one mile of Perryville by 1 Aug 1843 and $200 worth of work for brick laying, the other for 50,000 bricks to the same location for a wall and $200 worth of brick laying), three slaves; **Luke**, a black man about 22 years old; **Paulina**, a yellow or mulatto woman about 27 years old; and **Catharine**, child of sd **Paulina**. Sd Eli has completed the condition of the notes by execution of his note in place of sd Luther to John **Moore**, and for $25 cash. Signed Luther **Taylor**. Wit John W. **Noell**, Clerk. Rec 3 Dec 1842. [No. 1492]

1712. Page 374. 28 Nov 1842. Henry **Tucker** and Michael **Tucker**, execrs of Nicholas **Tucker** Senior, decd, to John N. **Tucker**. For the sum of $54.30, 43.44 acres, being the SW fractional, Sec 6, Twp 35 N, Rng 11 E. Executed as directed in the will of Nicholas **Tucker** Senior, to his son John N. **Tucker** (Probate Book 2:102). Signed Henry N. **Tucker**, Michael **Tucker**. Test James **Rice** (JP). Rec 3 Dec 1842. [No. 1493]

1713. Page 375. 30 Nov 1842. John N. **Tucker**, and Christina, his wife, to Leander **Tucker**. For the sum of $173, 43.44 acres, being the SW fractional 1/4, Sec 6, Twp 35 N, Rng 11 E as described in the preceding deed (4:374). Signed John N. **Tucker**, Christina **Tucker** (RD). Wit James **Rice** (JP). Rec 3 Dec 1842. [No. 1494]

1714. Page 376. 24 Oct 1842. James **Rice** to same. For the sum of $1, quit claim to ___ acres formerly belonging to Nicholas **Tucker** Sen., decd, being the undivided interest of John N. **Tucker** to the real estate of sd Nicholas, his father; and conveyed by sd John N. to sd **Rice** on 20 Jan 1840 (3:208). Signed James **Rice**. Wit John **Layton** (JP). Rec 3 Dec 1842. [No. 1495]

1715. Page 377. 5 Dec 1842. Valerio **Faina** to Morris **Block**. In consideration of debts, the trust described, and the sum of $1, deed of trust on one negro woman **Milly** about 30 years old and one negro boy **William** about 11 years old. Sd **Faina** executed three notes to sd **Block**, payable one day after date with 10% interest per annum; one dated 17 Dec 1841 for $205.38; one dated 16 Dec 1841 for $349.95; and one dated 2 Dec 1842 for $15.29. Sd **Faina** also owes a note of even date to Block & Avery for $148.93. If sd **Faina** fails to pay the notes, the property is to be sold at public sale by sd **Block**, to pay the debts. Signed Valerio **Faina**, Morris **Block**. Wit John W. **Noell**, Clerk. Rec 5 Dec 1842. [Marginal note: Full satisfaction received on 20 Apr 1853. Signed Morris **Block**. Test C. C. **Ellis**, Clerk.] [No. 1496]

1716. Page 379. 5 Dec 1842. Same to Ferdinand **Rozier** Junr. For securing a note and the sum of $1, 50 acres, part of a tract of 640 acres confirmed to John **Layton** Senr, decd, and since his death divided among his heirs; beginning at the most E corner of the original survey; and bounded in part by Rezin L. **Bishop** and a tract sd **Faina** purchased from the heirs of Joseph **Layton**, decd. Sd **Faina** owes a note for $450 to sd **Rozier**, due in 18 months and bearing 10% interest per annum. Signed Valerio **Faina**. Wit Geo. P. **Clark**, John W. **Noell**, Clerk. Rec 6 Dec 1842. [Marginal note: Full satisfaction received on 13 May 1856. Signed Ferdinand **Rozier** Jur. Test Charles C. **Ellis**, Clerk.] [No. 1497]

1717. Page 380. 12 Mar 1839. Valerio **Faina** and Matilda, his wife, to Henry **Caho**. For the sum of $10, 2 acres and 130 rods, beginning at the corner of sd **Caho**'s land on the NW line of John **Layton** Senior's survey; part of the land confirmed to John **Layton** Senior. Signed Valerio **Faina**, Matilda **Faina** (RD). Wit Reuben **Shelby**, JCC. Rec 6 Dec 1842. [No. 1498]

1718. Page 381. 6 Dec 1842. Augustine **Layton** to John **Layton** senr. For securing a note and the sum of $1, mortgage on one black mare, one dark bay or brown horse, one muly cow, one cow with horns, one red and white heffer, one yerlin heffer, on steer, 13 sheep, 19 stock hogs, 200 bushels corn, 1000 bundles oats, 700 bundles fodder, 200 lbs of tobacco, on buro, seven split bottom chairs, one plough, and one mans saddle. Sd John is security for sd Augustine in a note to Ferdinand **Rozier** Junr for $40.07. Sd Augustine also owes sd John a note dated 2 Oct 1842 for $109, payable in 12 months with 10% interest; is also indebted to Thomas **Riney** for $15. Signed Augustin **Layton**. Wit John W. **Noell**, Clerk. Rec 6 Dec 1842. [No. 1499]

1719. Page 382. 6 Dec 1842. William **Cobbs** to John W. **Noell**. For certain trusts and debts and the sum of $1, deed of trust on 40 acres entered by sd **Cobb**, being the NW 1/4, SE 1/4, Sec 2, Twp 34 N, Rng 10 E; one sorrel mare purchased at Noell & Tate's sale, about five or six years old next spring; one dark roan horse with blaze face about 15 years old; one yoke of oxen, one ox dark red and the other pale red; one cary plough & wheat fan; the undivided 1/2 of about 5000 pounds of a crop of tobacco; undivided 1/2 of about 500 bushels of corn; undivided 1/2 of eight stacks of oats and four stacks of fodder; and 1/2 of 25 bushels of wheat. All the personal property is on a farm belonging to the heirs of Cornelius **Cobbs**, decd, and now in the possession of William **Cobbs** and A. M. **Cobbs** as tenants of Anne **Cobbs**, Sarah **Cobbs**, and Elizabeth **Cobbs**. Sd William has executed two notes date to sd Sarah and sd Elizabeth; one of even date for $150, payable by 1 Jan next; the other for $8 due one day after date with 10% interest per annum. He is also indebted to sd **Noell** for the use of the late firm of Noell & Tate by two notes dated 19 Nov 1841, payable 12 months after date with 10% interest per annum, one for $3.88 with Daniel **Abernathy** as security, the other for

$43.50 with T. H. McAtee as security. Sd Noell is to sell the property if William Cobbs cannot pay the debts. Signed William Cobbs. Test John Layton (JP). Rec 6 Dec 1842. [Marginal note: Full satisfaction received on 25 Jan 1848. Signed John W. Noell for himself and for Sarah Cobbs.] [No. 1500]

1720. Page 385. 29 Aug 1842. Luther Taylor to Eli Taylor. For two notes, one for $335 to be discharged as brick delivered in or within one mile of Perryville by 1 Sep 1845 at $4.50 per thousand and one for $415 for brick to be delivered by 1 Jul 1846 at $4 per thousand, and the sum of $10; five horses; one yoke of oxen; seven cows; seven young cattle; 10 sheep; 35 hogs; one two-horse waggon and gear; one two-horse Dearborn or boggy and harness; one ox waggon and one ox cart; two ploughs; four log binding chains; four beds, bedsteads, and bedding; one buro, 1/2 doz cushion chairs and 1/2 doz cane bottom chairs; four tables; one brass clock; one large cupboard; one harrow; one cutting box; two wheelbarrows; 600 doz bundles oats; 15 acres of growing corn; 1 acre of potatoes; four saddles and bridles; 400 bushels of lime[?], 5 axes and one adds; one handsaw; one sledge; one crow bar; and 60,000 unturned brick. Signed Luther Taylor. Wit Edward M. Holden, John Layton (JP). Rec 7 Dec 1842. [No. 1501]

1721. Page 386. 9 Dec 1842. John Richardson and John Bridgman, partners in a carriage and waggon-making business, to John J. Hickey, all of Perryville. For the trusts mentioned and the sum of $1, deed of trust on Lot No. 78 on St. Marys St in Perryville, Lot No. 86 on West and South Sts in Perryville; all lumber and building materials on hand; one wardrobe; seven feather beds, bedding, and bedsteads; four wash stands; four tables; six sets knives & forks; six sets cups and saucers; four kettles; eight pots and ovens; 18 splits bottom chairs; three cows and calves; and one tavern bell and one tavern press. Sd Richardson & Bridgman owe 14 debts; one to Misses Sarah & Elizabeth Cobbs on 9 Dec 1842 for $50, one to Block & Avery for $220, one to Hertlich & Landry for about $162, one to Ferdinand Rozier Jr. dated 9 Dec 1842 for $38.78, one to F. Rozier & Co. dated 9 Dec 1842 for $50, one to John Logan by account for $50, one to Hyman Block for $15, one to Jacob L. Burrows by account for $10, one to Martin L. Moore & Isaac G. Whitworth for $8, one to Leonard Faith by account for $53, one to Joseph Shoults for $16, one to George Killian by account for about $120, one to Lee Campbell by account for about $30, and one to John C. Winebark for $25. Sd Hickey is to sell the property if Richardson & Bridgman do not pay the debts. Signed John Richardson, John Bridgman, John J. Hickey. Wit Ferdinand Rozier Jr., F. Rozier & Co., John W. Noell, Clerk. Rec 9 Dec 1842. [No. 1502]

1722. Page 388. 20 Sep 1842. Anthony Parres and Mary Ann, his wife, to John Richardson and John Bridgman. For the sum of $50, Lot No. 78 in Perryville. Signed Anthony Parres, Mary Ann (x) Parres (RD). Wit John F. Hase (JP). Rec 26 Nov 1842. [This is numbered No. 1481, out of sequence]

1723. Page 389. 10 Dec 1842. Claude Francois Guyot to Claude Emanuel Guyot. For the sum of $594.75, 1/3 part of two tracts; __ acres conveyed to him, F. F. Guyot, and F. X. Guyot by Catharine Lukefahr on 29 Dec 1841; and 30 acres of school lands purchased by Claude Francois Guyot, F. F. Guyot, and F. X. Guyot joining the same. Signed C. F. Guyot. Wit John W. Noell, Clerk. Rec 10 Dec 1842. [No. 1503]

1724. Page 389. 8 Dec 1842. Brice Young and Nancey, his wife, to John Moore. For the sum of $150, their undivided 1/8 part of 640 acres in Bois Brule Bottom confirmed to the heirs of Absolem Kinnison, decd; joining lands confirmed to John R. McLaughlin, Michael Burns, Dunks, John Smith's legal representatives, and James Burns. Signed Brice Young, Nancey (x) Young. Test Alfred L. Parks (JP). Rec 10 Dec 1842. [No. 1504]

1725. Page 391. 9 Dec 1842. William Taylor and Mary, his wife, to Reuben Shelby. For the sum of $70, part of Lot No. 63 in Perryville, beginning at the SW corner of the lot, and bounded by sd Shelby, Javaux, and St. Joseph St. Signed William Taylor, Mary (x) Taylor (RD). Wit John W. Noell, Clerk. Rec 10 Dec 1842. [No. 1505]

1726. Page 392. 3 Apr 1841. Martin Layton and Nereus Layton, admrs of the last will and testament of Zachariah Layton, decd, to John Hasher. For the sum of $12.50, Lot No. 76 on West St in Perryville. Signed Martin Layton, Nereus Layton. Wit Reuben Shelby, JCC. Rec 12 Dec 1842. [No. 1506]

1727. Page 393. 12 Dec 1842. John Hasher and Lavina, his wife, to Griswold W. Wheeler. For the sum of $12, N undivided 1/2 of Lot No. 76 in Perryville. Signed John Hasher, Leviner Hasher (RD). Wit John F. Hase (JP). Rec 13 Dec 1842. [No. 1507]

1728. Page 394. 10 Dec 1842. Richard Maddock Junr and Cisaly, his wife, of Perry Co. to Nathaniel W. Watkins and Greer W. Davis of Cape Girardeau Co., Mo. For the sum of $1200, mortgage on 200 acres in four tracts in Twp 35 N, Rng 9 E; 40 acres, being the SE 1/4, SE 1/4, Sec 35; 40 acres, being the NE 1/4, SW 1/4, Sec 35; 80 acres, being the W 1/2, SW 1/4, Sec 36 purchased by sd Maddock from John Hahn and Elizabeth, his wife; and 40 acres, being the SE 1/4, NW 1/4, Sec 35, purchased by sd Maddock from Richard Maddock Senr. Sd Maddock owes Watkins & Davis the debt by 10 Dec 1844, with 10% interest from this date. Signed Richard Maddock Jr., Ciely Maddock (RD). Wit Mark Brewer (JP). Rec 14 Dec 1842. [No. 1508]

1729. Page 395. 17 Dec 1842. Eli Taylor to John Logan. In consideration of the debts, liabilities, and trusts mentioned herein and the sum of $1, deed of trust on one negro man Luke about 22 years old, one negro woman Paulina, of a yellow complexion about 27 years old, and her child Catharine about 3 years old, and her infant son; four horses; five work oxen; seven cows; seven young cattle; ten sheep; 35 hogs; one two-horse Dearborn or buggy and harness; one ox waggon; two ploughs; four log binding chains; four beds, bedsteads, and bedding; one bureau; six cushion chairs and six cane bottom chairs; four tables; one brass clock; one large cupboard; one harrow; one cutting box and knife; two wheel barrows; four saddles and bridles; five axes and one adze; one hand saw; one sledge; one crow bar; and 60,000 bricks. The slaves are the same purchased from Luther Taylor and the personal property is the same purchased from Luther Taylor on 29 Aug 1842, except three of the oxen. Sd Eli owes several notes with sd Luther as security; one to John Moore dated 1 Dec 1842 for $643.25 with 10% interest from date; one dated 1 Apr 1843 for about $38 and another for $81 dated 1 Jul 1843 to Block & Avery; and one for $40 to Joseph Hertick of Ste. Genevieve Co., Mo.; one dated 1 Dec 1842 for $200 to John W. Noell; one executed 8 May 1841 to Perry Co. for the use of Congressional Twp 36, Rng 12 E for $100 with 10% interest to hold sd Noell harmless; one to Reuben Shelby for $80 to hold him harmless for a note to Robert

S. **Manning** for $42; and to hold sd **Noell** and sd **Shelby** harmless, one dated 1 Dec 1842 to sd **Noell** and one of even date to sd **Shelby**. If sd Eli does not pay the debts, then sd **Logan** is to sell the property to pay them, and hold sd **Noell** and sd **Shelby** harmless. Signed Eli **Taylor**, John **Logan**. Wit John **Layton** (JP). Rec 17 Dec 1842. [No. 1509]

1730. Page 398. 26 Dec 1842. Edward **Harter** to Christian **Oser**. For securing debts and the sum of $1, 80 acres, being the SE 1/4, SW 1/4 and SW 1/4, SE 1/4, Sec 25, Twp 34 N, Rng 10 E, subject to a mortgage dated 8 Aug 1842 from sd **Harter** to Jacob **Shoults** of New Orleans, La.; one sorrel mare with blaze face; one cow; two heffers; two small steers about one year old; 25 stock hogs; one small waggon and geer; two plows; one wheat fan; one mans saddle; one ladies saddle; two beds and bedding; two clocks; one close press; three tables; six chairs; two axes; two maddocks; three hoes; 800 bundles oats; and 300 bushels of corn. Sd **Oser** is to sell the property if the debts are not paid by 26 Dec 1846. Sd **Harter** owes eight debts by note; one to Joseph **Pratte** for $26.68; one to William **Dean** for $60, one to William **Tucker** for $35, one to Peter **Baker** for $22.50, one to Elizabeth & Sarah **Cobbs** for $7, one and an account to F. **Rozier**, one balance on a note to Henry **Ryan**, and one to Christian **Ozer** for $50. Signed Edward **Harter**, Christian **Oser**. Wit John W. **Noell**, Clerk. Rec 26 Dec 1842. [Marginal note: Full satisfaction received on 24 Jan 1843. Signed Christian **Oser** [in German]. Test J. W. **Noell**, Clerk.] [No. 1510]

1731. Page 399. 29 Dec 1842. Francis **Zeigler** and Ann, his wife, to Thomas **Faith**. For the sum of $110, Lot No. 64 fronting on Jackson St in Perryville. Signed Francis J. **Zeigler**, Ann **Zeigler** (RD). Test John **Layton** senr (JP), Leonard **Faith**. Rec 29 Dec 184[2]. [No. 1511]

1732. Page 401. 28 Dec 1842. Thomas **Kenny** to Cornelius **Manning** and Electius **Manning**. For securing three notes and the sum of $1, mortgage on 36.0475 acres, being the NE 1/4, NW 1/4, Sec 6, Twp 34 N, Rng 11 E; one yoke of oxen; one ox cart; five cows; two steers; one heifer; one bull; five last spring calves; 14 sheep; 300 bushels corn; 400 bundles fodder; one plough and geer; one bed and high post bedstead, bedding, etc.; one buro; and 24 hogs. Sd Kenny owes a note dated 10 Jun 1842 to sd Cornelius for $286.37 1/2, a note dated 11 Oct 1842 to sd Electius for $293, and a note dated Jun 1841 to sd Electius or the execr of Isidore **Moore** Senr, decd, for $50 with interest. The debts are due by 1 Jan 1846. Signed Thomas **Kenny**. Wit Mark **Brewer** (JP). Rec 29 Dec 1842. [Marginal note: Full satisfaction received on 7 Oct 1848. Signed Alexius **Manning**. Wit J. W. **Noell**, Clk.] [No. 1512]

1733. Page 402. 2 Jan 1843. Thomas J. **Tucker** to Josephus **Tucker**. For the sum of $1225, 205.25 acres, originally confirmed to Elisha **Crosby** as Survey No. 1007 in Twp 37 N, Rng 11 E; except 50 acres previously sold to John E. **Burgett** off the upper end on 27 Sep (4:58). Signed Thos. J. **Tucker**. Wit John W. **Noell**, Clerk. Rec 2 Jan 1843. [No. 1513]

1734. Page 403. 2 Jan 1843. Same to same. For securing a note and the sum of $1, mortgage on one black mare; one rone filly three years old; one iron grey horse about three years old; one rone colt one year old; two yoke of oxen; two cows and calfs; one two-year-old heifer; one three-year-old heifer; 50 hoggs; one ox cart; two plows and two sets plow geer; 700 bushels corn; one secretary; one clock; two tables; and one safe. Sd Thomas owes a note dated 2 Jan 1843 to sd Josephus for $396 with 10% interest, by 1 Jan 1845. Signed Thos. J. **Tucker**. Wit John W. **Noell**, Clerk. Rec 2 Jan 1843. [No. 1514]

1735. Page 404. 3 Oct 1842. Wm. P. **Belsha** and America, his wife, to Wm. C. **Reynolds** and Gideon H. **Baxter**. For the sum of $350, 50 acres, part of a survey confirmed to William **Hickman**; beginning at a corner on **McCasland**'s line. Signed William P. (x) **Belsha**, America (x) **Belsha** (RD). Test Alfred L. **Parks** (JP). Rec 3 Jan 1843. [No. 1515]

1736. Page 405. 5 Dec 1842. William **Thompson** to Jacob **Shaner**. For the sum of $69, mortgage on 80 acres, being the NW 1/4, SW 1/4, and the SE 1/4, SW 1/4, Sec 34, Twp 35 N, Rng 13 E; entered by sd **Thompson** on 20 Aug 1840, in Duplicate No. 7872. Sd **Thompson** owes a note of even date to sd **Shaner** in 12 months with 10% interest per annum. Signed William (x) **Thompson**. Wit A. M. **McPherson** (JP), Sally **McPherson**. Rec 3 Jan 1843. [No. 1516]

1737. Page 407. 12 Dec 1842. Thomas **Taylor** and Balbina, his wife, to James **Dunn**. For the sum of $15, 40 acres, being the NW 1/4, SE 1/4, Sec 33, Twp 35 N, Rng 10 E. Signed Thomas **Taylor**, Balbina (x) **Taylor** (RD). Test Mark **Brewer** (JP). Rec 3 Jan 1842. [No. 1517]

1738. Page 408. 10 Aug 1840. John **Peyton** and Elizabeth, his wife, to Samuel **Peyton**. For the sum of $125, 139.18 acres, being the SW fractional 1/4, Sec 30, Twp 34 N, Rng 14 E. Signed John **Peyton**, Elizabeth (x) **Peyton** (RD). Wit Augustus **Davis** (JP), Jacob **Kunce**. Rec 4 Jan 1843. [No. 1518]

1739. Page 409. 26 Dec 1842. Peter P. **Tucker** and Maryan, his wife, to Thomas J. **Miles**. For the sum of $200, 80 acres, more or less, being the S 1/2, NW 1/4, fractional Sec 36, Twp 36 N, Rng 10 E. Signed Peter P. **Tucker**, Maryan (x) **Tucker** (RD). Test John W. **Noell**, Clerk. Rec 6 Jan 1843. [No. 1519]

1740. Page 410. 10 Jan 1843. Peter **Tucker** Senior to James **Rice**. For the sum of $300, deed of trust on a slave **Harry**, about 24 years of age. Sd **Tucker** owes sd **Rice** a note of even date, due in 12 months with interest, excepting the sum of $70 for the labor of sd **Harry**. If the debt is not paid, sd **Rice** is to sell the slave. Signed Peter **Tucker** senior. Wit John W. **Noell**, Clerk. Rec 10 Jan 1843. [No. 1520]

1741. Page 411. 14 Jan 1843. Lewis **Dickson** and Martha C., his wife, to Joseph V. **Beauvais** and Ceron E. **Delassus**. For the sum of $520, a 2/7 part of three tracts once owned by Lewis **Dickson** at the time of his death; 320 arpens purchased from J. B. **Bossier** and Henry **Elliot** on 21 Jan 1820, bounded on the E by the Mississippi River, N by **Fisher**, and S by the heirs of Lewis **Dickson**; 640 acres confirmed to Lewis **Dickson**, decd, as Survey No. 1846; and 640 acres confirmed to Abraham **Armstrong** and purchased by Lewis **Dickson**, decd, at Sheriff's sale on 9 Jul 1819, bounded on the E by lands above and N by **Smith**. Lewis **Dickson** owns 1/7 as heir of his father Lewis **Dickson**, decd, and 1/7 by purchased from Dalinda **Clifton**, his sister, on 7 Nov 1842. Signed Lewis **Dickson**, Martha Caroline **Dickson** (RD). Proved by Reuben **Shelby**. Wit John W. **Noell**, Clerk. Rec 14 Jan 1843. [No. 1521]

1742. Page 413. 5 Jan 1843. James **Wadsworth** to Robert **Farrar** Senr. For acting as security for debts and the sum of $1, mortgage on one set of blacksmith tools, one two horse waggon, one sorrel horse, and one bay mare with one eye. Sd **Farrar** is security for sd **Wadsworth** in a note dated 25 Jun 1842 for $42.40 to Ferdinand **Rozier** Jr., and another note dated 14 Aug 1841 for $40 to George **Rutledge**, guardian of the heirs of the estate of Robert **Abernathy**, decd. Signed James **Wadsworth**. Wit John W. **Noell**, Clerk. Rec 16 Jan 1843. [No. 1522]

1743. Page 414. 8 Oct 1842. Joseph **Shoults** and Eliza R., his wife, to Valerio **Faina**. For the sum of $100, part of Lot No. 58 in Perryville, commencing 25 ft from the SW corner. Signed Joseph **Shoults**, Eliza R. **Shoults** (RD). Wit James **Rice** (JP). Rec 16 Jan 1843. [No. 1523]

1744. Page 415. 14 Jan 1843. Valerio **Faina** to John W. **Noell**. For securing four notes and the sum of $1, deed of trust on 96 1/4 acres and 24 poles, the N part of 640 acres originally belonging to John **Layton** Senr, decd, joining Joseph **Manning** part of the tract, on the S between the division line and the parallel of Zachariah **Layton**, excepting 2 acres sold to Henry **Caho**; Lot No. 30, the undivided 1/2 of Lot No. 20, Lot No. 11, and part of Lot No. 10 in Perryville, being purchased by sd **Faina** of the estate of Charles **Stewart**, decd (Lot Nos. 10 & 11); [five] negroes, **Mary Ann**, a yellow girl about 7 years old, **Emily** a girl about 4 years old, **Lucretia** about 4 years old, **Peter** a boy about 3 years old, and a girl child about 7 months old; one large bay horse; one sorrel horse; one rone colt; one bay colt; one yoke of black oxen, one yoke of red oxen; one ox waggon; one horse waggon; one Deborn carage and harness; one buro; one brass clock; one press; one sugar chest; one table; two sittees; one high poste bedstead; two steers two years old next spring; and one kill of brick containing about 30,000. John **Logan** is security for sd **Faina** in two notes; one to William **Manning**, guardian of Ellen **Caldwell**, infant heir of D. L. **Caldwell**, decd, dated 2 Jan 1843 for $309 with 10 % interest, payable in 12 months; one to Joseph **Simpson** for the benefit of the heirs of Charles **Stewart**, decd, dated 15 Jun 1842, for $217.25, payable in 12 months. Sd **Faina** also owes two notes to Edward **Walsh** of St. Louis Co., Mo.; one dated 1 Mar 1842 for $650 due in two years; and one dated 10 Jan 1843 for $575 payable in 18 months. Sd **Noell** is to sell the property if sd **Logan** has to pay the notes, or if sd **Walsh** requests the notes due him and sd **Faina** cannot pay them. Signed Valerio **Faina**. Wit John W. **Noell**, Clerk, John F. **Hase** (JP). Rec 18 Jan 1843. [Marginal note: Full satisfaction received on 18 Dec 1845. Signed John **Logan**. Test Jno. W. **Noell**, Clerk.] [No. 1524]

1745. Page 417. 20 Jan 1843. James **Riddick** to James D. **Brewer**, Joseph **Shoults**, and Valerio **Faina**. For holding the grantees harmless and the sum of $1, mortgage on one black roan mare with a dark colored colt; three cows and calves; three young cattle; one brass clock; eight sheep; two sows and pigs; four barrows; and about 100 bushels of corn. Sd **Brewer** is security for sd **Riddick** in a note to Alexius **Manning** dated 10 Dec 1840 for $73, payable 12 months after date; and sd **Shoults** and sd **Faina** are security for sd **Riddick** in a note to Perry Co. for the use of the inhabitants of Twp 36 N dated 15 Feb 1842 for $40, bearing interest at 10% per annum. Signed James **Riddick**. Wit John W. **Noell**, Clerk. Rec 20 Jan 1843. [No. 1525]

1746. Page 419. 23 Jan 1843. Valerio **Faina** and Matilda, his wife, to John **Logan**. For the sum of $75, part of Lot No. 58 in Perryville on St. Marys St, commencing 25 ft from the SW corner.

Signed Valerio **Faina**, Matilda **Faina** (RD). Wit John W. **Noell**, Clerk. Rec 23 Jan 1843. [No. 1526]

1747. Page 420. 23 Jan 1843. Josephus **Tucker** Senior and Nancy, his wife, to Marcus **Block** and Adolph **Block**. For the sum of $1361, 127.60 acres on the Mississippi River in Bois Brule Bottom; a tract conveyed to Thomas J. **Tucker** by Joseph **Pratte** and John **Logan**, commissioners to sell the real estate of the estate of Charles **Ellis**, decd, on 22 Jul 1841 (4:105); and taken off the S 1/2 of the portion sold by Thomas J. **Tucker** and wife to Josephus **Tucker**. Signed Josephus (x) **Tucker** senr, Nancy C. (x) **Tucker** (RD). Wit John F. **Hase** (JP). Rec 23 Jan 1843. [No. 1527]

1748. Page 421. 24 Jan 1843. Edward **Harter** to Jacob **Conrad**. For securing two notes and the sum of $1, mortgage on 80 acres, being the SE 1/4, SW 1/4, and SW 1/4, SE 1/4, Sec 25, Twp 34 N, Rng 10 E, subject to a mortgage to Jacob **Shoults** of New Orleans, La. dated 8 Aug 1842; one sorrel mare with blaze face; one cow; two heifers; two small steers about one year old; 25 stock hogs; one small waggon and gear; two ploughs; one wheat fan; one mans saddle; one ladies saddle; one clothes press; three tables; two beds and bedding; six chairs; two axes; two mattocks; three hoes; 800 bundles oats; and 300 bushels corn. Sd **Conrad** is security for sd **Harter** in a note to Peter **Baker** for $22.50, and another dated 24 Jan 1843 for sd **Harter** and Jno. M. **Bower** to Ferdinand **Rozier** Jr. for $112.41. payable four months after date. Signed Edward **Harter**. Wit John W. **Noell**, Clerk. Rec 24 Jan 1843. [Marginal note: Full satisfaction received on 30 Nov 1843. Signed Jacob **Conrad**. Test J. W. **Noell**, Clerk.] [No. 1528]

1749. Page 422. 8 Dec 1841. Sarah **Newberry** to Henry **Newberry**. In consideration of the love she has for her son, two tracts in Sec 28, Twp 35 N, Rng 12 E; 40 acres, being the [S]W 1/4, NE 1/4; and 80 acres, being the W 1/2, SE 1/4. Signed Sarah (x) **Newberry**. Wit Jas. B. **Martin**, Osbirn W. **Walker**, Robert T. **Brown** (JP). Rec 27 Jan 1843. [No. 1529]

1750. Page 423. 28 Jan 1843. Lewis **Mattingly** to George W. **Taylor**. For securing debts and the sum of $1, three gray horses; one sorrel mare; and one four horse waggon and gearing. Sd **Mattingly** owes three notes to sd **Taylor**; one dated 5 Jan 1842 for $35; one dated 4 Apr 1842 for $50; and one dated 19 Dec 1842 for $21. Signed Lewis **Mattingley**. Wit John W. **Noell**, Clerk. Rec 28 Jan 1843. [Marginal note: Full satisfaction received on 27 Jul 1844. Signed George W. **Taylor**. Test J. W. **Noell**, Clerk.] [No. 1530]

1751. Page 424. 19 Nov 1842. Charles **Hayden** and Matilda, his wife, to Henry **Caho**. For the sum of $500, Lot No. 75 in Perryville, on North St and Jackson St. Signed Charles **Hayden**, Matilda **Hayden** (RD). Wit John W. **Noell**, Clerk. Rec 28 Jan 1843. [No. 1531]

1752. Page 425. 27 Jan 1843. Ernst Henry **Voelker** to his wife Sophia Dorothea Amelia **Voelker**. For natural love and affection to his wife and the sum of $200, 40 acres, being the SW 1/4, SE 1/4, fractional Sec 29, Twp 34 N, Rng 10 E, entered by Christiana **Voelker** on 1 4 Nov 1837, Certificate No. 5351, and conveyed by her to sd Ernst on 2 Jun 1840 (3:331); 40 acres, being the SE 1/4, SE 1/4, Sec 10, Twp 35 N, Rng 12 E, entered by sd Ernst on 1 Aug 1838; all his household and kitchen furniture; all his stock horses, cows, cattle, sheep, and hogs; his crop of grain; and farming utensils. Signed Ernst Henry **Voelker**. Wit John F. **Hase** (JP). Rec 30 Jan 1843. [No. 1532]

1753. Page 426. 27 Jan 1843. Christiana **Voelker** to Sophia Dorothea Amelia **Voelker**. For the sum of $50, 36.40 acres, being the SE fractional 1/4, SE 1/4, Sec 29, Twp 36 N, Rng 10 E, patented on 6 Aug 1842 in Certificate No. 8519. Signed Christiana Johana **Voelkerin**. Wit Adam **Klein**, John F. **Hase** (JP). Rec 30 Jan 1843. [No. 1533]

1754. Page 427. 21 Jan 1843. Walter B. **Wilkinson** and Emilie, his wife, to Ferdinand **Rozier** Jr. For the sum of $150, the undivided 1/3 of 155.30 acres, being the NE fractional 1/4, fractional Sec 29, Twp 35 N, Rng 10 E; entered by Lewis **French** and Walter B. **Wilkinson**. Signed W. B. **Wilkinson**, Emily L. **Wilkinson**. Wit Firman A. **Rozier**, John W. **Noell**, Clerk. Rec 30 Jan 1843. [No. 1534]

1755. Page 428. 28 Jan 1843. Ferdinand **Rozier** Jr. and Harriet, his wife, to Ann (alias Mary) **Goff**, a woman of color. For the sum of $20, Lot No. 72 in Perryville. Signed Ferdinand **Rozier** Jr., Harriet **Rozier** (RD). Wit James **Rice** (JP). Rec 30 Jan 1843. [No. 1535]

1756. Page 429. 3 Feb 1843. Bartholomew **Murphy** and Ellen L., his wife, to Marcus **Block** and Adolph **Block**. For the sum of $20, Lot No. 44 in Perryville. Signed Bartholomew **Murphy**, Ellen (x) **Murphy** (RD). Wit John W. **Noell**, Clerk. Rec 3 Feb 1843. [No. 1536]

1757. Page 429. 4 Feb 1843. William **Winfield** to Robert L. **Philips**. For the sum of $480, 200 acres where sd **Winfield** now resides; confirmed to Tunis **Quick**, conveyed by him to John W. **Quick**, conveyed by the admr of John W. **Quick** to Peter R. **Pratte**, and by sd **Pratte** and wife to sd **Winfield**. Signed William **Winfield**. Wit John W. **Noell**, Clerk. Rec 4 Feb 1843. [No. 1537]

1758. Page 430. 13 Feb 1843. Martin L. **Moore** and Anna Regina, his wife, and Isaac G. **Whitworth** to Martin L. **Moore**. For the sum of $300, two lots in Perryville; Lot No. 73, deeded to sd **Moore** and sd **Whitworth** by Charles **Roy** on 1 Feb 1842; and part of Lot No. 32, beginning at the SE corner of Peter R. **Pratte**'s storehouse. Signed Martin L. **Moore**, Anna Regina **Moore** (RD), Isaac G. **Whitworth**. Wit John F. **Hase** (JP). Rec 13 Feb 1843. [No. 1538]

1759. Page 431. 13 Feb 1843. Same, same, and same to Isaac G. **Whitworth**. For the sum of $1500, Lot No. 7 in Perryville. Signed Martin L. **Moore**, Anna Ragina **Moore** (RD), Isaac G. **Whitworth**. Wit John F. **Hase** (JP). Rec 13 Feb 1843. [No. 1539]

1760. Page 432. 14 Feb 1843. Isaac G. **Whitworth** to Benjamin R. **Allbright** of Cape Girardeau Co., Mo. For the sum of $75, the undivided 1/2 of Lot Nos. 87, 88, & 89 in Perryville. Signed Isaac G. **Whitworth**. Wit John W. **Noell**, Clerk. Rec 14 Feb 1843. [No. 1540]

1761. Page 433. 18 Feb 1843. Joseph A. **Mossey** to William **Kline**. For securing a note and the sum of $1, mortgage on 160 acres, more or less, beginning at a white oak on the bank of Rock Spring Branch at the juncture of a small branch coming in from the SW NE corner of sd tract; also mortgaged to James **Rice** in a deed dated 26 Feb 1842 (4:160). Sd **Mossey** owes sd **Kline** a note of even date for $321.68, due with interest. Signed Jos. A. **Mossey**. Wit James **Rice** (JP). Rec 18 Feb 1843. [No. 1541]

1762. Page 434. 23 Dec 1842. Thomas **Wilkinson** to John **Wilkinson**. For the sum of $90, an undivided 1/2 of 76.41 acres on the Mississippi River, being the E fractional 1/2, SW 1/4, Sec 18, Twp 35 N, Rng 13 E. Signed Thos. **Wilkinson**. Wit Jas. **Rose**, Notary Public in Shelby Co., Tenn. Rec 6 Mar 1843. [No. 1542]

1763. Page 435. 23 Feb 1843. Joseph D. **Simpson** and Mary, his wife, to Joseph **Cissell**. For the sum of $150, mortgage on 233 acres in Twps 35 & 36, Rng 9 & 10, being the E end of Survey No. 2169 granted to Roland **Boyd**. Sd **Cissell** is security for sd **Simpson** in a note of even date to Ferdinand **Rozier** Jr. for $296, due in six months with 10% interest. Signed Joseph D. **Simpson**, Mary **Simpson** (RD). Wit John W. **Noell**, Clerk. Rec 8 Mar 1843. [No. 1543]

1764. Page 437. 8 Mar 1843. Stephen **Dolson** and Lucinda, his wife, to Lucas **Bonard**. For the sum of $60, 40 acres, being the SE 1/4, SE 1/4, Sec 35, Twp 35 N, Rng 10 E; purchased by sd **Dolson** at a sale of school lands at Nov 1838 Circuit Court term by Sheriff Hugh **Wells**. Signed Stephen **Dolson**, Lucinda **Dolson** (RD). John F. **Hase** (JP). Rec 9 Mar 1843. [No. 1544]

1765. Page 438. 25 Feb 1843. Thomas **Cochran** to William **Burns**. For the sum of $100, mortgage on one jackass eight or nine years old. Sd **Burns** is security for sd **Cochran** in a note to Alexander **Baily** dated 9 Jun 1841, payable the next Christmas, with 10% interest. Signed Thomas **Cochran**. Wit Barna B. **Burns**, Alfred L. **Parks** (JP). Rec 9 Mar 1843. [No. 1545]

1766. Page 438. [Page number is used twice.] 11 Mar 1843. Sylvarius **Layton** to Morris **Block** and Charles **Avery**. For securing a note and the sum of $1, deed of trust on 40 acres, being the SW 1/4, NW 1/4, Sec 17, Twp 34 N, Rng 10 E. Sd **Layton** owes Block & Avery a note of even date for $121.17 3/4, with 10% interest per annum, due one day after date; with the property to be sold if the note is not paid in 12 months. Signed Sylvarius (x) **Layton**. Wit John W. **Noell**, Clerk. Rec 11 Mar 1843. [No. 1546]

1767. Page 439. 12 Feb 1842. Thomas **Riney** and Sarah, his wife, to Evaristus **Riney**. For the sum of $150, two tracts in Twp 37 N, Rng 10 E; 61 acres, more or less, being the S part, NW fractional 1/4 and N part, SW fractional 1/4, Sec 27; and 16 acres, more or less, being the NE 1/4 fractional 1/4, fractional Sec 28, beginning at the SW corner of John **Greenawalt**'s survey and also bounded by Luke **Mattingly**. Signed Thomas **Riney**, Sarah (x) **Riney** (RD). Wit Henry **Drury** (JP). Rec 11 Mar 1843. [No. 1547]

1768. Page 440. 13 Mar 1843. Helen **Winfield**, wife of William **Winfield**, to Robert L. **Philips**. Relinquishment of dower rights to 200 acres originally confirmed to Tunis **Quick**, sd tract having been sold on 4 Feb 1843 (4:429). Signed Helen (x) **Winfield** (RD). Test J. W. **Noell**, Clerk. Rec 13 Mar 1843. [No. 1548]

1769. Page 441. 17 Mar 1843. Henry **Dean** to Ferdinand **Rozier**, Jr. For securing a note and the sum of $1, mortgage on three tracts in Sec 25, Twp 36 N, Rng 10 E: 55.28 acres, being the NE fractional 1/4; 39.8875 acres, being the NE 1/4, NW 1/4; and 2 1/2 acres, being purchased by sd **Dean** from Leo **Layton** and wife on 2 Oct 1841. Sd **Dean** owes sd **Rozier** a note of even date for

$164.61 with 8% interest per annum. Signed Henry **Dean**. Wit John W. **Noell**, Clerk. Rec 17 Mar 1843. [No. 1549]

1770. Page 442. 18 Mar 1843. Thomas H. **McAtee** to Robert S. **Manning**. For the sum of $80, mortgage on one large bay stable horse called Mark Antony. Sd **McAtee** owes sd **Manning** a debt, payable on demand. Signed Thomas H. **McAtee**. Wit John W. **Noell**, Clerk. Rec 18 Mar 1843. [No. 1550]

1771. Page 442. 25 Mar 1843. Guy **Elder** to Morris **Block** and Charles **Avery**. For the sum of $50, Lot No. 37 in Perryville. Signed Guy **Elder**. Wit John W. **Noell**, Clerk. Rec 27 Mar 1843. [No. 1551]

1772. Page 443. 1 Aug 1840. Julius E. **Parks** to Joseph **Parks**. For the sum of $50, 40 acres, being the NW 1/4, SW 1/4, Sec 8, Twp 34 N, Rng 12 E. Signed Julius E. **Parks**. Wit Elias **Barber** (JP). Rec 29 Mar 1843. [No. 1552]

1773. Page 444. 20 Mar 1843. Andres **Popp** and Amolia Rosena, his wife, to George **Helbert** [**Hilpert**]. For the sum of $50, 40 acres, being the SW 1/4, SW 1/4, Sec 21, Twp 34 N, Rng 13 E; entered by sd **Popp** on 28 Apr 1841, Duplicate No. 8151. Signed Andres **Popp**, Amolina **Poppin** (RD). Wit A. M. **McPherson** (JP). Rec 3 Apr 1843. [No. 1553]

1774. Page 445. 17 Mar 1843. Lutze **Grother** and Anna, his wife, to John Gottlieb **Goethe**. For the sum of $4.50, two parcels, part of 7.50 acres out of the NW 1/4, SW 1/4, Sec 22, Twp 34 N, Rng 13 E; sold by Henry C. **Bimpage**, admr of Johann George **Gube**, to sd **Grother**; 1 acre and 32 poles beginning at the NW 1/4 corner; and 1 rood and 10 poles off the S end. Signed Lutze **Grother**, Anna (x) **Grother** (RD). Wit A. M. **McPherson** (JP). Rec 3 Apr 1843. [No. 1554]

1775. Page 446. 11 Mar 1842. Joseph **Jenkins** and Elizabeth, his wife, to Robert **Jenkins**. For the sum of $100, 20 acres, more or less, being the W 1/2, SE 1/4, SW 1/4, Sec 23, Twp 34 N, Rng 13 E. Signed Joseph **Jenkins**, Elizabeth (x) **Jenkins**. Wit Cyrus **Henderson**, Augustus **Davis** (JP). Rec 3 Apr 1843. [No. 1555]

1776. Page 447. 25 Nov 1839. Thomas **Jinkins** and Mary, his wife, to Thomas **Swan**. For the sum of $200, 40 acres, being the SE 1/4, SW 1/4, Sec 23, Twp 34 N, Rng 13 E. Signed Thomas **Jenkins**, Mary (x) **Jenkins**. Test M. C. **Wilson**, Charles (x) **Swan**, Augustus **Davis** (JP). Rec 3 Apr 1843. [No. 1556]

1777. Page 448. 26 Oct 1842. Robert M. **Jenkins** and Lucy E., his wife, to Robert P. **Slaughter**. For the sum of $100, 20 acres, more or less, being the W 1/2, SE 1/4, SW 1/4, Sec 23, Twp 34 N, Rng 13 E. Signed Robert M. **Jenkins**, Lucy E. **Jenkins** (RD). Wit A. M. **McPherson** (JP). Rec 3 Apr 1843. [No. 1557]

1778. Page 449. 24 Feb 1843. George **Klugel** to Ernst Gerhard Wilhelm **Keyl**. For the sum of $308, 40 acres, more or less, being the SE 1/4, NW 1/4, Sec 26, Twp 34 N, Rng 13 E. Wit George **Klugel**. Test Gottlieb **Klugel**, Augustus H. **Doederleud**, John W. **Noell**, Clerk. Rec 3 Apr 1843. [No. 1558]

1779. Page 450. 30 Aug 1841. Louisa **Marbach** and Francis A., her husband, to George **Klugel**. For the sum of $150, 40 acres, more or less, being the SE 1/4, NW 1/4, Lot No. 2, [Sec ?], Twp 34 N, Rng 13 E. Signed Louisa **Marbach**, Francis A. **Marbach**. Wit Johann Gottlieb **Palisch**, Gottleeb **Klugel**, Augustus **Davis** (JP). Rec 3 Apr 1843. [No. 1559]

1780. Page 451. 28 Oct 1841. Robert C. **Powell** and Cyrinder A., his wife, to Rachel **Taylor**. For the sum of $186, two negro boy slaves, **Hillry** aged about 20 years, and **Ellic** aged about 12; both belonging to the estate of James Taylor, decd. Signed Robert C. **Powell**, Cyrinda Ann **Powell** (RD). Wit Perry **Evans** (JP). Rec 4 Apr 1843. [No. 1560]

1781. Page 451. 21 Dec 1842. Archibald M. **McPherson** and Sarah, his wife, to George Washington **Cowan**. For the sum of $45, 36.15 acres, being the E 1/2, W 1/2, NE 1/4, Sec 5, Twp 34 N, Rng 13 E; entered by sd **McPherson** on 19 Jun 1840, Duplicate No. 7819. Signed A. M. **McPherson**, Sally **McPherson** (RD). Wit Thomas M. **Blair**, Joseph **Cowan**, Augustus **Davis** (JP). Rec 4 Apr 1843. [No. 1561]

1782. Page 452. 26 Feb 1840. Benjamin **Davis** and Jane, his wife, Augustus **Davis**, Minervey and Eliza **Davis**, and Washington **Davis** to Sylvester **Young**. For the sum of $350, 80 acres, being Lot No. 2, NW 1/4, Sec 2, Twp 33 N, Rng 13 E. Signed Benjamin **Davis**, Jain (x) **Davis**, Augustus **Davis**, Manerva **Davis**, Eliza **Davis**, Washington **Davis**. Wit Elias **Barber** (JP). Rec 6 Apr 1843. [No. 1562]

1783. Page 454. 2 Nov 1836. Philip **Davis** and Margaret, his wife, of Jackson Co., Ill. to Sylvester **Young** of La. For the sum of $100, 80 acres, being Lot No. 1, NW 1/4, Sec 2, Twp 33, Rng 13 E; patented by sd **Davis** from the U. S. A. on 6 Nov 1823 (1:311). Signed Philip **Davis**, Margaret **Davis**. Wit D. H. **Brush**, Circuit Clerk of Jackson Co., Ill., Benjamin **Davis**. Rec 6 Apr 1843. [No. 1563]

1784. Page 455. 12 Apr 1839. George A. **Hamilton** to Fenwick J. **Hamilton**. For the sum of $100, 105 acres and some poles, bounded on the N by the dower land of his decd mother, W by public land, S by Lot No. 9, and E by Lot No. 6 & 7 owned by Leo **Fenwick** and Harrison **Young**, decd. Signed George A. **Hamilton**. Wit Robert P. **Slaughter**, Leo **Fenwick**, John W. **Noell**, Clerk. Rec 6 Apr 1843. [No. 1564]

1785. Page 456. 7 Apr 1843. Jefferson **Young** and Elizabeth, his wife, to Sarah **Young**. For the sum of $500, mortgage on about 44 acres in Brazeau Bottom on the Mississippi River, part of the original survey of George A. **Hamilton**, and the undivided 1/5 of Lot No. 2; 44 acres, more or less, the undivided 1/5 of Lot No. 3; 44 acres and some poles, the undivided 1/11 part of Lot No. 4; 65 acres and 88 poles, the undivided 1/5 part of Lot No. 7; undivided 1/6 part of the slaves belonging to the estate of Harrison **Young**, decd: **Darcas**, **Ann**, **Andy**, **Priscillia**, **Joseph**, **Andrew**, and **Sydua**; and all their right to any real and personal property of sd decd. Sd Jefferson owes sd Sarah a debt, due in 12 months with 10% interest per annum. Signed Jefferson **Young**, Elizabeth **Young** (RD). Wit R. P. **Slaughter**, A. M. **McPherson** (JP). Rec 10 Apr 1843. [No. 1565]

1786. Page 458. 29 Aug 1840. Fenwick J. **Hamilton** and Rebecca Ann, his wife, and Henry C. **Bimpage** and Mary Jane, his wife, to Merritt C. **Wilson**. For the sum or $45.87 1/2, 40 acres, more or less, being the SW 1/4, NW 1/4, fractional Sec 24, Twp 34 N, Rng 13 E. Signed F. J. **Hamilton**, Rebecca A. **Hamilton** (RD), Henry

C. **Bimpage**, Mary Jane **Bimpage** (RD). Wit Thomas **Swan**, Augustus **Davis** (JP). Rec 10 Apr 1843. [No. 1566]

1787. Page 459. 10 Apr 1843. John **OShea** to Thomas **Harte**. For the sum of $402.50, mortgage on a slave **Jack**, about 16 years of age. Sd **OShea** owes sd **Harte** a note of even date, due in 12 months at 10% interest per annum. Signed John **OShea**. Wit A. M. **McPherson** (JP), George **Caphart**. Rec 11 Apr 1843. [Marginal note: Full satisfaction received on 14 Apr 1845. Signed Thos. **Hartz**. Test Jno. W. **Noell**, Clerk.] [No. 1567]

1788. Page 460. 11 Apr 1843. Edward M. **Holden** to Ignatius G. **Beal** of St. Francis Co., Mo. For securing a note and the sum of $1, mortgage on one brown horse, one bay mare, one yoke of black oxen he purchased at the trustee sale of Joseph S. **Pease** as the property of George **McKinstry**, and one ox cart purchased from Richardson & Bridgeman. Sd **Holden** owes sd **Beal** $150, due in two years with 10% interest. Signed Edward M. **Holden**. Wit John W. **Noell**, Clerk. Rec 11 Apr 1843. [No. 1568]

1789. Page 461. 8 Mar 1843. John G. **Hemmon** and Mary R., his wife, to John Gottlieb **Burghart**. For the sum of $50, 40 acres, being the NE 1/4, NE 1/4, Sec 26, Twp 34, Rng 13 E; entered by Jacob **Gross** on 10 Aug 1841 in Certificate No. 7177, deeded by him to Gottlieb **Gross**, and by him to sd **Hemmon**. Signed John Gottfried **Hemmon**, Rosina Maria **Hemmon** (RD). Wit A. M. **McPherson** (JP). Rec 12 Apr 1843. [No. 1569]

1790. Page 462. 8 Mar 1843. John Gottlieb **Burkhart** and Alfrona, his wife, to John G. **Hammonn**. For the sum of $50, 40 acres, being the SE 1/4, SW 1/4, Sec 21, Twp 34 N, Rng 12 E; entered by Gottlieb **Burkhardt** on 22 Apr 1840, Duplicate No. 7698. Signed John Gottlieb **Burghart**, Alfrona **Burghardt** (RD). Wit A. M. **McPherson** (JP). Rec 12 Apr 1843. [No. 1570]

1791. Page 463. 20 Mar 1843. Gottleap Frederick **Gross** and Hannah Rosetta, his wife, to John Gottlieb **Hemmonn**. For the sum of $200, 40 acres, being the NE 1/4, NE 1/4, Sec 26, Twp 34 N, Rng 13 E; entered by Jacob **Gross**. Certificate No. 7177. Signed Gottlob Frederick **Gross**, Hannah Rosetta **Gross** (RD; proved by Michael **Nicher** and Anemann **Popp**). Wit A. M. **McPherson** (JP). Rec 12 Apr 1843. [No. 1571]

1792. Page 464. 13 Dec 1826. John **Cissell** to John B. **Bossier** of Ste. Genevieve, Ste. Genevieve Co., Mo. For the sum of $20, undivided 1/4 part of the NE 1/4, Sec 30, Twp 35 N, Rng 10 E, now owned in common by sd **Cissell**, **Bossier**, and Simon **Duvall**. Signed John **Cissell**. Wit Savinan **St. Vrain**, Jos. D. **Grafton**, Clerk. Rec 12 Apr 1843. [No. 1572]

1793. Page 465. 17 Apr 1843. James **Dunn** and Mary, his wife, to Ferdinand **Rozier** Jr. For the sum of $174, two tracts in Sec 18, Twp 34 N, Rng 11 E; 79.56 acres, being the W 1/2, SW 1/4; and 40.77 acres, being the S 1/2, Lot No. 2, NW 1/4; the N 1/2, S 1/2 of the same tract having been previously conveyed by sd **Dunn** to sd **Rozier**. Signed James **Dunn**, Mary **Dunn** (RD). Wit John W. **Noell**, Clerk. Rec 17 Apr 1843. [No. 1573]

1794. Page 467. 18 Apr 1843. Kunnegunda **Greener** to Michael **Fasold** and Alfred **Fasold**. For the sum of $325, two tracts in Sec 22, Twp 35 N, Rng 11 E; 40 acres, being the SW 1/4, SE 1/4; and 40 acres, being the SE 1/4, SE 1/4. Signed Kunnegunda (x) **Greener**. Test John W. **Noell**, Clerk. Rec 18 Apr 1843. [No. 1574]

1795. Page 468. 14 Apr 1843. Reuben **Shelby** and Mary, his wife, to Clemence **Landry**. For the sum of $200, part of Lot No. 61 on Jackson St in Perryville, beginning at the SE corner. Signed Reuben **Shelby**, Mary E. **Shelby** (RD). Wit John W. **Noell**, Clerk. Rec 14 Apr 1843. [No. 1575]

1796. Page 469. 22 Jan 1827. Simon **Duvall** and Mary, his wife, to John B. **Bossier** of Ste. Genevieve Co., Mo. For the sum of $20, an undivided 1/4 part of the NE 1/4, Sec 30, Twp 35 N, Rng 10 E; which 1/4 section is now owned in common by sd **Duvall** and sd **Bossier**. Signed Simon **Duvall**, Mary Ann **Duvall**. Wit John **Smith**, Paschal **Bequet**, James **Rice** (JP). Rec 19 Apr 1843. [No. 1576]

1797. Page 470. 19 Apr 1843. James **Stewart** to James **Rice**. For the sum of $50, his undivided share of the estate of Charles **Stewart**, decd, and his right to the shares of John Rosamont **Stewart**, decd, and Ann **Stewart**, decd, which was their part of the estate of their father Charles **Stewart**, decd. Signed James E. **Stewart**. Wit John W. **Noell**, Clerk. Rec 19 Apr 1843. [No. 1577]

1798. Page 471. 29 Apr 1843. Anna Clary **Welker** to Andrew **Welker**. For the sum of $150, one gray mare and one gray horse two years old this spring; one cow and calf; three sheep; and one note from William **Welker** for $100, dated 9 Apr 1842 at 10% interest per annum. Signed Anna Clary (x) **Welker**. Test William **Farrar** Senr (JP). Rec 1 May 1843. [No. 1578]

1799. Page 472. 18 Mar 1843. William J. **Tucker** and Elizabeth, his wife, to Enoch G. **Stone**. For the sum of $100, 40 acres, being the SE 1/4, SE 1/4, Sec 15, Twp 34 N, Rng 10 E. Signed William J. **Tucker**, Elizabeth (x) **Tucker** (RD). Wit James **Rice** (JP). Rec 1 May 1843. [No. 1579]

1800. Page 473. 15 Mar 1843. Claude F. **Guyot** to Seraphim **Bruchon**. For the sum of $50, 39.99 acres, being the SE 1/4, SE fractional 1/4, Sec 22, Twp 35 N, Rng 10 E. Signed C. F. **Guyot**. Wit John W. **Noell**, Clerk. Rec 3 Apr 1843. [No. 1553 is inserted here, out of sequence]

1801. Page 473. 6 May 1843. John **Layton** and Monica, his wife, to George W. **Scollay** of Montgomery Co., Ill. For the sum of $100.84, 7 acres, 3 roods, and 35 poles, exclusive of the road from Perryville to the seminary; beginning at the most S corner the survey of John **Layton** Senr; bounded in part by Louis **Layton**, Bernard **Layton**'s survey. Signed John **Layton** Senr, Monica (x) **Layton** (RD). Wit John J. **Hickey**, John F. **Hase** (JP). Rec 8 May 1843. [No. 1580]

1802. Page 475. 6 Feb 1841. James **Roseborough** and Julia, his wife, to Joseph **Lane**. For the sum of $1070, three tracts; the E 1/2, SE 1/4, Sec 36, Twp 35 N, Rng 12 E; the SW 1/4, SE 1/4, Sec 36, Twp 35 N, Rng 12 E; and the S 1/2, Lot No. 2, SW 1/4, Sec 31, Twp 35 N, Rng 13 E. Signed James **Rosebrough**, Julia **Rosebrough** (RD). Wit Elias **Barber** (JP). Rec 13 May 1843. [No. 1581]

1803. Page 476. 9 Jun 1834. Henry **Little** to Lot **Abernathy**. For the sum of $50, 40 acres, being the NW 1/4, SE 1/4, Sec 23, Twp 34 N, Rng 11 E. purchased by sd **Little** from the U. S. on 12 Dec

1833, Duplicate No. 1698. Signed Hy. **Little**. Wit J. **Abernathy** (JP). Rec 17 May 1843. [No. 1582]

1804. Page 477. 9 Jun 1834. Lot **Abernathy** and Margaret, his wife, to Elihu **Sides**. For the sum of $25, 20 acres, beginning on the NE corner of sd **Sides**' land, and bounded in part by Saml. L. **Moore** and Eliza **Sides**; part of 40 acres sd **Abernathy** purchased from Henry **Little** on 9 Jun 1834. Signed Lott **Abernathy**, Margaret **Abernathy** (RD). Wit J. **Abernathy** (JP). Rec 17 May 1843. [No. 1583]

1805. Page 478. 20 May 1843. Michael **Fasold** and Alfred **Fasold** to Kunnegunda **Greener**. For securing debts and the sum of $1, mortgage on two tracts in Sec 22, Twp 35 N, Rng 11 E; 40 acres, being the SW 1/4, SE 1/4; and 40 acres, being the SE 1/4, SE 1/4. Sd **Fasold**s owe sd **Greener** $300 by six notes for $50 each, dated 18 Apr 1843 with 7% interest per annum, and payable in one, two, three, four, five, and six years. Signed Alfert **Fasold**, Michael **Fasold**. Test John W. **Noell**, Clerk. Rec 20 May 1843. [Marginal note: Full satisfaction received. Signed John W. **Noell**, assignee of Kunnegunda **Greener**.] [No. 1584]

1806. Page 479. 7 Jun 1842. Last will and testament of Charles **Ingram**. To his son Benjamin Franklin **Ingram**: 500 acres purchased from **Cybert** (the mill tract) and all adjoining entries; 505 acres purchased from Charles **Harris**, agent for his brother; and slaves: **Jinny** and her children **William**, **Harriette**, **Adaline**, **David**, and **Sylvestus**, a woman **Martha** and her child **Mary**, and **Garrette**. To his son John Nelum **Ingram**: 600 acres on Brazo formerly belonging to Samuel **Anderson**; 80 acres purchased from John **Garner** S of Apple Creek; and slaves: **Joe** and **Sena** his wife, **Josiah**, **Amanda**, **Betsy**, **Berry**, **Charles**, and **Margaret**. To his son George Washington **Ingram**: 900 acres in Madison Co. purchased from Burwell **Porter** and William **Crawford** in two adjoining tracts, and slaves: **Charity** and her children **Betty**, **Antony**, **Sam**, **Wiley**, **Edmond**, **Andy**, Young **Presly**, and **Boson**. To his three daughters and granddaughters, Mary Ann **Edwards** living in La., Betsy **Clark** living in Ga., Polly **Law** in Ga., and his granddaughter in La., the slaves **Antony**, **Jerry** and **Letty** his wife, **Galon**, **Sarah** and her child **Isaac** and his wife and four children **Jefferson**, **Susan**, **Louisa**, **Julia** and **Sarah** and her child **John**, Old **Peter**, **Providence**, **John**, **Susa**, **Sylva**, **Nelly Ann**, **Ricey Feriba** and her child. The slaves are to be equally divided among his daughter and granddaughter Demaris **Ingram**, daughter of Wiley **Ingram**, decd. Also to Demaris **Ingram**: 640 acres, more or less, purchased at the estate auction of John **Carr**, decd, and four slaves: **Edmond**, **Luce**, **Elias**, and **Joe**. To his children and granddaughter: all his lands in La., to be sold, or equal distribution of sd lands. To Sally **Tricky**, daughter of Acy **Tricky**, decd: one negro child **Luce** and $250. To his wife Polly, who left his bed and board about 12 months ago without any just cause: $100 of his estate and $400 in place of what she received from her father's estate. His sons Benjamin F., John N., and George W. are to be sent to school or bound out to some good trade. His execrs are to find some good man to take charge of the farm and the saw and grist mill. His sons are to receive their legacies and an equal share of his stock and personal property at age 21, unless they "prove to be idle, indolent, immoral, and not economical," in which case they do not receive their bequests until they are reformed. Curus **Henderson**, Joseph **James**, and Sylvester **Young** are appointed executors. Signed Charles **Ingram**. Wit John **Peyton**, Samuel B. **McKnight**, Columbus **Price**, James **Rice**, County Court Clerk. Rec 22 May 1843. [No. 1585]

1807. Page 482. 5 May 1843. John R. **Layton** to Martin **Layton**. For securing two notes, mortgage on 230 acres in Survey No. 846 in Twp 35 N, Rng 10 & 11 E, confirmed to John **Layton** Senior; being the part devised by Zechariah **Layton**, decd, to his sons Nereus and Felix; and the same purchased by sd John R. Sd Martin is security for sd John R. in two notes bearing 10% interest per annum; one dated 24 May 1843 to Block & Avery of Perryville for $38.14, due in one day; the other dated 24 May 1843 to Perry Co. for $60.81. Signed John R. **Layton**. Wit James **Rice** (JP). Rec 25 May 1843. [Marginal note: Full satisfaction received on 26 Feb 1852. Signed Martin **Layton**. Test Charles C. **Ellis**, Clerk.] [No. 1586]

1808. Page 483. 26 May 1843. William D. **Harrington** of St. Louis, Mo. to James **Abernathy**. For securing a note and the sum of $1, mortgage on 160 acres, being the SE 1/4, Sec 4, Twp 34 N, Rng 11 E. Sd **Harrington** owes a note of even date to sd **Abernathy** for $300, due in 12 months with 10% interest per annum. Signed Wm. D. **Harrington**. Wit John W. **Noell**, Clerk. Rec 21 May 1843. [No. 1587]

1809. Page 485. 9 May 1843. James **Haydon** and Christeen, his wife, to Charles **Haydon**. For the sum of $100, 40 acres, being the NW 1/4, SW 1/4, Sec 32, Twp 34 N, Rng 11 E. Signed James **Haydon**, Christeen **Haydon** (RD). Wit Mark **Brewer** (JP). Rec 27 May 1843. [No. 1588]

1810. Page 486. 29 May 1843. John B. **Cissell** and Susannah, his wife, to James **Dunn**. For the sum of $200, 80 acres, more or less, being the SE 1/4, NE 1/4, and the NE 1/4, SE 1/4, Sec 33, Twp 35 N, Rng 10 E. Signed John B. (x) **Cissell**, Susannah (x) **Cissell** (RD). Wit James **Rice** (JP). Rec 29 May 1843. [No. 1589]

1811. Page 487. 27 May 1843. Robert C. **Powell** and Cerinda A., his wife, to James S. **Powell**. For the sum of $300, 120 acres in three 40-acre lots cornering on the center of fractional Sec 16, Twp 36 N, Rng 10 E; being Lot Nos. 5, 8, & 9. Signed Robert C. **Powell**, [Cerinda E (x) **Powell** (RD)]. Test Stephen **Sanders** (JP). Rec 31 May 1843. [No. 1590]

1812. Page 488. 6 May 1843. Robert H. **Ross**, execr of the last will and testament of John **Ross**, to William J. **McCombs**. For the sum of $411, two tracts in Sec 13, Twp 34 N, Rng 12 E; 80 acres, being the W 1/2, NW 1/4; and 40 acres, being the NW 1/4, SW 1/4; being entered by John **Ross**. Signed Robert H. **Ross**. Wit A. M. **McPherson** (JP). Rec 3 Jun 1843. [No. 1591]

1813. Page 489. 6 May 1843. William J. **McCombs** to Robert H. **Ross**. For the sum of $345, mortgage on the two tracts described in the preceding deed (4:488). Sd **McCombs** a note with 10% interest to be paid in six months. Signed William J. **McCombs**. Wit A. M. **McPherson** (JP). Rec 3 Jun 1843. [Marginal note: Full satisfaction received on 3 Nov 1846. Signed John E. **Ross**. Wit J. W. **Noell**, Clerk.] [No. 1592]

1814. Page 490. 26 May 1843. John **Merz** and Helenor, his wife, to Perry Co. for the use of the inhabitants of Congressional Twp 35 N, Rng 11 E. For securing a note and the sum of $1, mortgage on 114 1/4 acres in Sec 16, Twp 35 N, Rng 11 E; being the NE 1/4, SW 1/4, the SE 1/4, NW 1/4; and the SW fractional 1/4, NE fractional 1/4. Sd **Merz** owes a note of even date for $189.11 with 10% interest per annum, due by 26 May 1844. Signed John **Merz**,

Helena **Merz** (RD). Wit Andrew **Derr**, James A. **Nash**, John F. **Hase** (JP). Rec 5 Jun 1843. [Marginal note: Full satisfaction received on 1 Apr 1851. Signed Bernard **Cissell**, Treasurer of Perry Co. Test Charles C. **Ellis**, Clerk.] [No. 1593]

1815. Page 493. 1 Apr 1843. John R. **Martin** to Elias **Barber**. For the sum of $70, mortgage on 40 acres, being the NW 1/4, NE 1/4, Sec 36, Twp 35 N, Rng 12 E. Sd **Martin** owes a note to sd **Barber** bearing 10% interest, dated 19 Mar 1843 and due one day after date. Signed John R. **Martin**. Wit A. M. **McPherson** (JP). Rec 6 Jun 1843. [Marginal note: Full satisfaction received on 14 Apr 1845. Signed Elias **Barber**.] [No. 1594]

1816. Page 494. 22 May 1843. Robert **Hughey** to Robert **Wilson**. For the sum of $70, mortgage on one bay filly about three years this spring, one-year-old black horse colt, 12 hogs about 11 months old, one cow, and three sheep. Sd **Hughey** owes sd **Wilson** a bond of even date, due in 12 months with 10% interest per annum, or sd **Wilson** may sell the property. Signed Robert **Hughey**. Wit A. M. **McPherson** (JP). Rec 7 Jun 1843. [No. 1595]

1817. Page 496. 7 Jun 1843. Levi **Block** and Susan, his wife, of St. Louis, Mo. to Clemence **Landry**. For the sum of $40, Lot No. 82 in Perryville, fronting on South St. Signed Levi **Block**, Susan M. **Block** (RD). Wit Wm. **Ames**, Dep Clerk of St. Louis Co., Mo. Rec 12 Jun 1843. [No. 1596]

1818. Page 497. 8 Apr 1843. James S. **Powell** and Julia Ann, his wife, to Perry Co., for the use of the inhabitants of Twp 36 N, Rng 10 E. For securing a note and the sum of $1, mortgage on three tracts in Sec 16, Twp 36 N, Rng 10 E; 40 acres, being the NE 1/4, SW 1/4; 40 acres, being the NW 1/4, SE 1/4; and 40 acres, being the SE 1/4, NE 1/4. Sd **Powell** owes a note of even date for $173.50, with 10% interest per annum, due 8 Apr 1844. Signed James S. **Powell**, Julia A. **Powell** (RD). Wit to note J. M. M. **Powell**, James B. **Laville**, Samuel A. **Dixon**. Wit Stn. **Sanders** (JP). Rec 12 Jun 1843. [Marginal note: Full satisfaction received on 6 Jun 1846. Signed Reuben **Shelby**, Treasurer of Perry Co.] [No. 1597]

1819. Page 500. 3 Jun 1841. Lemuel H. **Powell** of Dubuque Co., Ioway Terr, to J. M. M. **Powell**. For the sum of $100, his 1/7 undivided part of 140 acres, a tract patented to Wm. **Powell**. Signed L. H. **Powell**. Wit Jos. **Griffith** sen, James S. **Powell**, John W. **Noell**, Clerk. Rec 12 Jun 1843. [No. 1598]

1820. Page 501. 12 Jun 1843. Matthias **Ricks** and Barbary, his wife, to Frederick **Recks** and Adolphus **Recks**. For the sum of $350 from sd Frederick and $380 from sd Adolphus, mortgage on land and personal property; 40 acres, being the SE 1/4, SE 1/4, Sec 19, Twp 34 N, Rng 12 E; 40 acres, a tract entered by Adolphus **Rix** senor, decd, and sold by Martin **Layton** and Leo **Moore** and Austin **Moore**, commissioners, to sd Matthias; one horse and mare; 10 cattle, two cows, four stears, two heifers, and two yearlings; 10 sheep; six hogs; one waggon; one wheat fan; one iron tooth harrow; one clock; one cupboard; one broad ax; and two pair of plow gears. Sd Matthias owes two notes payable one day after date; one to sd Frederick dated 15 May 1842; and one to sd Adolphus dated 4 Jun 1842. Signed Matthias **Rix**, Barbara **Rix** (RD). Wit William **Farrar** (JP). Rec 13 Jun 1843. [Marginal notes: Full satisfaction received on 13 Dec 1844. Signed Helen (x) **Rix**, widow of Adolphus **Rix**. Full satisfaction received on 11 Dec 1846. Signed Frederick (x) **Rix**. Wit John W. **Noell**, Clerk.] [No. 1599]

1821. Page 502. 12 Jun 1843. Robert T. **Brown** to Reuben **Shelby**. For the sum of $30, Lot No. 47 on Jackson St and South St in Perryville. Signed R. T. **Brown**. Wit John W. **Noell**, Clerk. Rec 14 Jun 1843. [No. 1600]

1822. Page 503. 23 May 1843. William **McCauley** to Bennett **McCauley**. For performing conditions as specified; three tracts in Twp 35 N, Rng 11 E; 63.91 acres, being the W 1/2, SW 1/4, Sec 11; 30.60 acres, being the NE 1/4, NE 1/4, fractional Sec 15; and 68 acres, more or less, that sd William purchased from Clement **Knot**, adjoining the first two tracts. Sd Bennett binds himself to make the following payments eight years after the death of William **McCauley**: to his brother James, $150; to his sister Elizabeth **Knott**, $150; to his brother John **McCauley**, $150 and a common bed and furniture when he marries; to his sister Theresa **McCauley**, $150 and a common bed and furniture when she marries; to his brother William **McCauley**, $150, one horse and saddle worth $75, a bed and furniture when he is age 21, and he is to raise Wm. **McCauley** and give him common education; to Josephine **Stewart**, $150 if she lives to be 18 years old, if not, the money to be paid to his brother William at age 21. This contract is to have no effect during the lifetime of William **McCauley** [Sr.], or if he sells the land. Signed Wm. **McCauley**, Bennett **McCauley**. Test John B. **Layton** Jr., John **Moore**, John W. **Noell**, Clerk. Rec 19 Jun 1843. [No. 1601]

1823. Page 505. 21 Jun 1843. William **Rutledge** to George Washington **Gresham**. For the sum of $435, three tracts in Twp 35 N, Rng 11 E; 40 acres, being the SE 1/4, NE 1/4, Sec 22; 40 acres, being the SW 1/4, NW 1/4, Sec 23; and 80 acres, being the NW 1/4, NW 1/4 and NW 1/4, SW 1/4, Sec 23. Signed Wm. **Rutledge**. Test John **Layton** Senr (JP). Rec 21 Jun 1843. [No. 1602]

1824. Page 506. 13 Jun 1843. George A. **Ross** and Phebe, his wife, Robert H. **Ross**, and John E. **Ross** to Solomon **Cline**. For the sum of $75, 40 acres, being the SW 1/4, NE 1/4, Sec 30, Twp 35 N, Rng 13 E; entered by George A. **Ross** on 28 Nov 1838. Signed Geo. A. **Ross**, Phebe **Ross** (RD), Robert H. **Ross**, John E. **Ross**. Wit William **Farrar** Senor (JP). Rec 22 Jun 1843. [No. 1603]

1825. Page 507. 22 Jun 1843. William **Rutledge** to Morris **Block** and Charles **Avery**. For the sum of $1 and securing notes, deed of trust on one fan mill; 15 hogs; two milch cows and calves; one two-year-old bay colt; one bay mare and colt; one sorrel horse called Fox; and one sorrel horse called Ball. Sd **Rutledge** owes two notes of even date and payable by 1 Oct next; one to sd **Block** for $48.72 1/2, due with 10% interest; and to sd Block & Avery for $59.31 1/2. Block & Avery are to sell the property if the debts are not paid. Signed William **Rutledge**. Wit John J. **Hickey**, Thomas M. **Blair**, John W. **Noell**, Clerk. Rec 22 Jun 1843. [No. 1604]

1826. Page 508. 3 Jun 1841. Peter **Brown** and Mary, his wife, to Stephen **Wimsett**. For the sum of $210, 40 acres, being the NW 1/4, NW 1/4, Sec 25, Twp 36 N, Rng 10 E; purchased by sd **Brown** at the land office. Signed Peter **Brown**, Mary (x) **Brown** (RD). Wit James **Rice** (JP). Rec 3 Jul 1843. [No. 1605]

1827. Page 509. 10 Jun 1843. Jackson D. **Taylor** to George W. **Taylor**. For the sum of $166.66, two negro boys, **Hillery** about 21 years old and **Elleck** about 12 years old, belonging to the estate of James **Taylor**, decd. Signed Jackson D. **Taylor**. Test Hannibal H. **Taylor**. Rec 4 Jul 1843. [No. 1606]

1828. Page 510. 20 Jul 1843. Edward M. **Holden** to Charles **Haydon**. For holding sd **Haydon** harmless and the sum of $1, mortgage on 10 sows and six barrows; and one yellow or cream colored horse that he got from ___ **Huston**. Sd **Holden** owes a note to Perry Co. for $100 with 10% interest, dated 25 Aug 1840; for which sd **Haydon** is security. Signed Edward M. **Holden**. Wit John W. **Noell**, Clerk. Rec 20 Jul 1843. [No. 1607]

1829. Page 511. 21 Jun 1843. Conrad C. **Ziegler** of Ste. Genevieve Co., Mo. to John F. **Brown**. For the sum of $50, quit claim to two tracts in Sec 31, Twp 36 N, Rng 10 E; 45.98 acres, being the SE fractional 1/4, and SE 1/4, SW 1/4; and 39.70 acres, being the NE 1/4, SW fractional 1/4; purchased by sd **Ziegler** at marshall's sale as the property of Robert T. **Brown** sen. Signed Conrad C. **Ziegler**. Wit Jesse B. **Robbins**, Clerk of Ste. Genevieve Co., Mo. Rec 22 Jul 1843. [No. 1608]

1830. Page 512. 12 May 1843. John **Carlisle**, late of Perry Co. but now of St. Louis Co., Mo., to Henry G. **Montfort**, trustee for Julia M. **Clark**, wife of Joseph P. **Clark**. For the sum of $1200, 85.06 acres, more or less, beginning on the Mississippi River at the upper corner of a tract sold by John **Kinnison** to William H. **Digges** and George **McKinstry** Junior; also bounded by **Sanders**, Alexander **McConnahue**'s survey, sd **Digges** & **McKinstry**; and part of a tract confirmed to sd **McConnahue**, and sold by him to sd **Kinnison**, and by him to sd **Carlisle** on 28 Sep 1841 (4:338). Julia **Montfort**, for love and affection to her niece Julia M. **Clark**, wife of Joseph T. **Clark**, wants to convey the tract to sd Julia M. for her sole use and benefit. Julia **Montfort** has provided her own money to purchased the tract, and Joseph T. **Clark** has agreed to abstain from interference with Henry G. **Montfort** regarding the trust. Signed John **Carlisle**, H. G. **Montfort**, Jos. T. **Clark**. Test Alfred L. **Parks** (JP). Rec 27 Jul 1843. [No. 1609]

1831. Page 515. 27 Jul 1843. John Conrad **Ocks** and Ann Catharine, his wife, to Christina **Ocks**, wife of John Michael **Ocks**. For the sum of $65, 40 acres, being the NW 1/4, SW 1/4, Sec 26, Twp 35 N, Rng 11 E. Signed Johann Conradt **Ocks**, Anna Katharine **Ocks** (RD). Wit John W. **Noell**, Clerk. Rec 27 Jul 1843. [No. 1610]

1832. Page 516. 23 Mar 1840. Commissioners to sell the real estate of the heirs of William **Beal**, decd, to Joseph T. **Abernathy**. For the sum of $1015.04 ($976 plus interest), 160 acres, being the SW 1/4, Sec 4, Twp 34, Rng 11 E. Sold in Jul 1838 at the decree of Circuit Court issued at Mar Term. Signed John **Logan**, John **Farrar**, Alonzo **Abernathy**. Wit Reuben **Shelby**, JCC. Rec 5 Aug 1843. [No. 1611]

1833. Page 517. 17 Aug 1843. John **Beinlein** and Margaret, his wife, to George **Gleinlein**. For the sum of $96, 40 acres, being the SE 1/4, NW 1/4, Sec 27, Twp 35 N, Rng 11 E. Signed John **Beinlein**, Margaret **Beinlein** (RD). Wit John W. **Noell**, Clerk. Rec 17 Aug 1843. [No. 1612]

1834. Page 518. 21 Aug 1843. John M. **Duvall** to G. W. **Wheeler**. In consideration of a promissory note, one light sorrel mare with a bald face, silver mane and tail, about 16 hands high and four years old 4 Jul last. Sd **Duvall** owes a note for $43.50 to sd **Wheeler**, dated 7 Jul 1842 and due one day after date. Signed John M. **Duvall**. Wit James White **Leal**, John W. **Noell**, Clerk. Rec 21 Aug 1843. [No. 1613]

1835. Page 519. 30 May 1839. Martin **Stephen** to Christ. Gottfried **Schlimpert** and Joh. Geo. **Gube**. For the sum of $50, assignment of Certificate No. 6809 for 40 acres, entry No. 1613, and the SW 1/4, NE 1/4, Sec 23, Twp 34 N, Rng 13 E; issued by Ralph **Guild**, Receiver. Signed Martin **Stephen**. Wit Hy. C. **Bimpage**, Frederick C. **Hase**, Clerk. Rec 29 Aug 1843. [No. 1614]

1836. Page 520. 20 Jun 1843. Clement **Vessels** and Catharine, his wife, to Charles **Miles**. For the sum of $250, 40 acres, being the SW 1/4, SE 1/4, Sec 14, Twp 36 N, Rng 10 E. Signed Clement **Vessels**, Catharine **Vessels** (RD). Test Stephen **Sanders** (JP). Rec 1 Sep 1843. [No. 1615]

1837. Page 522. 4 Sep 1843. William **Shannon** by Sheriff Henry **Caho** to Jas. **Herald**. For the sum of $35.41 in back taxes and interest, 640 acres in Bois Brule, assessed for 1825 & 1826. Signed Henry **Caho**, Sheriff. Test John W. **Noell**, Clerk. Rec 4 Sep 1843. [No. 1616]

1838. Page 522. 4 Sep 1843. The widow **Lockhart** by Sheriff Henry **Caho** to Levi C. **McDaniel**. For the sum of $1.85 in back taxes and interest, 40 acres in Survey No. 1884 in Twp 36 N, Rng 11 & 12 E, assessed for 1841. Signed Henry **Caho**, Sheriff. Test John W. **Noell**, Clerk. Rec 4 Sep 1843. [No. 1617]

1839. Page 523. 4 Sep 1843. Charles **Hempstead** by Sheriff Henry **Caho** to Elisha **Belsha**. For the sum of $8.48 in back taxes and interest, 375 acres on the Mississippi River, assessed for 1827. Signed Henry **Caho**, Sheriff. Test John W. **Noell**, Clerk. Rec 4 Sep 1843. [No. 1618]

1840. Page 524. 4 Sep 1843. William **McCauley** by Sheriff Henry **Caho** to Morris **Block**. For the sum of $3.87 1/2 in back taxes, interest, and costs, Lot No. 43 in Perryville, assessed for 1833. Signed Henry **Caho**, Sheriff. Test John W. **Noell**, Clerk. Rec 4 Sep 1843. [No. 1619]

1841. Page 525. 5 Sep 1843. The widow **Lockhart** and Wm. P. **McArthur** and others by Sheriff Henry **Caho** to Henry L. **McArthur**. For the sum of $20.95 in back taxes, interest, and costs, two tracts; 382.81 acres in Survey No. 1844, Twp 36 N, Rng 11 & 12 E, assessed to sd **Lockhart** for 1831 & 1835; and 255 acres in Cinque Hommes Twp, assessed to Wm. P. **McArthur** and others for 1825 & 1826. Signed Henry **Caho**, Sheriff. Test John W. **Noell**, Clerk. Rec 5 Sep 1843. [No. 1620]

1842. Page 526. 4 Sep 1843. William **McLane** by Sheriff Henry **Caho** to Andrew **Doerr**. For the sum of $1.49 in back taxes, interest, and costs, 1/2 of Lot No. 42 in Perryville, assessed for 1833. Signed Henry **Caho**, Sheriff. Test John W. **Noell**, Clerk. Rec 4 Sep 1843. [No. 1621]

1843. Page 527. 2 Sep 1843. Andrew **Doer** to Philip **Doer**. For love and affection he has for his son and for his better support and divers other causes and considerations, 106 acres, more or less, where sd Andrew now lives in Twp 35 N, Rng 11 E; including 40 acres, being the SW 1/4, SW 1/4, Sec 17; and 40 acres, less 14.87 acres sold to Frederick **Sutterer**, a portion of the NW part of the NW 1/4, Sec 20; all the growing crops (about 25 acres of corn, 10 acres of wheat in the barn); 13 neat cattle; one yoke of oxen; six horses; 21 sheep; 18 hogs; four beds and bedding; one cupboard; one bureau; two tables; one horse waggon; and one ox waggon with four plows and gears. Sd Philip agrees to support his father, provide him with good and wholesome food, and clothing adapted to his situation in life, and to provide him convenient and suitable dwelling and lodging, and take care of him in sickness, and pay all expenses thereof, and to protect, provide. for and support sd Andrew as a dutiful son would provide for and support his father. Sd Philip also agrees to pay $125, one horse, and one cow each to the other children of sd Andrew: Frederick, William, Christian, Augustine, and Lewis; and will allow them to reside with him until they turn age 21, and provide them with food, clothing, a proper education, and support and maintenance. Signed Andrew **Doer**, Philip **Doer**. Test James **Rice** (JP). Rec 9 Sep 1843. [No. 1622]

1844. Page 529. 6 Sep 1843. Andrew **Doer** to Morris **Block**. For the sum of $3.62 1/2, 1/2 of Lot No. 42 in Perryville, purchased by sd **Doer** from the Sheriff on 4 Sep 1843, to pay back taxes for 1833. Signed Andrew **Doer**. Wit John W. **Noell**, Clerk. Rec 9 Sep 1843. [No. 1623]

1845. Page 530. 8 Sep 1843. Various owners by Sheriff Henry **Caho** to James **Rice** and John W. **Noell**. For the sum of $40.02 in back taxes, interest, and costs; the following tracts:

To whom assessed	Acres	Survey/part	Sec	Twp	Rng	Years taxes due
Able, Ezekiel	136.28	81		36	10	1828, 1829, 1832
Bogy & Shannon	255.21	2063		36&37	11	1828
Elias **Coen**	40.28	89		36	10	1835, 1836, 1837
Andrew **Cox**	96.28	90		36&37	10	1835, 1836, 1837, 1839
Lewis **Coyteaux**	425.35	965		36	10&11	1836, 1837, 1839, 1840, 1841
John M. **Daniel**	80	W 1/2, NW	20	35	13	1835
Jno. **McClannahan** legal reps.	170.14	661		36	11	1828, 1832, 1835, 1840, 1841
James C. **Moore**	Lot No. 12 in Perryville					1835, 1836
William **McLane**	Lot No. 88 in Perryville					1835, 1836
Joseph **Schnarbush**	Lot No. 13 in Perryville					1833

Signed Henry **Caho**, Sheriff. Test John W. **Noell**, Clerk. Rec 4 Sep 1843. [No. 1624]

1846. Page 531. 8 Sep 1843. Various owners by Sheriff Henry **Caho** to John W. **Noell** and James **Rice**. For the sum of $39.49 in back taxes and interest, the following tracts:

To whom assessed	Acres	Survey/part	Sec	Twp	Rng	Years taxes due
Samuel **Burrows**	80	W 1/2, NW	25	35	11	1841
David **Bollinger**	1/4 part of Lot No. 55 in Perryville, S side					1840
David **Crips**	276.50	2186		36	10&11	1837
Jacob **Clotfelter**	49 (part)	W 1/2, SW	4	34	12	1840, 1841
Edward **Durning**	80	E 1/2, SE	33	34	11	1839, 1840, 1841
James **Dodson**	100	440		37	11	1841
Josiah **Ellis**	150	440		37	11	1841
Jacob **Fowler**	44	E corner 356		36	11	1840, 1841
Joseph A. **Mossey**	W side of Lot No. 56 in Perryville					1841
Thomas **Madden**	140	2144		37	10	1840
John **Nurgan** Jr.	135	2142		36	10&11	1839, 1840, 1841
John **Thomas**	74	NWSE&NESE	24	36	11	1841
Nathan **Vanhorn**	80	4NW	1	33	12	1840
James B. **Wilson**	143.01	NW frac	1	34	12	1840

Signed Henry **Caho**, Sheriff. Test John W. **Noell**, Clerk. Rec 9 Sep 1843. [No. 1625]

1847. Page 532. 11 Sep 1843. Patrick **McAtee** to Henry **McAtee** Senr. In consideration of the premises and the sum of $1, mortgage on one bead, bedstead, and bedding; one buro; one chest of drawers or press; one clock; one ladies saddle; one mans saddle; all the corn now growing; one sorrel filly two years old next spring; 18 hogs; two cows, one red and the other pided; two steers, one red and the other pided; one pided heifer; and one yearlin bull, one yearlin steer, and one yearlin heffer, all of a red color. Sd Patrick owes sd Henry a note for $211 with interest, dated 1 Nov 1842 and payable in two years. Signed Patrick **McAtee**. Wit Jno. W. **Noell**, Clerk. Rec 11 Sep 1843. [No. 1626]

1848. Page 533. 18 Sep 1843. James **Rice** and John W. **Noell** to William B. **Burgett**. For the sum of $4.50, 96.28 acres in Survey No. 90, Twp 36 & 37, Rng 10 E; sold by Sheriff Henry **Caho** on 4 Sep 1843 for taxes and penalties assessed to Andrew **Cox** for 1835, 1836, 1837, & 1839. Signed James **Rice**, John W. **Noell**. Wit John F. **Hase** (JP). Rec 18 Sep 1843. [No. 1627]

1849. Page 533. 18 Sep 1843. Leo **Layton** and Mary Magdalean, his wife, to Bennett **Spalding** of Ste. Genevieve Co., Mo. For the sum of $270, 36.35 acres, part of the SE 1/4, NW 1/4, Sec 25, Twp 36 N, Rng 10 E. Signed Leo **Layton**, Mary Magdaline (x) **Layton** (RD). Wit Joab W. **Burgee**, JCC, Michael **Spalding**. Rec 23 Sep 1843. [No. 1628]

1850. Page 534. 29 Jun 1843. Luther **Taylor** to Eli **Taylor**. For the sum of $150, 35 acres, more or less, beginning on the boundary of Perryville near the center of Main St, and bounded in part by Bernard **Layton**; conveyed by sd Luther and wife by deed of trust to John **Logan** on 30 Nov 1842 (4:367). Signed Luther **Taylor**. Wit John W. **Noell**, Clerk. Rec 25 Sep 1843. [No. 1629]

1851. Page 536. 16 Sep 1843. Andrew **Doer** to Henry **Doer**. For the sum of $1, love and affection to his son, and for his better support and maintenance, 40 acres, being the NW 1/4, SW 1/4, Sec 21, Twp 36, Rng 11 E; entered at the land office by Thomas **Stewart**. Signed Andrew **Doer**. Wit James **Rice** (JP). Rec 25 Sep 1843. [No. 1630]

1852. Page 536. 2 Sep 1843. Charles **Tucker** and Trecy, his wife, to Leander **Tucker**. For the sum of $87, 254 acres, more or less, a tract owned by Nicholas **Tucker** at the time of his death; 200 acres of which was confirmed to Josephus **Tucker** and the balance purchased from the U. S. A. Signed Charles **Tucker**, Tresy (x) **Tucker** (RD). Wit John **Layton** (JP). Rec 27 Sep 1843. [No. 1631]

1853. Page 537. 2 Oct 1843. Philip **Roff** and Appollonia, his wife, to John **Hoffman**. For the sum of $50, mortgage on 80 acres, being the E 1/2, NW 1/4, Sec 11, Twp 34 N, Rng 10 E. Sd **Roff** owes a note of even date to sd **Hoffman**, with interest of 10% per annum until paid. Signed Philip **Ruh**, Appollonia Reelspeyer **Ruh** (RD). Wit James **Rice** (JP). Rec 2 Oct 1843. [No. 1632]

1854. Page 539. 12 Oct 1843. Amzi **Osborn** by Sheriff Henry **Caho** to Andrew **Derr**. For the sum of $1, two tracts; 400 arpens, more or less, at the mouth of Apple Creek, including a steam mill and other buildings, purchased by sd **Osborn** from John **Logan**; and 248.35 acres in Sec 32, Twp 34, Rng 14 E. Sold on 14 Feb 1843 on an execution issued by Circuit Court on 31 Oct 1842 on a judgment issued 5 Jul 1838 against sd **Osborn** and for Alpheus **Gurney** for the use of Singleton H. **Kimmel**, for $382.45 debt, $39.83 3/4 damages, and costs. Signed Henry **Caho**, Sheriff. Wit John W. **Noell**, Clerk. Rec 12 Oct 1843. [No. 1633]

1855. Page 540. 8 Apr 1843. Robert **Black** and Sarah, his wife, to Perry Co. for the use of the inhabitants of Twp 36 N, Rng 12 E. For securing a debt and the sum of $1, mortgage on 80 acres in Twp 34 N, Rng 12 E; being the NE 1/4, NW 1/4, Sec 8; and the NE 1/4, SE 1/4, Sec 5; as per Certificate Nos. 1774 & 1825 issued 17 Dec 1837. Sd **Black** owes a note of even date to Perry Co., due by 8 Apr 1844 with 10% interest from date, for $1096.33, with William **Farrar** and Ransom A. **Little** as security. Signed Robert **Black**, Sarah (x) **Black** (RD). Test William **Farrar** (JP). Rec 13 Oct 1843. [Marginal note: Full satisfaction received on 5 Feb 1847. Signed Reuben **Shelby**, Treasurer. Test John W. **Noell**, Clerk.] [No. 1634]

1856. Page 543. 13 Oct 1843. Roland **Boyd** Senr. and Roland **Boyd** Junr. by Sheriff Henry **Caho** to Felix **Valle**. For the sum of $100 paid to Joseph D. **Simpson**, former sheriff, 406 acres, more or less, the W end of a tract granted to Roland **Boyd** Senr as Survey No. 2169. Sold on an execution issued 14 Sep 1841 by Circuit Court, on a judgment issued 29 Jul 1841 against sd **Boyds** and in favor of Timothy Davis & Co. for $312.50 debt, $69.50 damages, and $7.21 costs. Signed Henry **Caho**, Sheriff. Test Jno. W. **Noell**, Clerk. Rec 13 Oct 1843. [No. 1635]

1857. Page 546. 13 Oct 1843. Joseph **Pratte** and Emanuel **Pratte** by same to same. For the sum of $5.50, Lot No. 21 on St. Marys St and Spring St, and Lot No. 22, both in Perryville. Sold on an execution issued 17 Oct 1842 by Circuit Court, on four judgments issued 15 Oct 1842 against Joseph **Pratte**; one in favor of John **Siter**, Richard **Price**, Joseph **Price** Junr and John **Cook** for $1500.19 debt and $318.79 damages; one in favor of Alexander **Price**, Thomas S. **Newlin**, and Benjamin **Marshall** for $642.74 debt and $136.58 damages; one in favor of Lewis V. **Bogy** for $1567.50 damages; and one in favor of Bernard **Pratte** for $2562.50 damages. Also issued on two judgments against Emanual & Joseph **Pratte**; one in favor of Wayman **Crow**, Joshua **Tevis**, John C. **Tevis**, and Phocian R. **McCreary** for $706.72 damages; and one in favor of Timothy M. **Bryan**, John **Redman**, and Isaiah B. **Heylen** for $726.85 damages. Signed Henry **Caho**, Sheriff. Test Jno. W. **Noell**, Clerk. Rec 13 Oct 1843. [No. 1636]

1858. Page 548. 13 Oct 1843. Joseph **Pratte** and Emanuel **Pratte** by same to John W. **Noell**. For the sum of $15.25, Lot No. 32 in Perryville, except that part sold by P. R. **Pratte** and wife to Martin L. **Moore** and Isaac G. **Whitworth**. Sold on the conditions described in the preceding deed (4:546). Signed Henry **Caho**, Sheriff. Test Jno. W. **Noell**, Clerk. Rec 13 Oct 1843. [No. 1637]

1859. Page 551. 10 Oct 1843. John **Logan**, admr of Joel **Kinnison**, decd, to John **Moore**. For the sum of $100 paid by Robert **Moore** to sd **Kinnison**, 80 acres in Bois Brule Creek in Bois Brule Twp, part of 640 acres confirmed to Absolom **Kinnison**. Joel **Kinnison** paid a bond of $200 to execute a deed for the tract, but died before doing so; and he was entitled to the tract as one of eight heirs of his father Absolom **Kinnison** senr, decd. Robert **Moore** assigned the bond to John **Moore** on 8 Jul 1843. Executed on order of Circuit Court issued on 10 Oct 1843 in the case of John **Moore**, complainant, vs. sd **Logan** as admr of Joel **Kinnison**, decd. Signed John **Logan**, admr. Wit John W. **Noell**, Clerk. Rec 13 Oct 1843. [No. 1638]

1860. Page 553. 13 Oct 1843. Peter R. **Pratte** and Emanuel **Pratte** by Sheriff Henry **Caho** to Bernard S. **Pratte**. For the sum of $53, 991.09 acres in Perry and Ste. Genevieve Cos., being Lot No. 4 of a league square confirmed to the heirs of Francis **Valle**. Sold on 14 Feb 1843 on an execution issued by Circuit Court on 3 Dec 1842, in a case decided on 14 Oct 1842 against sd **Prattes** and in favor or Joseph S. **Pease**, Lewis G. **Irving**, and Henry L. **Pease**, for $98.57 damages with 10% interest, with costs. Signed Henry **Caho**, Sheriff. Wit John W. **Noell**, Clerk. Rec 13 Oct 1843. [No. 1639]

1861. Page 556. 13 Oct 1843. Ransom A. **Little** and Mary, his wife, to George **Rutledge**, guardian of the minor heirs of Robert **Abernathy**, decd. For securing a note and the sum of $1, mortgage on the NE fractional 1/4, Sec 2, Twp 34 N, Rng 11 E. Sd **Little** owes a note to sd heirs, dated 4 Sep 1843 for $217.05 with 10% interest per annum, payable in 18 months. Signed Ransom A. **Little**, Mary (x) **Little** (RD). Wit William **Farrar** (JP). Rec 14 Oct 1843. [Marginal note: Full satisfaction received on 10 Feb 1849. Signed William **McCombs**, execr of Franklin **Abernathy**. Guardianship was transferred to sd **Abernathy** by the admr of George **Rutledge**, and sd **Abernathy** is now decd.] [No. 1640]

1862. Page 558. 12 Oct 1843. Walter B. **Wilkinson** by Sheriff Henry **Caho** to Ferdinand **Rozier** Jr. For the sum of $20, two tracts; 160 acres, being the NW 1/4, Sec 13, Twp 35 N, Rng 12, entered by Joseph **Brazeau**, sd **Wilkinson**, and Francis **Wilkinson**; and 155.30 acres, being the NE fractional 1/4, Sec 29, Twp 35 N, Rng 10 E. Sold on 3 Apr 1843 on two executions issued by Circuit Court; one issued 20 Oct 1842 against sd **Wilkinson** and in favor of Joseph S. **Pease**, Lewis G. **Irving**, and Henry L. **Pease** for costs, dated 12 Oct 1842; the other issued 26 Oct 1842 against sd **Wilkinson** and Peter R. **Pratte** and in favor of Lyman B. **Shaw**, assignee of P. E. **Blow** for $184.10 debt, dated 16 Jun 1842. Signed Henry **Caho**, Sheriff. Wit John W. **Noell**, Clerk. Rec 14 Oct 1843. [No. 1641]

1863. Page 560. 14 Oct 1843. Joseph **Pratte** and Emanuel **Pratte** by Sheriff Henry **Caho** to Valerio **Faina**. For the sum of $2, the undivided 1/2 of Lot No. 20 in Perryville. Sold on 11 Apr 1843 on the conditions described in 4:546. Signed Henry **Caho**, Sheriff. Wit Jno. W. **Noell**, Clerk. Rec 14 Oct 1843. [No. 1642]

1864. Page 563. 27 May 1843. Thomas **McAtee** by Sheriff Henry **Caho** to Joseph **Sutterer** by his agent James **Rice**. For the sum of $7.50, about 7 acres in the SE 1/4, SW 1/4, Sec 1, Twp 34 N, Rng 10 E; deeded by sd **Sutterer** and wife to sd **McAtee**. Sold on 12 Apr 1843 on an execution issued by Circuit Court on 22 Dec 1842, against Thomas **McAtee** and in favor of Augustine **Layton**, assignee of M. Barringer & Co. for $10.37 1/2 debt and damages, with costs, in a case heard 1 Oct 1842 before James **Rice**, JP for Cinque Hommes Twp. Signed Henry **Caho**, Sheriff. Wit Jno. W. **Noell**, Clerk. Rec 14 Oct 1843. [No. 1643]

1865. Page 564. 23 Oct 1843. John W. **Noell** and Mary A., his wife, to Elizabeth **Thurman**. For the sum of $100, 200 acres in Survey No. 1868 confirmed to William **Hickman**; purchased by sd **Noell** at Sheriff's sale on 17 Jun 1842; and all the undivided interest held by Archibald **Thurman** and wife. Signed John W. **Noell**, Mary A. **Noell**. Wit James **Rice** (JP). Rec 23 Oct 1843. [No. 1644]

1866. Page 565. 23 Oct 1843. Elizabeth **Thurman** to William **Belsha**. For securing a debt and the sum of $1, mortgage on 200 acres as described in the preceding deed (4:564), being her undivided right to that part of the survey owned by the late Andrew **McCasland** and William **McCasland**. Sd **Thurman** owes sd **Belsha** $50, due in six months. Signed Elizabeth (x) **Thurman**. Wit Jno. W. **Noell**, Clerk. Rec 23 Oct 1843. [No. 1645]

1867. Page 566. 14 Oct 1843. Andrew **Derr** to Albert **Jackson** of Jackson, Cape Girardeau Co., Mo. For the sum of $10, undivided 1/2 of two tracts; 400 arpens, more or less, at the mouth of Apple Creek, on which there are a steam mill and other buildings; and 248.35 acres in Sec 32, Twp 34, Rng 14 E, purchased by sd **Derr** of the Sheriff on 12 Oct 1843. Signed Andrew **Doer**. Wit John F. **Hase** (JP). Rec 28 Oct 1843. [No. 1646]

1868. Page 567. 8 Apr 1843. Franklin **Farrar** and Mary R., his wife, to Perry Co., for the use and benefit of the inhabitants of Twp 34 N, Rng 11 E. For securing a debt and the sum of $1, mortgage on 80 acres, being the SW 1/4, NE 1/4, and the SE 1/4, NW 1/4, Sec 16, Twp 34 N, Rng 11 E. Sd **Farrar** owes Perry Co. a note for $443.08, dated 8 Apr 1843, with John **Farrar** and Moses **Farrar** as securities, due in one year. Signed Franklin **Farrar**, Mary R. **Farrar** (RD). Wit Levi **Moore**, William **Farrar** (JP). Rec 28 Oct 1843. [No. 1647]

1869. Page 570. 8 Apr 1843. Harley D. **Abernathy** and Sarah, his wife, to same. For securing a debt and the sum of $1, 40 acres, being the SW 1/4, NW 1/4, Sec 15, Twp 34 N, Rng 11 E. Sd **Abernathy** owes a note to Perry Co. for $321.46 with interest, dated 8 Apr 1843, with Ransom A. **Little** and Alonzo **Abernathy** as securities, due in one year. Signed H. D. **Abernathy**, Sarah **Abernathy** (RD). Wit William **Farrar** (JP). Rec 28 Oct 1843. [Marginal note: Full satisfaction received on 23 Mar 1853. Signed Bernard **Cissell**, Treasurer.] [No. 1648]

1870. Page 573. 28 Oct 1843. George **Brown**, heir of Ann **Brown**, who is heir or Charles **Brewer** Sr., decd, to Mark **Brewer**. For the sum of $15, all his right to the estate of Charles **Brewer** Sr., especially 153 acres, more or less, being the NE 1/4, Sec 5, Twp 34 N, Rng 11 E. Signed George (x) **Brown**. Test Jno. W. **Noell**, Clerk. Rec 28 Oct 1843. [No. 1649]

1871. Page 574. 8 Feb 1827. Francis **Janis** and Odile, his wife, to John B. **Bossier**. For the sum of $20, one undivided 1/4 part of __ acres, being the NE 1/4, Sec 35, Twp 35 N, Rng 10 E; now owned in common by sd **Janis** and sd **Bossier**. Signed Francois **Janis**, Odile **Janis** (RD). Wit Paschal **Bequet**, J. V. **Littlejohn**, Clerk of Ste. Genevieve Co. Court. Rec 31 Oct 1843. [No. 1650]

1872. Page 575. 10 Oct 1843. William J. **McCombs** and Sally, his wife, to Napoleon B. **McCombs**. For the sum of $250, 78 acres, more or less, being the W 1/2, NW 1/4, Sec 13, Twp 34 N, Rng 12 E, and the N part of a tract formerly belonging to John **Ross**; beginning at the Brazeau Creek. Signed William J. **McCombs**, Sally **McCombs** (RD). Wit A. M. **McPherson** (JP). Rec 4 Nov 1843. [No. 1651]

1873. Page 576. 9 Nov 1843. E. W. **Geer** and Letitia Ann, his wife, to William **Mackey**, all of Ste. Genevieve Co., Mo. For the sum of $175, their undivided part of three tracts in Twp 36 N, Rng 10 E; 25.91 acres, being the SW fractional 1/4, Sec 10; and 53.95

acres, being the NE fractional 1/4 and the N 1/2, S fractional 1/4, Sec 9, conveyed by Francis **Clark** and wife to F. A. **Kent**, Jerome **Merit** and E. W. **Geer** on 20 Jun 1840 (3:504); and 156.92 acres, being the NW fractional 1/4, fractional Sec 10, conveyed by John M. M. **Powell** and wife to sd **Kent**, sd **Merit**, and sd **Geer** (3:505). Signed E. W. **Geer**, Latitia Ann **Geer** (RD). Wit George **Vessells** (JP), Sinai **Kinnison**. Rec 16 Nov 1843. [No. 1652]

1874. Page 578. 21 Nov 1843. Joseph W. **Layton** and Malania, his wife, to Henry J. **Layton**. For the sum of $50, 40 acres, being the SW 1/4, NE 1/4, Sec 36, Twp 36 N, Rng 10 E. Signed Joseph W. **Layton**, Malania (x) **Layton** (RD). Test Thomas **Stewart**, John **Layton** Senr (JP), Levi **Moore**. Rec 23 Nov 1843. [No. 1653]

1875. Page 579. 21 Nov 1843. Same and same to same. For the sum of $100, two tracts in Sec 36, Twp 36 N, Rng 10 E; 40 acres, being the NW 1/4, SE 1/4; and 40 acres, being the NE 1/4, SW 1/4. Signed Joseph W. **Layton**, Malania **Layton** (RD). Wit John **Layton** Senr (JP). Rec 23 Nov 1843. [No. 1654]

1876. Page 580. 21 Nov 1843. Joseph W. **Layton** to Adolph **Rix**. For securing two notes and the sum of $1, mortgage on one dark bay stable horse, one dark brindled bull seven years old last spring, one pided yellow and white cow, two small steers year olds last spring, one waggon and gearing, one clock, all the corn now standing on the premises he occupies, eight shoats, one press, one broad axe, one barrell sugar, one sack of coffee, two plows and two sets of plow gears, one man saddle, and one side saddle. Sd **Layton** owes two notes bearing 6% interest to Mary **Watkins** and assigned sd **Rix**; one dated 21 Oct 1843 for $144 and payable in four years; the other dated 21 Oct 1843 for $118 and payable in three years. Signed Joseph W. **Layton**. Test Thomas **Stewart**, John W. **Noell**, Clerk. Rec 23 Nov 1843. [No. 1655]

1877. Page 581. 10 Nov 1841. J. M. M. **Powell** and Harriet, his wife, Robert C. **Powell** and Sarinda, his wife, James S. **Powell** and Juliann, his wife, and James B. **Laville** and Mary B., his wife to William R. **Thompson**. For the sum of $500, five undivided 1/7 parts of 140.33 acres, being the NE fractional 1/4, Sec 10, Twp 36 N, Rng 10 E; patented to William **Powell**, decd, on 1 Jan 1831. Signed James B. **Laville**, J. M. M. **Powell**, Robert C. **Powell**, Mary B. **Laville**, Sarinda (x) A. **Powell** (RD), Harriet **Powell** (RD), James **Powell**, Juliann **Powell** (RD). Wit Rebecca **Wright**, George **Vessels** (JP), Alfred L. **Parks** (JP). Rec 24 Nov 1843. [No. 1656]

1878. Page 583. 30 Oct 1843. John **Logan** to Ferdinand **Roner**. For the sum of $305, 150 acres, part of a survey confirmed to Clement **Knott**, beginning at the S corner of land owned by William **McCauley**, decd; conveyed by sd **Knott** to James **McCauley** on 28 Apr 1838, and conveyed by him to Charles **Stewart** (since decd) on 11 Mar 1840, and purchased by sd **Logan** at the sale to partition the land of sd **Stewart**. Signed John **Logan**. Wit John W. **Noell**, Clerk. Rec 28 Nov 1843. [No. 1657]

1879. Page 584. 2 Dec 1843. Francis H. **Wilkinson** and Julia, his wife, to Thomas **Riney**. For the sum of $60.78, 40 acres, being the SW 1/4, SW 1/4, Sec 16, Twp 36 N, Rng 10 E. Signed Frcs. H. **Wilkinson**, Julue M. **Wilkinson** (RD). Wit John F. **Hase** (JP). Rec 9 Dec 1843. [No. 1658]

1880. Page 585. 1 Dec 1843. Joseph **Winkler** and Roceaner, his wife, to Joseph **Folts**. For the sum of $100, mortgage on 40 acres, being the SW 1/4, NW 1/4, Sec 22, Twp 34 N, Rng 12 E, Certificate No. 7502; one rone mare and one black mare; one yoke of work stears; one cow; and three heifers. Sd **Winkler** owes a debt with interest to sd **Folts**, due in 12 months. Signed Joseph **Winkler**, Roceaner **Winkler** (RD). Wit William **Farrar** senor (JP). Rec 9 Dec 1843. [No. 1659]

1881. Page 586. 6 Dec 1843. Thomas **Stewart** to Anselm **Winfield**. For securing two notes and the sum of $1, mortgage on one wooden clock; two pair of fancy bedsteads; four feathers beads; four small square tables; one folding leaf table; one set of windsor chairs; three barrels of whiskey; one of brandy; one of swete wine; one of gin; one dozen of cherries in brandy; one of muscat wine; one doz lemon syrup; and four dozen of claratt. Sd **Stewart** owes sd **Winfield** a note for $22, dated 12 Jun 1843 and payable one day after date with 6% interest; and sd **Winfield** is security for sd **Stewart** for $60 in a note payable at the Branch of the Bank of Missouri at Jackson, dated 28 Nov 1843. Signed Thomas **Stewart**. Wit John W. **Noell**, Clerk. Rec 13 Dec 1843. [No. 1660]

1882. Page 588. 9 Dec 1843. John **Richardson** and John **Bridgeman**, trading as Richardson & Bridgeman, to Reuben **Shelby**. Supplement to deed of trust to John J. **Hickey**. John J. **Hickey** has since deceased, and sd **Shelby** is appointed trustee, as agreed by all parties to the original deed of trust, and is to sell the property on the first Monday of Jan next. Signed John **Richardson**, John **Bridgeman**, Block & Avery, F. **Rozier** Jr., F. **Rozier** & Co., Hertick & Landry, Leonard **Fath**, Charles **Hayden**, John **Logan**, Sarah **Cobbs**, Elizabeth **Cobbs**, J. L. **Burrows**. Reuben **Shelby**, trustee, is not responsible for the personal property. Signed Reuben **Shelby**. Wit John W. **Noell**, Clerk. Rec 13 Dec 1843. [No. 1661]

1883. Page 589. 13 Dec 1843. Lewis **Moore** to George **Hose**. For the sum of $1, mortgage on one yoke of white and red steers, seven years old next spring; one ox cart; one gray mare 13 years; one iron gray mare six years old; one iron gray mare four years old next spring; four cows and calves; 17 sheep; 29 hogs; one two-year-old bull, red and white; one set of carpenter's tools; 2500 weight of tobacco in the leaf; all the corn raised in the present season; 17 acres of wheat sown in Sep on the farm where he now resides; and one stack of wheat in the sheaf. Sd **Moore** owes sd **Hose** a note of even date for $150, at 6% interest per annum. Signed Lewis **Moore**. Wit John F. **Hase** (JP). Rec 14 Dec 184[3]. [No. 1662]

1884. Page 590. 14 Dec 1843. William D. **Harrington** and Emily Ann, his wife, of St. Louis, Mo. to Francis L. **Jones**. For the sum of $450, their 1/4 part of all the land entered by the legal representatives of William **Burns**, decd. The land is described in a deed from Jesse **Dickson** and Barbary, his wife, to sd **Jones**, dated 4 Apr 1842 (4:180). Signed Wm. D. **Harrington**, Emily A. **Harrington** (RD). Test David C. **Waters**, Alfred L. **Parks**, JCC. Rec 18 Dec 1843. [No. 1663]

1885. Page 591. 20 Dec 1843. Joseph **Winkler** to Martin **Layton**. For securing two notes, mortgage on one bay horse nine years old; two heifers two years old, one red and one red and white; one black and white cow eight years old; 14 sheep; six hogs; one ox cart; and all the increase of sd stock. Sd **Winkler** owes sd **Layton**

two notes at 10% interest per annum; one for $21.60 by 4 Mar next; and one for $50 due in 12 months. Signed Joseph **Winkler**. Wit James **Rice** (JP). Rec 20 Dec 1843. [No. 1664]

1886. Page 592. 16 Dec 1843. Stephen **Winkler** and Tracy, his wife, to John **Foltz**. For the sum of $60, mortgage on 51.66 acres, being the E 1/2, Lot No. 7, NE 1/4, Sec 13, Twp 33 N, Rng 12 E; Certificate No. 7462 granted to Stephen **Winkler** on 26 Feb 1840. Sd **Winkler** owes sd **Foltz** a note dated Feb 1840, due one year from date. Signed Joseph [sic] **Winkler**, Therese **Winkler** (RD). Wit William **Farrar** (JP). Rec 21 Dec 1843. [No. 1665]

1887. Page 594. 15 Dec 1843. David **Lucky** of Brazo Twp to Wm. M. **Myers** and Lorenzo D. **Myers**. Release of Circuit Court judgment binding on the lands of sd Lorenzo; being 40 acres, the NW 1/4, SE 1/4, Sec 13 [Sec probably in error; Twp & Rng not given]. Signed David **Luckey**. Wit Wm. F. **Beek**, A. M. **McPherson** (JP). Rec 27 Dec 1843. [No. 1666]

1888. Page 594. 15 Dec 1843. Lorenzo D. **Myers** and Angelina, his wife, to Francis L. **Weber**. For the sum of $65, __ acres. being the NW 1/4, SE 1/4, Sec 22, Twp 34 N, Rng 13 E; entered by sd **Myers** on 2 Jun 1836, Duplicate No. 3327. Signed Lorenzo D. **Myers**, Angelina **Myers**. Wit A. M. **McPherson** (JP). Rec 27 Dec 1843. [No. 1667]

1889. Page 595. 26 Dec 1843. Robert T. **Brown** Jr. to Margaret **Holden**. For esteem and affection for his sister-in-law and the sum of $1, one sorrel horse about 10 years old, now in her possession. Signed Robert T. **Brown** Jr. Wit John **Carbrey**, JP in Ste. Genevieve Co., Mo. Rec 28 Dec 1843. [No. 1668]

1890. Page 596. 4 Dec 1843. John **Scudder** to William M. **Perrine**, both of Birmingham, Perry Co. For the sum of $10,000, 1105.51 acres, more or less, in Perry Co. and Cape Girardeau Co. in eight parcels; 400 arpens at the mouth of Apple Creek, known as Pere Menard Claim, conveyed to him by John **Logan** of Ill., by sd **Logan** to Amzi **Osborn**, and by sd **Osborn** to sd **Scudder**; 405.75 acres, being Tower Island in Twp 33 & 34 N, Rng 14 E; 40 acres, being Lot No. 2, NW 1/4, fractional Sec 5, Twp 33 N, Rng 14 E; 40 acres, being the E 1/2, Lot No. 1, and NW 1/4, Sec 6, Twp 33 N, Rng 14 E; 80 acres, being the Lot No. 1, NE 1/4, fractional Sec 3, Twp 33 N, Rng 13 E; 40 acres, being the NE 1/4, SE 1/4, Sec 3, Twp 33 N, Rng 13 E; 79.76 acres, being the NW 1/4, fractional Sec 7, Twp 33 N, Rng 14 E; and 80 acres, being Lot No. 1, NE 1/4, Sec 6, Twp 33 N, Rng 14 E. This is with the exception of Lot Nos. 1, 2 & 18, Block No. 8; Lot Nos. 9, 10, 11, 15 & 16, Block No. 12; Lot No. 12, Block 24; and Lot Nos. 7 & 8, Block No. 4. Signed John **Scudder**. Wit Michael **Onstadt**, Augustus **Davis** (JP), James **Rice**, County Court Clerk. Rec 1 Jan 1844. [No. 1669]

1891. Page 597. 2 Jan 1844. Same to same. For holding sd **Perrine** harmless as security for a bond and the sum of $1, mortgage on one pair of red oxen, yoke, and chain; one pair of brindle oxen, yoke, and chain; one ox with a lump on his face; one Durham bull 15 months old; one red cow and suckling calf, full blood Durham breed; one two year old heifer, red and white, called the Clay heifer, full blood Durham; one large black cow and calf of the Patent stock; 20 yearling calves; one three-year-old and two two-year-old steers; 41 cows of the common breed; ten heifers from one to two years old (making all together 85 cattle); one black saddle horse; one bay horse; one clay bank horse; one pair of timber wheels; one ox waggon; one ox cart; one pair of truck wheels; and one negro woman **Winny** and her children **Emiline** and **Joseph**. Sd **Perrine** is security for sd **Scudder** in a bond dated 7 Jan 1843, to enjoin Nicholas Noel **Distrihan** from selling sd **Scudder**'s land, and sd **Scudder** agrees to hold sd **Perrine** harmless in this matter. Signed John **Scudder**. Wit C. P. **Fulenwider**, Clerk of Cape Girardeau Co., Mo. Rec 2 Jan 1844. [No. 1670]

1892. Page 599. 1 Jan 1844. Rachel **Taylor** to Francis **Clark** and William S. **Laville**, commissioners to sell the slaves of James **Taylor**, decd. For securing a note, mortgage on a negro man named **Hillery**. Sd **Taylor** has purchased the man at public sale for $555, for which she executed a note to sd **Clark** and sd **Laville**, with Jackson **Taylor** as security. Signed Reachel (x) **Taylor**. Wit John W. **Noell**, Clerk. Rec 1 Jan 1844. [No. 1671]

1893. Page 599. 15 Apr 1843. Johann August **Sterzel** to Johann Carl August **Hochne**. For the sum of $300, two tracts; 76 acres, being the N 1/2, SE 1/4, Sec 26, Twp 34, Rng 13 E; less 4 acres deeded to Samuel Gottfried **Kaempfe**; and 16 acres, being the S part, W 1/2, NW 1/4, Sec 35, Twp 34 N, Rng 13 E, beginning at the SW corner of the NW 1/4 of Sec 35, and the same transferred to him by Henry C. **Bimpage**, admr of John George **Gube**, decd. Signed Johann August **Hochne** [sic]. Wit Johann Gottleib **Palisch**, Samuel Gottfried **Kaempfe**, Augustus **Davis** (JP). Rec 1 Jan 1844. [No. 1672]

1894. Page 600. 29 Nov 1843. John **Layton** senior to Reuben **Shelby**. For the sum of $120, mortgage on 50 acres, beginning at the SW corner of a tract confirmed to John **Layton** Junior; and bounded in part by land sold to John **Timon**. This tract is appropriated as the share of sd **Layton**'s daughter Maria **Gole**. Sd **Layton** has give a bond to sd **Shelby** on this day, payable in 12 months with 10% interest per annum. Signed John **Layton** senior. Wit Amatus **Layton**, John W. **Noell**, Clerk. Rec 1 Jan 1844. [No. 1673]

1895. Page 602. 30 Dec 1843. Samuel Gottfried **Kempfe** and Julian Christena, his wife, to John Diedrich **Wittler**. For the sum of $625, four tracts in Twp 34 N, Rng 13 E; 40 acres, being the SW 1/4, SW 1/4, Sec 26, entered by Samuel **Mathews** on 10 Feb 1837, and transferred to sd **Kempfe** on 18 Jul 1843; 40 acres, being the SE 1/4, SW 1/4, Sec 26; 10 acres, being the E 1/4, SE 1/4, Sec 27, transferred to sd **Kempfe** by John Gottloib **Palisch** on 2 Sep 1842; and 10 acres out of the NE 1/4, NE 1/4, Sec 34, commencing at the corner of Secs 26, 27, 34 & 35, and transferred to sd **Kempfe** by Carl Gottloib **Leibig** and Sophia, his wife, on 30 Dec 1843. Signed Samuel Gottfried **Kaempfe**, Juliana Christina **Kaempfe** (RD). Wit Frederich August **Uhlig**, C. H. **Wurkworth**, A. M. **McPherson** (JP). Rec 1 Jan 1844. [No. 1674]

1896. Page 603. 18 Jul 1843. Samuel **Mathews** of Cape Girardeau Co., Mo. to Samuel Gottfried **Kempfe**. For the sum of $150, 40 acres, being the SW 1/4, SW 1/4, Sec 26, Twp 34 N, Rng 13 E, Certificate No. 4954. Signed Samuel **Mathews**. Wit Johann Gottlieb **Palisch**, A. M. **McPherson** (JP). Rec 1 Jan 1844. [No. 1675]

1897. Page 604. 1 Jan 1844. James **Rice** and John W. **Noell** to Perry **Evans**. For the sum of $5.67, their interest in 140 acres in Survey No. 2144, Twp 37 N, Rng 10 E; purchased by them from Henry **Caho**, Sheriff, on 4 Sep 1843. Signed John W. **Noell**,

James **Rice**. Wit Joab W. **Burgee**, JCC. Rec 1 Jan 1844. [No. 1676]

1898. Page 605. 30 Dec 1843. Samuel Gottfried **Kempfe** and Juliana Christena, his wife, to Frederick Augustus **Uhlich**. For the sum of $30, 4 acres, commencing at the NE corner of the NW 1/4, SW 1/4, Sec 26, Twp 34 N, Rng 13 E; transferred by Henry C. **Bimpage**, admr of John Georg **Gube**, to John August **Serzel**, and sold by him to sd **Kempfe** on 15 Apr 1842. Signed Samuel Gottfried **Kampfe**, Juliana Christene **Kempfe** (RD). Wit A. M. **McPherson** (JP). Rec 1 Jan 1844. [No. 1677]

1899. Page 606. 15 Apr 1843. Johann August **Sterzel** to Samuel Gottfried **Kempfe**. For the sum of $16, 4 acres as described in the preceding deed (4:605). Signed Johann August **Sterzel**. Wit Johann Gottlieb **Palisch**, Johann Gottlieb **Hohne**, Augustus **Davis** (JP). Rec 1 Jan 1844. [No. 1677; number used twice]

1900. Page 607. 30 Dec 1843. Samuel Gottfried **Kempfe** and Juliana Christena, his wife, to Carl Gottleib **Leibig**. For the sum of $37.25, 10 acres out of the SW corner of the SE 1/4, SE 1/4, Sec 27, Twp 34 N, Rng 13 E; commencing 20 chains and 58 links W of the corner of Secs 26, 27, 34 & 35. Signed Samuel Gottfried **Kampfe**, Juliana Christene **Kempfe** (RD). Wit A. M. **McPherson** (JP), Fredrick August **Uhlich**. Rec 1 Jan 1844. [No. 1678]

1901. Page 608. 18 Jul 1842. Samuel **Mathews** of Cape Girardeau Co., Mo. to Carl Gottlib **Leibig**. For the sum of $150, 40 acres, being the NE 1/4, NE 1/4, Sec 34, Twp 34 N, Rng 13 E; Certificate No. 4846. Signed Samuel **Mathews**. Wit Johann Gottlieb **Palisch**, A. M. **McPherson** (JP). Rec 1 Jan 1844. [No. 1679]

1902. Page 609. 30 Dec 1843. Carl Gottloib **Leibig** and Sophia, his wife, to Samuel Gottfried **Kempfe**. For the sum of $37.25, 10 acres out of the NE corner, NE 1/4, NE 1/4, Sec 34, Twp 34 N, Rng 13 E; commencing at the corner of Secs 26, 27, 34. & 35; entered by Samuel **Mathews** and deeded to sd **Leibig**. Signed Carl Gottlieb **Leibig**, Sophia **Leibig** (RD). Wit A. M. **McPherson** (JP), Fredrick August **Uhlich**. Rec 1 Jan 1844. [No. 1680]

1903. Page 610. 2 Sep 1842. Johann Gottlieb **Palisch** and Johann Christiane, his wife, to Samuel Gottlieb **Kempfe**. For the sum of $100, two tracts in Twp 34 N, Rng 13 E transferred to sd **Palisch** by Henry C. **Bimpage**, admr of Johann Georg **Gube**, decd; 40 acres, being the SE 1/4, SW 1/4, Sec 26; and 20 acres, being the S 1/2, SE 1/4, SE 1/4, Sec 27. Signed Johann Gottlieb **Palisch**, Johanne Christiane **Palisch** (RD). Wit Johann Gottlieb **Hohne**, Carl Gottlieb **Leibig**. Augustus **Davis** (JP). Rec 1 Jan 1844. [No. 1681]

1904. Page 611. 2 Jan 1844. Robert L. **Phillips** to Andrew **Hoover**. For the sum of $550, 200 acres confirmed to Tunis **Quick**; conveyed by him to John W. **Quick**, by the admr of John W. **Quick** to Peter R. **Pratte**, by sd **Pratte** and wife to William **Winfield**, and by sd **Winfield** to sd **Phillips**; where sd **Hoover** now resides. Signed Robert L. **Phillips**. Wit John W. **Noell**. Clerk. Rec 2 Jan 1844. [No. 1682]

1905. Page 612. 12 Feb 1842. Trustees of Wittenberg to August Heinrich **Doderlein**. For the sum of $15, Lot No. 45 in Wittenberg, fronting on First St and Second St, and in between Lot Nos. 44 & 46. Signed Henry C. **Bimpage**, Friedr. Wilhelm Barthel, Christ Friedr. **Muller**. Wit F. L. **Hache**, Augustus **Davis** (JP). Rec 2 Jan 1844. [No. 1683]

1906. Page 613. 3 Jan 1844. James **Rice** and John W. **Noell** to William **Fugate** of Cape Girardeau Co., Mo. For the sum of $10, 150 acres, part of Survey No. 440, Twp 37, Rng 11; sold for taxes due in the name of Josiah **Ellis** on 4 Sep 1843 by Henry **Caho**, Sheriff. Signed James **Rice**, John W. **Noell**. Wit Mark **Brewer** (JP). Rec 3 Jan 1844. [No. 1684]

1907. Page 614. 2 Aug 1837. James **Bell** and Mary, his wife, to Morrits **Venners**. For the sum of $425, __ acres, being the W 1/2, NE 1/4, Sec 32, Twp 34, Rng 12 E. Signed James **Bell**, Mary **Bell** (RD). Wit Elias **Barber** (JP). Rec 3 Jan 1844. [No. 1685]

1908. Page 615. __ Dec 1843. William **Welker** to Andrew **Welker** and Jacob **Welker**. For the sum of $800, 160 acres, more or less, in Sec 35, Twp 34 N, Rng 11 E; 40 acres, being the SW 1/4, SW 1/4; the NE 1/4, SW 1/4; the NW 1/4, SW 1/4; and the NE 1/4, SE 1/4. Signed William **Welker**. Wit William **Farrar** (JP). Rec 4 Jan 1844. [No. 1686]

1909. Page 616. 6 Jan 1844. James **Rice** and John W. **Noell** to Caleb **Hattan**. For the sum of $75, 425.35 acres, being Survey No. 965 in Twp 36 N, Rng 10 & 11; purchased from Henry **Caho**, Sheriff, at a tax sale on 4 Sep 1843. Signed James **Rice**, John W. **Noell**. Wit Alfred L. **Parks** (JP). Rec 6 Jan 1844. [No. 1687]

1910. Page 617. 6 Dec 1843. John **Martin** Senior to Anderson **Cashion**. For the sum of $200, two tracts; 40 acres, being the NE 1/4, SE 1/4, Sec 25, Twp 35 N, Rng 11 E, conveyed by Marx **Adler** and wife to Richmond **Penny**; and 39.36 acres, being the NW 1/4, SW 1/4, Sec 30, Twp 35 N, Rng 12 E, entered by sd **Penny**, less so much as was conveyed by sd **Martin** and wife to the Baptist Church of Pleasant Grove on 11 Jan 1841 (4:467). Both parcels were conveyed by sd **Penny** to sd **Martin** on 16 Oct 1840. Signed John (x) **Martin** Senor. Test William **Farrar** (JP), James **Cashion**. Rec 8 Jan 1844. [No. 1688]

1911. Page 617. [Page number used twice.] 13 Jan 1844. Peter **Tucker** senior and Elizabeth, his wife, to Francis **Miles**. For the sum of $260, 121.27 acres in Sec 35, Twp 36 N, Rng 10 E; beginning at the NE corner and bounded in part by Joseph **Hagan**. Signed Peter **Tucker** senior, Elizabeth (x) **Tucker** (RD). Wit James **Rice** (JP). Rec 13 Jan 1844. [No. 1689]

1912. Page 618. 24 Jul 1841. Jacob **Kunce** to William **Peyton**. For the sum of $250, quit claim to 80 acres on the Mississippi River, being the SW 1/2, SE 1/4, Survey 2175 in Twp 34, Rng 14 E; and immediately below land granted to James **Hatchings** and confirmed to Walter **Fenwick**. Signed Jacob **Kunce**. Wit Augustus **Davis** (JP), Manerva A. **Davis**. Rec 13 Jan 1844. [No. 1690]

1913. Page 618. 14 Apr 1842. Daniel **Welker** and Rebecca, his wife, to Jacob F. **Rudisaile** and John G. **Rudisaile**. For the sum of $15, 1 1/2 acres, more or less, part of the SE 1/4, Sec 21, Twp 34 N, Rng 11 E; beginning at a black oak five inches in diameter; and bounded in part by Henry **Rudisaile**. Signed Daniel **Welker**, Rebecca (x) **Welker** (RD). Wit Reuben **Shelby**, JCC. Rec 17 Jan 1844. [No. 1691]

1914. Page 620. 17 Jan 1844. Joseph D. **Burns** to Jesse **Mitchel** of Cape Girardeau Co., Mo. For the sum of $41, three mules; one gray, one bay with crooked legs, and one small bay one. Signed Joseph **Burns**. Wit Royal **Thompson**, Osbirn W. **Walker** (JP). Rec 20 Jan 1844. [No. 1692]

1915. Page 620. 19 Jan 1844. Bede **Moore** and Verlinder, his wife, to James S. **Moore**. For the sum of $31.25, 25 acres, more or less, a portion of a tract confirmed to James **Berry**, and conveyed by him to Bede **Moore**; beginning on the line of James **Samuels**, and bounded in part by Lewis **Moore** and Austin **Tucker**. Signed Bede **Moore**, Verlinder (x) **Moore** (RD). Wit James **Rice** (JP). Rec 22 Jan 1844. [No. 1693]

1916. Page 622. 22 Jan 1844. Bridget **Hayden** to Firmin A. **Rozier** for the use of Ferdinand **Rozier** Jr. For securing debts and the sum of $1, deed of trust on two tracts in Twp 35 N, Rng 10 E; 9.24 acres, more or less, the S part of the SW fractional 1/4, Sec 1; and 69.31 acres, a portion of the W 1/2, NW 1/4, fractional Sec 12, reserving 9.24 acres in the W or NW part that contains the cleared land, orchard, spring, and improvements where sd **Hayden** now lives, and not to include the Malcom field. Sd **Hayden** owes Ferdinand **Rozier** Jr. $217.57 on account with 10% interest per annum: $145.89 on note and interest dated 7 Feb 1843, $12.41 store account, and $59.17 in a debt to School Twp No. 2. The debt in a note of even date is due by 22 Jan 1845, or sd Firmin is to sell the land to pay it. Signed Briget **Hayden**, Firmin A. **Rozier**. Wit James **Rice** (JP). Rec 23 Jan 1844. [No. 1694]

1917. Page 624. 23 Jan 1844. Lewis **Layton** to John **Layton** senior. For the sum of $1, mortgage on one gray horse three years old next spring, and about 13 hands high; one black horse two years old next spring; one red bob-tailed cow with a white back, five years old next spring; one red heifer three years old next spring; one yellow bull two years old next spring; two red heifers one year old next spring. Sd Lewis owes sd John a note for $10, payable two months after date. Signed Lewis **Layton**. Test James White **Leal**, Jno. W. **Noell**, Clerk. Rec 23 Jan 1844. [No. 1695]

1918. Page 625. __ Apr 1843. John **Martin** to Olly **Penny**, wife of Richmond **Penny**, and her heirs. For love and affection to his daughter, a negro girl **Marthy** with her increase. Signed John (x) **Martin**. Test A. M. **McPherson** (JP), Joseph D. **Simpson**. Rec 23 Jan 1844. [No. 1696]

1919. Page 625. 23 Jan 1844. John Gottleib **Burkheardt** to John Gottfried **Hemmon**. For the sum of $111, two tracts in Twp 34 N, Rng 13 E; 40 acres, being the NE 1/4, NE 1/4, Sec 26; and 3 acres, 1 rood, and 34 poles out of the SE 1/4, SE 1/4, Sec 23, commencing at the corner of Secs 23, 24, 25 & 26. Sd **Burkheardt** owes sd **Hemmon** a note, due two years after date with 6% interest from this date. Signed Johann Gottleib **Burkhardt**. Wit A. M. **McPherson** (JP), Frederick H. **Uhlich**. Rec 30 Jan 1844. [Marginal note: Satisfaction received on 7 Mar 1851. Signed Johann Gottfried **Hemmond**.] [No. 1697]

1920. Page 626. 31 Jan 1844. John B. **Pelletier** and Sally, his wife, to Firmin A. **Rozier** for the use of Ferdinand **Rozier** Jr. For securing notes and the sum of $1, deed of trust on two tracts; 71.56 acres, more or less, being the NE fractional 1/4, Sec 2, Twp 35 N, Rng 10 E; and 40 acres, more or less, being the SW 1/4, SW 1/4, Sec 36, Twp 36 N, Rng 10 E. Sd **Pelletier** owes Ferdinand **Rozier** Jr. $247.13 with 6% interest per annum in three notes, due on 31 Jan 1847; and sd Firmin is to sell the land if the debt is not paid. Signed John B. (x) **Pelletier**, Sally (x) **Pelletier** (RD). Wit James **Rice** (JP). Rec 31 Jan 1844. [No. 1698]

1921. Page 629. 5 Feb 1844. John W. **Cox** and Susan, his wife, to Andrew **Hoover**. For the sum of $290, 94.44 acres, being the E fractional 1/2, fractional Sec 33, Twp 36 N, Rng 11 E. Signed J. W. **Cox**, Susan (x) **Cox** (RD). Test Joab W. **Burgee**, JCC. Rec 6 Feb 1844. [No. 1699]

1922. Page 630. 6 Feb 1844. James **Rice** and Salina, his wife, to Felix **Rozier** and Walter F. **Mattingly**, trading as Rozier & Mattingly. For the sum of $85, 40 acres, more or less, being the undivided 1/2, N 1/2, NW 1/4, Sec 14, Twp 35 N, Rng 12 E; conveyed to sd **Rice** by Robert T. **Brown** junior on 12 Mar 1840 (3:281). Signed James **Rice**, Salina **Rice** (RD). Wit John F. **Hase** (JP). Rec 6 Feb 1844. [No. 1700]

End of Book 4.

Perry County Deed Abstracts - Name Index

___, Frederick S. 1197
___, Stephen 71
Abell, Jesse 40-41
Abernathy, Aaron 267
Abernathy, Albartus O. 1473
Abernathy, Alonzo 487, 603, 702, 707, 724, 733-734, 761, 766, 779, 811, 861, 866, 896, 935, 947, 1031, 1074, 1092, 1098, 1121-1122, 1199, 1210, 1250, 1274, 1279-1280, 1308, 1315-1316, 1329, 1344-1345, 1495, 1622, 1643, 1657, 1832, 1869
Abernathy, Ann Arpy 146, 232, 733-734, 839-840, 1027, 1277
Abernathy, Arpa 603, 724
Abernathy, Batte 1344
Abernathy, Bernice 779
Abernathy, C. D. 486
Abernathy, Calidonia 1473
Abernathy, Clayton D., children of 1473
Abernathy, Daniel 1719
Abernathy, Eligah B., heirs of 779
Abernathy, Elijah B. 761
Abernathy, Elizabeth 267, 603, 724, 761
Abernathy, F. A. 1605-1606
Abernathy, Fonzo 485
Abernathy, Francis (Franky) 603, 724
Abernathy, Franklin 1861
Abernathy, Harley D. 1869
Abernathy, J. 209-210, 410-411, 486, 523-524, 543, 1277, 1803-1804
Abernathy, James 603, 724, 1808
Abernathy, James D., heirs of 779
Abernathy, James F. 101, 935
Abernathy, James F., heirs of 603, 724
Abernathy, James S. 761
Abernathy, Jeremiah (Jere.) 779, 1344-1345
Abernathy, John H. 779, 861, 1344-1345
Abernathy, Jonas 232, 338, 453, 565, 724
Abernathy, Jones 487, 497, 603, 1093
Abernathy, Joseph A. 779
Abernathy, Joseph T. 1832
Abernathy, Joshua (Joshuah) 603, 610, 724, 728
Abernathy, Larkin 630
Abernathy, Lot (Lott) 1210, 1344-1345, 1803-1804
Abernathy, Margaret 1804
Abernathy, Martha 603, 724
Abernathy, Mary 603, 724
Abernathy, Nancy F. 1473
Abernathy, Patsy T. 779
Abernathy, Permalia (Permealea) 603, 724
Abernathy, Perneely L. 779
Abernathy, Robert 100, 146, 232, 333, 572, 603, 724, 733-734, 839, 1256, 1277, 1697
Abernathy, Robert, heirs of 1530, 1707, 1742, 1861
Abernathy, Sarah 1869
Abernathy, Sarah Ann 267
Abernathy, Starling G. 1473
Abernathy, Sufphronia 1473
Abernathy, Susanna 779
Able (Abel), Ezekiel 54, 59, 268, 309, 395, 687, 1200, 1845
Adams, John Quincy (J. Q.) 174, 233, 462, 792
Adinger, George H. 400
Adler, Elizabeth 1334
Adler, H. Jacob 1316
Adler, Mark 1036
Adler, Marx 1074, 1334, 1335, 1910
Ahlich, Frederich August 1181
Akin, John 36
Albright, B. R. 1188
Albright, Nancey 952
Aldridge, James P. 942
Aldridge, Louisa 942
Alexander, Jane S. 506
Alexander, William 506
Alfemous, Lewis 54
Allaire (Allair), Joseph 59, 67, 1476
Allaire, Rachiel 1476
Allan, Joseph 29
Allan, Rachel 29
Allbright (Albright), Benjamin 754, 952, 974
Allbright, Ann 750
Allbright, Benjamin 441, 523-524, 579, 689, 711
Allbright, Benjamin (Benjamine) R. 749-750, 1012, 1131, 1760
Allbright, Nancy 524, 579, 689
Allcorn, ___ 696, 735
Allcorn, Lydia 696, 735
Alldrige, James G. 731
Alldrige, Louisa 731
Allen, Almira 719, 742
Allen, Beverley (Beverly) 69, 143, 382, 477, 634, 770, 872
Allen, Celeste M. 985
Allen, Frank J. 824
Allen, Lydia 696, 735
Allen, Mahala (Mahaly) 426, 480, 719
Allen, Margaret 696, 735
Allen, Mrs. Thomas 442
Allen, Nancy 696, 735
Allen, Penelope 770, 872
Allen, Sally 479
Allen, Samuel 426, 479-480, 696, 719, 735, 819, 964, 1062
Allen, Thomas (Thos.) 42, 51, 114, 205, 293, 479-480, 662, 1059, 1066-1067, 1174, 1179
Allen, William (Wm.) 479-480, 664, 696, 719, 735, 742, 1317
Ames, Wm. 1817
Amoreaux (Amareaux), Benjamine C. 981-982
Amoureux, M. 51
Anders, Samuel 4
Anderson, Arashee 408
Anderson, David M. 633, 644, 865, 873
Anderson, H. 484
Anderson, Jane 408
Anderson, Jane F. 1225
Anderson, Margaret 408, 873
Anderson, Margaret A. 530
Anderson, Miles R. 530, 1101
Anderson, Miley 408
Anderson, Milless R. 384
Anderson, Pinkney 1225
Anderson, Pinkney K. 384, 530, 566, 1101
Anderson, Pinkney R. 408
Anderson, Samuel (Saml.) 8, 30, 530, 691, 1101, 1806
Anderson, Samuel A. Rickey 408
Anderson, Samuel, heirs of 408
Anderson, Thomas 408
Anderson, Thomas W. 530
Andrews, Elizabeth 1545
Andrews, Jms. 13
Andrews, Martin 1545
Anduze, Aristides (Aristideze) 74, 195-196, 990-991
Anselm (Anseleun), Terrice (Terice, Teriece) 1622, 1633
Anselm (Anseleun), Thomas 1622, 1633
Anstadt, Michael 959, 961
Anthony, B. 14
Ardery, Alexander 969, 1652
Armas, Christover de 195
Armour, David 128
Armstrong, Abraham 1297, 1691, 1741
Augustin, Gottleib 1389
Avery, ___ 1604
Avery, Charles (Chas.) 1332, 1534, 1698, 1766, 1771, 1825
Baber, Hiram H. 1191, 1340, 1447-1448
Bacher, John C. 1536
Bacher, Nancy 1536
Bailey (Baley, Baly), Alexander 468, 594-595, 696, 735, 916, 964, 967, 1051, 1765
Bailey (Baley, Baly), Margaret 594, 696, 735, 964, 1051
Bailey, J. B. 1019
Baker, Peter 1730, 1748
Baldock, George 1431
Balie, John Bte. 911
Ball, A. 59
Bankson, Daniel 250
Barada 226
Barber, Betsey 998
Barber, Elias 185, 328, 337, 365-366, 369, 400, 414-415, 429, 444, 473, 478, 482, 499, 518, 552-556, 566, 576, 580-

Barber, Samuel 576, 796
Barcroft, Elias (E.) 222, 231, 244, 252, 262, 268, 284-285, 305, 309, 321, 323, 343, 383, 395, 791
Barcume, F. 343
Barks, A. L. 1317
Barnhart, ___ 912
Barnhart, Christopher (C.) 231, 436, 1598, 1671
Barrett, John S. 569
Barringer, Eliza 656, 949, 979
Barringer, M. 1035
Barringer, Matthias (Mathias, Mats.) 407, 431, 456, 535, 542, 577, 584, 586, 610, 656, 775, 798, 949, 956, 979, 1072, 1141, 1294
Barringer, Mathias M. 949, 1141
Barringer, William 949, 1141
Barthel (Barthels), Friederich (Fred., Fredk., Frederick) Wilh. 1142, 1262-1263, 1360, 1363-1364, 1380, 1438, 1430, 1667, 1670, 1672
Barthel, Gottlieb 1409
Barthume, ___ 369
Barthume (Barchume, Barthieme, Barthume, Batheaum, Bearthune, Berthume), Francis (Francois) 72, 81, 83, 92, 118, 120, 193, 241, 459, 619, 629
Barthume, Francis [Jr.] 45
Barthume (Bartheamne, Bartheaum), Francis [Sr.] 45
Barton, Joshua 1, 3, 5, 7-11, 25, 80
Basher, John G. 975
Bates, Frederick 160
Baugh, Abner 544
Bausland, William H. 673
Bauvais, Vitale 33
Baxter, Gideon H. 1735
Beal, Ignatius G. 1788
Beal, James A. 1599
Beal, William, heirs of 1832
Beard, Isaac 131
Beasley, James 479
Beasly, James R. 742-743, 1029
Beatrix, Sister 511, 1235
Beauchemin, Joseph 226
Beauvais, Jean Baptiste Ste. Gemes 33
Beauvais (Beauvise, Bovie), Joseph Vitalle (Vital, V.) 595, 781, 821, 1081, 1324, 1741
Beauvais, Matilda 1324
Beauvais, Matilda V. 1081
Beauvis, St. Gemme 277-279
Beauvis, Vital, heirs of 277-279
Beebe, Charles 226
Beebe, Edward H. 226
Beebe, Mary H. 226
Beebe, Mary Lisa 226
Beebe, Sarah 226
Beebe, William 226
Beek, Wm. F. 1887
Behrle (Behrley), Moritz (Morritz) 1424, 1675

Behrle, Helena 1094
Beinlein, John 1833
Beinlein, Margaret 1833
Bell, Ann 1241
Bell, David 18-19
Bell, James 915, 1907
Bell, Mary 915, 1907
Bell, William 1241
Bellsha, Delilah 372
Bellsha, Ester 372
Bellsha, Jane 372
Belsha (Bellsha), John 804, 805
Belsha, America 1522, 1735
Belsha, Catharine Sr. 1523
Belsha (Bellsha, Belshey), Elisha 34, 135, 155, 357-359, 372(2), 834, 934, 1524, 1589, 1839
Belsha, Elisha [Jr.] 1126
Belsha, Elisha [Sr.], heirs of 1126
Belsha, Ferdinand 803, 1029, 1062, 1169
Belsha, Hester 609, 667
Belsha (Bellsha), James 372, 1126, 1522, 1525
Belsha (Bellsha), Jeramiah (Jeremiah) 372, 1126
Belsha (Bellsha), Jerry 372, 1126
Belsha, John 519, 609, 854
Belsha (Bellsha), Katharine 227, 248, 370, 564
Bellsha, Mary (Poley, Polly) 135, 358, 372
Belsha, Sarah 1523, 1525
Belsha, William 804, 933, 1047, 1866
Belsha, William P. (Wm. P.) 1328, 1522, 1735
Benedictine, Maria Theresia 1389
Benton, Thomas H. 196, 991, 994
Bequet, Paschal 1796, 1871
Bergmann (Bergeman, Bergman), George 877, 1322, 1545, 1619, 1625-1626, 1696
Bergmon, Ferdnand 1281
Bergt, Willhelm Adolph 1181
Bernes, James 485
Berry, Eliza Teresa 1662
Berry, James 357. 1915
Berry, William 23, 745, 1662
Berryman, Josias 322
Berthold, Odaria 206
Bertramm, Ludwig Ernst Edward 1325
Bertramm, Sophia 1325
Bertt, Christian Adolph 1181
Besan, Ciril 1306
Besand, John Claude 1491
Bess, Delila 592
Bess, John 592
Bess (Best), Joseph 376, 1490
Bess, Joseph, heirs of 592
Bess, Joshua 376, 592
Bess, Lawson 592
Bess, Mary 592
Bess, Ruey 592
Bessonnette, Joseph 226
Bey, Felix 1479

Bey, John Claude Cassimere 1538
Biddle, Thomas 196, 991
Bimpage, Henry Christoph (C., Christoper) 1026, 1065, 1142, 1159, 1262-1263, 1265, 1360-1423, 1430, 1503, 1534-1535, 1638, 1670, 1693-1694, 1774, 1786, 1835, 1893, 1898, 1903
Bimpage, Mary Jane 1503, 1534-1535, 1786
Bird, A. 77, 90, 158, 1107
Bird, Alfred 37, 39, 78-79, 133, 222, 285, 946
Bird, Amos 71, 270, 308, 346, 451, 475, 476, 522, 831, 939, 946, 1454, 1618
Bird, Gustavus 483
Bird, Gustavus A. 68, 71, 117-118, 120, 193, 241, 270, 421-422, 475, 939
Bird, Hannah L. 193, 421, 483
Bird, Penelope 144
Bird, Stephen 1148
Birntrie, ___ 1265
Bishop, Elizabeth 1555
Bishop, John M. 1555
Bishop, Rebecca (Rebeckah) 199, 208, 221, 381, 1255, 1310, 1542, 1578
Bishop, Rezin 294
Bishop, Rezin L. (Resin L.) 103, 139, 146-147, 199, 208, 216, 221, 266, 351, 381, 1158, 1208, 1255, 1310, 1542, 1555, 1578, 1716
Bishop, Thomas J. 1555
Bissonnette, Charles 226
Black, Elizabeth 1315, 1316
Black, Emily 422
Black, R. S. 882
Black, Robert 604, 627, 860, 1855
Black, Sarah 627, 860, 1855
Black, William 1093, 1315, 1316
Blackley, Godfrey 497
Blair, Thomas M. 1781, 1825
Bland, Harriet 1037
Bland, John 1037
Bland, Joseph 261, 270, 422, 694, 697, 811, 832
Bland, Joseph Jr. 1037
Bland, Joseph R. 22, 43, 53, 339
Bland, Joseph Sr. 1037
Bland, Joseph Sr., heirs of 1037
Bland, Nancy 1037
Bland, Sabrina 339, 396
Blanka, Martin 212-214
Blaylock, Elizabeth 1077
Blaylock, Thomas 1077
Bliss, Arthur M. (A. M.) 958-959, 1111-1113, 1214, 1253-1254, 1426
Bliss, Nancey 1214
Block & Avery 1534, 1715, 1721, 1729, 1807, 1825, 1882
Block, Adolph 1747, 1756
Block, Delia 508, 535
Block, H. 589
Block, Hyman (Himan, Hynman) 548, 578, 737, 754, 808, 842, 978, 980, 1005,

1012, 1099, 1162, 1272-1273, 1314, 1434, 1487, 1604, 1721
Block, Levi (Levy) 307, 353, 632, 739, 744, 750, 754, 807, 870, 891, 1067, 1071, 1434, 1487, 1575, 1817
Block, Marcus 1482, 1701, 1747, 1756
Block, Morris 952, 1012, 1222, 1534-1535, 1698, 1715, 1766, 1771, 1825, 1840, 1844
Block, Moses 1604
Block, Phineas (Phinias) 280, 508, 535
Block, Rozina (Risina) 1265, 1415
Block, Susan 1071, 1817
Blow, P. E. 1862
Boak, Michael Jr. 1225
Boak, Michael Sr. 1225
Bochamp 226
Bochlau, ___ 1265
Bochman, Johanne 1400
Bocktert, Maurice 381
Boeuf (Boeuff), Pierre Theodore (T.) 1446, 1539, 1560, 1689
Boeuf, Francois Flavier 1446, 1689
Boeuf, Malina 1689
Boeuf, Melanie 1539
Boggs, Lilburn W. 1340
Bogy (Boggy) & Shannon 268, 1845
Bogy, Joseph 277-279, 570
Bogy, Lewis V. 1060, 1857
Bogy, Marie 570
Bogy, Mary 278
Boice, Joseph 362
Bollinger, Adam J. 592
Bollinger (Bolinger), David 93, 433, 1846
Bonard, Lucas 1764
Bond, Samuel 746
Boner, William 458
Bonthelier, Francis 226
Boon, Benningsen 830
Born (Borne), Martin 1289, 1292
Born, Elizabeth 1292
Borrows, Samuel 587, 718, 841
Bosia, J. P. 1691
Bosier, J. B. 1297
Bosoni, John 212-214
Boss, Joseph 1124, 1153
Boss, Lieot (Lugarts) 1124
Bossier, John B. (J. B.) 550, 1741, 1792, 1796, 1871
Bossier, Martha 550
Bovie, Joseph V. 594
Bovus, ___ 24
Bower, Jno. M. 1748
Bowie, John J. 1476
Boyce, John 1349
Boyce, Sarah 1349
Boyce, William 147, 765, 839, 1256, 1651
Boyd (Boid, Boiyd), Roland (Rowland) 58, 66, 73, 938
Boyd, ___ 223
Boyd, Elijah 788
Boyd, Julia 643
Boyd, Julian 197

Boyd, Juliet (Julie, Juliett) 306, 326, 350
Boyd, R. 492
Boyd, Roland (Roling, Rowland) 197, 242, 293, 306, 326, 350-351, 643, 1763
Boyd, Roland Jr. 1466, 1856
Boyd, Roland Sr. 1466, 1856
Boyd, William 53, 132, 227
Boyd, William G. 788
Bozy, Josephy 240
Brady, ___ 570
Brady, Thomas 593
Brands, John 534
Branham, Wm. B. 506
Branstetter, Joseph 704
Brazeau, Caroline 816, 1499
Brazeau, Charles F. 816, 1499
Brazeau, Joseph 226, 1862
Bredell, Edward 788
Breedwell, Edward 1104
Breese, Sidney 1244
Brewer, Ann 220, 466
Brewer, Charles 1348
Brewer, Charles Jr. 1436
Brewer, Charles Sr. 1870
Brewer, James 62
Brewer, James D. 1745
Brewer, John 220, 466, 470
Brewer, Mark 491, 589, 596, 603, 680, 724, 732-734, 809, 888, 908, 973, 996, 1069, 1086, 1096, 1126, 1166, 1172, 1204, 1207, 1219, 1227, 1243, 1284, 1286, 1304-1305, 1344-1345, 1442, 1488, 1497, 1501-1502, 1517, 1548, 1564, 1571, 1589, 1595, 1601, 1656-1658, 1669, 1675, 1705, 1728, 1732, 1737, 1809, 1870, 1906
Brewer, Mary 1348, 1571
Brewer, Pius (Pious) 247, 312, 338, 439, 533, 1006
Brickey, J. C. 588
Brickey, John 588
Brickey, John C. 13
Brickey, John S. 1224
Bricky, Jno. S. 461
Bridgeman (Bridgman), John 1700, 1721, 1722
Bridgeman, John 1882
Bright, John 551, 930-931, 945
Brightson, ___ 1181
Brooks, John B. 969
Brooks, John T. 1652
Brooks, M. 477
Brooks, Mark 18-19, 24, 43, 77, 90, 240, 309, 568-570, 969, 1652
Brown, Ann 334-335, 364, 375, 504, 610, 685, 1177, 1870
Brown, Barnard (Bernard) 75-76, 178, 183, 334-335, 355, 363-364, 375, 420, 504, 610, 660, 1176-1177, 1191
Brown, Catharine (Catherine, Catiche) 282, 327, 367, 454, 829, 923, 985, 1217, 1473
Brown, Ethan A. 848, 1450
Brown, Frances V. 922

Brown, George 1870
Brown, James 660
Brown, James S. 1436
Brown, John F. 1829
Brown, John W. 1476
Brown, John Y. 1217
Brown, Joseph 276
Brown, Mary 1826
Brown, Nancy 660
Brown, Peter 1046, 1192, 1513, 1826
Brown, Precilla 1055
Brown, Rachiel 1476
Brown, Robert 1593
Brown, Robert T. (Robt. T., R. T.) 4, 5-6, 28-29, 54, 59, 61, 74, 90, 123, 126, 142, 144, 148, 157, 160, 163, 177, 181, 202, 225, 281-282, 325, 327, 351, 367, 378, 396, 454, 465, 593, 634, 643, 677, 829, 923, 985, 1008, 1173, 1177, 1217, 1297, 1473, 1618, 1749, 1821, 1829
Brown, Robert T. Jr. 895, 1133-1134, 1138, 1152, 1298, 1889, 1922
Brown, Robert T. Sr. 1064, 1138, 1507
Brown, Sarah 469
Brown, Thomas 529, 551, 1342
Brown, Thomas A. 1565
Brown, Thomas B. 1055
Brown, William 1152
Browning J. R. 324
Bruce, Amos J. 320
Bruchon, Seraphim 1800
Bruner, Ann 1044
Bruner, Elias E. 1044
Brunstrater, Joseph 1264
Brush, Daniel H. (D. H.) 607, 647, 1215, 1783
Bryan, Timothy 1857
Buck, Wilhelm Frederick 1414
Buckanan, Colonel 920
Buenger, J. Frederick 1693
Bull, William A. (Wm. A.) 429, 473, 499, 903, 1156
Bullitt, Celeste 985
Bullitt, George 985
Bullitt, Nancy 634, 985
Bunger (Binger), John Frederick 1181
Bunger, Christeni 1374
Bunger, Dr. 1265
Bunger, Friederich 1367
Burge, Nancy 184
Burgee, Anna 351
Burgee, Eleanor 351
Burgee, Elizabeth 564, 756, 875
Burgee, Joab 1541
Burgee, Joab W. (J. W.) 370, 426, 495, 520-521, 559, 564, 617, 693, 719, 721-722, 735, 755-756, 776, 789, 799, 811, 865, 875, 895, 897, 916, 918, 921, 1076, 1560, 1568, 1849, 1897, 1921
Burger, Ernst Moritz 1382
Burger, George 1418
Burget, John A. 1161
Burget, Nancy (Nancey), heirs of 913, 1044-1045

Burget, Peter L. 1045
Burgett, J. E. 1323
Burgett (Burget), John 77, 626, 876, 912, 1082, 1618
Burgett (Burget), John E. 520-521, 696, 735, 912-913, 1267, 1442, 1453, 1454, 1458, 1530, 1636, 1692, 1733
Burgett (Burget), John, heirs of 912, 1044-1045
Burgett (Burget), Mary 696, 735, 1454
Burgett, Mary 912-913
Burgett (Burget), Mary C. 520-521, 1636
Burgett (Burget), Nancy 522, 849, 876, 883, 913, 1453-1454
Burgett, William 912
Burgett (Burget), William B. 849-876, 1044-1045, 1848
Burghart, John Gottlieb 1789
Burkharett, ___ 1181
Burkhart, Alfrona 1790
Burkhart (Burkheardt), John Gottlieb 1790, 1919
Burklow, John D. 1037
Burns, A. 127, 426, 719, 722
Burns, Alvina 1102
Burns, Andrew 1182-1183, 1201
Burns, Andrew R. 1599
Burns, Barna B. 1765
Burns, Barnabas (Barnabus) 5, 10, 22, 25, 28, 34, 52, 57, 104, 137, 313, 334, 338, 347, 362(2), 397, 399, 523, 575, 754, 617, 689, 711
Burns, Barnabas, heirs of 578, 964
Burns, David 250, 256, 397, 399, 439, 468, 575, 682, 696, 719-722, 735, 902, 1236, 1353, 1504, 1610
Burns, Deza (Diza, Dizy) 603, 707, 724
Burns, Elizabeth 696(2), 735(2), 1183, 1561
Burns, Emily Ann 696, 735, 1561
Burns, Getty 1183
Burns, Henry 696, 735, 1037
Burns, James (Jas.) 250, 256, 338, 439, 442, 487, 603, 617, 696, 707, 721, 724, 735, 948, 1039, 1169, 1236, 1344-1345, 1610, 1690, 1724
Burns, James T. 1599
Burns, John 200, 232, 256, 347
Burns, John, heirs of 399
Burns, Joseph 1102, 1599
Burns, Joseph D. 762, 1031, 1331, 1914
Burns, Letitia 696, 735
Burns, Lucinda 721
Burns, Lydia (Lidia) 250, 696, 735
Burns, Margaret 362
Burns, Margaret J. 1236
Burns, Martha 578, 617
Burns, Martha Mulvine 523
Burns, Mary 362, 696, 719-722, 1059, 1561
Burns, Michael 52, 314, 362, 397, 399, 696, 719-722, 756, 799, 916, 921, 964, 1059, 1541, 1690, 1724
Burns, Michael, heirs of 735, 1560

Burns, Nancy 362
Burns, Rebecca 397, 399, 916
Burns, William 13-14, 362(2), 377, 397, 399, 523-524, 575, 578, 617, 689, 696, 711, 735-736, 754, 1039, 1062, 1173, 1182-1183, 1353, 1584, 1610, 1653, 1765, 1884
Burns, William [Sr.], heirs of 736
Burns, William B. 1085, 1504
Burns, William Jr. 948
Burns, William Sr. 1236
Burns, William (Wm.), heirs of 468, 914, 1173, 1561
Burrows, J. L. 1882
Burrows, Jacob L. 1613, 1677, 1721
Burrows, Samuel 1199, 1846
Burt, A. Jr. 320
Buts, Helena 704
Butz, Elizabeth 631
Butz, Martern 1460
Butz, Martin 631
Cadwallader, Isaac 81-82, 118, 204, 459
Caho, Henry 639, 752, 783, 900, 905, 909, 1011, 1014, 1083, 1208, 1226, 1258, 1270, 1666, 1673-1675, 1699, 1717, 1744, 1751, 1837-1842, 1845-1846, 1848, 1854, 1856, 1857-1858, 1860, 1862-1864, 1906, 1909
Caho, Maria 783, 905, 1083, 1270
Caldwell, ___ 429
Caldwell, David L. (D. L.) 4, 9, 12, 20, 24, 29, 35, 43, 47, 53, 58, 66, 88, 90, 105, 132, 139, 158, 181, 207, 241-242, 254, 259, 264, 270, 272-273, 277-279, 305, 338-339, 345, 385, 433, 439, 522, 567, 715, 831, 1453-1454, 1489, 1579, 1744
Caldwell, David L., heirs of 815
Caldwell, Ellen 1744
Caldwell, H___ 88
Caldwell, James 185, 489
Caldwell, James C. 132, 145
Caldwell, Logan 55
Caldwell, Margaret M. 405
Caldwell, May 489
Caldwell, Mecka 185
Caldwell, Polly Ann Elizabeth 351
Caldwell, Robert 29, 54, 132, 145, 1238
Caldwell, Rosannah 132
Callier, Daniel 1303
Cambron, Adela 1645
Cambron, Benjamin 1645
Cameron (Cambron, Cammeron), Elizabeth 965
Cameron (Cambron, Cammeron), James 859, 922, 965
Campbell, Lee 1721
Campbell, Samuel 59
Campbell, Samuel A. 915
Camster, Archibald (Archd.) 231, 615, 947
Camster, Archibald Sr. 564
Camster (Campster), George 29, 91, 112, 137, 227, 231, 240, 248, 317, 351, 370, 424, 564, 615, 623, 824, 947, 1151, 1184, 1212, 1533, 1674
Camster, Henry 227
Camster (Campster), Martha (Marthy) 227, 317, 615, 623, 824
Camster (Campster), widow 588, 608
Caphart, George 1787
Capper, James 232
Carbrey, John 1889
Carlisle, Joanna M. 1151, 1184
Carlisle, John 623, 944, 1151, 1184, 1355, 1674, 1680, 1830
Carns, Elizabeth 844, 846
Carpenter, Peter 1449
Carr, John 1806
Carr, William C. 235, 240
Carrico, Benjamin 1528
Carrico, Mary 1528
Cashion, Anderson 1910
Cashion, Anna 1281
Cashion, Cinthia 718
Cashion, James 1281, 1293, 1910
Cashion, Robert 718
Cashion, William D. 1563
Cassilly (Casley), Michael P. (M. P.) 821, 822, 1324
Cassilly, Sophia 821
Cassley, Edward B. 1463
Catlamy, Antoin Joseph 1480
Chambers, L. L. 788
Chandler, Amyd. 549
Chandler, Amzi 1583
Chartier, John P. 1603
Chesley, Alexander 37, 39
Chesley, Alexander C. 78-79
Chesley, Louisa Jane 79
Chouteau, Henry 770, 816, 872
Christy, James 1604
Christy, William T. 1604
Church, L. J. 672
Cissell, Ann 198, 492
Cissell, Ann M. 409, 763
Cissell, Bernard 223, 293, 490, 574, 790, 938, 965, 1814, 1869
Cissell, Clement 15, 198, 223, 492, 574, 763, 938, 965
Cissell, Elizabeth 1603, 1628
Cissell (Cissel), Francis 270, 421, 474, 939
Cissell, Francis R. 567
Cissell, Francis, heirs of 1037
Cissell, John 1792
Cissell, John B. 228, 283, 880, 893, 1239, 1624, 1810
Cissell (Cissel), Joseph 15, 125, 130, 354, 490, 536, 574, 674, 782, 937-938, 951, 1205, 1307, 1464, 1466, 1628, 1661, 1707, 1763
Cissell, Joseph Jr. 1053, 1640
Cissell, Joseph Sr. 1650, 1662, 1679
Cissell (Cissel), Lewis 4, 7, 139, 223, 293, 409, 574, 763, 765, 918, 1645, 1651
Cissell, Maria (Anne) 1651

Cissell, Mary 574(2), 1205, 1650
Cissell, Monica 490
Cissell, Nancy 574
Cissell, Susan 1239
Cissell, Susannah 1810
Cissell, William 492
Clark, ___ 173
Clark, Alfred L. 880
Clark, Betsy 1806
Clark, David 1462
Clark, Evaline (Eveline) 517, 1346
Clark, Francis (Francois) 88, 132, 142,
    395, 437, 517, 525, 560, 815, 1106,
    1211, 1238, 1346, 1469, 1489, 1532,
    1579, 1636, 1704, 1873, 1892
Clark, George P. (Geo. P.) 1346, 1716
Clark, H. 91, 112, 352
Clark, Henry 18-19, 88-89, 142, 227, 382,
    770, 911, 1211
Clark, Henry F. 1449
Clark, Henry J. 1476
Clark, James 37, 79, 133
Clark, Joseph T. 1830
Clark, Julia M. 1830
Clark, Lawrence 133, 889
Clark, Michael M. 1164
Claudet, O. 1577
Clendennin, Harvey 1655
Cleveland, Robert 371
Clifton, Catharine 1327
Clifton, Dalinda (Dalinder, Dolinda)
    1521, 1691, 1741
Clifton, Eli 1119-1120, 1122, 1123, 1133
Clifton, Isabella (Isabela) 1122, 1123
Clifton, Jacob 1326-1327
Clifton, James 1091-1092, 1110, 1116-
    1118, 1121-1123, 1274
Clifton, James [Jr.] 1329
Clifton, James [Sr.] 1329
Clifton, Mary 431, 471
Clifton, Milton 1121
Clifton, Rebeca 1092
Clifton, Warren 413, 431, 456, 471
Clifton, Wiley 1122
Cline, Daniel 371, 406, 622, 727, 1581
Cline, Daniel Sr. 860
Cline, Daniel U. 518, 602, 796
Cline, Dorcas H. (Darcus H.) 602, 796
Cline, Leah 622, 1581
Cline, Moses 1581
Cline, Samuel 1080
Cline, Solomon 915, 1824
Clodfelter, Elizabeth 836
Clodfelter, Jacob 1846
Clodfelter, Jacob Sr. 836
Clodfelter, John 693, 698-699, 836, 1057,
    1061
Clotfelter, Sarah 1057
Coale, Samuel A. (S. A.) 788, 1060, 1104,
    1644
Coale, Samuel A. & Co. 788
Cobb, Eleazar 740
Cobb, Thomas C. 1495
Cobbs, A. M. 1719

Cobbs, Alexander M. 956, 979, 1035,
    1084-1085, 1097, 1219, 1351
Cobbs, Anne (Ann) 543, 1719
Cobbs, Catharine 956, 1035
Cobbs, Cornelius 543
Cobbs, Cornelius, heirs of 1719
Cobbs, E. 903
Cobbs, Elizabeth 1719, 1721, 1730, 1882
Cobbs, Elizabeth L. 543
Cobbs, Samuel M. 1097, 1351
Cobbs, Sarah 1719, 1721, 1730, 1882
Cobbs, Sarah M. 543
Cobbs, William 1719
Cochran (Cockram, Cockrane), George
    57, 137
Cochran, James H. 1253
Cochran, James W. 226
Cochran, Jane 1253
Cochran, John 960, 1253
Cochran (Cockram), Mariah 57, 137
Cochran, Mary 1106
Cochran, Mary O. 871
Cochran, Robert Nathan (Robert N.) 871,
    915, 1148
Cochran, Thomas 1462, 1765
Cochran, Thomas, heirs of 1106
Cody, Elizabeth 1702
Cody (Coty), Thomas 48, 149, 296, 319,
    5311130, 1702
Coen, Elias 531, 1447, 1845
Coffman, Joseph 1427
Cogan, Elizabeth 1008
Cogan, James P. 1010
Cogan, Richard (Richd.) 509, 532, 587,
    594, 601, 611, 970-971, 1008, 1018
Cole, Philip 1039
Collier, Antoine Legis Gaspard 1557
Collier, Clotilda Virguire Faivre 1557
Collier, George 1618
Collier, Polly 208
Conen(?), Joab 431
Conners, John 534
Connor, Jeremiah (Jerh.) 2, 4, 38
Conrad, Jacob 375, 592, 610, 1748
Conrad, John L. 176, 500, 592, 881
Conrad, Peter 592, 1308
Conrad, Sally 610
Conrad, Sarah 1308
Conrad, William 1308
Cook, Alvan 294, 312, 318, 368, 378, 657
Cook, John 226, 1857
Cook, John D. 160, 164, 176, 188, 193,
    562-563, 573, 664, 1182
Cook, William F. (Wm. F.) 1163, 1543
Cooper, Henry W. 350
Cortise, Antonio 1245
Cortise, Susan 1245
Costner, Emanuel 1608
Cotner, George 621, 1128
Cotner, Sarah 1128
Cotten, Joab 485
Cotter, John 434
Coty, Lewis 24
Counsil, Daniel T. 77

Cource, Charles 1132
Courtois, Francis Victor (V.) 1498, 1515
Courtois, Jane Mary Felisete 1498
Cowan, George Washington (George W.)
    1635, 1781
Cowan, John Epee 1020, 1164, 1592,
    1593
Cowan, Joseph 1635, 1781
Cowan, William Bowie 1020, 1477
Cowen, Elias 314
Cox, Andrew 314, 883, 912-913, 1845,
    1848
Cox, Andrew Jr. 184, 723
Cox (Coxe), Andrew Sr. 184, 849
Cox, Benjamin 87, 148, 437, 488
Cox, Benjamin (Benjamine) Jr. 1301,
    1428-1429, 1582, 1697
Cox, Benjamin (Benjamine) Sr. 164,
    1301, 1429
Cox, Charmic L. 1261
Cox, Hosea 1338
Cox, James 1253-1254
Cox, John 184, 314, 723
Cox, John W. 1358, 1921
Cox, Margaret 1529
Cox, Mary 1254
Cox, Susan 1921
Cox, William 723, 758, 1167, 1338, 1529
Coyteaux, Lewis 1845
Cozens, William 85
Craig, James 917
Crane, Smith 645
Cranner, Gottfried 1406
Crawford, Ch. W. 1033
Crawford, William 1806
Crips, David 268, 529, 531, 696, 789-
    790, 799-800, 921, 1447, 1541, 1560,
    1846
Crips, James 531, 1447
Crips, Thereassa (Terecy) 529, 789, 799
Crockett, George 1149
Croper, James 226
Crosby, Elisha 1458, 1733
Crosley, ___ 476
Crow, Wayman 1857
Cull, Thomas 40-41
Cummen, Nancy 617
Cuningham, Wm. 482
Cunningham, Daniel 140
Cunningham, John P. 1164, 1592, 1631-
    1632
Curtis, H. B. 944
Cybert, ___ 1806
Dade, Johann Gottleib 1389
Dahmen, Francis Xavier, Rev. 212-214
Dahmen, Xavier 435
Dahmer, Francis Xavier 600
Daley (Daly), Michael 1219, 1234, 1351
Dallam, James 847
Dalson, Stephen 192
Daly, John T. 1288, 1560
Daly, M. 1339
Daly, Michael 1541, 1560
Daly, Rose 1351, 1560

Daniel, John M. 1845
Darnstedt, Gotchold 1390
Daugherty (Dougherty), John 517, 561, 835, 853, 884, 889, 906, 1072, 1218, 1221, 1598
Daumer, Johann Christ. 1418
Davie, Winstead 672, 1253
Davis, Augustus 369, 646, 777-778, 784-786, 812, 830, 857, 957-963, 1003, 1016-1017, 1057, 1065, 1111-1113, 1163, 1196-1197, 1214, 1231, 1252, 1254-1255, 1262-1263, 1333, 1354, 1363-1364, 1380, 1426, 1430, 1433, 1435, 1438, 1444, 1467, 1543, 1552-1555, 1562, 1597, 1670, 1694, 1738, 1775, 1779, 1781, 1782, 1786, 1890, 1893, 1899, 1903, 1905, 1912
Davis, Benjamin (Benjamine) 10, 16, 45, 54, 61, 72, 81-83, 92, 118, 159, 165, 167, 170, 175, 204, 229, 369, 404, 459, 646, 658, 692, 771-772, 856-857, 1016-1017, 1175-1176, 1214, 1230, 1627, 1663, 1782, 1783
Davis, Eliza 369, 1782
Davis, Elizabeth 404, 430
Davis, Erastus 368, 828, 946, 1566
Davis, Greer W. 333, 382, 406, 509, 781, 964, 1728
Davis, James 188, 277
Davis, Jane 857, 1782
Davis, Joseph B. 159
Davis, Manerva 1782
Davis, Manerva A. 1065, 1163, 1562, 1912
Davis, Margaret 1783
Davis, Margaret H. 159
Davis, Nancy (Nancey) 143, 164, 436, 849, 1301
Davis, Philip 72, 82, 1783
Davis, Sylvester 1783
Davis, T. 118, 368
Davis, T. & Co. 885
Davis, Timothy 67, 87, 142-144, 148, 164, 197, 308, 346, 436, 451, 475-477, 520, 561, 569, 585, 643-644, 694, 697, 723, 730, 770, 811, 831-832, 849, 872-874, 879, 883, 885, 889, 911, 913, 939, 946, 1037, 1301, 1449
Davis, Timothy & Co. 1466
Davis, Washington 857, 1782
Daviss, Eleanor 351
Dawlson, Stephen 590
Dean, Henry 466, 470, 1456, 1769
Dean, Teresa 983
Dean, William 983, 1730
Deaumee, ___ 1265
DeBow, James M. 812
DeBurgh, William 63
Deichmann, Johann Gottfried 1376
Delashmutt, J. J. 193
Delassus, ___ 344
DeLassus, Avarice 594
Delassus, Camille 787
Delassus, Cerant 787

Delassus, Ceron E. 1607, 1741
Delassus, Leon 787, 1051, 1068, 1081
Delassus, Louisa 787
Delassus, Odile 787
Dennichea, Joseph Sr. 39
Denny, Christian 226
Derr (see Doer)
Destrihan, Nicholas Noel 1354, 1891
Devee, Isaac 86
Devore, Isaac 36
Dezier, Lewis Paul 113
Dickerson, Emilie 173
Dickerson, Henry 815
Dickerson, William R. 815
Dickey, William 827
Dickinson, A. J. 1244
Dickinson (Dickason), Henry 24, 277
Dickinson, Lewis 1029
Dickinson, W. 504
Dickson (see also Dixon)
Dickson (Dixon), Barbara Rebeca 1297, 1561
Dickson (Dixon), Barbary 1584, 1884
Dickson (Dicson, Dixon), Jessee 468, 696, 735, 914, 964, 1091, 1173, 1297, 1440, 1561, 1584, 1884
Dickson, Lewis 1297
Dickson, Lewis [Jr.] 1691, 1741
Dickson, Lewis [Sr.] 1691, 1741
Dickson, Lewis, heirs of 1297, 1741
Dickson, Margaret 1007
Dickson, Marshal (Marschal, Marschal, Marshel) 736, 1173, 1297, 1561
Dickson, Martha Caroline 1741
Digges, William 1680
Digges (Diggs), William H. 1146, 1184, 1674, 1830
Diggs, Moses H. 1151
Diggs, William 1355
Diggs, William H. & Co. 1195
Distrihan (see Destrihan)
Divine, Nathaniel J. 549, 564, 609, 627, 655, 667, 479-480, 1201, 1565
Dixon (see also Dickson)
Dixon, Joe 561
Dixon (Dixkson), Joseph 730, 884-885
Dixon, Samuel A. 1818
Doderleud, Augustus H. 1778
Dodge, Henry 38, 66, 116, 222, 262, 687
Dodge, Thomas 113
Dodier 226
Dodson, James (Jas.) 343, 1846
Doederlein, August Henrich (August Henry, Aug. Henr.) 1361-1362, 1430, 1438, 1667, 1672, 1905
Doederlein (Dorderlein), Henrich. Aug. 1262, 1364
Doer (Deer, Derr, Doere, Doerr), Andrew (Andreas) 773, 1292, 1508, 1814, 1842-1844, 1851, 1854, 1867
Doer, Henry 1851
Doer, Philip 1843
Doere (Derr), Christina (Christeen) 773, 1508

Doharty, William H. 1472
Dolan, Dorsey F. 347
Doll, Francis Joseph 953
Doll, Joseph Francis 666
Doll, Mary 953
Dolle, John Hermon 1634
Dolson, Elizabeth 216
Dolson, Lucinda 1764
Dolson, Stephen 216, 848, 1699, 1764
Donald, ___ 1542
Donald (Donalds), Samuel T. 1255, 1578
Donelson, A. 848
Donelson, A. J. 1110, 1116-1120, 1326, 1450
Donnehue, J. 442
Donnohue, Daniel 122
Donohue, ___ 1574
Donohue, John 87, 148, 164, 531, 1300, 1429, 1437, 1448
Donohue (Donohowe, Donnohue), Joseph 47, 58, 66, 77, 122, 242, 892, 1618
Donohue, Mary 545
Donohue, Polly 47
Donohue (Donahue, Donnehoe, Donnohue, Donoho, Donohoe, Donohoo, Donohowe), Thomas (Thos.) 24, 47, 58, 66, 86, 158, 242, 281-282, 327, 372, 396, 422, 434, 436, 545, 716, 892, 906, 912, 946, 1072, 1218, 1449, 1476, 1598, 1671
Dorsey, Charles 1283
Dorsey, Louvecy (Louvesy, Louvice) 192, 256, 271, 300, 325, 696, 735
Dorsey, R. P. 611
Dorsey, Richard S. (Richd. S., R. S.) 134, 156, 192, 217, 246, 250, 256, 271, 299, 300, 325, 342, 398, 409, 412, 413, 416, 438, 447, 452, 454, 456, 460, 471-472, 481, 485, 494, 500-501, 509, 516, 522, 527, 533, 611, 696, 698, 735, 795, 984, 1149, 1283, 1473
Dorsey, W. 250
Dorsey, Washington 1149, 1283, 1424
Dossenbach, Francis 823
Doughty, James W. 1138
Doyle, H. Glen 134
Dropp, Sebastian 1352
Drury (Drewery), Henry 632, 1000, 1055, 1321, 1559, 1617, 1767
DuBourg, Bishop 330, 445
Dubourg, Lewis William 600
Dubourg, Louis William, Rev. 211-215
DuBourg, William, Rev. 435
Dubrenil, Susannah 226
Duffner (Dufner), Joseph 928, 933, 940
Duffner, Anna 933
Duggins, Elizabeth 947
Duggins (Duggin), Pouncey 615, 655, 947, 1656
Dumont, Charles 816
Dumphy (Dunphy), Mathew 331-332, 460
Duncan, Matthew 30, 116
Duncaster, Charles 168, 185, 393, 1230
Dunks, ___ 476, 1690, 1724

Dunks, Andrew 105, 142, 352, 382, 477, 872
Dunks, Andrew Sr. 18-19
Dunks, John 18, 142, 382, 770, 911
Dunlap, Douglas C. 1058
Dunlap, James 552-556, 637, 703
Dunn, Elizabeth 26
Dunn, James 1474, 1475, 1501-1502, 1512, 1571, 1573, 1639, 1737, 1793, 1810
Dunn, Mary 1475, 1512, 1793
Dunn, William 17, 26, 588, 608, 1115, 1496, 1537
Duplantier, Albert 1032
Duquette, Francis 226
Durning, Edward 444, 1846
Dutton, ___ 476
Dutton, James (Jas.) 32, 343
Duval, Caroline 1472
Duval, Jean Bte. 1472
Duval, Tresia 919
Duvall, ___ 130, 783, 1168
Duvall, Evaline (Eveline) 455, 765, 1200, 1300-1301
Duvall, Gabriel 838, 1005, 1487
Duvall, Gabriel M. 839-840, 892, 1027-1028, 1030, 1256, 1300-1301, 1302, 1428-1429, 1437, 1482, 1582, 1699
Duvall (Duvawl), John 34, 47, 144, 146-147, 155, 164, 357, 372, 533, 765, 834, 837-840, 892, 1256, 1277, 1300, 1429, 1437, 1697
Duvall, John Jr. 1676
Duvall, John M. 671, 1834
Duvall, John, heirs of 840, 1027, 1301-1302
Duvall (Duval), Joseph 147, 357, 455, 677, 687-688, 765, 839-840, 892, 919, 1027, 1200, 1300-1301
Duvall, Joseph Jr. 764, 1250
Duvall, Lewis 223
Duvall, Mary 472, 1054
Duvall, Mary Ann (Maryann) 919, 1796
Duvall, Matilda 1428-1429
Duvall, Rosanna 1250
Duvall (Duval), Simon 15, 61, 251, 354, 472, 574, 592, 1054, 1792, 1796, 763-764, 840, 919
Eason, Nancy 888
Eason, Reddick (Redick) 313, 715, 888
Eastman, E. H. 1020
Eastman, Martin L. 1477
Easton, R. 80
Easton, Rufus 32
Eddlemon, Henry 502
Eddlemon, Mary 502
Edinger, John P. 468
Edinger, John Phillip 1561
Edinger, Mary 468, 1561
Edwards, Mary Ann 1806
Eggers, Elisha 137, 248, 495, 718, 756, 799, 804-805, 814, 846, 875, 948, 1007, 1180, 1653
Eggers, Elizabeth 846

Egler, Jaque D. 226
Eisenschmidt, Barnhart 1420
Elder, Elizabeth 793
Elder, Emily 1658
Elder, George 1658
Elder, Guy 40-41, 197, 793-795, 1240, 1332, 1510, 1658, 1771
Elder, Guy T. 419
Elder, James G. 1658
Elder, John 1658
Elder, Joseph 1658
Elder, Mary M. 1658
Ell, John 1682
Ellias, Caroline 816
Elliott (Eliot), Henry 80, 86, 169, 215, 235, 240, 306, 919, 1297, 1691, 1741
Ellis, C. C. 1352, 1715
Ellis, Caroline 1499
Ellis, Charles 22, 32, 43, 77, 351, 1108, 1115, 1496, 1499, 1537, 1747
Ellis, Charles C. 1504, 1716, 1807, 1814
Ellis, Charles G. 1499
Ellis, Charles Sr. 306, 643
Ellis, Charles, heirs of 1499
Ellis, Josiah 1846, 1906
Ellis, Keziah 223
Ellis, Lunsford 197, 223
Ellis, Sarah 77, 1499
Ellis, Willis 348, 350, 606, 612-613, 1237, 1245, 1575
Elmore, James 780, 1015, 1624, 1675
Endras, Loranz 1682
Engest, Frederick 1390
English, ___ 351
English, Simeon 1212
English, Thomas B. 1547
Ensley, Olive 745
Ensley, Squire D. 670, 745
Enstis, George 990
Erstreicher (Erstricher), Isidore 411, 497
Erstricher, Gertrude 497
Estel, Andreas 1369
Estel, Johann A. G. 1638
Estes, Betsey 1007
Estes, Catharine 1007
Estes, Polly 1007
Estes, Reuben 1007
Etter, Chant. 1216
Evans, David 208, 1352
Evans, Diana (Dianna) 572, 1185, 1453, 1703-1704
Evans, Henderson 422
Evans, James 168, 283, 301, 314, 318, 318, 387-388, 509, 537, 601, 997, 1001, 1064, 1143, 1156, 1222, 1283, 1318, 1461, 1570, 1625-1626, 1673
Evans, James G. 1147
Evans, Jesse 442, 946
Evans, Owen 165
Evans, Perry 47, 169, 271, 560-561, 572, 730, 885, 1037, 1185, 1449, 1453-1454, 1550, 1566, 1703-1704, 1780, 1897
Evans, Susan M. 311, 657, 1143
Evans, William 410

Everett (Everetts), Burgett 1442, 1530
Everett, Catharine 1499
Everett (Everets, Everts), Jacob J. 240, 351, 424, 520, 522, 815, 1499
Faherty, Matilda 858
Faherty, Peter 579, 729, 858, 1099, 1487
Faina, ___ 1487
Faina (Fainia, Fiana), Matilda 698, 795, 808, 842, 978, 1717, 1746
Faina (Fainia, Frainna, Frinia), Valario (Valerio, Valero) 294, 419, 698, 795, 801-802, 808, 842, 978, 1239, 1556, 1585, 1715-1717, 1743, 1744, 1745, 1746, 1863
Faith (see also Fath)
Faith, Thomas 1731
Farquhar, James 262, 981
Farrar, Alonzo 1633
Farrar, Alphonzo 1524, 1526-1528
Farrar, Ann Arpy 1697
Farrar, Elizabeth 267
Farrar, Francis 603
Farrar, Franklin 638, 1868
Farrar, John 267, 603, 638, 702, 724, 732, 766, 902, 1832, 1868
Farrar, John B. 622
Farrar, Mary 603, 724
Farrar, Mary R. 1868
Farrar, Miles 487, 618, 638, 702, 732
Farrar, Miles Sr. 1522-1528
Farrar, Moses 405, 426, 603, 781, 819, 1302, 1437, 1582, 1697, 1868
Farrar, Robert 1074, 1098, 1687
Farrar, Robert A. 1605-1606, 1633
Farrar, Robert Sr. 1742
Farrar, Susan 1074, 1098
Farrar, William (Wm.) 603, 724, 1261, 1274, 1311, 1331, 1335, 1344-1345, 1471, 1521, 1523-1528, 1605-1606, 1633, 1820, 1855, 1861, 1868-1869, 1886, 1908, 1910
Farrar, William Jr. 1561
Farrar, William Sr. 1798, 1824, 1880
Farrot, L. 1032
Fasold, Alfred 1794, 1805
Fasold, Michael 1794, 1805
Fassett, Alfred 1618
Fassett, James 1618
Fassett, James & Co. 1618
Fassett, Theodore L. 1618
Fath (Faith, Fate), Leonard 1332, 1625-1626, 1646, 1721, 1731, 1882
Fechler, Gottlob 1225
Fenter, Christian 235
Fenwick, Ann 161
Fenwick, Benedicta 330, 510
Fenwick, Chloe (Cloe) 1024, 1052, 1159
Fenwick, E. 16
Fenwick, Evaline 691
Fenwick, Ezekiel 30, 163, 398, 478, 628, 691
Fenwick, George 109, 170, 264, 363, 658-660, 685, 943, 1175-1176, 1665, 1699
Fenwick, Isabella (Isabel) 478, 691

Fenwick, J. 391
Fenwick, J. C. 1503
Fenwick, James (Jas.) 140, 231, 1024, 1159
Fenwick, James J. 11, 16, 30, 50, 159, 161, 254, 288-290, 291-292, 385, 478, 616, 691. 767-768, 1101
Fenwick, James J., heirs of 1024
Fenwick, Joseph 16, 140, 214, 222, 268, 287, 292, 309, 398, 600, 628, 1581
Fenwick, Joseph Alexander 691
Fenwick, Joseph C. 1063
Fenwick, Joseph, heirs of 478
Fenwick, Julia (Benedicta, Juliana) 511-515, 985, 1235
Fenwick, Leo 30, 287-292, 467, 478, 731, 1024, 1062, 1063, 1101, 1157, 1319, 1534, 1784
Fenwick, Leo A. 769
Fenwick, Leo, Dr. 1503
Fenwick, Margaret 170, 943, 1175-1176
Fenwick, Martin 30, 231
Fenwick, Peggy 363
Fenwick, Rebeca 1157
Fenwick, Thomas (Tho., Thos.) 16, 30, 163, 206, 188-189, 398, 478, 628, 1603
Fenwick, Thos. 1101
Fenwick, Ulila 691
Fenwick, Walter 30, 985, 1912
Ferand, L. H. 195
Ferguson, James (Ja., Jas.) 622, 627, 631, 638, 702, 707, 718, 761, 779, 817, 820, 1036, 1123, 1132, 1264, 1327, 1334823, 860-861, 944, 955, 998
Ferguson, John 505
Ferrel (Ferrell), Ansel 23, 52, 114, 205, 604, 627, 1059, 1692
Ferrel (Ferrell), Esther 205, 627, 1059, 1692
Field, Maria 422
Finch, Elizabeth 914, 934, 1022, 1561
Finch, John P. 563-564, 609, 667, 804-805, 847, 901, 967, 1049-1050, 1587
Finch, Mary Ann 609, 667, 804-805, 967
Finch, Thomas J. (Thos. J.) 562, 847, 870, 907, 914, 934, 964, 1022, 1533, 1561
Fischer, Mariana 1095
Fisher, ___ 1297
Fisher, ___ 1741
Fisher, Jacob 1416
Fisher, Johann Fredk. 1416
Fisher, Joshua 306, 351
FitzGibbons (Fitz Gibbons, Fitzgibon, Fitzgiven), William 91, 112, 317, 424, 623, 1039, 1151, 1184, 1674
Flack, Fr. 1015
Fleck, Anthony (Anton) 704, 817-818, 823, 1186
Fleck (Flak), Elizabeth 637, 817, 823, 1186
Fleming, Baley 1090
Fleming (Flemming), George 30, 222
Flynn, ___ 222
Flynn, David 265, 341, 1055, 1078, 1259

Flynn, Elizabeth (Isabella) 1055, 1259
Flynn (Flinn), Isaac 240, 265, 341, 568, 1594
Flynn, Malissa 1636
Flynn, Mary 696, 735
Flynn, Mary C. 1636
Flynn, Nancey (Nancy) 865, 1115, 1267
Flynn, Sarah C. 1636
Flynn, William (Wm.) 132, 352, 401, 476, 520-522, 588, 607-608, 696, 701, 735, 788, 865, 873, 939, 1104, 1108, 1115, 1267, 1341, 1453-1454, 1636, 1644
Flynn, William [Jr.] 32
Flynn, William [Sr.] 32
Foltz (see also Volz)
Foltz, John 1886
Fonderheider, Casper H. 976
Ford, Timothy 810
Foster, Ezekiel 1090, 1344, 1345
Foster, James 408
Fowler, Hilliard 248-249, 261, 567
Fowler, Hiram 321
Fowler, Jacob 1846
Fowler, Naomah (Naomy) 249, 261
Fowler, Thomas 231
French, Charles 540
French, Joseph 931
French, Lewis 224, 318, 713, 747, 950-951, 1001, 1106, 1167, 1683, 1754
French, Mary 950
French, Polly 224
French, Silas (Silus) 540, 1075
Frenzil, Christian Gotlieb 1186
Frippell, Mason 1209
Fry, Philip 1682
Fugate, William 1906
Fulenwider, Caleb P. (C. P.) 1690, 1891
Gamble, Archibald (A.) 32, 38, 211, 421, 994
Garfield, Egbert B. 241
Garland, Hudson M. (H. M.) 1040, 1139, 1251, 1293
Garner, J. C. 324
Garner, John 1223, 1806
Garner, Louisa V. 1231
Garner, William (Wm., W.) 309, 337, 365, 700, 1101, 1231, 1444, 1520, 1673
Garrett, Peter R. 129, 136, 263, 634, 824, 1212
Garvey, Christopher 1584
Gaty (see Girty)
Gaylord, Guy 32, 1108
Geer, E. Woodbridge (W.) 1346-1347, 1873
Geer, Letitia Ann 1873
Geier, Natalie 1373
Geisel, Conrad 1416
Gener(?), John 1323
Generdeaux, Joseph 1148
Gholson, Thomas 68
Gilbert, Ealenor 351
Gile, James 830
Gill (Gile), George Washington 253, 672-673, 830, 1215

Gill, James 231, 252-253, 672, 1215-1216
Gill, M. L. 672
Gill, Mary 673
Gill, Mrs. 1158
Gill, Napoleon 253
Gill, Napoleon B. 1215-1216
Gill, Sarah 1215
Gill, Wm. 482
Gillespie, James 1655
Girade, Joseph 226
Girty (Gaty), Charity 91, 112, 448, 1039
Girty (Gaty), William 91, 112, 448, 461, 1039
Girty, William, heirs of 395
Gittar, John Grant 57
Glasscock, Elizabeth 726
Glasscock, Robert L. 725-726, 737
Gleinlein, George 1833
Glover, Peter G. 531
Goehring, Rosina 1418
Goethe, ___ 1265
Goethe, Johann Gottleib (John Gottlieb) 1397, 1774
Goff, Ann (Mary) 1755
Gole, Maria 1894
Goodman, Elizabeth 1585
Goodspeed, David 1164
Gottschelk, F. 1142, 1360
Govereau, Etienne Jr. 1245
Govereau, Etienne Sr. 1245
Govereau, Etienne Sr., heirs of 1245
Govereau, Mary 1245
Govereau, Susan 1245
Govero, Antoine 1618
Goverot, Caroline 1472
Goverot, Cecile 1472
Goverot, Etienne 1472
Graefe, Johann Christ. 1365
Grafton, Joseph D. (Jos. D.) 131, 235, 277-278, 325, 402, 477, 570, 677, 687, 709, 787, 843, 911, 992, 1245, 1792
Graham, ___ 1574
Graham, Geo. 166, 174, 233, 341, 446, 462, 792, 1490
Graham, J. P. 91, 112
Graham, John 88, 226, 277
Graibing, Hartmann 1417
Grass, Henry 918, 965
Grass, John 918
Grass, Joseph 918
Grass, Matilda 918
Gray, John W. 1555
Greenawalt, John Jr., heirs of 1127
Greenawalt, John Sr. 1127
Greenawalt, Joseph 1127
Greene, Lewis 370
Greene, Winneyfred 370
Greener (Grinner), John 1601-1602, 1629
Greener (Grinner), Kunnigunda (Kunnegunda) 1602, 1629(2), 1794, 1805
Greenewalt, Elizabeth 1007
Greenewalt, Frederick 1007
Greenewalt, Isaac 1007

Greenewalt (Greenawalt, Greenwalt), John 75, 170, 174, 182, 1039, 1767
Greenewalt (Greenawalt), John Jr. 1007, 1127
Greenewalt, John, heirs of 1007
Greenewalt, Matilda 1007
Greenewalt, William 1007
Greenier (Grenier, Greeny), Lewis 249, 474, 939
Greenier (Grenier, Greeny), Winifried (Winyfred) 474, 939
Greenvoll, Robert 768
Greenwault, John Jr. 1532, 1574
Greenwell, Robert 616
Greeny, Mary 65
Greeny, Vincent 65
Gregoire, Charles (Chs.) 394, 503, 538, 714, 882, 985, 1150, 1559
Gregoire (Grigoir), Charles Jr. 367, 403, 709
Gregoire, Eulila (Eulalia) 714, 1150
Gregoire, F. 1138
Gresham, George Washington 1823
Griffeth, Jas. 1579
Griffieth, Jos. Sr. 1819
Griffith, R. B. 1496
Grissom, Nelson 854
Gross (Groeste, Grosse), Gottlob Frederick (F.) 1181, 1196, 1197, 1791
Gross, Gottlieb 1789
Gross, Hannah Rosetta 1791
Gross, Jacob 1196, 1789, 1791
Gross, Sarah 1196
Grosse, Henrietta 1197
Grother, ___ 1265
Grother, Anna 1774
Grother, Lutze 1398, 1774
Gruber, Rev. 1265
Gube, ___ 1265
Gube, Johann George (Johann Gorge, John Georg, John George, Joh. Geo., J. G.) 991, 993, 1002-1004, 1016-1017, 1065, 1142, 1159, 1163, 1244, 1262-1263, 1360-1423, 1693-1694, 1774, 1835, 1893, 1898, 1903
Guild, Ralph 467, 1835
Guitar, Mary 89
Guitar, William 928, 940, 1009
Guitau, John 200
Guitau, Mary 200
Gurhz, R. Jno. 1044
Gurney, Alpheus 1854
Guthrie, W. M. 1244
Guyot, Claude Emanuel 1723
Guyot, Claude Francois (Claude F.) 1515, 1723, 1800
Guyot, Fernal Francois (F. F.) 1515, 1723
Guyot, Francois Xavier (F. X.) 1515, 1723
Haas, Sebastian 704
Hache (Hacke), Theod. F. L. 1552-1554, 1670
Hacher, John 1249
Hachne, F. L. 1905

Hacker, August Frederick 1372
Hagan, Agnes 1645
Hagan, Ann (Anne) 741, 929, 1502, 1572
Hagan (Hagin), Aquila (Acquila, Aequila, Aquilah, Equilla) 4, 20, 42, 48, 52, 56, 94, 114, 187, 205, 220, 338, 340, 373, 423, 439, 466, 470, 662, 792, 1059, 1174, 1179
Hagan, Benedict 481
Hagan, Benjamin 21, 50
Hagan, Elizabeth 56
Hagan, George W. 1645
Hagan, Helen 1501
Hagan, Isidore (Isadore) 726, 737, 1487, 1639
Hagan, James 544, 662, 776, 1079
Hagan, Jane 1585
Hagan, John 423
Hagan, Joseph 48, 187, 309, 319, 323, 336, 395, 791, 929, 1224, 1911
Hagan, Levi (Levy) 65, 140, 447, 929, 1501, 1573, 1639
Hagan, Mary 56, 220, 373, 423, 662, 1174, 1179, 1645
Hagan, Mary Ann 65
Hagan, Michael 15, 323, 336, 395, 791, 929, 1585
Hagan, Nancy 1645
Hagan, Pius (Pious) 492, 1645
Hagan, Vincent 1573, 1645
Hagan, Wilfred 1645
Hagard, Austin (A.) 667, 724
Hagard, John 667
Hager, Aaron 1516
Hager, Archibald L. 1563
Hager, Cyntha 986
Hager (Hagar), John 986-987, 1091-1092, 1114, 1132, 1261
Hager, Lucey 1091
Hager, Sally 1563
Hager, William 1563
Haggard, ___ 804
Hahn, Christian 376, 1023
Hahn, Elizabeth 878, 1023, 1728
Hahn, Eve 376
Hahn, John 176, 878, 1023, 1728
Hale (Haile), Thomas 427, 507
Hall, Abner 1439
Hall, Abner H. 552, 555, 637, 703
Hall, Abner, heirs of 555
Hall, Elizabeth 552-555, 637, 703
Hall, George 555-556, 637, 703
Hall, Harriet M. A. (Harriett M. A.) 555, 637, 703
Hall, Phebe 555
Hall, Seth 552, 553-556, 637, 703, 1057, 1061, 1439
Hamilton, Austin F. 16
Hamilton, Clara (Clair, Claire, Clare) 16, 30, 214, 287, 291, 386, 1052, 1063, 1140, 1144, 1157
Hamilton, Clare, heirs of 600
Hamilton, Clarissa 691
Hamilton, Eulila F. 768-769

Hamilton, Eulile (Eulia, Eulale, Ulila) 287, 288, 386, 600
Hamilton, F. J. 220, 373, 482, 662, 1174, 1319, 1578
Hamilton, Fanny 287
Hamilton, Fenwick 168, 254, 287, 385, 478, 731
Hamilton, Fenwick J. 206-207, 209, 210, 288-289, 292, 386, 580, 600, 614, 616, 691, 768-769, 1159, 1542, 1784, 1786
Hamilton, George 16, 600
Hamilton (Hamelton), George A. (Geo. A., G. A.) 16, 188, 209, 254, 268, 291, 309, 385, 386-388, 392, 452, 580, 614, 616, 691, 768, 1002, 1004, 1024, 1140, 1157, 1784, 1785
Hamilton, George A. [Jr.] 287, 292, 769, 1063, 1144, 1319
Hamilton, George A. [Sr.] 287, 292, 1063, 1144, 1319
Hamilton, George A., heirs of 287-292, 767, 769, 1052
Hamilton, J. F. 1003
Hamilton, James T. 1610-1611
Hamilton, Josiah 16
Hamilton (Hamelton), Josiah F. 30, 140, 168, 188, 254, 287, 292, 385-386, 580, 593, 600, 614, 691, 769
Hamilton, Leo 16, 600
Hamilton, Leo F. 206, 287, 290-291, 580, 616, 767, 769
Hamilton, Margaret M. 1611
Hamilton, Matilda 16, 207, 287, 290, 387, 580, 616, 768, 769, 1063
Hamilton, Rebecca Ann 1786
Hamilton, Ulila (Eulalie), Regis 206-207
Hamilton, Walter 16, 600
Hamilton, Walter F. 287, 290-291, 387-388, 452, 580, 614, 769
Hamilton, Walter J. 616
Hamilton, Wile 16
Hammilton, J. 991
Hammonn, John G. 1790
Hancock (Handcock, Hondcock), William 73, 85, 636, 1170, 1595
Handcock (Hancock), Nelly 1170
Handcock, L. C. 1170
Hanela, James 1663
Haneld, James 771-772
Hanford, Hy. 1182
Hanly, Mary 64
Hanly, Thomas 38, 49, 64
Hanson, John M. 607
Harbeson, George C. 448
Hardin, Henry C. 1201
Hardon, David 1048
Harrington, Emily Ann 1561, 1584, 1884
Harrington, William 986-987
Harrington, William D. 1561, 1584, 1808, 1884
Harris, Charles 1806
Harris, Hannah 861
Harris, Hezekiah P. (H. P.) 235, 248, 338, 439, 964, 1596

Harris, John 127
Harris, Mary A. 1002
Harris, Mary A. K. 855
Harris, Milton 1547
Harris, Moses 173, 224
Harris, Moses (Mosses) S. 325, 855, 1002, 1142, 1360
Harris, Thomas 159
Harrison, Ann 315-316
Harrison, Aris 13-14
Harrison, Aristides 315-316
Harrison, Benjamin (Benj.) 13, 231, 298, 404, 731, 942
Harrison, Benjamin, heirs of 315-316
Harrison, Julius (Julias) 13, 315-316
Harrison, Mary 13
Harrison, Richard 473
Harrison, William 13-14, 315-316
Harrison, William Henry 821
Hart, John A. 1254
Hart, Robert D. 122
Harte (Hartz), Thomas 245, 1787
Harter, Edward 589, 1095, 1637, 1730, 1748
Harter, Mary 1637
Harter, Mary F. 1095
Hartle, John 444
Hase, Augustin Zimmerman (Zimerman) 463, 539
Hase, Elizabeth 539
Hase, Frederick C. (F. C., Frederk. C., Fredk. C.) 106-107, 160, 228, 233, 241-242, 247, 250-251, 254, 257-258, 262, 264, 269, 273, 275-276, 283-285, 293-294, 297, 301-302, 305, 307-311, 314, 323, 326, 333-332, 342-343, 345-347, 349-351, 353, 356-357, 362-363, 372-374, 377, 383-386-388, 390, 393, 395-396, 403, 405, 437, 445, 468, 474-475, 488, 519, 522-524, 530-532, 535-538, 539, 540, 544, 548, 567, 571, 579, 585, 587, 590, 592-593, 595, 599-601, 608, 610-613, 630, 632, 636, 639-642, 654, 660, 693, 696, 670, 671. 674, 683-685, 689, 703-704, 726, 731, 735-738, 741, 744-745, 751, 754-755, 773, 780, 782, 788, 811, 814, 832, 860, 862-863, 881, 883, 891, 893-895, 910, 914-915, 917, 924-927, 930-932, 936, 939, 943, 950-952, 964-965, 970-971, 974-977, 980, 989, 997-998, 1001, 1004, 1007-1008, 1012, 1018-1019, 1029, 1038-1039, 1046, 1053, 1058, 1071, 1073, 1090, 1104-1105, 1108-1109, 1127, 1131, 1137-1138, 1141-1143, 1147-1148, 1156, 1159, 1161, 1169, 1181, 1187, 1191, 1238, 1265-1266, 1274-1275, 1292, 1318-1319, 1323, 1325, 1336, 1341, 1348-1349, 1351, 1360-1362, 1365-1379, 1381-1399, 1400-1425, 1431-1432, 1434, 1441, 1443, 1447-1448, 1452, 1456-1457, 1460-1466, 1469-1470, 1478, 1492, 1515, 1542, 1602, 1835

Hase, J. A. C. 543
Hase, James 294
Hase, James A. C. 437, 465
Hase, John C. 986-987, 1168
Hase, John F. 224, 700, 985, 1007, 1054-1055, 1072, 1082, 1090, 1114, 1143, 1191, 1208-1209, 1217-1224, 1250, 1283, 1330, 1359, 1671, 1676, 1682, 1686, 1688, 1695, 1698, 1707, 1722, 1727, 1744, 1747, 1752-1753, 1758-1759, 1764, 1801, 1814, 1848, 1867, 1879, 1883, 1922
Hasher, John 1314, 1726, 1727
Hasher, Lavina 1727
Hatchings, James 1912
Hattan (Hatten), Caleb 370, 1570, 1909
Haven, Rensselaer N. 1020
Hawkins, Austin 1147
Hawkins, Jacob 1164
Hawkins, John 110, 268, 383, 604
Hawkins, John, Maj. 198
Hawkins, Rebeckah 110
Hawkins, Thomas 687
Hay, John 645
Hayden, Benedict 170, 183
Hayden, Bridget 1469, 1916
Hayden (Haydon), Charles 1208, 1264, 1341, 1492, 1751, 1809, 1828, 1882
Hayden, Clement 40, 174, 182-183, 658, 685, 1046, 1176
Hayden, Clement [Jr.] 170, 658, 659, 1175
Hayden, Clement [Sr.] 170
Hayden, Clemment [Sr.], heirs of 1175
Hayden, Elenor 170
Hayden, Elizabeth 1469
Hayden (Haydon, Heydon), James 109, 123, 170, 1469, 1809
Hayden, Johanna 1469
Hayden, John 170, 685, 1469
Hayden, Margaret 1469
Hayden (Heydon), Mary 109, 170(2)
Hayden, Mary Ann 1469
Hayden, Matilda 1751
Hayden, Sarah 170
Hayden, Susan 40
Hayden, Susanna (Susanah, Susannah) 170, 182-183, 1175
Hayden, Thomas 170, 201-203, 234, 244-245, 258, 1038, 1469
Hayden, Thomas, heirs of 1469
Hayden (Haydon), William 504, 1229, 1469
Hayden, William R. 1257
Haydon, Christeen 1809
Hayes, Wm. J. 632
Haynes, John D. 1209, 1359
Hays, John (Jno.) 309, 414
Hayward (Haywood), Elijah 443, 510, 512-513, 1110, 1116-1120, 1278, 1326
Heakins, S. M. 145
Hebert, Valmont 1034
Heilmann, Christian August 1181
Heinig, Frederick 1417

Heinig, Johann Gottfried (Gottfried) 1181, 1423
Heinigan, John Gottfied 1181
Helbig, Gottlieb 1181
Hellard, David 565-566
Hellard, Mary 566
Hellard, Thomas 1569
Helling, Gottlieb 1181
Hemmann, Johann (John) Gottfried (Gotfrey, G.) 1094, 1100, 1197, 1296, 1789, 1919
Hemmon, Rosina Maria 1789
Hemmonn, John Gottlieb 1791
Hempstead, Albert G. 226
Hempstead, Charles 1839
Hempstead, Charles S. 226, 231
Hempstead, Christopher 226
Hempstead, Clarissa 226
Hempstead, Cornelia 226
Hempstead, E., heirs of 231
Hempstead, Edward 226
Hempstead, Edward L. 226
Hempstead, John 226
Hempstead, Joseph 226(2)
Hempstead, Mary 226
Hempstead, Samuel 226
Hempstead, Stephen 226(2)
Hempstead, Thomas 226(2)
Hempstead, William 226
Hemsted, ___ 667
Henderson, Curus 1806
Henderson, Cyrus 1775
Henderson, George 317, 558, 743
Henderson, James 73, 85, 1170
Henderson, John M. 568
Henry, John F. 25, 37, 39, 51, 69, 115, 138, 343, 437, 525
Henthston, Robert 38
Herald, Jas. 1837
Herman, Duncan N. 1477
Herrick, Ezekiel B. 71
Hertick & Landry (Herlich & Landry) 1721, 1882
Hertick, Joseph 351, 1729
Hervey, Ann 543
Heyenigen, Johanna Sophie 1181
Heyenigin, Johanna 1181
Heyle, Rev. 1181
Heylen, Isaiah B. 1857
Hickey, John J. 1659, 1721, 1801, 1825, 1882
Hickey, Sarah S. 1659
Hickman, ___ 370, 476, 564
Hickman, T. 343
Hickman, Theophilus 240, 568, 1594
Hickman, William 67, 128, 562-563, 573, 609, 667, 804-805, 847, 907, 934, 1022, 1328, 1596, 1735, 1865
Hill, Elizabeth 612, 1115
Hill, Isaac 313, 326, 350, 606, 612, 613, 788, 1104, 1115, 1125, 1504(2), 1505, 1644
Hill, Isaac, heirs of 1504
Hill, Louisa Ann 1504

Hill, Thomas W. 1504
Hilpert (Helbert), George 1773
Hinch, C. S. 371
Hinch, S. 393
Hinch, Samuel Sr. 268, 383, 408, 429
Hines, Christopher 462-463, 539
Hines, Joseph 175
Hines, Teresa (Treasa) 463, 539
Hinkle, Alexander 1264
Hinkle, Catherine (Catharine) 414, 453
Hinkle, Isaac 414, 453
Hinkle, Robert 453, 501
Hinklemann, Johann Christian 1383, 1387
Hinkson, ___ 768
Hinkson, Jane (Ginney) 13, 298
Hinkson (Hinkston), William 13, 185, 298, 315, 402
Hinkston, ___ 206
Hinkston, Mary 1101
Hinkston (Hinckston), Robert (Robt.) 64, 74, 196, 531, 580, 614, 616, 991, 1101, 1263, 1363, 1382-1387, 1389-1391
Hinton, John 1593
Hirst, Cynthia 1215
Hirst, John 1215
Hoar (Hoare), George 108, 130, 219
Hobbs, Samuel 351
Hobbs, William 351
Hochne, Johann Carl August (Aug.) 1381, 1893
Hochne, Johann Gottleib 1381
Hoffman, Anne 1484
Hoffman, Johanne Rosine 1409
Hoffman (Hofman, Hoofman), John 496, 780, 1015, 1484, 1630, 1853
Hogard (Hoggard), Austin (A.) 573, 603, 847, 907, 1022, 1462, 1596
Hogard, Elizabeth 847
Hogard, John 847
Hogard, Mary 907
Hogard, Wm. 847
Hohne, Johann Gottlieb 1694, 1899, 1903
Holden, Edward 1720
Holden, Edward M. 890-891, 1058, 1073, 1082, 1161, 1224, 1341, 1349, 1547, 1575, 1706, 1788, 1828
Holden, John 1058, 1134
Holden, Margaret 1889
Holly, David 68, 483, 1039
Holly, John 1039
Holmes, Joseph B. 1323
Holschen, Johann 1399
Holster, Felix 1321
Holster, Mary 1180, 1321
Holster, Peter 1180
Holster (Holzer), Peter Sr. 183, 516
Holston, Joseph 1212
Holston, Rosana 1212
Hooks, Wm. 135
Hooss, George 1294, 1625-1626
Hoover, Andrew 1904, 1921
Hore, George 124, 157, 412
Horine, Thomas 1037
Horine, Thomas M. 320, 422, 608

Hornbeck, Cornelius (Neal, Noel) 91, 112, 317, 395, 461, 1039, 1147
Horrel, Benj. 222
Horrel, John 222
Horrell, Elizabeth 1648
Horrell (Horrel), Henry 1199, 1648
Hortis, Joseph Jr. 226
Hose, George 1883
Hotop, Paul 444
Hough, Daniel 812
Houston, William 1164
Howard, James E. 1078
Howard, Wm. C. 1078
Howell, Rebecca 208
Hozard, Austin 519
Huddleston, Archibald 85, 606, 612, 1466
Hudson, George W. 919
Huepe, ___ 1265
Hueschel, Sophia 1255
Huff, Geo. 1523
Huffman, Polly 1229
Huffman, Solomon 1229
Hughes, James 484, 946
Hughes, John 827
Hughey, Elenor 1576
Hughey, John 718, 1052, 1091, 1133-1134, 1333, 1336, 1576
Hughey, John A. 690
Hughey, Milus 690
Hughey, Robert 1816
Hungerford, Wm. J. 1295
Hunsucker, George 1657
Hunt, Anthony 1284
Hunt (Hund), Eleanor (Elanor, Elenor) 523-524, 689, 711, 754, 1202, 1205, 1709
Hunt, John P. 1690
Hurst, John 830
Huston, ___ 1828
Huston, John 131
Hutchings (Hutchins), Barbary 378, 1130, 1330
Hutchings, Charlette 1478
Hutchings, Ignatius 1330, 1478
Hutchings (Hutchins), James 222, 309, 378, 1129-1130
Hutchings, John 1648
Hyatt, Miranda 351
Ilgin, George 1414
Ingram, Benjamin Franklin 1806
Ingram, Charles 530, 619, 629, 1806
Ingram, Demaris 1806
Ingram, George Washington 1806
Ingram, John Nelum 1806
Ingram, Mary 629
Ingram, Polly 1806
Ingram, Wiley 1806
Intres, Elizabeth 1545
Intres, Martin 1545, 1619
Irving, Lewis G. 1295, 1647, 1860, 1862
Jackson, A. 1293
Jackson, A. Jr. 1040
Jackson, Albert 1867

Jackson, Andrew 443, 510, 512-513, 515, 848, 1040, 1110, 1116-1120, 1278, 1293, 1326, 1450, 1490
Jackson, George 981
Jackson, George E. 262, 982
Jackson, James 1224
Jaeger, Charles 1484
Jaeger, Gottfried 1144
Jahn, Gottfried 1410, 1419
James, ___ 530
James, Elizabeth 154, 412, 413
James, Joseph 63, 166, 231, 290-291, 298, 305, 315, 404, 429, 465, 744, 768, 1101, 1806
James, Joseph Jr. 124-125, 130, 153-154, 157, 340, 412, 413, 428, 1130-1131, 1627
James, Joseph Sr. 531, 1448
James, Mary Elizabeth 1131, 1627
James, William 422, 691, 1143
Janis, Francis 1871
Janis, Odile 1871
Jarrott, Julie 278
Jarrott, Nicholas 278
Javaux, ___ 1725
Javaux, Catharine 1601
Javaux, Victor 1601
Jenkins, Am. 607
Jenkins, Elizabeth 1775
Jenkins, Joseph 1775
Jenkins, Lucy E. 1777
Jenkins, Mary 1776
Jenkins, Robert 1775
Jenkins, Robert M. 1777
Jenkins, Thomas 1776
Johnson, Burwell 1496, 1537
Johnson, Clotilda 881
Johnson, Henry 195, 881
Johnson, Hezekiah 32
Johnson, Isaac (Isac) 293, 938
Johnson, James C. 461
Johnson, Jane 881
Johnson, John 500, 881, 1194, 1312, 1660
Johnson, John G. 1685
Johnson, John J. 1187, 1586, 1609, 1668, 1685
Johnson, Joseph 881
Johnson, Lott 336
Johnson, Lucinda 881
Johnson, Margaret 718
Johnson, Mary 881
Johnson, Matilda 336
Johnson, Noble 718
Johnson, Priscilla (Precilla, Pricilla) 500, 881, 938
Johnson, Saley 881
Johnson, William (Wm.) 615, 623, 664, 1203
Johnston, Lot 319
Johnston, Thomas E. 1148
Jones, Alphonso C. 1032

Jones, Francis L. 559, 1032, 1033, 1034, 1183, 1198, 1220, 1358, 1529, 1561, 1584, 1884
Jones, Francis Leak 819, 954
Jones, Henry 188
Jones, Jno. Rice 64
Jones, John 13
Jones, John A. 957-958, 960-961, 963
Jones, John Rice 14, 46
Jones, Matt 1037
Jones, Nelson 819, 832
Jones, Nelson P. 1032, 1033, 1034, 1220
Jourdain, Frances 215
Joyce, W. 1034
Joyce (Joice), William (Wm.) 1032, 1198
Juden, Abbey (Abby) 558, 562-563, 573, 664, 743, 1182
Juden, G. W. 467
Juden, J. 467
Juden, John 1183
Juden, John Jr. 129, 136, 558, 562-563, 573, 664, 667, 742-743, 1182
Kaempfe, Juliana Christina(Juliann Christiane) 1694, 1895, 1898, 1900
Kaempfe, Samuel Gottfried 1893, 1895-1896, 1898-1900, 1902-1903
Kaempfe, Samuel Gottleib 1366, 1368, 1694
Kastner, Emanuel 1484
Keener, Francis 1170
Keener, James 1341
Keener, James F. 1170
Keesackers, ___ 226
Keizer, Lawrence 1257
Keller, George, heirs of 1015
Keller, George, heirs of 780, 1015
Kelly, ___ 222
Kelly, Ann 621
Kelly, James S. 310
Kelly, James Stidman 621
Kelly, Terrice (Tereice) 1622
Kelly, Timothy 588, 608
Kenaday, William P. 344
Kennedy, Sarah 89, 200
Kennedy (Kenedy), Thomas 436, 545
Kenner, Francis 73, 85
Kenney, Jno. B. 1634
Kennison (see Kinnison)
Kenny, Thomas 1732
Kent, F. A. 1873
Kent, Frederick A. 1346-1347
Kester, Isaac 85
Ketchum, Edward A. 1575
Keyle (Keyl), Ernst Gerard Wilhelm 1422, 1778
Keyte, Ann 301, 333, 509
Keyte, James 324, 333
Keyte, William 230, 232
Keyte, William A. (Wm. A.) 301, 324, 333, 433, 472, 532, 601, 611, 937
Keyte, William Augustus 509
Keyte, William H. 380, 601
Keyton, ___ 1595
Keyton, William 1170

Killian, Daniel 12, 119, 293, 423, 541
Killian, George 237-238, 260, 295, 342, 420, 445, 547, 653, 715, 1721
Killian, Matilda 342, 420, 445
Kimmel & Taylor 473, 624
Kimmel (Kimmell), Singleton H. 619, 624, 629, 646, 648, 780, 856, 1015, 1061, 1244, 1439, 1634, 1854
Kimmel, Caroline 405
Kimmel, Julia 405
Kimmel, Manning 405
Kimmel, S. H. 628, 635, 649-650
Kimmel, Sarah 856
Kimmel, Sarah G. 646, 1634
King, Geo. 18-19
Kingston, Robt. 231
Kinnerson, ___ 627
Kinnison, Abner 138, 351, 1212
Kinnison, Absolom(Absolem, Absolum) 57, 137-138, 181, 1690
Kinnison, Absolem, heirs of 1724
Kinnison, Absolum [Jr.] 344
Kinnison, Absolom Sr. 344, 1859
Kinnison, Alexander 1146, 1184
Kinnison, Alexander S. 1145, 1355
Kinnison, Elizabeth 1690
Kinnison, Hiram 1690
Kinnison (Kinneson), Joel 138, 227, 248, 370, 564, 696, 735, 799, 1859
Kinnison, John 57, 390, 969, 1039, 1145-1146, 1184, 1195, 1238, 1355(2), 1356, 1652, 1674, 1680, 1690, 1830
Kinnison, Louisa 138
Kennison, Mary 696, 735
Kinnison, Nicy (Nicey) Jane 1145, 1355-1356
Kinnison, Presley (Presly) 137, 344, 1212
Kinnison, Sinia (Sina) 390, 969, 1146, 1184, 1238, 1652, 1680, 1690, 1873
Kirkpatrick, Charlott T. 895
Kirkpatrick, William 875
Kirkpatrick, William C. 895, 1134
Klein, Adam 1753
Kleugle, George Sr. 1361-1362, 1402-1403
Kline, Adam 943
Kline, Samuel 1617
Kline, William 1761
Kline, William L. 1588
Klob (Klobe, Klop), Adam 877, 1322, 1625
Kluegle, George Jr. 1421
Klugel, George 1778, 1779
Klugel, Gottlieb (Gottleeb) 1778
Klugle, George Sr. 1392
Knott (Knot, Knotts), Clement 26, 34, 121, 150, 155, 357-358, 469, 675-676, 834, 850, 901, 1204, 1459, 1483, 1583, 1587, 1589, 1620, 1669, 1822, 1878
Knott, Elizabeth 469, 675, 850, 1459, 1822
Knott, Henry 1669
Knott, Hilarion 675
Knott, Hillary 551

Koeppel, Frederick Henning 1265
Kopple, Johann Frederick 1415
Kranner, Gottlog 1265
Kuhn, Johann Adam 1388
Kunce, Jacob 1738, 1912
Kunhert, Johann Christian 1386
Kunze (Kunz), Henry 995-996, 1227, 1243
L'Andreville, Andre 226
L'Esperance, ___ 226
L'homme, Constant 1539
L'homme, Victor 1539
Labeaume, Louis T. 1500
Lacey, Emely M. 189
Lacey, William P. (Wm. P.) 188-189
Lacey, Wm. 216
Lacroix, Joseph 226
Lacy, ___ 287
Ladd, C. J. 1061
Laffeirre, M. P. 816
Lalande, Alexis 226
Lamb, James L. 607, 701
Lamb, Susan H. 701
Lameth, Jn. Bp. 195
Land, John C. 1299
Landgraf, Christian Frederick 1181
Landry, Clemence 1795, 1817
Lane & Relfe 222, 231
Lane, Harvey 320, 421
Lane, Joseph 1802
Langlois, L. 33
LaPare, Martin 161
Lappin, James 820, 822, 1324
Laughlin, Garland 672-673, 830, 1215
Laughlin, Jane 830
Laveille, Joseph 885
Laville (Lavielle), James B. 1489, 1579, 1818, 1877
Laville, Mary B. 1877
Lavilie, William S. 1892
Laville, William T. 1532, 1574
Law, Polly 1806
Lawless, Luke Edward (L. E.) 38, 49, 74, 196, 991-993
Lawless, Virginia 196, 231, 531, 991, 994
Layton, ___ 686, 908
Layton, Amatus 1103, 1686, 1894
Layton, Andrew 1046
Layton, Ann Elizabeth 936
Layton, Anselm 1282
Layton, Augustine (Augustin) 539, 1075, 1287, 1425, 1718, 1864
Layton, Augustine A. 1612
Layton, Austin 834, 1348
Layton, Bede 936
Layton, Bernard (Barnard) 15, 21, 61, 124-125, 130, 141, 157, 302, 412, 425, 465, 481, 491, 531, 565, 642, 739, 751, 908, 989, 1154-1155, 1205, 1448, 1460, 1468, 1582, 1650, 1686, 1697, 1707, 1801, 1850
Layton, Cecilia 1585
Layton, Cecily 936
Layton, Christeen 1046

Layton, Christina 1103, 1538
Layton, Clotildia 1247
Layton, Elizabeth 27, 213, 215, 217, 238, 266, 269, 294, 380, 1470, 1486, 1585(3), 1684
Layton, Feliciann 1513
Layton, Felix 1046, 1513, 1684, 1807
Layton, Henry J. 1874-1875
Layton, Hillary (Hilary, Hillarey) 936, 1247-1248, 1485-1486, 1551
Layton, Hyacinthus A. 1549, 1580
Layton, Ignatius 27, 65, 130, 139, 162, 198, 213, 215, 217, 238, 266, 269, 294, 380, 420, 463, 531, 591, 601, 653, 763, 936, 988, 1025, 1250, 1287, 1348, 1448, 1468
Layton, Ignatius Jr. 1585
Layton, Ignatius Sr. 542, 546, 598, 1228, 1585, 1686
Layton, Ignatius, heirs of 936, 1348
Layton, James 296, 319, 361, 381, 680, 739, 834, 1046, 1058, 1600
Layton, John 7-9, 11, 17, 21, 26-27, 31, 42, 50, 62, 54, 111, 130, 135, 139-141, 146-147, 152, 161, 169, 173, 175, 182-184, 190-191, 199(2), 205, 208, 212-216, 217(2), 219-221, 223-224, 230, 234, 237-239, 243, 245-247, 256, 266, 271(2), 274-275, 295-296, 300, 304, 313, 318-319, 336, 338, 340, 355, 358-360, 364, 373, 375-376, 380-381, 392, 417, 423, 428, 431, 434-435, 438, 440, 466, 470, 490, 496, 526, 528, 534, 551, 572(2), 574-575, 583, 599, 659, 661-662, 680, 688, 696, 699, 713, 735, 739, 763, 782, 794, 800, 833-834, 837-838, 868, 878, 937, 988, 999, 1038-1039, 1046, 1075, 1129-1130, 1165, 1174, 1194, 1228, 1235, 1241, 1282, 1287, 1310, 1357, 1468, 1482, 1498, 1515, 1706, 1714, 1719, 1720, 1729, 1852
Layton, John [Jr.] 15, 1468
Layton, John [Sr.] 15
Layton, John Babtist (John B.) Jr. 675, 1822
Layton, John Baptist 110, 198, 389, 894, 936, 1470
Layton, John Baptist Sr. 1585, 1612
Layton, John Jr. 450, 546, 1702, 1894
Layton, John R. 330, 1590, 1684, 1807
Layton, John Sr. 284, 294, 361, 379, 381, 389, 450, 463, 469, 491-492, 526, 539, 546-547, 577, 591, 598, 605, 651-653, 929, 938, 991, 1023, 1046, 1056, 1084, 1088, 1103, 1126, 1141, 1178, 1213, 1256, 1330, 1538, 1585(2), 1684, 1686, 1702, 1716, 1717, 1718, 1731, 1744, 1801, 1807, 1823, 1874-1875, 1894, 1917
Layton, John Sr., heirs of 266
Layton, Joseph 110, 175, 198, 407, 598, 936
Layton, Joseph J. 1320
Layton, Joseph W. 1874-1876

Layton, Joseph, heirs of 266, 294, 1716
Layton, Leo 1046, 1456, 1769, 1849
Layton, Lewis (Louis) 1228, 1425, 1801, 1917
Layton, Lewis W. 1580
Layton, Lucey 175
Layton, Malania 1874-1875
Layton, Marcell 1046
Layton, Marcella 1213
Layton, Maria 1023, 1213, 1241, 1282, 1684, 1686
Layton, Martin 1046, 1273, 1288, 1337, 1461, 1487, 1700, 1726, 1807, 1820, 1885
Layton, Mary 61, 124-125, 130, 157, 175, 295, 330, 412, 491, 565, 739, 1046(2), 1178, 1348, 1468, 1585
Layton, Mary Austin 936
Layton, Mary Elenor 175
Layton, Mary Magdaline (Magdalen) 1456, 1849
Layton, Matilda 699, 936
Layton, Monica 438, 680, 937, 1165, 1686, 1801
Layton, Nereus (Nerius) 1046, 1273, 1288, 1337, 1487, 1513, 1590, 1684, 1700, 1726, 1807
Layton, Rosanna (Rosana) 936, 1250
Layton, Sarah 1046, 1603
Layton, Severious 936
Layton, Susanna 110, 1282, 1585
Layton, Sylvarius 1766
Layton, Thomas 12, 1046
Layton, Treasia (Tresa) 919, 1348
Layton, Vincent 1247
Layton, Vincent de Andre 936
Layton, Walter 15, 175, 1549
Layton, Wilfred (Wilford) 15, 98, 110, 364, 375, 407, 657, 1585, 1282
Layton, Zachariah (Zechariah) 15, 109, 179, 182, 295, 330, 420, 511, 599, 605, 659, 1046, 1178, 1273, 1288, 1337, 1487, 1513, 1585, 1684, 1700, 1726, 1744, 1807
Layton, Zachariah, heirs of 1046
Layton, Zachary 417
Layton, Zeno 1103
Leal, James White 1834, 1917
Leatherberry, William 22
Ledoux, Valery 969, 1652
Ledue, Mary Philip (M. Philip, M. P.) 196, 851-852, 1013
Lee, Charles 839, 1256
Lee, Elizabeth 720
Lee, Hiram 720
Lee, Richard B. 1631-1632
Legate, Samuel 672
Leggett, Henry L. 1520
Leibig, Carl Gottleib 1895, 1900-1902, 1903
Leibig, Sophia 1895, 1902
Leible, Johannes 1325
Lemley, G. A. 1253
Lesage, J. B. 226

Lesieur, Francis 226
Lewis, Little Berry 23
Lewis, Saml. W. 204
Lightner, Sam. 145
Lindsley, Joseph C. 962
Linn, Lewis F. 69, 115-116
Linn, William 68
Lirique, August 1034
Little, Alexander 1279-1280
Little, Fanny 1280
Little, Henry 485, 603, 935, 1803, 1804
Little, Mary 1861
Little, Polly 1316
Little, Ransom 603
Little, Ransom A. 724, 935, 1315-1316, 1855, 1861, 1869
Littlejohn, J. V. 1871
Lively, Wm. 45
Livinston, Richard M. 1295
Lober, Christian 1408
Lockard, James 68
Lockard, Mary 68
Lockard, William 483
Lockart, Elizabeth 844, 846
Lockhard, Mary 483
Lockhart, widow 268, 465, 1838, 1841
Loeber, Gotthilf 1265
Loeber, Henry 1265
Loeber, Martha 1265
Loeber, Rev. 1265
Loesch, John David 1181
Logan, Elizabeth 647, 700
Logan, James 159, 465, 493-494, 498, 531
Logan, John 36, 45-46, 54, 72, 81, 92, 117-118, 120, 173, 192-193, 276, 351, 372, 383-385, 405, 412, 460, 483-484, 499, 509, 522, 525, 530, 567, 571, 593, 620, 642, 647, 665, 696, 700, 735, 771, 777, 785, 799, 814, 832, 835, 851-852, 885, 925, 927, 984, 1007, 1018, 1073, 1106, 1109, 1127, 1134, 1137, 1148, 1160-1161, 1167, 1185, 1211, 1221, 1354, 1432, 1444, 1469, 1476, 1499, 1517, 1532, 1566, 1574, 1598, 1620, 1665, 1699, 1707, 1721, 1729, 1744, 1746, 1747, 1832, 1850, 1854, 1859, 1878, 1882, 1890
Logan, John Jr. 83, 88
Logan, John Sr. 81, 83, 92, 118, 120, 343, 369, 459, 619, 629
Logan, Maria (Marier) 72, 81, 83, 118
Long, ___ 1167
Long, ___ 169
Long, David 358
Long, Fanny 1654
Long, Margaret 845, 1653
Long, Newton 427, 845, 1653-1654
Long, Thomas 397, 399, 427, 845, 1067, 1653, 1655
Loper, Maria 632
Lorenz, Gottfred 1390
Lott, Jno. W. 1164
Lott, Peter 812

Lowrie, M. B. 1020
Luckey (Lucky), David 915, 1887
Lukefahr, Catharine 1497, 1515, 1723
Lukefahr, Henry 1564
Luriel, ___ 226
Lynn, Thomas 1298
Mabry, Benjamin 408
Mabry, Benjamin S. 429
Mabry, Delilah 408, 429
Mackey, William 1873
Maddin (Madden), Charles 418, 421-422, 457, 561, 588, 608, 716, 730, 828
Maddin, Caroline 422
Maddin (Madden), Israel 270, 421-422
Maddin, James 418
Maddin, Louisana 270
Maddin (Madden), Malachi 418, 422, 716
Maddin (Madden), Philip 421, 422, 716
Maddin (Madden), Thomas 32, 222, 320, 343, 395, 418, 588, 716, 1846
Maddin, Thomas Sr. 422, 457
Maddin, Timothy 608
Maddock Richard Sr. 1728
Maddock, Cisaly 1728
Maddock, Elizabeth 1025, 1213
Maddock, Richard 878, 988, 1595
Maddock, Richard Jr. 1172, 1728
Maddock, Richard Sr. 445, 1025, 1172, 1213, 1464, 1570
Maddox, Elizabeth 651
Maddox, Richard 653
Maddox, Richard Sr. 651
Maginnis, Edward 460
Maillard, John Jr. 1033
Maillard, John Sr. 1033
Maize, Gor. 193
Manning James Sr. 516
Manning Pius 1482
Manning, Alexius (Alexues) 141, 287, 630, 1745
Manning, Anastasia 224
Manning, Ann 398, 877, 1247, 1603, 1625, 1664
Manning, Anna 1004
Manning, Caroline 405
Manning, Clare 630
Manning, Clotildia 1247
Manning, Cornelius 287, 630, 1199, 1664, 1732
Manning, Electius 1732
Manning, Elenor (Elanor) 405, 768
Manning, Elizabeth 253, 405, 516, 1158
Manning, George 405
Manning, Hilarion 342, 547, 548
Manning, Hoyle 1247
Manning, J. 720
Manning, James (Jas.) 182-183, 224, 231, 253, 354, 672, 830, 1002, 1004, 1158-1159
Manning, James C. 405, 691, 727, 1581
Manning, John 580, 614, 616, 630, 806, 868, 877, 1065, 1142, 1322, 1357, 1360, 1625
Manning, John [Jr.] 1004

Manning, John [Sr.] 1004
Manning, John Jr., heirs of 224
Manning, John Sr. 224
Manning, Joseph 15, 60, 63, 139, 199, 213, 215, 304, 330, 381, 417, 428, 599, 652, 833, 1260, 1310, 1357, 1585, 1621, 1649, 1666, 1744
Manning, Joseph Jr. 1247
Manning, Joseph Sr. 303, 868
Manning, Margaret 392, 630
Manning, Margaret M. 405
Manning, Mark 16, 63, 141, 209, 392, 405, 630, 767
Manning, Mark L. 776, 1137, 1482, 1683
Manning, Martha M. J. 628
Manning, Martha M. S. 649
Manning, Mary 63, 139, 199, 304, 381, 428, 547, 776, 833, 1310, 1603, 1664
Manning, Matilda 630
Manning, Nancy (Nancey) 224, 406, 1001, 1294, 1304, 1322
Manning, Pius (Pious) 868, 1357, 1666
Manning, Robert (Robt.) 405, 452, 671, 851, 977, 1057, 1141, 1503, 1534, 1555, 1611
Manning, Robert S. 163, 224, 398, 406, 746, 747, 926, 950, 1001-1002, 1004, 1142, 1294, 1304-1305, 1360, 1442-1443, 1530, 1581, 1609, 1668, 1729, 1770
Manning, Sarah 1046, 1158
Manning, widow 206
Manning, Wilford 529, 684, 1342
Manning, William 373, 391-392, 398, 405-406, 449-450, 527, 621, 628, 635, 649, 650, 851, 1046, 1061, 1156, 1158, 1439, 1469, 1581, 1611, 1744
Manning, William, heirs of 405
Mansico, Samuel 57
Mansker, Nancy 137
Mansker, Samuel 137, 495
Marbach, Francis Adolph (A.) 1378, 1779
Marbach, Louisa (Louise) 1378, 1779
Marie, Joseph 226
Marksworth, Heinrich Gottfred Christian 1412
Marshall, Benjamin 1857
Marshall, John J. 1299
Marshall, Wm. B. 1533
Martin, Adam Moore (M.) 718, 820, 1324
Martin, Andrew 558
Martin, Catharine 1003
Martin, Elizabeth 820
Martin, George 366
Martin, George Washington (W.) 619, 629, 1003, 1016
Martin, James B. (Jas. B.) 1525, 1749
Martin, John 1311, 1918
Martin, John R. 1815
Martin, John Sr. 1335, 1910
Martin, Moses 998
Martin, Sarah 1525
Martin, Susanna 1311
Martin, William H. 1223

Massey, Joseph A. 1544, 1588
Massey, Joseph H. 923, 1660
Massey, Mos. A. 89
Massey, Sarah (Sally) 1583
Mathery, V. R. 701
Mathews, Samuel 1895, 1896, 1901, 1902
Matthews, G. W. 145
Mattingley (Mattingly), James 165, 170, 175, 224, 287-289, 467, 502, 514, 658, 678-679, 1028, 1030, 1176
Mattingley (Mattingly), James B. 738, 1342, 1676
Mattingley (Mattingly), Joseph B. 536, 746-747, 897, 950, 1076
Mattingley, Leo 1028, 1030
Mattingley (Mattingly), Maria 536, 713, 746-747, 897, 950, 1076
Mattingley, Matilda 746-747
Mattingley (Mattingly), William 224, 228, 283, 703, 924, 977
Mattingly, Elizabeth 224
Mattingly, Joseph 713
Mattingly, Lewis 1750
Mattingly, Luke 658, 1767
Mattingly, Mary 738, 1676
Mattingly, Nancy 224
Mattingly, Walter F. 1922
Mauche, Claude Joseph 1478
Maxey, E. H. 1045
Maxwell, James 116
May, Cessilia 1469
May, Elizabeth 1469
May, Hellen 1469
May, James B. 84, 221, 258, 264, 274, 297, 377, 432, 753, 1069-1070, 1171, 1307, 1679
May, John 70, 99, 156, 432, 1469 (2)
May, Maria 274, 297, 753
May, Martha Ann 1469
Mayes, Danl. 329
Mays, ___ 820, 822
McArthur, Henry L. 1841
McArthur, John 68, 226
McArthur, John M. 68
McArthur, Lewis L. 68
McArthur, Mary 882
McArthur, Mary Ann 68
McArthur, Theodosia M. 68
McArthur, William P. (Wm. P.) 68, 1841
McAtee, Ann 169
McAtee (McAttee), Henry 169, 286, 357, 834, 886-887, 1011, 1168, 1268-1269, 1275, 1280, 1285, 1340, 1442, 1530, 1616, 1847
McAtee, Henry Jr. 358-360, 1589
McAtee, Henry Sr. 800
McAtee, Maria (Mariah) 886, 1168, 1275, 1285, 1589, 1616
McAtee, Mary 887, 1530, 1646
McAtee, Patrick 1847
McAtee, T. H. 1719
McAtee, Thomas 867, 886-887, 966, 1011, 1014, 1040-1043, 1275, 1285, 1442-1443, 1530, 1646, 1770, 1864

McAtte, Mary Magdalen 1442
McBride, ___ 1577
McBride, Patrick 1166
McBride, Robert 903
McCall, Samuel 77
McCalop, James 1034, 1198
McCasland (McCausland), ___ 128, 573, 907, 1022, 1328, 1735
McCasland (McCaslin), Andrew 519, 1596, 1866
McCasland, Andrew M. 67
McCasland, Elizabeth 1596
McCasland, William 67, 128, 1866
McCaslin, H. D. 933
McCaslin, Henry 519
McCaslin, James 519
McCauley, Benedict 123, 199
McCauley, Bennett (Bennet) 927, 1208, 1310, 1664, 1822
McCauley, Charlotte 1310
McCauley, Elizabeth 927
McCauley, James 123, 199, 920, 968, 1168, 1204, 1208, 1310, 1822, 1878
McCauley, John 1822
McCauley, Rosanna (Rosana) 920, 968, 1204, 1310
McCauley, Theresa 1822
McCauley, William (Wm.) 123, 357, 381, 465, 469, 1204, 1208, 1309, 1840, 1878
McCauley, William [Jr.] 1822
McCauley, William Sr. 1822
McClanahan, Jms. 268
McClanahan (McClannahan), John (Jno.) 397, 696, 735, 1039, 1845
McClanahan, Lydia 696, 735
McCombs, Napoleon B. 1872
McCombs, Sally 1872
McCombs, William 1457, 1861
McCombs, William J. 1431, 1812-1813, 1872
McConniho, ___ 623
McConnohoe (McConahoe, McConahue, McConehau, McConnahue, McConnoahue, McConnoehie, McConoho, McConohoe, McConohue), Alexander (Alexr.) 54, 69, 91, 112, 255, 317, 329, 390, 424, 437, 506, 525, 1145-1146, 1184, 1299, 1355, 1674, 1680, 1830
McConnohue, Catharine 255
McConohue, A. 343
McCowley, James 850
McCowley, William 850
McCreary, Phocian R. 1857
McCuslian(?), James S. 1222
McDaniel, Levi C. 1838
McDaniel, Samuel 844, 846
McDaniel, Samuel C. 275, 372
McGennis (McGinis), ___ 217, 271
McGillycuddy, James 1161
McGinnes (McGennis, McGines, McGinnis), Edward 257, 294, 328, 331, 337, 349, 365-366, 534, 572, 1056, 1497

McGinnes (McGennis, McGinnis), Margaret (Margret) 328, 331, 366, 1056
McGinnis (Magenis), Arthur 64
McGinnis, Michael 1558, 1577
McGready, Israel (Isrial) 298, 315-316, 461, 716, 1101
McGuire, Susan 263, 558, 664, 743, 1182
McGuire, Thomas (Thos.) 1-3, 44
McGuire, William (Wm.) 55, 136, 263, 458, 558, 664, 742-743, 1182, 1183, 1201
McKay (McCoy), Michael 1458
McKee, Rhoda 1125
McKee, Thomas S. 1125
McKenelly, Hugh F. 906
McKinstry, Charles 1189-1190, 1295, 1500, 1647
McKinstry (McKinstrey), George 1151, 1295, 1355, 1647, 1788
McKinstry, George Jr. 1146, 1184, 1189-1190, 1195, 1500, 1674, 1680, 1830
McKlemarry, Lewis 255
McKnew, George 538
McKnight, ___ 570
McKnight, Samuel B. 1806
McLain (see also McLane)
McLain, ___ 1203, 1709
McLain, Alby 110
McLain, Alfred 780
McLain (McLane), Alfred A. 706, 825-826, 1015
McLain, Allen 1026
McLain, Alley 657, 1154
McLain (McClane, McLane), Edward 425, 537, 843, 974-976, 989, 1010, 1026, 1155
McLain (McLane), Elenor (Ellen, Ellin) 843, 974-976, 1010, 1155
McLain, Lemanow 1026
McLain, Samuel F. 825
McLain, Sarah 825-826
McLain (McClane, McLane), Walter 425, 537, 989
McLain (McClain, McLane), William 15, 98, 125, 130, 141, 175, 198, 425, 465, 537, 657, 661, 681, 1154, 1205, 1650, 1707, 1842, 1845
McLain (McLaine), William H. 825-826, 1194
McLane (see also McLain)
McLane, Alley (Ally) Louisa 425, 681
McLane, J. R. 648-649, 717, 836
McLane, James 68, 320, 421-422, 474-475, 483, 716
McLane, John 740, 903
McLane, John Anson (A.) 229, 415, 499
McLane, Lucey (Alley) 175
McLaughlin, John Roff (R.) 439, 1236, 1610, 1690, 1724
McLaughlin, M. 693
McLean, James 270, 939
McLease, James 270
McMahann, Robert 1458
McNair, Alexander 1-11, 25, 44

McNeely, Ezekiel 402
McNeil, Henry 1655
McNew, George 613, 788, 1104, 1115, 1505, 1644
McNew, Louisiana 613, 1115
McPhearson, Robert 1439
McPherson (McPhearson, McPierson), Archibald M. (A. M.) 1352, 1439, 1514, 1569, 1576, 1581, 1635, 1667, 1672, 1736, 1773, 1774, 1777, 1781, 1785, 1787, 1789, 1790-1791, 1812-1813, 1815-1816, 1872, 1887-1888, 1895-1896, 1898, 1900-1902, 1918, 1919
McPherson, Sarah (Sally) 1736, 1781
McSherry, Edward 882
Meagher, Ambrose 335
Meane, W. 484
Melton, Rebecca 1501
Melton, Stephen 1501
Menard & Valle 1559
Menard, Angelique 484, 946
Menard, Pierre 33, 484, 550, 911, 946, 1217, 1354, 1559
Menn, B. 255
Merechal, Leander 1445
Merechal, Rose 1445
Meredith (Merideth), Daniel 89, 427, 759, 760, 1654
Meredith, Isaac (Isaak) 89, 200, 347, 479, 696, 735, 760, 1047-1048, 1317
Meredith, Mrs. 570
Meredith, Roland 55, 86
Meredith, Roland, heirs of 345
Meredith, Sarah 696, 735, 1317
Merideth, F. C. 643
Meridith, Daniel Jr. 954
Merrit (Merit), Jerome 1346-1347, 1873
Merry, Catharine M. 1013
Merry, Samuel 1013, 1164
Merz, Helena 1814
Merz, John 1814
Messersmith, Henry 882
Meyer, Joseph 1352
Michael, ___ 783
Michael, James 583, 744
Michaels, James Jr. 526
Middleton, Robert 633, 644-645
Middleton, William 106-107, 1429
Mihlfeld, Michael 1511, 1546
Mihlfeld, Susannah 1546
Milburn, Jas. H. 1644
Miles, Caroline 1710
Miles, Cecelia (Cecili) 41, 111
Miles, Charles 928, 933, 940, 1009, 1048, 1506, 1836
Miles, Elizabeth 27, 165, 243
Miles, Felix 1313, 1710
Miles, Francis 194, 243, 1911
Miles, Henry 70, 111, 165, 190, 297, 1054, 1469
Miles, Joseph 41, 111, 165, 194, 243, 269, 1054, 1260, 1357, 1551, 1666
Miles, Joseph Jr. 1075
Miles, Josiah 1589

Miles, Leo 1054
Miles, Mark 719, 759, 760, 954, 1047
Miles, Mary 1054
Miles, Nicholas 27, 165, 243, 988, 1025, 1250, 1287, 1348
Miles, Rosana 1075
Miles, Thomas J. 1739
Millard, ___ 476
Millard, Henry 69
Millard, Josiah 1458
Miller, Andrew 13, 315-316
Miller, C. Ch. W. 1003
Miller, Catharine (Cathrine) 13, 315-316
Miller, Elizabeth 610
Miller, George 24
Miller, H. 134
Miller, John W. 322
Miller, Joseph 375, 610, 1484
Miller, R. J. 267
Miller, Rebecca 24
Miller, Sophia 1325
Minor, Jas. L. 1558
Missouri, State of 49, 55, 488, 1340, 1558
Mitchel (Mitchall), Archibald (Archabald) 430, 499, 530
Mitchel (Mitchall), Eliza 430
Mitchel, Jesse 1914
Mitchel, Matthew D. 430
Mitchell (Mitchel), Robert 430, 499
Mitchell, Solomon 1691
Mitchel, Thomas B. 430, 690
Modglin, John 326
Mogran, John, heirs of 90
Moll, Joseph 1264
Monroe, James 166, 341, 446
Montfort, Henry G. 1830
Montfort, Julia 1299
Montgomery, Jordan J. 855, 1002
Moore, ___ 1011
Moore, Ann 70(2), 432, 1247, 1567
Moore, Anna Regina 1758-1759
Moore, Austin 302, 1461, 1603, 1820
Moore, Barbara 70, 1069
Moore, Bede (Beed) 34, 84, 155, 225, 297, 357, 442, 669, 834, 1025, 1213, 1247, 1485, 1551, 1915
Moore, Berlinder 669
Moore, Cecelia (Cecily) 806, 988, 1069
Moore, Christina 1603
Moore, Elizabeth 70, 936, 988, 1069, 1679
Moore, Elizabeth, heirs of 1469
Moore, Eulalia (Eulila) 936, 988, 1603
Moore, Ignatius 70, 753, 1069, 1469, 1679
Moore, Isidore (Isadore, I.) 2, 4, 27, 70, 95, 121, 139, 157, 199, 209, 210, 229, 302, 307, 356, 362, 381, 464, 630, 682, 755, 800, 875, 890, 895, 936, 984, 988, 1025, 1204, 1213
Moore, Isidore [Jr.] 1603
Moore, Isidore Jr. 1079, 1651
Moore, Isidore Sr. 1603, 1628, 1664, 1732

Moore (More), James (Jas.) 56, 70(2), 84, 190, 220, 252, 297, 464, 1014, 1083, 1088-1089, 1213
Moore, James [Jr.] 806, 839, 877, 1038, 1256, 1568, 1625
Moore, James [Sr.] 806, 839, 877, 1038, 1256, 1568, 1625
Moore, James C. 42, 96, 114, 230, 239, 245, 340, 466, 470, 531, 984, 1603, 1845
Moore, James J. 357, 377, 450, 676, 806, 834, 1069
Moore, James Jr. 84, 264, 297, 1567
Moore, James N. 172, 597, 1025, 1246, 1320, 1488
Moore, James S. 1915
Moore, James Sr. 1069-1070
Moore, James Sr. 48, 187, 222, 244-245, 258, 274, 379, 432, 449-450, 527, 753, 1240 1240, 1307, 1679
Moore, James Sr., heirs of 1469
Moore, Jno. M. 515
Moore, John 165, 190, 286, 360, 1126, 1248, 1256, 1603, 1690, 1711, 1724, 1729, 1822, 1859
Moore, John B. 1200
Moore, Jos. A. 433
Moore, Joseph Sr. 70
Moore, Leah 302, 307, 464, 988, 1213, 1603
Moore, Leo 362, 464, 1461, 1603, 1820
Moore, Levi 1868, 1874
Moore, Lewis 65, 161, 169, 680, 868, 1883, 1915
Moore, Lewis William 1603
Moore, M. L. 605, 1519
Moore, Maria 70
Moore, Martin J. 228, 283, 865, 1174, 1179, 1603, 528, 543, 551, 725, 737, 1085, 1481, 1531, 1591, 1618, 1721, 1758, 1759, 1858
Moore, Martin Lindsay 1488
Moore, Martina 1603
Moore, Mary 1015, 1079
Moore, Matilda 70, 274, 1469
Moore, Nancy 1179
Moore (Moor, More), Nicholas 27, 84, 190, 238, 297, 445, 651, 988, 1320
Moore, Nicholas, heirs of 1025
Moore, Rebecca (Rebeca, Rebeckah) 56, 230, 239, 470, 984
Moore, Robert 1859
Moore, Sabina 70
Moore, Sally 597, 1025, 1246, 1320
Moore, Samuel Lewis (Saml. L.) 464, 1096, 1603, 1804
Moore, Sarah 165, 190, 1488
Moore, Stephen Theodore 1603
Moore, Sylvester 597
Moore, Thomas 70, 527, 1038
Moore, Verlinder 1247, 1485, 1551, 1915
Moore, Verlinger 1025
Moore, William 70, 449, 1025, 1069, 1105, 1568

Moore, William C. (Wm. C.) 496, 1015, 1194
Moore, William G. 780
Moranville, John 63, 652
Moranville, John B. 428, 833, 1621
Mordock, ___ 947
Mordock, Alexander 67
Moredock, James 604, 627, 1692
Morehead, John 208
Morehead, William 208
Morgan, A. 343. 395
Morgan, Archibald (Archabald) 22, 43, 90, 105, 265, 352, 418, 457, 645, 730, 1107, 1108-1109
Morgan, Benajah 53, 90, 339
Morgan, David 90, 1007
Morgan, Elizabeth 53, 339
Morgan, John 53, 90, 105(2), 142, 281-282, 327, 434, 585, 633, 644, 694, 697
Morgan, John Jr. 352
Morgan, John Sr. 352, 865, 873, 1532, 1574
Morgan, John Sr., heirs of 873
Morgan, Joseph 459, 857
Morgan, Martha 105
Morgan, Patsy 281
Morgan, Saml. 231
Morgan, Solomon (Sol.) 18-19, 222, 268, 270, 352, 421-422, 474, 476, 522, 865, 873, 1453-1454
Morgan, Susan 1007
Morin, ___ 226
Morin, Antoine 226
Morrill, Edward J. 703
Morris, Elizabeth 844, 846
Morris, Hannah 585, 697, 811, 832
Morris, John (Jno.) 23, 606, 612-613, 643, 738, 906, 1107, 1115
Morris, Thomas 694, 697
Morris, William 22, 43, 133, 339, 560, 585, 694, 697, 811, 832, 1109, 1704
Morrison, Andrew 710
Morrison, David W. 690, 1471
Morrison, Eliner J. 1471
Morton, James G. C. 903
Mossey, Joseph A. 1761, 1846
Motherley, Wm. 1298
Muhlfeld, Matilda 1695
Muhlfeld (Muhlfelt), Michael 869, 1491, 1695
Muhlfelt, Susannah 1491
Muller, Christian Friedrich (Fred., Fredk.) 1142, 1360, 1413, 1430, 1670
Muller, Christian Gottfried 1388
Mullerin, Sophia 1401
Munn, Julius de 1518
Murdock, ___ 615
Murdock, Alexander (Alexr.) 226, 268, 383-384
Murdock, James 344
Murphey, ___ 978
Murphey, B. 980
Murphy, Bartholomew (Bartholimew) 300, 332, 460, 1027, 1487, 1756

Murphy, Elleaner 460
Murphy, Ellen L. 1756
Murphy, William 489
Murray (Murry), Joseph 695, 710, 718, 1471
Murray, Mary 695, 710, 718
Musick(?), Thomas Roy 226
Mutlins, John 1685
Myers, Angelina 1888
Myers, Elijah Asbury 1233
Myers, James 663, 1271, 1276
Myers, James Garner (James G.) 1230-1232, 1233, 1276
Myers, Joanna 1271, 1276
Myers, Lorenzo Dow (D.) 1514, 1520, 1887, 1888
Myers, Samuel Miller (Samuel M.) 1231, 1233
Myers, William Marion (William Marrion, William M., Wm. M.) 1231, 1233, 1514, 1520, 1887
Mylius, ___ 1265
Nagle, James 218
Nash, James A. 1814
Nasslien, Aran 1601
Naumann, ___ 1181
Neal, Marcella 1690
Negro Slaves (see also the Slave Index)
Negro Abelina 885
Negro Abraham 362
Negro Adaline 1806
Negro Adiel 126
Negro Agnes 1603
Negro Alexander 1064
Negro Amanda 1806
Negro Anderson 362
Negro Andrew 1785
Negro Andy 1785, 1806
Negro Ann 1785
Negro Antony 1806(2)
Negro Aron 1064
Negro Aura 28
Negro Austin 36, 46
Negro Ben Dainold 202
Negro Berry 1806
Negro Betsy 1806
Negro Betsy (Betsey) 36, 46
Negro Bett 467
Negro Betty 1806
Negro Bill 495
Negro Binday 495
Negro Bob 127
Negro Boson 1806
Negro Caroline 1064
Negro Catharine 1706, 1711, 1729
Negro Catharine 28, 126
Negro Celeste 840
Negro Chaney 1064
Negro Charity 1806
Negro Charles 1806
Negro Charles 28, 201
Negro Cortase 1032
Negro Darcas 1785
Negro David 1806

Negro David 840
Negro Dianah 467
Negro Dick 203
Negro Dick 860
Negro Dieueha(?) 1604
Negro Edmond 1806(2)
Negro Elias 1806
Negro Elizabeth 362
Negro Elizabeth 840
Negro Elleck 1827
Negro Ellic 1780
Negro Emaly 1032
Negro Emiline 1891
Negro Emily 1427
Negro Emily 1744
Negro Fillis 1033
Negro Flora 1143
Negro Frances 1659
Negro Francis 840
Negro Frisby 28
Negro Gabriel 126
Negro Galon 1806
Negro Garrette 1806
Negro Georg 998
Negro George 1212
Negro George 202
Negro Georges 1032
Negro Grace 28
Negro Grandison 16
Negro Hannah 761
Negro Harriet 1032, 1034
Negro Harriett 1198
Negro Harriette 1806
Negro Harry 1034
Negro Harry 1198
Negro Harry 1740
Negro Henry 1032-1034, 1064
Negro Henry 1198
Negro Henry 16, 126
Negro Henry 1603
Negro Hillery 1827, 1892
Negro Hillry 1780
Negro Hinney (Pinney?) 786
Negro Isaac 1032
Negro Isaac 1806
Negro Isaac 362
Negro Jack 1033, 1059
Negro Jack 1787
Negro Jack 36, 46
Negro James 1032, 1064
Negro Jefferson 1806
Negro Jerry 1806
Negro Jim 127
Negro Jim Evon 201
Negro Jinny 1806
Negro Joe 1033-1034
Negro Joe 1198
Negro Joe 1806(2)
Negro John 1033-1034
Negro John 1198
Negro John 1806(2)
Negro John 467
Negro Joseph 1785
Negro Joseph 1891

Negro Josiah 1603, 1692
Negro Josiah 1806
Negro Julia 1806
Negro Julia (July) 36, 46
Negro Juliann 840
Negro Kate 1032
Negro Kitty 1034
Negro Kitty 1198
Negro Leah 133
Negro Leah 1427
Negro Lett 16
Negro Letty 1806
Negro Lloyd 467
Negro Lorenzo 362
Negro Louisa 1806
Negro Louise 28
Negro Luce 1806(2)
Negro Lucey 1032
Negro Lucile 1064
Negro Lucinda (Linda) 1603, 1692
Negro Lucretia 133
Negro Lucretia 1744
Negro Lucretia 840
Negro Lucy 1603
Negro Lucy 201
Negro Luke 1706, 1711, 1729
Negro Marceler 126
Negro Margaret 1210
Negro Margaret 1603
Negro Margaret 1806
Negro Maria 201
Negro Maria 520
Negro Martha 1806
Negro Marthy 1918
Negro Martin 362
Negro Mary 1032, 1053
Negro Mary 1806
Negro Mary 28
Negro Mary Ann 1744
Negro Mary Annah 1143
Negro Melinda 840
Negro Milly 1715
Negro Milly 267
Negro Minerva 840
Negro Minty 202
Negro Minty 467
Negro Morrough 1440
Negro Mylat(?) 71
Negro Nace 202-203
Negro Nathan 1064
Negro Nathan 885
Negro Ned 16
Negro Nelly 202
Negro Nelly Ann 1806
Negro Orange 1032
Negro Oretia 71
Negro Patsey 495
Negro Paul 1064
Negro Paul 126
Negro Paulina 1706, 1711, 1729
Negro Peg 467
Negro Penelope 840
Negro Peter 1064
Negro Peter 1744

Negro Peter 936
Negro Peter, Old 1806
Negro Phillis 1034
Negro Phillis 1198
Negro Phoebe 840
Negro Phrisby 28
Negro Piere 1064
Negro Pierre 28(2)
Negro Polette 1064
Negro Polly 467
Negro Presly, Young 1806
Negro Price 251
Negro Priscilla 1785
Negro Providence 1806
Negro Qually 1032
Negro Ransom 761
Negro Reachel 31
Negro Ricey Feriba 1806
Negro Romulus 1032
Negro Rose 1032
Negro Sally 1059
Negro Sam 1806
Negro Sam 202
Negro Sam 495
Negro Sam 840
Negro Sarah 1806(2)
Negro Sarah 202
Negro Sarah 840
Negro Sena 1806
Negro Sonter 1033
Negro Sophia 1427(2)
Negro Stephen 362
Negro Susa 1806
Negro Susan 1427
Negro Susan 1806
Negro Sydua 1785
Negro Sylva 1806
Negro Sylvestrus 1806
Negro Sylvia 362
Negro Tenet 1032
Negro Tenna 1198
Negro Tharesa 1064
Negro Therese 28
Negro Tinna 1034
Negro Voluntine 28
Negro Wiley 1806
Negro William 1715, 1806
Negro Willis 1033-1034
Negro Willis 1198
Negro Winny 1891
Neil, Hugh 206
Newberry (Newbery), William M. 511, 550
Newberry, Henry 1749
Newberry, Sarah 1434, 1749
Newberry, Thomas 1434
Newberry, William M. 264
Newlin, Thomas S. 1857
Newmiller, John J. 1693
Newsom, ___ 272
Newsom, Elizabeth 876
Newsom (Nusam), H. B. 86, 570
Newsom, Henry B. 55, 148, 225, 345, 1238

Newsom, James 24, 1007
Newsom, James Jr. 1238
Newsom, John Sr. 77
Newsom (Nusom), Jonas (Jones) 1127, 1532, 1574
Newsom, Jones [Sr.] 969, 1652
Newsom, Jones Jr. 277, 969, 1652
Nicher, Michael 1791
Nichol, James 585
Nicholas, James 832
Nicholas, Mary Ann 832
Niemann, Frederick 1401
Nitzschker, Michael 1401
Noell & Tate 1012, 1719
Noell (Noel), Joel W. 924
Noell, John 543, 810
Noell, John W. (Jno. W., J. W.) 543, 629, 785, 810, 813, 857-858, 945, 1012, 1021, 1099, 1194, 1197, 1213, 1249, 1307, 1322, 1333, 1353, 1358, 1425, 1435, 1467, 1487, 1493, 1499, 1505-1506, 1511, 1518, 1529, 1544, 1547, 1549, 1556, 1563, 1570, 1573, 1575, 1578, 1579, 1580, 1583, 1586, 1587, 1592, 1594-1600, 1596, 1602, 1604, 1607, 1612-1613, 1615-1616, 1618-1621, 1621, 1623-1626, 1629-1632, 1635-1636, 1638-1639, 1641-1643, 1645, 1648-1649, 1656-1657, 1659-1660, 1665-1666, 1673-1675, 1683, 1685, 1687-1689, 1699-1700, 1707-1711, 1715-1716, 1718, 1719, 1721, 1723, 1725, 1729, 1730, 1732, 1733-1734, 1739-1742, 1744, 1745-1746, 1748, 1750-1751, 1754, 1756-1757, 1760, 1763, 1766, 1768-1771, 1778, 1784, 1787-1788, 1793-1795, 1797, 1800, 1805, 1808, 1813, 1819, 1820-1822, 1825, 1828, 1831, 1833-1834, 1837-1842, 1844-1845, 1846, 1847, 1848, 1850, 1854-1860, 1862-1864, 1865, 1866, 1870, 1876, 1878, 1881-1882, 1892, 1894, 1897, 1904, 1906, 1909, 1917
Noell, Mary 1613
Noell, Mary A. 1021, 1249, 1865
Noell, Mary Ann 1656-1657
Nolson, James 1264
Nonning, Gottfried Jr. 1404
Nonning, Gottfried Sr. 1404
Norfolk, James H. 355, 401
North, Ralph 1058
Notrebe, Charles F. 1472
Noyes, Michael J. 810
Nurgan, John Jr. 1846
Nurse, George 1213
O'Bryan, Margaret 1235
O'Connor, Chatharine 450
O'Connor (O'Conner), John 70, 268, 309, 377, 450, 569
O'Meara (Omeara), Daniel 741, 924, 1464, 1572
O'Shea, John 1008, 1787
O'Brian, Beatrix 599

O'Bryan, Margaret 511
O'Meara, Elizabeth 741
Oakless & Clark 285
Ocks, Ann Catharine 1831
Ocks, Christina 1831
Ocks (Ox), Conrad 1102, 1599
Ocks (Ockes), John Conrad 1619, 1831
Ocks, John Michael 1831
Odin, J. M. 1498, 1577
Odin, Jean Marie 435
Odin, John 1166
Odin, John M. 266, 294, 600, 999, 1056
Odin, John, Rev. 212
Oklap, John 37, 78-79, 116, 133
Oklap, Louisa Jane 37, 78, 133
Old, Joshua J. 750
Oliver, ___ 570
Oliver, Thomas (Tho., Thos.) 28, 33, 37, 69, 79, 85-87, 115-116, 131, 133, 143, 240, 568
Olmstedt, Michael 1113
Onstadt, Michael 1890
Osborn, Amzi 635, 647, 648-650, 692, 700, 771-772, 777-778, 784-786, 812, 851-852, 1019, 1156, 1444, 1477, 1854, 1890
Osborn, Esther 692, 778
Osborn (Osborne), Esther H. 635, 771-772, 784-785, 963, 1663
Osborn (Osborne, Osburn), Henry S. 962, 1111, 1214, 1252, 1254, 1354, 1433
Osborn, Nancey 1354
Oser, Christian 1251, 1730
Otto, ___ 1265
Otto, Johann Gottfried 1396
Otts, Mr. 1265
Overfield, F. T. 743
Pain, Gabriel Gagne 1710
Painter, Lewis 485
Painter, Philip 73
Palisch, Johann (John) Gottleib (Gottlieb, Gottloib) 1016, 1017, 1065, 1361-1362, 1368, 1371, 1376, 1380, 1694, 1779, 1893, 1895-1896, 1899, 1901, 1903
Palisch, Johanne Christiane 1903
Panier, Paul Peter 1479
Paquin, Joseph 327, 434-435, 600, 1234, 1235, 1260, 1485-1486
Paquin, Joseph, Rev. 212, 282
Parent, Etienne (Etinne) 1245, 1472
Parker, Alfred L. 328
Parker, Francis 226
Parks, A. L. 374, 844-846, 854, 1009, 1328
Parks, Alfred 627
Parks, Alfred J. 1201
Parks, Alfred L. 337, 742, 803, 907, 921, 928, 933-934, 940, 1022, 1047-1048, 1062, 1067, 1145, 1522, 1529, 1654, 1680, 1692, 1724, 1735, 1765, 1830, 1877, 1884, 1909
Parks, Hallyburton (Haleyburton) 1093, 1569
Parks, Haly B. 337

Parks, Jane 1093
Parks, Joseph 1446, 1772
Parks, Julius E. 820, 1772
Parres (Pairs, Pares, Parrs), Anthony 601, 1226, 1288-1289, 1339, 1465, 1508, 1698, 1722
Parres, Mary 1289
Parres, Mary Ann 1698, 1722
Partlett, Samuel 1583
Patterson, Alexander 181, 347, 845, 1653
Patterson, Alexander [Jr.] 89, 427
Patterson, Alexander [Sr.] 89, 427, 1654
Patterson, Alexander Jr. 507, 1654
Patterson, Alexander Sr. 200, 507
Patterson, John 89, 227, 248, 507, 907, 934, 1328
Patterson, John Jr. 1022
Patterson, Nancy 248, 427, 507, 1653
Patterson, Rachel 1317
Patterson, Rebecca 89
Patterson, William 89(2), 507, 1317, 1654
Paul, R. 49
Paulding, ___ 1354
Paulding, William 1647
Pease, Giles 1449
Pease, Henry L. 1295, 1647, 1860, 1862
Pease, J. S. & Co. 1138, 1295
Pease, Joseph S. 1295, 1500, 1647, 1788, 1860, 1862
Pease, Joseph S. & Co. 1647
Peers, Jno. D. 185
Pelletier, John B. 1920
Pelletier, John B. Sr. 1623
Pelletier, Sally 1623, 1920
Penny, Cullen 414, 453, 1569
Penny, Darcas 453
Penny, Olive (Olly) 1036, 1335, 1918
Penny (Peney), Richmond 1036, 1261, 1286, 1334-1335, 1910, 1918
Penny, William 1286
Pepin, Louis 1245
Pepin, Mary 1245
Pernshe(?), ___ 184
Perrin, Caleb H. (C. H.) 1533, 1636
Perrin, Mrs. 570
Perrine, Esther 777-778, 812
Perrine, William M. 959, 1890-1891
Perry Co., Commissioners of the 3% Fund 549
Perry County 921, 1085, 1350, 1611
Perry, William 1575
Perryville, Commissioners of 93-104, 108, 149-153, 162, 167, 171-172, 177-180, 219, 234, 236, 246, 260, 280, 299, 303, 349, 433, 493, 528, 661, 663, 688, 728-729, 837, 1066, 1129
Petit, Louis 990
Pettett, Jacob 185
Pettis, Spencer 226
Pettit, Elizabeth 451
Pettit (Petitt), George (Geo.) 308, 451, 1559
Pettit, James N. 730, 879
Pettit, Rachel A. 879

Pettus, Wm. G. 44
Petukin(?), John 211
Peyton, Elizabeth 1738
Peyton (Payton), John 797, 1738, 1806
Peyton (Payton), Samuel 797, 1738
Peyton, William 1912
Pfau, Gustave (Gustav, Gustavus) 1142, 1360, 1375, 1638
Phelps, Thomas 1039
Phelps, Timothy 461, 1147
Philips, Joseph 1589
Philips, Redman 1555
Philips, Timothy 448
Phillips (Philips), Elizabeth 557, 1555, 1641
Phillips (Philips), James 135, 358, 557, 1059, 1605, 1641
Phillips, Jane 351
Phillips, Mary 1299
Phillips (Philips), Robert L. 1432, 1757, 1768, 1904
Phillips, William B. 506, 1299
Piett (Piet), John 1260, 1659, 1666
Pinkerton, Adam 718
Pinkerton, Ann 718
Pinkerton, David 718, 968
Pinkerton, Dizah 718
Pinkerton, Elizabeth 718
Pinkerton, Ellenor (Ellen) 718
Pinkerton, Henry 718
Pinkerton, John [Jr.] 718
Pinkerton, John Sr. 718
Pinkerton, Margaret 718
Pinkerton, Sarah 718
Pinkerton, William 718, 781
Pinkston (Pinksten), David 427, 507
Poims, Pierre 226
Polk, John 119, 322
Polk, William 119
Polk, William Jr. 119
Polk, William Sr. 322
Pope, Edward P. 1299
Popp, Amolia Rosena 1773
Popp, Andres 1773
Popp, Anemann 1791
Poppits (Poppitz), Johann Christian 1383, 1391
Porter, Burwell 1806
Powel, Henry 322
Powell, Cerinda A. (Cyrinda Ann) 1780, 1811
Powell, Harriet (Harriot) 1347, 1489, 1877
Powell, J. M. M. 1489, 1579, 1818-1819, 1877
Powell, James S. 1489, 1811, 1818-1819, 1877
Powell, John M. M. 1347, 1873
Powell, Julia Ann (Juliann) 1489, 1818, 1877
Powell, Lemuel H. 1579, 1819
Powell, Robert C. (R. C.) 874, 1432, 1489, 1566, 1780, 1811, 1877

Powell, Sarinda (Serinda) 1489, 1566, 1877
Powell, William (Wm.) 272-273, 1489, 1579, 1819, 1877
Powers (Power), Jeffrey 590, 1157, 1168, 1451-1452, 1469, 1572
Powers, Elizabeth 1452
Pratiot, Charles 226
Pratiot, Edward H. 226
Pratiot, Susan 226
Pratte, Bernard 970, 1618, 1857
Pratte, Bernard S. 1481, 1860
Pratte, Celeste 1481
Pratte, Emanual 1064
Pratte, Emanuel (Emanual) 1064, 1598, 1618, 1671, 1857-1858, 1860, 1863
Pratte, J. 541, 949, 1141
Pratte, J. & Son 926
Pratte, Jane 1481
Pratte (Pratt), Joseph (Jos.) 201, 346, 572, 591, 604, 714, 774-775, 853, 985, 1064, 1064, 1150, 1160, 1218, 1499, 1550, 1559, 1591, 1618, 1730, 1747, 1857-1858, 1863
Pratte, Joseph & Son 977, 1618
Pratte, Louisa 787
Pratte, Marie 985
Pratte, Mary 774-775
Pratte, Mary Louisa (Louise, L.) 774-775, 904, 1531, 1556, 1591
Pratte, Mary Valle 604
Pratte, Peter 1618
Pratte (Pratt), Peter R. (P. R.) 403, 420, 541, 549, 572, 575, 591, 610, 696, 712, 735, 748, 750, 774-775, 787, 790, 799, 807, 841, 902, 904, 945, 949, 1006, 1028, 1127, 1141, 1427, 1469, 1483, 1531, 1548, 1556, 1591, 1620, 1757, 1858, 1860, 1862, 1904
Pratte, Roseman 816
Prem, John 231
Preston, Ann 34
Preston, George 34, 205, 557, 662, 696, 735, 934, 1007, 1059, 1105-1106
Preston, George, heirs of 1105
Preston, J. 1168
Preston, James 34, 1059, 1105-1106, 1583
Preston, Jonathan (Johnathan) 135, 286, 358, 360, 839, , 1256, 1589
Preston, Jonathan, heirs of 1583
Preston, Mary 696, 735, 1059, 1105-1106
Prevalet, Augustin Melchior 1538
Price, Alexander 1857
Price, Columbus 705, 827, 1806
Price, Darcus 518
Price, John 351
Price, Joseph Jr. 1857
Price, Lydia 705
Price, R. H. 226
Price, Richard 1857
Price, Stephen 1298
Price, William 489, 518, 530, 602, 1472
Primm, John 1148

Primo, Paul 226
Prims, Paul 226
Propst, George 1162
Propst, Hannah 1162
Prost, Jean Antonie 1452
Pucket, Dr. 623
Puckett, A. H. & Co. 1195
Puckett, Alfred 890
Puckett, Alfred H. (A. H.) 302, 368, 406-408, 418, 420, 426, 432, 495, 681-682, 755, 875, 895, 948, 1151, 1184, 1195, 1238, 1533, 1567, 1614, 1674, 1709
Puckett, Alfred Harrison 424
Puckett, Emily 682
Puckett, Emily B. 368
Pusey, Nathan (Nathen) 474, 476, 567, 939
Quarles, Elizabeth 405
Quarles, T. 32
Quick, J. W. 486
Quick, John 485
Quick, John W. 416, 487, 855, 901-902, 1353, 1483, 1587, 1620, 1757, 1904
Quick, Julia 1353
Quick, Nancy 121, 486, 901
Quick, Tunis (Tunas) 121, 154, 416, 486, 901-902, 904, 1483, 1587, 1620, 1757, 1768, 1904
Rabold, John C. 1615
Ragland, Elias 531
Ragland, Elvis 301
Ragsdale, William H. (Wm. H.) 1034, 1220
Ramsey, Thomas 32
Ranney, J. 398, 405
Ranney, Johnson 458, 567
Ranny, Wm. C. 458
Ray, James 18-19
Reardin, Landon 538
Reardon (Riardon, Riorden), Robert (Robt.) 348, 367, 394, 403, 538
Reardon (Reiorden, Riorden), Lucretia (Lucinda) 348, 367, 503, 1496
Reardon, William 348, 503, 538
Rease, Roland 953
Recks, Frederick 1820
Reddick (Riddick), James 652, 833, 1357, 1621, 1649, 1666, 1745
Reddick, Mary 652
Redford, William 885
Redman, John 1857
Reed, Benjamin 50, 65, 654
Reed, Elosius (Locious) 50, 65
Reed, James 62
Reed, Lucy 62
Reed, Matilda 50, 65
Reed, William 50
Reed, William M. 62, 65
Reeves, Bennet A. 1292
Reid, James B. 1331
Reid, John 1198
Renner, Michael 1162
Retherford, Joseph 944
Rex, William 348, 394, 714

Reynolds, Robert 128
Reynolds, Th. 1558
Reynolds, Wm. C. 1735
Rhodes, Bernice 811
Rhodes, Cornelius 31, 70, 1158
Rhodes, Henry J. 84, 245, 274, 1070, 1469
Rhodes, Jedthson (Jedson) 222, 244, 297
Rhodes, Joseph 811, 1259
Rhodes, Mary 1158
Rhodes, Matilda 84, 245, 274, 1469
Rhyne, Elizabeth 1608
Rhyne, Joel 1484
Rhyne, Peter 1608
Rhyne (Rine, Ryne), Thomas (Thos.) 635, 1148, 1688
Rice, Elianor 1112
Rice, Francis 1070, 1594
Rice, J. 735
Rice, James (Jas.) 48, 258, 264, 274, 297, 419, 425, 441, 449, 460, 464, 487, 527, 529, 536, 541-542, 551, 557, 575, 578, 584, 586-587, 591, 594-595, 597, 620, 656, 665-666, 668-669, 675, 681, 686, 696, 708, 711-712, 725, 728-729, 746-753, 758-760, 764-765, 781, 790, 798-799, 806-807, 819, 831, 839-841, 849-850, 858, 867, 870, 881, 890-892, 900-902, 904, 908, 917, 919, 924, 926, 937, 939, 945, 953-954, 967, 977-978, 981-983, 986-987, 1000, 1006, 1010, 1025, 1027-1028, 1038-1039, 1059, 1064, 1068-1070, 1079-1080, 1087, 1089, 1097, 1102, 1105-1106, 1136, 1138, 1146, 1152, 1157-1158, 1160, 1165, 1171, 1183-1184, 1189-1190, 1192, 1195, 1202, 1236, 1239, 1242, 1246-1248, 1272, 1290-1291, 1294-1295, 1300-1302, 1306-1307, 1309-1310, 1312, 1314, 1320, 1322, 1332, 1337-1338, 1342, 1353, 1358, 1453-1455, 1458-1459, 1464-1465, 1483, 1487, 1494, 1504, 1505, 1510, 1516, 1536, 1540, 1541, 1544, 1546, 1551, 1565, 1567, 1568, 1571, 1575, 1585, 1588, 1590, 1609-1610, 1612, 1614, 1623, 1628, 1636-1637, 1640, 1643, 1649, 1651-1652, 1662, 1664, 1668, 1677-1679, 1690, 1701, 1707, 1712, 1713, 1714, 1740, 1743, 1755, 1761, 1796, 1797, 1799, 1806, 1807, 1810, 1826, 1843, 1846, 1848, 1851, 1853, 1864, 1865, 1885, 1890, 1897, 1906, 1909, 1911, 1915-1916, 1920, 1922
Rice, Sabina 258, 1069, 1922
Richard, Alexr. 85
Richardson & Bridgeman 1721, 1788, 1882
Richardson, Allen Burns 1048
Richardson, John 1700, 1721, 1722, 1882
Richte, Johann Christ. 1411
Richter, ___ 1265
Richter, Christian 1387
Richter, Frederick 1417

Richter, Gottlieb 1387
Richter, Johann Christ. 1377
Riley, Ann (Anna) 170, 658, 1158, 1175
Riley, Benedict 58, 170, 258, 440, 658, 1158, 1175
Riley, Henry (Henrey) 1142, 1158, 1255, 1360, 1542, 1578
Riley, Henry, heirs of 1158
Riney, Evaristus 1767
Riney, Sarah 75, 295, 440, 605, 813, 1339, 1767
Riney, Thomas 61, 75-76, 151, 179, 228, 283, 295, 325, 420, 440, 605, 658-659, 813, 919, 932, 1175-1179, 1339, 1718, 1767, 1879
Riordan, Elizabeth 403
Rix (Recks), Adolph 704, 823, 1461, 1820, 1876
Rix, Adolphus Sr. 1820
Rix (Ricks), Barbara (Barbary) 1153, 1820
Rix, Frederick 1171
Rix, Helen 1820
Rix (Ricks), Mathias 1153, 1171, 1461, 1820
Roady (Rhody, Rody), Moses 1206, 1271, 1272
Roady (Rody), Hetty 1188, 1272, 1487
Roady (Rody), Moses 1188, 1487
Roark, Amos 348, 394, 403
Roark, Amos, heirs of 815
Roark, James 314, 723
Roark, Lucinda 723
Roark, Martha (Marthy) 538, 723
Roberts, Abraham 874
Roberts, Benjamin 17
Roberts, Catharine 722
Roberts, David 722
Roberts, Elizabeth 696, 722, 735
Roberts, James 722
Roberts, Michael 722
Roberts, Nancy 874
Roberts, Sophrona 722
Robertson, George 329
Robertson, Nathaniel P. 329
Robertson, Thomas Bollinger 211
Robidoux, Josoph 226
Robins (Robbins), Jesse B. 1507, 1537, 1545, 1829
Robinson, ___ 69
Robinson, Drucilla (Drusilla) 712, 748-749, 751, 754-755, 890
Robinson, George (Georg) 255, 506
Robinson, John 682-683, 711-712, 748-749, 751, 754-756, 875, 890, 895, 1487
Robinson, N. P. 506
Robinson, Thomas 1426
Rodney, Martin 36, 46
Rodney, Thos. S. 36
Rolfe (Rolf), James H. 268, 320, 421, 461
Rolfe, Mildred 320
Rolira, Joseph 434
Roman, A. B. 990
Roner, Ferdinand 1878

Rosati, Joseph 106-107, 435, 600
Rosati, Joseph, Rev. 211-214
Rose, Jas. 1762
Roseborough (Rosebrough), James 518, 1802
Roseborough, Julia 1802
Ross (Rosse), George P. 552-556
Ross, George A. 637, 703, 998, 1824
Ross, George Anthony 955
Ross, Hanah W. 818
Ross, Hannah 998
Ross, Ibby 998
Ross, Jane L. 998
Ross, Jenny 998
Ross, John 473, 817-818, 955, 998, 1812, 1872
Ross, John E. 998, 1824
Ross, John, heirs of 998
Ross, Peggy 998
Ross, Phebe (Febby, Pheby) 703, 955, 1824
Ross, Rachel R. 998
Ross, Robert H. 998, 1812-1813, 1824
Ross, Sada 576
Ross, Zenas N. 576, 998
Roth, Celestia 990
Rowark, Amos 538
Roy, Charles 757, 1519, 1758
Roy, Mary M. 1519
Rozier & Mattingly 1922
Rozier, Adolphus 992
Rozier, Constance 677
Rozier, F. 1730
Rozier, F. & Co. 1721, 1882
Rozier, F. Jr. 1882
Rozier, Felix 1922
Rozier, Ferdinand 454-455, 584, 798, 930, 1089, 1188, 1446, 1627
Rozier, Ferdinand [Sr.] 677
Rozier (Rozer), Ferdinand (F.) Jr. 583, 656, 677, 981-982, 1014, 1035, 1187, 1219, 1226, 1303, 1445, 1475, 1512, 1587, 1612, 1616, 1621, 1623, 1649, 1668, 1716, 1718, 1721, 1742, 1748, 1754, 1755, 1763, 1769, 1793, 1862, 1916, 1920
Rozier, Ferdinand Sr. 1507
Rozier, Firman (Firmin) Andrew (A.) 1621, 1754, 1916, 1920
Rozier, Harriet 798, 1303, 1446, 1755
Rucker, Christina 1713
Rudisaile (Rudisel), Henry 678-679, 1913
Rudisaile, Jacob F. 1913
Rudisaile, John G. 1913
Rudisel, Elizabeth 678-679
Rug, Philip 1695
Ruh (Roff), Appollonia 1853
Ruh (Roff), Philip 1853
Ruland, John (Jno.) 993, 1060, 1151, 1164, 1693
Russell, ___ 1297
Russell, James 120
Russell, William 80, 86, 231, 240, 343, 568

Rutledge, Caroline (Frances C.) 732
Rutledge, Charles C. 809, 1495
Rutledge, Francis C. 809
Rutledge, George 101, 603, 724, 732-734, 866, 1278-1280, 1344, 1345, 1530, 1707, 1742, 1861
Rutledge, Jonas A. 732, 809, 1463
Rutledge, Mary Ann 1495
Rutledge, Sarah Ann (Saraann, Susann) 603, 734, 866, 1344
Rutledge, Susanna (Susana) 733, 1279
Rutledge, William (Wm.) 920, 1823, 1825
Ryan, Henry 1730
Saddler, Hugh M. 986-987
Saddler, Hugh McFail 1114
Saddler, Zachariah 986
Sadler, Alfred 671
Sadler, Alfred F. 926
Sadler, Elvirittia (Elvrittia) 1605-1606, 1641-1642
Sadler (Saddler), James 1006, 1077, 1465
Sadler, John 1606, 1641, 1642
Sadler, Joseph 1605-1606, 1641-1642
Sadler, Lucretia 645
Samuels, James 26, 222, 262, 981-982, 1915
Sanders, ___ 1830
Sanders, John H. 329, 506
Sanders, Polly 329
Sanders, S. S. 1216
Sanders, Stephen (Stn.) 173, 1811, 1818, 1836
Sanders, Thomas 390, 1355, 1680
Sanford (Sandford), Hy. 382, 822, 1355-1356
Saulnier, Edmond 195-196
Saunders, John A. 69
Saunders, John H. 255
Saupin, Johanne Rosina 1389
Savarre 226
Scarborough, Edward B. 1044-1045
Schaumburg, Joseph W. 1477
Scherer (Schearer), Francis 438, 526
Schlimpert, Christian (Christ.) Gottfried 1016, 1017, 1385, 1835
Schlimpert, Traugott 1388
Schmidt (Schmit), Johann 1392-1394
Schmidt, Bernard 1395
Schmidt, Carl 1265
Schmidt, Christian 1265
Schmidt, Dr. 1265
Schmidt, George Jochinn 1408
Schmidt, Gothwirth 1265
Schmidt, Gottfried (Gottfred) 1265, 1325, 1410
Schmidt, Gottlob 1406
Schmidt, Johann (John) 1026, 1421
Schmidt, John Bernhard 1265
Schmoele, Anthony 1630
Schnebert, Ferdinand Willhelm 1181
Schnider, Adam Gothelf 1296
Schnider, Sophia 1263, 1363
Schnurbusch (Snowbush), Elizabeth 514

Schnurbusch (Snerbush, Snowbush), Francis 374, 514
Schnurbusch (Schnarbush, Schnerebush, Schnowbush, Snerbush, Snearbush, Snobush, Snowbush), Joseph 102, 444, 465, 511, 514, 531, 1235, 1448, 1845
Schools, Francis 257
Schrimp, Nicholas 1675
Schubert, Johann Gottfried 1386
Scollay, George W. 1801
Scollay, Leonard 1659
Scott & Allen 911
Scott, Aeson 645
Scott, Charles 371, 393
Scott, Evan 636
Scott, George 670
Scott, Harriet 477
Scott, J. F. 990
Scott, John 64, 74, 143, 278-279, 382, 467, 477, 669, 687, 872, 911, 992
Scott, Maria Ann 670
Scott, Obadiah 371, 393
Scott, Polly 371, 393
Scudder, John 624, 646, 692, 771, 777-778, 784, 785-786, 812, 851-852, 957-961, 963, 1013, 1019, 1111-1113, 1156, 1214, 1354, 1359, 1426, 1444, 1597, 1663, 1890-1891
Scudder, Rebecca (Rebeca) 624, 772, 778, 957-961, 1111-1113, 1354, 1426, 1663
Scudder, William H. (W. H.) 624, 692, 957, 962, 1252, 1426, 1433, 1597
Searcy, ___ 570
Searcy (Searsey), Rosanna (Rosannah) Wallace (W.) 86, 132, 259, 503
Searcy (Searsy), William (Wm., W.) 22, 86, 240, 259, 277, 352, 394, 436, 451, 457, 476, 503, 517, 545, 560-561, 568, 604, 625-626, 633, 644, 694, 697, 714, 723, 730, 828, 835, 853, 873-874, 876, 879, 883-884, 889, 912-913, 1007, 1150, 1167, 1185, 1200, 1211, 1259, 1267, 1346-1347, 1532, 1574, 1703-1704
Seargent, Sally 265
Seems, Felix 572
Seibert, Daniel 1457
Seibert, George 459, 1333
Seibert (Seybert), Henry 72, 81-82, 92, 117-118, 120, 204, 241, 404, 459, 593, 619, 628-629
Seibert (Saibart), Katharine (Catharine, Cathariner, Katharina, Kathran) 82, 92, 459, 619
Seible, Jacob 1415
Seible, John 1415
Seissall, Francis 261
Seissall, Naomah 261
Sepaugh, David 1550
Serzel, John August 1898
Severingen & Bredell 788
Severingen, James T. 788

Shaner (Sheaner), Jacob 731, 797, 941-942, 989
Shaner, Elizabeth 404
Shaner, Henry 229
Shaner, Jacob 231, 298, 316, 404, 1026, 1157, 1435, 1514, 1543, 1736
Shaner, John 404, 408, 731, 942
Shaner, John, heirs of 731
Shaner, Louisa 731, 942
Shannon & Boggy 309
Shannon, George A. 1594
Shannon, Susan 569
Shannon (Shanon), William 55, 86, 240, 343, 345, 568-570, 1594, 1837
Shaw & Larkin 1138
Shaw, Allen 1198
Shaw, Jane 922, 1312
Shaw, Johnathan 864
Shaw, Lyman B. 1862
Shaw, Malinda 864
Shaw, William 922, 1312
Shearman, Patrick 64
Shelby, Ezra 1154-1155, 1428-1429, 1437, 1582, 1697
Shelby, Mary 1068, 1089, 1291
Shelby, Mary E. 1084, 1497, 1516, 1795
Shelby, Reuben (Reubin, R.) 620, 641, 665, 668, 682-683, 686, 689, 711, 752, 757, 774-775, 783, 801-802, 808, 813, 842, 866-867, 869, 877, 886-887, 898-899, 904-905, 908, 909, 910, 920, 949, 956, 966, 968, 979, 1005, 1011, 1041, 1021, 1030, 1035, 1051, 1056, 1068, 1073, 1076, 1077, 1081-1083, 1084, 1085, 1087, 1088, 1089, 1099, 1106, 1152, 1154-1155, 1160, 1162, 1166, 1168, 1188, 1205-1206, 1219, 1226, 1229, 1234, 1249-1250, 1257-1258, 1260, 1270, 1273, 1281, 1285, 1288-1289, 1290-1291, 1303, 1313, 1322, 1324, 1339, 1348, 1350, 1428-1429, 1436-1437, 1441, 1445, 1446, 1465, 1475, 1479-1482, 1485-1486, 1491, 1493-1494, 1497, 1498, 1503, 1508-1509, 1510, 1512-1513, 1515, 1516, 1519, 1530, 1531, 1534-1535, 1539, 1557, 1560, 1582, 1586, 1591, 1607-1609, 1611, 1613, 1621, 1641, 1646, 1649-1650, 1661, 1678, 1697, 1708, 1710, 1717, 1725, 1726, 1729, 1741, 1795, 1818, 1821, 183, 1855, 1882, 1894, 1913
Shelby, Sarah 686
Shelby, Sarah A. 668, 683, 711
Sheppard, John 365
Sherry, Clare 287, 388
Sherry, John 287
Shery, Clarissa 691
Shery, John B. 691
Shlimpert, Johanne Sophia 1384
Shoults, Berthena 1521, 1526
Shoults, Eliza 869
Shoults, Eliza B. 535, 577, 584, 586
Shoults (Sholts), Eliza R. 1509, 1743

Shoults (Shoultz), Elizabeth 229, 293, 340
Shoults, Elizabeth R. 1242
Shoults, Emely Jane 499
Shoults, Francis 415, 499
Shoults, Franklin 499
Shoults, J. 775
Shoults (Shults), Jacob 696, 735, 948, 1169, 1239, 1624, 1637, 1730, 1748
Shoults (Shoultz), John 229, 415
Shoults, John Alfred 499
Shoults, John, heirs of 499
Shoults, Joseph 197, 221, 239, 293, 304, 326, 340, 508, 535, 546, 577, 584, 586, 656, 668, 683, 751, 798, 869, 888, 938, 979, 1058, 1141, 1242, 1509, 1511, 1622, 1686, 1721, 1743, 1745
Shoults, Mary 696, 735, 1169
Shoults, Micajah 1521, 1526
Shoults, Sarah 499
Shufford, John 1210
Shull, Samuel 440-441
Shurlds, H. 437
Shurlds, Henry 465, 488, 498, 525
Sides, Elihu 1804
Sides, Eliza 1804
Simms, Felix 1470
Simpleton, W. C. 1151
Simonds, N. 222, 231
Simpson, Joseph 1744
Simpson, Joseph D. 490, 492, 938, 965, 1359, 1460, 1462-1466, 1536, 1592, 1594-1600, 1628, 1631-1632, 1640, 1763, 1856, 1918
Simpson, Mary 1640, 1763
Sims, Anna (Ann) 863, 894
Sims, Felix 862-863, 894
Sipe, Elizabeth 589
Sipe, John 589
Siter, John 1857
Slader, Thomas P. 1149
Slattery, Cornelius M. (C. M., Cornl. M., Corns. M.) 1-4, 15, 23, 26, 31, 34, 44, 48-49, 54-56, 58, 59-61, 63, 65, 66-67, 70-71, 73-78, 84, 86, 89, 93-110, 112, 114, 118-119, 121, 123-127, 132, 139, 141-142, 144, 148-157, 160, 162-163, 165, 167, 168, 170-173, 175, 177-180, 189, 194, 198, 200-203, 207-208, 218, 234-236, 356, 391, 401, 493, 1175
Slattery, Lucretia 218
Slaughter, Evaline 1144
Slaughter, Evaline (Evalina) M. 706, 1232, 1667
Slaughter, James P. 388
Slaughter, Robert P. (R. P.) 705-706, 1024, 1052, 1063, 1140, 1144, 1232, 1319, 1435, 1552-1554, 1667, 1672, 1777, 1784-1785
Smaltz (Smalts), Lewis 1455, 1540
Smaltz (Smalts), Philip 1455, 1540, 1564
Smith, ___ 429, 1297, 1741
Smith, Allen R. 1078
Smith, Bernard (Barnard) 363, 1176

Smith, Eliza Elvira 1216
Smith, Henry C. 268
Smith, James W 185, 489
Smith, Jane 607, 699, 1078
Smith, Jno., reps. 343
Smith, John 38, 64, 226, 231, 699, 739, 1556, 1594, 1690, 1724, 1796
Smith, John Jr. 1548
Smith, John Sr. 80, 86, 235, 240, 568, 1039
Smith, Julius C. 1556
Smith, Julius H. 1548
Smith, Lucinda 185
Smith, Nathaniel B. 1216
Smith, Rachiel 1476
Smith, Reuben (Rubin) 38, 64, 196, 991
Smith, Robert 86, 235
Smith, Samuel 607, 701
Smith, Thomas P. 506
Smoot, Elizabeth 585
Smoot, Mathew 585
Souter, Joseph 1646, 1511
Spalding, Anne 590
Spalding, Bennett 1849
Spalding, Richard Fenwick (F.) 70, 590, 1450, 1470
Spalding, Samuel 505
Spaulding, Louisa 1665
Spaulding (Spalding), Michael 596, 1014, 1665, 1699, 1849
Speer, John W. 1164
Sprigg, J. T. 71
Springer, Charles 1101
Sproede, Frederick (Fredrich, Fredk.) 1252, 1370, 1433, 1467
Sproede, H. C. Bertha 1467
St. Ledger, Joseph de 496
St. Vrain, Savinien (Savinan) 484, 1792
Starnes, Peter 1688
Starr, James 1096, 1336
Stearns, John 845
Steel, James 1644
Steele, James C. 365
Steizle, Johann August 1379
Stemmer, Jacob 1327
Stephens (Stephen), Martin 1244, 1835
Stephenson, Alexander H. 1148
Stephenson, John 871
Stephenson, William 508, 810
Sternes, John 1655
Sterzel, Johann August 1893, 1899
Steuger, David 1039
Stevens, F. M. 465
Stevenson, Elizabeth 915
Stevenson, James M. 915
Stevenson, John L. 915
Stevenson, John, heirs of 915
Stevenson, Margaret A. 915
Stevenson, Sarah Ann 915
Stewart (Steward), Charles 801-802, 808, 843, 890, 898, 932
Stewart (Steward), Mary Jane 801, 898
Stewart, ___ 1058
Stewart, ___ 1224

Stewart, Ann 1797
Stewart, Charles 498, 1155, 1202-1203, 1207-1208, 1241-1242, 1258, 1487, 1709, 1744, 1797, 1878
Stewart, Charles [Jr.] 927
Stewart, Charles [Sr.] 927
Stewart, Charles Sr. 1204, 1309-1310, 1492
Stewart, Charles, heirs of 927, 1744
Stewart, Christeen 927
Stewart, Elizabeth 927
Stewart, Isabella (Isabela, Isabelle) 932, 1086, 1207
Stewart, Isabella (Isabell) T. 899, 909, 1492
Stewart, James 927
Stewart, James E. 1797
Stewart, John 131
Stewart, John Rosamont 1797
Stewart, John W. 51-52, 256
Stewart, Josephine (Josiphean) 927, 1822
Stewart, Lydia (Lidia) 52, 696, 735
Stewart, Margaret 927
Stewart, Mary 927
Stewart, Mary Ann Jane 927
Stewart, Robert C. 883
Stewart, Robert M. C. 625-626, 633, 644-645, 1349
Stewart, Rosamore 927
Stewart, Sally 626, 633
Stewart, Samuel 969
Stewart, Sarah 644, 883, 1349
Stewart, Sarah Ann 927
Stewart, Sipreon 927
Stewart, Thomas 897-899, 905, 909, 927, 932, 945, 954, 1086, 1207, 1226, 1242, 1318, 1337, 1492, 1851, 1874, 1876, 1881
Stewart, William 927
Stokes, George W. 1472
Stone, Enoch G. 1799
Storlin, Johanne Sophia 1386
Strickland (Stricklin), James 731, 942
Strickland (Stricklin), Margaret 942
Stringer, Greenbury Ridgely 211
Stringer, John 211
Strother, George F. 87
Stua_te, Samuel 1652
Stuart, Alexander 226
Stuart, Charles 471, 494, 640, 683
Stuart, David 131
Sturdevant (Studivant), Homer 396, 545
Sturdevant, Zar Sr. 545
Sturdivant, Betsey 424
Sturdivant, George 623, 1151, 1184
Sturdivant, George Washington 317, 424
Sturdivant (Sturdevant), Harriet (Harriatt) 396, 545
Sturdivant, Ira 396
Sturdivant (Sturdevant), Rachel 158, 396, 545
Sturdivant, Washington G. 396
Sturdivant, Zar 158, 396, 906, 1072, 1115, 1218
Sturdivant (Sturdevant), Zar Jr. 396, 545
Sulnier, Edmund 991
Sults, Jacob 1633
Suterer, Susannah 1546
Sutterer (Sudderer, Sutterr), Frederick 773, 1843
Sutterer (Suterer), Joseph 1546, 1864
Sutton, Rachel 29
Sutton, Reubin 29
Swan, Charles 580, 1157, 1776
Swan, Elizabeth J. 1160
Swan, George 1543
Swan (Swann), Henry 665, 1160
Swan, James 1562
Swan, James F. 1569
Swan, John 315-316
Swan, Mary 315-316
Swan, Nancy 1569
Swan (Swann), Richard 581-582, 1569
Swan, Thomas 1543, 1776, 1786
Swank, Anthony (Anton) 1352
Swank, Tresey 1352
Swanwick & Homes 1062
Swanwick, Francis 1323
Swearingen (Sweringen), James T. 1104, 1537, 1644
Sweringen, Martha Jane 1644
Sweringer & Bredell 1060
Swift, Jno. 1634
Talbot, Sarah 519
Talbot, William 519, 1596
Tate, Henry C. C. (H. C. C.) 810, 1012, 1021, 1643, 1657
Tatum, Jacob 882
Taylor, ___ 1487
Taylor, Balbina 807, 973, 1480, 1737
Taylor, Druscilla 1227
Taylor, Eli 1705-1706, 1711, 1720, 1729, 1850
Taylor, George W. 1750, 1827
Taylor, Hannah 620, 757, 808, 842, 978, 1006, 1202, 1306, 1661, 1701, 1707, 1708
Taylor, Hannibal H. 1827
Taylor, Jackson 22, 43, 1107, 1108, 1109, 1892
Taylor, Jackson D. 1827
Taylor, James (Jas.) 374, 457, 560, 624, 646, 650, 730, 828, 836, 851, 884, 1109, 1156, 1703-1704, 1780, 1827, 1892
Taylor, John B. 996-997, 1227, 1243
Taylor, Joseph W. 1705
Taylor, L. 486
Taylor, Levinia 1705
Taylor, Luther 356, 571, 620, 642, 708, 717, 757, 801-802, 808, 842, 978, 1006, 1202, 1246, 1306, 1341, 1441, 1509, 1517, 1519, 1650, 1661, 1701, 1705-1707, 1708-1709, 1711, 1720, 1729, 1850
Taylor, Mary 666, 752, 802, 908, 1011, 1014, 1088, 1441, 1678, 1725
Taylor, Pricilla 997
Taylor, Rachel 560, 884, 1780, 1892
Taylor, Thomas 596, 807, 972-973, 1480, 1737
Taylor, widow 561, 1704
Taylor, William 596, 639, 666, 686, 752, 774, 783, 802, 887, 908, 953, 983, 1011, 1014, 1083, 1088, 1291, 1441, 1678, 1725
Taylor, William W. 296, 1702, 1705
Tendall, Rueben 261
Tenz, Ernest Moritz 1667, 1670, 1672
Tenz, Friedericke Eleonore 1672
Tevis, John C. 1857
Tevis, Joshua 1857
Tharp (Thorp), Ann 155, 758
Tharp (Thorp), Lewis 155, 263, 758, 759-760, 954, 1105, 1583
Theiz, Conrad 1415
Thieme, ___ 1265
Thirth(?), Phillip 1198
Thomas, ___ 227
Thomas, Claiborne S. 128-129, 136, 263
Thomas, David 784
Thomas, Edm. P. 329
Thomas, Eliza Ann 128
Thomas, Frances 128
Thomas, John 1846
Thomas, Judge 248
Thomas, R. S. 2, 6
Thomas, Richard S. 67-68, 120, 128
Thompson, James 169, 355, 364, 442, 1106, 1167, 1185, 1282, 1655
Thompson, John 558-559, 803, 917, 925, 1029
Thompson, John A. 762
Thompson, Louson 1331
Thompson, Mary 559, 803
Thompson, Royal 762, 903, 1031, 1101, 1331, 1914
Thompson, Thomas 997
Thompson, William 1298, 1736
Thompson, William R. 1877
Thorp (see Tharp)
Thurman (Thurmond), Archibald 519, 1596, 1865
Thurman (Thurmond), Elizabeth 519, 1596, 1865-1866
Tiercorot, Gregoire 226
Timon, J. 514
Timon, John 330, 417, 651-653, 680, 1260, 1621, 1894
Timon, John, Rev. 990-991, 994
Tornatore, Jean Baptiste 435
Tornatori, John B. 434
Townsend, John (Jno.) 231, 240, 268, 309, 395, 568, 687, 1200
Tricky, Acy 1806
Tricky, Sally 1806
Trimble, John 716
Trotter, Robert 815, 859, 864, 922-923, 1125, 1138, 1170, 1179, 1193, 1237, 1240
Trudeau, Zeno 1245
Tucker, A. H. 612
Tucker, Allieus 158

Tucker, Andrew H. 240, 348, 788, 906, 1060, 1104, 1115, 1644
Tucker, Andrew Henry 606
Tucker, Ann 355
Tucker, Apolnerius 419, 795
Tucker, Atticus 828, 884, 906, 1072, 1115, 1218, 1496, 1537
Tucker, Austin 1915
Tucker, Charles 1053, 1852
Tucker, Charles J. 419
Tucker, Christina (Christeney) 12, 859, 1645
Tucker, Eleanor 12, 191, 373, 379, 391, 793
Tucker, Elizabeth 654, 674, 1053(2), 1228, 1799, 1911
Tucker, Ellen 606, 788, 906, 1104
Tucker, Francis 12, 20
Tucker, H. 486
Tucker, Henry 73, 85, 171, 394, 538, 606, 1053, 1087, 1170, 1595
Tucker, Henry N. 1712
Tucker, Henry Sr. 612
Tucker, Hillrey 1053
Tucker, Isaiah 401
Tucker, James 12, 35, 48, 187, 1485
Tucker, James F. 526, 899-900, 905, 1226
Tucker, James H. 40-41
Tucker, James Sr. 319, 336, 669
Tucker, James T. 353
Tucker, Joana 1053
Tucker, John 12, 183, 186-187, 269, 359, 373, 668, 1053, 1341
Tucker, John N. 1087, 1136, 1712, 1713, 1714
Tucker, John P. 62, 596, 1530, 1681-1682
Tucker, John Sr. 981-982
Tucker, John T. 966, 1442
Tucker, John W. 859, 1645
Tucker, Joseph 35, 70, 85, 180, 792, 794, 1206, 1247, 1510, 1551
Tucker, Joseph [Jr.] 12, 379, 419
Tucker, Joseph Sr. 12, 20, 35, 48, 61, 186(2), 187, 191, 373, 379, 389, 391(2), 419, 793, 919, 1240, 1658
Tucker, Joseph Sr., heirs of 795
Tucker, Josephus (Josephius) 190, 355, 364, 788, 1104, 1115, 1237, 1282, 1603, 1628, 1640, 1644, 1733-1734, 1852
Tucker, Josephus Sr. 1747
Tucker, Leander 1053, 1482, 1713-1714, 1852
Tucker, Lewis 215, 1053
Tucker, Maria 419
Tucker, Mary 12, 361, 389, 419, 500, 794, 951, 966, 1053, 1136, 1192, 1226, 1614, 1677
Tucker, Mary Ann (Maryan) 194, 900, 1305, 1739
Tucker, Michael 27, 212, 598, 965, 1025, 1053, 1087, 1135-1136, 1139, 1180, 1250, 1287, 1348, 1628, 1712
Tucker, Mr. 70
Tucker, N. B. 80

Tucker, Nancey 1115, 1237
Tucker, Nancy C. 1747
Tucker, Nicholas 12, 35, 70, 110, 187, 190, 194, 379, 794, 1240, 1510, 1640, 1852
Tucker, Nicholas P. 782
Tucker, Nicholas Sr. 1053, 1136, 1192, 1277, 1712, 1714
Tucker, Nicholas Sr., heirs of 1053
Tucker, Nicholas, heirs of 1087, 1603
Tucker, Peter 12, 15, 20, 228, 1287, 1468
Tucker, Peter J. 379, 389, 419, 674, 909, 950-951, 1001, 1086, 1207, 1226, 1240, 1304-1305, 1318, 1337, 1614, 1677
Tucker, Peter P. 361, 800, 1739
Tucker, Peter Sr. 654, 674, 1053, 1228, 1250, 1348, 1627, 1740, 1911
Tucker, Peter T. 191
Tucker, Phoebe 1505
Tucker, Ralphael 186-187
Tucker, Sarah (Sary) 12(2), 20, 170, 182, 354, 401, 596, 684-685, 782, 1175, 1499, 1682
Tucker, Sarah Ann (Sarahann) 419, 1206
Tucker, Sarah W. 1458
Tucker, Stephen 636, 1053, 1170, 1341, 1595
Tucker, Susannah (Susanah) 12, 447
Tucker, Thomas 12, 60, 63, 161, 186, 373, 391-392, 408, 446-447
Tucker, Thomas J. (Thos. J.) 532, 546, 593, 1458, 1499, 1504, 1733-1734, 1747
Tucker, Treacey (Tarecy, Treasy) 12, 35, 48, 1852
Tucker, William 12, 17, 31, 109, 170, 182, 354, 544, 684-685, 1175, 1617, 1730
Tucker, William J. 1799
Tuland, Jno. 624
Turine, Etienne 1270
Tuttle, Margaret 132, 259
Uhlich, Frederick H. 1919
Uhlig (Uhlich), Frederick August 1895, 1898, 1900, 1902
Uhlig, August 1181
Uhlig, Christian Frederick 1390
Underhiner (Underiner), Joseph 998, 999
Underwood, James 176
Underwood, Jemerson(?) 176
Underwood, Thomas 176
United States of America 166, 174, 233, 341, 437, 443, 446, 462, 488, 510, 512-513, 515, 792, 848, 995, 1040-1043, 1049-1050, 1110, 1116-1120, 1135, 1139, 1251, 1266, 1268-1269, 1278, 1293, 1326, 1450-1451, 1474, 1490, 1681
Valie, Charles C. 218
Vallars, Anthony 1324
Valle, Catharine 985, 1217
Valle, Celeste 985
Valle, Charles 714

Valle, Charles C. 6, 126, 203, 367, 402, 709, 829, 985, 1559
Valle, Emilie 28, 985
Valle, Felix 787, 1856, 1857
Valle, Fivis 6
Valle (Valley, Valli), Francis 28, 116, 126, 538, 634, 1618
Valle, Francis [Jr.] 1618
Valle, Francis, heirs of 1559, 1860
Valle, Francois 1217
Valle, Francois Jr. 985
Valle, Francois Sr., heirs of 985
Valle, Frans. (Frs.) 394, 403
Valle, John Bate. (Bte., B.) 33, 550, 787, 1217
Valle, Julia 985
Valle, Louis 787
Valle, Marie 774-775
Valle, Mary 985
Valle, Melanie (Milanie) 367, 402, 709, 714
Valle, Odile 787
Vallee, John Bte. 1559
Valli, Frois 116
Van Buren, A. 972, 1135, 1139, 1251, 1266, 1268-1269, 1451, 1681
Van Buren, M. 1049-1050
Van Buren, Martin (M.) 972, 995, 1041-1043, 1049-1050, 1135, 1139, 1251, 1266, 1268-1269, 1450-1451, 1474(2), 1681
Van Buren, Martin [Jr.] 1041-1043
van Dorin, John (J.) Livingston 1209, 1359
Vanburkelos, ___ 351
Vanhorn (Vanhorne), Nathan 1148, 1846
Vash, R. E. 483
Venable, Charles 870, 1090
Venable, John 870
Venners, Morrits 1907
Vesells, Marier 685
Vessels (Vessells), Hillary 789-790, 1000
Vessels (Vessells), Monica 790, 1000
Vessels, Catharine 1000, 1506, 1836
Vessels, Charles 409, 632, 1342, 1617
Vessels, Charles, heirs of 738, 1000, 1055, 1080
Vessels, Clement 1000, 1506, 1836
Vessels (Vessells), George (Geo.) 617, 1489, 1570, 1873, 1877
Vessels, George M. 1080
Vessels, Isabella 1055
Vessels, Mary 1080
Vessels, Precilla 1055
Vessels, Rosella 1617
Vistler (Weistler), Henry 1557
Vistler, Mary 1557
Voelker, Christiana Johana 1752, 1753
Voelker, Christiane 1193
Voelker, Ernst Henry 1752
Voelker, Henry 1193
Voelker, Louise 1423
Voelker, Sophia Dorothea Amelia 1752-1753

Vollant, A. 1298
Volz (Folts, Fulse, Fultz), Joseph 374, 1094, 1095, 1880
Volz (Fultz), Helanna B. 1094
Vonderheide, Henry Casper 1536
Vonderlick, Gotlieb 1124
Wade, Isaac 624
Wadsworth, James 1696, 1742
Wadsworth, Rebecca 1696
Wadsworth, Seburn 1696
Wagner, Martin 1073
Walker, Addison (Adison) 547, 858
Walker, Elizabeth 1290
Walker, Jesse R. 910, 1290
Walker, Mary 548
Walker, Maryann 1099
Walker, Osbirn W. 1691, 1696, 1749, 1914
Walker, Rufus (Ruffus) 978, 980, 1487
Walker, W. 1687
Walker, William (Wm.) A. 1099, 1487
Walker, William Addison 548
Walsh, E. 611
Walsh, Edward (Edw.) 149, 151, 419, 608, 970, 971, 1018, 1224, 1462, 1518, 1744
Walsh, Isabelle 1518
Walsh, J. 611
Walsh, J. & E. & Co. 1138
Walsh, Jas. B. 1647
Walsh, John 608, 970, 971, 1018, 1224, 1462, 1518
Walsh, John & Edward & Co. 1462
Walsh, T. 118
Walter, James 944
Walter, Michael Sigmund 1414
Warren, Elizabeth 516, 1607
Warren, Michael 17
Warren, William Y. K. 1607
Warthen, Elizabeth 1167
Wash, Robert 226
Water, Joab Jr. 249
Waters, ___ 272
Waters, D. C. 1522
Waters, David C. 1212, 1884
Waters, Elizabeth 1212
Waters, Henry G. 351
Waters (Watters), James L. 132, 1212
Waters, Joab 170, 175, 186-187, 200, 208, 251, 261, 265, 272-273, 281, 306, 333, 338, 344, 370, 372, 439, 658, 676, 715, 1175-1176
Waters, Joab [Sr.] 249
Waters, Joab Jr. 89, 351
Waters, Joab Sr. 54, 89, 160, 165, 181, 225, 345, 351, 401, 643
Waters, Joab, heirs of 1212
Waters, John 351, 756
Waters, Maj. 1039
Waters, Margaret 1212
Waters, Polly Ann 261
Waters, Polly Ann Elizabeth 132, 351
Waters, Richard J. 1212
Wathen, Juliana 417, 599, 1235, 1260

Watkins & Davis 1728
Watkins, David 360
Watkins, Mary 1876
Watkins, Nathaniel W. 1728
Watson, John C. 944
Watson, Joseph B. 1135, 1451
Watters, Robert 1212
Watters, Theodore 1212
Watts, Rebeca 1092
Watts, W. G. 1264
Watts, William 1092
Watts, William T. 718
Weber, Francis L. 1888
Weber, Maria D. 1405
Weindhalf, John Henrich 1181
Welker, Andrew 1798, 1908
Welker, Anna Clara 410-411, 1798
Welker, Clara 497
Welker, Daniel 678-679, 1913
Welker, David 312, 896
Welker, Eli 1527
Welker, George 443-444
Welker, Henry 312, 400, 501
Welker, Jacob 1908
Welker, John 501-502, 896, 1096
Welker, Mary 896
Welker, Rebecca 1913
Welker, William 896, 1798, 1908
Wells, Hugh 491, 631, 851, 970-971, 1018-1019, 1052, 1147, 1156, 1209, 1217-1224, 1424, 1460, 1550, 1764
West, Britten 85
Wheeler, Griswold W. (G. W.) 1314, 1727, 1834
Whitaker, Hardy H. 673
White, M. 1198
White, Mary 862, 1284
White, William H. 1284, 1313
White, William Henry 862-863
Whiteaker, John 672
Whitingberg, Rene 485
Whitledge, Francis 1343
Whitledge, John 415, 1343
Whitledge, Lyna Harrison 1343
Whitledge, William 229
Whitledge, William F. 415
Whittenburg, Irenius (Irenus, James) 638, 655, 702, 766, 947
Whitworth, Isaac 974
Whitworth, Isaac G. 1131, 1481, 1519, 1531, 1591, 1618, 1721, 1758-1760, 1858
Whybark, John C. 1660
Wiggins, Levi 231
Wilcox, James 1109
Wilhelm, Catharine 1615
Wilhelm, John 973, 1491, 1615
Wilkinson, ___ 820, 822
Wilkinson, Emilie (Emaly) 218, 985, 1481
Wilkinson, Emilie L. 1754
Wilkinson, F. 1138
Wilkinson, Francis 1862
Wilkinson, Francis H. 1064, 1879

Wilkinson, J. J. 181
Wilkinson, John 695, 1762
Wilkinson, Joseph P. 922
Wilkinson, Julia M. 1879
Wilkinson, Thomas 695, 1762
Wilkinson, W. 60, 113, 197, 225, 240, 253, 259, 260, 279-280, 286, 299, 303, 306, 325, 327, 334-335, 355, 367, 371, 433, 455, 663, 793, 829
Wilkinson, Walter 6, 28-29, 59, 139, 181, 201-203, 218, 282, 396, 730, 985, 1066, 1082, 1350
Wilkinson, Walter B. (W. B.) 625, 970, 1030, 1071, 1267, 1302, 1341, 1436, 1476, 1478, 1481, 1671, 1754, 1862
Wilkinson, Walter Bernard 457
Williams, Andrew 1298
Williams, Benjamin 1240
Williams, Caleb 208
Williams, John 77, 310, 944
Williams, Theophilus (Theofiles) 371, 393, 429, 489, 530, 602, 1101
Williams, Thomas 1034
Willis, Ths. 847
Willis, Wiley 1253
Wilson, Benjamin 130, 189, 247, 530, 533, 571, 582, 639, 640-642, 708, 717, 1203, 1707, 1709
Wilson, Elizabeth 1100
Wilson, Elizabeth J. 1562
Wilson, James B. 1846
Wilson, James S. 1268-1269
Wilson, Jane 582, 717, 1203
Wilson, John M. 847
Wilson, Joseph S. (Jos. S.) 972, 995, 1041-1043, 1049-1050, 1266, 1474, 1681
Wilson, M. C. 1776
Wilson, Margaret A. 530
Wilson, Merritt (Merit) C. 1562, 1786
Wilson, Pertelus 817, 1100, 1183, 1186
Wilson, Rachel 581, 690
Wilson, Robert 499, 518, 530, 581, 690, 941, 1816
Wilson, T. 1078
Wilson, Thomas 127
Wimsatt, Elenor 834
Wimsatt (Wimsett), James 311, 676, 834, 1323
Wimsatt (Wimsett), Joseph Z. 358-359, 1589
Wimsatt, Joseph Z., heirs of 311
Wimsatt, Joseph Zachariah 34, 97, 123, 155
Wimsatt, Mary 311, 357, 359, 676
Wimsatt (Wimsett), Robert 123, 311, 357, 676, 834
Wimsatt, Susanna 834
Wimsett, Stephen 1826
Winebark, John C. 1721
Winfield, Anselm 1881
Winfield, Elenor (Eleoner) 286, 318, 360, 505

Winfield (Windfield), Helen 549, 758-760, 880, 893, 1239, 1483, 1768
Winfield, James 236-237, 342
Winfield (Windfield), Jonas (Jona) 286, 318, 360, 505, 1168
Winfield, Jones 950
Winfield (Windfield), William 505, 549, 758-760, 880, 893, 904, 954, 1239, 1483, 1620, 1757, 1768, 1904
Winkler, Ignatius 704, 740
Winkler, Joseph 1880, 1885, 1886
Winkler, Roceaner 1880
Winkler, Stephen 1128, 1886
Winkler, Therese 1886
Wiseman, Joseph R. 534
Wiseman, Joseph V. 999
Wittenberg, Commissioners of 1142
Wittenberg, Trustees of 1430, 1438, 1552-1554, Trustees of 1905
Wittler, John Diedrich 1895
Wonderlich, Johann Carl 1407
Woodruff, William B. (W. B.) 403, 606, 612-613, 906
Woods, Christy & Co. 1604
Woods, James 1604
Woods, James A. 1576
Woods (Wood), Robert 618, 1604
Woolford, Frederick 308, 436, 451
Woolford, John 636, 864
Worth, William 1693
Wright, James W. 442
Wright (Write), Rebecca (Rebeca) 892, 1489, 1877
Wright, T. 144
Wright, Thomas 47, 122
Wunderlich, ___ 1265
Wurkworth, C. H. 1895
Wurmb, Johanne von 1693
Wurmb, Maria von 1265
Wurmb, Mrs. von 1265
Wurmb, Sarah von 1265
Wurmb, Theobald von 1265
Yaeger, Adolph 1630
Yaeger -- see Jaeger
Yarber, Nelson 1687
Yarber, Sally 1687
Yarborough, Nelson 1098
Young, Brice 495, 1724
Young, David B. 122
Young, Elizabeth 1785
Young, Harrison 189, 207, 209-210, 254, 287, 386-388, 1784, 1785
Young, Harrison, heirs of 1024, 1063, 1157
Young, Jefferson 1785
Young, Nancey 1724
Young, Sarah 1052, 1140, 1144, 1157, 1785
Young, Sylvester 1782, 1806
Zacher, Ernst William 1671
Zeibig, Carl Gottleib 1371, 1694
Zeigler (Ziegler), Francis J. 878, 1165, 1459, 1600, 1731
Zeigler, Ann 1731

Zeigler, Conrad 911
Zeigler (Ziegler), Conrad C. (C. C.) 1060, 1104, 1224, 1507, 1644, 1829
Zeigler, Elvina C. 1507

Perry County Deed Abstracts – Location Index

__, Madison Co. 1806
AL, Lauderdale Co. 1032
AR, Arkansas Co. 1472
AR, Hempstead Co. 1216
AR, Pulaski Co. 888
Arkansas 1476
Army, U. S. 819
Bank, Branch of Missouri 66, 87, 1881
Barrens, The 121, 264, 377, 1585, 1603
Barriere des Noyers, St. Louis Co., MO 226
Bay de Roy, Lincoln Co., MO 226
Bottom, Bois Brule (Bobruly, Boisbrula, Bois Brulla, Bois Brulle, Boyee Rule, Brul's) 18-19, 22, 29, 32, 43, 53, 55, 57-59, 66-69, 77-78, 80, 86, 90, 122, 128-129, 131, 133, 137-138, 181, 200, 255, 261, 265, 269, 272-273, 277-279, 281-282, 306, 320, 329, 339, 344, 346-347, 351-352, 382, 399, 418, 422, 424, 427, 457, 474-477, 483, 506-507, 517, 519, 560-563, 567-570, 585, 588, 604, 608, 615, 617, 623, 627, 633, 643-645, 667, 694, 697, 730, 766, 788, 803-805, 811, 816, 824, 828, 831-832, 835, 845, 853, 873-874, 879, 884-885, 889, 892, 911, 913, 939, 946-948, 969, 1007, 1039, 1060, 1104, 1106-1109, 1115, 1127, 1151, 1169, 1184, 1189-1190, 1195, 1212, 1221, 1238, 1297, 1299, 1355-1356, 1432, 1462, 1476, 1489, 1496, 1532, 1537, 1541, 1566, 1574, 1579, 1594, 1610-1611, 1644, 1652-1653, 1674, 1690, 1692, 1704, 1724, 1747, 1837
Bottom, Brazeau (Brazo) 254, 1157, 1534-1535, 1785
Bottom, Mississippi 386-387, 767, 1052, 1140, 1144
Bottom, Rush 1561, 1884
Branch, Joseph Tuckers Spring 175
Branch, Rock Spring 923, 1544, 1588
Cahla 1265
Calumet, Pike Co., MO 226
Church, Lutheran 1362, 1383, 1392, 1484
Church, Methodist Episcopal 486, 1344
Church, Pleasant Grove Baptist 1311, 1910
Church, Presbyterian of Brazo 518
Church, St. Josephs 1235
Claim, Menard 1444
Claim, Pierre Menard 1890
College, Lutheran 1181
Congregation, German Lutheran 1430, 1438
Connecticut 226

Convent of St. Joseph 511
Convent, Bethlehem 330, 417, 510-513, 1235
Convent, St. Michaels, Madison Co., MO 511
Court, Cape Girardeau Co. Circuit 1324
Court, Circuit 1-2, 74, 142, 163, 168, 235, 241, 254, 264, 291, 308, 338, 345, 385, 405, 439, 499, 530, 532, 551, 567, 575, 578, 592-593, 617, 696, 735, 767-769, 780, 851, 915-917, 970-971, 1015, 1018-1019, 1039, 1106, 1156-1157, 1217-1224, 1424, 1460-1466, 1469, 1483, 1493, 1499, 1560, 1592, 1594-1600, 1631-1632, 1636, 1673-1674, 1764, 1832, 1854, 1856-1860, 1862-1864, 1887
Court, Circuit in Chancery 600-601, 822, 1142, 1208, 1262-1263, 1360-1400-1423, 1583
Court, Circuit of Washington Co., Mo. 1147
Court, County 3-4, 7-9, 346-347, 356, 475, 527, 599, 831, 902, 904, 939, 1028, 1038, 1090, 1127, 1160, 1212, 1271, 1274, 1276, 1342, 1353, 1460, 1494, 1494, 1541-1542, 1548, 1610, 1643
Court, Lincoln Co. Circuit in Chancery 226
Court, Lousiana 4th District 1034
Court, Missouri Supreme 64
Court, Scott Co., Mo. 448
Court, St. Francois Co. Circuit 1209, 1359
Court, Ste. Genevieve Co. 982
Court, Ste. Genevieve Co. Circuit 54, 148, 242
Creek, Apple 1439
Creek, Apple 54, 72, 81-83, 92, 118, 120, 140, 159, 163, 214, 222, 231, 241, 312, 318, 369, 415, 459, 478, 484, 511, 589, 619, 624, 629, 646-647, 700, 740, 771, 777, 785, 851, 852, 950, 1015, 1061, 1148, 1209, 1304, 1354, 1439, 1806, 1854, 1867, 1890
Creek, Apple, north fork 713
Creek, Bennets 351
Creek, Bobs, Lincoln Co., MO 226
Creek, Bois Brule (Boisbruley, Bosprule) 272-273, 314, 397, 544, 658-659, 687, 815, 1007, 1127, 1176, 1200, 1238, 1859
Creek, Brazeau (Braseau, Brasoe, Brazaw, Braze, Brazoe, Brazo, Brazou, Obrasaw, Obraso, Obrazeau, Obraso, Obrazo, Obrzoe) 12, 16, 20, 38, 49-50, 60, 64, 74, 166, 185-186, 195-196, 209, 218, 224, 231, 290-

291, 298, 305, 315, 371, 373, 391, 393, 402, 404-405, 408, 430, 435, 489, 530, 731, 767, 915, 942, 990, 992, 994, 1002, 1065, 1142, 1230, 1360-1361, 1430, 1438, 1514, 1806, 1872
Creek, Campsters 588
Creek, Cape Cinque Hommes 1468, 1697
Creek, Cinque Hommes (Cape Cinque Hommes) 68, 87, 125, 147-148, 164, 222, 262, 266, 464, 469, 483, 765, 982, 984, 1582, 1585, 1603
Creek, Costerd (Custerds) 326, 350
Creek, Indian 161, 337, 365-366, 398, 566, 628, 710, 998
Creek, McClanahans (McClenahans, McChlanehans) 42, 51-52, 147, 169, 205, 397, 765, 1059, 1167, 1185
Creek, McClanahans, south fork 26
Creek, Meat 478
Creek, Omete (Au Mete River, Meete River) 1008, 1507
Creek, Ramseys, Pike Co., MO 226
Creek, Saline 116, 175, 191, 212, 222, 238, 244, 269, 283, 326, 350, 445, 634, 651, 653, 669, 674, 709, 829, 951, 985, 988, 1025, 1170, 1228, 1287, 1320, 1466, 1612
Creek, Saline, Cedar Fork of 73, 1595
Creek, Saline, south fork 27, 85, 110, 198, 223, 228, 293, 363, 367, 394, 403, 490, 492, 503, 538, 606, 612-613, 714, 919, 938, 965, 1245
Creek, Saline, west fork 598
Creek, Silver 208
Creek, St. Laurent (Laurant, Lorent, Louret) 71, 158, 184, 231, 545, 723, 849, 883, 906, 1072, 1218
Creek, St. Lero 1618
Devils Oven 253
District, Ste. Genevieve 24, 85, 109, 442
Eicherberg 1265
Falls of the Big Rocks 170
Flat, Poplar 406, 1581
Fork, Cedar 73, 1170
Fork, Cedar of Saline Creek 1595
Fork, Thompsons 169, 1167, 1185
Fund, Road and Canal 921, 1587
Georgia 1806
Hotel, Planters (New Orleans) 1354
IA, Dubuque Co. 1579, 1819
IL, Brownsville 483, 672-673, 830
IL, Chester 625, 730, 816
IL, Jackson Co. 344, 484, 494, 607, 647, 672-673, 700, 719-720, 722, 830, 1057, 1183, 1215, 1444, 1555, 1783
IL, Kaskaskia 484, 672-673, 946, 1216
IL, Montgomery Co. 1801

Illinois 193, 1216, 1354
IN, Albany 519
IN, Floyd Co. 519
Indiana 131
Island, Cape Cinque Hommes 131, 819, 1183
Island, Horse 32, 521, 626, 816, 939, 1039, 1259
Island, Sandy 777, 852
Island, Tower 1890
Island, Township 1013
Isle, Town 1354
Kentucky 131, 1039
Kleinentrsdorf(?) 1265
KY, Barren Co. 1431
KY, Bourbon Co. 506
KY, Campbell Co. 393, 436
KY, Christian Co. 115
KY, Clarke Co. 122
KY, Henry Co. 329
KY, Hickman Co. 1283
KY, Jefferson Co. 1299
KY, Lexington 134
KY, Livingston Co. 847
KY, Louisville 1299
KY, Madison Co. 208
KY, Marion Co. 505
KY, Mason Co. 506
KY, Nicholas Co. 329
KY, Scott Co. 391
KY, Washington Co. 41, 110, 186, 198
KY, Woodford Co. 392
LA, Avoyelles Parish 1078
LA, Catahoula Parish 145
LA, East Baton Rouge Parish 1033-1034
LA, Iberville Parish 990
LA, Jefferson Parish 1354
LA, Lafayette Parish 352
LA, New Orleans 195, 211, 812, 953, 1039, 1111, 1252, 1254, 1298, 1354, 1433, 1477, 1637, 1730, 1748
LA, New Orleans Parish 195
LA, Pointe Coupee Parish 969, 1652
LA, St. James Parish 196
LA, St. Landry Parish 18-19
LA, Upper 1245
LA, West Baton Rouge Parish 1034, 1198
Lake, Newsoms 272-273
Land, seminary 855
Landing, Baleys 944
Landing, Pratte's 1618
Landing, St. Marys 436, 451, 476, 694, 697, 879, 883, 913
Landing, Watters 1318
Louisiana 892, 1783, 1806
Louisiana, Upper 1039, 1603
MD, Frederick Co. 351
Mill 636, 1170
Mill Gregoires 503
Mill on Bois Brule Creek 544
Mill, Bishops 435
Mill, Logans 593

Mill, Noell's and Tate's 1643
Mill, steam saw 851
Mill, Tuckers 283
Mills, Brown & Valles 367
Mississippi 812
Missouri 1-11, 24, 44, 46, 49, 55, 71, 160, 222, 242, 244, 252, 262, 285, 305, 321, 323, 345, 383-384, 437, 465, 488, 498, 593, 791, 882, 1033, 1191, 1504, 1558, 1600
MO, Altenburg 1362
MO, Dresden 1362, 1368
MO, Neideifrohne 1362
MO, Selitz 1362
MO, Wittenberg 1362
MO, Altenburg 1265, 1325
MO, Altenburg
Lot No. 2 1406
Lot No. 3 1406
Lot No. 4 1421
Lot No. 5 1416
Lot No. 6 1415
Lot No. 7 1415
Lot No. 8 1415
Lot No. 9 1410
Lot No. 11 1392
Lot No. 12 1392
Lot No. 13 1416
Lot No. 14 1416
Lot No. 15 1417
Lot No. 16 1406, 1417
Lot No. 17 1418
Lot No. 19 1418
Lot No. 20 1419
Lot No. 21 1417
Lot No. 22 1421
Lot No. 23 1420
Lot No. 24 1421
Lot No. 25 1421
Lot No. 26 1421
Lot No. 27 1394
Lot No. 28 1406
Lot No. 29 1403
Lot No. 30 1421
Lot No. 31 1411
Lot No. 32 1413
Lot No. 33 1412
Lot No. 34 1414
Lot No. 35 1414
Lot No. 36 1396, 1421
Lot No. 37 1395
Lot No. 38 1395
Lot No. 39 1403
Lot No. 40 1403
MO, Benton 707, 732
MO, Birmingham 777-778, 1111, 1426, 1890
MO, Birmingham
Block No. 4, Lot No. 7 1426, 1890
Block No. 4, Lot No. 8 1426, 1890
Block No. 8, Lot No. 1 959, 1890
Block No. 8, Lot No. 2 959, 1890
Block No. 8, Lot No. 18 1113, 1890
Block No. 10 771, 1663

Block No. 11 772
Block No. 12 1597
Block No. 12, Lot No. 9 1111, 1890
Block No. 12, Lot No. 10 1111, 1890
Block No. 12, Lot No. 11 1111, 1890
Block No. 12, Lot No. 15 961, 963, 1890
Block No. 12, Lot No. 16 961, 963, 1890
Block No. 12, Lot No. 17 960, 1252-1254
Block No. 12, Lot No. 24 1112
Block No. 24, Lot No. 12 1890
Block No. 24, Lot No. 13 958, 1214
Block No. 24, Lot No. 14 958, 1214
Block No. 25 957
Block No. 25, Lot No. 17 1597
MO, Bois Brule 585, 694, 697, 865
MO, Brazeau 998
MO, Cape Girardeau 820
MO, Cape Girardeau Co. 30, 36, 67, 119-120, 128-130, 136, 138, 176, 188-189, 197, 208, 229, 263, 317, 337, 382, 414, 453, 458, 468, 473, 485, 533, 558, 562, 573, 615, 621, 623, 628, 634-635, 639, 648-649, 664, 699, 705-706, 708, 717, 739-740, 762, 822, 824-827, 836, 852, 861, 878, 903, 948, 1031, 1128, 1148, 1156, 1162, 1194, 1203, 1212, 1292, 1324, 1331, 1354, 1356, 1439, 1463, 1484, 1547, 1576, 1660, 1690, 1728, 1760, 1867, 1890-1891, 1896, 1901, 1906, 1914
MO, Chariton Co. 333
MO, Cinque Hommes 483
MO, Crawford Co. 1644
MO, Desden 1265
MO, Frohna 1181
MO, Jackson 1867, 1881
MO, Jefferson City 231, 284, 693
MO, Jefferson Co. 204, 226, 459, 1599
MO, Lincoln Co. 226
MO, Madison Co. 113, 322, 511, 550, 1685
MO, Marion Co. 855, 1002
MO, Paitzdorf 1265
MO, Perry Co. 5-6, 61, 160, 225, 330, 522, 549, 712, 790, 841, 911, 921, 1097, 1236, 1460, 1493-1494, 1541, 1587, 1611, 1745, 1814, 1818, 1855, 1868-1869
MO, Perryville 130, 257, 264, 324-325, 571, 620, 639-641, 668, 683, 686, 708, 715, 751, 783, 801-802, 808, 842, 885, 890-891, 945, 949, 978, 980, 1058, 1071, 1073, 1155, 1160, 1203, 1205, 1224, 1242, 1318, 1487, 1534-1535, 1701, 1707, 1709, 1711, 1720-1721
MO, Perryville
Lot No. 3 108, 124, 157, 412
Lot No. 4 303
Lot No. 5 178, 504, 1191

Lot No. 6 167, 178, 335
Lot No. 7 472, 532, 611, 970, 1481, 1707-1708, 1759
Lot No. 8 162, 380, 532, 611, 971, 1518, 1708
Lot No. 9 95, 302, 368, 682, 755, 875, 890-891, 895, 1058, 1134, 1224, 1708
Lot No. 10 103, 192, 216, 221, 340, 413, 431, 456, 471, 869, 1511, 1744
Lot No. 11 99, 156, 192, 216, 221, 340, 413, 431, 456, 471, 1744
Lot No. 12 96, 239, 340, 413, 431, 456, 471, 1202, 1709, 1845
Lot No. 13 102, 192, 216, 221, 465, 531, 1448, 1845
Lot No. 14 179, 1178
Lot No. 15 102, 192, 216
Lot No. 16 465, 493-494, 498, 531, 898, 932, 1339, 1698
Lot No. 17 236-237, 342, 547-548, 1487
Lot No. 18 180, 698
Lot No. 19 162, 531, 693, 699, 1448
Lot No. 20 531, 739, 1448, 1548, 1556, 1591, 1618, 1744, 1863
Lot No. 21 260, 420, 1591, 1618, 1857
Lot No. 22 178, 375, 610, 1591, 1618, 1857
Lot No. 23 728
Lot No. 24 153-154, 465, 486
Lot No. 25 108
Lot No. 26 108, 179
Lot No. 27 96, 230, 509, 531-532, 611, 1018, 1517, 1707
Lot No. 28 172, 1246, 1707
Lot No. 29 234, 531, 1448
Lot No. 30 180, 1744
Lot No. 31 162, 542, 1141, 1294
Lot No. 32 179, 295, 420, 1531, 1591, 1618, 1758, 1858
Lot No. 33 95, 302, 307
Lot No. 34 104, 523-524, 689, 711-712, 748-750, 754, 952, 1012, 1487
Lot No. 35 178, 334, 399, 575, 578, 793
Lot No. 36 180, 793, 1332
Lot No. 37 180, 1771
Lot No. 38 661, 681
Lot No. 39 663
Lot No. 40 171, 1504
Lot No. 41 528, 725-726, 737, 1487
Lot No. 42 98, 465, 657, 1222, 1842, 1844
Lot No. 43 97, 311, 465, 1222, 1840
Lot No. 44 331-332, 349, 460, 1756
Lot No. 45 837-838, 1005
Lot No. 46 152, 1222
Lot No. 47 177, 465, 1821
Lot No. 48 303-304
Lot No. 49 100, 232, 301, 333
Lot No. 50 149, 531, 1702, 1705
Lot No. 51 149, 296, 1705

Lot No. 52 234, 356, 1707
Lot No. 53 219
Lot No. 54 455, 677, 688
Lot No. 55 433, 1846
Lot No. 56 93, 333, 433, 1846
Lot No. 57 280, 508, 535, 577, 584, 586, 656, 798, 956, 979, 1035, 1509, 1661
Lot No. 58 104, 313, 888, 1207, 1242, 1509, 1661, 1743, 1746
Lot No. 59 152, 937
Lot No. 60 299-300, 460
Lot No. 61 101, 724, 866, 1795
Lot No. 62 101, 724, 866
Lot No. 63 94, 423, 541, 774, 908, 910, 1084-1085, 1097, 1219, 1290-1291, 1351, 1678, 1725
Lot No. 64 150, 1459, 1600, 1731
Lot No. 65 177, 465, 1473
Lot No. 66 179, 813, 1178, 1613
Lot No. 67 857, 1249, 1314
Lot No. 68 151, 440-441, 579, 858, 1099, 1487
Lot No. 69 246, 325, 454, 677
Lot No. 71 219
Lot No. 72 219, 1129-1130, 1627, 1755
Lot No. 73 533, 717, 757, 837, 1519, 1758
Lot No. 74 533, 717, 837, 1006, 1591, 1618
Lot No. 75 465, 729, 1751
Lot No. 76 605, 1046, 1726-1727
Lot No. 77 179, 605, 1046, 1337, 1677
Lot No. 78 179, 605, 1046, 1288-1289, 1292, 1508, 1721-1722
Lot No. 80 663
Lot No. 81 1028, 1030, 1350
Lot No. 82 1066-1067, 1817
Lot No. 83 837, 1027
Lot No. 84 219
Lot No. 85 1066-1067, 1071, 1350
Lot No. 86 179, 605, 1046, 1700, 1721
Lot No. 87 425, 661, 974, 1760
Lot No. 88 425, 661, 974, 1760, 1845
Lot No. 89 1129-1131, 1760
Lot No. 91 425, 661, 1010
Lot No. 92 425, 661, 976
Lot No. 93 425, 661, 975, 1536
Lot No. 94 149
Lot No. 95 663, 1276
Lot No. 96 179, 605, 1046, 1273, 1487
Lot No. 97 179, 605, 1046
Lot No. 99 663, 1271-1272, 1487
Taylor & Faina's addition 808
Taylor & Faina's Addition, Lot No. 1 1487
Taylor & Faina's Addition, Lot No. 2 1487
Taylor & Faina's Addition, Lot No. 3 1487

Taylor & Faina's Addition, Lot No. 5 1708
Taylor & Faina's Addition, Lot No. 6 1708
MO, Pike Co. 226, 508, 810
MO, Port Perry 1500
MO, Potosi, Lot No. 54 226
MO, Potosi, Lot No. 68 226
MO, Potosi, Lot No. 104 226
MO, Saline Co. 1033
MO, Scott Co. 91, 112, 707, 732, 769, 1039, 1690
MO, Shannon Co. 1593
MO, St. Charles 226, 1487
MO, St. Charles Co. 226
MO, St. Francis Co. 185, 427, 489, 507, 1359, 1653, 1788
MO, St. Louis 2, 4, 38, 87, 195-196, 226, 324, 421, 457, 483, 608, 611, 647, 700, 787-788, 812, 962, 993, 1013, 1138, 1265, 1298, 1518, 1584, 1593, 1602, 1618, 1647, 1659, 1808, 1817, 1884
MO, St. Louis Co. 38, 80, 161, 211, 226, 288, 419, 624, 646, 770, 795, 816, 851-852, 872, 971, 992, 1002, 1164, 1537, 1644, 1693, 1744, 1817, 1830
MO, Ste. Genevieve 30, 68-69, 126, 226, 1559, 1792
MO, Ste. Genevieve Co. 12-13, 16, 18-20, 32, 33, 38, 59, 64, 66, 71, 76-80, 86-87, 90, 115-116, 131, 133, 143, 184, 201, 212-214, 224, 253, 277-279, 308, 346, 368, 371, 393, 402, 418, 421-422, 436, 451, 454-455, 457, 477-478, 537, 550, 561, 568-570, 588, 594-595, 612, 634, 643, 669-670, 677, 687, 691, 709, 787-788, 843, 872, 874, 911, 985, 991-992, 1004, 1039, 1104, 1107-1108, 1143, 1200, 1245, 1341, 1346-1347, 1427, 1429, 1436, 1449, 1476, 1496, 1507, 1537, 1545, 1575, 1618, 1639, 1691, 1729, 1792, 1796, 1829, 1849, 1860, 1873, 1889
MO, Ste. Genevieve Co., Saline Township 788
MO, Washington Co. 13, 315-316, 320, 422, 448, 461, 588, 608, 693, 698, 716, 981, 1020, 1101, 1618
MO, Wittenburg 1142, 1159
MO, Wittenburg
  Lot No. 30 1553, 1667
  Lot No. 39 1438
  Lot No. 42 1435, 1554
  Lot No. 43 1670, 1672
  Lot No. 45 1905
  Lot No. 46 1435, 1552
  Lot No. 51 1430
MS, Adams Co. 1058, 1134
MS, Marshall Co. 672-673
MS, Vicksburg 255, 1151, 1161
MS, Warren Co. 255, 568, 1044-1045

MS, Yazoo Co. 1149
NC, Lincoln Co. 267
New Market 351
NJ, Essex Co. 784
NJ, Monmouth Co. 1112
NY, New York 1647
OH, Cincinnati 821
OH, Hamilton Co. 821
Ohio 396
PA, Philadelphia 1439, 1618, 1634
PA, Pittsburgh 32, 1020
Pond, __igg 77
Ponds. Beaver 226
Prairie. Brooks 86, 570
Prairie, Grand, St. Louis Co., MO 226
Receivers Certificate No. 481 608
River, Mississippi 12-14, 16, 20, 22,
    29-30, 43, 47, 50, 54, 57-58, 62, 66,
    86, 89, 91, 112, 122, 133, 137, 142-
    143, 181, 185-186, 188, 200, 206-
    207, 209, 222, 224, 226, 231, 235,
    240, 242, 281, 285, 287-291, 306,
    317, 320, 327, 329, 344, 347, 373,
    378, 387, 390-392, 405, 421, 424,
    434, 448, 451, 468, 479-480, 484,
    489, 506, 522, 561, 588, 594-595,
    608, 615, 623, 624, 627, 646, 672-
    673, 691, 716, 816, 819-820, 822,
    824, 830, 892, 944, 947, 1002, 1037,
    1063, 1065, 1107-1108, 1142, 1144,
    1146, 1151, 1157-1158, 1183-1184,
    1189-1190, 1195, 1209, 1212, 1215-
    1216, 1231, 1255, 1267, 1297, 1299,
    1318, 1355, 1360, 1444, 1453-1454,
    1458, 1534-1535, 1541-1542, 1561,
    1618, 1674, 1680, 1691-1692, 1704,
    1741, 1747, 1762, 1785, 1830, 1839,
    1884, 1912
River, Saline 1472
River, Whitewater 119, 322, 500, 881
Road, Farmington 1660
Road, Flynns Ferry 642
Road, Perryville to the Seminary 1801
Road, Ste. Genevieve to Cape Girardeau 187
Run, tanyard 703
Salien, Mississippi 1039
Salt Licks, Edward Reaves 1033
Salt Works, Dodges 1039
Saxony 1181
School Lands 1558
Seminary 213
Seminary, St. Marys 730, 990, 1165
Seminary, St. Marys of the Barrens 435
Settlement, Barren 17, 190, 245, 358, 360
Settlement, Brazeau 49
Settlement, German Lutheran 1361
Spring, Nicholas Tuckers 110
Spring, Pond 61
Spring, Sweat House 321
Steamboat *Pawnee* 944
Steamboat *Little Red* 1298
Survey No. 81 268, 309, 1845

Survey No. 86 1598, 1671
Survey No. 87 716
Survey No. 88 343
Survey No. 89 531, 1447, 1845
Survey No. 90 1845, 1848
Survey No. 117 1462
Survey No. 118 735, 756
Survey No. 142 439, 1236, 1610-1611
Survey No. 147 343, 437, 525
Survey No. 196 1472
Survey No. 356 1846
Survey No. 364 1255, 1542, 1578
Survey No. 377 395, 461, 1147
Survey No. 440 343, 1846, 1906
Survey No. 442 278-279
Survey No. 447 1238
Survey No. 661 268, 1845
Survey No. 662 338, 399
Survey No. 663 696, 921
Survey No. 830 1466
Survey No. 840 428, 833, 1621
Survey No. 844 284
Survey No. 845 215
Survey No. 846 1807
Survey No. 852 309, 323, 395, 791
Survey No. 855 419, 791, 795, 1658
Survey No. 864 268, 383-384
Survey No. 865 531, 1263, 1363,
    1382-1387, 1389-1391
Survey No. 868 806, 1038, 1567-1568
Survey No. 956 919
Survey No. 958 982
Survey No. 965 1845, 1909
Survey No. 1007 1499, 1733
Survey No. 1131 574
Survey No. 1158 468
Survey No. 1243 268, 309, 1581
Survey No. 1244 268
Survey No. 1275 1691
Survey No. 1310 1636
Survey No. 1844 465, 1841
Survey No. 1845 343, 459, 619
Survey No. 1846 1691, 1741
Survey No. 1866 477
Survey No. 1867 343
Survey No. 1868 1596, 1865-1866
Survey No. 1884 268, 1838
Survey No. 1886 343, 1594
Survey No. 2062 170, 174
Survey No. 2063 268, 309, 1845
Survey No. 2099 268
Survey No. 2109 268, 383-384
Survey No. 2112 166
Survey No. 2129 425, 989
Survey No. 2130 1004
Survey No. 2137 377, 432, 449-450,
    527, 753, 1069-1070, 1307, 1469,
    1679
Survey No. 2142 1846
Survey No. 2144 1846, 1897
Survey No. 2146 437, 1301, 1428
Survey No. 2147 1301
Survey No. 2155 1691
Survey No. 2169 1763, 1856

Survey No. 2170 268, 1603, 1628, 1640, 1664
Survey No. 2173 1065, 1142, 1159, 1360
Survey No. 2175 309, 378, 1912
Survey No. 2179 298, 315
Survey No. 2186 268, 529, 531, 1447, 1846
Tanyard 556
Tanyard, Logans 257, 509, 831
Terre Blue 351
TN, Campbell Co. 1495
TN, Shelby Co. 1762
TN, Wilson Co. 408, 429
Tower, Grand 16, 30, 287-290, 378, 1158
Township 10 S, Range 4 W
  Section 23 672-673, 830, 1215
  Section 24 672-673, 830, 1215-1216
Township 32 N, Range 9 E
  Section 10 1595
Township 33 N, Range 11 E
  Section 1 780, 1484, 1634
  Section 4 1162, 1675
  Section 6 780
  Section 33 1634
Township 33 N, Range 12 E
  Section 1 1343, 1846
  Section 2 903, 1019, 1148
  Section 3 621, 740, 1128
  Section 4 229, 499
  Section 5 552-553, 555, 1061, 1439
  Section 6 414, 453, 1634
  Section 13 1886
Township 33 N, Range 13 E
  Section 1 635, 648, 692, 852, 1156
  Section 2 159, 309, 856, 1782-1783
  Section 3 635, 649, 852, 1156, 1354, 1433, 1890
Township 33 N, Range 14 E
  Section 5 624, 646, 692, 771, 784, 797, 1013, 1209, 1354, 1359, 1890
  Section 6 635, 650, 692, 784, 852, 962, 1156, 1354, 1890
  Section 7 635, 649, 852, 1156, 1890
Township 34 N, Range 8 E
  Section 23 1194, 1586, 1668, 1685
  Section 24 500, 881, 1187, 1312, 1586, 1609, 1668, 1685
Township 34 N, Range 9 E
  Section 11 1020, 1164, 1237, 1592-1593, 1632
  Section 12 1676
  Section 14 763-764
  Section 29 592, 1490
  Section 33 376, 1023
Township 34 N, Range 10 E
  Section 1 807, 972-973, 1275, 1442, 1491, 1530, 1646, 1864
  Section 2 590, 848, 1450-1452, 1557, 1719
  Section 3 1188, 1206, 1303, 1665
  Section 5 1075
  Section 7 1164, 1592-1593, 1631

Section 11 1695, 1853
Section 12 752, 867, 966, 1275, 1285, 1442, 1530, 1646
Section 13 1475, 1564
Section 14 983, 1540
Section 15 1799
Section 17 1766
Section 21 1308
Section 25 1637, 1730, 1748
Section 26 1515
Section 29 1752
Section 35 1020, 1515

Township 34 N, Range 11 E
Section 1 809, 1315-1316, 1463, 1495
Section 2 603, 935, 1344-1345, 1861
Section 3 732
Section 4 1808, 1832
Section 5 1465, 1870
Section 6 995-997, 1077, 1227, 1516, 1732
Section 7 1616
Section 9 1268-1269, 1278-1280
Section 12 707, 809, 855, 1353, 1463
Section 13 1603
Section 15 1603, 1869
Section 16 1340, 1603, 1648, 1868
Section 17 1648
Section 18 1474-1475, 1512, 1793
Section 19 318, 536, 747, 950, 1001, 1304-1305
Section 20 505, 880, 893, 1239, 1624
Section 21 678-679, 1603, 1913
Section 22 502, 1603
Section 23 1096, 1803
Section 24 1603
Section 28 678-679, 1229, 1257
Section 32 1809
Section 33 1846
Section 34 589, 1095, 1608
Section 35 896, 1908
Section 36 410-411, 497, 780, 896, 1527-1528, 1634

Township 34 N, Range 12 E
Section 1 1333, 1576, 1846
Section 2 622
Section 4 1846
Section 5 860, 1855
Section 6 1274
Section 7 1093
Section 8 860, 1772, 1855
Section 12 430, 1495
Section 13 1457, 1812-1813, 1872
Section 15 710, 1471
Section 17 1326-1327
Section 19 1153, 1171, 1264, 1820
Section 21 1296, 1790
Section 22 491, 1460, 1880
Section 26 337, 365-366
Section 27 565-566, 631, 999, 1225, 1352, 1460
Section 28 328, 374, 817-818, 1094, 1100, 1124, 1186
Section 30 704, 823

Section 31 400, 501, 511, 513-514, 552, 555, 1235
Section 32 552, 554, 556, 637, 703, 836, 1057, 1061, 1439, 1622, 1633, 1907
Section 35 1615

Township 34 N, Range 13 E
Section 3 1017
Section 4 1635
Section 5 941, 1635, 1781
Section 6 576, 796, 827, 1196
Section 7 518, 602
Section 9 871, 915
Section 10 1391, 1393
Section 11 1393
Section 13 1361
Section 14 1163, 1263, 1361, 1363, 1393
Section 15 1026, 1393
Section 16 404, 731, 942
Section 20 1422-1423
Section 21 1395, 1398-1399, 1773
Section 22 1244, 1395, 1397-1398, 1407-1409, 1514, 1520, 1774, 1888
Section 23 1244, 1262-1263, 1362-1371, 1543, 1693-1694, 1775-1777, 1835, 1919
Section 24 1159, 1562, 1584, 1786
Section 25 1543
Section 26 1197, 1368, 1370, 1372-1380, 1467, 1638, 1778, 1789, 1791, 1893, 1895-1896, 1898-1899, 1903, 1919
Section 27 1223, 1396, 1400-1402, 1405-1406, 1895, 1900, 1903
Section 28 1395, 1402, 1404
Section 29 727, 1581
Section 32 727, 1581
Section 33 1404
Section 34 1003, 1016, 1380, 1895, 1901-1902
Section 35 1379, 1381, 1893

Township 34 N, Range 14 E
Section 30 797, 1738
Section 6 1144
Section 32 692, 785, 797, 852, 1854, 1867
Section 33 1013

Township 35 N, Range 9 E
Section 14 1125, 1504-1505
Section 23 1125, 1504
Section 29 864
Section 35 1020, 1172, 1631, 1728
Section 36 176, 878, 1728

Township 35 N, Range 10 E 1429
Section 1 1192, 1916
Section 2 1623, 1920
Section 8 1645
Section 12 886-887, 1011, 1014, 1040-1043, 1083, 1088-1089, 1234, 1260, 1916
Section 13 417, 511-512, 515, 1011, 1083, 1088-1089, 1208, 1235, 1260, 1309

Section 14 510-511, 1235, 1260
Section 15 988, 1025, 1213
Section 16 1020, 1477
Section 22 1800
Section 23 862-863, 1284
Section 26 534, 1056, 1497-1498
Section 27 741, 782, 1464, 1502, 1571, 1681-1682
Section 28 1020, 1164, 1592-1593, 1631
Section 29 1549, 1754, 1862
Section 30 1792, 1796
Section 30 550, 1792, 1796
Section 33 1020, 1164, 1592-1593, 1737, 1810
Section 34 446-447, 894, 1241, 1258, 1270, 1330, 1445-1446, 1470, 1478, 1480, 1501, 1539, 1573, 1639, 1689
Section 35 1056, 1103, 1166, 1497, 1538, 1558, 1764, 1871
Section 36 596, 666, 953, 1306, 1441, 1479

Township 35 N, Range 11 E 1429
Section 6 1053, 1102, 1135, 1712-1713
Section 11 1822
Section 12 1607
Section 13 1607
Section 14 655
Section 15 1822
Section 16 1814
Section 17 1322, 1625, 1843
Section 18 233, 1266, 1705
Section 19 462-463, 539
Section 20 773, 1251, 1843
Section 22 1601-1602, 1629, 1794, 1805, 1823
Section 23 920, 968, 1823
Section 25 443-444, 718, 841, 1074, 1098, 1334-1335, 1687, 1696, 1846, 1910
Section 26 638, 1031, 1331, 1599, 1831
Section 27 1833
Section 28 1281, 1293, 1545, 1619
Section 29 1149, 1424
Section 31 1546
Section 32 1021, 1643, 1656-1657
Section 34 733-734
Section 35 487, 702, 1036, 1199

Township 35 N, Range 12 E
Section 5 1114
Section 7 1605-1606, 1641-1642
Section 8 986
Section 10 594-595, 1752
Section 11 594-595, 781
Section 13 1132, 1862
Section 14 1008, 1119-1120, 1122, 1123, 1152, 1922
Section 15 1118, 1122
Section 18 967, 1049, 1051, 1068
Section 19 967, 1050-1051, 1068
Section 20 1116, 1121
Section 21 870

Section 22 1090
Section 28 1110, 1329, 1749
Section 29 1117
Section 30 1091-1092, 1311, 1335, 1910
Section 32 1521
Section 35 1569
Section 36 581-582, 690, 1802, 1815
Township 35 N, Range 13 E
Section 18 695, 820, 1324, 1762
Section 20 468, 736, 914, 1173, 1561, 1845, 1884
Section 21 618, 1522-1526
Section 26 1139, 1232
Section 27 705-706, 825-826
Section 30 955, 1824
Section 31 1802
Section 34 1673, 1736
Section 35 1233
Section 36 1231, 1233
Township 36 N, Range 9 E
Section 3 745
Section 23 670, 1662
Section 26 1662
Township 36 N, Range 10 E
Section 9 1193, 1346, 1873
Section 10 1346-1347, 1873, 1877
Section 14 1506, 1836
Section 16 1811, 1818, 1879
Section 22 409, 684, 738, 1000, 1055, 1080, 1342, 1590, 1617
Section 25 1769, 1826, 1849
Section 26 17, 1080
Section 29 859, 1753
Section 31 1152, 1829
Section 32 922
Section 33 470
Section 35 654, 1911
Section 36 407, 1739, 1874-1875, 1920
Township 36 N, Range 11 E
Section 3 874
Section 4 623, 1151, 1184, 1189-1190, 1195, 1674
Section 10 874
Section 19 776, 1076
Section 21 905, 909, 1086, 1226, 1851
Section 22 899-900
Section 23 824
Section 24 557, 803, 1029, 1059, 1846
Section 25 1456
Section 29 1079
Section 31 286, 360-361, 1168
Section 33 1358, 1921
Section 36 1220
Township 36 N, Range 12 E
Section 6 742
Section 16 136, 549, 558-559, 664, 758
Section 17 136, 743, 1317
Section 18 1529
Section 20 940
Section 21 263
Section 22 136, 426, 819, 1182, 1201
Section 23 426, 819
Section 26 136, 1182-1183
Section 30 928, 933, 1009, 1047-1048
Township 36 N, Range 13 E
Section 19 821, 1324
Township 37 N, Range 10 E
Section 27 1767
Section 28 1767
Section 35 517, 835, 1221, 1432, 1566, 1703
Township 37 N, Range 11 E
Section 17 521, 607, 701, 1636
Section 18 625-626
Section 19 626, 1078, 1259
Section 20 607, 701, 1636
Section 27 341
Section 28 240, 568, 879, 1594
Section 32 897, 1086, 1614
Section 33 879
Township 38 N, Range 6 E
Section 26 797
Township 39 N, Range 14 E
Section 6 784
Township, (Cape) Cinque Hommes 844, 846, 859
Township, Big Sandy 692
Township, Bois Brule 25, 88, 105, 142-143, 173, 200, 225, 227, 242, 248-249, 261, 345, 370, 421, 439, 521, 549, 564, 573, 633, 664, 756, 847, 897, 907, 921, 934, 1022, 1105, 1328, 1859
Township, Brazeau (Aubrazeau, Brasoe, Brazo, Brazoe) 163, 188, 274, 398, 405, 408, 429, 458, 593, 628, 710, 733-734, 1101, 1264, 1555, 1561, 1884, 1887
Township, Cinque Hommes 10-11, 23, 31, 44, 61, 63, 75, 106-107, 114, 130, 139, 157, 165, 191, 194, 216, 221, 225, 243, 253, 264, 274, 294, 381, 632, 922, 924, 977, 1193, 1219, 1287, 1456, 1841, 1864
Tract, Allen 181
Tract, Donohoe 912
Tract, Fenwick 1603
Tract, Gillard 588, 608
Tract, Grand Glaise 394, 403, 709, 829
Tract, Hempstead 1692
Tract, Hill 452, 1144, 1319, 1534-1535
Tract, mill 1806
Tract, old mill 912
Tract, Orphan 1585
Tract, Pr_aria 77
Tract, Roark & Reardon 714, 1559
Tract, Round Pond 240, 568
Tract, Seminary Mill 651, 653
Tract, Sweat House Spring 831
Transylvania, University of 134
VA, Fort Monroe 559
VA, Jefferson Co. 1260
WI, Ioway Co. 882

Wisconsin Terr. 882
Woodyard, Vitals 1298

www.ingramcontent.com/pod-product-compliance
Lightning Source LLC
Chambersburg PA
CBHW081356290426
44110CB00018B/2393